The Child Care
Professional

The Child Care Professional

Karen Stephens

Early Childhood Specialist
Director of ISU Child Care Center
Lecturer in Child Development
Illinois State University,
Normal, Illinois

GLENCOE
McGraw-Hill

New York, New York;   Columbus, Ohio;   MIssion Hills, California;   Peoria, Illinois

Contributing Writers

Sheila Platter
Assistant Principal for Instruction and Curriculum
Garland High School
Garland, Texas

Judy Marks
Child Care Occupations Instructor
North Valley Occupational Center
Los Angeles Unified School District
Mission Hills, California

Technical Reviewers

Bonnie J. Bucher
Director
Proctor Hospital New Horizons Employee
  Child Care Center
Peoria, Illinois

Linda B. Daniels, M.S.
Early Childhood Education Consultant
Ohio Department of Education
Columbus, Ohio

Linda R. Glosson, Ph.D.
Home Economics Teacher
Wylie High School
Wylie, Texas

**Constance G. Mueller,
M.S., R.D.**
Instructor, Foods and Nutrition
Illinois State University
Normal, Illinois

Educational Reviewers

Tanya Benson
Lake City High School
Coeur D'Alene, Idaho

Angela Lattuca Croce
Mira Mesa High School
San Diego, California

Betty Jo Jordan
West Virginia Department of Education
Charleston, West Virginia

Judy Marks
North Valley Occupational Center
Los Angeles Unified School District
Mission Hills, California

Darla Jean Olberding
North High School
Evansville, Indiana

Texanita Louise Randle
Wichita High School South
Wichita, Kansas

Janice Scholz
Office of Applied Technology and Vocational Education
Brevard County
Melbourne, Florida

Glencoe/McGraw-Hill

A Division of The **McGraw·Hill** *Companies*

Send all inquiries to:
Glencoe/McGraw-Hill
3008 W. Willow Knolls Drive
Peoria, IL 61614-1083

ISBN 0-02-675772-9

Printed in the United States of America

5 6 7 8 9 10 11 12   003   02 01 00 99 98 97

Table of Contents

Special Text Features

Charts and Highlighted Topics

THE CHILD CARE PROFESSION

CHAPTER

Reflections

"'These children need a role model.' That's what they told me when I first applied for a job at the child care center in my neighborhood. I was seventeen, needed part-time work, and didn't really care what kind of job I had. Many of the kids in the center didn't have a father figure at home. And they wanted me to be a father figure? What experience did I have for that? Well, I've learned. I help out with all sorts of activities in the center, but the outdoor activities are the best. I like to keep my kids on track (now I think of them as mine). People say I set a good example for them, and they need that. This is the kind of work I want to do after graduation. Men are needed in the child care field. I'm not sticking with it for that reason, though; I'm sticking because I like it."

—Andy

Chapter 1

Families and Child Care

CHAPTER OBJECTIVES

- Explain why the need for child care services has grown.

- Compare and contrast custodial, developmental, and comprehensive child care.

- Compare and contrast the different options in child care.

- Identify factors that promote quality in a child care program.

- Analyze issues in child care.

Terms to Learn

- au pair
- child care
- curriculum
- developmentally appropriate curriculum
- early childhood
- early childhood education
- environment
- extended families
- gender role
- nanny
- nuclear family

Dave couldn't believe the change in his daughter. He watched as four-year-old Holly skipped toward him, holding a special creation that looked like it had been made from part of an egg carton. Holly was beaming. "Look, Daddy!" Holly said with pride as she held out her art project. "I made it for you. Teacher said it has pretty colors. Can we put it on the table when we eat dinner?"

"Of course, we can," Dave replied, drawing Holly close for a hug. "I think it's great." As they left the child care center, Holly chattered happily about her day. She talked about Ms. O'Keefe and Mr. Millen, two of her favorite teachers. She also described a musical game that she had played with her friends.

"She's so happy here," Dave thought to himself. "And to think— only a few weeks ago, she seemed like a different child. She had so little to say when I picked her up, and it seemed like she was always tired and grumpy. I'm so glad I found another child care program for her. It has made such a difference—for her and for me."

QUALITY COUNTS

Good child care does make a difference. **Child care** is *the broad term that describes any situation in which children are provided with supervision, support, and sometimes training by individuals outside the child's immediate family.* For a parent who entrusts the care of a child to others, the quality of that care is critical. Can you imagine what it would be like as a parent to leave your child with people you don't trust? How would you feel if you thought your child was not happy or not receiving proper care from the people you were paying for child care service? How would you find quality care? These are very real questions that families face. The demand for more and better child care has grown significantly over the last few decades, and it will continue to do so. Identifying and insuring quality child care is a common goal.

THE GROWTH OF CHILD CARE

Throughout the early periods of history in America, child care was uncommon. If used at all, arrangements were usually made with nearby family and friends. Since **extended families** often lived together, child care for them was built right into the family setting. These families, *which include relatives other than parents and children,* did not usually need others for child care.

Times of war were the exception. The need for child care did surface when parents and other adult family members joined the war efforts. During World War II, for example, many women left their homes to work in the factories, where they helped build defense equipment and supplies. Because of women's presence in the work force, the national government and defense factories created child care centers to care for the children of employed women. Once World War II ended and men came back to the jobs, women returned to their homes, and most of the child care centers closed.

During the 1950s, many families fit a pattern that was typical after World War II. The **nuclear family,** *consisting of a mother, father, and their children,* was common. In many of these families, father went off to work while mother kept the household running smoothly. If you have ever watched a television program from the 1950s, you may have seen images that reflected those times; however, change was ahead.

One of the changes that has affected the way in which families handle child care has been in the extended family. These families have become less likely to live in the same household. Often they have moved far apart, eliminating the convenience of built-in child care. Although some families are returning to this pattern of living, it is still much less common than it was throughout the early years of American history.

Another change evolved during the 1960s as new attitudes about the roles of men and women at home and at work emerged. Ideas about gender roles broadened. A **gender role** is *the behavior and responsibilities expected of a man or woman in the family and society.* Gradually, more women became employed outside the home, a trend that has continued for every decade since the 1960s. Currently over 50 percent of preschoolers have a mother who works outside the home. By the year 2000, the National Academy of Sciences estimates that 70 per-

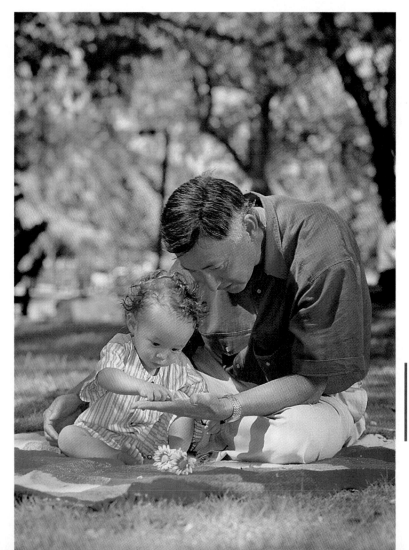

Child care for extended families who live together is built into the family setting. These families include relatives other than parents and children.

With more women in the workforce, the need for child care services has increased significantly. What special challenges do working parents of young children face?

cent of preschoolers will have mothers in the labor force. Although having a parent at home automatically supplied child care in the past, that situation just isn't as common anymore—for several reasons.

The Need for Two Incomes

Many families today depend on the incomes of both parents simply to provide food, shelter, and education for their children. In families with both parents

employed, many of the families would live in poverty if one parent stayed home. When both parents are employed outside the home, they usually need help with the care of young children.

More Single Parents

Both mothers and fathers raise children alone today. The number of single mothers, however, is far greater. After divorce, women rather than men more commonly have custody of the children. When unplanned pregnancy occurs and the parents do not marry, the same situation is likely—the mother usually cares for the child. Since the rates of divorce and teen pregnancy are high, so is the number of single parents who have a need for child care while they attend school, look for a job, or go to work.

Career Interests

Some people are highly motivated to have a career. Both family and employment offer them needed fulfillment. Leaving a career to care for children, even temporarily, may result in lost promotions and income as well as other setbacks. Some people who have a career find that they are better parents when they have the outside stimulation of a job.

furnish a place for the child to be supervised while basic needs are met. They may provide food and make sure children get the rest and exercise they need. Activities are limited and informal, with no planned program.

Developmental Care

Many programs go beyond custodial care. An interest in helping children develop properly is the reason. **Early childhood,** *those years between birth and age eight,* is a critical time for development. Children learn so much during the first years of life. Development moves at a fast pace, and personalities are shaped. If developmental delays occur, a child may have trouble catch-

DIFFERENT APPROACHES TO CHILD CARE

As the need to have child care has increased, providers have created different approaches to help meet the need. No two children are exactly alike. No two families are exactly alike. Therefore no one type of care is right for all families. Parents need child care options that suit their situations. They must choose from programs that provide everything from custodial, to developmental, to comprehensive care.

Custodial Care

As you explore the types of child care that are available, you will find some providers who give only custodial care. In other words, they

The early childhood years are important ones. Experiences shape each child's development and personality.

ing up. Problems may continue and become greater over time. How can child care professionals address this situation? Programs that focus on developmental care are the answer. Educational opportunities that promote good development are stressed with this type of care.

Early childhood education is the term applied to those *child care programs that promote development through formal teaching and learning experiences for children up to age eight.* Many of the child care programs you will read about, observe, and perhaps even work in someday include education of the child as part of what they offer. More and more emphasis is being placed on education in the child care setting.

Many parents want programs that give their children educational opportunities. Families are turning to early childhood education to provide their children with a better start toward success in future schooling. Often such programs are used by families who need child care but also want the experience to have educational and social benefits. Some families simply feel their children need the stimulation offered by early education. Such programs are particularly useful to disadvantaged children who need help in catching up developmentally with other children.

Comprehensive Care

Child care programs that supply a range of additional services fall into the category of comprehensive care. These programs meet the basic needs of children and also promote good development. The difference is in what else they provide. Programs may include medical care for children. They may also supply parent education and training. Such classes teach parents about many topics, including nutrition, raising children, infant care, discipline, and caring for special needs children. Some programs even have exercise classes for parents.

SPECIFIC CHILD CARE OPTIONS

*T*he availability of good child care has not kept up with the demand. On the positive side, however, society is recognizing that the need is real. In response, child care programs are increasing in number, kind, and quality.

Before selecting a program, families look for what they need. Whether part-time, full-time, custodial, or educational, they look for places where children will be lovingly and safely cared for. Parents want the right match between child and program. Some options are described below. You will read more about many of these in other chapters.

- *Child Care Centers.* These programs, which often have multiple classrooms, operate all day long but allow parents to use them part-time if necessary. Child care centers usually serve children from six weeks to twelve years of age. Some specialize in certain age categories. Transportation to and from school is generally provided for school-age children. Child care centers may be sponsored by a religious organization, public school, or a private owner. Some are for-profit businesses that operate as a chain in many locations across the country.

- *Family Day Care Homes.* This form of child care usually operates all day, serving children from six weeks to twelve years of age. Some limit the ages they will take. The provider is someone who adapts his or her own residence for the service. Family day care homes tend to be less structured than child care centers. Many parents choose them because they like the homelike atmosphere for their children and the longer hours of operation that some provide.

- *Infant/Toddler Child Care Centers.* Children from six weeks through two

The family day care provider is someone who adapts his or her own residence for service. Many parents choose them because they like the homelike atmosphere for their children.

years of age are served in these programs. They may be housed in a child care center that serves older children. Full- or part-time service is possible.

- *Before- and After-School Programs.* These programs give school-age children a place to go before and after school while their parents are working. They usually operate from about 6:00 a.m. to 9:00 a.m. and reopen from 3:00 p.m. to 6:00 p.m. Transportation to and from school is often provided.
- *Preschool/Nursery Schools.* Most programs of this type operate for a half day two to three times a week. They emphasize educational services to stimulate children's overall development.

- *Pre-Kindergarten Programs.* Sponsored by both public and private schools, these programs are designed to prevent school failure. Programs

Most nursery schools and preschools have limited schedules. What might be the advantages and disadvantages of this arrangement?

may be half-day or full-day. Three- to five-year-old children identified as being at risk of academic failure may be enrolled free of charge.

- **Corporate Child Care Centers.** These child care programs are offered by employers for their employees. They may be located in the company's building or in a nearby location. They often charge a lower rate than parents might pay in other programs. As these become more common, studies show that they have many benefits for child, parents, and company.

- **In-Home Child Care.** Some parents prefer to have their child cared for in their own home. Care may be provided by someone trained in child care or someone with no formal training. One option is care by a nanny. A **nanny** is *trained in child care and then employed to come into the home to care for children.* Sometimes nannies live with the family and receive free rent and food as part of their wages. Other times the nanny goes to the child's home in the morning and leaves each evening. Another option is an **au pair** (oh PARE). *This is a young person who comes from one country to live with a family in another country.* Au pairs exchange housework and child care for room and board.

- **Montessori Preschools.** These programs are based on the teachings of Maria Montessori, an Italian physician who worked with children in the early 1900s. Montessori brought new insights into how children learn, supplying materials that enabled children to master tasks in a step-by-step sequence. She promoted independence by emphasizing order and education in the preschool environment. Most Montessori programs operate on a half-day basis.

If you were hiring someone to provide full-time child care in your home, what qualities and characteristics would you look for?

- **Head Start Programs.** Created in the 1960s, Head Start is a federally funded program that primarily serves four-year-olds. It focuses on comprehensive services for low-income families. Although some Head Starts provide full-day care, most provide half-day programs.

- **Early Childhood Programs for Children with Special Needs.** Usually sponsored through public schools, these programs serve children birth to five years of age. Classrooms may include children who

Building Professional Skills

A Positive Attitude

WHAT IS A POSITIVE ATTITUDE?

Whether it's your personal or professional life, a positive attitude makes a difference in how you are viewed by others and what responses you get. With a positive attitude, you look at the bright side of things. You see the good more often than the bad, focus on achievement rather than failure, smile more than frown, build instead of tear down, and believe rather than doubt. Your actions and your words reveal your attitude to others. A positive attitude is often like a magnet, drawing others to you because they like being around you.

A Positive Attitude in Action

"I know we can do it," Delores said to the steering committee at her church. "The children in this neighborhood need it. So many of them are alone after school. Their parents just don't have any options. Why just the other day, a mother told me how scared her five-year-old was when some older kids threatened him and chased him home. The boy's mother was upset. She was angry about what happened and guilty because she wasn't there. This shouldn't be happening to these children. We've got a huge basement that's empty after school. I say let's give it a try."

Delores Jacobs watched as the committee members listened to her words. Soon a lively discussion was going on about what the church could do to set up an after-school program for children in the neighborhood. Repeatedly, Delores chimed in with words of enthusiasm. She suggested names of people who might help them. She was realistic about the problems, but she had answers for those who were negative.

"I think Delores has something here," Robert Lindsey said, "and we seem to be catching her spirit. What are we here for if it isn't to offer support to people who need it?" Delores smiled as she had visions of her dream becoming reality.

Your Analysis

1. How did Delores display a positive attitude?

2. What outcomes may be a result of Delores' attitude?

3. What might have happened if Delores were not a positive person?

4. How do people develop positive and negative attitudes?

5. Do you see yourself as more positive or negative? Describe two examples that support your analysis.

6. What might a person do to become more positive?

The early years of development are especially critical for children with special needs. Such children may be in specialized programs or may be included in any early childhood program.

have early diagnosis of such disabilities as cerebral palsy, birth defects, autism, behavioral disorders, Down syndrome, and hearing impairment.

- ***Child Care for Children Who Are Ill.*** Staffed with early childhood caregivers and nurses, these programs care for children who are mildly ill. Children who are recuperating from contagious diseases, such as chicken pox, use these programs. Hospitals often provide this care.

- ***Crisis Nurseries.*** Crisis nurseries are provided as a way to prevent child abuse. Parents who feel they are overstressed and at risk of abusing their children may use a crisis nursery. These programs operate on a 24-hour basis. They are usually funded by the United Way and other social service agencies. Crisis nurseries are seldom found in small communities.

- ***Parent Cooperatives.*** Some parents get together to sponsor a play group or preschool of their own. Parents take turns doing such tasks as secretarial work and caring for children.

- ***Other Programs.*** Where specific needs arise, other types of programs are created. Mother's Day Out programs, often sponsored by religious organizations, provide a few hours of child care each week for parents who need a little free time. Malls and health clubs may have drop-off care for their patrons. Respite care provides time off for parents of special needs children. These are a few examples of additional types of care that communities provide.

WHAT IS QUALITY?

Whatever type of care parents choose for their children, they still want it to be high quality. All it takes is one frightening story about a bad child care experience to raise parental concern. Infants and young children can't explain what their lives are like in a child care setting. It is up to adults to make sure that children are safe and happy. This is why an increased effort has been made to bring regulation and quality to the growing child care industry.

Suppose you were going to help your family find child care for a younger brother or sister. What characteristics would you look for to identify a quality program? The rest of

A positive child care environment is reflected in the behavior and attitudes of children and caregivers. What signs do you see here that this environment is a positive one?

Children need times and places for eating, sleeping, toileting, and cleaning up. They also need assistance with these. The health and safety of children depend on careful attention to the basics.

A Suitable Environment

When you walk into a child care center, you get an impression about the environment. The **environment** is *everything—objects, conditions, atmosphere—that*

this text will help you answer that question, but some of the key qualities are introduced here. If you decide to work in the child care field, you will be responsible for learning many specific ways to provide a quality program in all of these areas.

The Basic Needs

It's first things first when taking care of children. Before you can think about entertaining or teaching children, what would you have to plan for? The basics, of course.

A positive child care environment draws children in. The furniture, equipment, supplies, and toys all work together to stimulate the children's senses, invite them to learn, and encourage success. How would you rate this classroom?

makes up the surroundings. In a positive environment, what you see is inviting to the eye. Well-chosen furniture, equipment, supplies, and toys, all in appropriate quantity, make a contribution. The environment is more than just seen, however. It is also felt. A sense of warmth and order comes within a positive environment. A close look at the personalities and actions of employees and children reveals much about a center's environment.

A Well-Planned Curriculum

A well-planned curriculum points to quality. The **curriculum** is *a long-range plan of activities and experiences for children.* Many of the activities help children with their development. Children go through predictable stages of development, but at different rates. For example, Noel's teacher knows that he will learn to tie his shoes. She also knows the age at which he is most

likely to have the skills to do so. What she doesn't know is *exactly* when he will learn. Part of good curriculum planning for Noel and other children his age includes providing activities that allow them to practice the skills they need in order to be able to tie their shoes.

A well-planned curriculum provides many learning opportunities. Research in child development reports that children learn best by exploring with their senses—sight, hearing, touch, taste, and smell. For this reason, activities should give children opportunities to explore with *all* their senses, not just one or two.

The ability to plan appropriate activities depends on having an understanding of how children develop. When *activities include those that are geared to different levels of ability and development*, the program has a **developmentally appropriate curriculum.**

A well-planned curriculum has variety. That is, the planners strive to educate the

Exploration is an exciting as well as interesting part of a child's life. Those who plan curriculums include activities that give children opportunities to explore.

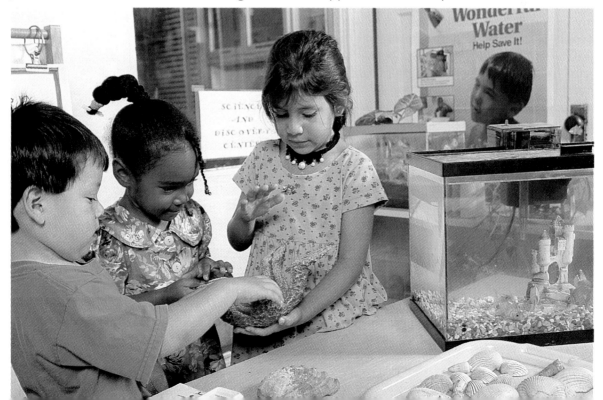

"whole" child. Activities address all areas of development—social, emotional, intellectual, physical, and moral.

An Organized Daily Schedule

In a quality program, the daily schedule provides children with a sense of security. The children can rely on a pattern that stays about the same every day. Although specific activities change daily, a basic schedule that is familiar makes children more comfortable and contributes to better behavior. Daily schedules do vary from one classroom to the next. Infant rooms have separate plans for each individual baby. Gradually, as they grow older, children learn to adapt to a schedule established for the group.

Being in group care for eight to ten hours a day demands a lot of energy from children. A well-organized schedule has time for quiet, as well as active, play.

Appropriate Discipline

"An ounce of prevention is worth a pound of cure." You've probably heard that saying before. How might you apply it to disciplining children? In a quality child care setting, people who work with children avoid many difficulties by taking steps to prevent problems from happening in the first place. What makes them successful? For one thing, they study discipline techniques to learn what works best with children. They use a positive approach with children. They also set up clear and simple rules. They plan schedules and activities that run smoothly. In addition, they think ahead about how to deal with behavior problems that might occur and take action when there is a need.

Parental Involvement

Bridging the gap between home and the child care setting is important to children. The more consistency and cooperation, the better. Although parents are the first teachers of children, they team up with professionals in child care to provide what is needed. Children feel more comfortable when parents and staff members work in harmony. A child care program that avoids contact and input from parents is not a quality one.

Often parents have particular concerns about the care and guidance given to their children. They try to choose a program that fits their beliefs about child care. They may have opinions and requests that the personnel in a good program will want to understand.

A quality program has child care professionals who can help parents. They often

In this corporate child care center, the father is able to spend some time with his child during the day. Parents need to be in touch with what goes on in their children's lives.

Tip FROM THE Pros

Some parents may believe that they don't have something special enough to share with their child's class. As a child care professional, you can encourage all parents to explore what they have to offer. Then include them. A parent who demonstrates how to hammer a nail so that it goes straight into a piece of wood has something just as interesting to share with children as the parent who is an accomplished artist.

serve as role models when parents watch them guide children's learning and behavior. They can be advisors when parents ask for suggestions on selecting toys or some other child-related issue.

Good child care professionals bridge home and program by inviting parents to become involved. Some ask parents to volunteer in the classroom. Others invite parents into the classroom as special visitors, especially when a particular skill, talent, or interest can be shared with the children. Newsletters and family potluck suppers are just two ways that a good program might use to help build a strong bond between family and staff.

Record Development

New abilities in children develop on a daily basis. Professionals in a quality program keep notes on each child's development. Some use checklists to record children's developmental achievements, such as the date when a one-year-old takes that first step.

Note-taking isn't the only way to record children's development. Some centers also save samples of children's work and use video recorders. The information recorded is used to evaluate development and report to parents. With so much going on in a child care setting, observations cannot be entrusted to memory.

A Professional Staff

Research and information on children and child care is not static. In other words, it is always changing, with new ideas and information regularly introduced. A quality child care program has professionals who continue their growth by reading books and journals. They attend conferences and workshops and share information with other employees. By enrolling in child development and early childhood education classes, they also promote their professional growth. A well-trained and caring professional staff

Two-year-olds need constant attention and guidance. That requires additional staff and increases the cost of care.

is probably the key ingredient when it comes to quality in child care.

Staff size is important too. When a program does not have an adequate number of staff members, children don't get the attention and care they need. The number of children one person can be responsible for varies according to the ages of the children. For infants and younger children, a larger staff is required.

Learning More about Quality

What you have just read about quality only skims the surface. In each area described, many techniques and efforts can help produce a quality child care program. You will find many ideas throughout this text. Much of what you will read is about preschoolers, those children from ages three to five. This is the age group handled by the majority of child care programs. Information about children who are younger and older, however, is also important. You will find specific discussions on these other age groups—infants, toddlers, and school-age children—featured throughout the text.

A LOOK AT THE ISSUES

The subject of children and child care is sometimes emotional. That's because certain questions concerning child care are controversial. People want what is best for children, but they don't always agree on the right approach to take. Answers are not easily reached when you look at both sides of the issues. Can you see varying points of view on the issues described below? What compromises and solutions can you offer to these questions?

- ***Does the creation of child care programs promote the breakdown of the family?*** Some people believe that it does, saying that child care programs allow parents to turn away from their responsibilities. For example, they would criticize parents who put their children in child care when they have a career by choice rather than economic necessity. Other people say child care services help many single parents and dual-income families who would otherwise struggle to give their children adequate care when they have to be employed. Hoping for a return to the 1950s style of family life doesn't seem to be realistic. Today's world is different and requires new approaches to managing as a family. Most people would agree that the strength of families is a serious concern in society. What they don't always agree on is the methods for keeping families strong and healthy.

- ***What price, if any, is paid by placing children in child care at a very young age?*** Research is contradictory on this issue. Some people believe that children can thrive even with early placement in child care. Others believe that a child needs the ongoing presence of a parent for a period of time during the early years. Such factors as the quality of a program, the condition of the family environment, the time involved, and the child's age and personality probably influence the answer to this question. Research also shows that the consistent presence of one individual as the primary caregiver in a program makes a significant difference in the child's well-being.

- ***When and how should a child's formal education begin?*** The demand for child care has created pressure on public and private schools to provide longer kindergarten programs, pre-kindergarten, and programs that extend the day. Some people are concerned that such programs put too much pressure on children. Others believe that children can benefit from programs that are well planned and provide what children may not be able to get otherwise.

- ***How can families get the quality child care they need?*** Quality programs have been slow in coming. Some child care situations are still inadequate. The number of quality programs is growing. Quality child care, however, usually comes with a high price, making it inaccessible to many. Often the people who need it the most can least afford it. Creative ways of funding child care may be the answer, including grants to private businesses as well as other methods.

Controversial problems are not easily solved in society. It takes time, experience, and the sharing of ideas. People who care about children, including parents and child care professionals, will be at the forefront, looking for solutions that make sense.

CHILDREN, THE FUTURE, AND YOU

*I*f you decide to work in the child care field, you will be in charge of the most valuable resource society has—children. Properly raised and cared for, children are able to raise their own families someday in that same caring manner. When children have positive experiences as they develop, they grow into adults who make contributions to society rather than tear it down. People who love children and want to insure a good future for them are needed in the field. What better reason can there be to aim for a career in child care? If you want to help children get a good start, then the child care field may be just the place for you.

Not everyone agrees about the impact of child care on children, families, and society. There is agreement that children in child care deserve and need the best care possible.

Chapter 1 Review

Chapter Summary

- Parents who need supplemental care for their children often use child care services.
- Economic and social changes have caused an increased need for child care services.
- Efforts are being made to improve the regulation and quality of the child care industry.
- Early childhood professionals have many responsibilities when providing quality child care.
- Child care professionals continually further their growth by keeping up-to-date on research and information about children and child care.
- Parents and child care professionals look for solutions to the emotional and controversial subject of children and child care.

Reviewing the Facts

1. What is child care?
2. Why is quality child care important?
3. Give three reasons for the increased need for child care services.
4. Compare and contrast custodial, developmental, and comprehensive child care programs.
5. Which type of child care program would be most suitable for the child in each of the following situations: (a) a child with a strep infection; (b) an eleven-year-old child whose single parent gets home at 5:30 p.m.; (c) a three-year-old with Down syndrome; (d) a child whose parents choose to employ someone to provide care in their own home?
6. What are the fundamentals of quality child care?
7. What are the ingredients of a well-planned curriculum?
8. Describe a developmentally appropriate curriculum.
9. Identify four controversial issues concerning child care.

Thinking Critically

1. Have you read or heard about any child care situations that were not favorable for children? If so, share the examples with the class. Were the situations resolved? How?
2. Describe a good child care situation with which you are familiar. What gives it quality?
3. Do you or any of your classmates have memories of child care experiences? Describe what these situations were like and any impact they had.
4. Share your point of view on each of the issues described in the chapter.
5. Suppose you were talking to an employed parent who feels guilty about having to use child care services. What would you say to the parent?

Activities and Applications

1. **Resource File.** Begin a resource file of brochures from different early childhood programs.
2. **Interviewing Parents.** Interview several parents who use child care services. What do they like about their child care arrangement? What would they change?
3. **Volunteering.** Volunteer to work in an early childhood classroom for a day. Record your thoughts and feelings at the end of the day. Was it what you expected? What did you like? What surprised you?

Chapter 1 Review

SCHOOL TO WORK

Your Professional Portfolio

From school to work. What does that mean? It means that you have an important transition ahead. Moving from the school world to the world of work takes adjustment. It also takes good preparation. The work you do in school not only helps prepare you for future jobs, but it can also be used to help you land the job that you want. Many students today build portfolios, or collections, of the work they do in a class. One way they use these is to show their capabilities to a prospective employer. You will discover more about portfolios and how to build one as you complete this course. Pay particular attention to the portfolio project ideas in the box like this one at the end of each chapter. If you do, you will be better prepared to make your own transition from school to work in the future.

Observing and Analyzing

First Steps to Observing

How often do you look at what is going on around you without really seeing? It's easy to do. Your thoughts may be elsewhere, or you simply might not have the habit of noticing things. As you begin this course, now is the time to check up on your skills in this area.

To learn about children, you need to observe them. Later in this text you will read about conducting formal observations of children. For now, just take some first steps. Watch children whenever opportunities arise. For practice, watch any situation, even when children are not involved.

Your early observations in this course can be casual ones. Use the ideas that follow to help you begin polishing this skill:

- **Make the decision to watch.** You are probably not in the habit of watching for the sake of watching. In other words, events go on around you all the time, but you may not make a conscious decision to pay close attention. Try that now. Notice a situation that is going on and decide to focus on all aspects of it.
- **Look for details.** It's easy to come away from an event without remembering exactly what you saw. Did you notice clothing? What expressions did the people display? What gestures were used? What was the setting like? Check yourself later to see what you remember.
- **Listen as well as look.** Participating can make observing more difficult. If possible, step back from what is going on and keep quiet. Then you can focus on listening. Learn to concentrate on what you hear without feeling that you have to get involved.
- **Ignore distractions.** Distractions can be the downfall when you want to be observant. It's like running out to the concession stand during a movie and missing some key scenes. When you return, you've lost track of what is going on. You need a complete and accurate understanding of what you see in order to make your observation useful. Practice watching without letting other people, noises, and events get in the way.

As you become a more disciplined observer, you may find that this skill is useful to you in many ways, not just in learning about children. You might perform better on tests. You might learn to see and appreciate simple things. What other possibilities are there?

Chapter 2

Your Role in Child Care

CHAPTER OBJECTIVES

- List the rewards and drawbacks of working in the child care field.

- Describe qualities people need to be an early childhood professional.

- Identify career possibilities in the child care field.

- Determine what the training and education requirements are for careers in the child care field.

- Explain what the CDA credential is.

- Assess your own suitability for a career in the child care field.

Terms to Learn

- CDA advisor
- child care resource and referral specialist
- child development associate (CDA) credential
- child development consultants
- compassion
- director
- early childhood professionals
- home visitor
- portfolio
- resourcefulness
- spontaneity

think this might be it," Maria thought as she left the job fair. "I think I've figured out what I want to do." A feeling of excitement swelled inside her as the thoughts began to run through her mind. Her feelings of uncertainty were quickly slipping away. Resolve was setting in.

Maria loved children. As a babysitter, she was always in demand. She never *just* spent time with the children in her care. She got involved with them, leading them in games and teaching them. That's why the children always begged their parents to call Maria when they needed a sitter. Working with children was not only fun for Maria, but it was rewarding too. "This makes sense," she thought.

As Maria headed for home, the job possibilities shown in the child care display at the job fair ran through her mind. Would she like to take care of children? What if she obtained more education? She might even become a teacher. The feeling that she had a direction to follow was a good one. She had some thinking to do and questions to explore with her counselor, but the possibilities excited her.

WORKING WITH CHILDREN

Knowing what you would like to do when you enter the work world *is* a good feeling. Through the job fair, Maria's thoughts about her future became clearer. The fact that you are reading this text may indicate that you have some interests similar to Maria's. Do you think you might like to work with children? As with any career, there are rewards as well as drawbacks to consider.

The Rewards

Above all else, just being around children can be rewarding. Children make you feel needed and special. They accept your faults and draw upon your strengths. Children are open-hearted and affectionate. Forgiveness comes easily to them. Children usually don't hide what they are thinking or feeling. Their honesty and directness is endearing to most adults—and sometimes amusing as well as embarrassing. After all, the little boy who innocently asked why the teacher's teeth were crooked wasn't aiming to hurt the teacher. He just wanted to know.

As a child care professional, you can make a real difference in the lives of young children. Through your efforts, children can learn skills like independence and cooperation. You can help build a strong foundation from which children develop into healthy, well-adjusted, caring adults. Children face

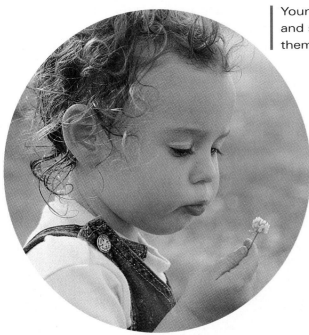

Young children find delight in their world and share it with the adults who care for them.

writer, actor, and storyteller, all rolled into one. You are a trusted counselor and nurse as you comfort hurt feelings and tend to bruised knees.

Each child care professional chooses the field for his or her own reasons. Most would agree, however, that a love of children is at the top of the list.

The Drawbacks

As with any job, you have to be realistic. Examining the drawbacks helps you figure out what you can accept and what you can't.

Working with young children can be draining, emotionally and physically. Anticipating and meeting so many needs may cause stress. Some of the responsibilities are not glamorous. Wiping noses, changing diapers, and cleaning up spills are simply part of the daily routine.

People who work with children are exposed to many minor childhood illnesses, such as colds, flu, and chicken pox. On the plus side, most caregivers eventually build strong resistance to the diseases that can be caught from children.

Not all child care programs are adequately funded. For this reason, wages tend to be low and fringe benefits minimal. Money for classroom materials may also be limited. Many efforts are being made in the field to improve the wage situation. To attract and keep quality employees, salaries must be reasonable. At the same time, services cannot be so costly that the parents who need them cannot afford the fees.

Working with young children often requires long hours. People who work directly with the children spend about eight hours per day on the job, with two fifteen minute breaks. Staff members may eat lunch

some tough situations today. Some come from families that are troubled by problems connected with alcohol, abuse, divorce, or economic difficulties. These children, perhaps even more than others, need the support of skilled caregivers. People who work with children feel proud when they contribute to a better future by addressing the needs of society's children.

Working in an early childhood program helps you stay young. Have you ever taken a glimpse of the world through a child's eyes? You will take less for granted if you do. To a small child, the discovery of a butterfly, an insect, a flower, or a pebble is a wonder. Any of these could create new interests in you, too, as you rediscover them through a child's eyes and mind.

Working with children is seldom boring. Although there is a consistent daily schedule, creative teachers make sure no two days are just the same. Teaching allows you to use many talents and skills. As you prepare and conduct activities, you are an artist, scientist, musician, mathematician, dancer, with the children. Planning and preparation is usually done in the evenings or on weekends. Time off must be planned carefully, since children must be constantly supervised, and substitutes are not always easy to find.

At times children and their families go through crisis. Illness and death in the family are examples. Resulting behavior problems may pose an extra challenge. Worry about a child may last well beyond the end of the work day. The strain, however, is diminished by the good feelings that come when you are able to help a child get through difficult times.

Many of the responsibilities you have while caring for children may not be especially fun, but they are necessary. As on any job, less pleasant tasks, such as cleaning up spills, are handled best with a positive attitude.

PORTRAIT OF A PROFESSIONAL

When thinking about a career in child care, you need to think about whether the job appeals to you, but there's another question to ask. Do you fit the job? To be a child care professional, you need certain qualities. As you read on, think about how well suited you are.

Appreciation of Children

From what you've read so far, you can see that no one could work well with children without having an appreciation for them. Spending time with children means communicating on a different level than you do with adults. Although you have contact with parents and other child care employees, much of your time as an employee in the child care field is spent with children. You have to want that.

Working with children every day requires real enjoyment of being with them. You will learn from them as they learn from you.

THE MULTICULTURAL CLASSROOM

Every early childhood program is a multicultural one. That means the children who enroll are from differing family origins. They represent many cultures and ethnic groups. To get along in society, children must first get along with each other. This is where you come in. As a child care professional, your mission in promoting multiculturalism has two components.

First, you must create a classroom that has a multicultural perspective. The objects children see and the activities they participate in can often have a multicultural base—if you plan that way.

Throughout this text, you will find many suggestions for promoting understanding among all people. You will also learn ways to help children be proud of their heritage.

Second, you must set an example for the children. Children mimic the attitudes and actions of adults. When you are tolerant and open-minded about people of all types, you help children adopt these attitudes. When you accept a child, the other children are more likely to be accepting also. There is room for nothing less as you prepare children for the future.

Appreciating children means participating in activities *with* them, not just watching. Physical contact, such as holding hands and having a child sit on your lap during a story, is part of the job in an early childhood program. Warm relationships are built with children as you listen to their ideas and feelings.

Energy

Children have a high energy level. That means that early childhood professionals need good physical and emotional stamina in order to keep up with them. Caregivers have to stay one step ahead of children, or a classroom quickly gets out of control.

Sense of Humor

A sense of humor is useful in many situations. With children around, humor is common. Their antics and laughter match their level of development. Children love it when you are ready and willing to laugh and be a bit zany with them. You need a serious side that takes care of business and gives steady support, but children also appreciate a more casual side that lets loose and has fun when the occasion is right.

A child care professional is careful, of course, to laugh *with* children, but never *at* them. Children often do and say things that are funny from an adult point of view, but the children don't understand why. Laughter at times like this can hurt a child.

Your sense of humor comes in most handy with children when the unexpected happens. When things don't turn out as you planned or mistakes are made, a willingness to laugh and enjoy the turn of events makes you and the children feel at ease.

Patience

What could be more important to someone who works with children than patience? Children make mistakes. They are often slow at doing things because they haven't perfected their skills yet. Acceptable behavior may not have been mastered. They are

Most children love to giggle, laugh, and have fun. The better able you are to understand children's sense of humor and to join in once in a while, the better you will be at working with them.

still learning self-control, and following rules requires new understanding and effort. You have to be prepared to repeat directions frequently and give many reminders. You will also be continually asked to give explanations. As any parent will tell you, "why?" is a young child's favorite question.

Compassion

Compassion works together with patience. A person with **compassion** *recognizes when others are having problems and wants to be of help.* Children need adults who try to understand and accommodate them. What may seem like a trivial fear or worry to an adult may be critical to a child. Compassionate adults calmly and gently help children with problems that arise.

Many problems are routine ones. A child who hits may simply need help with learning to handle anger more appropriately. A shy child can be shown how to ask to join in a game. Other children need more compassion. As you work with children, you might meet a child who has a serious disease, developmental delays, or a traumatic family life. Special compassion and skills are needed in such situations.

Flexibility

Because children are so different and unpredictable, they can surprise you. Children have spontaneity. **Spontaneity** (SPAHN-tuh-NAY-uh-tee) is *acting impulsively, or without taking time to use thinking and reasoning skills.* Since you never know what will happen next with children, you need to be flexible. A person who can't stand disruptions in routine would have a hard time working with children.

Creativity

People who think creatively are needed in child care. The activities you plan and the way you carry them out will be much more interesting and effective if you are creative. Children don't want to do the same things in the same way over and over again. They enjoy creative experiences, and they learn from them.

Resourcefulness

Resourcefulness is *an ability to find the ways and means to do something.* Just

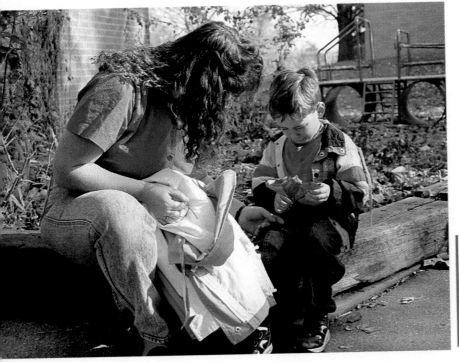

Understanding the intensity of a child's feelings is a key to compassion. Brian shed these tears when his favorite leaf was torn. As a caregiver, how would you have reacted?

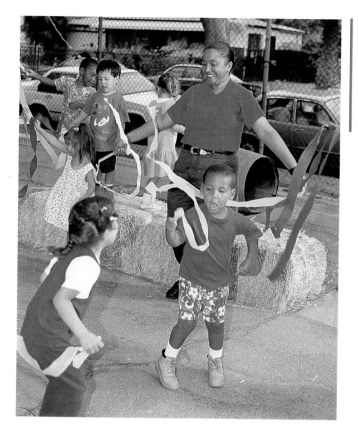

Children learn more and enjoy life in the child care setting more when their days include interesting activities. It takes a creative person to come up with new ideas that bring pleasure as well as opportunities to develop skills.

of these problems? The resourceful person finds opportunities where others give in to obstacles. Resourcefulness enables people to make things happen and get things done.

Sociability

Working in a child care program is a very social job. The schedule allows you little time to be by yourself. In addition to the constant interaction with children, you also work with parents and coworkers. A person who relates well to others, using good communication skills, does better than one who prefers to be alone.

think about what you might need if you were working with children. A low budget could mean that you need supplies and equipment that you can't afford. A child with special problems might need professional help. If you work with disadvantaged children, you might see a need for warm winter coats and mittens. If you were planning a special event, you might need volunteers. How would you solve all

A successful child care program depends on every employee working well with children, parents, and other staff members.

Dedication

WHAT IS DEDICATION?

Devotion, loyalty, and self-sacrifice are words that are often linked to the word dedication. When you are dedicated to a job, you have strong feelings about the value of the job and your desire to do it well. A dedicated person tries not to settle for second best and often contributes personal time, energy, and resources in order to do a job right.

Dedication in Action

Karl took a long look around the room. The walls were covered with rows of pages from coloring books. "Is this *all* the children have been doing?" he wondered. The children in the center had certainly done plenty of coloring. He saw no evidence of other art projects, nothing that would have called for more creativity.

It was Karl's first day on the job. "Things are going to change," he said to himself. Karl's predecessor was gone, and Karl was eager to get to work. "They seem bored," he noticed as he watched the children. "Maybe that's why there is so much bickering. With some

work, we can turn that around too."

In the evening Karl pored over some activity books. He found ideas that would be good for the week and put aside others to include in his plans for the future. After gathering some materials together, Karl headed for the store to buy a few additional items. As he drove, his thoughts were on the center and how he might make improvements. He remembered reading about a particular early childhood course in the university catalog. "I'll check into that on the weekend," he thought. "I need all the help I can get."

Your Analysis

1. List examples of Karl's dedication.

2. Compare Karl's approach to his job with what his predecessor's seemed to be.

3. How will the children be affected by Karl's dedication?

4. How would you have to feel about a job in order to be dedicated to it?

Commitment

Every child care professional should feel a sense of commitment. This means that you are dedicated to doing your best for the children in your care. You *don't* settle for doing the job halfway. You *do* take classes, read related journals, attend conferences, and share ideas with coworkers. You *do* research, plan, and prepare well. Most of all, you care about the children and are dedicated to having a positive effect on their lives.

CAREER OPPORTUNITIES

*I*f you and child care are a good match, why not explore the opportunities available in the field? There may be more of these than you realize.

As a group, *people who work in early childhood programs* are called **early childhood professionals.** Children usually view anyone who spends time with them in the center as a teacher. Actually, all the people who make up the child care team may have any of several titles. They may be called teachers, caregivers, child care workers, teacher's assistants, and teacher's aides. Different levels of training, as defined by each program, are generally required for specific titles. The people who work with children must be able to communicate effectively and work well together. Although there are many other jobs related to the child care field, the focus in this text is on working directly with the children in a preschool setting. You will see the term "teacher" used often throughout the text in that connection.

While the majority of the people in the child care field work directly with the children, some have other positions. A key person in most child care settings is the director. The **director** of a program *may work with children but has the primary*

Those who choose the child care field as a career can expect to spend considerable time working directly with children. To a preschooler, anyone who works with them is likely to be thought of as a "teacher."

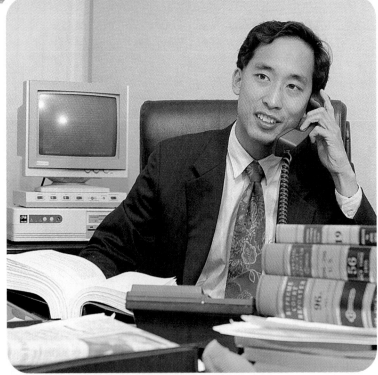

Many people combine an interest in children with other skills in choosing a career. A pediatrician, for example, must be an expert in both child development and medicine. A lawyer might specialize in cases related to children.

Where the Jobs Are

Where might you find a job in the child care field? Here are some ideas:

Battered women's shelters

Child care centers

Child care centers on Native American reservations

Child care law centers

Child care resource and referral agencies

Children's activity coordinator for cruise ship

Crisis nurseries

Departments of human services

Early childhood professional organizations

Elementary schools

Employer-sponsored child care programs

Family education agencies

Head Start

High school lab schools

Homeless shelters

Hospital pediatric units (child life therapy)

Hospitals with sick bay child care services

Mental health agencies

Migrant worker programs

Montessori preschool programs

Nurse/nurse practitioner

Nursery schools

Parks and recreation programs

Phone-a-Friend (hotline for children alone before and after school)

Prisons with in-house child visitation

Programs sponsored by religious organizations

PTA

Salvation Army

State boards of education

United Way

University lab schools

U. S. military bases

Visiting Nurses Association

YWCA, YMCA

---

responsibility of management. The director manages daily operations and guides the staff. Large programs may have a **home visitor**, *a parent educator who goes into a child's home to teach the parent how to guide the children's learning and to answer parents' questions.* A **child care resource and referral specialist** *works mainly on the telephone as a counselor with parents.* Referral specialists assist parents in choosing child care arrangements. Companies that create and market toys, clothing, and equipment for young children employ **child development consultants.** These individuals give child development advice to people who create children's products.

Child care is a fast-growing field. There is a need for lawyers who specialize in child care law and architects who specialize in designing child care center buildings. Publishing companies employ people with child development background to edit and review child care textbooks.

These are not the only opportunities for you in child care. A look at the lists above and on page 48 will give you a sampling of the kinds of places that employ people in child care and some ideas about positions.

Developing Your Portfolio

Making Your Schoolwork Count

Suppose you were an employer interviewing people for a job. The first candidate, Terry, interviews well. Terry describes several work experiences, giving you details about projects developed on previous jobs. Chris also interviews favorably, having projects to talk about too. During your conversation, Chris opens a binder, revealing neatly displayed photographs and actual examples of completed work. You notice how well organized and neat the binder is. You are impressed by the projects shown, observing that they are thorough and creative. It's time to decide who you will hire. Based on what you know, what is your decision?

Employers make decisions like this regularly. When they don't know applicants personally, they look for every clue that will help them choose the right person. When interviewing for the job, Chris stood out because of something extra—a portfolio.

A **portfolio** is *a collection of actual examples of a person's work, put together to show his or her capabilities. The examples are assembled in a binder, folder, or some other type of container that allows for simple, attractive presentation.* You can present a portfolio to a potential employer, as Chris did, or use it to help gain entry into an education or training program.

What goes into a portfolio is not the same for everyone. A journalist could clip his or her best articles and mount them in a binder. An artist might take photographs of certain works to place in an album. As a potential employee in the child care field, you can use the work you do in this course to create a portfolio. At the end of the chapters in this text you will find suggestions for projects that are suitable. You may find other activity ideas there that would also make good portfolio entries. Follow the instructions of your teacher, and include ideas of your own if you like.

Building a portfolio is an ongoing process of evaluation and refinement. To build your portfolio, save your work during the course. As the work you do is evaluated by you and your instructor, make improvements. Sometimes even good work can be better. By continually examining your efforts, you can eliminate some items and include others in order to shape your portfolio.

You will also see what progress you are making in the course. Once you have selectively created a portfolio that satisfies you, your teacher may want to evaluate it as a whole.

Start now to develop a portfolio of your best work in the child care field. If you do, you will make your schoolwork count when you move into the work world.

What Could You Be?

Not everyone who has a job associated with children is a teacher. Have you ever thought about any of these alternatives?

Adoption counselor

Amusement park guide

Architect specializing in child care settings

Art, music, or dance instructor

Athletic coach or assistant

Author of children's literature

Child care law attorney

Child custody mediator

Child development specialist for toy corporations

Children's librarian

Children's museum staff member

Children's photographer

Children's television programmer

Family life educator

Family therapist

Illustrator of children's literature

Newspaper or magazine columnist writing about children

Owner of children's clothing store

Pediatric dentist

Pediatrician

Textbook author

Writer for children's magazines

EDUCATION, TRAINING, AND EXPERIENCE

*I*f you decide to work in the child care field, how will you prepare for the job? The answer depends on which job you seek and where you live. In the United States, there is no uniform standard required for education, training, and experience. Each state establishes its own requirements. As you would guess, different job titles have different requirements. To find out about the requirements for your state, contact the local agency that licenses or regulates child care centers. (Programs in the public schools usually have higher requirements.

How Much Education Is Needed?

HIGH SCHOOL DIPLOMA	TWO-FOUR YEARS OF COLLEGE*
Teacher's aide Teacher's assistant Bus driver Cook Custodian Receptionist Secretary Bookkeeper	Nanny Teacher in child care center Home visitor Center director Assistant director Child care resource and referral specialist
BACHELOR'S DEGREE* **(Four Years of College)**	**MASTER'S DEGREE*** **(Four Years of College Plus Graduate School)**

Parent educator
Educational coordinator
Dietitian
Nutritionist
Family and consumer sciences instructor
University lab school instructor
Parent involvement coordinator
District manager of child care center
    chain
Play therapist in pediatric hospital
    program
Representative for child and adult care
    food program
Licensing specialist
Director of child care resource and
    referral agency
	University or college instructor
	Author of professional journal articles
	Legislative lobbyist
	Social worker
	School psychologist
	Child care consultant
	Music therapist
	Researcher
	Attorney in child care law firm
	Architect with firm specializing in child
	    care settings
	Director of play therapy in hospital

* Specializing in Early Childhood and/or Child Development

The CDA Credential

*I*n some professions, people can earn credentials that show they are qualified for the work they do. The child care field has a credential that may be of interest to you. It was developed in the 1970s when people became concerned about the quality of child care programs. They wanted to make sure that people who care for children have the education and training they need to make them competent caregivers.

The **child development associate (CDA) credential** is *awarded to an applicant after the person demonstrates competency skills in specific areas of child care.* These six areas are listed and described in the Appendix at the back of your text. Both on-the-job experience and course work are required as part of this national credentialing process. A **CDA advisor** *counsels candidates and provides specific training for the credential.*

Many states now require that certain employees have a CDA credential in order for a program to be licensed. You may not need the credential if you plan to obtain a four-year college degree, but you should check to see if it would be useful in connection with whatever goals you set for yourself.

You can apply for a CDA credential once you become eighteen. You must also have a high school diploma or the equivalent. Information about the CDA credential can be obtained from the Council for Early Childhood Professional Recognition, 1341 G Street, NW, Suite 400, Washington, DC 20005-3105.

These requirements can be obtained from your State Board of Education.)

Few, if any, jobs in child care accept less than a high school degree. For specialized positions, advanced education (beyond high school) is required. For teachers, at least two years of college education, specializing in child development, is usually necessary. Two to four years of college may be required of directors. Programs that employ an educational or program director may require a master's degree for the position. The chart on page 49 gives you an idea about the education needed in some states for certain positions in early childhood.

Tip FROM THE Pros

*A*re you interested in volunteering to work with young children? Check to see if there is a social service hotline in your area. They can give you ideas about who needs volunteers.

As you plan for your future, remember that better jobs and better pay are definitely linked to education. In addition, you can work more effectively with children when you have the knowledge that education provides. Setting educational goals is worthwhile. Having something to aim for is the first step to achievement and the rewards it brings.

While formal education and training in high school and college are very valuable, firsthand experience with young children is also an excellent way to learn how to teach and care for young children. By serving as a volunteer or teacher's aide, your training can begin today.

Education and training are keys to success in a child care career. They can help you work more effectively and open doors to opportunities.

Answering these questions will help you decide on a direction. What follows then is action. Talking to people who are knowledgeable about the child care field can provide you with information and ideas. Making plans for any education and training that you need will set you on the right path for your goal. Learning more about children should always be your aim. The rest of this text is a good place to start as you explore your role in child care.

It's your future. Isn't it worth taking the time to do the research needed to make the right career choice?

GETTING READY

*T*he child care field awaits you if you are interested. As the need to serve children and their families grows, the opportunities also grow. The course you are now taking can be a foundation for you, leading toward further education or training and eventually a career.

In her book, *Careers with Young Children—Making Your Decision*, published by the NAEYC (National Association for the Education of Young Children), Judith Seaver advises those who are serious about a child care career to ask themselves:

- Why do I want to work with or for young children?

- What are my skills and abilities?

- What degree of involvement with children is best for me?

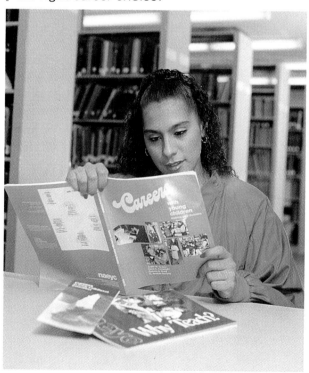

Chapter 2 Review

Reviewing the Facts

1. List four rewards and four drawbacks of working with young children.
2. List six personal characteristics of successful child care professionals.
3. Why is a sense of humor important when working with young children?
4. Define spontaneity. How does being flexible help when working with young children?
5. What is resourcefulness? Describe a resourceful person.
6. Describe at least four positions in the child care field that *do not* involve direct contact with children.
7. What are the training and education requirements for each of the following: (a) teachers; (b) directors; (c) educational or program director?
8. How is a CDA credential earned?
9. What are three questions you should ask yourself when deciding on a child care career?

Thinking Critically

1. Could some aspect of a job be negative to one person and positive to another? Explain.
2. Of all the qualities a person needs for working with children, as listed in the chapter, which one do you think is most important? Why?
3. Suppose the child care field employed many people who did not really enjoy children. What might the impact be on families and society?
4. What do you think would be most enjoyable about working with children?

Activities and Applications

1. **Newspaper Research.** Read the classified section of your newspaper. What opportunities in the field of early childhood are listed? What requirements for education and training are identified?
2. **Career Analysis.** Make two columns on a sheet of paper, labeling them "Reasons Why the Career Is Right for Me" and "Reasons Why the Career Is Wrong for Me." Then under each column list as many reasons as you can think of why a career in the child care field would work for you and why it wouldn't. What do you conclude?

3. **Preparing Questions.** Make a list of questions you would like to have answered about working in the child care field. Then as you complete this course, collect the answers you are looking for and keep a written record of them.

SCHOOL TO WORK

Your Professional Portfolio

Choose three qualities you have that would help you work effectively with children. How could you present these? You might simply write an explanation of each one. You could make a poster or take snapshots that illustrate how you display these qualities. You might even ask responsible people who know you well to write descriptions of how they see the qualities in you. When your project is finished to your satisfaction, save it for possible inclusion in your finalized portfolio.

Observing and Analyzing

Observing Careers

Even if you have narrowed down your career choice to knowing you want to work with children, you may still have some decision making to do. This chapter has shown you that there are many specific job possibilities in the child care field. How will you decide which direction is the right one for you?

This is where observation skills can come in handy. From week to week, you will find yourself in many circumstances where people are working with, or for, children. These are perfect opportunities for you to observe what the jobs are like. You can explore your own interests by noticing the actions of others. Pay attention to what you see. Ask yourself the questions below in order to discover whether or not the career is one you might enjoy:

- What is the work setting like? Is it appealing to you?
- What responsibilities do you see employees performing? Are they ones you would enjoy?
- What problems or difficulties do you see occurring? Would you mind encountering them? Given the right skills, could you handle them?
- How would you describe employee attitudes toward the job? Analyze both positive and negative situations to determine what is causing them. What would your reaction be under the same circumstances?

Choosing the right career requires more exploration than just observation. On the other hand, that's a good place to start. When you make it a point to take notice, you may discover many possibilities that are worth a second look.

Meet Ella Simpson, a child care referral specialist at a child care resource agency. Her primary job is advising parents on how to find and select quality child care. Based on information gathered from parents, she refers them to area child care options that would best meet the family's needs. In this interview, Ella describes the importance of her job and why she finds it rewarding.

Why did you choose this career?

"I find great satisfaction in helping parents make sure their children are cared for properly. The referrals I make are based on individual families' needs, such as the age of the children, how much money parents can afford to pay for child care, and the need for public transportation. I also respond to special requests and situations. For instance, some parents prefer child care in a person's home; others prefer center-based care. Parents may have a disabled child who needs child care providers with specialized training. All of this information is taken into account before I provide referrals."

What education and skills do you need?

"Most referral agencies require specialists to have at least a two-year associate's degree in a field related to children. Many require a four-year bachelor's degree in social work, child development, or early childhood education. In my position understanding how children grow and develop is important. I also need to be aware of the child care programs that are available. Parents trust me to match their child to the appropriate service.

"Communication skills are necessary in my job. I need to be an alert listener. The ability to communicate clearly with people from all different backgrounds is a real asset. I find the ability to speak both English and Spanish very helpful.

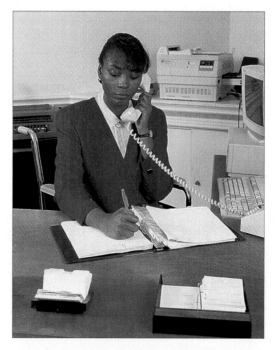

"I've always been a 'people person,' so talking with parents is a pleasure. I understand the hard choices they face when making child care arrangements. Some parents call our agency when they are unhappy with their child care provider. I'm sympathetic to their concerns, which helps them relax and calmly plan ways to solve their problem.

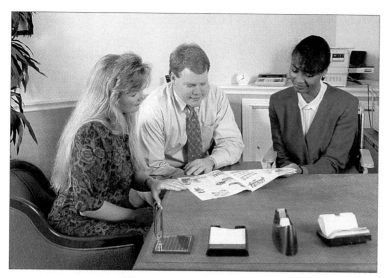

"Most referral agencies use computers to organize and maintain information about local child care programs. My computer skills are very valuable."

What is a typical day on the job like?

"I work mornings and afternoons three times a week. Two days a week I work afternoons and evenings until 8:30 p.m. This is so parents who work daytime hours can use our services.

"Most days begin with listening to our answering machine. Then I return calls to parents who left requests for services. Between callbacks I accept new phone calls, which can last up to half an hour. While doing this, I take detailed notes on the type of care parents want. During our conversation, I give tips on what to look for in quality care, stressing that the child care choice is their personal decision. After the conversation, I enter the information into the computer. The computer matches available options with the family's specific needs. Then I mail out a list of child care options, including brochures and educational literature on the importance of quality child care.

"I spend about four hours a day on the telephone. The other hours I may spend organizing our lending library of toys and books, developing new brochures for parents, or speaking to civic groups on opening new child care programs. Like other professionals, I attend staff meetings, complete paperwork, and participate in child care conferences."

What is most challenging about your job?

"The hardest part is not having enough child care enrollment slots for all the children who need care. Finding care for infants and school-age children is especially challenging. With more parents working outside the home, the demand for child care services is growing. Telling parents that there are no available child care spaces for their child is very hard."

What do you like best about your work?

"It's gratifying when a parent calls to say I helped find just what they needed for their child. Quality child care is a big worry for families; it's good to ease their anxiety."

SHARE YOUR THOUGHTS

1. If you were a referral specialist, how would you describe quality child care to parents?
2. What questions would you ask parents to determine the type of child care they need or prefer?
3. Why is it important for a referral specialist to have good communication skills?
4. What part of being a referral specialist sounds most interesting to you? What part would you like the least?

CHILD GROWTH AND DEVELOPMENT

CHAPTER

Reflections

"Even though classes and textbooks teach lessons about children, sometimes the best ones are learned through real-life experiences. That happened to me one morning during my first week on the job. Clarissa, who looked to be about age five, was not happy. I watched as she obstinately refused to take off her coat, repeatedly saying 'no' to the teacher. A picture started forming in my mind about Clarissa, and it wasn't a complimentary one. I even made a comment to another teacher about Clarissa's behavior. 'Do you know how old Clarissa is?' the teacher asked me. As I shook my head, she replied, 'She's almost three.' I know my eyes widened and my mouth dropped open. Clarissa's behavior didn't match her appearance at all, but it did match her age. I vowed then and there that I would never again be so quick to judge. That's one decision that has helped me greatly in my work with children."

—Ming

Chapter 3

Basic Principles of Development

CHAPTER OBJECTIVES

- Explain why understanding child development is important.

- Identify child development theorists.

- Identify and briefly explain the areas of development.

- Describe some principles of development.

- Analyze the impact of heredity and environment.

- Explain how self-esteem affects development.

- Recognize and be able to make objective observations.

Terms to Learn

- cephalocaudal
- child development
- cognitive development
- emotions
- maturation
- motor skills
- proximodistal
- self-concept
- self-esteem
- sequence
- values

Kendra Taylor glanced at the faces of the children in her story group. All the children were close in age. Their attention was focused on Kendra. She was holding a surprise box, from which she was about to pull a special item that would introduce the story she planned to read. The children were eager to discover what would emerge from the box—all except one child.

Even though he was the same age as the rest, Jackson just didn't react as the others did. "Why isn't he interested in the story?" Kendra wondered. Again, she had lead him to the story group, while the rest of the children quickly moved there on their own. Jackson often seemed only remotely interested in the stories Kendra read. What was humorous to the other children had little effect on him. Something just didn't seem right. Of course, each child had his or her own personality, habits, and characteristics, but the picture of Jackson that was forming in Kendra's mind was causing her concern. It was time to talk to the rest of the staff. They would compare observations and explore whether or not Jackson needed some special help. Kendra knew that taking action now could mean a great deal to Jackson in the future.

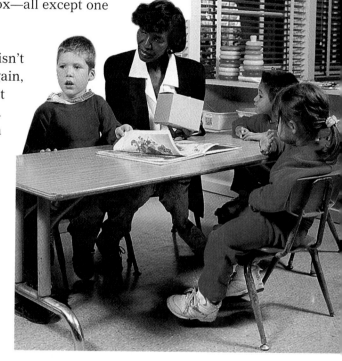

UNDERSTANDING DEVELOPMENT

Kendra Taylor is a teacher in a child care program. One of the things that makes her especially effective in her job is her understanding of children. If you were in Kendra's position, how would you decide whether Jackson has a problem that needs diagnosis and treatment? Coming to such conclusions is not easy, but Kendra uses her knowledge and understanding of child development to help her.

Child development is *the pattern of change that occurs as children grow from birth to adolescence.* The study of child development includes descriptions of how, when, why, and in what order changes

occur. When you understand what a child's capabilities should typically be at different age levels, you know what to expect from the child. You notice when a child is developmentally ahead and needs extra challenges. You also notice when something is not right.

For example, someone who isn't aware of the age at which children usually put complete sentences together may not notice that a child is having language problems. Undiagnosed, the problem gets worse. Other problems arise, and the child suffers further developmental difficulties. An alert observer, on the other hand, sees what is happening and seeks help that enables the child to improve his or her language skills and move forward developmentally.

The people who work in child care today have an especially large responsibility for monitoring the development of children. With so many parents employed, more children than ever before are spending time in group care settings. A caregiver may spend more waking hours with a child than the parents do. For this reason, child care professionals must keep a sharp eye on how children are progressing. Knowledge helps provide the confidence they need to handle children correctly.

THE CONTRIBUTION OF THEORISTS

Much of what is known about children and their development is the result of years of study by many researchers. Hundreds of years ago children were thought to be miniature adults. Few realized their special needs and characteristics. As interest in children and a desire to make their lives better grew, so did the need for information about them. To learn more, researchers developed and tested theories, a standard method of scientific research. They observed children and reached conclusions. Attitudes toward children have been shaped by what people discovered. The way society handles children has been strongly influenced by those who study child development.

Many researchers, or theorists, have contributed to the body of knowledge about children that exists today. As might be expected, the impact of some research has been greater than that of others. The conclusions reached have not always been accepted by everyone. Over time some theories have been replaced by newer ideas. The result over the years, however, has been an increased understanding and appreciation of children.

Certain theorists stand out when it comes to the study of children. Take a look at the chart on pages 62-63. There you will find information on several past and present theorists. You might even recognize some of the names. As you read further in this text, you will learn more about the work of some of these individuals. Keep in mind that these people are just part of the picture. Researchers at universities and elsewhere are continually exploring topics that relate to children. Through the efforts of all, people learn more and more about enriching the lives of children and the families that support them.

In 1921 Swiss researcher Jean Piaget began to study how children learn. His 50-year effort in this area has made a significant contribution to what is understood about intellectual development.

AREAS OF DEVELOPMENT

*I*n order to study children effectively, researchers look at specific topics. You, too, will be able to understand child development better if you look at the parts that make up the whole. Child development is often broken down into these areas of development: physical, intellectual, emotional, social, and moral. In this unit of the text, you will see how children change at different ages in each of these areas.

Physical Development

Physical development includes the growth of the body as well as its abilities. Growth in height and weight is an obvious aspect of physical development. Growth is most dramatic during infancy and adolescence. As children develop physically, they gain new abilities. *Those abilities that depend on the use and control of muscles* are called **motor skills.**

Coordination and balance accompany physical development. Learning them poses many challenges for children. Think what it would be like if you tried to walk a tightrope for the first time. Would you be shaky and

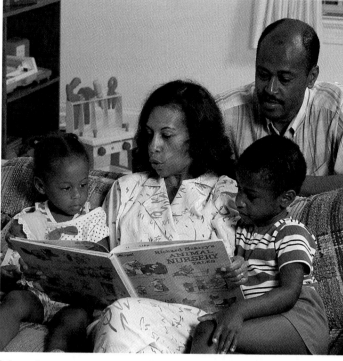

In what ways can reading to children help their intellectual development?

insecure? Would you fall? Children experience these sensations over and over again as they try out new physical skills and work toward mastering them.

Intellectual Development

Intellectual development, which is often called **cognitive development,** *occurs as children learn to think, understand, reason, and use language.* Although the learning process is still not fully understood, research has provided much knowledge about what takes place. Infants enter the world

Physical skills develop with age and practice. Why is this toy a good choice for improving motor skills?

Child Development Theorists

Jean Piaget (1896-1980) Swiss psychologist, biologist, and educator	Piaget believed that human cognitive development is a result of adaptation to the physical environment. This adaptation results in organized patterns of behavior and perception. Through observation of children, Piaget identified how the development of a child's thought processes and intellect proceeds through a series of stages.
Lawrence Kohlberg (1927-1987) Cognitive development theorist	Kohlberg's theory describes stages in the development of moral reasoning. Each level of development reflects the relationship between the self and society's rules and expectations. The lowest level relates to obedience and avoidance of punishment, and the highest level relates to conscience and ethical principles.
Erik Erikson (1902-1994) Psychoanalytical theorist	Erikson studied the development of personality by dividing life into stages of psychological crisis. Erikson believed that personality characteristics are developed according to how each individual adapts at each stage.
Alfred Binet (1857-1911) Psychologist; devised first intelligence test	Binet believed that intelligence increases with age, and is reflected in how children make judgments, understand the meanings of words, and solve problems. Binet's test showed the relationship between chronological age and mental age. A revised version of this test is called the Stanford-Binet Intelligence Scale, an IQ test.
Urie Bronfenbrenner (1917—) Developmental psychologist and professor at Cornell University	Bronfenbrenner believes that behavior and development should be observed in natural settings over long periods of time. Bronfenbrenner defines the ecology of human development as a reciprocal relationship between the self and a complex ecological environment.
Benjamin Bloom (1913—) Psychologist	According to Bloom, 50 percent of adult intelligence is achieved by age four, making early childhood education the most important time in a child's life. Bloom's Taxonomy ranks thought processes from the least to the most difficult cognitive levels and gives examples of tasks at each level.
Maria Montessori (1870-1952) Italian physician and educator	Montessori believed that children actively construct their own knowledge by using their senses. The Montessori method of teaching stresses that children learn at their own pace and level of development. Montessori preschools use specially designed materials that encourage individual learning through stimulation of the five senses.

Jerome Bruner (1915—) Psychologist	Bruner developed a structured educational program based on Piaget's hierarchy of stages. Bruner believes that a theory of development must be linked to theories of knowledge and of instruction to have merit. Bruner's theory of instruction suggests that intellectual development occurs in successive steps of representation. These stages are not linked to the child's chronological age, and environmental factors affect the rate at which children progress through the stages.
Rudolf Dreikurs (1897-1972) Family educator and child psychologist	Dreikurs maintained that an attempt to understand why a child misbehaves is important when providing guidance. Parents and caregivers must learn to observe a child objectively rather than seeing their own difficulties. Dreikurs developed techniques that allow children to experience the actual consequences of misbehavior.
Haim Ginott (1922-1973) Psychologist	Ginott believed that children should be allowed to express their feelings, so they can recognize and face their emotions. In his book *Between Parent and Child*, Ginott gives specific suggestions on how to help children become aware of their feelings and to handle emotional outbursts.
B. F. Skinner (1904-1990) Psychologist and behavioral theorist	Skinner's research of operant conditioning used a number of experiments to illustrate how learning is influenced through positive and negative reinforcement. Skinner believed that in order to achieve desired behavior from children, parents should reward or punish existing behavior.
Sigmund Freud (1856-1939) Psychoanalytical theorist and founder of psychiatry	Freud believed that personality develops through a predictable pattern of psychosexual stages. As children move through each of these stages, the source of pleasure moves to different areas of the body. Freud believed that emotional or psychological problems in adulthood are related to a child's satisfaction or dissatisfaction with how basic needs are met in each stage.
Anna Freud (1895-1982) Daughter of Sigmund Freud and analyst for Erik Erikson	Freud's work with mentally disabled children was influenced by the psychoanalytic theorists. She believed that all children go through normal stages of psychological development, and psychoanalysts must fully understand these stages through direct observation of children. In London in 1938, Freud established the Hampstead Child Therapy Course and Clinic, which treats children with mental disabilities and trains workers in childhood therapy.

ready and eager to learn, relying mostly on their senses—sight, hearing, taste, smell, and touch. The early years bring rapid changes in a child's knowledge and thinking abilities. Throughout childhood, complex intellectual processes are gradually developed, including the ability to analyze, evaluate, and solve problems.

Emotional Development

As children develop emotionally, they acquire *feelings about themselves, others, and the world*. These feelings are called **emotions.** Some emotions are associated with positive (good) feelings and others with negative (bad) feelings. Happiness and contentment, for example, are positive, and anger, fear, and frustration are negative. Both positive and negative emotions are experienced by everyone at one time or another.

When emotional development is at its best, children experience more positive emotions than negative ones. Positive emotions indicate that children feel good about themselves and what is going on in their lives. Children who have plenty of positive feelings are likely to be emotionally well adjusted.

Even though part of living means having negative emotions, children learn to understand and manage them as they develop. They discover that negative emotions are acceptable, and sometimes expected, under certain circumstances. For example, sorrow over a loss and anger over mistreatment are justifiable. What children need to learn is how to handle such emotions appropriately and recover from them.

Good emotional development depends heavily on the treatment a child receives. For example, children learn to give affection when they receive it. They learn to think favorably of themselves when people around them are supportive and loving. They learn to treat others well when they are treated well. Emotional development is very complex. As you learn more about it, you will see how important the role of a caregiver is in this area.

Very young children express their emotions—both positive and negative—very openly. Older children have better emotional control.

Social Development

As children discover how to relate to other people, social development takes place. They learn the skills they need to get along with people and to fit into society. Many interpersonal skills are part of social training. Children learn to play together, share, and trade. They discover how to settle fights with words, rather than hitting, kicking, pushing, or biting.

When children develop socially, they begin to understand that society has rules to live by. Getting along well means identifying and obeying the rules. Children also learn to care about the feelings and thoughts of oth-

Group play activities give children a chance to develop and practice social skills.

ers as they try to see issues from different points of view.

Proper social development serves children well. With it, they are liked and accepted by many people. Without it, they may feel isolated and different.

Moral Development

Moral development is closely linked to social development. Moral development comes as children begin to understand and act according to what is right and wrong. They develop *beliefs and attitudes about what is important.* These are called **values.** Families teach many values, and religion and society teach them too. In any case, what children learn has social impact

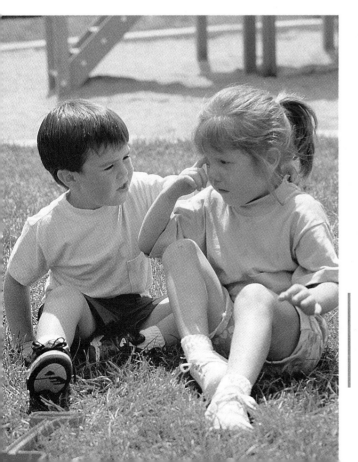

because it affects how they interact with other people.

In most child care settings, moral guidance is based on such widely held values as respect, sharing, and friendship. Families and religions don't necessarily agree on all moral issues and values. Learning basic societal values, however, is an important part of moral development in early childhood. With a sensitive approach, the child care professional can handle this aspect of development effectively.

Part of moral development is learning values. Certain basic values can be promoted in the child care setting. A child who learns to care and become involved when someone else is hurting is adopting the values of respect and compassion for others.

Knowledge

WHAT IS KNOWLEDGE?

You must have knowledge in any field in order to succeed. In child care you cannot recognize progress, encourage development, and identify problems unless you know how and when development takes place. Through study and experience, people gain the knowledge they need. Knowledge is a necessary resource for making decisions and taking action.

Knowledge in Action

"Never overlook the simple solutions." This statement from her nursing school days always seemed to pop back into Minda Rahami's mind. As a nurse, she divided her time among several schools in the community. As she completed some paperwork on nine-year-old Bernadette, that often remembered thought momentarily came to her again.

Bernadette's father Luke had come in personally to see her a few weeks ago. He was very concerned about the changes he was seeing in Bernadette. "She used to be a good student," Luke had explained to Ms. Rahami, "but now it takes her all night to finish a simple homework assignment, and she complains that her teacher doesn't give them enough time to finish their work. Bernadette says the other children tease her about being a 'slowpoke.' She's been complaining about headaches, and now she doesn't feel good enough to go to school on some days. I don't know what the problem is, but I am worried. She used to love school, and now she dreads it."

"Let me have a talk with her," Ms. Rahami suggested to Luke, "and then I'll get back to you. We may want her to have a physical exam."

Later, as Ms. Rahami talked with Bernadette and watched her carefully, she had a thought. "Bernadette, we're going to give you a little eye test. I'm going to have you look at some shapes on the wall, and you can tell me what you see."

Several weeks later, with a new pair of glasses, Bernadette was again enjoying school. Her headaches and unhappiness had disappeared. Luke was happy, too, and grateful that he had found someone capable to turn to for help.

Your Analysis

1. Why does Ms. Rahami need to be knowledgeable in her work with children?

2. What knowledge did Ms. Rahami use to help solve Bernadette's problem?

3. Explain how this situation illustrates the concept that growth in one area affects the development of other areas. Give specific examples.

DEVELOPMENTAL PRINCIPLES

*T*o understand development, you need to be aware of certain principles. As you observe children, you will see examples of all the principles described here.

Development Is Interrelated

You can study the different areas of development separately, but you can't isolate them in real life. Inevitably, one area has impact on another.

Suppose you were helping a young child learn self-feeding skills. This is a physical skill that requires the use of small muscles in the hand. How successful would the child be without intellectual skills too? With each attempt at self-feeding, the child uses trial and error to learn a little more. Gradually,

thinking abilities combine with physical skills to help the child master the goal of self-feeding.

As you think about other specific examples, you will see how all areas of development fit together. Because the different areas stimulate and reinforce each other, problems in one area can affect others. Likewise, promoting development in any area has a positive effect on total development.

Development Is Similar for All

Development follows a similar pattern for everyone. Whatever a child's background, development occurs in approximately the same way for all. Even children from different parts of the world go through the same stages. For example, all children sit before standing, and stand before walk-

Skills in Action

Physical Development. Jason and Joe utilized physical skills to place each block precisely.

Intellectual Development. The building process—from planning to choosing appropriate blocks—depended upon intellectual skills. How are they using the structure?

Social Development. The boys worked together to plan, make, and use the building. They may also have learned their building skills by playing with other children.

Emotional Development. Persistence is needed to finish a project, especially if problems arise.

Although you will learn what an "average" child of a certain age can do, in reality each child develops at his or her own rate. These children are all the same age. What variations in physical growth can you identify?

ing. Unless there are problems, such as a physical or mental disability, everyone eventually develops similar skills and behaviors. *The gradual process of development as each stage unfolds* is called **maturation.**

Rates of Development Are Individual

The interesting thing about development—and the challenging part for caregivers—is that it doesn't occur at exactly the same rate for every child. All children experience growth and develop new abilities at a pace that is unique to each individual.

If rates of development are different, then how can a caregiver tell when a child should be learning a new skill or reaching a new growth level? Researchers have found that patterns of development are predictable, especially during early childhood. They report on the abilities of the "average" child, but what does "average" mean? In mathematics, when you average the numbers 5, 6, 8, and 9, what do you get? The answer is 7, a number that is not even in the original list. If these were children's ages, the average age of the group would be seven, yet not one child is seven. An average, therefore, gives information, but it is not exact.

Labeling Developmental Stages

*O*ften when you read about children and child development, terms like "infant," "toddler," and "preschooler" are used to identify developmental stages. The problem with such labels is that not everyone uses them in the same way. You may find, for example, that "toddler" refers to ages twelve to twenty-four months in one reference and twelve to thirty-six months in another. In this text, the labels for developmental stages refer to these age ranges: infants—birth to twelve months; toddlers—twelve to thirty-six months; preschoolers—ages three to five; and school-age children—six to twelve years.

These stages provide an organized way to study child development. Because children change so much at each stage, however, the descriptions you will read in the chapters ahead are often tied to specific ages within each range.

As you study children and their development, be alert for variations. The labels you find in other references may differ somewhat from the ones used in this text. That doesn't matter. What does matter is the ages that are described. What matters even more is understanding that the descriptions and guidelines are only general ones.

As an example, child development researchers have noted that the "average" child walks at twelve months of age. This means that at least half of the children researchers observed had accomplished this skill by twelve months. The other half did so after that age. Children who walk at ten months of age are not abnormal. Neither are children who walk at fourteen months. Knowing that most children walk around the age of twelve months is simply a guidepost to help you assess whether children are developing properly. When a child is significantly outside the average pattern and possibly other problems are noted, investigation is in order. The child may need assistance with development.

Sometimes the same child may experience different rates of development in different areas. For example, in one family the decision was made to wait an extra year before their child entered kindergarten. The child had strong abilities intellectually but didn't seem ready socially for a school experience. A year later the child's social development had caught up, and the child was much better prepared to enter school.

Researchers have found that boys tend to develop more slowly than girls. Generally, boys' development lags from two to six months behind girls of the same age. The causes of this difference in rate of development are still unknown. Understanding the difference, however, helps caregivers react more appropriately to children of both genders (male and female).

Avoiding Comparisons

People who care for children need to guard against evaluating development in a judgmental way. Children who develop certain skills more quickly than others are not superior, just as those who lag a bit behind are not inferior. Eventually, most children catch up and master the same skills. Comparing children or making them feel inadequate or better only leads to trouble.

Development Is Ongoing

Although development is emphasized in the early years of life, it does not stop at a certain age. Sometimes the pace is slower than at other times, but development still continues. Because people change throughout life in many ways, the process is often referred to as *life-span development*. You have seen examples of this—a young adult who becomes independent; an adult who seeks a career change; an older person who gains wit and wisdom. All of these, and more, are part of the total picture that makes up development. There can be no denying, however, that helping a child get off to a good start developmentally sets the stage for satisfying development over a lifetime.

Development Is Sequential

Could you spell a word if you didn't know the letters of the alphabet? Of course, the answer is "no." In the same way that you learned the alphabet before you learned to spell, the skills that children learn during development build upon those acquired earlier. Development follows an orderly **sequence**, or *step-by-step pattern*. Several principles describe in general the sequences of development as shown in the illustration below.

Sequences of Development

From Top to Bottom ▲

Children progressively master body movement and coordination from the head downward. This is called the **cephalocaudal** (SEF-uh-luh-KAWD-ull) principle of development. First children can lift their head and then the trunk of their body. Eventually they coordinate their whole body in order to walk.

From Center to Outside ▼

Children develop from the center of their body outward. Development progresses from the spine to the arms and legs and then to the fingers and toes. This is called the **proximodistal** (PRAHK-suh-MOE-DISS-tull) principle of development. Children can use their shoulders and swing their arms in large circles before they can coordinate and maneuver their wrists and fingers.

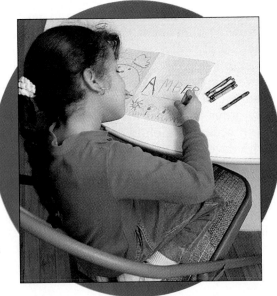

WHAT AFFECTS DEVELOPMENT?

You only need to look at the children you know to see that development doesn't bring about the same results for each one. What reasons can there be for all the differences that occur in how children develop? Sometimes circumstances of birth have an effect. A child may be born with abnormalities. Problems during prenatal development or the birth process itself may result in developmental difficulties. Injury or illness during the early years of life may also interfere.

While these situations do not occur with all children, two factors do: heredity and environment. Each has a strong impact on how children develop. Together, they bring up a question that has fascinated researchers for a long time. Which has the greater influence on children, heredity or environment?

Heredity and Environment

Children are born with a biological makeup that defines what they are like. This biological makeup, called *heredity,* is received from parents at conception. *Environment* also shapes what a child is. Environmental influences are external, including such things as people, surroundings, and experi-

From Large to Small

Children develop control over large muscles before small muscles. For example, children can run and jump before they are able to throw or catch a ball accurately.

From General to Specific ▼

Development progresses gradually from general to specific. Attempts to acquire new abilities start out simple and become increasingly complex. For instance, children jump up and down with both feet before being able to hop on one foot. Running comes first and skipping later. Babies make sounds before learning to form specific words.

ences. How much influence do heredity and environment have on people? Can one overcome the other? Though scientists and researchers have been studying heredity and environment for many years, they still don't have all the answers.

People who believe that heredity and environment are limiting have a tough time explaining some situations. They forget about the child who finds ways to overcome an inherited disability and the person who becomes highly successful in life despite limited resources while growing up. For the child care professional, looking at the possibilities is better than focusing on any limitations caused by heredity *or* environment. If you see limits in children, they will see them too. You have the opportunity to help children develop as fully as possible. Frustrating them by expecting

Tip FROM THE Pros

Sometimes you help build self-esteem in children in little ways that you are hardly aware of. Self-esteem builders can become habits if you consciously make the effort until they are automatic. Try these: smiling at children; making eye contact; giving a pat on the head or shoulder; using positive words, like "great try" or "good job"; listening one-on-one whenever possible.

too much is not the answer, but encouraging them onward and upward toward new goals is. Children need positive experiences for good development. They can often make great strides with your help. You may be surprised at what can happen when you believe in a child's capabilities.

Self-Esteem

Suppose that a new toy has been placed on the playground at a child care center. It is a colorful, heavy-duty bicycle with two wheels. Jarod sees the bicycle for the first time, and he can't wait to try it out. He jumps on and makes several clumsy attempts to ride. He laughs at his mistakes and forgets about the spills, determined that he will master this new challenge. Bill also sees the bicycle. Inside he yearns to ride it, but something tells him not to try. He is sure he will fall. Instead of taking a turn, he stands back to watch. Eventually he walks away, with a feeling of disappointment inside.

In this situation, Bill and Jarod illustrate a principle that should be foremost in your thinking: children need a good self-concept and high self-esteem in order to develop and function well in the world.

Self-concept is *the picture individuals carry in their mind of who they are, what they can do, and what they are like.* Self-concept is developed through interaction with people and surroundings. Many

Positive interactions help children build a positive self-concept. With very young children, parents and other caregivers have the greatest influence.

researchers believe a child's self-concept is basically formed by age six.

Self-esteem is *how much people do, or do not, like the picture they have of themselves.* It is a sense of self-worth. Self-esteem may be high, low, or anywhere in between. When people feel good about themselves, they are said to have high self-esteem. Children who are developing high self-esteem are positive and optimistic. They enjoy trying new things and meeting new people.

When children think negatively about themselves, they have low self-esteem. They avoid trying something new because they expect to fail. If they don't try, however, opportunities for the positive input they need from caregivers are limited. If they try and do fail, low self-esteem is reinforced. Sometimes children don't work very hard in school because they think too poorly of themselves. Success isn't consistent with their self-concept or self-esteem.

Throughout this book, ways to build self-esteem will be identified. How children are cared for, parented, educated, and disciplined affects self-esteem. Providing experiences that build high self-esteem is the best gift you could ever give a child. It is a key factor in fostering good development.

OBSERVING CHILDREN

All that you learn about children and their development comes to life when you see the principles in action.

Practice promotes your observation skills. Now is the time to start. As you progress through this course, look for opportunities to watch children in a more thoughtful manner than you ever have before. Begin in little ways, looking for the signs of development that you will read about in this unit. You will have observation assignments, but you can practice on your own. Every effort you make in this area will contribute toward making you a more effective child care professional in the future.

THE MULTICULTURAL CLASSROOM

Are individuality and confidence traits that you would encourage children to develop? Very likely your answer is "yes." Like many others, you may believe that these qualities are part of high self-esteem. Not everyone agrees.

In some Asian countries, for example, children are taught that conformity is better than individuality. Not conforming can mean defiance or not fitting in. A sibling who strives to be "like" a brother or sister rather than "different" gains respect. Not drawing attention to yourself is preferred.

Likewise in these cultures, a child who demonstrates confidence may seem lacking in modesty. Since modesty is highly valued, confidence is not.

As a child care professional, you need to be sensitive to the viewpoints of other cultures. Children can be confused by contradictions. Learn about the cultures represented in your classroom. You may want to modify the way you handle some situations. Talk with parents. Invite them to observe the program, where they can see your methods in action. When both sides develop understanding, everything goes more smoothly.

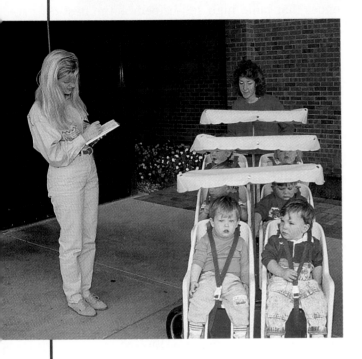

wrote objectively and one, subjectively. An *objective* expression uses facts without the interference of personal feelings or prejudices. A s*ubjective* expression, on the other hand, reflects personal judgments. Which of these terms describes the way Rachel handled her observations? If you said "objective," you are right. Rachel described what happened without interpreting and evaluating. Note how Todd conveyed his opinion, not just what he saw, when he reported on the scene.

When you observe children, use Rachel's example. You should write objectively. Objective observations do not reach conclusions. They simply record facts that can

Rachel and Todd were watching the children in a center from a corner of the room. As they observed, a scene involving two children unfolded. Later, Rachel and Todd finalized their notes on what they saw. Study carefully what each of them said:

Rachel: "Sherise got angry and stood up. Her face became red. She turned to Felipe and said in a harsh tone, 'Those are my crayons! You can't use them.' She grabbed a crayon from Felipe's hand and sat back down to continue working on the picture she was drawing. Felipe walked away without a word."

Todd: "Sherise suddenly displayed aggressive behavior as she confronted Felipe over the use of materials at the art table. Felipe was pretty meek about it. Sherise showed that she is a domineering child."

Todd and Rachel wrote in very different ways about what they observed. One

Objective or Subjective?

Can you recognize objective writing? Analyze each of the following pairs of statements, deciding which ones are objective and which are subjective:

- Tim was afraid to enter the child care center.
- Tim had a look of fear on his face as his father led him through the door of the center.

- The children walked in several directions around chairs, tables, and toy shelves in order to get to the story circle.
- The furnishings in the center were poorly arranged.

- Lee grabbed the clay from Marta's hands.
- Lee showed his nasty nature while sitting next to Marta during the art activity.

- Two samples of children's artwork decorated the walls of the center.
- There wasn't enough artwork displayed in the center.

- Bethany was too frustrated to finish her project.
- Bethany tried to apply glue to the paper airplane three times before giving up.

later be interpreted by professionals who have the necessary expertise. Often professionals, those well trained in child development, medicine, psychiatry, or psychology, use many observations to reach conclusions about a child. Only when they have carefully documented observations that are truly objective can they reach accurate conclusions.

As you build your observation skills, learn to be objective. Like the professionals, you may eventually be called upon to analyze and reach conclusions about the behavior of children. With objective observations, you will be better able to build a true picture of a child and provide the right support.

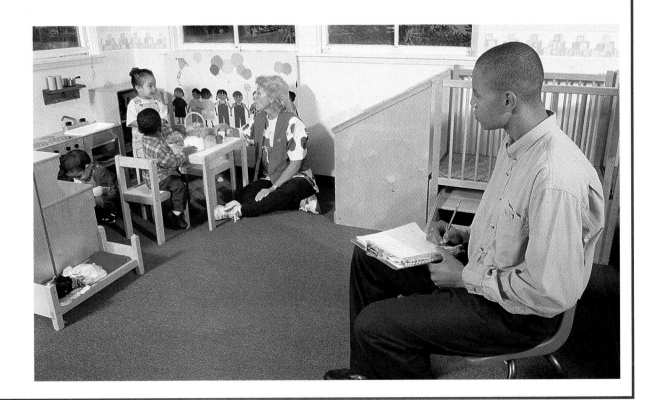

Chapter 3 Review

Chapter Summary

- To guide and care for children appropriately, knowledge of child development is required.
- Many theorists have contributed to knowledge about children and their development.
- Child development can be divided into different areas of study.
- Development includes many changes in the way children look, act, feel, and function.
- The different areas of development affect each other as children grow and change.
- Even though development follows a similar pattern for everyone, children have individual styles and rates of development.
- Children develop in predictable step-by-step sequences that build on each other.
- Heredity and environment influence development.
- Self-esteem affects development.

Reviewing the Facts

1. Why is it important for those who work with children to understand child development?
2. Name three theorists and briefly describe their contributions to the body of knowledge about child development.
3. List and briefly describe the five areas of development.
4. List five principles of development.
5. Can you accurately predict when a child will accomplish a developmental skill? Explain your answer.
6. Should the child who develops at a slower pace than others be considered inferior to the rest? Explain your answer.
7. Explain four principles that describe the sequential nature of development.
8. Is potential limited by heredity and environment? Explain your answer.
9. Why do caregivers need to help children develop high self-esteem?
10. Explain the difference between objective and subjective observations.

Thinking Critically

1. If a child care professional has limited knowledge of child development, what impact might this have on the children under his or her care?
2. How are multiple areas of development related to each of these skills: (a) walking; (b) grasping objects; (c) speaking; (d) learning independence.
3. Which do you think has greater impact on a child, heredity or environment? Explain.
4. Could the self-esteem level of a child care professional have an effect on the children in his or her care? Explain.

Activities and Applications

1. **Theorists.** Choose a theorist to research. Prepare a paper or give an oral report to the class.
2. **Values.** Work with a partner to list values that might be acceptable to teach to all children in a child care setting. Compare your list with those of others.
3. **Self-Esteem.** Observe young children in a public

setting, such as a mall or park. Make a list of specific behaviors that show high self-esteem.

4. **Analyzing Heredity and Environment.** Make a list of traits and abilities you believe you have inherited from your parents. Then write down any traits and abilities that you believe have been influenced by your environment. Do any items fit in both lists? Summarize your observations.

Your Professional Portfolio

Develop a self-esteem checklist for evaluating the self-esteem of preschoolers. You might use a question format, including such items as: Does the child participate willingly in activities? Does the child play with other children? Is the child able to complete tasks regularly with reasonable success? Refine the checklist as you complete this course and include it in your portfolio.

Observing and Analyzing

Studying Children's Development

The study of children's development is not limited to the classroom. Sometimes simple, everyday situations provide a spontaneous opportunity to observe the concepts you have studied in your classroom. Here are some ideas:

- **A Trip to the Park.** Observe the playground area designated for young children. Look at the types of equipment and watch how children use each one. What motor skills are demonstrated by children of different ages as they use the swings? If there is a large climbing apparatus that has multiple functions, such as a jungle gym, crawling tubes, climbing net, and slide, describe the difference in mastery of motor skills between the youngest and oldest participants. Do they all use the jungle gym and slide the same way?

- **Restaurants.** When you visit restaurants, fast food or other types, note what provisions are made for children. What accommodations does the restaurant offer for children who are too small for the chairs? Booster seats and high chairs? Why do the younger children create more spills and messy areas? What motor skills does the child need to eat the meals sold specifically for children? If there is an outdoor play area, why are some areas age- or size-restricted? How does the design of the tables, chairs, and play area relate to the children's development?

- **Watching Television.** Observe commercials shown during children's programs. What kinds of products are advertised? What appeals are used? How might self-esteem be influenced when children see items they want and later get? What if they do not get what they see and want?

- **The Toy Store.** Observe a selection of toys in a toy store to identify those that promote different types of development. Which toys focus on these different areas of development: physical, intellectual, social, and emotional? In what ways do some toys promote multiple areas of development? Which toys, if any, have very little value in promoting development?

Chapter 4

Understanding Infants

CHAPTER OBJECTIVES

- Identify and define reflexes infants have at birth.

- Identify signs of physical, intellectual, emotional, and social development in infancy.

- Describe the sensorimotor period as presented by Piaget.

- Describe three types of temperament and explain how temperament affects personality development.

Terms to Learn

- attachment behavior
- bonding
- egocentric
- eye-hand coordination
- infancy
- nurture
- object permanence
- perceptual motor skills
- reflexes
- sensorimotor period
- stranger anxiety
- temperament
- vocalizations

For ten-month-old Jacob, a shopping trip to the supermarket was an adventure. It was also an opportunity for development.

First, his nanny Andrea held his hands while she walked him to the front door of the house. Then she swooped him into her arms while he squealed with delight. Jacob loved the feeling of walking, although he couldn't quite manage it on his own yet. Even at his young age, he was eager to move in the direction of independence.

As they drove to the supermarket, Andrea talked animatedly to Jacob. She pointed to objects outside the car and asked him many questions that he didn't yet have the ability to answer. At the supermarket she strapped him into the child's seat in the shopping cart and pushed him up and down the aisles, all lined with brightly colored boxes and cans. He grasped at the smooth paper labels as Andrea held up two cans and asked, "Which shall we buy, Jake—these dark red kidney beans or these bright green peas?" He liked her smile of approval as he tried to imitate some of the sounds she was making.

Jacob's senses were called into action as they roamed the supermarket. In some parts of the store, he could feel the colder temperatures. In one section he smelled some unusual but interesting aromas. He was fascinated by the cashier's face as she leaned over the counter to coo and smile at him, but he was happiest when Andrea picked him up and held him again.

On the drive home, Andrea peeled a banana and let Jacob gnaw on a small piece as he watched the passing scenery from his car seat. The banana tasted good, he decided, and it was soft and sticky between his fingers. That, too, was a wonder. The world, it seemed, was full of wonders.

THAT AMAZING FIRST YEAR

To many caregivers, the conversion of a helpless, crying newborn to an active, inquisitive, babbling one-year-old happens so fast that they hardly have time to enjoy each momentous step along the way. The process occurs in twelve months, but so much goes on that people often look back and wonder how much they missed noticing.

Infancy is often defined as *the time between birth and twelve months of age*. The remarkable changes that take place make up the most concentrated period of accelerated growth and development in a person's life.

PHYSICAL DEVELOPMENT

Rapid growth and development require energy. To help sustain them, very young infants sleep up to seventeen hours a day and require frequent feedings. Generally, infants come into the world weighing between six and ten pounds (2.7 and 4.5 kg). They are usually about 20 inches (51 cm) long. By the end of their first year, most babies weigh about 22 pounds (10 kg) and are 30 inches (76 cm) long. Of course, inherited qualities from a mother and father influence this growth.

An infant's head grows rapidly. Open spaces in the bones of the infant's skull, called *fontanels*, allow for the growth of the quickly developing brain. The bones of the skull gradually grow together, and the open spaces are usually closed by eighteen months.

At six months, baby teeth begin to appear. By two years of age, all twenty baby (or *primary*) teeth are usually present.

Presence of Reflexes

All humans are born with **reflexes**, or *instinctive, involuntary reactions to a stimulus, such as a noise or touch.* Infants have

Frequent feedings and plenty of rest help infants grow rapidly.

Insuring Safety

The largest fontanel on an infant's skull is located on the top of the head. It is often called the "soft spot." Until this area becomes covered by the bones of the skull, the possibility of injury is present. Although the overlying skin is tough, any sharp or hard blow to the head could cause internal injuries. Caregivers need to be especially cautious about protecting an infant's head during the time that this "soft spot" exists.

*A*s new teeth push through an infant's gums (a process called *eruption*), the child is said to be teething. This is very painful for babies and usually difficult for their caregivers as well. Infants may cry and become cranky during eruption, which lasts from two to ten days for each tooth. They may even run a slight temperature. Caregivers can ease teething by giving infants teething biscuits and teething rings filled with ice water. The gnawing action and ice water help relieve the pain. During teething, caregivers need extra patience and understanding.

certain reflexes that function only for the first months of life. After that, intellectual and physical growth allow for voluntary action.

Reflexes that infants have are:

- Startle reflex—throwing out the arms and legs in response to a loud sound or sudden movement.
- Rooting reflex—turning toward a touch on the cheek or lips and beginning to suck.
- Grasping reflex—automatically closing the hand when the palm is touched.

- Babinski reflex—fanning the toes when the bottom of the foot is stroked.
- Other reflexes—making a walking motion when held up with the feet touching the floor, and appearing to swim when held horizontally in water.

To understand how reflexes work, suppose that you are working in an infant care center. You are preparing to feed three-week-old Elisha her formula when you accidentally drop the bottle on the floor. Elisha responds with the startle reflex. She throws out her arms and legs when she hears the

What purpose might the rooting reflex serve?

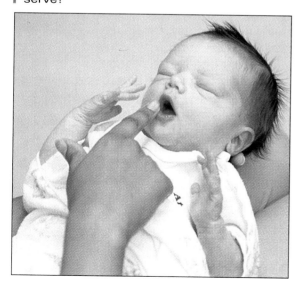

How would you feel, as a parent, if your newborn firmly grasped your finger? What effect might this have on your emotional attachment to the baby?

loud sound. As you pick Elisha up, the touch of the blanket on her face triggers the rooting reflex. She turns toward the blanket and begins to suck. Then while feeding her, you touch the palm of her hand, and her hand automatically closes. Within just a few minutes, you have seen three common reflexes present in infants.

Sensory Development

At birth, babies are equipped with all of their senses. They can see, hear, taste, feel, and smell. Within the first week of life, these senses quickly become more refined.

Newborn babies hear well enough to distinguish the voices of those caregivers who spend the most time with them from the voices of others. Vision is not clear at birth, but it improves within weeks. Soon, infants prefer looking at a human face, or picture of a face, that is held about 12 inches (30.5 cm) from their eyes. They enjoy brightly colored objects and patterns with contrasting colors. Their visual *perception*—learning about something through the senses—is not yet developed enough for them to follow objects with their eyes or to reach for objects.

Babies sense differences in taste. They prefer sweet over plain tastes. Limiting sweet food and drinks is necessary, however, as part of a caregiver's interest in providing healthful meals and snacks. When solid food is offered at about six months, babies often spit out the new food simply because the taste and texture are new.

Within the first two weeks of life, babies can recognize the unique scent of their mother. They gradually learn the scents of other family members as well.

Babies feel differences in texture. In fact, some babies are so sensitive that they become cranky and cry if dressed in clothing of a texture they dislike.

Motor Development

At birth, babies are completely dependent on others. They cannot lift or hold up their own head, roll over, sit up, or stand. Physical strength and movement improve quickly, however. Muscular development eventually gives infants *mobility*, allowing them to move from one place to another. The chart on page 83 lists major motor developments during the first year of life.

Motor development influences, and is influenced by, other types of growth. Curiosity, a sign of intellectual growth, motivates infants to become increasingly mobile. Sitting up allows babies to make eye contact, which encourages social growth.

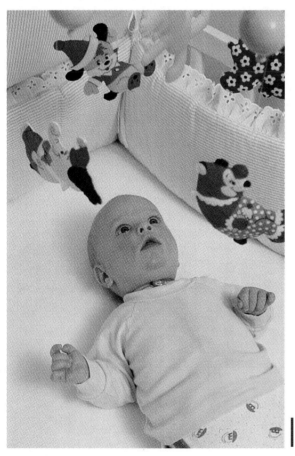

Even in the first months of life, infants need sensory stimulation for normal development.

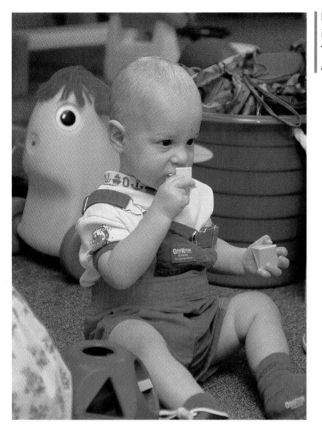

Improving eye-hand coordination gives an infant additional ways to explore the world. These blocks, for example, are seen, touched, and tasted.

Walking and self-feeding have a similar effect.

As babies progress physically and intellectually, they acquire **perceptual motor skills**—*skills that require the coordination of vision, intellect, and movement.* Climbing up a step is a perceptual motor skill. The child must see the step, judge the height, and lift his or her hands and knees. A related skill is **eye-hand coordination,** *the ability to move the hands and fingers precisely in relation to what is seen.* Infants begin to develop eye-hand coordination around three or four months of age. They can see a toy, reach for it, and grasp it successfully. Eye-hand coordination continues to develop throughout childhood.

Motor Development during Infancy

AGE	MOTOR DEVELOPMENT
Two months	Lifts head and chest when lying on stomach
Four months	Sits erect in arms of adult; reaches for objects
Six months	Grasps objects; rolls self over
Eight months	Thrusts arms and legs out and squirms to push self forward; pulls self up
Ten months	Crawls on hands and knees; walks with help of adult
Twelve months	Stands, sometimes walks alone; picks up small objects between thumb and forefinger; begins self-feeding

INTELLECTUAL DEVELOPMENT

How do people acquire thinking skills? Much research has gone into this question. The work of cognitive theorist Jean Piaget has provided much insight into how children learn. He identified four periods that people go through as they develop intellectually from infancy through adulthood. The chart on this page shows these. Additional explanations of these periods will be found throughout the chapters in this unit. The first one, the sensorimotor period, is described here, since it applies to infants.

The Sensorimotor Period

Piaget used the term **sensorimotor period** (sents-ree-MOH-tur) to describe the time frame during which infants develop their intellect. *During this period, from birth to age two, infants and one-year-olds learn by using their senses and motor abilities to gain information about the world.* As you can see in the chart on page 85, the sensorimotor period is subdivided into stages. Children learn by touching, tasting, smelling, and hearing. For instance, the principle of cause and effect is learned when an infant sees that pulling a string on a toy will make the toy move. If the child moves forward while pulling the string, the toy follows. This and similar types of learning usually begin between seven and eight months of age.

At around nine months, Piaget found, most children acquire an intellectual ability called **object permanence.** *This is the understanding that an object continues to exist even when out of sight.* Children discover that although a person or object disappears from view, it will be back. Before object permanence develops, you can cover a child's toy with a scarf and the child's interest shifts to something else. After object permanence develops, the child deliberately removes the scarf to find the toy.

Piaget's Periods of Cognitive Development

PERIOD	DESCRIPTION
Sensorimotor Period Birth to age two	Babies learn primarily through their senses and their own actions. Behavior is primarily motor.
Preoperational Period Age two to seven	Children start to think symbolically and imaginatively. They rely less on motor abilities and more on thinking to direct behavior.
Concrete Operations Period Age seven to eleven	Children use logical thinking, relating it to actual (concrete) objects and experiences.
Formal Operations Period Age eleven through adulthood	Children think logically, but now with the ability to apply it to ideas that are abstract and hypothetical (unreal).

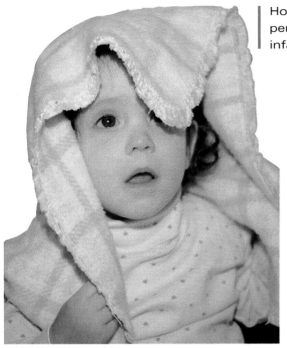

How is playing peek-a-boo related to object permanence? How would a very young infant react?

As intellect increases, children begin to analyze, make associations, and form predictions. At one year, for example, Dane learned that the rattle of keys in the front door lock meant that his mother or father had come home. His smiles and excitement at seeing his parent strengthened the bonds between them, aiding Dane's emotional development.

The Role of Language

Language plays a large role in developing intellectual abilities. Children understand language long before they can speak it well

Stages of the Sensorimotor Period

STAGE AND APPROXIMATE AGE	CHARACTERISTICS
1—Birth to one month	Practices inborn reflexes; does not understand self as separate person.
2—One to four months	Combines two or more reflexes; develops hand-mouth coordination.
3—Four to eight months	Acts intentionally to produce results; improves eye-hand coordination.
4—Eight to twelve months	Begins to solve problems; finds partially hidden objects; imitates others.
5—Twelve to eighteen months	Finds hidden objects; explores and experiments; understands that objects exist independently.
6—Eighteen to twenty-four months	Solves problems by thinking through sequences; can think using symbols; begins imaginative thinking.

THE MULTICULTURAL CLASSROOM

The point has been made that language is an important part of intellectual development. What happens, then, to the infant who comes to a child care program where the language spoken is different from the one heard at home? Such situations are easier to manage than you might think.

Children are amazing. They learn quickly that there are two ways of saying things. Because they are ready to absorb anything new and because they haven't had time to get used to handling only one language, accepting two ways of saying "me," "cup," and "cracker" is often easy for them. Many caregivers make it a point to learn certain words and phrases in the child's own language. This helps insure that important messages get through. Obtaining a bilingual dictionary with an English pronunciation guide helps ease communication with the child and family.

themselves. By six months of age, children can understand some spoken words, such as "mommy" and "daddy." By one year, children can usually speak several words. By eighteen months, two-word sentences are common; by age two, complete sentences can be formed.

Even very young babies benefit when you talk to them. Although they do not understand the words, they soon make **vocalizations**—*sounds that imitate adult language.* When adults respond to vocalizations, infants begin to learn that wants and needs can be expressed through language. Eventually, they learn specific ideas. Understandable spoken language isn't far behind.

EMOTIONAL DEVELOPMENT

*I*nfants experience such emotions as discomfort, distress, and happiness. As children develop, feelings become more specific. Excitement, joy, frustration, and anger are evident. These emotions are much easier to identify and manage after an infant learns language skills.

Bonding

Throughout a baby's first year of life, almost from the minute of birth, an important emotional development is taking place—bonding. **Bonding** is *forming a strong attachment to, and preference for, the primary caregivers.* This is usually a parent or parents. Secondary bonding can take place with other caregivers. A sign that bonding has occurred is **attachment behavior.** *The infant shows signs of pleasure when the caregiver appears and signs of distress when that person leaves.* Babies who smile and gurgle with delight when their caregivers enter the room and cry or fuss when these individuals leave are testimony to attentive, involved caregivers.

Bonding is necessary for development of good self-esteem. According to theorist Erik Erikson, children develop a sense of trust or mistrust based on the quality of early experiences with caregivers and with their environment. If needs for food, warmth, and comfort are met consistently, infants devel-

A baby who is cuddled during feeding gains a sense of security and trust, as well as the food needed for physical health. How else can caregivers foster self-esteem in infants?

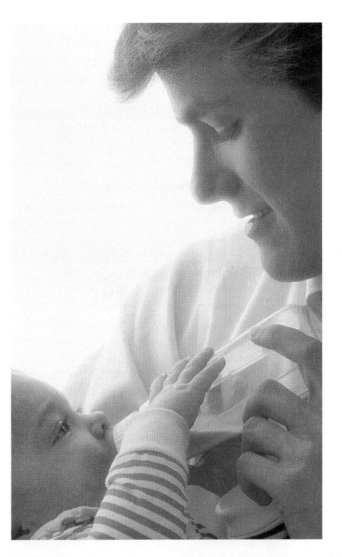

op a sense of trust. If these needs are not satisfied consistently, they develop a sense of mistrust. They see the world as a threatening and unpredictable place. The earlier children develop trust in others and in their environment, the better their emotional health. Responsive, reliable, and stable caregivers in the earliest months of life are critical for the development of trust. Positive social development cannot take place until babies experience a trusting relationship that allows them to bond with their primary caregiver.

Development of Personality

How children develop personality characteristics is a fascinating topic. While the process is not completely understood, research has given clues to the mystery.

Personality begins during infancy. Hereditary traits form the basis for personality, which continues to be influenced by experiences with the environment. Reactions from caregivers in a child's life affect personality. Interactions with people

Starving for Attention

An extreme example of how development in one area affects growth in another is failure to thrive, which is also called *marasmus*. Babies with this condition fail to grow normally. While the condition can be caused by physical problems or poor nutrition, it can also be due to a lack of social and emotional interaction. The infants have not been held, played with, or spoken to, even though their physical needs have been met. When older, these children may be unable to care for others and form lasting personal relationships. As a caregiver, you need to be able to identify infants with health problems so that help can be sought. Although failure to thrive is relatively uncommon, knowing that it can occur will enable you to take action if necessary.

and the environment, however, do not completely explain how personality develops.

From the day they are born, children have distinctively different ways of approaching the world. *A person's inborn style of reacting to the environment* is known as **temperament.** Temperament has a strong impact on personality.

Identifying Temperaments

The work of doctors Stella Chess and Alexander Thomas in the 1960s and 1970s resulted in the identification of three categories of temperament: difficult, easy, and slow-to-warm-up. These temperaments contribute to the development of different personality traits.

According to Chess and Thomas, easy children adjust quickly to changes in their routines. They are responsive to stimulation, tend to be sociable, and smile frequently. They have few problems with eating or sleeping. Their relaxed outlook on life often makes them easy to care for.

Slow-to-warm-up children can also be outgoing and sociable, but they usually need more time to adjust to new people and new situations. Often these children are prematurely labeled as "shy." Slow-to-warm-up chil-

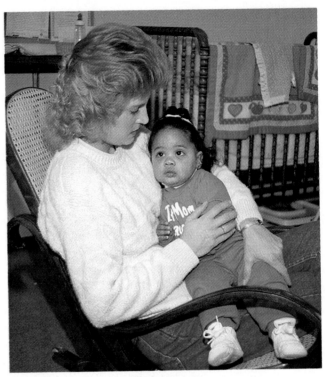

Caregivers can help children who are slow-to-warm-up prepare for changes and experience success with new situations. Such children need frequent reassurance.

dren require notice when changes are made. They may be hesitant to begin new activities. With time and experience, this hesitance lessens.

Difficult children can be more challenging, but they are *not bad*. They simply have an approach to the world that requires more patience from caregivers. Difficult children often have digestive and sleeping problems. They do not adjust well to changes in routine. They can be negative, and they need lots of support when trying something new. Difficult children become overstimulated

A nurturing caregiver can make real contributions to children's lives.

and frustrated easily, often causing them to withdraw from contact. Caregivers may misinterpret withdrawal as dislike. These children also often have a high activity level. They experience emotions intensely and sometimes unpredictably.

While no child is completely one temperament or the other, children do exhibit a general pattern of behavior that is consistent with one category more than another. Knowledge of temperament does not allow you to change a child, but it does help you better understand children's behavior. Individual temperament helps explain why children raised in the same family can develop very different personalities.

As you work with children, remember that the terms for temperament used by Chess and Thomas are only tools to use in objectively analyzing children. Remove judgment from your thinking as you use them. For example, "difficult" in this use only describes a set of characteristics. A "difficult" child may very well turn out to be an outstanding attorney or a competitive athlete. You can provide positive support to a child of any temperament when you understand that these terms help you learn how to work with children, not how to feel about them.

SOCIAL DEVELOPMENT

Do babies have friends? Can infants love their parents? In the strictest sense, babies are not capable of these types of relationships, any more than they are capable of walking or adding numbers. As with other areas of growth, however, the foundations of social development—the ability to form relationships with others—are laid during infancy.

Piaget believed that during the first year of life, children's thinking is **egocentric** (ee-go-SEN-trick). *They see everything only from their own point of view.* During infancy, for example, children do not play cooperatively with each other. They may show interest in another baby but only as they would another object. They do not perceive the baby as another person. It is impossible for them to understand how anyone else thinks or feels.

It takes several years of social experiences to help children grow beyond egocentrism. Emotional development is linked to this process. When infants learn to trust caregivers, they learn to value a social relationship. They discover that they can depend on others for assistance. They become secure in their relationships. Positive social skills are further developed when such routines as feeding, diapering, and bathing are pleasant experiences.

How can labeling a child as "difficult" be harmful to the child? How can understanding a child's temperament be helpful?

Stranger anxiety is a sign of intellectual growth. If an infant experiencing this fear is in child care, what steps might the staff take to minimize the baby's anxiety?

Stranger Anxiety

The fear of unfamiliar people, usually expressed by crying, that many infants develop is called **stranger anxiety.** It becomes common as object permanence develops, usually around nine months of age. By then, children are able to distinguish between strangers and caregivers. They may scream if a stranger tries to pick them up.

Children usually grow beyond stranger anxiety by twelve or fifteen months of age. Because of this fear, parents are advised to avoid placing children in a new child care setting when they are between the ages of eight and fifteen months.

TAKING TIME TO NURTURE

As you reflect on all the development that takes place during the first year of life, you can see that the changes are remarkable. Infants have so many challenges to meet. Imagine what would happen to an infant who is often ignored. Will he or she build muscles and become skilled at using them if left lying in a crib all the time? Will the child learn sounds that are seldom heard? Will the child feel loved when touching and holding are limited?

Obviously, developmental problems are likely when caregivers do not nurture a child. To **nurture** (NUR-chur) means *to provide love, support, attention, and encouragement.* Caregivers who are generous with their time and willing to take the extra steps that are needed give a child the best possible start in life.

How Can You Recognize Good Health?

While growth rates vary, all infants show certain signs when they are in good health. To help you identify healthy children, look for these signs:

- Clear, bright eyes.
- Steady increases in height and weight.
- Smooth, soft skin.
- Glossy hair.
- Appropriate muscular control for the age.
- Doesn't tire easily.
- Quick, definite movements.
- A generally happy, active, and curious disposition.

Building Professional Skills

Good Judgment

WHAT IS GOOD JUDGMENT?

Good judgment is the ability to make wise decisions. Using intellectual skills, such as reasoning and thinking about consequences, is part of good judgment. A person develops good judgment through experience and increased understanding of individuals and their abilities. You don't acquire good judgment overnight. It comes with practice as you continually refine your decision-making skills. With good judgment, you can resolve any number of challenging situations.

Good Judgment in Action

Rosa walked through the park, pushing eight-month-old Jerome in his stroller. The two four-year-old girls that she cared for in her family day care home were walking beside her. As they strolled, Rosa recognized a group of older women from her neighborhood, who were out for their morning walk.

"Rosa!" they called. "Is that the Sandburg boy? Can we see him?" They gathered around the stroller and bent down to see Jerome. Jerome began to fuss and whimper.

Rosa took a step forward, moving herself into Jerome's line of vision. "He's a little shy with new people. I think he wants a little room."

"Oh, are you sure?" asked Mrs. Atherton.

"When my granddaughter was that age, she loved to be held and cuddled. Everyone remarked that she was such a sweet baby." Mrs. Atherton reached out to stroke Jerome's cheek. Jerome shrieked and thrashed his arms in front of his face.

"I'm sorry, Mrs. Atherton," Rosa apologized, "but like I said, he's not comfortable with strangers. He'll probably be a little friendlier in a few months. I'm sure you'll understand if we go on with our walk today."

A few seconds later, Rosa stopped in a quiet spot beneath a tree and squatted down with the girls beside the stroller. "You're okay, little guy," she soothed Jerome. "You just don't want to be passed around like a hot potato, do you? You've got your own way of dealing with people, and that's just fine."

Your Analysis

1. How did Rosa show good judgment? Give specific examples.

2. What might have been some consequences if Rosa had not used good judgment in this situation?

3. Identify some everyday situations that you face in which good judgment helps you.

Chapter 4 Review

Chapter Summary

- Infancy is a time of rapid growth.
- Infants are born with certain reflexes.
- Senses are quickly refined during infancy.
- Greater mobility comes as infants develop motor skills.
- Intellectual development takes place when babies are allowed to explore their environment with senses and motor skills.
- Bonding and the development of trust are needed for emotional health.
- Studies show that children are born with different temperaments.
- The foundation for future social relationships is built during infancy.
- An infant who is nurtured gets a good start in life.

Reviewing the Facts

1. What is infancy?
2. Briefly describe physical growth during infancy.
3. What are reflexes? Describe three reflexes infants have when they are born.
4. Describe how infants gradually gain mobility.
5. At approximately what age can an infant: (a) sit erect in the arms of an adult; (b) reach for and grasp objects; (c) begin self-feeding with finger foods?
6. Describe sensorimotor learning. What well-known theorist developed research on cognitive development?
7. Define and give an example of object permanence.
8. Explain the meaning of bonding. Why is bonding important?
9. Briefly describe the three types of temperaments identified by Chess and Thomas.
10. What is stranger anxiety? When is it most intense?

Thinking Critically

1. A baby enjoys trying to grasp objects. What types of toys allow the baby to practice this skill? What could you make that would serve this purpose?
2. Why might a talkative person be good at working with infants?
3. What could a child care professional do to help when parents miss out on certain "firsts" in the child's life?
4. How do you explain a baby's sensitivity to different tastes, smells, and textures? What purpose might it serve?
5. What dangers might there be in labeling a child as difficult?
6. How would you handle situations that involve stranger anxiety?

Activities and Applications

1. **Motor Development.** Observe and compare the motor skills of a two-month-old and a six-month-old. What physical progress has the older infant made?
2. **Judging Ages.** With a partner, find magazine pictures that show infants. Try to judge the ages of the infants pictured, applying your knowledge of development.
3. **Nurturing.** Videotape a parent (or a child care student) playing with an

infant. Review the tape several times. Cite specific examples of ways that the parent's involvement stimulates the child's physical, intellectual, emotional, and social development.

4. **An Important Point.** Complete the following sentence in writing. "I believe a very important point to remember about infant development is . . ."

Your Professional Portfolio

As an addition to your portfolio and for your own personal use, begin a resource list to develop as you complete this course. Include resources that would be useful to you as an employee in the child care field. You might include the names of books, magazines, newsletters, companies that provide toys and equipment, and agencies. Include reviews of selected resources.

Observing and Analyzing

Studying Infant Development

To understand how infants develop you need to observe them. Although your classroom experiences will provide excellent information, to observe infants up close is to really understand how complex and fascinating they are.

Observing infants requires considerable concentration. Although infants may appear to be accomplishing little in their day-to-day experiences, their minds and senses are taking in everything in their environment. You will need to watch carefully to see what is going on. Through observation, the differences and similarities between infants will be more apparent.

- **A Newborn Nursery.** If your local hospital will allow visitors, look for the name labels on each crib and record the heights and weights of the infants. What is the range?
- **A Look at Proportions.** Observe a sleeping newborn and compare the size of the hand in relation to the face. How large is the hand when placed on the cheek? Place your own hand on your face to see the difference in proportions as compared to the infant. How long is the infant's arm in relation to the head? If you raise your arm above your head, how far does your elbow reach? Observe a child who can walk and see if the head-body proportions are the same as those you have seen in younger children.
- **Bonding.** Look for opportunities to observe the relationship between infants and their caregivers. What signs of bonding do you see? What kind of voice is used? How is a crying infant comforted? How does the caregiver interact with the infant during feeding, diaper changing, and playtime?

Chapter 5

Understanding Toddlers

CHAPTER OBJECTIVES

■ Describe major physical developments in toddlers.

■ Identify significant signs of intellectual, emotional, and social growth in toddlers.

■ Explain the impact of role models on children.

■ Explain why the two-year-old stage can be particularly trying for children and adults.

■ Describe an environment that promotes sound emotional development.

■ Explain the impact of play on social development.

■ Identify ways to promote responsibility in toddlers.

Terms to Learn

- accommodation
- assimilation
- attention span
- autonomy
- concepts
- fine motor skills
- gross motor skills
- parallel play
- preoperational period
- role model
- self-help skills
- solitary play
- toddler

This was the part of the afternoon that Barbara Taylor enjoyed the most. On days when the weather was nice, she got out the special wagon that was equipped to hold four children from her child care center. It had high sides, small benches with backs, and seatbelts to hold the children in place.

As she snapped the belts closed, she gave each child a quick hug. She got several in return. The children loved these outings too. The fresh air felt good, and it was an opportunity for a change of pace.

Barbara walked casually, pushing the wagon in front of her. As they traveled along, she talked to the children and pointed out things they saw on the way.

When they got as far as the park, she unloaded the children from the wagon, so they could do some exploring. "Let's look at this," she said to them. "What do you think we might find under this rock?" The children crouched down beside the rock, ready for discovery. From experience they knew Barbara could find interesting things. "Are you ready?" she asked, building a little suspense for what she hoped to find. Her fingers gripped the side of the large rock as she began to lift it gently. All eyes were on the rock.

CHANGES AND CHALLENGES

What an exciting time for learning is presented by the toddler stage. Whether it's the hidden surprises under a rock or the textures and flavors of new foods, children at these ages are ready to absorb all the information they can.

Toddler is the term commonly given to *a child between the ages of twelve and thirty-six months*. Toddlers are in a transition stage. They are no longer infants, but they are eagerly beginning to increase their skills so they can be more independent. This can be a confusing and frustrating time for children—as well as the adults who care for them.

PHYSICAL DEVELOPMENT

Watch a fifteen-month-old walk and you'll see why children this age are called toddlers. Learning to stand erect, they often appear a bit bowlegged. Their stomachs stick out, and they "toddle" from side to side. By eighteen months, they are much improved at the art of balance. Once they reach age two, their bodies begin to slim down and take on the appearance of a more mature child.

Flexibility

WHAT IS FLEXIBILITY?

Having flexibility means that you can change plans easily. You are not set in a rigid way of doing things. Flexibility can also be a mental quality, when you are able to see a situation from a different viewpoint and with a different attitude. Flexibility is an important quality for getting along with others and resolving conflicts.

Flexibility in Action

Carolyn had the scene set up perfectly. Eighteen-month-old Tobias sat quietly on the table in front of a pale blue background. He babbled happily at his mother, who stood just out of the camera's range holding up Tobias' favorite doll. Suddenly his expression changed. His lip curled down, and he began to squawk and then wail. "Mama!" he cried, as he shifted to his hands and knees. "I don't understand," his mother said helplessly. "He loves this toy. It always makes him happy."

"That's okay," said Carolyn cheerfully. "These things always take longer than you planned." She had been a professional child photographer for a long time, and she was prepared. She showed Tobias items from a big box of toys and stuffed animals. Nothing held his attention. Then he caught sight of one of her photography magazines.

It was the latest issue. Carolyn hadn't read it yet, but she decided to let Tobias hold it anyway. Gleefully, he latched onto the magazine and patted the pages. Several pages tore as he pulled on them. He was so amused that he hardly noticed when Carolyn snapped his picture.

"I can always buy another one," she chuckled to herself later, picking up the scattered pages, "or tape this one back together." Tobias's expression that she had caught on film was worth much more than the price of a magazine.

Your Analysis

1. How did Carolyn show flexibility in her job?

2. Why do you think flexibility is an important quality for child care professionals?

3. Can a person be too flexible? If so, what might be some negative consequences of this?

4. How might a caregiver's flexibility affect a child's social and emotional development? Would the effects be mostly positive or mostly negative? Explain your answer.

Average Heights and Weights of Toddlers

AGE	HEIGHT	WEIGHT
One Year	30 in. (76 cm)	22 lbs. (10 kg)
Two Years	34 in. (86.5 cm)	28 lbs. (13 kg)
Three Years	38 in. (96.5 cm)	32 lbs. (14.5 kg)

Physical Growth

After infancy, growth in height and weight slows for toddlers. The chart above shows approximate heights and weights for children from one to three. These numbers can vary greatly for individual children.

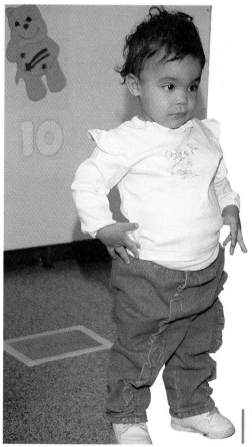

Body proportions gradually change along with height and weight gains. An infant's head is relatively large in comparison to the rest of the body, and arms and legs are short. With physical growth, children take on more mature proportions.

Because less fuel is needed for growth, appetites decrease during the toddler years. Two-year-olds can feed themselves with a fork and spoon but often show less interest in eating and may dawdle over food. Likewise, although teeth come in rapidly between eighteen and twenty-four months of age, children do not always chew their food properly. Instead they may gulp their food to finish meals as quickly as possible. For safety reasons, food should still be served in very small pieces to prevent choking.

Motor Development

Motor development and coordination advance quickly during this time of life. Improving **gross motor skills**, *skills that use the larger muscles of the back, legs, shoulders, and arms*, gives children new physical abilities. Learning to walk gives them greater independence.

From twelve to eighteen months, children begin to climb. At first, climbing up stairs is

The toddler stage is one of dramatic changes and development.

easier than climbing down them. By age two, however, this skill is mastered as well. Older toddlers love to climb over, around, on top of, and through obstacles in their path. They become more skilled at running, hopping, and jumping.

Between eighteen and twenty-four months of age, children begin to push themselves on wheeled toys. By the end of their second year, they are able to pedal a tricycle or similar pedal-type vehicle.

Toddlers are also refining their **fine motor skills**, *those that require use of the smaller muscles of the fingers, wrists, and ankles.* These skills contribute to improved eye-hand coordination and other perceptual motor skills. Children learn to stack blocks, string beads, and put together simple puzzles. Twelve- to eighteen-month-olds can stack two to four blocks and join a two-piece puzzle. Between eighteen months and thirty-six months, children become adept at doing simple six-piece puzzles and can build towers of about eight blocks.

Development of small muscles and increased eye-hand coordination also enable

Fine motor skills improve throughout the toddler stage. Caregivers need to provide both opportunities for play and appropriate toys.

toddlers to turn the pages of a book one at a time and to scribble with a crayon. By age two, they can turn doorknobs and even work a television remote control, as well as feed themselves.

Insuring Safety

Toddlers may try to practice their climbing skills even when it is unsafe. Be careful that children do not make "stairs" from pieces of furniture, from chairs and tables or countertops, or from drawers and cabinets.

Toilet Training

Children around age two are physically and intellectually ready to begin toilet training. Most are gaining control of the muscles that stop as well as start elimination. Intellectually, they are learning to recognize bodily sensations that precede elimination and to understand the use and purpose of a toilet or potty chair.

Children are generally able to use a regular toilet by the age of two or three. Some children are trained by eighteen months, but this is rare. Girls tend to master the skill earlier than boys.

INTELLECTUAL DEVELOPMENT

*D*iscovery is a big part of intellectual development. For example, Corey was walking with his two-year-old nephew Ozzie around the neighborhood when Ozzie became excited. He pulled Corey over to a huge oak tree and pointed at the small objects scattered beneath it. Ozzie squatted down and gazed at one. He picked it up and held it close to his eyes, fingering the smooth exterior and rough cap. He pressed it to his nose and wrinkled his nostrils. Finally he looked inquiringly at Corey, holding the puzzling object up to him.

"Acorn," Corey said slowly. "That's an acorn."

Like Ozzie, other toddlers continue to grow intellectually through sensorimotor development. Because they learn by doing and by using their senses, they need many hands-on experiences. They need freedom to

explore their environment. In order to develop their thinking skills, they need time to satisfy their curiosity. Children have a keen sense of wonder and are fascinated by the simplest things. A child's desire to explore can easily conflict with an adult's desire to follow a tight schedule. That's why adults have to be sure they provide adequate time for a child's investigations. Observing the wonders of the world stretches a young child's mind. Adults who patiently respond to "Why?" and "What's that?" are rewarded with an enthusiastic learner.

Knowledge develops through other means also. Children use trial and error, repetition, and imitation. They observe adults closely and copy their behavior. They even begin to adopt attitudes that adults have. *A person whose behavior and attitudes are imitated*

Toddlers want to try. They may be slow and they may make a mess, but they need opportunities to test and practice their skills. The patient adult builds self-esteem and helps skills develop by allowing the child to try.

by others is called a **role model.** Caregivers are especially powerful role models for children. If you were working with children, what kinds of attitudes and behavior would you want them to learn from you? How would you make sure the children learn them?

Unlike infants, older toddlers do not often explore objects by putting them in their mouth. For this reason, the health and safety concerns that go along with this habit are reduced.

Attention Span

Toddlers are slowly developing an increased **attention span,** which is *the ability to focus on a specific activity for a period of time.* Attention span generally increases with age. It is also affected by the child's interest in the activity and the activity's developmental appropriateness. Think of the last time you read a dull story or attempted to solve a problem that was beyond your abilities. Was it easy or difficult to stay focused on what you were doing? Children, likewise, are more apt to stay with an activity that provides a reasonable challenge without boring or frustrating them. This helps make the experience a positive one and encourages learning.

Memory

At about nine months Nadia began to look for objects that were removed from view. She realized that the objects still existed even though she couldn't see them. You will recall that this concept is called object permanence. What ability do you think Nadia needed for this understanding? The answer is memory. Memory is the ability to recall images and information. Without memory there would be no learning. If an experience left no impression, it could not affect or improve future thoughts and behavior. When Nadia could remember what she saw, she was better able to understand that the objects out of view still existed.

Memory begins to develop in infancy and grows rapidly over the next two years. Toddlers begin to have memory of actual events. Two-year-olds can remember a parent who has been absent for several weeks. They can repeat bits of favorite rhymes and stories and tell about experiences after returning from a walk.

Symbolic Thinking

Once a child has the ability to remember, the stage is set to develop a more advanced thought process—symbolic thinking. With symbolic thought, children understand that one thing can stand for something else. They learn to use images, art, and language as symbols to represent objects, events, and concepts.

Why is attention span considered such a key skill for intellectual development?

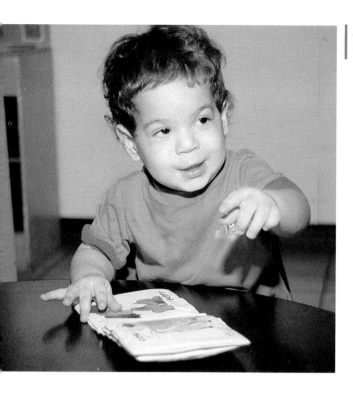

As symbolic thought develops, toddlers become more interested in simple books.

ing and creating. The development of symbolic thought is a significant milestone in intellectual development.

Language Development

Command of more refined language skills fosters incredible intellectual development from ages one to three. Children who at twelve months said only a few words quickly acquire vocabularies of up to 50 words. Babbling continues as children gradually grasp the meaning of their native language.

Eighteen-month-olds respond to questions that are answerable with a "yes" or "no." They identify parts of the body by pointing to them when named. They follow simple directions, such as "Hand me the ball." Communicating with signals that use

Symbolic thought is characteristic of Piaget's second period of intellectual development—preoperational. The **preoperational period** *covers ages two to seven. In this period children start to think symbolically and imaginatively. They rely less on motor abilities and more on thinking to direct behavior.* Intellectually toddlers are beginning to move out of the sensorimotor period and into the preoperational one. A two-year-old may show signs of symbolic thinking, although this ability develops much more fully after toddlerhood.

Because they are starting to think symbolically, many older toddlers enjoy make-believe play. It's not unusual to see a two-year-old holding "conversations" with the use of a wooden block "telephone" or sitting inside a cardboard box that has become a vehicle.

Imagination and creativity are natural outgrowths of symbolic thought. When children begin to think symbolically, they show first signs of the human potential for invent-

"Where is your ear?" Toddlers understand more words than they can speak.

THE MULTICULTURAL CLASSROOM

Regardless of cultural background, most children provide certain widely understood clues that give messages about their needs. A drowsy child needs a nap. A crying child needs attention, perhaps a dry diaper or a hug. A child who is tugging on his or her pants may need to go to the bathroom. Not all messages are as easily communicated.

When children come from different ethnic backgrounds and if they speak another language, caregivers need information that will enable them to respond appropriately to children. A home language survey can help. Parents fill out this form along with other enrollment forms. On it they explain how the family refers to common terms, such as sleep, eat, look, hit, milk, doll, urinate, and bowel movement. Phonetic spellings are helpful. Even in a preschool of all English speaking families, two dozen different words might be used in connection with toilet use, plus a variety of words used to describe the related body parts. A home language survey can help prevent frustration for children and caregivers as they communicate.

the hands, arms, head, or face—gesturing—begins at this age.

Many two-year-olds have a growing vocabulary of 50 to 300 words. They can name familiar objects. More understandable speech includes three- to four-word sentences. Their ability to follow increasingly complex directions, such as "Put the ball inside the box," shows they have begun to understand prepositions as well as nouns.

Conceptual Development

The ability to understand **concepts**—*general ideas formed from other information*—increases rapidly with emerging language skills. Concept development and language development build on each other. The more concepts children encounter, the more words they need to label them. The more words children understand, the more concepts they are able to identify and label.

When labeling concepts, children usually begin by using broad generalizations. One word, to them, has a wide variety of meanings. As their experiences increase, they gradually learn that concepts have limits.

Piaget used two terms to help explain how children absorb information and attempt to make sense of it. Through **assimilation**, children *take in new information and try to make it fit with what they currently know and understand*. When the information doesn't fit, another process takes place—accommodation. With **accommodation**, children *change their thinking to make the new information fit*. Cognitive development is a continual process of balancing new information with existing concepts in order to reach more accurate understandings. In the following example, you can see how this process was used by Anwar to expand his thinking.

Two-year-old Anwar was watching a neighbor's new pet. He observed that the animal was covered with white fur that had black spots. It had four legs, two eyes and ears, a nose, and a long tail swinging from side to side. As Anwar petted the animal, his father repeated, "Doggie. Pet the doggie gently."

The next day, Anwar and his father were driving past a farm. Anwar saw a black-and-white cow in the field. He pointed and exclaimed, "Doggie! Doggie!" Anwar was using assimilation to try to incorporate something new with what was already familiar to him.

"That's a cow," his father explained. "Look how big the cow is."

Anwar was confused. After all, the animal was spotted. It had four legs, two ears and eyes, and a nose. There was even a long, swishing tail at the end.

"Doggie!" he repeated.

Given time and experience, Anwar learned to identify cows. He observed important differences, such as shape, size, and other features, that distinguish a cow from a dog. Through the process of accommodation, Anwar altered his thinking to make the new information fit.

By age two, children begin noticing similarities and differences. They match and sort very simple items that look alike. Children begin to recognize shapes and sizes. For example, many can work a puzzle with four pieces that have different shapes. This abili-

ty is a critical early step that precedes learning to read language symbols.

Toddlers also begin to understand opposite concepts. They start to see the relationship between such terms as hot and cold, hard and soft, and up and down.

Cause and effect continues to hold fascination for them. When playing hide-and-seek games, they become more methodical as they think about where and how to look for the hidden person or object. This means they are learning to solve problems, a complex intellectual skill.

EMOTIONAL DEVELOPMENT

Toddlers are only beginning to develop emotional control. They are still prone to impulsiveness and quick mood swings. You may have heard people talk about the "terrible twos." Some children try adult patience more at this age than at any other. Children may be cheerful one minute and screaming dramatically the next. Understanding what a child may be like and knowing that the stage will pass can make working with children of this age easier.

For the most part, when the basic needs of toddlers are met, they are very pleasant and cooperative. Sudden shifts in mood and behavior are more a result of individual temperament. Problems may stem from frustration. The child is struggling to learn and

Toddlers are often frustrated by their limited abilities. Parents and other caregivers need to be understanding and patient.

do more, but not all the abilities are present yet. When their grasp of language is inadequate, children may resort to whining and crying. As their language skills improve, toddlers are better able to communicate their wants, needs, and feelings. Some of the frustrations they have are eliminated. They also gradually learn to identify and manage their feelings more appropriately. When there is stability in home life and the caregiving environment, any trying emotional times of the two-year-old stage are likely to subside.

Development of Autonomy

According to Erikson, toddlers are developing a sense of **autonomy** (aw-TAHN-uh-mee), or *independence*. They start to see themselves as separate from their caregivers. They want to be self-governing. Indeed, they need to learn this task in order to overcome doubts about themselves and move forward with their personal development.

You will see children take many opportunities to assert their independence. Frequently they exclaim "No!" to what seems like everything and everyone. They often resist cooperating in routines they used to enjoy, such as eating and bathing. They are sensitive about being bossed, shown, helped, or directed. Doing exactly the opposite of what is wanted happens frequently. If you ask a child of this age to give you something he or she is holding, the child will often run off with the object instead.

By showing patience and offering as many reasonable choices as possible, caregivers can make the progress toward autonomy easier for child and adult alike. Watching them practice their reasoning and decision-making skills can be a fascinating, and even humorous, study.

Appearance of Fears

Looking back on your own childhood, do you recall having fears that were very real but now seem ridiculous and irrational? Perhaps it was water, spiders, or monsters. This is a common experience for toddlers. Their fears may range from storms to birds to being alone in a room. They are often frightened by strange figures dressed up in larger-than-life costumes, such as Santa Claus and the Easter Bunny.

Fear arises for several reasons. Some are very good ones. You wouldn't want children to be unafraid of jumping from a high wall or petting a wild animal. Healthy fear contributes to children's safety.

Fear may develop from lack of experience. For a young child who has never been in a wading pool,

Animals intrigue toddlers but may also frighten them. How are this child's parents handling the situation?

stepping into water a foot deep may be very frightening. Some fears are irrational or stem from misconceptions. Others are learned from other children and adults. For example, Marco's older brother cringed and turned away whenever he saw a spider. What do you think Marco's reaction to spiders was?

For toddlers, some fears are partially a result of intellectual as well as emotional development. As children become more aware of the outside world, they realize they are vulnerable to danger. Life is scarier away from the shelter of the family. In addition to causing fears, this realization can also produce mixed emotions about becoming an independent being.

When fears do arise, toddlers are usually calmed when caregivers are close at hand. Children overcome fears with patience, understanding, and emotional support from caregivers. It often helps to talk with children about fears. If a child fears storms, explain that rain is needed for flowers to grow. If an older child fears climbing, *gradually* introduce the child to different heights on climbing structures. Pushing children to overcome fears all at once usually backfires. It results in a more—and not less—fearful child. Most fears pass with time and experience if handled in a supportive, understanding manner.

Importance of Security

A sense of security continues as a primary emotional need for toddlers. Stable routines and rituals help fulfill this need. As creatures of habit, children feel more secure and relaxed when their daily schedule and environment are reliable and predictable.

Tip **FROM THE** *Pros*

*T*oddlers find rules and limits especially frustrating. Wherever possible, create a "can-do" environment that encourages children's participation. Use nonbreakable tableware, and allow children to take turns helping to set the table for meals. Let them help sort and put away toys. Such tasks also strengthen intellectual skills.

Only when they experience this sense of security are they free to take chances with exploration. In this way, emotional development affects intellectual development.

SOCIAL DEVELOPMENT

*S*ocial development in very young children progresses more slowly than other areas of development. It takes time for children to establish social relationships with *peers* (people their own age) and those who are not primary caregivers.

Beginning at age two, children can participate in groups of up to eight, but only for short periods. They may enjoy group singing for five minutes or listening to a short story with others in a group. The primary focus of social interaction, however, continues to be parents, siblings, and other caregivers. In the child care setting, children are most comfortable sharing time with a caregiver in a small group that includes only two or three children.

At age two, children begin making friends. They often show kindness when someone is hurt or crying. From this age, children increasingly like snuggling with a buddy in a cozy space. Friendships bloom after the age of three.

Play and Social Development

For children, play is the primary mode for interacting with the world. It is their "work." Through play, they stretch their abilities and expand their understanding of concepts. They spend hours poking, prodding, and

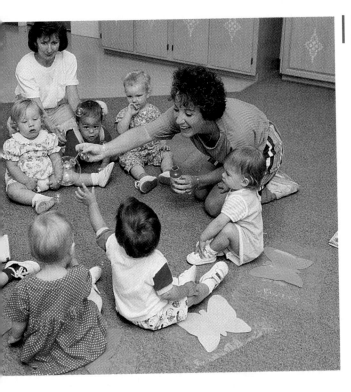

How can brief group activities benefit toddlers?

manipulating objects. They engage in delightful banter with caregivers. Play is the best method of learning throughout the early childhood years.

From eighteen to twenty-four months, children still engage mostly in **solitary play**. They *play alone rather than with other chil-* *dren*. They are interested in other children, but more out of curiosity than a desire to form friendships.

Between twenty-four and about thirty months, children engage in **parallel play**. You will see them *playing near each other but not with each other*. Two children of this age might investigate a toy together at the same time, but each acts independently of the other. A small group of toddlers might all play with the same caregiver at the same time. The interaction, however, is taking place primarily between the caregiver and each separate child, not among the children.

As they approach age three, children gradually begin interacting with other children of about the same age, usually for limited periods of time. Parallel play continues to be their main style of interaction. Two or three children of this age may play dress-up in the same area but only occasionally join in each other's play theme.

Learning Social Rules

Toddlers are beginning to understand the concepts of limits and rules. Not until age

Let's Pretend

Pretend play and make-believe can make important contributions to the intellectual, social, and emotional development of toddlers. Through make-believe, children practice symbolic thinking. They "see" tea in empty plastic teacups and cookies on empty plates. A sheet "becomes" a cape or dress. They also learn social skills, even before cooperative play begins. By assuming the roles and feelings of their make-believe characters, children teach themselves empathy. They learn to look beyond themselves and into the lives of others. Pretend play also satisfies children's emotional need for security by allowing them to be in control. When they "heal" a stuffed animal patient or "teach" a class of dolls, they feel a sense of power and competence not usually experienced in their real lives.

three do these concepts become part of everyday behavior.

By age two, language has developed well enough for caregivers to set a few, very simple rules for children and offer very brief reasons for them. Rules should relate primarily to safety.

Social skills, such as using table manners, sharing, and cooperating, develop slowly. Plenty of opportunities to develop these skills should be provided, but remember that the process is slow. The best way to teach positive social behavior is to provide good examples.

Developing Responsibility

Even at this early age, children are forming a sense of responsibility. You can encourage responsibility (as well as independence) by allowing children to develop **self-help skills.** *These are skills that allow children to help take care of themselves and their personal needs.* Self-help skills that are appropriate for toddlers include getting dressed, putting away toys, washing hands, and brushing teeth.

Responsibility, of course, is more than just self-care. Children need to learn how to take on responsibility as they interact with others too. When approached properly, toddlers take pride in what they do to be helpful. Setting napkins around the table, for example, may seem like a small job to you, but a two-year-old takes it seriously and is proud when given recognition for the accomplishment. If the napkins are crooked, that doesn't matter. Adults have to react with sensitivity. Self-esteem grows when you say something like "Chelsea put the napkins on the table all by herself." Self-esteem suffers when you do the job over again because it isn't up to adult standards.

A patient adult takes the time needed to encourage responsibility. When children become responsible for themselves and learn to be helpful to others, they develop a

sense of belonging and importance. Thus, social development contributes to emotional development.

A NOTE OF UNDERSTANDING

*T*oddlers may seem like human bundles of contradictions. For every time they are cheerful, spontaneous, enthusiastic, and helpful, there is likely to be a time when they are negative, argumentative, and obstinate. Knowing how they grow can help you understand their moods and behavior. You can then help them deal with the challenges of this stage, channel their budding abilities, and take a positive step toward maturity.

Learning self-help skills can build a toddler's self-esteem. Think about how you might go about teaching one specific skill. How could you make it fun to learn?

Chapter 5 Review

Chapter Summary

- The rate of physical growth for toddlers slows.
- Curiosity fosters intellectual development.
- Toddlers can remember actual events, and they have an increasing attention span.
- Symbolic thinking, creativity, and imagination are important intellectual developments that begin at this age.
- Toddlers strive to develop autonomy.
- Seemingly irrational fears are common to toddlers.
- Toddlers need a sense of security.
- Toddlers engage in solitary and parallel play.
- Children this age can begin to understand simple rules and to develop a sense of responsibility.

Reviewing the Facts

1. Give the age at which the average child is likely to do each of the following: (a) begin to climb; (b) pedal a tricycle; (c) stack three blocks; (d) stack eight blocks; (e) scribble with a crayon; (f) turn a doorknob.
2. What three things must occur before a child can be expected to learn to be toilet trained? At what age do children become toilet trained?
3. What is attention span? Identify three factors that affect attention span.
4. What is symbolic thinking? Explain how symbolic thinking is related to play toddlers enjoy.
5. Explain why a toddler might say "doggie" when looking at a cat.
6. What is autonomy? Describe the behavior of a child who is trying to achieve autonomy.
7. What types of fears do toddlers experience? What are some possible causes of these fears? Should they be made to face their fears? Why or why not?
8. What can be done to help give toddlers a sense of security?
9. Describe solitary and parallel play.
10. How can you help a toddler develop a sense of responsibility?

Thinking Critically

1. How might newfound mobility affect a toddler's intellectual growth? What about social growth?
2. Using terms that you have learned in this chapter, explain what is happening when a toddler sees a water tower from the car window and calls it a balloon.
3. Why might a two-year-old have feelings of frustration? What behavior might display this sense of frustration?
4. What choices would you allow children to make concerning what they eat, what they wear, and what activities they pursue?
5. Suggest two rules you might set for toddlers. What reasons for obeying these rules would you give them?

Activities and Applications

1. **Handling Curiosity.** Write five "why" questions two-year-olds might ask and five responses that would satisfy their curiosity.
2. **Understanding Fears.** Imagine you are a two-year-old encountering a

new situation, such as starting day care or meeting a large dog. Write a paragraph describing your fears and anxieties from a child's viewpoint.

3. **Categorizing Toys.** Using a toy catalog or advertisements, make a list of those that would help develop gross motor skills and fine motor skills. If you wish, create a poster for each type.

Your Professional Portfolio

Begin a glossary of terms that you want to learn and remember for use in your work with children. Start with selected vocabulary terms from this unit of the text. Include definitions and examples of how the terms are used. Add to the glossary as your study continues, using terms from the text and from other sources. If possible, keep your work in a computer file that can be regularly updated. Place the glossary in your portfolio.

Observing and Analyzing

Toddlers—An Observation Challenge

Observing busy, energetic toddlers can be a challenge, especially when you are watching a group of them all at once. The challenge is worth taking, however, because the physical activity of toddlers can teach you much about overall development. Try these observation ideas in order to discover more about toddlers:

- **Attention Span.** How long can a toddler stay focused on one activity? In order to observe attention span in toddlers, don't observe the entire group. Instead, choose three toddlers, one who is barely walking, one who has some mastery of walking, and one who is taller and heavier than most of the others. At a designated time when all three are in the same area, record what activity each one has selected and how long each child stays at each activity. Continue to follow the same three toddlers for an hour, if possible. Which activities held their attention for the longest amount of time, and why?

- **Sleep/Awake Comparison.** In a program that includes infants (not yet walking), observe and record the sleep/awake hours of three infants of about the same age. Then do the same for three toddlers. The differences between the two groups will be more obvious if they are least a year apart. Compare the information. What similarities and differences are there between the two groups' sleep/awake patterns?

- **Self-Help Skills.** Mealtime provides an excellent opportunity to observe infants' and toddlers' attempts at self-help skills, however messy. Take notes on their abilities in these areas: eating with fingers, holding utensils, holding a cup, "fingerpainting" with food, and any other self-help skills attempted. How are these early attempts handled by the caregiver? Is the child encouraged to continue or immediately cleaned up? Which is the better solution? What progress do you see from infancy to toddlerhood?

Chapter 6

Understanding Preschoolers

CHAPTER OBJECTIVES

- Identify signs of preschoolers' physical, intellectual, emotional, social, and moral development.

- Describe what children understand in Piaget's preoperational period of intellectual development.

- Explain how caregivers should react when preschoolers stutter or make grammar and pronunciation mistakes.

- Explain the role of accomplishment in developing a preschooler's self-esteem.

Terms to Learn

- centration
- classification
- conscience
- conservation
- cooperative play
- dramatic play
- empathy
- gender identity
- initiative
- one-to-one correspondence
- preschoolers
- rational counting
- rote counting
- seriation
- stereotype

"**T**omorrow I go to kindergarten," Zachariah proudly announced to his preschool teacher.

"It won't be long, Zack," Sheri Morrison responded casually, "but not tomorrow. You have to finish preschool first. When summer is over, you can go to kindergarten."

Zack looked concerned. "But it's my birthday tomorrow. I want to go to school with my sister," he said with frustration. "My mother said I could."

Mrs. Morrison looked at Zack for a long moment. She wondered why he was so sure about this. "Zack," she said gently, "why do you think you should go to kindergarten tomorrow?"

"It's my birthday tomorrow," Zack repeated impatiently. "I'll be five. My mother told me I could go to kindergarten when I'm five."

Mrs. Morrison held back the amusement she felt. She placed her hand on Zack's shoulder. "Come over here, Zack. Let's look at the calendar and see if we can find the day when kindergarten begins. I think you will still be five when that day comes. That's going to be a special day, isn't it? What do you think it will be like?"

Distracted from his concerns, Zack followed Mrs. Morrison to the calendar. He did wonder what it would be like. Maybe Mrs. Morrison would tell him.

THE PRESCHOOL AGE

By the time children reach preschool age, they have learned so much, yet the process has only just begun. Much more development is ahead. Anyone who works with preschoolers will tell you that surprises are an everyday occurrence. Preschoolers haven't figured everything out yet, but like Zack, they are trying. This quality alone can make them refreshing, amusing, and exciting to be around.

Children three, four, and five years old are commonly referred to as **preschoolers**. This term tells you something about children of this age. They are getting ready to learn and interact with others in a school setting. The physical, intellectual, emotional, social, and moral development children experience during the preschool years is necessary for success both in and out of the classroom.

PHYSICAL DEVELOPMENT

Physical growth during the preschool years is slow and gradual, which keeps the appetite small. The chart on page 112 shows the average heights and weights of children at different preschool ages. Because preschoolers consume such small amounts, making sure that what they eat is healthful is essential. Adequate vitamins, minerals, and other nutrients are needed.

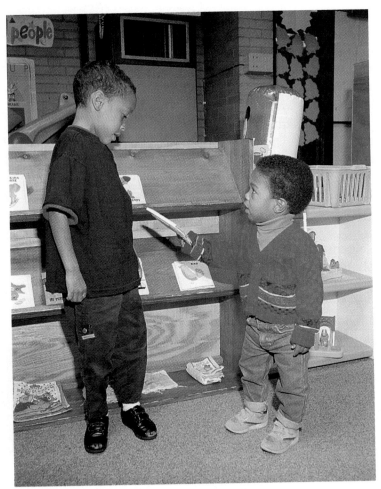

By their fourth year, preschoolers show obvious physical differences from toddlers. How do these changes in height, weight, proportion, and posture influence physical abilities?

As children of this age grow, their bodies appear less baby-like. Body fat is reduced, and most growth occurs in the muscles and bones. Posture becomes erect. The neck lengthens, the shoulders widen and flatten, and the once protruding stomach flattens as well. Legs become proportionally longer.

Motor Development

Preschoolers grow increasingly active as new physical and motor abilities rapidly emerge. These skills gradually become refined and complex. By age five, preschoolers can run fast and powerfully and can balance when walking on a beam.

Each year, physical skills develop more fully. Three-year-olds ride tricycles. Five-year-olds can usually ride bicycles. At three, children like to move and sway to music. By five, they can learn specific rhythms and dances. A three-year-old can throw a ball. A five-year-old can also catch a ball.

Preschoolers have mastered control of their bodies, so they can move in a variety of

Average Heights and Weights of Preschoolers

AGE	HEIGHT	WEIGHT
Three years	38 in. (96.5 cm)	32 lbs. (14.5 kg)
Four years	41 in. (104 cm)	36 lbs. (16 kg)
Five years	44 in. (112 cm)	41 lbs. (18.6 kg)

What skills are needed for a preschooler to successfully master climbing equipment?

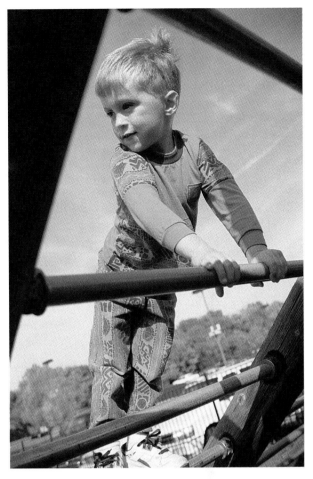

ways. They hop, gallop, and run. They zigzag while running and change directions with increasing ease. Climbing is a favorite activity of preschoolers. The older they become, the more challenging the structures they try to climb.

Perceptual Motor Development

Preschoolers become more skilled in eye-hand coordination and fine motor skills. Three-year-olds learn to use crayons and paintbrushes to create pictures. By five, they can draw and paint letters and shapes too. These are important first steps in learning to read and write. Other activities that develop perceptual motor skills include simple cooking tasks. For example, they can help spread peanut butter on vegetables. An enjoyable woodworking skill for a preschooler is pounding nails.

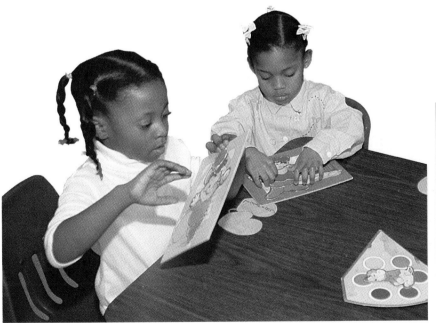

Preschoolers learn to coordinate what they see with the use of their hands. They see the shape of a puzzle piece, look for the shape on the puzzle, and then move the piece with hands and fingers until it fits into the right place. This is perceptual motor development.

INTELLECTUAL DEVELOPMENT

*D*uring the preschool years, children's intellectual abilities also become more refined and complex. Attention span lengthens. Children gradually develop more elaborate thought processes.

The Preoperational Period

Although Piaget's preoperational period began during the toddler years, by the time children are preschoolers, the characteristics of this period are much more evident. With their increasing ability to think symbolically, children readily add new concepts to their understanding.

Classification and Centration

Preschoolers are beginning to learn **classification**. They can *mentally group objects into categories according to similarities.* Thus, they can separate a mixed set of cards with pictures of cats and dogs into two smaller groups of just cats and just dogs.

Preoperational thought, however, limits children to *focusing on only one characteristic at a time,* what Piaget termed **centration**. Younger preschool children, for example, can sort objects by color alone. They can find all the red items in a group of toy cars, trucks, and airplanes. Not until children are almost six can they pick out only the red cars. Considering two characteristics at once is very hard for preschoolers.

Seriation

Around age five, children begin to become capable of **seriation**, *organizing objects according to increasing or decreasing size.* As with classification, their understanding is very limited. If you give a three-year-old ten blocks and say, "Line these up from biggest to smallest," the child may put a large block beside one of the smallest ones. The child will not be able to see the relationship between the sizes of all ten blocks for several more years.

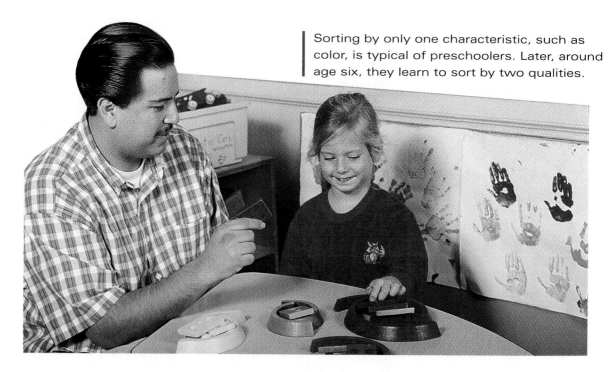

Sorting by only one characteristic, such as color, is typical of preschoolers. Later, around age six, they learn to sort by two qualities.

Numbers and Counting

Children in the preoperational period are just beginning to understand numbers and counting. Often two-year-olds are capable of **rote counting**—*reciting numbers in order without understanding that each number represents a specific amount.* If asked to bring three balls, a child who could only count by rote might bring one ball or ten balls. When counting by rote, preschoolers may count some objects more than once and some not at all.

The understanding that, when counting objects in a group, each item is counted once and only once is called **one-to-one correspondence.** Children must comprehend this mathematical concept before they can count accurately. When one-to-one correspondence is grasped, **rational counting**—*the understanding that the last number counted in a group represents the entire number of objects*—is possible.

Preschool children also have difficulty with the idea of time. While they may have learned the difference between "now" and "later," more detailed concepts are too abstract for their limited understanding.

Conservation

A preschooler's understanding is limited by what is seen, making some concepts difficult to grasp. Note how this is illustrated by the following description of what happened when four-year-old Maya tried to interpret what she saw.

Maya was watching as Chantal poured equal amounts of juice into identical glasses for Maya and her twin brother Angel. Since the children were going to take their drinks outside, Chantal decided to pour the juice into plastic cups. Chantal poured Maya's serving into a shorter, wider cup and Angel's into a taller, skinny one. When Chantal handed the children their juice, Maya looked inside the cups and asked, "Why does Angel get more than I do?"

Although she had seen that their servings were equal before, *now* Angel seemed to be getting more because the juice line was higher in his glass. Even if Chantal had poured the juice back into the original glasses, Maya probably would still not have understood that the amount of juice remained constant regardless of which glasses were used. *The understanding that an object's physical dimensions remain the same even when its appearance changes* was termed **conservation** by Piaget. This concept is beyond children in the preoperational period.

Development of Language

Scientists are not completely sure how language is acquired. Language expert Noam Chomsky believes part of the human brain is specially designed to learn language. Provided the brain has developed properly, children then learn their native language from their environment. They are quickly praised by adults for first making sounds, then words, and finally sentences.

With this encouragement and reinforcement, language blossoms during the preschool years. The average three-year-old has a vocabulary of 300 words. Four-year-olds speak about 1500 different words. By five years of age, an average child speaks 2200 words. As with most age groups, preschool children understand more words than they can speak. Language also becomes more expressive during the preschool years. Children use facial expressions, tone of voice, and more gestures to convey meaning. The language of older preschoolers can be surprisingly similar to that of adults.

Children develop language ability more quickly when provided with good examples. Talking and reading to children daily helps them expand their language use and comprehension. For instance, a three-year-old may simply say, "My ball." An adult can

Preschoolers use facial expressions both unconsciously and on purpose. In both situations, they give clues to what a child is feeling or thinking.

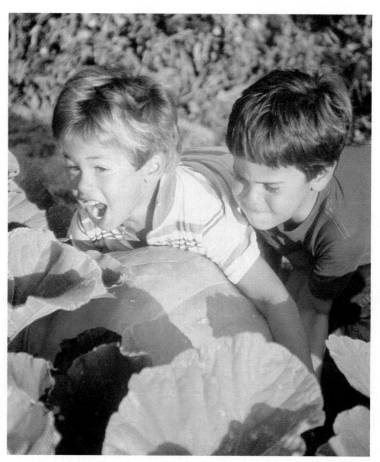

encourage more complex language by responding, "Yes, that is your big, red ball. Show me how you can bounce the ball." Children should be encouraged to ask questions and tell stories or jokes.

Grammar and Pronunciation

Gradually, children learn rules for grammar and pronunciation. This often causes some confusion. When Ashley was three, for example, she tried to form plurals in the best way she could. Since she commonly heard "s" on the ends of words

From the Mouths of Babes

*L*anguage development involves more than learning new words. It is also learning the effect of those words. Children quickly discover that using certain words and phrases produces a desired response in others, especially adults. They don't necessarily understand what they are saying, but they enjoy the attention it brings them.

If adults laugh when children use obscene language, the children interpret the response as approval. They don't recognize the crudeness of their own words. The same principle applies when children say "I hate you!" if someone makes them angry. They don't truly hate, but the forceful-

ness of that word produces a strong reaction. It gets the adult's attention.

In neither instance is the child misbehaving. Both cases are the result of partial development. The child has learned the power of language itself before understanding the specific words.

that were made plural, she used this knowledge to form the plural of the word "foot." She referred to her feet as "foots." Later, as she became more aware of the exceptions to the rules, her "foots" became "feet."

When working with children, be careful how you handle their grammar and pronunciation mistakes. Criticism hurts them. Since children learn by hearing, casually rephrase the child's statement to provide the correct model and continue the conversation. Focusing on content rather than on grammar or speech mechanics encourages children to use language. In turn, language usage promotes development.

Stuttering

During the preschool years, most children learn to speak clearly; however, mispronunciation of some sounds is to be expected. Some preschoolers have problems with stuttering. They may leave long pauses between words or repeat a sound or word many times before continuing a sentence. This is not "true" stuttering. It is the natural result when thinking ability exceeds speaking ability. Once speaking abilities catch up with thinking abilities, this speech pattern usually subsides. By not making an issue of it, caregivers preserve the child's self-esteem. If children stutter past age six or seven, they are usually referred to a speech therapist for evaluation.

EMOTIONAL DEVELOPMENT

Preschoolers experience an increasing range of emotions, including loneliness, disappointment, anticipation, and sympathy. Development of language helps preschoolers identify their many new feelings.

Better control over feelings is a positive achievement that occurs during the preschool years. With increasing language skills, preschoolers are able to identify feelings and vent their emotions appropriately with words, rather than by hitting or pushing. Emotional self-control leads to more cooperative social behavior.

In what ways does reading to young children encourage development?

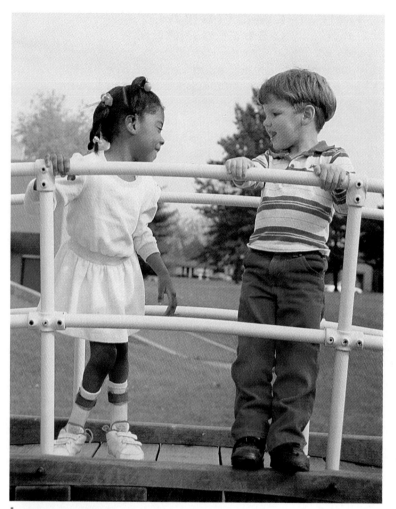

Friendships help preschoolers become less egocentric. They begin to be able to see things from another person's perspective.

Though often self-centered, preschool children begin to develop **empathy**. *This is the ability to recognize and understand the feelings of others.* Preschool children begin to help others without expecting a reward. This emotional development paves the way for making friends, fostering further social development.

Preschoolers may still have a variety of fears. Most of these will pass with time and more experience.

Development of Self-Esteem

Around the preschool age, feelings of self-esteem become more distinct. Preschoolers' self-esteem comes largely from their pride in the physical and intellectual skills they have worked so hard to achieve. They often ask for attention when climbing, running, or hopping. "Teacher, see what I can do!" is frequently heard in a child care center. Preschoolers also enjoy demonstrating their intellectual skills. They may name the colors they see or recite the alphabet repeatedly.

*M*any preschoolers cope with fears and insecurities, by clinging to *items of attachment.* These objects provide a feeling of familiarity and stability. You may want to allow children to bring a favorite toy or a "security blanket" into the child care setting if they want to. By respecting this need, you contribute to their comfort. Most children give up the attachment as they grow more confident and socially skilled.

Patience

WHAT IS PATIENCE?

Patience is the willingness to tolerate a trying situation. Sometimes it is simply the willingness to wait for a desired event. When you are patient, you can put aside your own concerns for the moment in order to do what needs to be done first. A patient person sees that some things are more important even though other options might be more personally satisfying.

Patience in Action

Valeska was ready to bake muffins for the children in her family day care home. It was early in the morning and, so far, only four-year-old Jamie had arrived for the day. Jamie was eager to help bake.

"I can do that!" Jamie exclaimed as Valeska began measuring the flour.

"Okay," Valeska agreed. She held the measuring cup while Jamie slowly, carefully filled it by the scoopful with flour.

"Let me!" Jamie cried when Valeska started to mix the ingredients. Valeska glanced at the clock as she watched Jamie stir the mixture in the bowl with awkward but determined strokes. The other children would start arriving soon. After a few stirs, she gently took the mixing spoon from Jamie. "I think you've about got it," she said.

"What else can I do?" Jamie begged.

Feeling a bit rushed, Valeska reached for the box of colorful, paper baking cups and handed a small stack to Jamie. "Here. You can put these in the pan for me," she said, showing Jamie how to do the first one.

Jamie set to work, carefully separating and placing the cups in the muffin pan. As Valeska watched, she noticed that the little girl was deliberately placing cups of the same color in individual rows. She had a row for each of the pink, blue, and green cups.

"That's very good, Jamie," Valeska told her, smiling. She pulled a silver baking cup from the box. "You're a very helpful assistant. I think we'll let you fill this cup with batter to make a special muffin just for you."

Your Analysis

1. How would you describe Valeska's ability to be patient? Give two examples that show patience.

2. How might an impatient person have reacted to Jamie?

3. What effects would an impatient approach have had on Jamie? How do you think Valeska's approach affected Jamie?

4. Why do you think patience is an important quality in a child care professional?

5. Why is it sometimes difficult for adults to be patient with children?

6. Are you a patient person? How might you go about making any necessary improvements?

Self-esteem also increases as preschoolers develop their self-help skills. They like to take care of themselves and their personal needs. Preschoolers want to "do it myself." Three-year-olds can begin lacing shoes. With practice, five-year-olds can tie them. By four, children are efficient at dressing themselves. Four-year-olds can eat neatly and use proper manners.

As the list of accomplishments grows for preschoolers, they are excited by the feelings of independence and self-worth that result. According to Erikson, these feelings give rise to a sense of **initiative** (ih-NIH-shuh-tiv)—*motivation to accomplish more.* Children feel good about what they learn to do and therefore try to accomplish more in order to increase the good feelings. As a result, preschoolers are very willing to be helpful. They especially like contributing to the group. In the classroom, they can pick up toys, water plants, set the table, feed animals, and help pass out name cards.

SOCIAL DEVELOPMENT

*B*efore the preschool years, most social interactions for children are centered around adults. By three years of age, peers increase in importance.

The Role of Play

Three-year-olds like to play in small groups of two or three. By five, children enjoy playing in groups of five to eight. Through play, preschoolers develop social skills. They learn to get along and trade with each other. They gain the willingness to give in a little in order to reach compromises. They can also negotiate, or bargain, for what they want. Preschoolers become more comfortable joining in activities with others and suggesting their own. They learn to capture other children's interests with their play

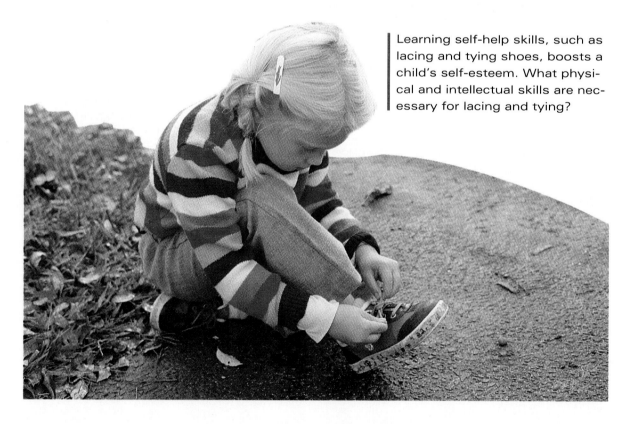

Learning self-help skills, such as lacing and tying shoes, boosts a child's self-esteem. What physical and intellectual skills are necessary for lacing and tying?

Conflicts occur frequently among preschoolers. Use good judgment in deciding whether and how to intervene.

ideas. This enables them to engage in **cooperative play**—*playing together and agreeing on play themes and activities.*

When given many opportunities to play, children become skilled in forming relationships. Learning how to form relationships helps children create a support system of friends during all stages of life.

Forming Friendships

By four, children begin to form close friendships with one or two other children, whom they refer to as their "best friends." By five years of age, children form close-knit groups of preferred playmates. They can be cruel in their rejection of anyone who is not in their "group."

Preschoolers often "bribe" other children into friendship. A child might offer to let another child play with a favorite toy on the condition that they become best friends. These friendships are usually temporary. Preschoolers may have a different "best friend" every day of the week. After age six, friendships become more stable.

Dealing with Conflict

When conflicts arise between preschoolers, it is often over toys or personal property. Preschoolers can be very territorial. Children in group care often need to be reminded of which toys are the program's and which belong to individuals. When children are allowed to bring personal items

What are the benefits of dramatic play? How can adults encourage dramatic play activities?

from home, caregivers may ask that they bring only items that are easily shared, such as books and tapes. Individuals who have trouble sharing are often asked to keep personal belongings in their own private storage space so that disagreements don't occur.

Around four or five years of age, some children begin to use name-calling. They often direct silly, crude, or hurtful names at others. Some of this can be ignored by adults. If it becomes too frequent or intense, however, caregivers should firmly tell children that name-calling will not be allowed because it hurts people's feelings. In addition, caregivers themselves must be good role models by never calling children names.

Development of Identity

Around age three, children begin to notice that boys and girls are physically different. This is the beginning of **gender identity**, *the awareness of being male or female.* A person's appreciation for his or her own gender is an important part of good emotional health, including the development of self-esteem.

One way children develop gender identity is through **dramatic play**, *the imitation of real-life situations.* They might play house or play school. During dramatic play, children often pretend to be adults. Through this type of play, children learn about themselves as well as about others. Dramatic play allows them to explore the wide range of roles and careers that grown men and women have. Seeing both women and men in caregiving roles further emphasizes this lesson.

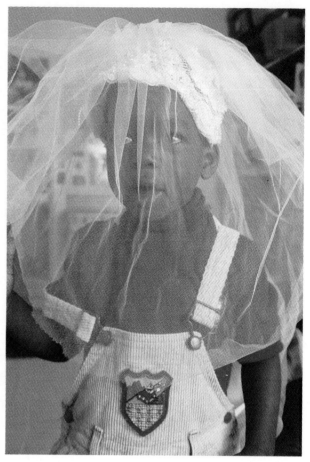

Preschoolers also become aware of differences in racial and ethnic backgrounds. They need to take pride in their own heritage and respect the heritage of others. These attitudes are encouraged when books, posters, music, and foods in the program represent many different cultures. It is also helpful if caregivers are from different cultural backgrounds.

Gender and racial stereotypes do not belong in any early childhood program, or anywhere else, for that matter. A **stereotype** is *a preset idea about a person or group of people based solely on one characteristic, such as gender, nationality, race, or religion.* A stereotype may be true of a few people in the group, but it is not true of all. For example, saying that all blondes are dumb is simply not true. Moreover, such statements can be hurtful. In addition, the statements often affect the thinking and attitudes of people. When stereotyping is not allowed, children can feel proud of who they are and more confident about developing their potential.

MORAL DEVELOPMENT

Children aged four and under have no real sense of right or wrong. They choose some actions and avoid others based on the understanding of consequences. They drink their juice because it makes a parent happy. They don't hit others because it results in punishment.

By age five, children begin developing a **conscience** (KAHNT-shunts). This means

they start to form *attitudes about right and wrong that guide their behavior*. They continue to base behavior on consequences; however, they also experience feelings of guilt when they believe they have behaved inappropriately or displeased an adult. Preschoolers can be very serious about right and wrong. They eagerly tell an adult whenever they see someone break a rule.

THE NEXT STEP

Growth in the preschool years is dramatic and exciting. As preschoolers become more mobile, as their vocabulary grows, as they learn to play with others, they can no longer be called "babies." They are in fact ready for the next major step in life: the beginning of formal education.

THE MULTICULTURAL CLASSROOM

At the preschool age, children are beginning to recognize similarities and differences and are very curious about things that are new to them. This is the ideal time to integrate activities with a cultural theme into the curriculum. Here are some ideas for ongoing, not just occasional, use:

- **Dress-Up Clothing.** Find sources of clothing, shoes, hats, and accessories that represent different cultures. You might receive donations from religious organizations and cultural centers. Also check thrift shops and catalogs.

- **Housekeeping Corner.** Supply an assortment of ethnic cooking tools. Include ethnic food containers, as long as they are safe for play. Plastic repli-

cas of ethnic foods can be obtained from some school supply companies.

- **Doll Area.** Handmade and store-bought dolls should represent many cultures and have appropriate clothing. Include male and female dolls. Dolls that depict older as well as younger ages add to dramatic play too.

- **Books and Music.** Sources for books and music are the public library, community cultural centers, early childhood organization chapters, and school supply catalogues. A travel agency might be a good resource for some items, including posters and brochures. By circulating the collection between classrooms, a limited budget can be stretched.

Chapter 6 Review

Chapter Summary

- Growth rate is slow and gradual during the preschool years.
- Motor development improves during the preschool years. Perceptual motor skills are also becoming more refined.
- Piaget described preschoolers' intellectual development as the pre-operational period.
- Preschoolers rapidly expand their vocabulary and expressive language skills.
- Preschoolers have better control over their emotions. They may still have a variety of fears.
- Self-help skills and other physical, as well as intellectual, accomplishments enhance preschoolers' self-esteem.
- Play is important to social development.
- Social development includes the ability to make friends, keep friends, and deal with conflicts with peers.
- Preschoolers are developing a sense of gender, racial, and ethnic identity.
- Preschoolers begin to develop a conscience.

Reviewing the Facts

1. Give three examples of how a preschool child's physical abilities develop from age three to five.
2. Describe the characteristics of the preoperational period of intellectual development.
3. How should you handle children's grammar and pronunciation mistakes?
4. Describe the type of stuttering that is common in many preschoolers. What is usually the cause of their stuttering?
5. What is empathy? How does this emotional development affect social development?
6. What is initiative? Why does Erikson believe preschoolers strive to develop initiative?
7. Describe the relationship between children's self-esteem and their physical and intellectual accomplishments.
8. What is cooperative play?
9. What is gender identity? Describe how children often develop gender identity.
10. What is a conscience? At what age does it begin to develop a conscience?

Thinking Critically

1. Why might caregivers tend to discourage preschoolers from learning self-help skills?
2. Should preschoolers be discouraged from bribing other children into friendship? From accepting such an offer? Explain your answer.
3. Do you think preschoolers should be allowed to resolve some conflicts among themselves, without adult intervention? Is so, what types of conflict? If not, why not?
4. What type of environment encourages initiative in preschoolers? What activities are provided? What other traits are promoted? What is the attitude of caregivers?
5. Do you think caregivers might promote stereotypes without realizing? Explain.

Activities and Applications

1. **Friendship.** Question several five-year-olds about friendship. Ask them to define "friend." Have them tell what they

Chapter 6 Review

think a good friend is and does. Write a paragraph that summarizes your findings.

2. **Moral Development.** With a partner, write a skit in which a five-year-old must make a moral decision commonly faced by preschoolers. Have the character describe his or her feelings, thoughts, and reasoning as the decision is made about what to do.

Your Professional Portfolio

Begin to accumulate a list of outstanding children's books that you would like to use if you work with children someday. Read and review the books as you add them to your list. Use suggestions from librarians, your instructor, and other sources to get your list started. Keep the list in your portfolio and develop it as you complete this course.

Observing and Analyzing

Observing the Preschool Child

Once children reach the preschool age, observing becomes even more interesting. Language skills have developed to a level that is easily understood by most observers. The following observation ideas will help you focus on some of the preschooler's growth achievements:

- **Dramatic Play.** The area of the center that is used for dramatic play or housekeeping can be an ideal place to get well acquainted with preschoolers. While staying within hearing range but as much out of sight as possible, observe the roles children play. Listen carefully to what they say. How do the youngest play and interact in this area? How is the play of the older children different?

- **Preoperational Stage.** Find an opportunity to observe preschoolers while they are using molding clay. The teacher gives all of the children fairly equal amounts. Do any of the children ask for more in order to have as much as another child? When the children start to roll, pound, and create objects from their clay, listen carefully to their comments about who has the most and the least. What other activities are available for developing the principle of conservation?

- **Perceptual Motor Development.** Look at the drawings done by a group of three- to five-year-olds. Record some of the details you notice, especially of people. Look for facial expressions, fingers, necks, clothing, and body proportions. What details distinguish the drawings of a three-year-old from those of a five-year-old?

SCHOOL TO WORK

Chapter 7

Understanding School-Age Children

CHAPTER OBJECTIVES

- Describe the physical and intellectual development of school-age children.

- Explain how improved motor and perceptual motor skills influence school-age children's activities.

- Analyze the impact of puberty, self-esteem, competition, fear, stress, and rules on school-age children.

- Compare and contrast friendship among preschoolers to that of school-age children.

Terms to Learn

- concrete operations period
- depth perception
- diversity
- growth plateau
- hormones
- industry
- inferiority
- puberty
- school-age children
- stress

Approaching Whittier Elementary School for an orientation meeting, Marc Caruso saw that he'd arrived during recess. Next semester he would be a student teacher at the school, and he was about to learn more about his assignment. Even before he could see the playground, he could hear the sound of children.

"Bet I can run faster than you!"

"Oh, Brian, you're such a show-off!"

"Aileen, want to come over after school tonight?"

As he rounded the corner of the building, Marc saw a display of energy and emotion. A group of girls and boys played a boisterous soccer match on a grassy field. Three children went for the ball at once and sprawled in a shrieking, giggling tangle of legs. At the basketball hoop, four children dribbled, passed, and shot the ball, while a fifth "announced" the game into his fist. On the swings, three children sat close together, heads hung in solemn conversation. One girl reached toward the girl in the center and hugged her around the shoulders. The girl in the center began to smile and wipe her eyes.

Marc took a deep breath. As a young teacher-to-be, he was filled with a range of emotions: excitement, enthusiasm, uncertainty, caring. "From the looks of it," he thought to himself, "I'm not the only one."

THE SCHOOL-AGE YEARS

Whether on the playground or anywhere else, school-age children are an interesting mixture of emotions and energy. Working with them presents new challenges.

As with any age group, you need to understand school-age children in order to work well with them. **School-age children** *include a wide range of ages, from six to twelve.* Because children change so much during those years, it helps to break the ages down for discussion. In this text, school-age means children who are six to ten. References to older children means eleven to twelve.

Development Continues

Imagine that you are hiking up a steep and winding trail. Halfway to the end you start to feel winded. You slow your pace for a while to replenish your energy reserves and then push off again with renewed vigor. The school-age years are similar. After a half-dozen years of rapid growth, school-age children ease off the pace. Physically, they level off before the final surge toward maturity. Socially, they strengthen friendships. Intellectually, emotionally, and morally, they begin to feel the expectation to act more like adults than children. Even more than in other stages of life, growth in school-age children points to greater development to come.

PHYSICAL DEVELOPMENT

Younger school-age children are in a **growth plateau.** They have reached *a period of relatively slow and steady growth.* Children in this age range continue to build muscles and bone and to develop a longer, leaner appearance.

The chart below shows approximate heights and weights for children from ages six to eight. Throughout this period, boys are a little heavier than girls. By age eight, however, girls catch up with boys' weights.

At five or six years of age, children begin losing their baby teeth. Gaps left by missing teeth may temporarily affect speech, causing some children to lisp—"s" and "z" may sound like "th." By ten, these children have many of their adult teeth.

Signs of Puberty

Around age twelve (slightly younger for girls), children undergo a surge of growth. This marks the beginning of a new, even more dramatic kind of physical development, a transition stage of life. Older chil-

Compared with infants and toddlers, school-age children grow more slowly. Individual children of the same age can still vary significantly in size.

Average Heights and Weights of Six- to Eight-Year-Olds		
AGE	**HEIGHT**	**WEIGHT**
Six Years	46 in. (117 cm)	45 lbs. (20.4 kg)
Seven Years	48 in. (122 cm)	50 lbs. (22.7 kg)
Eight Years	50 in. (127 cm)	55 lbs. (25 kg)

Nutrition and the School-Age Child

Getting proper nutrition can be a challenge for school-age children. Most children who have been taught healthful eating habits continue to follow them. However, a number of factors in their increasingly independent lives begin to present obstacles.

Television viewing can be a problem. Watching television encourages an inactive lifestyle. Also, foods advertised during children's programming tend to be high in sugar, fat, and sodium but low in other nutrients. These factors contribute to childhood obesity. Obesity is defined as being 20 percent or more over a healthful weight. In children, it is linked with heart and respiratory disease, diabetes, and poor self-esteem. The number of obese children in the United States has increased by 50 percent in the last 20 years.

Active children, too, may have poor eating habits. They may become so involved with school, friends, and other interests that they do not make time for nutritious eating and end up "eating on the run." Their food choices then tend to be limited and not always healthful.

A small number of school-age children suffer from eating disorders. These are caused in part by society's emphasis on thinness as a desirable quality and partly by anxieties over growing up.

Children with eating disorders often resort to starving themselves or forcing themselves to vomit after meals in order to lose or avoid gaining weight. Young athletes, especially gymnasts and wrestlers, may be encouraged to diet to stay small or to compete in a particular weight class.

Caregivers have less control over what school-age children eat, but they can still help children make nutritious food choices. They can teach young children healthful eating habits. They can also be careful of the messages they send children about food, eating, and dieting.

---

dren end childhood and begin **puberty**, *a stage when boys and girls undergo a series of physical changes and begin to develop into men and women who are able to reproduce.* Puberty is the result of an increase in **hormones**, *growth-regulating chemicals that are produced by the body and carried in the blood.* Puberty leads to adulthood.

Girls may experience the onset of puberty six months to a year younger than boys. Hormones that cause girls to menstruate begin to be secreted, usually around ages ten to twelve but sometimes as late as age fourteen. Girls begin to weigh more than boys as their body fat increases slightly. This is normal and healthy for girls during puberty. At this time, it is not unusual for girls to pass up boys in height as well.

Once boys are well into puberty, their heights and weights surpass those of girls. Boys develop more muscle tissue, which adds considerable weight. The growth of facial hair is another development. Also as a result of male hormone production, boys experience a change in their voices. Their voices may frequently "crack" or sound squeaky until permanently lowering in pitch.

A Sense of Humor

WHAT IS A SENSE OF HUMOR?

Having a sense of humor lets you see the lighter side of a situation. You still recognize problems, and you know when a serious approach is needed. At the same time, you realize that many problems are less threatening and easier to deal with when you can find a way to laugh about them.

A Sense of Humor in Action

"I hate my nose!"

"I'll never be as tall as the other boys."

"Why can't I be pretty like my sister?"

Every day, Gwen heard self-critical remarks like these from her sixth-graders. She wished she could make them understand that what they were experiencing was only temporary. Eventually their bodies would grow in all the ways they were supposed to. Not everyone would be as tall or as pretty as each would like, but that didn't matter either.

One day Gwen came to class with bright orange hair and a big red nose. Two of her teeth appeared to be missing, and a wart had sprung up on her face overnight. She wore enormous shoes, a green-and-blue plaid skirt, and a purple blouse.

At first the students greeted her with stunned silence; a few began to giggle.

"What are you looking at?" she asked innocently.

"You look . . . funny," said one.

"You look *weird*," corrected another.

"Oh?" Gwen acted surprised. She sat on her desk and raised her oversized feet. "I rather like the way I look."

They started talking then about appearances, and why people look as they do, and what makes some people unhappy with their looks.

"Does it really matter whether I have orange hair—" she pulled off the wig—"or brown? Does it make me a better teacher? Or a better person?" Her eyes met a room full of smiling, understanding faces. She smiled back.

"Whatever they learn this year," she thought, "nothing else could be more important."

Your Analysis

1. How did Gwen show a sense of humor in dealing with this problem?

2. What might have been some consequences if Gwen had tried to discuss the matter seriously? Do you think a serious approach would have been more effective or less? Explain your answer.

3. Might there be negative consequences of looking at a problem humorously? If so, explain what these might be.

4. Describe a time when you faced a problem with humor.

For both boys and girls, the high level of hormone production during puberty can cause intense mood swings. Also, new oils are produced that can lead to acne, oily hair, and body odor. Older school-age children must pay extra attention to hygiene and grooming.

Motor Development

School-age children perfect the skills they need for body control. Large muscles now work in unison, improving coordination. By age ten, all types of gross motor movement, such as galloping and leaping, are possible. School-age children often like to challenge their bodies with daring feats of climbing and risk taking.

Control over small muscles is most often fully achieved by age seven or eight. Their ability to control muscles in the wrists, hands, and fingers enables children to handle writing instruments, a skill they need for school participation. Playing a musical instrument also requires the control of these small muscles.

As both genders experience increased muscle strength and coordination, as well as improved perceptual motor skills, they become more involved in team games and sports. These activities require quick movements, coordination of the body, and **depth perception**, *the ability to judge distance and see objects in perspective.* With perceptual motor development come many new opportunities to challenge the body. Younger school-age children can learn to skate, play T-ball, and snow ski. By ages eight to ten, many can play hockey, dodge ball, and baseball with skill.

Both genders participate in rough and tumble play, but you may notice that more boys choose this type of play. After eight to ten years of age, girls may be as active in sports as boys, but many do not roughhouse as much. Caregivers need to be cautious

Sports both require motor skills and improve them. What motor skills are needed to play baseball?

about pushing children into activities that are traditionally considered "male" or "female." Children will be happier when they are allowed to pursue hobbies and interests that suit their personalities rather than gender stereotypes.

INTELLECTUAL DEVELOPMENT

*T*he ability to create, analyze, and evaluate ideas progresses rapidly during the school-age years. According to Piaget, school-age children are no longer bound to learning through their senses, as were preschool children in the preoperational period of development. They are now in what Piaget termed the **concrete operations period** of development. *This is a period of intellectual development during which children (ages seven to eleven) think logically. In other words, they use valid reasoning to think things through. They relate logic to actual objects and experiences.* With greatly improved thinking processes, children have a better grasp of complex concepts.

Once they have reached the concrete operations period, children can grasp the principle of *conservation.* Remember Maya, who in the last chapter thought the quantity of juice changed after it was poured into a different glass? As a school-age child, Maya understands that the volume, or quantity, of a liquid does not change just because the shape of the glass holding it does. School-age children can also consider several variables at one time. This allows them to classify and order different categories of objects, important skills when studying math and science.

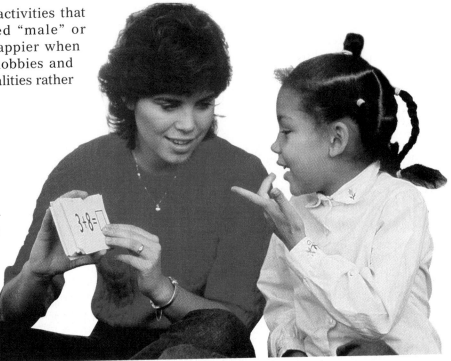

Why is it difficult for many young school-age children to learn basic math skills?

Complex concepts become clearer in the concrete operations period. Children can understand and calculate the passage of time. School-age children can remember the past, consider the present, and anticipate and plan for the future.

Although children in this period are beginning to think logically, they still learn best by direct experience. The younger the child, the more dependent he or she is on handling or seeing material objects in order to solve problems. For example, seven-year-old Dana cannot mentally subtract 3 from 19. When given buttons to use as a visual cue, however, she can count 19 buttons, remove 3, and see that 19 minus 3 leaves 16. As Dana progresses through the concrete operations period, she will need fewer and fewer visual or sensory cues to analyze and solve increasingly complex problems.

Many children use computers for both learning and play. For children with disabilities, such as those that limit movement or speech, computers play an important role in everyday life.

Curiosity about a wide variety of topics is characteristic of school-age children. By ten, they have mastered the basic language skills of speaking, reading, comprehending, and writing. They understand basic mathematical concepts and can apply them to solving problems. These skills enable school-age children to explore new subjects. More detailed explorations of biology, geography, and social studies are possible. Their abilities to create and analyze ideas, as well as to plan, also allow children to try such hobbies as woodworking, crafts, and cooking.

Word Power and Mind Power

Development of language skills in school-age children reflects overall intellectual growth. What signs of intellectual development do you recognize in the progression of language skills below?

SIX TO SEVEN YEARS
- Learns to print capitals and small letters.
- Learns short vowel sounds and common consonant and vowel blends.

- Reads a simple book alone.
- Recognizes common word endings, such as -er and -ing.

EIGHT TO NINE YEARS
- Prints all letters and begins to learn script (handwriting).
- Reads aloud fluently.
- Writes a simple story alone.
- Begins to use a dictionary.

TEN YEARS AND OLDER
- Writes in script automatically.
- Reads for information and writes a simple factual report.
- Begins to use indexes, appendices, and footnotes to find information.
- Learns to use prefixes and suffixes to identify meanings of words.

EMOTIONAL DEVELOPMENT

Although you may not remember much about your own years as a preschooler and younger, you may have memories about your school-age years. What were your emotions like? If you were typical as a young school-age child, you had a wide array of emotions, and you had the ability to express them. Language skills, refined during the preschool years, allow school-age children to express their emotions frequently and more clearly than ever before.

School-age children understand the viewpoints of others better; however, they don't always agree with others. True discussions and debates begin to surface during the school-age years.

School-age children further develop empathy and begin to feel compassion. With empathy improved, they are better able to recognize and understand the feelings of others. As *compassion* is added, they are able to sympathize with another's feelings and difficulties. Their increased empathy and newfound compassion inspire school-age children to become part of a campaign to better the world. They may join causes, perhaps aiming to help animals or preserve the environment.

School-age children can be very sensitive and sentimental. It is not unusual for them to cry over a sad movie or book. Properly channeled, all these traits can lead to the development of good citizens and caring adults.

Development of Self-Esteem

By age six, most children have established a clear identification with their own gender. They have developed strong ties to their family and cultural background. All of this helps them form a stable and secure self-concept.

Self-confidence and pride are reinforced by new physical accomplishments. In addition, the ability to converse on a more mature level often allows school-age children to participate more fully in adult conversations. Increasing attention from adults adds to building the self-esteem of school-age children.

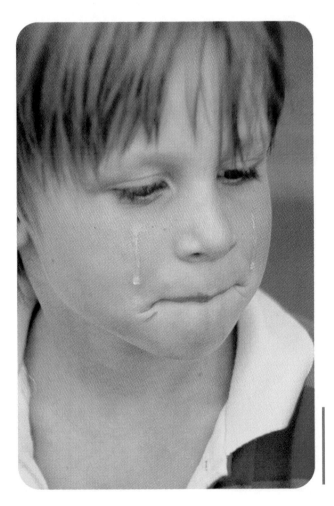

Learning emotional self-control is not easy. What emotions does society tell us are acceptable to show openly? Which are considered unacceptable? Do you agree with these attitudes?

According to Erikson, school-age children strive to develop a sense of **industry**. This is *the desire to perform skills, succeed at tasks, and make social contributions.* School-age children want to put their energy to use. Erikson claimed that if school-age children are not able to feel productive, they will develop a sense of **inferiority,** *a feeling of not having met expected standards.* Feeling inferior greatly damages self-esteem. School-age children need to be provided with many opportunities for success in their interactions with peers—games, sports activities, and group projects, as well as in learning situations—in order to prevent feelings of inferiority from developing.

Many, but not all, children enjoy competitive activities. In some cultures, cooperation is emphasized, not competition. What effects do you think this would have?

Competition

The issue of competition among school-age children has been widely debated. Think back to the competitive activities that you participated in as a child. Your impression of how they affected you will influence your thinking about how much competition you believe is good for children.

School-age children begin to compare themselves to other people. As they progress through the school years, they experience more emphasis on competition in sports and school subjects. Looking at what others can do and comparing that to their own skills is only natural. Trying to measure up can be a challenge, but it can also be a disappointment.

Many people see healthy, reasonable competition as good for children. It motivates them to do their best and helps them assess their individual abilities as compared to the group. Competition can refine skills and talents. Participating in team competition rewards children for cooperating with others and recognizing their contributions.

Excessive emphasis on competition—the idea that winning is more important than enjoying the activity—can be harmful. Some children may focus more on their weaknesses than their strengths. This also damages self-esteem. Children may avoid participating in activities for fear of failure, thereby hindering their development. To avoid these situations, many teachers emphasize cooperative games over competitive games, especially in the early school-age years. Helping children identify their own strengths and take pride and pleasure in them is better than making comparisons.

Change in Fears

When children reach school age, they usually let go of the more specific fears that they had at the preschool age. They are not as likely to be afraid of things like dogs and storms. Instead, their increased reasoning powers allow for anxieties that are more vague but every bit as troubling.

School-age children are fearful of not belonging to a group. They are afraid of being teased and criticized by children and adults. They often worry that they won't have friends. They sometimes imagine that others are talking about them behind their back. They fear being different, which could result in not being accepted.

Many school-age children fear failure. They hate the thought of disappointing parents, teachers, and other respected adults.

Some school-age children worry about world events that are beyond their control, such as war, earthquakes, famine, and drought. The fact that they are better able to understand other points of view probably contributes to this concern for problems in the world. These children are able to think more abstractly and are less egocentric. Thus, they begin to worry about people other than themselves and family members.

All of these fears are very real to school-age children. Adults should take them seriously and not make fun of children for having them. Giving children opportunities to talk about their fears is helpful. If fears become very exaggerated and irrational, caregivers may wish to consult mental health professionals.

Increased Stress

You've probably heard people long for "the good old days," a time when life seemed more simple and enjoyable. Increasingly, this is true for school-age children.

Stress is present at every stage of life. **Stress** is *mental and physical tension and strain caused by problems, pressures, fears, or unsettling changes.* School-age children have always had their own particular sources of stress. They must devote hours of energy toward developing new intellectual and physical skills. They must concentrate for long periods of time during the school day. They may face the added stress of fears or excessive emphasis on competition.

School-age children these days may also have less relaxation time at home. A typical schedule is group care from 6:00 a.m. to 9:00 a.m., school until 3:00 p.m., and group care again until 6:00 p.m. Many have organized activities that take up some of their evening

The fear of being excluded is very real during the school years. Dressing and acting like everyone else are often keys to popularity. How could the experience of being excluded by others be harmful? Could it be helpful?

time. The leisure hours left for family and friends are often limited.

Family and personal problems can also greatly increase stress. Illness or injury, the addition of a sibling, and the divorce of parents can all make children tense and strained.

Children show stress in many ways. They may develop fatigue, apathy, and even depression. Some children become easily angered, aggressive, and disobedient. Such signs as biting their nails and pulling out their eyelashes also point to stress. Teachers and caregivers should watch for these signals and consult with parents and mental health professionals when necessary.

Approaching Puberty

Older school-age children have additional emotional challenges. Developmental transitions are hard at any age, but especially so for school-age children

---

> ### *Tip*
> **FROM THE**
> ### *Pros*
>
> *T*o better understand school-age children, try to find schoolwork, letters, a diary, and other mementos from your own childhood. These can give you insights into their attitudes and behavior.

---

approaching puberty. It's not uncommon for older school-age children to behave differently from day to day. One day they are struggling to be an adult; the next day they are clinging to the security of childhood. Their increased desire for privacy can add to their moodiness. At these times, children need patience and respect. They need plenty of chances to talk about their new feelings, as well as reassurance that what they are experiencing is not unusual.

SOCIAL DEVELOPMENT

*F*rom preschool to school age, the way friendships are handled changes. During the school-age years, friendships become more lasting and meaningful. They are formed because children sincerely appreciate the characteristics of another person rather than because of convenience or personal gain. Feelings and values are shared during the school years. This "bonding" results in friendships. Younger school-age children have many friends of both genders. By seven or eight years of age, children prefer friends of the same gender.

School-age friendships remain fairly stable despite periodic conflicts. Squabbling seems to be just another part of being friends. Socially competent school-age children know how to be close and nurture friendships.

Think about a special friend you had while growing up. How did that relationship make a difference in your life?

When school-age children make friends, it is sometimes at the expense of other children. An "us versus them" attitude sometimes exists. School-age children do have the capacity for great sensitivity. Their growing concern for acceptance by peers, however, can lead them to be cruel toward those who are not considered "friends." They can engage in unmerciful teasing and sometimes even hurt other children physically.

If teasing or physical conflict occurs, caregivers should firmly communicate that it is not acceptable. Child care programs should be a haven where children are protected from verbal and physical abuse.

Recognition of Diversity

Diversity is *the term often used today when talking about all the qualities people have that make them different from one another.* By the time children reach the school-age years, they are aware of differences. They see variations in gender, race, culture, and physical and mental abilities. They observe the way other people react to differences and easily adopt similar attitudes.

You are probably aware of what can happen when differences are the basis for dislike. Racial problems, gang violence, and simple rejection from a social group are all examples. These situations hurt individuals—as well as society.

Children need to grow up with positive attitudes toward differences. Differences should be discussed openly and honestly. A child care program that integrates children from many different economic levels and social and cultural backgrounds helps school-age children accept and enjoy diversity. An environment that not only acknowledges, but also celebrates, differences helps school-age children become compassionate, tolerant, and accepting.

MORAL DEVELOPMENT

With intellectual and social development comes moral growth. Younger school-age children are very concerned about rules. They continue to obey them to earn rewards and avoid punishment. They also begin to see that rules are needed for people to live together peacefully. They may not always follow the rules, but they do know that they are necessary. With development of

In life children will meet and work with people of many different backgrounds. Help them to see people as individuals, not stereotypes.

THE MULTICULTURAL CLASSROOM

Preadolescent children are often embarrassed to draw attention to themselves. They may prefer to blend in or even be anonymous. Promoting acceptance and understanding of all ethnic backgrounds means taking a sensitive approach with children of this age. Here are some ideas for creating an atmosphere of sharing and caring:

- **Mapping Origins.** Put a large world map on the bulletin board. Use map tacks to indicate the birthplace of each child and possibly parents or grandparents. This is also a great tool for teaching about world news.

- **Star of the Week.** Set up a list for use in featuring one child each week on a special bulletin board. Include a current photo and a "star questionnaire" that has information filled in about the child's favorite television show, book, hobbies, sports, foods, etc. Other photos of family, pets, and home may be added when possible. Cover the entire bulletin board with a sheet of acrylic or plastic to protect photos.

- **Sharing Thoughts.** During group time, an occasional survey allows the children to understand each other better and discover ways that they are similar. Some suggested topics include fears, likes and dislikes, ideas for room improvements, and group decisions, such as plans for a field trip. Decision-making is also a hands-on lesson in democracy.

conscience, children like to make sure everybody else obeys the rules as well.

Awareness of rules and their purpose allows children to develop and participate in group games. The games may focus on intellectual skills and have rules that must be obeyed. Children might play card games or such physical games as hopscotch and soccer. Playing fairly takes on great importance to school-age children.

As children become older and develop stronger personal relationships, they are more likely to feel outside pressure when deciding between right and wrong. They are highly influenced by the expectations of family, peers, teachers, and other influential groups. The ideas children have about right and wrong may vary according to whatever group is most important to them.

Limited though it is, this developing sense of morality makes school-age children different from younger children. They are slowly discovering their ability to make their own decisions and control their actions.

APPROACHING ADULTHOOD

You might think of the school-age years as the last act in the stage drama of childhood. Much has to be learned and resolved before the curtain falls. When it rises again, the main characters will be as close to adulthood as to childhood. They need a firm foundation to fulfill this most challenging of roles. When children get what they need from skillful, concerned caregivers, they can approach and eventually manage adulthood with confidence and competence.

Chapter 7 Review

Chapter Summary

- Younger school-age children (six to ten years old) are in a growth plateau. Older school-age children (ages eleven to twelve) are approaching, or experiencing, a growth spurt and the beginning of puberty.
- Motor and perceptual skills develop rapidly during the school-age years.
- School-age children are in the concrete operations period of intellectual development.
- Self-esteem can suffer if children do not experience successes.
- Competition, fears, stress, and puberty affect emotional development.
- School-age children form deep and meaningful friendships.
- Social rules are important for school-age children.
- The developing sense of morality in a school-age child is used to help the child make decisions and control actions.

Reviewing the Facts

1. Define puberty. Describe the physical changes that take place during puberty for males and females.
2. Briefly describe the motor development of school-age children and how this development affects the activities they enjoy.
3. Discuss some of the abilities displayed in the concrete operations period of intellectual development.
4. Explain Erikson's beliefs about the relationship between industry and inferiority concerning school-age children.
5. Describe both the positive and negative effects of competition on emotional development. How is competition best handled?
6. How and why do school-age children's fears differ from preschooler's? Give examples.
7. What is stress? What stresses are common in the life of a school-age child?
8. How does puberty affect school-age children's emotional development?
9. What is the basis for friendship in the school-age years?
10. How do attitudes about rules change in the preschool years? How does this affect game-playing?

Thinking Critically

1. How might the physical changes associated with the approach of puberty make school-age children feel different from their peers? What effect might this have on self-esteem?
2. Do you think school-age children today are pushed into becoming adults before they are ready? If so, what evidence of this do you see? What might be some causes? How can the problem be combated?
3. Why do you think some school-age children tease or exclude others? What can be done to prevent this?
4. What kinds of situations do you think help build a school-age child's self-esteem? Do they have to be ones that involve other children? What happens that allows self-esteem to grow?

Activities and Applications

1. **Motor Skills.** With a partner, compile a list of activities that would help school-age children develop gross motor skills, fine

motor skills, and depth perception. Make a separate list for each type of development.

2. **Stress.** In newspapers and magazines, find articles and advertisements related to the stress and pressure school-age children face today. Discuss which types of stress are inevitable and which can be avoided.

SCHOOL TO WORK

Your Professional Portfolio

Begin a collection of ideas for cooperative games. Talk to others and consult references that include such games. (You might record these on index cards.) Then create a cooperative game of your own to include in the collection. As you write descriptions of the games, explain them as accurately as possible, so that you can use them easily if you work with children someday. Keep the file in your portfolio.

Observing and Analyzing

Gaining Insight on the School-Age Child

If you were in charge of guiding the activities for school-age children, what might be one of your most challenging tasks? It could be planning activities that hold their interest as well as assist their development.

School-age children cover a wide range of ages. The six-year-old just out of kindergarten won't have the same interests or abilities that the twelve-year-old has. Knowing what works at each age level is a skill you can build through study and observation.

Whenever you are around children in this age range, pay attention to what abilities they have. Take note of the activities that they enjoy and how they benefit from them. If possible, visit a school-age program. As you observe, use these questions to guide your thinking:

1. What ages are grouped together?
2. Which activities are intellectually challenging?
3. Which activities are physically challenging?
4. What kinds of projects and activities enhance the child's self-esteem?
5. What are the most and least popular activities?
6. What options do children have when they do not wish to participate in the planned activities?
7. Describe the attention span of the children you observed. How did it affect their activity?
8. What, if anything, caused interference in any of the activities?
9. What contributed to the effectiveness of activities?
10. What changes would you recommend to improve this program?

Career Profile

Meet James Lee, a pre-kindergarten teacher in a public school. James helps children at risk of academic failure improve their readiness for kindergarten. James teaches morning and afternoon sessions of twelve four-year-old children. He is assisted by one aide and one parent volunteer.

Why did you choose this career?

"I began working with children as an aide in a Head Start program. While working there I earned my CDA credential and was placed in charge of my own classroom. That experience got me interested in being a teacher. I learned about pre-kindergarten teaching jobs at a conference of the NAEYC. Although I loved Head Start, I thought it would be exciting to work in other areas of early childhood education."

What education and skills do you need?

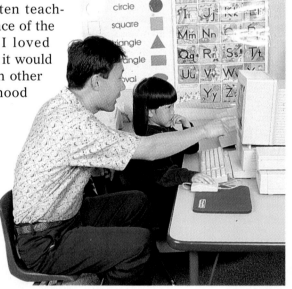

"For this job, the public school system requires a bachelor's degree in early childhood education. Part of my coursework in college helped me learn how to teach children with special needs. That training has been very useful, since many of the children in the program have learning problems or other difficulties. I also attend several conferences each year.

"To be an effective pre-kindergarten teacher, it's important to know typical child development. I must be able to observe and document development that is different or unusual in each child.

"Curriculum planning is a big part of my job. I'm responsible for coming up with creative activities to stimulate intellectual, emotional, social, and physical development.

"Communication skills are important, too. I talk frequently with parents about how their children are progressing. Outside of class I conduct parent conferences, home visits, and write a weekly newsletter.

"To encourage parents to read to their children at home, I organized and manage a lending library. Like many aspects of my job, this requires close attention to detail."

142

What is a typical day on the job like?

"As all good teachers do, I arrive about half an hour early to review plans and prepare for the day. At 8:00 a.m. I meet the first group of children as they arrive on the bus. Throughout the morning the children play in learning centers and participate in planned activities, such as baking mini-pizzas or playing with magnets. I move from one small group to another guiding children's learning. I also spend individual time with children when needed.

"Some days a speech therapist comes into the classroom. Many of my children have language delays, so the speech therapist and I work together to stimulate language development.

"After the morning session ends at 11:30, I have a quick lunch and catch up on paperwork. Some days I use this time to telephone parents, make field trip arrangements, and record information about children's development for their file. At 1:00 p.m. the process starts all over again. My afternoon class leaves at 4:30. I use the last hour of each day to develop lesson plans and attend to other program details."

What is most challenging about your job?

"Some children need more help than I can give them. For instance, one child was very aggressive toward the other children. Nothing I did could stop the behavior. I tried to convince the parents to go for family counseling, but they were too embarrassed to seek help."

What is your favorite part of being a pre-kindergarten teacher?

"I love seeing children bloom after attending our program! After just a few short months, children who barely spoke begin to speak in complete sentences. Children who were quiet and afraid to play with others often end up being leaders by the end of the year. By helping children develop in the early years I believe I'm helping prevent possible school failure. That makes me feel really proud of my job!"

SHARE YOUR THOUGHTS

1. What would be the benefits of having only twelve children per classroom?
2. What information would be important for teachers to include in parent newsletters?
3. What part of being a pre-kindergarten teacher sounds most interesting to you? What part would you like least?

THE CHILD CARE CENTER

CHAPTER

Reflections

"I guess you could say it was a dream come true for me. When I first saw this old building, I just knew I could turn it into the preschool I had always wanted to have. The structure was sound, and the layout of the building was just right. All it needed was a little work. Well, I was right about the 'work' and wrong about the 'little.' Some friends helped me get started. We planned, scrubbed, sanded, pounded, and painted. It took a lot of effort. It also took getting over some financing and licensing hurdles, but it was worth it. The Morning Glory Preschool is a great place for children to spend time. It's lively, loving, and interesting—and for me, it's finally a reality."

—Miriam

Chapter 8

Operating an Early Childhood Program

CHAPTER OBJECTIVES

- Give examples of program philosophy statements and goals.

- Describe different types of early childhood programs.

- Assess the impact of licensing laws and other regulations.

- Explain the roles of director, staff, advisory board, and parents.

Terms to Learn

- advisory board
- liability insurance
- licensing laws
- philosophy
- policy
- program goals
- self-correcting
- staff-to-child ratio

That's my favorite part of the classroom," Lilly Brazelton said as she pointed to the art center. "There's just something about art activities that allows us to put so much of the program philosophy into action."

Lilly was doing something that she really enjoyed—showing off her early childhood program to an inquiring parent. As the director, Lilly was proud of what they accomplished, and she loved introducing new children and their parents to the program.

"Watch Mr. Gasparini work with the children, and you'll see what I mean," Lilly went on. "These little ones don't worry about whether they have artistic talent or not. They just want to try things. They have to learn to listen to Mr. Gasparini first. We believe communication is important. Then they practice all kinds of other skills—everything from fine motor skills, to sharing, to creativity. Mr. G makes sure they feel good about what they do. If that isn't a self-esteem booster, I don't know what is. When the children help clean up, they learn responsibility. I could go on and on, but you can see why I like art activities so much."

Mrs. Alvarez smiled in response to Lilly's enthusiasm. She was quickly getting good vibrations about this place. The program philosophy was becoming clear to her as she listened to Lilly speak, and she liked what she was hearing. "I could feel comfortable leaving Conrad here," she thought to herself. She was well on the way toward making a decision.

PROGRAM PHILOSOPHY

*I*f there is one element that can be called the core of any early childhood program, it is the philosophy of that program. The **philosophy** of an early childhood program *describes general beliefs, concepts, and attitudes the program has about how children learn and how the program should serve and educate young children.* A sample program philosophy is shown on page 149. Principles like these are what guide the operation of a program. They are what parents look for in hopes of finding a program that fits with their own thinking.

Lilly Brazelton and her staff have a clear idea about the philosophy of their program. Because they do, their actions reflect that philosophy in the activities they plan and the way they handle the children. When Lilly introduces people to her program, she talks freely about what goes on, showing the link between philosophical principles and the activity in the center. In any well-managed early childhood program, you might hear a director like Lilly describe a program by saying something like, "We believe that . . ." You know then that you are learning about their philosophy.

PROGRAM GOALS

*P*rogram goals are an outgrowth of philosophy. Once the general philosophy is established, program goals that support the philosophy can be set up. **Program goals** *identify basic skills, concepts, and attitudes to be developed and encouraged in children.* They are usually more specific than philosophical statements. While philosophical statements talk about beliefs that the program holds, the program goals spell out what children should gain because of these beliefs. For example, a program might expect children to:

- Gain high self-esteem and a positive attitude.
- Learn self-help skills that lead to independence and responsibility.
- Develop positive social skills, such as cooperation and sharing.
- Learn problem-solving skills.
- Develop gross and fine motor skills.
- Improve communication skills, including listening, speaking, reading, and writing.
- Develop curiosity about the world.
- Improve creative thinking and playing abilities.
- Gain respect, acceptance, and understanding of the rights and feelings of others.
- Learn how to handle and store play materials properly.

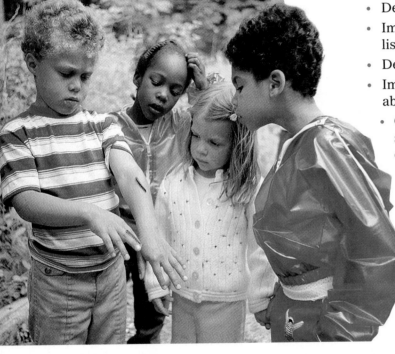

Writing down program goals helps make sure they are achieved. How might these children's teacher follow up on their curiosity about caterpillars?

*A*s a child care professional, you can do a better job when you have a clear idea of the program philosophy. Ask about philosophy before you take a job. Then you will know whether you agree with the principles and can support them in your work. Knowing the philosophy improves your communication on the job too. When you understand why the program operates as it does, you are better able to discuss qualities of the program with parents and other staff members.

A Sample Program Philosophy

*B*elow are some of the beliefs that guide program development in one specific child care center:

- Children need many sensory, concrete, hands-on learning experiences.
- Different children have different learning styles, rates of learning, and developmental levels.
- The classroom should be designed to nurture curiosity, exploration, and investigation.
- Children need time for independent activity as well as cooperative effort.
- The curriculum should evolve from the interests and needs of children enrolled in the classroom.
- Activities should address the development of the whole child, including physical, intellectual, social, emotional, and moral development.

- The classroom and teacher-child interactions should encourage problem-solving and creativity.
- Children learn best when allowed to explore and arrive at answers and understand concepts through their own process of thinking. Trial and error is an acceptable means of trying to make sense of the world.
- Parent involvement is desirable and, in fact, necessary in order to enhance the overall development of the young child.
- Because a child's self-esteem is very precious, teachers are employed who like, respect, and enjoy children, and who delight in the milestones of development that take place in the early years of life.

EARLY CHILDHOOD PROGRAMS

*W*hen you examine early childhood programs, you will notice both similarities and differences. That's to be expected. Each program aims at providing a safe environment in which children can develop and learn. However, their sponsors and the reasons why they were created are not the same. Moreover, the philosophies behind them are different.

Some of the early childhood programs you were introduced to in Chapter 1 are described more fully in the text that follows. As you read, think about what philosophies guide each one.

Child Care Centers

You may sometimes hear the term "child care center" used in a general sense to describe almost any type of child care facility. However, the term also has a more specific meaning. In this more specific sense, child care centers (also called *day care centers*) have as their primary purpose the care of children whose parents must work or attend school during the day. Many child care centers also provide learning activities for children, even though education is not generally the main goal.

Child care centers are typically open from 6:00 a.m. to 6:00 p.m. to accommodate parents' schedules. This means that they serve breakfast, lunch, and two snacks each day. Because days are long, nap time is part of the schedule.

Some child care centers serve only two- to six-year-olds. Increasingly, however, centers take children from six weeks to twelve years of age. Centers vary in size, with enrollments ranging as high as 200 children.

One quality that sets child care centers apart from each other is their sponsorship. Sponsors of child care centers include religious organizations and social service agencies. Originally, these organizations set up centers primarily to serve children from low-income families. Today families of all economic levels use the centers these organizations maintain. The federal government provides money to centers that serve low-income families. This is called Title XX funding.

When different organizations put programs in motion, each center takes on its own unique qualities in structure and program. Often principles that the organization operates under are reflected in the center's philosophy and goals.

Corporate Centers

One specific type of child care center that you have read about is provided by some corporations, either on or close to the parents' workplace. A corporation may operate the center itself or contract with someone else to manage it.

As with any issue, the need for on-site child care is accompanied by a mixture of opinions. Corporations want to keep employees happy, loyal, and productive. Providing on-site care has been shown to contribute to all of these, making work and family life easier to manage for employees in many companies. The cost of providing on-site care, however, is high. Not all companies can afford the expense, and when they do, they want to be sure it is worthwhile. When companies provide benefits, they tend to look for those that are useful to many employees.

Not all employed parents favor on-site care. They may prefer another center, one that has a different program or is closer to home. Some couples find that using on-site care puts the burden of transportation and attention on only one of them—the person who works at the site.

Serving nutritious meals and snacks is a responsibility child care programs must take seriously. What might happen if children are routinely fed inadequate or poor quality food?

It is often difficult for parents who work at night or on weekends to find quality care for their children. This hospital operates an on-site child care program that accommodates its employees' work schedules.

Despite the negatives, many reports about on-site care are favorable. The experience of Myra Abraham typifies what people like about on-site care. Since Myra's company provides care, she didn't have to spend time hunting for a program for her child. Her schedule runs smoothly, since she just brings Grant to work with her and doesn't have to rush to pick him up. Having him close by for regular contact and in case of illness eases her mind. For reasons like these, the interest in on-site child care is likely to continue.

As an alternative to on-site care, some companies offer vouchers to employees. These coupons are worth a certain amount of money toward child care services selected by the family.

Laboratory Schools

Some universities, colleges, and high schools provide child care for students and employees. These centers usually serve as laboratory schools to help students who are studying child development or early childhood education learn more about children. Many of the students who work and study in lab schools go on to find careers in the child care field.

Because lab schools are the training ground for future child care professionals, many are at the forefront of what is going on in the field. Children often receive care, education, and guidance based on the latest research and methods. While the atmosphere may be different from those centers in the "real" world, they make an excellent learning environment for children and students.

Profit and Nonprofit

Child care centers sponsored by religious organizations, corporations, and many schools and universities are usually *nonprofit* (also called not-for-profit) operations. This means that there are no stockholders who receive money from income earned by the child care center. Money earned by a nonprofit child care center goes back into the center budget or into savings for future use. Staff members receive salaries in nonprofit centers just as they do in others.

Some centers are created for the purpose of earning a profit. *For-profit* child care centers may be privately owned by individuals or by large child care corporations. Profit-earning centers provide income for the own-

What might be the advantages and disadvantages of a for-profit child care center?

ers. The largest chain of child care centers in the United States is Kinder-Care™. They have over 1,000 child care centers. Surplus money earned goes into the child care budget but also to stockholders and other investors.

Preschools

Preschools are set up for the main purpose of providing educational services to children from three to five years of age. Preschools are often used by families to give children extra stimulation and experiences prior to formal education. Children also have a chance to learn social skills as they spend time with other children.

Preschool is usually scheduled for 2 1/2 hours in the morning or afternoon. Children generally attend two or three days per week. With the short preschool schedule, employed parents may find enrolling a child in preschool inconvenient unless they can work out transportation as well as child care for the rest of the day.

Different organizations sponsor preschools. Sometimes religious organizations manage them or provide space for them. Preschools may also be owned by private individuals. Thus, there are both for-profit and nonprofit preschools.

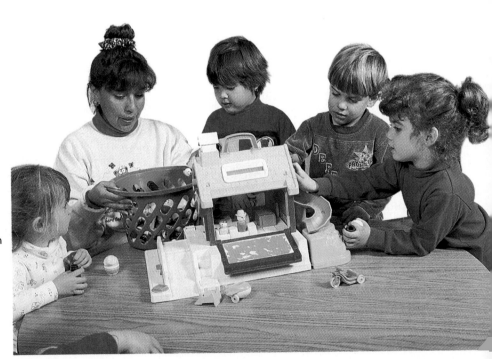

In a preschool setting, children ages three to five learn as they play. This type of program is often chosen by families who do not need an all-day child care provider.

Parent Cooperatives

As you may recall, some parents join together to form and run their own preschools, called parent cooperatives. They usually follow a schedule similar to other preschools.

In a cooperative, the parents hire a teacher, determine the goals, and set the rules and procedures to be followed in the preschool. Since parents are in charge, the philosophy behind the program reflects their ideas and attitudes. Child care professionals who work in the preschool conform to this philosophy. Although disagreements can occur, often a bond forms as teachers and parents work closely together toward the same goals.

Cooperatives typically require parents to work in the preschool a few hours every month. They may assist the teacher and do administrative work. This helps keep the costs lower and gives the teacher more time to spend working with the children.

Head Start

As part of President Johnson's *War on Poverty*, Head Start was created in the mid-1960s. The philosophy behind this program was clear and remains so today. Because children who live in low-income environments often have limited opportunities, many enter school not as well prepared as other youngsters. Catching up is difficult and, in fact, may never happen. To counteract this situation, Head Start aims to do just what the name suggests—give children a "head start." When young, disadvantaged children are given experiences they might otherwise miss, these children have a better chance of succeeding educationally and ultimately breaking the poverty cycle.

Serving primarily four-year-olds, Head Start is designed to foster intellectual as well as emotional, social, and physical growth. Besides educational programming, Head Start coordinates such services as health and dental care. Specialists plan meals and snacks that provide children with a healthful diet. Those in charge of the program know that only when children feel good and are alert and healthy can they focus on intellectual tasks.

Head Start also requires parents to get actively involved in their child's education. For children under four years of age, Head Start employs home visitors to teach parents

Participating in a Head Start program may help these children succeed in school and in life.

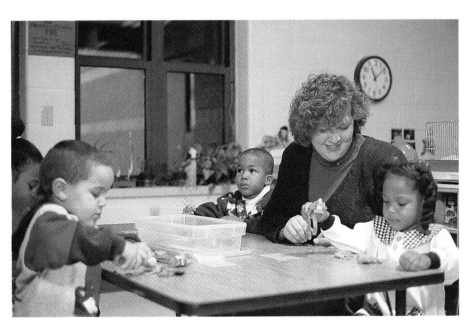

how to educate and care for children in the home. By getting involved, parents have a better chance at fulfilling their role as the primary teacher in a child's life.

Head Start programs may operate for a half or full day. Because the program is federally funded, no fees are charged to children and families who are accepted into the program.

Head Start has been subject to many evaluations over the years. Most reports show positive outcomes. Higher IQs and greater school achievements have been demonstrated when children in the program were compared to those who were not but had similar backgrounds. The economic benefits to society have also been studied. In general, for the children involved, Head Start reduces the need for remedial education, welfare, and the justice system. For all of these reasons, Head Start has become a significant contributor to early childhood education.

Pre-Kindergarten Programs

Head Start is not the only program designed specifically to prepare children for school. Some children who are not economically disadvantaged can also be at risk of academic failure when they enter school. Factors other than low income that are associated with poor performance include slow development, lack of language skills, and premature birth.

Public and private schools offer pre-kindergarten programs that are designed to prevent school failure by remedying problems early. Three- to five-year-olds are served by these programs. Pre-kindergarten programs differ from Head Start in that they are open to all children, not just those who are economically disadvantaged.

Pre-kindergarten classes are usually half-day and free of charge in public schools. Most pre-kindergartens operate only during the school year. Parent involvement, including home visits, is heavily stressed.

Montessori Programs

From Chapter 1, you know that Montessori programs originated with the philosophy and teachings of Dr. Maria Montessori. She lived in Italy from 1870 to 1952. Montessori's philosophy has influenced all of early childhood education. Maria Montessori was one of the early pioneers in the study of how children learn. She theorized

In Montessori programs, real-life experiences are used as learning experiences.

that children learn best by being active and by doing. She believed in self-education and that children should "learn how to learn." Preschools that follow the Montessori philosophy encourage independent learning and stress learning by doing and learning through the senses.

Montessori developed many of her own educational materials. Each of these materials is designed to teach a specific lesson, and each must be used only in the prescribed manner. Children are shown by the teacher how to use the materials and are then left to practice and master the lesson independently. Materials for lessons are **self-correcting**. This means *the child gets immediate feedback after correctly (or incorrectly) finishing the task.* Materials are organized from simple to complex, so children progress to increasingly challenging tasks.

The role of the teacher in a Montessori preschool is much less active than in a traditional classroom. The teacher observes children to determine their needs, chooses proper educational materials, and then quietly demonstrates to each child how to use the new materials. There is little talk from the teacher. Montessori felt that children should be motivated by the inward satisfaction that is gained when a job is well done.

Montessori schools usually serve three- to six-year-olds, but a few enroll children from infancy through eight years. Teachers receive one year of Montessori instruction before they can teach. Montessori schools may be for-profit or nonprofit.

Programs for Children with Special Needs

Finding child care for children who have special needs—physical, intellectual, emotional, or social disabilities—can be a challenge for parents. Some centers lack personnel with specialized training to care for special needs children. They may also lack needed equipment and space in the building.

For the protection of special needs children and their families, federal laws require that public centers enroll these children. Private centers are not required to do so, but they must be able to prove why they can't. The costs involved in renovating a building or hiring specialized staff may be the deciding factors.

Children with physical, intellectual, or emotional disabilities can benefit from inclusion in an early childhood program. Their peers benefit, too.

When a special needs child is enrolled, teachers work closely with parents to make sure all goes well. Social service agencies, such as the Easter Seals Society, can be helpful resources when integrating a child with special needs.

Remember that children with special needs are children first. They have most of the same needs, wants, and feelings as children without disabilities. Their presence brings an opportunity for all children to learn more about diversity and develop qualities of compassion and empathy.

KEYS TO OPERATING SMOOTHLY

By this time, you are well aware that early childhood programs come in all shapes and sizes. Regardless of format, however, no early childhood program can run well without paying attention to certain key components.

Suppose that a plan for setting up a program is in place. The sponsors know what type of program they want and have developed the philosophy to guide it. What else must be done to insure that the program operates smoothly?

Licensing

In most situations, an early childhood program cannot operate until it is licensed by the state. State **licensing laws** outline *rules and regulations that programs must follow*. These rules set minimum standards that protect children's safety and well-being. As part of the licensing process, facilities are inspected to make sure they meet all building, fire, and health codes.

Licensing laws cover hundreds of issues. For example, they specify minimum space requirements and the number of staff members needed for the children at the center. It is generally accepted that there should be a minimum of 35 square feet (3.3 square meters) of indoor space and 75 square feet (7 square meters) of outdoor space for each child. Exceptions may exist depending on the ages of children. Licensing laws also cover such things as the number of required emergency exits, the number of toilets, the types of outdoor fencing, and the minimum qualifications of program personnel.

Licensing laws vary widely from state to state. To find out what the licensing standards are in your state, call the Chamber of Commerce. Ask for the name, address, and telephone number of the appropriate licensing agency.

Before a program is set up, a careful look at licensing can help determine whether a plan is realistic. Modifications to a building can be costly. People who establish programs look at potential expenses carefully before moving ahead.

One of the controversial aspects of licensing is the question of how far requirements should go in regulating child care programs. For the protection of children, careful regulation is critical. On the other hand, unnecessary requirements that place a heavy financial burden on providers can cause them to end, or never begin, operation. A sensible balance is needed in order to keep quality programs going.

A program director has many responsibilities, ranging from recruitment to licensing. What key skills or qualities would be most important for this position?

Leadership

A successful program relies on good leadership. Child care programs employ directors to serve this function. Directors are administrators and managers. They are usually responsible to a board of directors or an owner. Some directors own their own programs. In small programs, directors may teach part-time in a classroom. Programs that enroll more than 85 children usually have an assistant director in addition to one who is full-time.

As the director of a program, Bill Thorndike finds that the most time-consuming part of his job is supervision of all personnel. He recruits, interviews, and hires employees. He must also make sure new personnel are trained. For good communication, he generally holds weekly staff meetings. This allows time to assess and cope with issues before they become big problems. An additional part of his responsibilities includes formally evaluating staff members at least once per year.

Directors work with teachers to plan, implement, and evaluate learning programs and other activities based on the program's goals and philosophy. In addition, they are responsible for financial management—preparing yearly budgets and reviewing them frequently. Organized bookkeeping is necessary in order to keep track of incoming money, such as parent fees, and outgoing expenses, such as ordering supplies

and equipment. The director also makes sure the facility, the physical building that houses the program, meets all licensing laws and other regulations.

Directors talk frequently with parents as they bring their children to the center and pick them up. In addition, they use newsletters, notes on the parent bulletin board, and parent handbooks to communicate center policies and procedures to parents.

Staffing

Besides the director, how many people do you think it might take to staff an early childhood program? At first glance, you might think only of the teachers. Depending on program type and size, however, the staff could be much larger.

There are a variety of job opportunities in early childhood programs. Each staff member is a key to a program's success.

Cooperation

WHAT IS COOPERATION?

Cooperation is the willingness and ability to work with others to achieve goals. It means accepting the knowledge, authority, and assistance of others, as well as contributing your own skills to make the effort a successful one.

Cooperation in Action

"I'll start the water boiling," Walter said as he placed the large kettle on the range. "They'll be happy today."

Casey Alexander, the head cook, smiled. She said, "They always are when it's spaghetti and meatball day." Walter was Casey's assistant in the kitchen of a large preschool program. Together they had prepared the meatball mixture earlier in the day. Then Casey had started the sauce while Walter rolled the meatballs. While Casey cooked the meatballs, Walter cleaned the counter, utensils, and cookware they had used.

"Smells good," Virginia said as she entered the kitchen. Virginia was a parent volunteer in the preschool. She was ready to set the tables for lunch.

"It looks like we need some more napkins. Do you have another package?" she asked.

Casey opened the door to the storage area. "Here you go," she responded, handing Virginia a package of napkins.

The door opened again as Fran Daniels, the program director, walked in. "Will you still have time to go over next month's menu this afternoon?" she asked Casey. "I'd like to finalize it with you and Darlene today if possible. Then you can call in your food orders."

Casey nodded. She liked working with Darlene. As a dietitian, Darlene had taught Casey a lot about nutrition. Good nutrition at a reasonable price was their aim in the preschool.

"I'll be back to help with cleanup after lunch," Virginia said as she went out the door.

"Good! Then I'll just go home," Casey joked. She had a way of making people laugh. She reached out to stir the spaghetti sauce, returning to the business at hand. They had a meal to get on the table.

Your Analysis

1. Identify the individuals who cooperate in the meal program. What skills and knowledge does each bring to the process?

2. What might be some consequences if Casey tried to do all the work herself?

3. What personal traits or attitudes make it easier to cooperate with others?

Staff members are needed in the classrooms. In addition to teachers, teacher's aides may also be employed to work with children.

Food service requires a full- or part-time cook. Larger programs, such as Head Start, employ a dietitian to plan menus with a cook. A *dietitian* is a person who has been specially trained to educate people about healthful foods. Kitchen aides may be hired to assist cooks.

Other personnel positions that may be needed include a bus driver, a bus monitor, a nurse, a custodian, a social worker, a parent education coordinator, an educational program director, a home visitor, and a speech therapist. All personnel are responsible to the director.

Educational qualifications and experience needed for positions vary from state to state. Of course, programs have the right to set staff qualifications higher then licensing laws require. Individual programs create job descriptions for all personnel.

What are some specific ways a high staff-to-child ratio benefits the children? How would it benefit the staff?

Staff-to-Child Ratios

A **staff-to-child ratio** is *the number of personnel in relation to the number of children in a classroom.* For example, a 1-to-5 ratio means there is one caregiver for every five children. States establish minimum staff-to-child ratios to make sure there are enough adults available to evacuate children safely in case of an emergency, such as a fire. High staff-to-child ratios also help insure that children are well supervised and getting the attention and care they need. Some programs employ more staff members than state licensing laws require.

As you read in an earlier chapter, the necessary number of caregivers to children is higher when younger children are enrolled. Infants require much more individual attention than preschoolers or school-age children. Infant rooms usually have at least one caregiver to every three or four infants. One caregiver might be assigned to a group of three to five toddlers. In contrast, it is not unusual for a group of five-year-olds to have two teachers for 20 children.

When staff members are highly qualified, they may be able to manage larger groups of children. The smallest group size possible, however, is always the best choice.

Legal Responsibilities

No parent would want to place a child in a program that did not have the health, safety, and well-being of children as its top priority. Before beginning operation, a program must meet all local, state, and federal laws and regulations. This is the director's responsi-

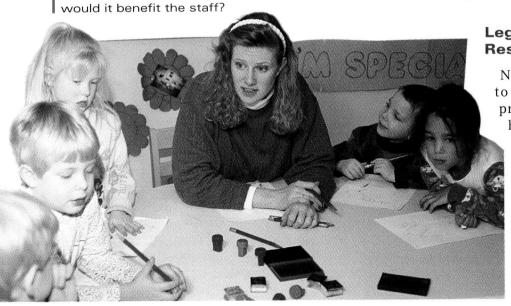

bility. For example, the director must make sure that fire alarms are in working order and that evacuation procedures are established.

Directors also advise staff members of their legal responsibilities to young children. For instance, many states require child care personnel to report suspected child abuse to state authorities. Therefore, the director must arrange for the education of all personnel about the procedures to follow when reporting this information.

Centers should have **liability insurance** that covers employees, enrolled children, visitors, and people on or around the site. This means that *if the program is found responsible for an injury or damages that occur at the center or in connection with*

An advisory board can bring additional expertise, as well as parental viewpoints, to a program. What kinds of people do you think would make positive contributions to an advisory board?

center activity, insurance will cover costs involved in any resulting lawsuit. Medical costs for injury can be included in this insurance. Insurance to cover the cost of theft or damage to the facility as the result of storms or fire should also be purchased.

Liability insurance policies are difficult to read and understand. Individuals who are in charge of a program need to ask an insurance agent about coverage for certain situations. They must think about field trips, food-related illnesses, damage to property owned by a landlord, transportation of children, and kidnapping of a child by a parent who doesn't have legal custody of the child.

Advisory Board

Smooth operation relies on expert input and willing workers. Many early childhood programs, especially nonprofit programs, find this kind of help in an advisory board. An **advisory board** *is a group of people, often parents, community members, or people in early childhood careers, who help directors develop and implement center policies.* Advisory boards usually consist of seven to twelve members. A **policy** *is a statement of rules or guidelines that guide the actions and decision making of an organization.*

Parental Involvement

Involving parents is beneficial for a program. Confident child care professionals welcome their input and assistance. A good staff has nothing to hide from parents and appreciates the fact that parents can help make a good program even better. How might this happen?

For one thing, many parents are often eager to provide materials and supplies. They can also be a financial resource. For example, some might be willing to help with a fund-raiser that helps the program cut costs.

THE MULTICULTURAL CLASSROOM

In the multicultural classroom, making everyone feel comfortable may take an extra effort. What can you do to make all families feel welcome? Since language is the first barrier that can separate families of different cultures, that's a good place to start.

Most early childhood programs have flyers, brochures, and building signs available to the public. To serve families that are not primarily English speaking, post bilingual signs and circulate bilingual flyers. This is the best welcome mat you could offer.

Some programs provide enrollment forms that have been translated. A phone call to a community cultural or religious center may help you locate assistance in translating vital documents. They may also provide contact with people who can translate at future meetings. If the school offers parent meetings to discuss important topics, such as child abuse, home safety, and community problems, all families should have the opportunity to participate. The effort you put forth can make the difference in preventing people from feeling alienated by a lack of communication.

Extra hands can make operating a program much easier. Involving parents as volunteers lessens the load on staff members and makes parents feel needed. Parents enjoy volunteering when they have time to give. Among the tasks they can do are: assist with children's activities, organize family events, make repairs to toys and equipment, create a newsletter, handle paperwork, share hobbies and knowledge with children, and help with setup and cleanup in the center. Like everyone else, parents are busy people. Giving them an opportunity to choose from different levels of commitment may make them more willing to volunteer.

Before parents can do a job, they need information and perhaps training. Planning a special meeting to welcome and inform them is a good idea. Showing appreciation for their efforts makes them more willing to help again.

Getting involved is beneficial not just to the program but to parents as well. Parents who are involved tend to feel more committed and supportive of a program. They have a better understanding of what goes on, including any limitations and problems experienced by the program.

MANY DETAILS AHEAD

As this chapter comes to an end, you might think that the subject of operating an early childhood program is closed. In truth, it has just begun. Being in charge of children is a huge responsibility. The other chapters in this unit offer much more that you need to know about how programs are set up and managed so that children are well cared for. The rest of this text includes information that applies to many different kinds of programs for children from birth to school-age. However, the main focus is on programs that provide both care and educational experiences for children ages three to five.

Chapter 8 Review

- At the core of any early childhood program is its philosophy. Program goals are an outgrowth of that philosophy.
- There are many kinds of early childhood programs. Their characteristics vary because of who sponsors them, why they were created, and the philosophies.
- Some early childhood programs make money for the owners as well as serve children and their families.
- Early childhood programs must meet state licensing laws. These laws vary from state to state.
- In order to operate smoothly, early childhood programs need a director for leadership and a skilled staff.
- Parents can contribute much to the operation of an early childhood program.

Reviewing the Facts

1. What purpose does the philosophy of an early childhood education program serve?

2. What is the function of program goals? Give five examples.

3. For what purpose were child care centers created? How does this affect their operation?

4. What reasons do corporations have for providing and not providing on-site child care?

5. Explain the difference between a profit and non-profit organization.

6. How are preschools different from child care centers?

7. What services do Head Start programs provide? Describe the children served in Head Start.

8. Who sponsors pre-kindergarten programs? Describe the children served in these programs.

9. Briefly describe the characteristics of a Montessori program.

10. What are licensing laws?

11. Summarize the responsibilities a director has in an early childhood program.

12. List six staff positions other than director that an early childhood program might have.

13. Describe three ways a parent could be beneficially involved in an early childhood program.

Thinking Critically

1. Why is it important to understand the philosophy of an early childhood program before becoming an employee?

2. Explore points of view on the following issues:

   a. A large company announces that the child care center it provides on site will be closing. Describe possible points of view of the company, a parent with a child currently enrolled, and an employee who has no children.

   b. A child care center is barely staying in business when new licensing rules require the center to make costly improvements to the facility. Describe possible points of view of the licensing agency, the center owners, and the parents of children in the center.

Activities and Applications

1. **Math Practice.** Suppose you are setting up a child care program that will enroll 75 children. The ratio of teachers to children will be 1 to 5. How

many teachers will you need to hire? How many teachers will you need if you decide that 15 of the 75 children will be infants, requiring a ratio of 1 to 3?

2. **Licensing.** Obtain licensing information for child care programs in your state. With a group of classmates, evaluate the regulations. What is the reasoning behind specific regulations? What would you add or eliminate? Why?

SCHOOL TO WORK

Your Professional Portfolio

Professionals sometimes develop their own philosophy about their career: why the work is valuable; their attitudes and beliefs about the work; and what they feel their approach to the job should be. Putting your philosophy into words compels you to think about the significance of your chosen career and your role in it. Assuming that you will work in child care, write your own personal philosophy on working with children.

Observing and Analyzing

Observing How Programs Operate

First-hand observation is the best way to see how early childhood programs operate. If you are able to visit several different programs, so much the better. Use the ideas below to discover the scope of child care in your community:

- **Comparing Programs.** Observe two different programs that provide child care, such as Head Start, corporate child care, a parent cooperative, pre-kindergarten, or a Montessori program. Make a chart to compare the following characteristics: age range, number of children, fees, staff salaries (not always revealed), profit or nonprofit status, hours of operation, staff-to-child ratio, provision for special needs children, and minimum educational requirements for teachers and aides. Also inquire about the philosophy of each of these programs. Create a bulletin board by combining the information in your chart with that of your classmates. Compare results. Include philosophy statements in the bulletin board display and analyze their similarities.

- **What Agencies Provide.** If possible, spend a morning or an afternoon at a resource and referral agency or a child care licensing office. Observe the tasks of the staff. What knowledge about child care programs do the people who staff these agencies need in order to serve their clients? Ask for brochures, current legislation, and any other pertinent information to share in class.

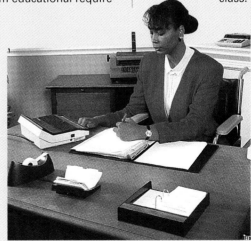

Chapter 9

Providing an Appropriate Environment

CHAPTER OBJECTIVES

- Identify principles to use in planning early childhood environments.

- List and describe the kinds of learning centers.

- Explain the purpose of learning centers.

- Describe how learning centers are set up in the classroom.

- Explain how to choose equipment, materials, and toys wisely.

- Be able to evaluate an early childhood environment.

Terms to Learn

- cubby
- custodial needs
- isolation room
- learning centers
- nontoxic
- sanitized
- toxic
- traffic pattern

Now this is what I like to see," Irene Sullivan thought to herself as she gazed around the room. The preschool was buzzing with activity, but it was the kind of noise she always enjoyed hearing.

"Teacher, teacher, look! Our tower's getting tall!" Michelle called out to Irene. The cardboard block tower certainly was growing. Irene could see that it was about to tumble, but that was half the fun—watching the blocks fall to the carpet.

Not surprisingly, the tower came down, accompanied by squeals of delight. Two children in another corner of the room turned to look. One was wearing a large, floppy hat that nearly covered her face. Her dress hung in folds on the floor, and her oversized high-heeled shoes barely showed. A long feathery scarf completed Erika's outfit. After watching the excitement over the block tower, Erika folded her arms across her chest in the most adult manner she could put together and shook her head. "Those children are just too-oo noisy," she said to the little girl beside her.

As Irene continued to walk around the room, she stopped to admire a painting that Rob was hanging on the clothesline to dry. "What pretty, bright colors you used, Rob," she said. "Are they your favorites?"

"No," Rob replied. "I didn't paint with my favorite colors because I didn't want to use them all up."

Irene chuckled to herself as she began to get ready for a science activity. "There's never a dull moment," she thought.

INSIDE THE CENTER

*I*magine for a moment that you are walking into a child care center or preschool. What do you think you will see? If the classroom has been carefully planned and equipped, you could come upon a scene similar to the one just described. You might notice that the children are participating in different activities. Because the atmosphere is inviting, a sense of warmth and enjoyment is present. Behavior problems are minimal. None of this comes about by chance. It comes with careful planning.

PLANNING THE ENVIRONMENT

*B*ecause child care facilities come in many shapes and sizes, what you discover inside isn't always the same. The physical space, whether several rooms or one large one, must be arranged so that similar functions can be carried out. When planning how to use space for a child care program, think about these principles:

- Does the plan meet program goals?
- Will the needs of all the children be served?
- Will the staff's needs be met?
- Does the plan encourage parental involvement?

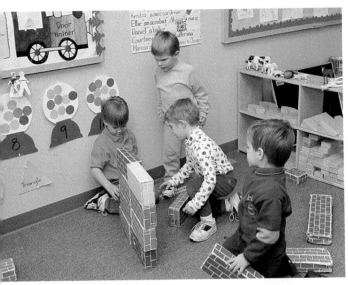

When children work and play in interesting environments, they are more likely to behave well. Activity is constructive, not destructive. Children are less likely to be bored and frustrated, both of which can lead to inappropriate behavior.

Meeting Program Goals

The environment created in a child care facility has a strong impact on the staff's ability to meet program goals. With goals in mind, you can plan effective use of space.

Independence is one example of a goal that a program might promote. The aim is to create an environment that helps children become independent. In one center, after the children finish painting, the teacher hangs the smocks in a storage room. In another center, the children hang up their own smocks on hooks that have been placed within easy reach. Which technique do you think promotes independence? The children who hang up their own smocks are actually learning more about doing for themselves. Planning the environment with independence in mind helps make the goal achievable. The information below gives more ideas for linking the environment to program goals.

Meeting Program Goals

Here are some ideas for promoting program goals in the early childhood classroom. Can you add other goals and techniques to the list?

STRONG SELF-ESTEEM
Display children's work. Provide toys and equipment that match the children's age and developmental level. Enable children to make choices.

SOCIAL SKILLS
Provide toys and activities that encourage children to play and work together.

PROBLEM-SOLVING ABILITY
Supply toys and materials that can be used in many creative ways. Blocks are an example.

LANGUAGE SKILLS
Place an interesting assortment of books at children's eye level. Label toys, equipment, and storage locations.

LARGE MUSCLE DEVELOPMENT
Include space for active play, making sure it is separate from quiet areas. Provide equipment and activities that require the use of the whole body.

SMALL MUSCLE COORDINATION
Provide toys and activities that encourage children to use their fingers and hands to practice small motor skills.

Planning for Development

Physical Development. All developmental areas are addressed when a child care environment is planned. Often one activity promotes different kinds of development. When Kevin paints, he develops his fine motor skills, which is part of his physical development.

Emotional Development. Painting also contributes to emotional development. Kevin uses his artwork to express emotions. He feels good about what he can do, especially when a caregiver recognizes his efforts.

Intellectual Development. Kevin's intellectual development progresses as he acquires new information. He learns the names of colors and begins to recognize different shapes. His creative abilities are tapped as he expresses himself artistically.

Social Development. Painting might also be part of Kevin's social development. This could happen in several ways—talking to a caregiver about his artwork, showing his painting to other children, and displaying his art during open house.

Meeting the Needs of Children

Everything you have learned about how children develop can be useful when planning space for a child care program. What a preschooler needs is quite different from a school-age child's needs. A preschooler will be frustrated if activities and toys are not age-appropriate. A school-age child won't be comfortable in a preschool setting. Understanding what a child is like at each stage of development enables you to provide a program that is not only satisfying and safe for children but also provides opportunities for growth.

Remember to plan for all areas of development. As you can see from the illustration above, even one activity can be handled so that several types of development are addressed.

Custodial Care

In planning space for children, physical needs are high priority. These **custodial needs** include *toileting, hand washing, eating, napping, and resting.*

Toileting and hand-washing areas have child-size toilets and

Tip **FROM THE** *Pros*

When arranging classroom space, bend down to a child's level. How does everything look from a child's viewpoint? Is it inviting? You may not know for sure until you try this.

These cots are conveniently stored. The storage space used is minimal, which is often a concern in a child care setting.

sinks mounted low enough for children to reach. If necessary, a small stool can be stored close by. Mirrors are best placed at children's eye level.

Meal service is provided on low tables that can be used for play activities throughout the rest of the day. Chairs should be a comfortable size for children. Hard-surfaced flooring, such as tile or wood, under eating tables makes cleanup easier.

Full-day programs provide cot space for napping. By moving classroom equipment from the middle of the classroom, you can make space to set up cots. Equipment mounted on casters simplifies this job. When not in use, stack cots away from play space so children do not climb on them.

Children who become ill need a place to wait for their parents. A separate **isolation room** provides the child with *a cozy, comfortable place to rest when sick.* Children can be away from the curious eyes of other children, and illnesses are less easily spread. An adult must always be present with a child in an isolation room.

FOCUS ON INFANT/TODDLER PROGRAMS

The environment for infant and toddler programs differs somewhat from preschool programs. Because of diaper changing, proper ventilation and easy access to diaper disposal areas are necessary. Changing tables should be the proper height to limit caregiver back injuries. Hand-washing sinks should be close by in order to limit the spread of organisms that cause diseases. Low windows allow toddlers to see the outside world. A warm room adds to the children's comfort.

Specialized equipment is needed for infant/toddler classrooms. Also, infants and toddlers need more toys than just baby rattles. Think how much pleasure and discovery these youngsters can get from other types of toys. A few possibilities are mobiles; cradle gyms; toys that squeeze, pull, push, stack, and snap; nesting barrels; and sorter boxes.

Insuring Safety

When electrical appliances are present in the child care facility, caution is the byword. Such devices can be a hazard. Improperly placed cords are easy for children and adults to trip over. A small child might grab a dangling cord, pulling an appliance from a shelf or counter. Try taping cords to the wall so that they are out of reach. Electrical shock is possible when an appliance is kept near water. Place appliances in safe locations. Also, put protective covers over electrical outlets that are within the reach of children. Always take the safe approach, making sure cords and appliances are correctly handled.

Storage

Children arrive each day with an assortment of belongings and treasures. They may bring coats, hats, extra sets of clothing (for use in case of spills and toileting accidents), and special items for "show and tell." Many programs provide a cubby for each child. A **cubby** is *a small space for storage of personal items*. Often cubbies resemble small lockers without doors. Placing

them near an entrance makes them convenient to use.

Cubbies can be identified by printing each child's name in bold letters over or under the cubby. Children who can't read their names need a snapshot of themselves posted beside each cubby. In some centers parents tape a family photo inside the cubby, both for identification purposes and so the child can see it when feeling lonely.

Children with Special Needs

Early childhood programs must be willing and able to serve children with special needs. An environment that is planned with foresight is more easily adapted when a special needs child enrolls. Wider classroom pathways accommodate wheelchairs and devices that aid walking. Ramps provide access to classrooms. Depending on a child's disability, some modifications may need to be made in restrooms and eating areas. Many other adaptations are possible, depending on the particular disability. By working closely with families, caregivers can meet the needs of all children, including those with special needs.

Meeting Staff Needs

To perform their duties effectively and efficiently, staff members also have certain needs. When space is planned with staff members in mind, their jobs are easier and more enjoyable. A good working environment helps keep staff morale high. In turn, their attitude toward the children is more likely to be positive.

Directors need a private office for conducting confidential business. Important files and records are kept here. The director's office is usually placed near the entrance so the director can monitor who comes and goes in the center.

Teachers need storage space for classroom materials, such as art supplies. A quiet location where they can take breaks is helpful. They also need space for storing personal belongings and teaching materials.

The kitchen staff needs space and equipment for food preparation and storage. Custodians keep cleaning equipment and supplies in a locked closet, since many cleaning supplies can be **toxic** (*poisonous*).

Meeting the Needs of Parents and Visitors

In a child care facility, an entrance that is inviting and convenient for parents as well as children helps get every day off to a better start. Parents sign the children in and out at a check-in table. A bulletin board at the entrance is useful for posting items of interest. You might see articles on parenting, newsletters, and menus for the week or month.

Many programs have an observation window. On the classroom side, this looks like a mirror. From the other side, however, parents and child development students can observe the children without being seen.

Some early childhood programs have a parents' room. This provides space for relaxation and often includes a lending library of parenting books. Parent support groups may meet here.

THE CLASSROOM

Large or small, every child care program has space for the activities that keep children constructively busy throughout their stay. This is the area, often called the classroom or playroom, where children spend most of their time. The size of the classroom space dictates how many children the program can serve.

People who plan child care facilities pay special attention to the classroom space. What would you do to make such areas pleasing, safe, and easy to use for children

Staff members function best when they have proper facilities. This kitchen enables employees to prepare tasty, nutritious meals in an efficient manner.

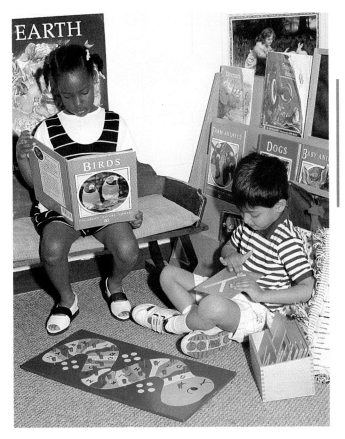

A learning center should entice children to participate. It should also enable children to see exactly where to return the toys and materials they use. This is one way to promote organization skills. Books displayed openly at eye level create interest. Children can clearly see where they should be stored when done.

Learning centers provide an organized way to arrange space and manage the activity in a center. Specifically, they:

- Direct children to activities and focus their attention.
- Allow children to learn by doing, while working at their own pace.
- Provide opportunities for independent and small group play.
- Distribute children throughout the classroom, minimizing conflicts and noise in any one area.

and staff? Wall colors that are warm and bright and area rugs contribute to a pleasant atmosphere. Windows also add brightness. What matters even more is how space is arranged and what is contained within.

Learning Centers

The classroom area of a well-planned child care program is divided into learning centers. **Learning centers** are *areas clearly defined for specific types of play.* Each learning center is organized around a theme or curriculum topic, such as blocks, art, or science. Each is suited to the age of the children who will use it.

A child care program may not be able to offer every type of learning center that is possible. Budget and space can be limiting. Most programs, however, do try to include certain learning centers as a core. These are centers for art, language arts, dramatic play, social studies, music, science, math, blocks, and active play. Other learning centers, such as woodworking and computers, can be added to the program as space and resources allow. The size and scope of each learning center also depends on space and resources.

Many preschoolers are becoming familiar with computers. A touch screen makes this educational game easy to use.

Arranging Learning Centers

A typical child care classroom is a large rectangular room. Deciding how to arrange the learning centers within the room can be a challenge. You want each area to be distinct from the others, yet for safety reasons, they all need to be visible to supervising teachers. When space is limited, combining or rotating learning centers works well. An example of how the learning centers are arranged in one preschool is shown on pages 174-175. You will learn much more about the contents and use of these centers later in the text.

When learning centers are well marked, children understand the limits for play. Most areas need at least three boundaries. For instance, a block center can be placed in a corner of the room. The two walls make automatic boundaries. A block storage unit can serve as a third "wall." Colored tape on the floor can also divide play spaces. A piano might separate the music area from the art center.

Learning centers can be arranged so that children have a degree of privacy when

Focus ON SCHOOL-AGE PROGRAM

After a long day at school, the school-age child may be ready for either action or a little time to rest and recover. A well-equipped play yard scaled to the children's size and abilities helps release pent-up energy after sitting all day. A quiet corner with a bean bag chair and books is good for relaxing. When children have homework to do, they need a place to complete it.

Even though they are gone much of the day, school-age children still need a storage place for their belongings. Jackets and coats, as well as school books and supplies, can be stored in lockers or another handy location.

needed. Lofts (platforms raised a few feet off the ground) allow children to get away from more boisterous activities and be "alone." Books, puppets, and puzzles are used in this area. Large wooden crates (checked for splinters and protruding nails) can provide a small enclosure that is comforting to children. If you drape a colorful bedsheet over a table, children can cuddle up underneath. Add floor pillows and this space becomes cozy and inviting to young children. Although areas like these are aimed at giving children a chance for privacy, adults must still be sure that children are supervised at all times.

When arranging space, consider *the direction of movement that children take as they go from one part of the classroom to another.* This is called the **traffic pattern.**

Well-planned traffic patterns limit congestion from the time children enter until they leave the center.

Outdoor Play

Although an indoor area is included for some active play, an outdoor area extends this learning center. Play yards may be equipped with climbers, low slides, and soft-seated swings. Children enjoy sand and water activities as well as gardening. They need accessories that challenge them to develop their large motor skills. Many programs provide balls, hoops, tricycles, wagons, balance beams, and scooters. A boundary, such as a fence, surrounds the outdoor play area to keep children from wandering away.

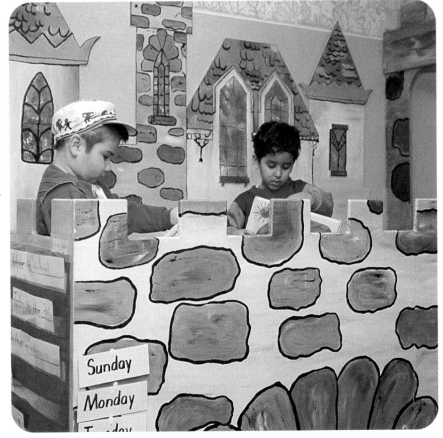

Even a few steps up into a loft can give a child a sense of privacy. Note that these children can still be observed by caregivers as they read.

The Learning Center Plan

Blocks

The block center is rich with learning opportunities. For a classroom of 20 children, 400 blocks are recommended. Placing the block center on a carpeted area helps reduce noise. Toy vehicles and plastic zoo and farm animals add to the enjoyment.

Science

The science center encourages children to investigate the world through their senses. A low table displays science collections. Magnifying glasses, balance scales, and magnets aid children's investigations.

Math

Math concepts, such as matching, sorting, comparing, counting, and classifying, are explored in the math center. Concepts related to color, size, and shape are also developed.

Music

As expected, musical instruments are part of this center. Tambourines, finger cymbals, triangles, and drums are all possibilities. Records and audio tapes are also located in the music center.

Art

The art center allows for creativity and imagination. The center should be uncarpeted and near a water source. Children may draw, paint, and paste. They might work with dough, clay, fabric, wallpaper scraps, and cardboard.

Active Play

Here children exercise their large muscles and develop coordination. Children might play with bean bags or streamers. Well-supervised areas for climbing, tumbling, and sliding are desirable.

Language Arts

This center, which includes social studies, lures children into the love of speaking, listening, reading, and writing. A quiet area with good lighting, it might contain a rocking chair, large pillows, and bean bag chairs for comfort.

Dramatic Play

In the dramatic play center, children use child-size furnishings, dress-up clothes, dolls, and stuffed animals to act out the world as they see it. Props are changed to reflect changing themes.

175

CHOOSING TOYS AND MATERIALS

*O*nce you have the space arranged for learning centers, you need the right toys and materials to put in them. Use good judgment, knowledge of children, and creativity when deciding. Good choices promote learning. Poor choices can create safety hazards and increase behavior prob-

lems. Some questions to ask when selecting toys and equipment are listed below. The following guidelines will also be helpful when making choices:

- ***Toys and materials should be appropriate for children's ages and abilities.*** Four-year-olds can use blunt scissors with supervision. The same scissors, however, would be unsafe for a two-year-old.

Selecting Equipment and Toys

*C*areful thought pays when choosing equipment and toys. You are likely to be more satisfied with your selections when you ask questions like these before choosing:

- Is the item safe? Metal, wood, and plastic edges should be rounded rather than sharp. Paint should be nontoxic. **Nontoxic** means *not poisonous.* Some paints and other finishes contain ingredients that are toxic, especially to young children who may chew on them.

- Will the item withstand heavy or rough use by a group of up to 20 children? Is it durable?

- Will the toy be easy to clean? Can it be **sanitized**, or *cleaned in a way that will kill the organisms that can cause illness?*

- Can children of different ages use the toy?

- Does the toy encourage cooperative play rather than aggressive, or even violent, play?

- Can more than one child use the item at a time?

- Does your classroom have storage space for the item?

- Can the item be used in more than one way? Will it generate creativity?

- Does the item encourage children's active involvement rather than passive observation? Will it hold a child's interest?

- Will children learn basic concepts while playing with the toy? Will it support program goals? Will it reinforce curriculum themes and objectives?

- Will the toy allow for sensory learning?

- Would both girls and boys enjoy the toy? Is the toy free of racial, cultural, and gender stereotypes?

- Are children likely to have fun with the toy?

THE MULTICULTURAL CLASSROOM

Sensitivity is a good guide when choosing multicultural toys and other items for the early childhood classroom. Will just anything work? The answer is "no." Some books, posters, puppets, and dolls may be insulting. They may show stereotypes of different cultures. They may focus only on historical images, rather than today. They may be inaccurate representations. Before you include an item in the classroom, examine how it depicts the culture. Would you feel good about having the item in the classroom if the culture were yours? If the item passes your inspection, include it along with others. Make multiculturalism ongoing, with many items visible and usable every day. A single doll or poster that appears only on certain holidays teaches children that multiculturalism is here today and gone tomorrow. That's not reality.

Safety is a high priority when choosing toys and materials. What evidence do you see that safety is a concern in this activity?

- ***Provide a variety of materials.*** Children need variety and novelty to keep their interest. They become bored if offered the same learning materials every day. Rotate items regularly, maintaining a balance between familiar items and new ones.

- ***Include materials that children can look at, touch, listen to, smell, and sometimes taste.*** Such materials enable children to use all their senses for learning.

- ***Materials should include different cultures.*** Children's books, puppets, dolls, and posters can reflect many ethnic groups. Activities using foods, customs, and music of multiple cultures make learning interesting and exciting.

- ***Provide enough materials so children can comfortably share.*** Having too few materials frustrates children and sets the stage for fights. The younger the children, the more important it is to have duplicate toys.

PLANNING FOR QUALITY

Wherever you work in child care, there are likely to be improvements you want to make. Sometimes resources are limited. Even small spaces, however, can be carefully arranged to make the most of them. With knowledge and a little ingenuity, you can make the environment work well for you and the children in your care.

Toys should be suitable for the children's age. Has that guideline been taken into consideration in this setting?

Building Professional Skills

Management

WHAT IS MANAGEMENT?

On many jobs, the ability to be a good manager is vital. What does it mean to be a good manager? The person who knows how to use resources to accomplish goals is likely to manage well. This skill is useful in many situations.

Management in Action

Ted Hargrove sighed with discouragement. After only two weeks on the job at the Sunshine Child Care Center, he was running out of materials. He was responsible for the art and woodworking centers, and his budget was limited. "It's time to do something," he thought to himself.

With determination, he started to make a list. "What do I need and where can I get it?" were the two questions that guided his list making. When the list was complete, he was ready for action.

It wasn't long before the art and woodworking centers were in good shape again. Ted had placed an article in the center newsletter, asking parents for donations of computer paper, scraps of wallpaper, leftover fabric, cardboard, and any other materials that might be useful for art projects. The response had been terrific. A trip to the lumber yard had yielded free scrap lumber. He was able to get assorted nails and screws as a donation from a hardware store. "That was easy on the budget," Ted thought. "Now what else can I find?"

Your Analysis

1. What was Ted's goal?

2. What resources did Ted use to meet his goal?

3. What might have happened if Ted had not used his management skills?

4. How might management skills help in the situations below?

   • Many of the toys in a preschool need repairs.

   • Children enter a center from two doors, causing confusion as the center opens.

   • Several child care workers seem to be unhappy on the job.

Chapter 9 Review

Chapter Summary

- Basic principles guide the planning for how space is used in a child care facility.
- Program goals should be addressed through use of space in the classroom.
- Classrooms should be planned to allow for the space and equipment needed to meet children's custodial needs.
- Space should be designed according to children's ages and stages of development. Children with physical disabilities or limitations may have special space needs.
- The handling of space must also take into consideration the requirements of staff, parents, and visitors.
- Classrooms contain learning centers that are suited to the age of the children. They provide an organized way to arrange space and manage activities.
- Boundaries define the areas of learning centers.
- Outdoor as well as indoor play can address the need for children to be active.
- Toys and materials must be carefully chosen.

Reviewing the Facts

1. What four principles guide the planning of space in a child care program?
2. What helps make goals achievable in a child care program?
3. What are custodial needs?
4. Why does a child care facility need an isolation room?
5. For what is a cubby used?
6. Why is a good working environment needed for staff members?
7. Of what use is an observation window in a child care program?
8. What is a learning center?
9. List nine typical learning centers.
10. List five guidelines for choosing toys and materials.
11. What special features are needed in an infant/toddler program? In a school-age program?

Thinking Critically

1. What signs would indicate to you that the environment in a preschool was poorly planned?
2. In what ways might the arrangement of a child care center teach the children organization skills?
3. Why is behavior likely to be better in a well-planned child care environment?
4. Do you agree or disagree with this statement: a good learning center is expensive to equip. Explain your answer.
5. What would you do if a parent donated splintered blocks and plastic building bricks that were cracked to the program?

Activities and Applications

1. **Evaluation Checklist.** Imagine that you are the parent of a preschool child who is going into a child care program. Develop a checklist that you would use to determine the quality of a program's environment.

2. **Entry Design.** Using words and drawings, design an entry area for a child care program. Include the traffic pattern, furnishings, and equipment.

3. **Choosing Supplies and Equipment.** Review at least two catalogs of early childhood equipment and supplies. Make a list of the items you would purchase to equip one learning center. Calculate the total cost.

SCHOOL TO WORK

Your Professional Portfolio

How would you design a child care classroom? Try your hand at becoming a designer by drawing your own layout for the learning centers in a preschool program. Include labels to show the centers and the contents that you would include. Also indicate the main traffic patterns. Place the completed design in your portfolio.

Observing and Analyzing

Evaluating Environments in Early Childhood Programs

Observing child care environments can tell you much about a program's effectiveness. More than one visit may be needed. First, examine the facility to see how space is used. Find out about the program goals and look at how state licensing requirements are met. Finally, examine the effectiveness of learning centers.

To observe environments, choose one or more of the locations listed below. Be sure to telephone ahead to schedule your visit. Ask for printed information about the program.

After observing, write a one- to two-page summary of what you saw. If you visit more than one location, describe the similarities and differences in the programs. Then share results with other students in your class. How do your observations compare and contrast?

- **Observing Preschools.** Observe a preschool classroom both before the children arrive and while children are there. Notice what kinds and sizes of furniture are in the room. Is the furniture appropriate for children in this age group? Where and how is it arranged? Does the classroom have learning centers? If so, what are they and how are they arranged? How is the traf-

fic flow between centers? Can the children move freely? Describe the kinds of equipment you find in the learning centers. What large muscle equipment is available for children for indoor and outdoor use? What health and safety measures do you see?

- **Observing Child Care Centers.** Observe at a child care center both before the children arrive and while children are there. Look for the same information described above for preschools.

- **Observing Family Day Care Homes.** Observe at a licensed family day care home, realizing, of course, that this type of child care program will differ from a larger program. Spend some time talking with the child care provider when children are not present. What licensing requirements are necessary? What amount of space is required for the number of children served? How are children's needs met for active and quiet play and for large motor and small motor play? How is the space arranged for children? What equipment is available? How are health and safety requirements met?

Chapter 10

Keeping Children Safe

CHAPTER OBJECTIVES

- Explain who has responsibility for children's safety.

- Develop an effective safety policy.

- Describe the safety forms used in an early childhood program.

- Identify and explain how to eliminate safety hazards.

- Explain how to promote safety with children.

- Describe what should be done during medical, fire, and weather-related emergencies.

- Assemble a first aid kit.

Terms to Learn

- accident log
- accident report form
- cardiopulmonary resuscitation (CPR)
- emergency treatment waiver form
- Heimlich maneuver
- liable for negligence
- prevention
- safety hazards
- safety policy
- syrup of ipecac

As far as I'm concerned," Nick Turner said, smiling at Melinda, "every child in here is an accident waiting to happen." Nick chuckled as he gave his newest employee the introductory tour of the child care center. "You know how children are. They love to explore. They don't think about danger. They're energetic but not well coordinated. And they just don't have the knowledge and experience that adults have. That's why we do everything we can to keep them safe."

As Melinda followed Nick around, she noticed some of the signs of safety in the center. Fire extinguishers and smoke detectors were on the walls of every room. "That's the medicine cabinet," Nick said as he pointed to a cupboard in the nurse's office. "There's a first aid kit and medications in it, but it's always locked. I'll show you where the key is."

A few minutes later Nick and Melinda were in the play yard, where six preschoolers were having fun. The yard was surrounded by a sturdy fence with a gate and lock. "This looks like a nice, safe play area," Melinda commented.

At that moment, one child ran across the grass and bumped another one, sending her into tears. "I guess that's one thing we can't completely control," Nick said to Melinda, shrugging his shoulders as he gave the child a hug. "Even though we do our best, we can't always protect them from each other."

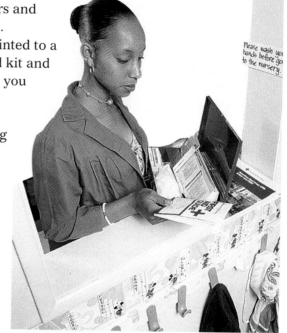

SAFETY—WHOSE RESPONSIBILITY?

Proper safety in an early childhood program is everyone's business—the director, teachers, teacher's aides, cooks, bus drivers, and custodians. A safe environment comes about with careful planning and continuous attention.

The very nature of children makes them prone to injury. They are excitable and impulsive; they act first and think later. Their curiosity and enthusiasm urge them to explore and investigate. Unfortunately, however, they are not able to anticipate threats to their safety.

As an example, at one preschool, three-year-old Angelo caught a glimpse of a butterfly floating by a window. He was just about to climb onto the windowsill to get a better look when his teacher gently redirected his attention to a poster with butterflies on it in the science center.

Child care employees have a legal as well as a moral obligation to watch for children's safety. No one can care for children without taking this responsibility seriously.

Individual state governments establish minimum safety standards in their child care licensing laws. This is the government's contribution to insuring children's safety in child care situations.

Everyone who works in a program must know and follow the program's safety policy. An effective policy not only includes all major areas of safety, but also identifies specific procedures to insure safety.

Additional regulations affecting child care include fire marshal codes, building safety codes, and health department codes. These regulations represent the community's role in protecting young children.

Safety is of supreme importance in child care programs. If child care professionals do not prevent or handle accidents to the best of their ability, they could be held **liable for negligence.** This means they could be *held accountable in a court of law for neglecting to prevent an accident or to handle an emergency in a responsible manner.* Early childhood programs should carry liability insurance to cover costs if sued for injuries. Some staff members choose to carry personal professional liability insurance when they are not covered by the employer's insurance.

DEVELOPING A SAFETY POLICY

*T*o make their commitment to safety clear to everyone, program directors develop a **safety policy.** *This policy states the rules and procedures to follow to insure children's physical and emotional well-being.* A safety policy must address many areas of concern, including:

- Maintaining a safe facility.
- Toy safety.
- Rules for children's conduct.
- Positive methods of discipline to prevent questions of child abuse.
- Transportation safety.
- Safety inspections.
- Emergency procedures.
- Evacuation procedures.

Staff training manuals should include the written safety policy. This should be reviewed with employees when they begin work. Some programs provide in-service (on-the-job) training on the rules and procedures to follow. Employees may be asked to sign a paper stating that they have read and understand the safety policy.

Safety policies should also be clearly identified in parent information materials. This helps reassure parents that their children will be carefully and responsibly looked after at all times. It also informs parents of their role in complying with safety rules.

SAFETY FORMS

*I*n following safety policy, staff members need to be familiar with the forms that they have to fill out as they work with children. These forms apply to:

- *Injuries.* All incidents involving injury, no matter how minor, must be recorded on an accident report form and an accident log immediately after a child is treated. The **accident report form** is *used to record specific information about any accident involving a child.* It should include the child's name, injury date, and time of injury; names of witnesses to the injury; the classroom location of the injury; equipment or products involved; the cause of the injury; the type of injury; who gave the first aid and what they did; and any action taken by a doctor or dentist. This form is placed in the child's file. An **accident log** is used to keep a written record of all injuries as they happen. Logs may be used to record other types of information as well. Explanations are written in the log (perhaps a notebook or clipboard) on a day-to-day basis. This documentation can be referenced later if questions or problems arise.

- **Suspected Abuse.** Any suspected cases of child abuse or neglect must be documented and reported. Chapter 11 includes more about this subject.

- **Releasing Children.** Children may leave the program *only* with their parents, unless parents have signed a waiver that gives their permission for someone else to pick up the child. In addition, many programs request a picture of any other person that the parents authorize for pickup. Before the child can be released, the person who picks up the child must show a form of identification that indicates his or her name.

- **Emergency Treatment.** An **emergency treatment waiver form** must be filled out for each child. *This statement, signed by a parent or legal guardian, gives the program permission to secure emergency medical treatment for a sick or injured child.* It usually states that no emergency treatment will be given to a child without parent/guardian consent except in a life-threatening situation. Also included on the form are: telephone numbers of parents or guardians at home and at work; times when they can be reached at these numbers; additional people to contact when the parent or guardian is unavailable, including telephone numbers and relationship to the child; and the name and telephone number of the child's medical care provider.

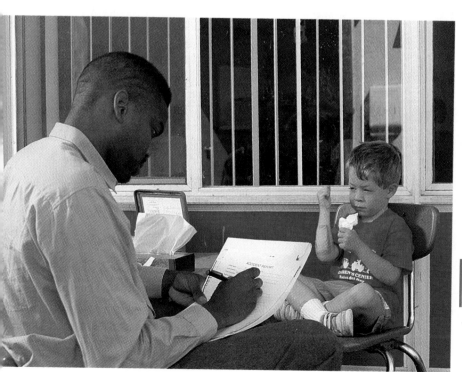

Give two reasons for documenting accidents in writing.

THE MULTICULTURAL CLASSROOM

Educating staff and parents about safety and emergency procedures can be especially difficult when working with people of diverse backgrounds. They may have been taught standards and procedures that are different from the policies in your program or community. Home remedies and cures for such things as burns, headaches, insect bites, hiccups, and upset stomachs are not the same everywhere. To build understanding, one solution is to invite specialists or a panel of experts to discuss these topics, handle the questions and answers, and make suggestions in a nonjudgmental way. You might include the information in a parent orientation meeting.

Children need to learn safety rules and the reasons behind them. Frequent reminders will be needed.

PREVENTING ACCIDENTS AND INJURIES

By definition, **prevention** means *taking action to keep something from happening*. Of course, no child care program is completely free of accidents. With prevention, however, the number and severity of incidents can be limited.

Possibly the single most important precaution regarding safety is to *supervise children at all times*. Never leave a child unattended.

Another way to prevent accidents is to anticipate problem situations. By understanding child development and children's behavior, caregivers can reduce the risk of mishaps. Knowledge makes them aware that what is perfectly safe for a four-year-old may be hazardous for a one-year-old. Teachers should never assume children will use toys and equipment in appropriate ways. They should ask themselves, "How else might some children use this item?"

Keen observation is also important for accident prevention. Always be on the lookout for **safety hazards**. These are *items, conditions, and situations that could put*

Building Professional Skills

Common Sense

WHAT IS COMMON SENSE?

Common sense is a combination of experience, observation, and reasoning skills. It allows you to see actions and aspects of a situation that might cause problems and to take steps to avoid them. It also helps you deal with a problem in a logical, rational manner. Common sense is the practical use of your thinking skills.

Common Sense in Action

"We'll have an 'outside' day when we can really enjoy it," Javier told the children. He was as disappointed as anyone by the unexpectedly cold and cloudy weather. He had promised his preschoolers that they could work on their art projects and eat lunch outside that day. True, most of them had jackets, but he felt the sudden change in the weather would be especially uncomfortable when they weren't used to it.

Although disappointed, the children accepted his decision and began to work on their art projects. After a while, however, one girl began to complain of a headache. Javier sent her to the school nurse, who called the girl's father. After lunch, two boys also said they had headaches, and stomachaches as well. They, too, were sent home.

Javier was starting to worry. "What could be making the children sick?" he wondered to himself. "The graham crackers I gave them as a snack were from the same box I used yesterday. Their art supplies are all nontoxic and haven't caused problems before. And the two boys brought their lunches from home, so they ate different things. What's going on?"

An idea came to mind. "Is this the first time the furnace has been on since last winter?" he asked the school custodian.

"Yes, it is," the custodian replied, "but I wish the weather had held off. I haven't had a chance to clean the furnace yet."

Javier took his suspicions to the school director, who immediately called the utility company. Tests of the air showed that the furnace was giving off unusually high levels of some fumes—not dangerous, but enough to make some younger children sick. Immediate steps were taken to correct the situation. "We're all grateful for your alertness, Javier," the director said to him. "You just might have prevented something worse from happening."

Your Analysis

1. What was Javier's first common sense decision?

2. How did knowledge of children's health help Javier discover the cause of their illness?

3. What might have happened if Javier had not pursued his concerns?

4. What can people do to improve their common sense?

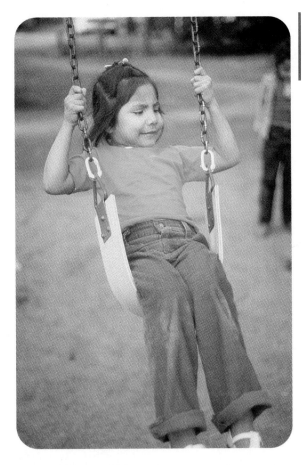

A safe outdoor play area gives children an opportunity to develop new skills. How could you minimize the possibility of injury from a swing set?

children in physical or emotional danger. Hazards can be found in indoor and outdoor play areas, on field trips, and even on short walks. In fact, wherever you find children, there is a potential for mishaps.

Environmental Safety Precautions

Indoor and outdoor play areas and learning centers should be inspected daily for safety hazards, as suggested in the information below and on page 189. Toys, equipment, and facilities should be checked for wear and damage. Such hazards as torn carpeting and exposed wiring should be reported for immediate repair. Keep children away from these until repairs are made. Litter, especially glass, should be disposed of quickly. Full safety inspections, using a checklist, should be conducted frequently.

Outdoor Safety Precautions to Take

- Surround play yards with at least four-foot tall (1.25 m) fencing with a locked gate.

- Choose climbing equipment that is the right size for children's height and abilities.

- Check equipment frequently for splinters, jagged edges, and rusted metal.

- Place padding underneath and around climbing and swinging equipment to cushion falls.

- Locate swing sets away from the traffic pattern so children running by aren't injured.

- Make sure shrubs, bushes, and trees do not have leaves and berries that could be poisonous if eaten.

- Provide safety goggles and nonelectric tools in the woodworking area.

- Supervise wading pools constantly. Surround pools with a locked fence.

- Choose soft, grassy areas for play space; provide cement or asphalt for wheeled toys.

Indoor Safety Precautions to Take

- Use only nontoxic materials in art projects and in the science center. Remember that some plant leaves and berries can be poisonous if eaten.

- Provide only round-tipped scissors.

- Take special care with electricity, particularly when cooking with electric appliances and playing with electric and battery-operated toys. Make sure wires are not frayed and batteries are not leaking. Cover all unused electric outlets.

- Provide appropriate padding under climbing equipment.

- Provide handrails on stairways.

- Use nonslip rugs on hard floors.

- Lock the staff's personal belongings in a closet or cabinet. This applies especially to purses, which may contain such hazards as fingernail files, scissors, pocket knives, and matches.

- Label potential poisons and lock them out of children's reach. This includes cleaning preparations, aerosol sprays, drain cleaners, and even medicine. (Some children like the taste of flavored medicines, which may result in overdose.)

- Place decals at children's eye level on low windows and sliding glass doors. This helps children be aware of the glass and keeps them from running into or even through it.

- Bolt tall toy shelves to the wall to prevent them from toppling onto a child.

- Make sure water temperature in bathrooms is warm, not hot, to prevent burns.

- Do not allow children in kitchen and garage areas.

Toy Safety

Suppose you were buying a stuffed animal for an infant nursery. Would you choose one with sewn-on button eyes or one with embroidered eyes? This is the kind of safety decision you make routinely when stocking a center with toys. The button-eyed animal is a poor choice because the eyes could come off and be swallowed by an infant. Here are some tips that will help when choosing toys:

- Select toys that are appropriate for the ages of children you care for.
- Read labels and catalog descriptions for age recommendations before purchasing toys.

- Check all toys for sharp edges by running your fingers carefully over the edges of the toys. By law, new toys that are to be used by children under eight should be free of sharp glass, sharp points, and metal edges.

- Examine labels to be sure that plastic toys are shatterproof and nonflammable.

- Make certain that painted toys and art supplies are labeled nontoxic.

- Check to be sure that toys, and any removable parts from toys, are not small enough to swallow or inhale. For children under the age of three, these items should be no smaller than the approximate size of a child's fist.

Children need to learn new skills but in a safe way. Safety scissors, for example, minimize the possibility of injury.

• Avoid toys with long cords or strings for use by infants and toddlers. If a cord becomes wrapped around the neck, the child may strangle.

When programs have children of different ages, older and younger children should play with their toys in separate areas. Teach the older ones to keep their toys away from younger children. Storage areas for these toys should also be out of the range of young children.

To manage toy safety, a program might assign the responsibility to one employee. For example, as part of her morning routine before the children arrive, Fala examines the toys stored on shelves and in crates. She removes anything broken, making note of the repairs to be made. Fala rarely finds broken toys anymore, since the teachers have encouraged the children to bring broken toys immediately to them. This makes Fala's job easier, and the center is a safer place.

Focus On INFANT/TODDLER PROGRAMS

Infants and toddlers are especially vulnerable to safety hazards and emergencies. Because they cannot communicate their difficulties or get themselves away from danger quickly, adults are needed for good supervision.

Fires require especially quick action when infants are involved, because they must be transported away from the danger. For speed, caregivers often put several infants in one crib with wheels and rapidly move them to safety. This is much quicker than carrying two infants out at a time.

Infants and toddlers put everything in their mouths. Therefore, rattles and shaker toys must be sturdy so small beads inside do not fall out.

Movable pieces of equipment used around infants and toddlers must have locking wheels so they stay in place. Doors on low cabinets should be equipped with childproof locks to prevent injury and poisoning.

Transportation Safety Precautions

Child care facilities sometimes provide transportation for field trips and to and from home or school. Many precautions must be taken to make sure that children are protected. These include:

- Conducting safety inspections on vehicles.
- Making sure all drivers are legally licensed to drive a large vehicle.
- Equipping vehicles with seat belts and carseats.
- Providing an adult bus supervisor.
- Having a first aid kit in each vehicle.
- Making sure all vehicles are equipped with a working two-way radio, flashlight, fire extinguisher, and city map with the location of hospitals clearly identified.

Tip FROM THE Pros

Keeping track of children can be a challenge on a field trip. Try using safety pins to fasten the name tags to the backs of children's shirts. When name tags are on the children's backs, they are less likely to be torn off and lost.

Field Trip Safety Precautions

Since field trips may take you to places not specifically designed for children, they offer added safety concerns. You can plan for these. For example, when Dominic was arranging a field trip to a fire station, he toured the station beforehand and talked with the fire chief to identify any safety hazards they might encounter. Prior to the field trip, he told the children (and also the staff and parent supervisors) about these hazards and the rules they would follow to prevent possible accidents. Dominic also made sure that he collected the permission forms signed by the children's parents or legal guardians before the trip. In addition, he took all emergency treatment waiver forms with him.

At any field trip site, vehicles should be parked in a safe, off-street area as children

Field trips can provide wonderful opportunities for learning, but they require careful planning and extra supervision to insure safety. An alternative is bringing the community to the children. These preschoolers have been eagerly awaiting the policeman's visit.

enter and exit them. Each child should wear a name tag identifying the child care facility's name and telephone number. Inviting parents or other adults on the field trip increases supervision and can add to the enjoyment.

PROMOTING SAFETY WITH CHILDREN

Children can learn about safety in many ways. As with other behavior, role modeling by adults is one of the best teachers. Children also learn safety concepts in the classroom. They can create posters on safety practices and listen to stories about safety. Field trips can reinforce safety practices too. Visits to the fire station, hospital, and doctor's office emphasize the importance of being careful. Children also learn about safety when taking part in safety inspections with teachers.

When talking to children about safety, speak in positive terms. Stress good safety habits, rather than listing all of the "don'ts." Here are some simple safety rules children should be taught to follow:

- Walk indoors. Running is for outside.

- Play with toys carefully. Give broken toys to a teacher.
- Stack hard blocks only to (the child's) shoulder height. (Higher buildings might topple on children.)
- Settle conflicts with words, not by hitting, biting, pushing, or throwing toys.
- Tables and shelves are for games and toys, not for climbing.
- Stay with the teacher when on walks or a field trip.
- Ask permission before going to the play yard.
- Obey safety rules when using art supplies, cooking utensils, and woodworking tools.
- Be careful when playing on riding toys. Try not to bump into other children or into their toys.
- Tell a teacher right away if a stranger comes into the classroom or play yard.
- Tell a parent, teacher, or good friend who is an adult if anyone touches you on a private area of your body.

Learning what to do in an emergency situation gives children confidence. This is one of a series of activities to help these children learn and remember fire safety rules.

FOCUS **O**N SCHOOL-AGE PROGRAMS

School-age children enjoy rough-and-tumble play, which means they are likely to get scrapes, bumps, and bruises. With this age group, plan games that allow children to use their physical energy without getting hurt. Some games school-age children want to participate in, such as tackle football, can be dangerous to muscles and bones. Program rules should not allow these sports. Such games as touch football, dodgeball, catch, and relay races tend to result in fewer injuries.

Although rare, some school-age children experiment with drugs, alcohol, and cigarette smoking. Changes in behavior may indicate a child's involvement. You might notice withdrawal from friends or a change in friends, a change in grades or attitude toward school, or outbursts of violent or destructive behavior. A teacher should keep a watchful eye for behavior signals and report them to parents.

EMERGENCY PROCEDURES

How do you react in an emergency? Not everyone responds in the same way. Emergencies can cause pain and confusion, especially when people are not prepared for them. Establishing, reviewing, and practicing emergency procedures can help staff and children remain calm and respond quickly to any emergency.

Emergency procedures should be outlined in staff training manuals and reviewed regularly during staff meetings. The child care staff should take part in ongoing safety training to instruct them on emergency techniques.

Children should also be prepared for emergencies. Such information as fire escape routes should be prominently posted in halls and classrooms. The telephone numbers for the fire, police, and weather stations; hospital; ambulance service; child abuse hotline; and poison control center

should be listed next to every telephone. In many areas, 911 can be dialed to summon emergency medical technicians and other emergency help. Children as well as staff members should practice emergency procedures regularly.

In an emergency, children look to adults for guidance and comfort. The calmness that comes from being prepared and knowing what to do can literally be a lifesaver.

Handling Medical Emergencies

Even when prevention is practiced conscientiously, accidents and injuries do occur. A confident, appropriate response is much more likely when you have thought ahead of time about what to do and you know the basic procedure to follow.

In any medical emergency, the first rule is to stay calm. Determine how severe the injury is. Decide what kind of on-site care is appropriate and whether professional treatment is needed.

When Injuries Are Minor

Often injuries are minor and can be quickly treated. For bumps and bruises an ice pack minimizes swelling; a scraped knee may require thorough cleaning with soap and water, a mild antiseptic, and a bandage. First aid training gives employees the knowledge to treat simple injuries.

Certain supplies are needed to handle minor injuries. Blankets and towels should be available. Each classroom should also have a first aid kit that is easily accessible to teachers yet out of the reach of children. In addition, a kit should be available outdoors and taken along on field trips. First aid kits contain these items: a first aid book, bandages, gauze pads and strips, adhesive tape, thermometers, flashlight, tongue depressors, cotton balls, blunt scissors, liquid soap, dis-

posable latex gloves, tweezers, and syrup of ipecac (IH-pih-kak).

Syrup of ipecac is *a substance that, when swallowed, causes vomiting.* Remember that syrup of ipecac is recommended only in some cases of poisoning. Call the poison control center before you give syrup of ipecac to a child. Some poisons may cause more damage to a child's esophagus and mouth when vomiting forces the substance back up.

When Injuries Are Serious

If a child requires professional medical treatment, the teacher should stay with the child and administer any appropriate first aid while someone else calls an ambulance or other emergency assistance. The child's parents should then be called, and the medical treatment waiver should be obtained from the child's file. If parents do not arrive in time, a teacher should go to the hospital with the child.

Occasionally an injury is life threatening, requiring immediate attention. Staff members should be certified in infant/child **cardiopulmonary resuscitation (CPR)** (CAR-dee-oh-PULL-muh-NAIR-ee ree-SUH-suh-TAY-shun). This is *a life-saving technique used when the heartbeat and/or breathing has*

Bumps, bruises, and scrapes are common injuries for young children. Supplying sympathy and comfort is as important as giving first aid.

The Heimlich maneuver is used when a child over age one (or an adult) is choking. Only use it if the child is conscious but cannot speak or cough. Stand behind the child and make a fist with one hand. Press the thumb against the child's abdomen just beneath the rib cage. Grasp your fist with your hand. Give quick, upward thrusts until the object is dislodged.

stopped. Gentle puffs of air are given to the person while forcing the heart to pump blood by applying gentle pressure to the chest. CPR can be used for suffocation, electrical shock, choking, drowning, and heart failure. CPR, which should only be administered by trained people, can keep the person alive until professional help arrives. The American Red Cross, along with many hospitals, provides excellent first aid and CPR training.

Choking

An important technique to remedy choking in adults and children over one year of age is the **Heimlich maneuver** (HIME-lick muh-NOO-vur). *With this technique, pressure on the body is used to dislodge an object that is blocking air through the windpipe or throat.* A diagram that shows and explains how to use the Heimlich maneuver should be posted in the eating area, and staff members should be trained to use the procedure. This maneuver should not be used on infants because of the possibility of internal injury. A different first aid procedure is used for infants.

Poisoning

Poisoning is a very serious medical emergency and one of the greatest hazards to children. The chart on page 196 contains a list of some poisonous subtances. Signs that may indicate poisoning are:

- Burns around or in the mouth and throat.
- Vomiting from swallowing poisons or chemicals.
- Burns or rash on the skin from direct contact with poisons or chemicals.
- Burning or irritation of the eyes or blindness caused by poisons or chemicals coming in contact with the eyes.
- Choking, coughing, headache, nausea, or dizziness from inhaling fumes, sprays, or poisonous gases.

Examples of Poisonous Substances

PLANTS
English ivy

Daffodil bulbs

Rhubarb leaves

Holly berries

Poison ivy and oak

Contact: swallowing and skin

MEDICINE
Aspirin

Sleeping pills

Tranquilizers

Vitamins

Cold and allergy preparations

Contact: swallowing

CLEANING PRODUCTS
Ammonia

Laundry detergent

Bleach

Drain and toilet bowl cleaners

Disinfectants

Furniture polish

Contact: swallowing, skin, eyes, and inhaling

PERSONAL CARE PRODUCTS
Shampoo

Soap

Nail polish and nail polish remover

Perfumes and aftershave lotions

Mouthwash

Rubbing alcohol

Sunscreens and lotions

Contact: swallowing, eyes, and inhaling

MISCELLANEOUS PRODUCTS
Insecticides

Insect repellant

Paint thinner

Paint

Mouse poison

Contact: swallowing, skin, eyes, and inhaling

If poisoning is suspected, quickly try to determine the cause. Remember that emergency procedures described on product labels are not always correct. Instead of using them, immediately call a poison control center and follow their directions. Be prepared to give the following information when you call:

- Symptoms the child is displaying.
- Child's age and weight.
- Substance that poisoned the child, if you know.
- When and how much poison was ingested, if it was swallowed.

- The list of ingredients on the product container, if possible.

Handling Fire Emergencies

Fire extinguishers should be located in each classroom and in the kitchen and laundry area. All staff members should be trained in using them. In the event of a fire, sound the alarm at the first sight of smoke or flames.

Fire evacuation diagrams should be posted in each classroom. The diagram should include arrows showing the directions to take to reach exits. By making sure there are clear pathways to exits, evacuation time can be kept to a minimum. Fire drills should be held monthly, often along with the assistance of the fire department. Staff and children will react more calmly, quickly, and correctly if the drill has been practiced repeatedly and children are familiar with the sound of the alarm. Record the time of each drill and identify any problems that need to be solved. Take attendance sheets outside during the drill and make sure all children arrive at the planned destination. Always use the same destination.

Handling Weather Emergencies

Weather emergencies include electrical storms, tornadoes, hurricanes, blizzards, and floods, depending on geographic location. Some teachers also have to plan earthquake procedures.

Safety procedures vary according to the emergency. The fire department or weather station can give you recommended responses to specific types of severe weather. Here are some general rules that apply to weather emergencies:

keep in touch w/

- Keep battery-operated radios and flashlights readily accessible.
- Post directions to rooms designated as shelter areas.
- Take shelter at the first sound of an alarm and remain there until the all-clear signal is given.
- Take attendance immediately after reaching shelter and try to locate missing children as quickly as possible.

YOUR RESPONSIBILITY

When a parent places a child in a child care program, there is trust. The parent believes that you will do everything in your power to keep the child safe and to respond correctly if a problem arises. As a child care professional, you owe that kind of dedication to every child. There may be no better way to take responsibility for the safety and well-being of children than thinking of each child as your very own.

As a teacher, would you know how to react if a tornado warning sounded? Regular drills help children and teachers practice what to do.

Chapter 10 Review

Chapter Summary

- One of the most important responsibilities of any child care program and of its staff is to keep children safe.
- Child care facilities have safety policies stating rules and procedures to follow to insure safety.
- Prevention is the key to safety.
- Hazards to children's safety are everywhere. Children should be supervised at all times.
- The child care staff is responsible for identifying safety hazards and preventing accidents.
- Children learn about safety through adults' examples, classroom lessons, field trips, and taking part in safety inspections.
- First aid training is helpful in handling many medical emergencies. First aid kits should be readily accessible.
- Staff members should be thoroughly trained in procedures to follow during fire and weather emergencies, as well as a wide variety of medical emergencies. Training and practice should be ongoing.

Reviewing the Facts

1. What does "liable for negligence" mean?
2. What areas of concern are included in a safety policy?
3. Briefly describe three safety forms that are used in child care programs.
4. What is the link between prevention and safety hazards?
5. List four indoor and four outdoor safety precautions.
6. Give four tips for choosing safe toys.
7. Cite four safety precautions for field trips.
8. List five safety rules that children should learn.
9. What is the first rule to follow in a medical emergency?
10. List eight items that should be included in a first aid kit.
11. When and by whom is CPR administered?
12. What information must be given when calling a poison control center in the event of poisoning?
13. Why are fire drills necessary?

Thinking Critically

1. One of the children at your lunch table becomes very quiet. His eyes are wide and watery. His face is turning blue. He keeps grabbing his throat. Describe what you would do.
2. What specific things could you do to keep children calm in an emergency situation?
3. Predict the consequences of failing to pay regular attention to safety details in the early childhood classroom. How might this affect the children, the program, and the staff?
4. Do you think it is possible to make children overly concerned about their own safety and well-being? How would you instill a healthy awareness of safety without making children afraid?

Activities and Applications

1. **Investigating Equipment.** Investigate types of padding available to use with outdoor climbing equipment. List the pros and cons of each.

2. **Demonstrating Fire Extinguisher Usage.** Prepare a demonstration on how to use fire extinguishers.

3. **First Aid Kit.** Compare the costs of commercially prepared first aid kits to the cost of putting together a first aid kit on your own. Do commercially prepared kits supply all the items necessary for an early childhood classroom?

4. **Safety Pledge.** With a partner, write a pledge that every child care professional could make as a commitment to the safety of children in a child care setting.

SCHOOL TO WORK

Your Professional Portfolio

Prepare a checklist that could be used to evaluate the safety conditions in an early childhood classroom. Include environmental safety, medical safety, transportation safety, etc. Place the completed checklist in your portfolio.

Observing and Analyzing

Checking for Safety

The numerous inspections that are required to license child care programs are usually safety-based. In other words, safety is the most significant factor in licensing a facility, and the inspector's name attesting to this fact should be in plain view on the posted license. To discover more about how child care programs manage safety, observe some programs and analyze what you discover.

- **Licensing.** Visit a child care program to examine licensing requirements. Where is the license posted? Is it within view of visitors? Count the number of children in the building. Is this number less than, or more than, what is shown on the license? Is the license current? Is all of the other information on the license accurate? What are some of the repercussions if the license is not correct or has expired? Should the families be told? Why or why not?

- **Safety Preparedness.** While visiting an early childhood program, observe the classroom(s) for safety preparedness. Look for the method used to cover electrical outlets, the way appliance cords are kept safely out of the way, how cleaning supplies are stored, safety measures in the play yard, and the locations of smoke alarms. Do you see other signs of preparedness? Keep looking. Can you find an emergency evacuation plan posted on a wall in each classroom? What about emergency phone numbers, including the poison control center? Do you see an emergency drill schedule? These are all signs that the child care setting is a safe one.

Chapter 11

Promoting
Good Health

CHAPTER OBJECTIVES

■ Describe how to maintain a healthful environment in a child care setting.

■ Explain practices used to monitor illnesses.

■ Describe concerns that arise when children have special health conditions.

■ Discuss health problems associated with weather, abuse, neglect, and emotion.

■ Assess the health procedures used in a child care program.

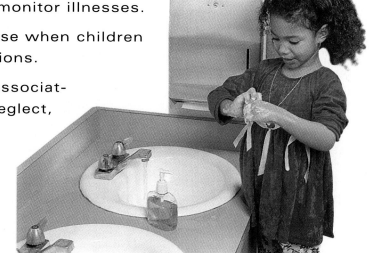

Terms to Learn

- antibodies
- child abuse
- child neglect
- communicable diseases
- grand mal seizure
- immune system
- immunization
- infectious diseases
- noncommunicable diseases
- pathogens
- petit mal seizures
- vaccine

But it hurts," Alex complained, holding his arms over his stomach. He had a look of pain on his face.

Ms. Jasper, the new teacher's aide, watched as Mr. Morgan knelt to talk to Alex.

"Stomachaches aren't fun, are they?" Mr. Morgan asked him. Then he put his arm around Alex's shoulders and gave him a little hug. "Did I tell you how much I like your shirt? What kind of horse is that on the front?"

Alex looked down at his shirt and started to explain what kind of horse he thought it was.

"You know, Alex, I think we have a book about all kinds of horses. Some horses have patches of black and white. They're called pintos. Have you ever seen one?"

Alex seemed to have forgotten his pain. In a short time he was totally absorbed in the pictures of horses in the book Mr. Morgan found for him.

"He wasn't really sick, was he?" Ms. Jasper asked.

"No," Mr. Morgan replied. "I've learned to tell when Alex just needs a little attention. Sometimes that's his way of getting it. We have to be careful though. When you're responsible for children, it pays to take things seriously. I watch all the children closely. We have some who think they're sick when they're not and some who don't tell you they're sick when they are. Getting to know all of them well helps."

TAKING HEALTH SERIOUSLY

Safety is not the only part of children's care that deserves close attention. Health does too. As anyone who works with children knows, physical illnesses are common, and emotional problems can also cause concern.

Child care professionals take their responsibilities toward children's health seriously. Not only do they aim to provide a healthful environment, but they also keep accurate records on the health of children. They establish practices and procedures designed to prevent illness and limit its spread. These are covered in staff training workshops, staff manuals, parent handbooks, and newsletters. Above all, child care professionals become knowledgeable about the care that children need so they can take the right steps when physical, as well as emotional, health problems arise.

CHILDREN AND DISEASE

*C*hildren are subject to many **infectious diseases.** *These illnesses are caused by organisms that enter the body and damage tissue.* The *disease-causing organisms* are called **pathogens** but are more commonly known as germs. Bacteria and viruses are two kinds of pathogens.

Some infectious diseases are *passed from person to person.* Called **communicable diseases**, they include colds and the flu. Chicken pox and strep throat are other examples.

Communicable diseases spread easily, especially among children in group settings. Many pathogens are present in fluids from the nose, mouth, lungs, and eyes. Thus, coughing, sneezing, and simple contact enable certain illnesses to pass from one child to another. Everything touched—toys, drinking glasses, infant teething rings, bedding, food, books, and other people—becomes a possible source of illness. Some disease-causing organisms are found in feces and urine as well as blood. In these cases, too, contact with the sources can result in the spread of disease. Changing diapers and caring for injuries, for example, pose a risk when not handled properly.

Other infectious diseases do not pass from person to person. These are **noncommunicable diseases**. Some are transmitted by way of food, animals, and insects. Such conditions as ear infections and diaper rash are also noncommunicable.

The Immune System

Have you ever wondered why children get sick so easily? One reason is that a child's **immune system** is not as well developed as an adult's. *This bodily system produces antibodies that resist disease. When released into the blood,* **antibodies** *help destroy pathogens.* Until immune systems develop and children learn how to protect themselves better against illness, caregivers have to do all they can to keep children healthy.

HEALTH PRECAUTIONS

*A*s you can see, putting children together in groups is an invitation to illness. Only by paying particular attention to what goes on within the environment can limits be put on the spread of disease.

Healthful Air

Although they aren't visible, the organisms that cause diseases are often in the air. Breathing puts them in the air, and a cough or a sneeze propels them through the air.

One way to limit the spread of communicable diseases in a child care program is to teach the children good health habits.

Knowing this, many child care professionals take some basic precautions. Kristin, for example, spoke to the custodian in her center about proper air circulation and ventilation. She wanted the air to be as clear of pathogens as possible. As long as weather permitted and pollution was not a problem, she let the children play outside for a while each day. Indoors, she kept the children spread out in small groups. She even spaced cots a few feet apart during nap time. She also made sure the children covered their mouths when they sneezed or coughed and washed their hands afterwards.

Cleanliness

Cleanliness not only makes the environment look better and feel more comfortable, but it also helps reduce the presence of disease-causing organisms. Classrooms should be cleaned nightly by a custodian. Special attention must be given to bathrooms and diapering areas, drinking fountains, and kitchen and meal service areas. Classroom walls and floors should also be cleaned on a regular basis.

Doing laundry is part of the cleanliness routine. Cot covers, blankets, sheets, pillowcases, and pillows should be washed weekly or whenever they become soiled due to toileting accidents or illness. To limit the exchange of illnesses, children should each be assigned a crib or cot complete with personal bedding. Cots should be labeled with children's names. Kitchen towels, cloths, and aprons should be laundered daily. Children's dress-up clothes, puppets, stuffed animals, and lounging pillows require regular cleaning.

Standards of cleanliness apply outdoors too. Make sure sandboxes are covered nightly to prevent animals from depositing their waste there. Climbing equipment and swinging tires must have drainage holes to prevent standing water. Mosquitoes, which can carry harmful diseases, breed in standing water. Part of your job as a child care professional is to insure that all cleanliness tasks are performed as needed.

Sanitizing

Sanitizing is essential. Toys and equipment need regular sanitizing. The health department has information on how to sanitize items. Eating tables should be washed and treated with a sanitizing solution before and after each meal. Diapering surfaces must be sanitized before and after each use. A sanitizing solution frequently used in child care programs is one part bleach mixed with four parts water.

Tables where children eat need to be sanitized before and after meals and snacks. What are some other situations that might call for sanitizing surfaces during the day?

Hand Washing

The most important step in keeping children and staff free of communicable diseases is frequent and thorough hand washing. Children and staff should wash hands before and after preparing or eating meals and snacks, and after coughing, sneezing, and toileting. Staff members must also wash their hands before and after diapering. Everyone should wash after such play activities as sand or water play, finger painting, and using clays and doughs. The information below shows the proper method for thoroughly washing hands.

Washing areas should be easily accessible. Ideally, washing areas are provided in the classroom, in restrooms, in kitchens and staff lounges, and outdoors . All washing facilities should have *liquid* soap and *disposable* paper towels. Bar soap and cloth towels can spread illnesses.

You can teach children good health practices, such as hand washing, through classroom activities and daily routines. Monitor them as they wash so that you can guide their technique. Posters, signs, and bulletin boards educate and remind everyone. Most importantly, be a good role model by following the hand washing rules yourself.

Universal Precautions

All of the precautions you have just read are essential for limiting the spread of disease. A few additional ones, sometimes called universal precautions, should be taken during specific procedures. Because some disease-causing organisms are present in blood, urine, and feces, the universal precautions should be taken whenever you might come in contact with these. Whenever you change diapers, help with toileting, or treat an injury, always wear a fresh pair of

Steps for Proper Hand Washing

Turn on warm water.

Rub your hands vigorously, using liquid soap.

Wash all surfaces, including the backs of hands, wrists, between fingers, and under fingernails.

FOCUS ON INFANT/TODDLER PROGRAMS

Infants and toddlers are especially vulnerable to illness. They have had little time to build a strong immune system. To decrease the risk of illness, infants should consistently have the same caregivers. Frequent rotation of caregivers increases exposure to disease-causing organisms.

Infants are especially vulnerable to illnesses involving diarrhea. Severe diarrhea can cause dehydration, which can be fatal for infants.

Giardia (jee-ar-DEE-uh) is a common disease in infants that results in diarrhea. It is spread through poor sanitary practices. It can be passed from child to child when caregivers do not clean children's or their own hands after diapering, as well as through toys an infected person has touched. Proper diapering and hand washing are the best ways to prevent the spread of giardia and other disease-causing organisms.

Since infants and toddlers constantly put toys in their mouths, daily toy sanitation is another important means of avoiding illness. Some programs put toys in a large mesh bag and put this in the dishwasher for sanitizing. Others hand wash toys in a bleach solution at the end of each day.

4 Rinse well.

Turn off the water using a paper towel, not your clean hands.

6

5 Dry hands with a paper towel.

Building Professional Skills

Thoroughness

WHAT IS THOROUGHNESS?

Thoroughness means doing a job well and completely. When you are thorough, you pay attention to details; you believe that "little things mean a lot." You don't assume that someone else will finish your work or hope your lack of attention won't be noticed. Diligence and commitment are part of thoroughness.

Thoroughness in Action

"You must have too much time on your hands," Rene said to her friend Joanna. "Every time I come over here it seems like you're cleaning something."

Joanna laughed. "Not really," she replied. "It's just part of my work. I have to make sure the children that come to my home are protected. If I don't spend some time each day getting things done, I'll have a problem—and so will the little ones."

It was true. Joanna did spend some time every day on cleanup in the rooms used for her family day care home. Every evening she dry-mopped floors and vacuumed carpets. She checked under furniture for potentially dangerous objects. She made sure the windows were securely locked and none of the panes were cracked. She also cleaned the restroom. Every other day she dusted the blinds and window sills and wiped down the chalk ledges along the blackboard. She even cut off the loose strands on the edges of an area rug.

"This is a place for children to grow and learn and be happy," Joanna added as she stopped to look at Rene. "If health and safety aren't high priority, then my home won't be right for them, and that's important to me. Give me ten more minutes to finish cleaning this hamster cage, and we'll head for the movie. You see, I don't spend *all* my time cleaning."

Your Analysis

1. Identify the actions that demonstrate Joanna's thoroughness. Explain why each task is important and tell what might happen if she neglected to do it.

2. How is respect for yourself and your work related to thoroughness?

3. Think of an activity you enjoy or a service you use regularly. How often do you think about the individuals whose work makes the activity or service available? What might this say about their thoroughness on the job?

disposable latex gloves. The materials used to clean up body fluids should be disposable too. Paper towels, tissues, and diaper wipes are possibilities. Once used, place these in a plastic bag and then in a plastic-lined, covered trash container.

Many centers have special procedures for handling materials that contain blood. Check on these and follow them closely. Often such materials are labeled as medical waste and disposed of separately. The container must be kept out of children's reach.

Next, clean any surfaces—walls, floors, diapering areas—with soap and water and sanitize with a disinfectant. Then remove gloves by pulling them off inside out. Place the gloves in a plastic bag, tie it closed, and dispose of it properly. Gloves should only be used once. To complete the process, thoroughly wash your hands with liquid disinfectant soap under running water for at least ten seconds.

in order to comply with health codes and licensing requirements. In addition, careful monitoring enables caregivers to make accurate reports to parents.

Health Checks and Screenings

Health checks are routine procedures used to spot health problems. Usually they are conducted by the staff each morning as children arrive. This practice allows symptoms to be discovered in the early stages, when an illness is most treatable and can be kept from spreading.

Most programs conduct informal health checks. Caregivers take note of children's appearance, attitudes, and behavior. They check for physical signs of ill health. A rash, blisters, watery eyes, harsh coughing, inflamed throat, fever, or discharge from the nose or mouth could sig-

MONITORING ILLNESS

*E*ven in the best of environments, illnesses still occur. Child care professionals monitor illness for several reasons. They need to protect children from each other's illnesses and to care for sick children appropriately. They also need to keep track of health information

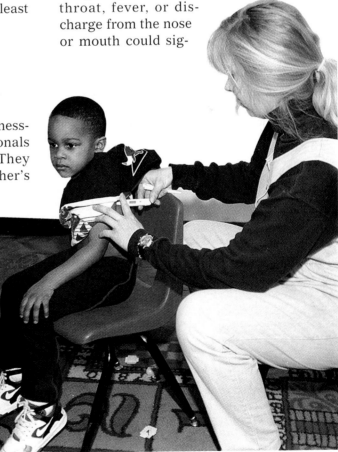

A child who shows possible signs of illness during a health check may need additional evaluation. Johnathon did not have a temperature and stayed for the day's activities.

FOCUS ON SCHOOL-AGE PROGRAMS

School-age children may experience less sickness than younger children. With more exposure to different illnesses, they have better developed immune systems.

School-age children often resist going to the doctor, even when very sick. With these children and their parents, emphasize the importance of regular medical checkups.

During the early school years, vision and hearing problems become more apparent. Signs of vision problems include holding a book very close to the face or avoiding reading entirely. Hearing problems may be indicated if a child often seems to ignore directions. If children exhibit these behaviors, a vision and hearing screening should be recommended.

nal illness. Unusual behavior, such as tiredness, crankiness, and whining, may too. All signs that concern teachers should be discussed immediately with the parent and recorded in the child's file. Some programs employ a part-time nurse to conduct daily health checks.

Screenings are examinations usually given to a group of children to look for one specific health problem. Those children who have the problem can then be referred for special treatment.

Screenings for vision and hearing problems are usually started at age three—earlier if problems are suspected. Some children are checked for diseases they might have inherited, such as blood diseases. Lead poisoning, which can cause serious illness and brain damage, is another condition that can be detected with screening.

As a rule, early childhood programs do not provide health screenings, but they do educate parents about how to locate this service in their community. Screenings may be conducted by a physician or the health department.

Restricting Attendance

A child or staff member who has a communicable illness may have to be absent temporarily. Restricting attendance helps protect others from becoming ill. Most programs establish specific guidelines, often with the help of the health department, so that parents and staff understand when attendance is not acceptable. A child who shows symptoms specified in these guidelines should rest in the isolation room until taken home by a parent or guardian. The guidelines also specify when a person who has been ill may return. For example, one guideline might be: "Children and staff must be fever-free for a 24-hour period before resuming attendance."

Notifying Parents

When such communicable diseases as measles and chicken pox occur, all parents of children in the program should be notified. Alert them by sending letters that identify:

- The illness or condition.
- Associated symptoms.
- Time that elapses before symptoms become apparent.
- Typical length of the illness.
- Suggested treatment.
- Point when a child can safely return to the classroom.

Certain communicable diseases should be reported to the health department for tracking of possible epidemics. Measles, mumps, and chicken pox are typical outbreaks that require reporting.

Maintaining Health Records

Health records are a protection for everyone involved in a child's care. Child care professionals need them to become informed about a child's health status. Parents use them to provide important information about their child's health. These records include:

- ***Physician's Reports.*** Most states require a physician's exam stating that a child is free of any serious communicable diseases upon entering a program. Proof that the child has had a negative tuberculosis test may also be required. In addition, immunization records should be included. Through **immunization**, children are *given a vaccine that protects them from particular diseases.* A **vaccine** is *a small amount of a disease that is introduced into the body, usually by injection, so the body can build a resistance to it.* A sample immunization schedule is on page 210. The physician's report is kept in the children's files. Similar health records for staff members are also kept on file.

THE MULTICULTURAL CLASSROOM

If you can't read a child's health record, it won't do you much good. Moreover, if parents can't read health bulletins sent out by your program, that won't do them much good either. Any time language barriers may get in the way of important communication, translation is needed.

Health forms need to be completed by someone who can write in the primary language used by the program professionals. Often this will be English. Before sending letters home regarding head lice, chicken pox, Halloween candy warnings, and other precautionary topics, be sure those who need the message will receive it. Making arrangements with someone who can do translations for you on a regular basis is a good idea.

Communication is difficult enough when people speak the same language. A little foresight can eliminate some of the problems when people speak different ones.

How can requiring a physical exam before a child enters child care benefit both the child and the child care program?

- **Health Histories.** Health histories are provided by parents and guardians. They give information about the child's developmental growth. Any allergies, medications needed, and medical problems or injuries experienced before, during, or after birth are also listed. This information is confidential and should be shared only with a child's direct-care staff. Some programs employ a nurse to collect and interpret health histories.

Recommended Immunizations

RECOMMENDED AGE	IMMUNIZATIONS	COMMENTS
Birth	Hep B	Timing for certain immunizations may vary according to doctor's advice. Some are given within a recommended age range. Certain follow-up immunizations are affected by the time at which earlier ones are administered.
One month	Hep B	
Two months	DTP, OPV, Hib	
Four months	DTP, OPV, Hib	
Six months	Hep B, DTP, OPV, Hib	
Twelve months	DTP, Hib, MMR, Var	
Four to six years	DTP, OPV, MMR	

Hep B=Hepatitis B
DTP=Diphtheria, tetanus, pertussis
   (whooping cough)
OPV=Oral polio vaccine

Hib-Meningitis, pneumonia, infections
   (Hemophilus influenza type b)
MMR=Measles, mumps, rubella
Var=Chicken pox (varicella zoster virus)

- *Emergency Forms.* These forms are kept in file for every child and staff member. They list the telephone numbers and addresses of people to be contacted in case of emergency. The physician and preferred hospital are also noted. For those who have special health conditions, emergency treatment procedures are needed. Duplicate forms may be kept in the classroom for quick teacher reference.

- *Medication Forms.* The licensing laws in some states put restrictions on administering medicine in child care settings. Programs that do administer medication set up a system to insure that children receive the correct dosage. Parents complete and sign a medication permission form that indicates the exact time, amount, and method of dosage, as well as any side effects the medication may have on the child. When staff members give the medicine, they indicate that on a log and sign their entry.

MILD ILLNESSES

Simple illnesses are common in any child care setting. For example, a mild cold without fever may not keep a child at home. Special arrangements may need to be made for some children, especially if medication is to be administered. Mildly ill children may need a restricted diet, extra rest, or restricted activity. Teachers, teacher's aides, and cooks need this information.

Some children with asthma use an inhaler to deliver medication directly to the respiratory system. As with all medications, strict guidelines must be followed to protect both the child and caregiver.

SPECIAL HEALTH CONDITIONS

Unfortunately, not all illnesses are simple ones. Some children have conditions that require special attention. Information about care and medication should be noted on enrollment applications and discussed with parents.

When caring for children with special problems, child care professionals look for signs of a child's needs. They must be sensitive to the child's feelings and find ways to avoid setting the child apart as "different."

Every special health situation has its own set of concerns. A few of the ones you might encounter are described here. The more knowledge you have about these and other conditions, the better able you will be to handle children competently.

Asthma

Asthma (AZ-muh) is a respiratory condition characterized by recurring attacks of

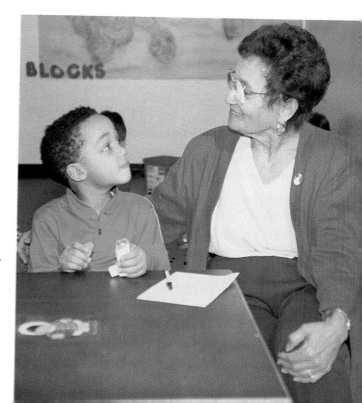

shortness of breath. Coughing, wheezing, and whistling breathing are other common symptoms. Asthma attacks may last for a few hours or for weeks. What brings on an attack is not the same for everyone. Dust, weather changes, strenuous exercise, smoke, or pets can be the problem. Parents can tell you about specific triggers that their children have. To help treat asthma, keep children with asthma away from what causes attacks. Sometimes medication is needed.

Allergies

An allergy is an unusual reaction to a substance that most people can tolerate. The substances cause a reaction when eaten, breathed in, or touched. Allergic reactions include nasal congestion, coughing, wheezing, asthma, frequent sneezing, a rash, eye irritation, upset stomach, and diarrhea. Hundreds of substances may trigger allergic reactions, including foods, animal fur, insect stings, dust, pollen, and mold. Some allergic reactions are treated with medication. You can help prevent allergic reactions by keeping children from trigger substances and by maintaining cleanliness standards for the program. Follow parents' directions for treatment of allergic reactions. If an allergic reaction is severe, call the child's physician right away.

Head Lice

Head lice are very small insects that live close to the scalp on human hair. Lice are usually identified when lice eggs, called *nits*, are found. Nits are typically spotted at the back of the neck, behind the ears, and on the top of the head. Signs of lice include itching at the roots of the hair and small red bite marks on the scalp.

Children and adults get lice by using the personal items of someone who is already infected. Sharing a comb or hat might result in transmittal. Acquiring lice has nothing to do with cleanliness, race, gender, or income level.

While very inconvenient and uncomfortable, head lice are easily treated. You as a child care worker should alert parents and other staff members as soon as an outbreak of head lice is discovered. Doctors can provide advice on treating them. Public health departments also provide written materials that outline methods for containing the spread of head lice throughout the child care program.

Epilepsy

Epilepsy is a disorder in which the electrical rhythms of the central nervous system are disturbed, resulting in seizures. There are two major types of seizures—petit mal and grand mal. With **petit mal seizures** (puh-TEE mahl), the person has only *a few seconds during which consciousness is clouded and possibly a few muscles twitch.* A child who is having a petit mal seizure may stop in the middle of an activity, "freeze" in position, and stare blankly; his or her eyelids may flutter. A **grand mal seizure** is *a complete loss of consciousness with stiffening, jerking, or thrashing of the body.*

If a child in your care has a seizure, follow the guidelines on the next page. Afterward, the child will not remember what happened. Sleep is common after a grand mal seizure.

Medication is often prescribed for epilepsy. When caring for children with epilepsy, observe and record any changes in behavior. Report changes to parents as they occur.

Tip FROM THE Pros

As a reminder to staff members about which children have food allergies, place a large chart with that information in the meal service area. Be sure to identify the names of children and their specific food allergies on the chart.

Handling Seizures

Petit Mal Seizure. Be alert for signs of this type of seizure. The child may simply stop and stare blankly, unaware of what is happening. If the child is in a dangerous location—crossing the street, for example—gently guide him or her to safety. Otherwise, you need not do anything. The seizure lasts only a few seconds.

Grand Mal Seizure. If a child falls to the ground, stiffens, and jerks uncontrollably, remain calm. Guide the child to a safe position on the floor, if possible. Clear the area to allow room for thrashing. Place a pillow beneath the child's head, and turn the head to one side to allow saliva to drain out. *Do not put anything in the child's mouth.* This can cause injury or fatal choking. If a seizure lasts for more than five minutes or the child goes from one seizure to another, contact the child's physician

Diabetes

Diabetes (dy-uh-BEET-eez) is a condition in which the body does not produce enough of a chemical called insulin. Insulin helps the body store and use foods (especially starches and sugars) for energy. Diabetes is usually controlled by medication plus a special diet.

Diabetics need to eat at regular intervals, with snacks and meals at the same time every day. This helps keep insulin and blood sugar at the proper levels. A poor or late meal or excessive exercise may cause an

What steps would you take to insure that a child with diabetes eats snacks and meals when needed?

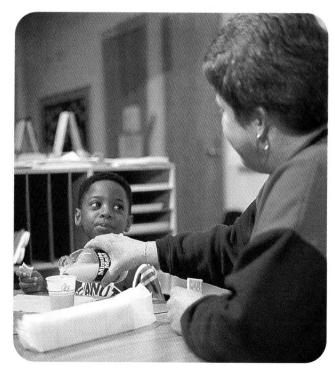

insulin reaction. For example, after a busy morning of outdoor play, the snack at one preschool was served late. Erica, a four-year-old diabetic in the program, became weak, pale, and sweaty. She started trembling and complained of dizziness and headache. Her teacher gave her a glass of orange juice and some crackers to help counteract this reaction. If her teacher hadn't responded to Erica, the child might have lost consciousness and gone into convulsions.

If you are caring for a diabetic child, keep in close contact with parents regarding treatment. Keep juice and crackers on hand and make sure that meals are served regularly. Exercise should not be excessive.

Sickle-Cell Anemia

Sickle-cell anemia is an inherited blood disorder accompanied by attacks of pain in the arms, hands, feet, legs, and abdomen. Infection or injury can make these attacks more likely to occur. Organ damage can result.

Because children with sickle-cell anemia are very vulnerable to infections, only those with a mild case of the disorder should be in group care. Upon enrollment, you should discuss with parents any specialized care that may be required.

Drug-Exposed Children

Serious effects have come to children from their mothers' drug use. Such drugs as cocaine, crack (a highly purified form of cocaine), and heroin enter a baby's blood stream through the umbilical cord and through breast milk. The number of affected children has become very high in this country, making it very likely that you, as a child care professional, will encounter them in your work.

Drug-exposed children have many problems, some that are lasting. Drugs alter their development. Resulting difficulties are phys-

ical as well as emotional. To care for these children, you need a special combination of skills, knowledge, and compassion. Training can help you meet the challenge. Contact the health department in your area for resources.

HIV and AIDS

Human Immunodeficiency Virus (HIV) is a virus that attacks and gradually weakens the body's immune system. Over time the affected person has frequent illnesses from exposure to disease-causing organisms that a healthy immune system would easily fight off. This cycle of repeated illness from infectious disease is called Acquired Immune-Deficiency Syndrome (AIDS). People with AIDS die from diseases that others usually survive, such as pneumonia and influenza. At this time, there is no known cure for AIDS.

The topic of AIDS is a sensitive one. Misinformation and emotions have fueled the fires of controversy for many people. If you become knowledgeable and think logically, you can take what precautions are necessary and manage without undue concern.

Acquiring HIV

First, you need to understand that HIV is not transmitted through the casual contact that is common with children in a group setting. Touching, hugging, and sitting on a lap do not result in the transmittal of HIV. This has been proven. The virus cannot be caught by touching an infected person's tears, perspiration, or saliva.

Then how is the virus acquired? HIV is a delicate virus than can live only in certain body fluids. It is transmitted through blood, semen, vaginal secretions, and breast milk. No evidence exists that it is transmitted through any other body fluids. HIV is acquired when infected body fluid enters

By using universal precautions in situations that call for them, you are safeguarding yourself and the children in your care.

directly into the body and reaches the blood of an uninfected person. Sexual activity is the most common method of transmission. Entry through a break in the skin is also possible.

A child may acquire HIV in any of the following ways:

- From an HIV-infected mother during pregnancy or delivery.
- Through contact with infected blood by transfusion or through an open wound or sore.
- During breastfeeding with an HIV-infected mother.
- Through sexual abuse by an HIV-infected abuser.

As you can see, the chances of transmittal are extremely small. Because AIDS is a deadly disease, however, people realize that taking precautions against even the smallest risk is necessary. Thus, those who work in child care programs, and in many other jobs, follow all the precautions described earlier, including the universal ones, in order to reduce risk and help put minds at ease.

Enrollment of Children

Because of the limited risk of a child passing on HIV in group care, the Americans with Disabilities Act of 1990 protects children who have the virus. This law makes it illegal to deny enrollment in a program to children because they are infected with HIV.

At this time, parents are not required by law to reveal a child's HIV-infected condition. You may not know whether a child in your program has the disease. Because the virus is not always actively attacking the immune system, HIV-infected children may not have any noticeable symptoms.

When you do know that a child has HIV, confidentiality is critical. Telling others about such cases can result in discrimination against a child and his or her family. Information about HIV-infected children is generally limited to the main caregiver and the director of the program. Written permission must be obtained from the parents if a child care employee wants to discuss the case with the child's medical doctor.

HIV-infected children benefit from early childhood care and education just as other children do. However, parents of children with AIDS should be cautioned about the risks of group care. Group care exposes children to typical childhood communicable diseases. Because HIV-infected children have very weak immune systems, these illnesses may be quite serious for them. HIV-infected children should not attend group care when there is an outbreak of communicable disease at the child care facility.

Keeping Up-to-Date

What you have just read about HIV and AIDS reflects current knowledge about the disease. Research is ongoing, so new developments are always possible. You need to stay informed so that you know if additional information suggests different approaches to take. The health department in your area can keep you up-to-date on this subject.

Hepatitis B

Hepatitis B (hep-uh-TY-tuhs) is an infection of the liver. Its symptoms include jaundice (a yellowing of the skin and whites of the eyes), nausea, fever, and loss of appetite. Hepatitis B can be transmitted from one person to another through blood, bodily fluids containing blood, genital fluids, and saliva. It cannot be transmitted through casual body contact. Because of this, health professionals say the risk of contracting Hepatitis B in a child care setting is extremely low. Health practices for preventing the spread of Hepatitis B include the universal precautions.

WEATHER-RELATED HEALTH PROBLEMS

Diseases are not the only threat to health. Sometimes weather is the cause. Playing outside can be good for children, but very cold or very hot weather can pose a threat to their health.

Hypothermia, a serious condition in which the body's temperature gets dangerously low, can occur if children are out in very cold weather for extended periods of time. *Frostbite*, the freezing of body tissue, can occur if parts of the body—especially feet, hands, face, and ears—are not well protected from the cold. Even if dressed in warm and waterproof clothing, children may still become frostbitten if allowed outside for long periods in severely cold weather. Signs of frostbite include numbness and white or grayish-yellow skin.

In hot weather, *heat exhaustion* becomes a concern. Heat exhaustion is dizziness and fatigue caused by the loss of fluid and salt due to intense per-

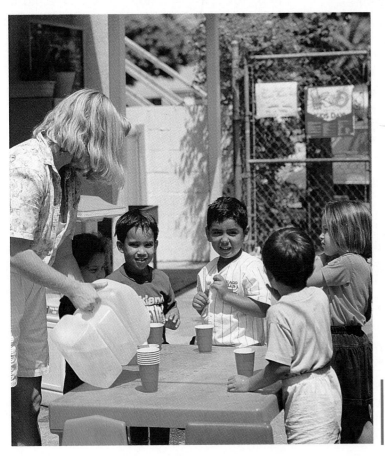

Children playing outdoors in hot weather need extra water. What other precautions might you need to take?

Insuring Safety

Moderate amounts of sunlight are not harmful to children; however, they should wear sunscreen on exposed skin to prevent burning. A sunscreen with at least an SPF number of 15 is needed for the best protection. Children with very fair complexions may also need to wear a hat or cap to protect the scalp and face from sunburn.

spiration. Children who show symptoms of heat exhaustion should be given fluids and allowed to rest in a cool place. You can prevent heat exhaustion by not allowing children to play outdoors for extended periods during very hot weather. Play areas should be as shaded as possible. Encourage children to drink water frequently to replace water lost through perspiring.

Sunburn can be a problem during any season of the year. When playing outdoors, children should wear a sunscreen. Talk to parents about any skin sensitivities that their children may have. You might want to ask each child's parent to supply an appropriate sunscreen.

If any of these conditions arise, refer to a first aid manual for treatment. Medical clinics and health departments can also provide assistance.

CHILD ABUSE AND NEGLECT

It's sad but true that many people in society do harm to children, sometimes their own. Called child abuse and neglect, these conditions are too common in society. They demand the attention of all people who work in the interest of children. Child abuse and neglect happen in all neighborhoods and to children of all races and economic backgrounds.

Child Abuse

Child abuse occurs when *nonaccidental injury is inflicted on a child. The injury may be physical, sexual, or emotional in nature.* As a child care professional, you need to know the signs of child abuse, as listed on page 218. Any signs noted should be documented in the child's records.

Physical abuse often results in visible injury to the child's body. You might notice bumps, bruises, burns, welts, cuts, or unexplained sensitivity. Since children frequently injure themselves through their own activity, how can you tell the difference between abuse and a routine injury? Watch for severe injury, repeated injuries, and indications from the child that something out of the ordinary may have occurred.

Sexual abuse occurs when a person older than the child uses the child to fulfill his or her own sexual desires. Sexual abuse is not limited to sexual intercourse. Genital exposure, touching personal body parts, and other inappropriate sexual acts with young children are also sexual abuse. Often comments young children make are clues to what has happened.

Emotional abuse is generally committed when an adult chronically says things that hurt a child. The hurtful language may be foul, vulgar, or demeaning. Children who experience ridicule, tormenting, and inhumane teasing by a parent or caregiver are considered to be emotionally abused. Emotional abuse may also include placing unreasonable demands on a child to perform beyond his or her capabilities or failing to provide a child with affection and emotional support. Encouraging children to engage in illegal behavior, such as stealing, using drugs, and prostitution, is also considered emotional abuse. Emotional abuse is evidenced by a child's behavior. Emotional abuse can severely lower self-esteem so that a person has difficulty functioning throughout life.

Child Neglect

Child neglect is *the failure to provide a child with the basic necessities of life, including food, clothing, shelter, and medical care.* Because young children cannot care for themselves, they need reliable attention from adults. A child who is neglected may be left without adult supervision for hours, days, or weeks at a time. Neglect puts a child's health and safety at risk. If you notice habitual lack of adequate cleanliness, nutrition, sanitary shelter, clothing, medical care, or dental care, you may be seeing signs of neglect.

Reporting Abuse and Neglect

States have laws that require those who work with children to report circumstances that might involve abuse or neglect. You are required to make a report whether it involves a parent or a fellow staff member. It is your professional responsibility to act in good faith and report only those conditions that cause you to have genuine fear for a child's health or welfare.

Reporting usually means calling a child abuse hotline or notifying the child welfare agency. You will want to obtain the correct telephone number and post it next to classroom telephones and on the parent bulletin board. The number should be handy for you, other staff members, and parents.

All states have agencies that investigate suspected child abuse and neglect. They protect children and provide help to the family.

Prevention

Recognizing and reporting cases of suspected child abuse can help put an end to existing abuse. Other efforts may help prevent it from happening in the first place.

Signs of Possible Child Abuse

*T*he following signs in children may indicate child abuse:

- Unexplained injuries.
- Evidence of malnutrition or dehydration.
- Evidence of repeated skin injuries or bone fractures.
- Unusual sexual knowledge for the age of the child.
- Evidence of being given inappropriate food, beverages, or drugs.
- Appearance of unusual fear.
- Differences in emotional makeup from other children—low self-esteem.

By learning normal developmental patterns and really getting to know the children in your care, you can more easily recognize the signs that a child is experiencing problems.

Although there are no excuses, certain factors seem to be associated with abuse. Parents and others who abuse or neglect children often suffer from low self-esteem. Many have poor coping skills. They may lack knowledge about parenting and appropriate care, causing them to put unrealistic expectations on children.

Some child care programs offer evening workshops for adults to deal with these issues. The programs address such topics as parenting, human growth and development, alternative forms of discipline, and ways to cope with stress. Support groups are also helpful. In your role as a child care professional, you may also refer people to community resources, including such groups as Parents Anonymous.

Staff Protection

Regrettably, incidents of child abuse have occurred in low-quality child care programs. Children need to be protected from this rare occurrence, and staff members need to be protected from false accusation. To eliminate any questions about conduct with children, make sure you always supervise them with another adult present. This is especially important during nap time, toileting, outdoor play, and bus runs. Also remove locks from bathroom doors and install observation windows in all classrooms. You are safe from possible accusations of physical, verbal, or sexual abuse when another employee is with you and can verify that your behavior was appropriate.

CHILDREN'S EMOTIONAL HEALTH

*L*ife isn't always easy for children in today's world. Some have divorced or alcoholic parents. Some have experienced the deaths or illnesses of family members. Sadly, children also know violence—in their homes and their neighborhoods. Any of these can lead to stress, even in young children. To recognize when children are having difficult times, look for the signs listed below. Although some of these may signal other problems, these are often associated with stress:

- Unusual aggression or laziness.
- Complaints of a pounding heart. This may be caused by elevated blood pressure. If this is the case, suggest that parents have their child's blood pressure checked by a doctor.
- Unusual anxiety or fear.
- Nervous tics or habits, such as twisting hair.
- Stuttering or other speech difficulties that have not been present earlier.
- Trouble falling asleep or staying asleep.
- Changes in appetite or regular complaints of an upset stomach.

- Unwillingness to try new things.
- Withdrawing from activities and other children.
- Displaying a sense of hopelessness.

When you discover that a child has problems, what can you do to help? The first step is to listen. Listening to children's thoughts, fears, and feelings is a good way to help children with their emotional needs.

Secondly, talk to them. Remind them of their own past successes in coping with certain stressful situations. Children relate well to their own personal experiences. To build their confidence, praise children when they successfully cope with a stressful situation. Life events often make children feel powerless and out of control. These feelings undermine coping ability. Children need reinforcement from you. Give them as much decision-making power and control over their daytime experiences as is developmentally possible.

Another technique is to provide books and tapes on problems that children face. Reading about going to the hospital, divorce, and moving gives children ideas for coping and makes them feel that they are not alone in the experience.

In addition, provide children with a predictable and consistent routine. This helps them gain a sense of stability and security.

Finally, work closely with parents in helping children through stressful situations. Parents may not realize what children are feeling unless you document and share the signs with them. If necessary, professionals can be consulted. In some cases, you may need the help of doctors, psychologists, law enforcement workers, or social workers.

Reading appropriate stories is just one way to help a child cope with a stressful situation. What are some others?

IN YOUR HANDS

*M*anaging the health concerns of a group of children is a serious responsibility. As you have seen, it is much more than simply wiping a nose now and then. In the child care setting, each child has health needs that are common to all, yet each one also has unique needs to be attended. Without the support of adults, children cannot achieve good physical and emotional health. As a child care professional, children are, indeed, in your hands.

Helping Children Cope with Death

*C*hildren experience death in many ways. A friend or family member may die. A pet may die. Children even see death through violence in neighborhoods and on the news. How would you help a child cope with death? Unless you think ahead, you may not be prepared.

Age affects how children perceive death. Under the age of three, they tend to have little or no understanding of the idea of death. They may grieve for the loss, but they don't realize what has happened. At four, children have some vague notions about death. They see the connection with sadness. A five-year-old may think that death is reversible. At this age, they don't accept the idea that death happens to everyone. Some, however, are just beginning to recognize the finality of death. This recognition becomes clearer by age six or seven. Not until about age nine or ten do children recognize that death is inevitable. Sometime during the preteen years, children are ready to deal with the reality of death.

Regardless of their level of understanding, children do experience grief. They recognize loss and they sense sorrow. If a relationship was close, the death has greater impact. A child's personality and emotional needs affect how the child responds to the loss and copes with it.

As a caregiver, you can give support to children who are grieving. Remember that they may not have the language skills to tell you how they feel. Play with them and notice what they express through play. You could ask a child to draw a self-portrait. Then say, "Tell me about the boy (or girl) in the picture." Puppets and storytelling may also give clues to what is going on in a child's mind. Through play, the child releases stress and finds ways to deal with emotions.

A grieving child needs attention and love. Talk with the child, giving truthful responses to any questions. Remember that phrases like "passed away" and "fallen asleep" are inaccurate and confusing for children. Consider the child's age as you talk and listen. A child who doesn't seem to care may simply lack understanding. Watch for fears that might develop. For example, a child may fear the death of another loved one after a death has occurred. Reassurances can help. You might also look for quality books that help children understand and cope with death. These, along with your sensitive but matter-of-fact approach, can help the child see that life goes on—even after death.

Chapter 11 Review

Chapter Summary

- Staff, children, and parents must all know and practice procedures that contribute to the good health of children.
- Providing a healthful environment helps limit the spread of disease.
- Health checks should be conducted each morning when children arrive.
- Parents should be notified about outbreaks of communicable diseases.
- Before enrolling, children should be examined by a physician and should be up-to-date on all immunizations.
- Programs should plan strategies for caring for mildly ill children.
- Knowledge about special health conditions helps the child care professional handle children with these conditions correctly.
- Child care professionals are required by law to report cases of suspected child abuse.
- Helping children cope with special emotional situations is part of the child care professional's responsibilities.

Reviewing the Facts

1. What is a communicable disease?
2. Why do children, in general, get sick more easily than adults do?
3. Why is proper circulation and ventilation of air necessary in an early childhood classroom?
4. Why do cleanliness habits and routines need to be practiced?
5. What are two ways to teach children about hand washing?
6. Describe the universal precautions to take when taking care of children.
7. Briefly describe three types of health records collected when children are in group care.
8. What are allergies?
9. What precautions can a child care professional take to help prevent insulin reactions?
10. How is HIV transmitted?
11. Identify two weather-related health problems and tell how each can be prevented.
12. Describe the three different kinds of child abuse.
13. Explain three techniques for helping children handle problems that affect their emotional health.

Thinking Critically

1. Why do child care professionals take their responsibilities regarding children's health very seriously?
2. How would you help a child who has an ongoing health problem feel like he or she is no different from other children in the group?
3. Some children are brought to child care when they are too ill to be there. Why do you think this happens? What approach should child care professionals take?
4. Which do you think would be easier to identify and prove, emotional or physical abuse? Explain your answer.

Activities and Applications

1. **Health Article.** Write a short article on a children's health issue for a parent newsletter.
2. **Inspection Chart.** Assume you are a child care worker. Put together a cleanliness inspection chart for the child care center. Develop a rating system for determining whether

a cleanliness routine was performed effectively.

3. **Job Shadow.** Contact a social worker or law enforcement worker who specifically handles cases involving children. Make arrangements to "shadow" the person for a day and observe the work. What qualifications must they have to do what they do? What personal characteristics make these individuals effective?

SCHOOL TO WORK

Your Professional Portfolio

Young children often need to be reminded about procedures that are routine to adults. Prepare a bulletin board that shows the steps for effective hand washing. Use simple pictures that young children can easily understand. Laminate the pictures so the board may be saved for future use. After writing directions for placing the pictures on the bulletin board, place the pictures and directions in your portfolio.

Observing and Analyzing

Making Health Observations

Young children pick up the organisms that cause illness so easily. Your understanding and appreciation for this fact will increase when you make some simple observations.

- **Placing Objects in the Mouth.** Observe one or more children age one or two informally in a public setting or in a center. For one hour count how many objects are placed in or on the mouth. Also record what happens to the objects during play and when the child loses interest or is redirected.

- **Touching the Face.** Watch three- to five-year-olds in a public setting or center. Record the number of times their hands go to their mouths and noses within a one-hour period.

- **Staff Habits.** Visit a preschool classroom and observe the hygiene habits of the staff. Do they wash hands after wiping noses, before preparing snacks, after fixing hair, and in any other situations that might require it?

What conclusions do you reach from these observations? What suggestions do you have for improving health management in the settings you observed?

Chapter 12

Handling Schedules and Routines

CHAPTER OBJECTIVES

- Explain what a schedule is and describe some considerations when developing one.

- Describe why and how certain common routines are incorporated in the daily schedule.

- Explain why and how transitions are used.

- Assess schedules, routines, and transitions observed in child care settings.

Terms to Learn

- choice time
- job board
- job jar
- personal hygiene
- routine
- schedule
- self-directed
- sphincter muscles
- teacher-directed
- transition

The melody was certainly "Here We Go 'Round the Mulberry Bush," but the words were different. As Emile approached the four-year-olds' room at the child care center, he heard the children singing. Quietly entering the room, he saw a group of children picking up blocks and stacking them neatly on a toy shelf. "This is the way we pick up the blocks, pick up the blocks, pick up the blocks . . . ," they sang as they worked. The children were cheerful and cooperative. They worked independently.

Emile sat in a chair in the corner of the room to wait for direction from one of the teachers. He was a new volunteer in the center. Seeing him, Mrs. Patterson walked over and sat beside him.

As the blocks were put away, the children began to flow in groups of two and three to a large rug. They sat in a circle, gazing expectantly at their teacher Miss Osterlund, who sat at one side of the circle with a storybook. She watched the children finish their task but gave no directions.

While waiting patiently for all the children to arrive, Miss Osterlund began to sing "The Itsy Bitsy Spider," using hand motions with the words. The children on the rug sang with her and mimicked the motions. When everyone was present, Miss Osterlund held the book so the cover could be seen. The face of a large, cartoon spider smiled cheerfully at the children.

"She makes it look so easy," Emile whispered to Mrs. Patterson. "Are they always this well behaved?"

"It doesn't happen by accident," she replied with a smile and a shake of her head. "In time, you'll see what I mean. I've got so much to tell you about what makes it work."

IT'S NO ACCIDENT

Mrs. Patterson was right. When the activity in an early childhood program is calm and orderly, it's no accident. Skillful child care professionals use knowledge and effort to make things go smoothly. What do they know that helps them? How could you achieve the same results if you were a child care professional? The answer begins with a well-planned schedule.

SCHEDULES

Imagine what life would be like without schedules. A **schedule** is *a plan for how time will be used; it places events in the order they will occur and indicates how long each event will last*. Transportation systems run with schedules so that people can easily get where they need to go. Businesses have schedules that enable employees to create products and provide services. You have schedules that tell you when and where you have to be.

Schedules bring order to life. In an early childhood program, the schedule accounts for how the hours will be spent from the time children arrive until they leave. A schedule includes the basics, not details. In other words, time for science might be shown on the schedule, but the specific procedure to follow for an activity is not. A sample schedule that might be used with preschoolers is shown on page 227.

Schedules keep things running smoothly for several reasons. For one thing, there's no need to spend time deciding what to do next. With a schedule in place, such decisions have already been made. In addition, children feel more comfortable with a schedule that has a similar pattern each day, giving them something familiar to rely on. A schedule also contributes to better behavior. Children who already know what comes next are less likely to get sidetracked by their own ideas. Fewer questions arise, and confusion is less likely. A schedule makes children feel independent. As *they respond on their own without having to be told what to do*, they become **self-directed**.

Creating a Schedule

No single schedule works for every child care program. Although some patterns may be similar, each schedule is planned according to the program's characteristics. All of the following affect schedules:

- *Philosophy and Objectives of the Program.* For example, if a program emphasizes intellectual development, ample time is allowed in the schedule for activities that promote this type of development.

In this center, children take turns being the "helper" for various parts of the schedule, such as snack time and circle time. They identify their responsibilities by finding their pictures.

- *Length of the Program.* Obviously, more activities can be included in a longer schedule than in a shorter one. Setting priorities is necessary.
- *Children's Ages.* Older children have longer attention spans and less need for rest, yet younger children need more assistance. These affect the amount of time needed for activities.
- *Size of the Program.* A large program requires grouping of children. The schedule must allow for rotation of activities and locations. The more children a teacher must help, the more time will be needed for each activity in the schedule.
- *The Facility.* A small center may have multipurpose rooms that require careful scheduling for efficient use.

A workable schedule doesn't just happen. It takes forethought to avoid pitfalls. For example, if you schedule outdoor activity early in the morning during the summer,

Sample Schedule

TIME	ACTIVITY
7:30 a.m.—8:30 a.m.	Arrival and breakfast
8:30 a.m.—9:15 a.m.	Free play in learning centers
9:15 a.m.—9:30 a.m.	Cleanup and choice time
9:30 a.m.—10:00 a.m.	Small group activities
10:00 a.m.—10:30 a.m.	Toileting and hand washing; Snack time
10:30 a.m.—11:00 a.m.	Outdoor play
11:00 a.m.—11:45 a.m.	Free play in learning centers
11:45 a.m.—12:00 p.m.	Music time
12:00 p.m.—12:30 p.m.	Toileting and hand washing; Lunch
12:30 p.m.—12:45 p.m.	Toothbrushing, toileting, and hand washing
12:45 p.m.—1:00 p.m.	Story time
1:00 p.m.—2:30 p.m.	Nap time
2:30 p.m.—3:00 p.m.	Wake up from nap; Quiet play
3:00 p.m.—3:30 p.m.	Toileting and hand washing; Snack
3:30 p.m.—4:00 p.m.	Story time and singing
4:00 p.m.—4:30 p.m.	Outdoor play
4:30 p.m.—5:30 p.m.	Choice time; Small group activities
5:30 p.m.—5:45 p.m.	General cleanup
5:45 p.m.—6:00 p.m.	End-of-day activity

what happens several months later in a climate that has cold, snowy winters? During this season, the weather may be too cold for children to be outdoors in the early morning hours. Here's another question. What will you plan for children who arrive at different times during the first half hour of the day? Some activities are not easy to join once they have already begun. Also, what do you do when the weather forces a change in plans? Unless an alternative schedule is familiar to all, confusion takes hold. Answering questions like these as you plan a schedule is much easier than dealing with problems when they arise.

Energy Levels

Another consideration in scheduling is managing the energy levels of children.

FOCUS ON INFANT/TODDLER PROGRAMS

All infants operate according to their own sleep, diapering, and feeding schedules, which vary greatly from child to child. As new parents will tell you, attempts at getting infants to follow any schedule other than their own are usually unsuccessful. Instead, caregivers must identify the schedule that best meets the infant's needs.

They can do this by learning to interpret the moods and body language of the child. For example, you might notice that an infant squirms or cries just before needing a diaper change. Rubbing the eyes may indicate the need for a nap. Although infants cannot talk, they offer many signals as clues.

Outdoor play gives children a release for their energy. What alternative activities might be planned for days when the weather prevents outdoor play?

Children need a balance between quiet and active play. Time for activities like running and jumping is just as important as time for putting together a puzzle or creating a work of art. Tired children don't cooperate. Restless children won't settle down. Balancing restful times with energetic ones helps control behavior problems.

Compare planning the daily schedule to riding a bicycle over a hill. As you start out, riding is smooth and leisurely. The further you ride up the hill, the more energy you expend until you reach the peak. After you reach the crest of the hill, your activity level decreases until you reach the bottom of the hill, where a leisurely pace resumes.

This pattern should be reflected in the morning and again in the afternoon when planning children's activities. For example, the schedule for a full day at one child care center starts out slowly and calmly with breakfast. The activity level gradually increases toward the middle of the morning, when the most active play occurs. After active play, children switch to quieter activities while preparations are made for the midday meal. Children need to relax and become more calm as they get ready for their meal. The early afternoon is reserved for nap time. After napping, the activity level gradually increases toward midafternoon. As the time nears for children to go home, the activity level decreases again. Children play quietly in learning centers until someone arrives to take them home.

ROUTINES

Although important, schedules only set the stage for what goes on each day in an early childhood program. Something else is needed to put the schedule into action. Clear and predictable routines do just that. A **routine** is a *regular, expected procedure that is followed in order to accomplish something*. For example, the schedule includes times for arrival, toileting, naps, dressing for outdoor play, meals, and departure. Each of these needs a routine that is familiar and consistent.

A routine may be short or long. It usually includes steps that are followed the same way each time the routine is used. Sometimes signals, such as ringing a bell, are incorporated in the routine to help children know when to take certain steps.

Like the schedule, daily routines add a sense of security to children's lives. They

FOCUS ON SCHOOL-AGE PROGRAMS

Because many older children have very structured schedules during school hours, they need a flexible schedule in the child care setting. This age group needs time after school to relax from the demands of studies and extracurricular activities. A healthful snack followed by optional play activities should be offered. Often these children are mature enough to make decisions about what they want and need to do. Child care professionals can give guidance toward making good decisions.

Building Professional Skills

Dependability

WHAT IS DEPENDABILITY?

Dependability is reliability, a "you-can-count-on-me" attitude. You depend heavily on so many things—from alarm clocks and automobiles to friendships—that you may take them for granted. Sometimes it's only when these things don't work as expected—when cars won't start, when friends forget promises—that you realize how important dependability is, in both your personal and professional life.

Dependability in Action

It was almost 9:00 a.m. on Thursday, and Margo had not arrived. Even though the children in the preschool could not yet tell time, they knew when it was time for Margo to appear. "Where is Miss Margo?" one of the children asked. "Isn't she coming?"

Once each week Margo Cummings visited the preschool. She was an accomplished storyteller who always came with books, props, and puppets for story time. This week, however, 9:00 a.m. neared with no sign of Margo. The teacher was about to announce a different activity when Margo burst into the room. She looked flustered and disheveled from hurrying but quickly became composed and smiling when she saw the children.

"Miss Margo's here!" they squealed. "Did you bring your toys? Is it a good story today?"

"Well, of course!" she laughed, and Thursday morning story time went on to be its usual success.

Later, Margo explained her lateness to the teacher. "The water was out in our apartment building, so we had to drive to a friend's house to get ready for work. Then we ran into a construction area, so traffic was backed up."

"You could have canceled," the teacher said. "We would have understood."

Margo smiled, looking at the children. "*Some* of you would have," she said.

Your Analysis

1. What did Margo mean by her last statement?

2. How would you describe Margo's sense of dependability?

3. Did lack of dependability play any role in Margo's lateness? How?

4. Is dependability the same thing as punctuality, or is it something more? What else do the children count on Margo for?

5. What do children learn about dependability when they follow schedules and routines?

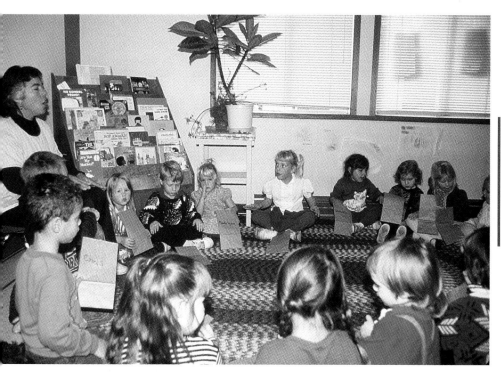

"Circle Time" is common in early childhood programs. In this center, the children quickly form a circle by sitting around the edges of the rug.

know what to expect and when. They also know what is expected of them. As they adapt to specific routines, children gain confidence and become more independent and organized. Their self-help skills improve. Accomplishing daily tasks introduces them to the good feeling that comes when goals are reached. Moreover, they learn patience and persistence.

Routines are an important tool for teachers. They provide orderliness and discourage conflict, which helps save valuable learning time and contributes to a calm environment. In addition, when daily routines become like habits, children can pay more attention to learning. Skilled teachers integrate learning opportunities into routines.

To be effective, routines should be established according to the age and developmental abilities of children. Presenting them clearly to children enables them to follow the routines with ease. As you will see from the following descriptions of certain common routines, careful thought goes into making them workable.

Arrival Routines

The arrival routine sets the tone for the day. It should be positive and inviting. Those in charge of a program set up a consistent pattern that fits their specific needs. The manner in which children are transported to the facility and the arrangement of classrooms and entryway affect how the arrival routine is structured. The illustration on pages 232 and 233 shows what an arrival routine might be like.

Some children have a hard time separating from their parents during arrival. Leaving a personal item, such as a scarf, may ease the lonely feeling. If separation is difficult, a short parting is usually best. Advise parents to be honest and matter-of-fact with the child. A quick hug, kiss, and wishes for a good day can be shared. The parent should then leave. Discourage parents from disappearing while the child isn't looking. After noticing that the parent is gone, the child will feel tricked. This can cause more fear and insecurity.

If a child cries when a parent leaves, it is usually for only a few minutes. Denying children's feelings by telling them not to cry or to act more grown up is not productive. Instead, show your understanding by saying, "It's hard for you to let Dad go this morning, isn't it?" Offer a tissue to wipe tears. Casually invite distressed children to join an activity whenever they feel better.

Personal Hygiene Routines

When children learn skills that contribute to personal hygiene, life in an early childhood program is simpler. **Personal hygiene** (HI-jeen) is *keeping the body clean in order to promote good health and prevent illness.*

In addition to hand washing, young children can also learn to comb or brush their hair. Teach every child to use a personal comb, not anyone else's. This prevents the spread of such conditions as head lice.

By age two, children can begin to care for their teeth with a toothbrush. Children should routinely brush their teeth after

An Arrival Routine in Preschool

A. Sign in In many programs the arrival routine begins with some technique for monitoring attendance. When parents accompany children, they might use a sign up sheet. ▶

B. Greeting Arrival time is happy and positive when a friendly greeting comes from a staff member. Bend or kneel at the child's level and smile warmly. Use the "treasures" children bring, such as a favorite stuffed animal, to start conversations. You can show interest and respect by asking questions and listening attentively.

breakfast and lunch. When teachers brush along with the children, they act as role models for practicing good dental care. Children can also be motivated to brush by placing a mirror at their eye level. Children love to watch themselves while they brush.

Children should learn to use facial tissues for blowing the nose. Learning to blow out rather than in is not easy for young children. With practice, however, the skill is eventually acquired. Encourage children to blow their own nose by having tissues readily available. After blowing, children should dispose of used tissues and wash their hands.

Teaching personal hygiene routines is one key to controlling the spread of disease. Facial tissues should be used once and thrown away. Why is hand washing afterward so important?

C. Storing Items Include time during arrival to store personal belongings. Cubbies can hold small items. Jackets and coats might hang on hooks. Children learn independence as they perform these tasks on their own. ▶

D. Health Check As children enter the classroom, this is a good time for an informal health check. Pay attention to the appearance of children in order to spot any problems. ▲

E. Conversation Time An arrival routine can end with teachers and children gathered in a group to discuss the upcoming day's activities. A good way to begin this conversation time is to sing a familiar greeting song. ▲

Toileting Routines

Children usually begin to learn about responsible toileting when they reach age two. By this time the **sphincter muscles** (SFINK-tur), *which surround certain body openings and have the ability to close them*, are developed in most children. These muscles enable children to control bowel movements and urination. Because the age of readiness can vary, however, caregivers need to be cautious about pushing children too soon. With close communication between parent, child, and staff members, the learning process goes more smoothly.

Patience is especially useful when children are in the process of learning. They may resist or be upset if toileting becomes a battleground between child and adult. Calm, quiet assistance from caregivers is needed. Accidents do happen and must be handled without hurting the child's feelings or causing embarrassment.

At this stage of development, teachers should assist children in sitting on the toilet (or potty chair). Independent toileting is made easier if pants can be easily pulled down. Clothing that is difficult to remove, such as bib overalls, may contribute to toileting accidents.

Observant teachers notice how children behave when they need to use the restroom—some children may tug at their clothing and others may press their legs together tightly. Clues like these help teachers know when to remind children to use the restroom. Reminders about using toilet paper properly and washing hands thoroughly after flushing should be made.

Even children who have already mastered toileting need frequent opportunities to use the restroom. Regular times should be set aside for this routine. Some schedules include time before the morning snack, after lunch, before and after naps, and following the afternoon snack. In addition, children should feel free to use the toilet whenever necessary.

Dressing Routines

At age two, young children can begin to put on some of their own clothing. Slip-on pants and pullover shirts and dresses are easier to manage successfully in the beginning. By age four, children should require little assistance. For example, if a child needs help with zipping a jacket, you could start the process and let the child finish it. This encourages self-sufficiency. Remember that heavy winter coats and boots are a challenge to put on (even for adults). Children appreciate extra time and patience when learning to manage these garments.

One creative teacher instructed children to lay their snowsuits on the floor before

Marissa has learned to put on her coat by placing it on the floor, finding the armholes, and flipping the coat over her head.

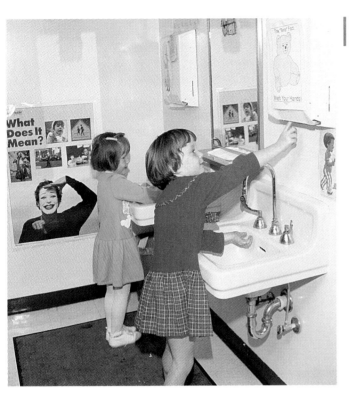

How can children be encouraged to practice routines they learn in child care at home?

els, and bibs for each child. Place protective floor covering beneath feeding chairs.

At age two, children can sit independently at meals, using small chairs at low tables. Their attempts at self-feeding are more successful by this time, but spills are still frequent. Keep paper towels nearby so children can clean up their own spills.

As children develop, they can practice new skills associated with mealtime. If small bowls and utensils are offered, two-year-olds can begin to serve themselves and put food on their own plates. Small pitchers for pouring milk and juice are manageable by age three. Children age two and older can pass out napkins, set nonbreakable plates and drinking glasses on the table, and help with minor cleanup after the meal. Creating centerpieces and placemats is another way children can contribute to the mealtime routine. By complimenting children when they accomplish these tasks, you help boost their self-esteem.

putting them on. The children sat on the snowsuits and put their feet and legs into the legs of the snowsuits. Then they stood up to put on the rest of the snowsuit.

Mealtime Routines

Meal and snack times include hand washing. This is the standard beginning and ending to these routines.

Self-feeding skills develop over time. First attempts begin at about nine months of age, when children begin drinking from a cup. Since young children like to explore their food, and because their aim isn't well developed, this stage of self-feeding is very messy. Be sure to provide washcloths, towels, and bibs for each child. Place protective

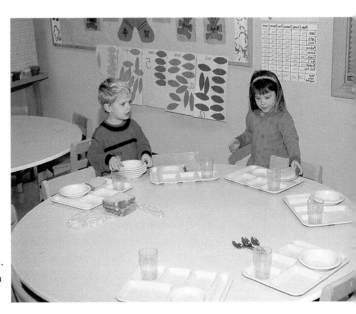

Children can help set the table for meals. What other skills can be learned through meal times?

Routines and rituals at nap time help children fall asleep more easily. Even if children can't sleep, the quiet rest time helps restore energy.

Nap Time Routines

Young children need adequate sleep to maintain healthy bodies. A daily schedule usually allows 30 to 90 minutes of nap time. Children age five and older may not need as much sleep as younger children, but they do need at least a short rest period. Most states require a nap time in their licensing laws.

Nap time should be the same each day. It usually follows lunch. While one teacher helps children brush teeth and toilet, another sets up cots throughout the room. Each child needs a personally labeled cot. For familiarity, each cot should be placed in the same place

THE MULTICULTURAL CLASSROOM

Multiculturalism can be incorporated in classroom routines. Here are some ideas:

- **Names.** Names are often linked to culture, making some difficult to pronounce and spell for those who are not familiar with them. Names are a vital part of identity. Arrival time is a good time to greet children by name, making sure that you pronounce them correctly.

- **Greeting Songs.** Add variety to the greeting songs each morning by learning some in different languages. Check music stores and school supply catalogs for tapes.

- **Learning Center Labels.** Identify the learning centers with labels in other languages. Parents can assist with this.

- **Snack Time.** For snack time, ask parents to bring a favorite food in their family that is linked to their heritage.

- **Nap Time.** Nap time can be a "trip around the world" with the soothing sounds of Tchaikovsky, Chopin, Brahms, Beethoven, Mozart, Prokofiev, Ravel, Debussy, Strauss, Bach, Wagner, Segovia, Bizet, Rossini, and more. The library might have classical collections, or parents might loan theirs or provide funds to buy tapes.

- **Departure Time.** At departure, say goodbye multiculturally. Send children on their way with "sayonara," "adios," "ciao," "salaam," "aloha," "shalom," "adieu," and "bonsoir."

every day. For safety, there should always be at least two adults present in the room during nap time.

Nap time can be scary for young children. Teachers should make it as comfortable as possible. Reading a story in a dimly lit room with a ceiling spotlight on the teacher creates a calming mood. After the story, relaxing music can be played throughout the nap.

Rituals often help children fall asleep. Rituals are actions that are repeated regularly. When used at nap time, a ritual becomes a signal for sleep. Some children need a back rub or a foot massage to relax them. Other children want a favorite stuffed animal, book, or blanket to hold.

Departure Routines

At the end of the day, try to plan a calm reunion between children and parents. Schedule the same type of activity for the end of each day. This helps children antici-pate when parents will arrive. Favorite activities include storytelling, working with puzzles, and singing. A good-bye song signals the day's end.

Some children easily leave child care at the end of the day. Others find it frustrating to have their play activities ended. Help parents understand that these children are not really unhappy about going home. They simply need a little more time to "shift gears." You might suggest that parents plan to do a short activity with their children before going home.

At the end of the day, parents should sign their children out on an attendance sheet. While they are doing this, encourage children to put toys away. Personal items, such as art projects, can be collected. Briefly talk to parents about their child's day. This should be a positive experience, not a time to unload all of the day's problems. If there are issues to be discussed more thoroughly, suggest a parent conference.

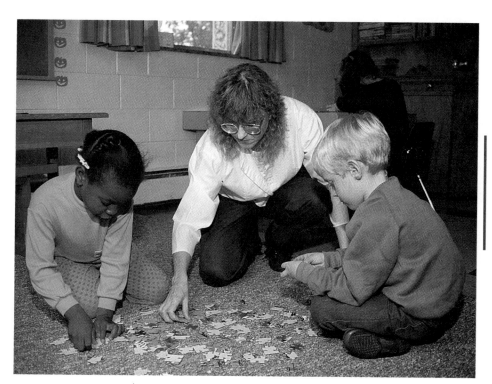

Why is working with others on a puzzle a better choice for an end-of-day activity than an art project?

LEARNING ACTIVITIES

All of the routines you have just read about are a regular part of the schedule, but they are not the whole schedule. To complete a schedule, play and learning activities are included. These are the theme activities that take place in the learning centers of the classroom. They are the heart of most programs.

While some activities may be scheduled for every day, others are not. Story and music times are likely to be daily events. Such activities as science and woodworking might be rotated into the schedule. An activity can have a routine linked to it, totally or in part. For example, a specific routine helps manage story time. Art, on the other hand, might have variations in routine, depending on the project. You will learn about how to plan and carry out many different kinds of play and learning activities in later chapters.

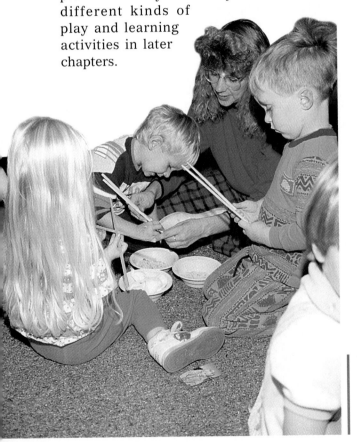

TRANSITIONS

Any time you put a group of preschoolers together, things can easily get out of control. When do you think this might be most likely to occur? One of these times is when children are switching from one activity to another. Just think what might happen if twenty four-year-olds were sent to the restroom all at once to wash their hands. Without guidance, confusion could result. Transitions can help manage situations like this.

A **transition** is *a short activity or technique used to help guide children smoothly from one activity or event to another*. It directs children's behavior so the teacher doesn't have to explain repeatedly what to do. By giving children something to focus on, their minds and bodies are less likely to wander elsewhere. A transition also provides the time young children need to make the mental shift from one activity to another. Good teachers become skilled at using effective transitions.

Transition Signals

Just as you know what it means when the bell rings in your school, young children can respond to sounds and visual cues that tell them what is coming next. No instructions are needed when the same transition signal is used in the same way on a regular basis. Here are some examples:

- Play a simple melody on the piano when it's time to pick up toys.
- Jingle some chimes to signal nap time.

Trying to pick up objects with chopsticks is more difficult than it looks. Can you identify at least two things children might learn through this activity?

"Let's walk like elephants over to the table for a snack. What do you think elephants would like to eat?" Transitions help children move from one activity to another smoothly.

Why do you think using visual cues or sounds to signal a transition is often more effective than telling children it's time to change activities?

- Flicker the lights off and on to help build anticipation for story time.
- Play a recording of a drum roll to signal a particular activity.

Children in Motion

If you want a large group of children to move from one area to another, you may not be able to let them all go at once. Allowing children to leave a few at a time is a useful technique.

Clay Tucker, a preschool teacher, knew he couldn't send all twenty children to the restroom at once before snack time. Instead, he asked the children wearing red shirts to wash their hands. While he supervised in the restroom, the teacher's aide led the others in a song. As the first group left the restroom and went to the snack tables where a parent volunteer supervised them, the aide asked children wearing blue shirts to wash their hands. This process continued until all the children had been to the restroom and arrived at the snack tables.

To keep this technique fresh, many themes can be used. You might use types of clothing, patterns on clothing, or letters in children's names. Can you think of others? With this method, effective teachers make the transition process a listening and thinking game.

Here's another technique to help children change locations. When asking children to go from outside to inside, ask them to move like gorillas, rabbits, or robots. This method is particularly effective because it focuses children's attention. They are more likely to make it from one place to another without becoming distracted.

Tip
F R O M   T H E
Pros

*I*f not used daily, transition songs and rhymes are easy to forget. Record your favorites on index cards and file for future reference. You might want to structure your file by such themes as seasons, holidays, colors, animals, and insects.

Starting Activities

As a new activity begins, doing something special that captures children's interest can draw them in. For example, at the beginning of music time, some teachers use cards that have the title of a different children's song on each one. Children pick a card randomly from a pile, and the class sings the song chosen. Children enjoy the sense of surprise that comes with this transition. Using a prop that catches the eye and arouses the curiosity of children is another possible way to begin an activity.

Cleanup Transitions

Transition techniques can motivate children to clean up at day's end. A job board is one such device. A **job board** *shows jobs that children should do.* A different cleanup activity, such as washing paint brushes or putting away tricycles, is identified on each section of the board. The board is laid flat on the floor. A child tosses a bean bag onto the board and then completes the task indicated by the bean bag's position on the board.

A **job jar**—*a container filled with pieces of paper that show pictures of activities*—serves the same purpose as a job board. Each child draws a piece of paper from the jar and completes the job indicated. Some teachers include special "jobs," such as "hug a friend."

Choice Time

One unique transition activity is choice time. **Choice time** is *a transition technique that lets children decide which activity they would like to participate in next.* This tran-

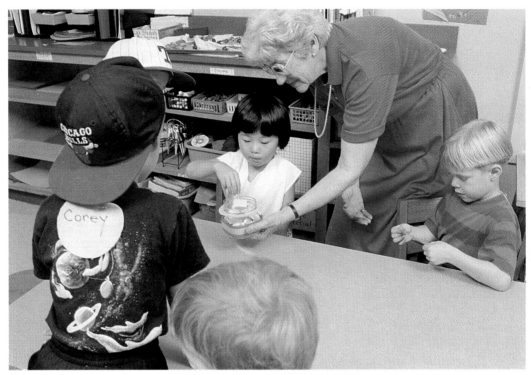

Using a job jar or job board to determine cleanup responsibilities helps make this part of the routine more interesting. What other ways might cleanup be handled?

sition helps children develop decision-making skills and builds responsibility, independence, and self-direction. It is generally conducted twice each day.

Prepare for choice time by dividing a large board that can hold hooks into areas for each learning center in the classroom. Hang a specific number of hooks in each area according to the number of children that can play in that area at a time. For example, there might be six hooks for the art area and four for the science area.

Before choice time begins, teachers describe the activities that are available in each learning center. In most cases, these activities are **teacher-directed**. That is, *the teacher leads and supervises the children.* Each child selects an activity by hanging a symbol or name tag on a hook in one of the areas. Once the choice is made, the child moves directly to that area.

PUTTING THE PIECES TOGETHER

Within the framework of a schedule, so much goes on. When a schedule works well, you can bet that some thoughtful planning has taken place. Putting the pieces of a schedule together carefully helps insure that children will be happy and better behaved and that adults will be more relaxed and able to do a good job. This is reason enough for taking the time and effort needed to build a schedule that contributes to smooth operation rather than hinders it.

Chapter 12 Review

Chapter Summary

- A well-planned schedule is helpful to everyone in an early childhood program.
- Different programs have schedules that suit their specific needs.
- In creating a schedule, activities should be arranged so that the energy level of children is taken into consideration.
- Routines are established for arrival, toileting, naps, dressing for outdoor play, meals, and departure.
- Child care professionals can make arrival easier for children. A personal greeting for each child helps children get the day off to a good start.
- Nap time is required by the licensing laws in many states.
- Many different ideas for transitions can be used by child care professionals to make the schedule operate smoothly.

Reviewing the Facts

1. When the atmosphere in an early childhood program is calm and orderly, what might this indicate?
2. What is a schedule and why is it useful?
3. List five factors that affect the creation of a schedule.
4. How does the energy level of children affect scheduling?
5. What is a routine?
6. How do both children and teachers benefit from the use of routines?
7. Since some children fear separation from parents at arrival time, what are some suggestions for handling this situation?
8. List four tasks that are incorporated in personal hygiene routines.
9. What are three reminders that caregivers need to make in connection with toileting?
10. What important step should begin and end the routines for meals and snacks?
11. Suggest three ideas for making nap time easier for children.
12. What is a transition?
13. Explain how each of the following could be used as transitions: signals; music; job boards; job jars; and choice time.

Thinking Critically

1. If a five-year-old child asked for help with buttoning a coat, how would you respond? Explain your reasoning.
2. When using a job board, you notice that a few children always manage to land the bean bag on the most desirable activities. What would you do?
3. Predict what could happen in the following situations: nap time is not scheduled at the same time each day; toileting is not scheduled at consistent times throughout the day; time for hand washing is limited; outdoor play is scheduled right before children depart for the day.
4. Do you think it's possible to make schedules and routines too rigid? Explain your reasoning.

Activities and Applications

1. **Developing a Schedule.** Create a daily schedule. Identify routines and when they take place. Where will you need to include transition ideas?

2. **Creating Transitions.** With a partner, create original transition ideas. Share these with other partnerships and analyze the ideas, looking for ways to improve them.

3. **Designing Instructional Posters.** Design three posters to help children remember daily routines, such as washing hands, flushing the toilet, and using a tissue for blowing the nose.

SCHOOL TO WORK

Your Professional Portfolio

What types of transitions work best for you? You will find some that are very effective and others that are not. Develop a card file for transition activities that you like. Use index cards to record each transition idea, specifically describing each one. Organize your file by category, such as choice time and nap time. Place the file in your portfolio.

Observing and Analyzing

Comparing Techniques in Different Facilities

As with many other aspects of early childhood programs, the best way to understand routines and transitions is to visit facilities to see examples of how these techniques are implemented. To see them in action, visit a program that fits each of the following types: family day care, a small preschool (one room), and a large child care center (several classrooms). In observing each, take notes on routines and transitions that are used. Later, compare and contrast what you discovered, using the questions below. Then prepare a written summary of your observations.

Routines
- What routines did you see used in each setting?
- Were any routines shared by all three programs? If so, which ones?
- Why are some routines different and some similar from one program to another?
- Did you see any ways that routines might be improved?

Transitions
- What transitions did you see used in each setting?
- Did any program rely more heavily on the use of transitions than the others? If so, why?
- How effective were the transitions? Which ones worked better than others?
- What suggestions do you have for improvement?

Chapter 13

Food for Young Children

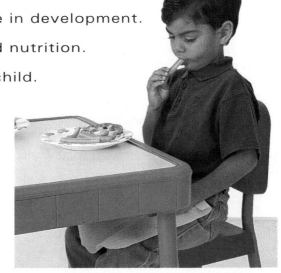

CHAPTER OBJECTIVES

■ Define nutrition and explain its role in development.

■ Identify nutrients required for good nutrition.

■ Plan balanced menus for a young child.

■ Outline important considerations in meal planning for young children.

■ Describe proper food safety and sanitation practices.

■ List meal service guidelines.

■ Plan nutrition education activities.

Terms to Learn

- Child and Adult Care Food Program (CACFP)
- deficiency
- Food Guide Pyramid
- health inspectors
- nutrients
- nutrition
- perishable
- sanitation
- Women, Infants, and Children (WIC) Program

want to stir the batter first!"

"Okay, but I get to mix in the pumpkin."

"Miss Lydia, could I add the cinnamon?"

Lydia Torres knelt at the low table, surrounded by five-year-olds in aprons. She looked at the eager faces, noticing one child who said nothing. "I think it's Michael's turn to help," she said. "We'll let him add the cinnamon."

For a moment, all talking stopped. Six pairs of eyes focused on Michael's trembling hand as he carefully lifted the measuring spoon with the cinnamon in it. Without realizing, Lydia held her breath, hoping that Michael would get the cinnamon where he wanted it to go. A look of intense concentration was on Michael's face as he moved the spoon slowly toward the bowl. Just past the rim, the spoon jiggled, sending the cinnamon streaming into the mixture. "You did that very well, Michael," Lydia said quietly, looking him right in the eyes and smiling.

"Are we going to have the pumpkin bread for a snack?" one child asked as the chatter resumed.

"Can we taste it before we bake it?"

"Look, it's turning orange!"

Lydia responded to each excited comment. "Who can tell me why pumpkin is good for us?" she asked as she looked around the circle. Although Michael still said nothing, she noticed a different expression on his face. There was the hint of a smile and a new brightness in his eyes. It made her feel good inside. "Michael may enjoy this pumpkin bread more than any of the others do," she thought.

FOOD FOR HEALTH, LEARNING, AND FUN

Most children are fascinated by food, especially when they can help prepare it themselves. Wise teachers capitalize on children's interest in food. Exposure to a variety of foods and food experiences helps children develop positive attitudes toward eating properly. In turn, eating properly enhances children's well-being. Those who are responsible for children need to understand how proper nutrition and nutrition education can improve the lives of young children.

THE BASICS OF GOOD NUTRITION

Nutrients are *the substances which are found in food and used by the body to function, grow, repair itself, and produce energy.* **Nutrition** is *the process through which the body utilizes the nutrients in food.*

Some nutrients provide energy for activities, such as running or playing a computer game, and for essential body processes, such as pumping blood and digesting food. Other nutrients help keep the body working smoothly. Without the right balance of many different nutrients, the body cannot produce the energy it needs. It cannot function properly and has less resistance to illness.

Good nutrition is especially important in the early years. It provides the foundation for children's normal physical growth. Proper early growth and development are critical to having a long, healthful life.

Nutrition affects intellectual development as well. To function properly, the brain must receive important chemicals from nutrients on a regular basis. Most of the brain's growth occurs in the first two years of life. Research has shown that well-nourished children learn better.

Children also enjoy better emotional health when properly fed. They feel healthier and have a more positive outlook on life. Their ability to combat fatigue, depression, and everyday stress is enhanced. Healthy, well-nourished children are more likely to feel good about themselves and enjoy life.

Components of Good Nutrition

Evidence of poor nutrition can be observed in many ways. One caregiver, for example, noticed that a child in her preschool seemed tired all the time. In a conversation with the child, she learned that he seldom had breakfast. When the boy's parent's were asked what he typically ate for supper, the response was, "His favorite is a jelly sandwich, potato chips, and a soda." No wonder the child's body did not have energy. It wasn't being fueled properly.

For good health, the body needs six types of nutrients: carbohydrates, proteins, fats, vitamins, minerals, and water. Each plays a unique role in developing a healthy body.

- *Carbohydrates* (car-boh-HI-draytes). These are the body's main source of energy. They also help the body make the best use of proteins and fats. Good sources of carbohydrates include fruits, vegetables, and grain products (such as whole-grain breads and cereals, rice, and pasta).

- *Proteins.* These nutrients help the body make new cells and repair injured ones. They are necessary for growth and to fight off disease. Meat, poultry, fish, eggs, and dairy products provide complete protein—protein the body can readily use. Complete protein can also be obtained by eating the right combination of foods from plant sources. Simply combine dry beans, dry peas, or peanut butter with grains, nuts, or seeds. For example, peanut butter and whole-wheat bread together provide complete protein.

Food provides the nutrients children need for energy, growth, and good health.

- *Fats.* Fats provide energy and carry some vitamins that regulate body processes. They are also needed for healthy skin. Fats are obtained from meat, vegetable oils, whole dairy products, egg yolks, nuts, margarine, mayonnaise, and salad dressing.
- *Vitamins.* These nutrients help keep the body working properly and help other nutrients do their jobs. They include vitamins A, C, D, E, and K, as well as the B vitamins (a group of eight nutrients). Each vitamin has specific jobs to do. For example, vitamin A protects the eyes, contributes to healthy skin, and helps provide resistance to disease. Vitamins are found in varying amounts in a wide variety of foods—grain products, fruits, vegetables, dairy products, meat, fish, poultry, eggs, dry beans and peas, and nuts.
- *Minerals.* Helping regulate body processes is the function of minerals. They also become a part of the body's bones, tissues, and fluids. Many different minerals—including calcium, phosphorus, iron, potassium, and sodium—carry out specific functions in the human body. Eating a wide variety of foods helps the body get all of these important minerals, as well as the other nutrients it needs.
- *Water.* Water is essential for life. You can live for several days or even weeks without food, but only about three days without water. Water is present in every cell of the body. It delivers nutrients throughout the body, serves as the body's cooling system, and helps the body eliminate waste.

Providing Balanced Nutrition

As you have seen, many different nutrients play a role in maintaining good health. These nutrients work as a team. The body needs specific amounts of each.

Too Much of a Good Thing

Concerns about nutrition often focus on whether people get enough nutrients. In some cases, however, getting too much of a nutrient is also cause for concern. Here's why health experts recommend going easy on fat, sugars, and sodium.

- **Fat.** Although fat is an essential nutrient, eating too much fat can lead to overweight. It has also been linked with heart disease and cancer in adults. Health experts recommend that, except for infants and toddlers under age two, people limit the amount of fat they eat.
- **Sugars.** Such foods as candies, cookies, cakes and other desserts, and some breakfast cereals often contain large amounts of added sugars. When children (or adults) fill up on these sweets, they may not eat enough of the other, more nutrient-dense foods they need for good health. The high calorie content of these foods can also contribute to overweight. In addition, eating too many sugary foods can lead to tooth decay.
- **Sodium.** Most Americans get much more sodium than they need. It is found mainly in processed foods and in table salt. Cutting down on sodium may help some children avoid high blood pressure when they become adults.

Food Pyramid

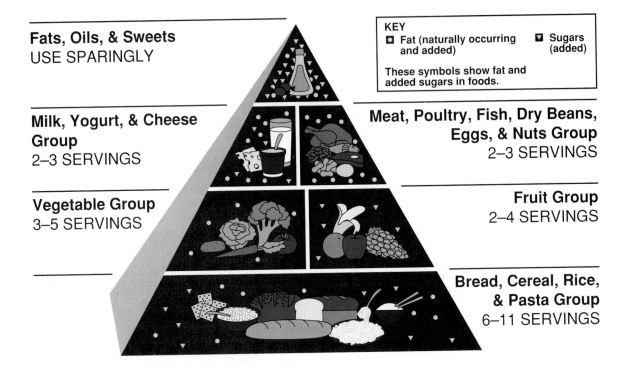

Fats, Oils, & Sweets
USE SPARINGLY

KEY
◻ Fat (naturally occurring and added)   ▼ Sugars (added)

These symbols show fat and added sugars in foods.

Milk, Yogurt, & Cheese Group
2–3 SERVINGS

Meat, Poultry, Fish, Dry Beans, Eggs, & Nuts Group
2–3 SERVINGS

Vegetable Group
3–5 SERVINGS

Fruit Group
2–4 SERVINGS

Bread, Cereal, Rice, & Pasta Group
6–11 SERVINGS

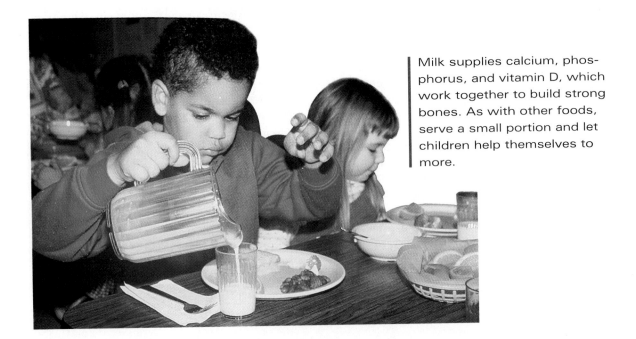

Milk supplies calcium, phosphorus, and vitamin D, which work together to build strong bones. As with other foods, serve a small portion and let children help themselves to more.

If children are lacking in one or more nutrients, especially over long periods of time, they can develop serious health problems. For instance, a **deficiency** *(severe shortage)* of vitamin D can lead to rickets, a disease in which bones soften and may become deformed. A deficiency of iron can cause a type of anemia. Children with this condition are tired, pale, and weak and have poor appetites. Getting too much of some nutrients, such as fat, sugar, and sodium, can also lead to health problems in later life.

For good health, children need a variety of nutritious foods daily. These foods should be chosen with care to insure that they provide the right balance of nutrients.

The Food Guide Pyramid

One way to plan balanced, nutritious meals and snacks is with the help of the **Food Guide Pyramid**, *a guide to daily food choices based on the recommendations of nutrition experts.* The Food Guide Pyramid organizes food into five main groups according to the nutrients they contain. Children and adults need foods from each of the following groups every day:

• Bread, Cereal, Rice, and Pasta Group
• Vegetable Group
• Fruit Group
• Milk, Yogurt, and Cheese Group
• Meat, Poultry, Fish, Dry Beans, Eggs, and Nuts Group

These food groups are shown in the pyramid diagram on page 248. The small tip of the pyramid represents Fats, Oils, and Sweets. Foods in this category are not essential for good health and should be used sparingly. They include butter, margarine, salad dressings, jelly, honey, syrup, pastries, doughnuts, and candy bars.

Although some fats and oils are needed for growth, the amounts required are easily obtained through eating foods from the five main groups. Children under age two, however, are growing very rapidly. The fat in the foods they consume is needed for growth. Milk, especially, should be whole, *not* low-fat, for children at this very young age.

Servings for Young Children

The five main food groups are equally important to health; however, they are not needed in equal amounts. The Food Guide Pyramid shows a range of recommended daily servings for each group. Generally, young children should have at least the lowest number of servings in the range. Older children's needs usually fall in the middle of the range. The needs of adults vary depending on how active they are.

Serving sizes for young children are smaller than those for adults. That's because young children have small stomachs that cannot hold much food at a time. For example, a preschooler might be served half a slice of bread at dinner instead of a whole slice. Some nutritionists recommend serving about one tablespoon (15 mL) of each food choice per year of a child's age. A serving of vegetables for a three-year-old might be about 3 tablespoons (45 mL). One exception is milk. Children need the same amount of milk per day as most adults—at least 2 cups (500 mL). This amount can be divided into several small portions.

A child should not be forced to eat large portions at mealtime. Offer small amounts at first, and then let the child have more if he or she is still hungry. Between meals, offer nutritious snacks. Children need snacks to keep up their energy and provide additional servings from the food groups.

Children's food needs vary from day to day, depending on how active they are and how rapidly they are growing. In general, the important thing is not how much children eat, but what they eat. As long as foods from the five food groups are eaten, the child is probably getting adequate nutrition.

FOOD SERVICE IN CHILD CARE PROGRAMS

*T*he type of meal service provided by a child care program depends on the hours of operation and the age of the children. A full-day program might provide breakfast, lunch, and one or two snacks. If a program is open later hours, an evening meal may also be provided. Half-day preschools might provide one meal and perhaps a snack.

When programs provide full food service, they usually employ a person to plan menus, purchase food, and prepare meals. This person may be a nutritionist or dietitian. In other programs, teachers may take on some or all of the responsibility for planning, preparing, and serving meals and snacks.

Menu Planning

When planning menus for a child care program, three important questions must be considered: Will the meal or snack be nutritious yet within the budget? Will it be easy and safe for children to eat? Will it appeal to children?

Meeting Nutrition Requirements

Most state licensing regulations set minimum standards for meal service in child

Providing food for children goes beyond satisfying their hunger. During the hours they attend a child care program, the responsibility for children's nutritional needs rests with the program's staff.

care programs. These standards insure that menus meet children's nutritional needs.

The U.S. government has developed a set of general guidelines for use in its child nutrition programs. They are shown below.

Nutrition Guidance for the Child Nutrition Programs

- Offer a variety of foods.
- Serve meals that help maintain a healthy body and weight.
- Offer meals low in fat, saturated fat, and cholesterol.
- Serve plenty of vegetables, fruits, and grain products.
- Offer and use sugars only in moderation.
- Offer and use salt and sodium only in moderation.
- Promote an alcohol- and drug-free lifestyle.

Meal Pattern for Children

BREAKFAST	CHILDREN 1-2 YEARS	CHILDREN 3-5 YEARS	CHILDREN 6-12 YEARS
Milk, fluid	1/2 cup	3/4 cup	1 cup
Juice or **fruit** or **vegetable**	1/4 cup	1/2 cup	1/2 cup
Bread and/or **cereal**			
Enriched or whole-grain bread	1/2 slice	1/2 slice	1 slice
Cereal: Cold dry or	1/4 cup[1]	1/3 cup[2]	3/4 cup[3]
Hot cooked	1/4 cup	1/4 cup	1/2 cup
MIDMORNING OR MIDAFTERNOON SNACK (SUPPLEMENT)			
(Select 2 of these 4 components.)			
Milk, fluid	1/2 cup	1/2 cup	1 cup
Meat or **meat alternate**	1/2 oz.	1/2 oz.	1 oz.
Juice or **fruit** or **vegetable**	1/2 cup	1/2 cup	3/4 cup
Bread and/or **cereal**			
Enriched or whole-grain bread	1/2 slice	1/2 slice	1 slice
Cereal: Cold dry or	1/4 cup[1]	1/3 cup[2]	3/4 cup[3]
Hot cooked	1/4 cup	1/4 cup	1/2 cup
LUNCH/SUPPER			
Milk, fluid	1/2 cup	3/4 cup	1 cup
Meat or **meat alternate**			
Meat, poultry, or fish, cooked (lean meat without bone)	1 oz.	1 1/2 oz.	2 oz.
Cheese	1 oz.	1 1/2 oz.	2 oz.
Egg	1	1	1
Cooked dry beans and peas	1/4 cup	3/8 cup	1/2 cup
Peanut butter or other nut or seed butters	2 Tbsp.	3 Tbsp.	4 Tbsp.
Nuts and/or seeds	1/2 oz.[4]	3/4 oz.[4]	1 oz.[4]
Vegetable and/or **fruit** (two or more)	1/4 cup	1/2 cup	3/4 cup
Bread or **bread alternate**, enriched or whole grain	1/2 slice	1/2 slice	1 slice

[1] 1/4 cup (volume) or 1/3 ounce (weight), whichever is less.
[2] 1/3 cup (volume) or 1/2 ounce (weight), whichever is less.
[3] 3/4 cup (volume) or 1 ounce (weight), whichever is less.
[4] This portion can meet only one-half of the total serving of the meat/meat alternate requirement for lunch or supper. Nuts or seeds must be combined with another meat/meat alternate to fulfill the requirement. For determining combinations, 1 ounce of nuts or seeds is equal to 1 ounce of cooked lean meat, poultry, or fish.

Caution: Children under five are at the highest risk of choking. The USDA recommends that any nuts or seeds be served to them in a prepared food and be ground or finely chopped.

Metric Conversions (approximate): 1 Tbsp.—15mL; 1/4 cup—50mL; 1/3 cup—75mL; 3/8 cup—90 mL; 1/2 cup—125mL; 3/4 cup—175 mL; 1 cup—250 mL; 1/3 oz.—9 g; 1/2 oz.—14 g; 3/4 oz.—21 g; 1 oz.—28 g.

One federal child nutrition program is the **Child and Adult Care Food Program (CACFP).** This is *a federally funded program that helps provide healthful meals and snacks in child and adult care facilities.* In order to receive money and commodity food from the CACFP, programs must serve meals that meet federal nutrition guidelines. The meal pattern established by the CACFP is shown on page 251.

Teachers who plan menus for child care programs should learn about proper nutrition by reading nutrition books and enrolling in an early childhood nutrition course. Here are some tips for making sure the foods served are nutritious:

- Choose fruit and vegetable juices that are 100 percent juice, with no added sweetener.
- Serve fruits and vegetables raw when possible. Valuable nutrients can be lost during cooking. When you do cook fruits and vegetables, choose such methods as microwaving, steaming, or simmering in a small amount of water. Avoid overcooking.
- Choose low-fat dairy products for children over age two.
- Serve only lean meats. To reduce fat, bake or broil meats instead of frying.
- Choose whole-grain breads, crackers, and cereals. Whole-grain products are usually more nutritious, and they provide fiber, which helps keep the digestive tract working normally.
- Encourage children to drink small amounts of water frequently throughout the day. Of course, water is also present in juices and milk, but the best source is plain, natural water from the tap or drinking fountain.

The extra challenge in planning a nutritious menu comes with making it economical too. Since budgets are usually tight in child care programs, a practical approach to planning and purchasing foods is necessary. Buying fresh produce that is in season, purchasing in quantity, and taking advantage of sales are techniques used to keep in line with the budget.

Making Foods Easy to Eat

Young children are just learning to use eating utensils. To make eating easier, include some finger foods, such as carrot sticks or apple slices.

Serve children's food in small pieces. Large chunks of meat, vegetables, or fruit may be difficult for them to chew and could cause choking. Children may need to be reminded to eat slowly and chew food thoroughly.

Avoid serving young children nuts, popcorn, grapes, hot dogs, and hard candies. These foods can easily be inhaled and cause choking. In case of choking, use the Heimlich maneuver (explained in Chapter 10). A poster showing how to perform the Heimlich maneuver should be displayed in every eating area.

Making Meals Appealing

Imagine sitting down to a meal in which every food item is sweet—or everything is tart. You probably wouldn't enjoy it. As do most adults, children like a mixture of flavors in a meal. Their taste buds are sensitive, however, so foods should be only

Tip FROM THE Pros

*U*se your imagination to make food more fun and appealing for children. Cut slices of meat or cheese into stars or animal shapes. Make a boat out of a sandwich, using a toothpick to hold a paper sail. Turn a pancake into a funny face by adding banana slices and raisins to form eyes, nose, and mouth.

Cutting or arranging food into fun shapes can boost children's interest. What else about this snack makes it a good choice for young children?

monotony. For instance, broccoli may be part of a salad for one meal. The next time it is served, it may be steamed as a side dish or eaten raw with a dip as a snack.

A sample child care menu is shown below. How well do you think it fulfills the goals of nutrition, ease of eating, and appeal to young children?

Special Considerations in Meal Planning

Some children may be unable to eat certain foods because of allergies or other medical problems. In addition, religious beliefs may call for avoiding certain foods or food combinations. Be sure to ask parents about any such restrictions that may apply to their child. Keep a convenient record of these restrictions to consult when planning meals.

lightly seasoned. Including bright colors and different shapes on the plate adds eye appeal. For even more interest, serve foods with different textures—soft and creamy, hard and crunchy, chewy, or crisp.

Prepare foods in a variety of ways to encourage new food choices and avoid

Sample Menu

BREAKFAST
Sliced banana

Corn flakes

Milk

MIDMORNING SNACK
Pineapple juice

Whole-wheat toast

LUNCH
Baked chicken

Mashed potatoes

Carrot sticks

Roll

Milk

AFTERNOON SNACK
Milk

Bean and cheese burrito

THE MULTICULTURAL CLASSROOM

Food offers an excellent way to introduce children to other cultures. Although menus should include foods children are familiar with, introducing those from other cultures broadens their horizons.

One interesting way to ease young children into an appreciation of different foods is to let them smell the seasonings associated with certain foods. The children may recognize cinnamon, basil, oregano, garlic, black pepper, and vanilla, but nutmeg, paprika, chili powder, cilantro, and cumin might not be as

familiar. Encourage the children to discuss what these seasonings smell like, and allow tasting. Sprinkle some of the spices into dough or make a spice collage on a paper plate. The next time the children are introduced to a food with an unfamiliar aroma, they may be more willing to give it a try.

Adding ethnic foods little by little during snack time is another good idea. Serving bagels, tortillas, lavosh (Armenian bread), scones, wontons, and pizza is a good start.

Food Safety and Sanitation

Food that is spoiled or tainted with bacteria can cause serious illness in children and adults. Anyone preparing to serve food must be trained in food safety and sanitation practices. **Sanitation** means *practicing cleanliness to prevent the spread of illness and disease.*

Harmful bacteria and other disease-carrying agents can easily spread from unclean hands or equipment to food. To limit the spread of these agents, food handlers must wash their hands with hot, soapy water before beginning food preparation. They must take care not to cough or sneeze on the food. Like all others in the center, they must wash their hands after coughing, sneezing, blowing their nose, or using the restroom. In addition, hand washing is necessary after handling raw meat, poultry, fish, or eggs. Equipment that touched the raw food, such as cutting boards and knives, must also be scrubbed in hot, soapy water before being used for other foods.

All dishes and utensils must be sanitized after each use. This is usually done in dishwashers, using very hot (170°F [77°C]) water to kill bacteria. Eating areas and food preparation areas must be cleaned with a sanitizing solution before and after each use. Serve food on clean dishes, not the same dishes that were used for raw food.

In addition to cleanliness, proper temperatures for storing and serving food are necessary. Many foods are **perishable**, which means *they will spoil if not refrigerated or frozen.* That is because bacteria multiply rapidly at room temperature. Cold temperatures limit the growth of bacteria. High temperatures used in cooking food destroy many harmful bacteria.

To maintain proper food temperatures, follow these guidelines:

- Make sure the temperature inside the refrigerator is between 32°F and 40°F (0°C and 4°C). Keep the freezer at 0°F (-18°C) or lower.
- Never let frozen food sit at room temperature to thaw. Instead, let it thaw in the refrigerator. You may also use a microwave oven to defrost the food, as long as you cook it right away.

Building Professional Skills

Responsibility

WHAT IS RESPONSIBILITY?

People show responsibility by proving they can be trusted with important obligations. Responsible people don't need constant supervision; they carry out their duties without being told. They are also willing to accept the blame when they make mistakes. Responsibility is an important part of maturity.

Responsibility in Action

It was afternoon snack time in the child care center where Nolan and Clarisse worked as aides. Mrs. Andrews, the food service manager, took Nolan aside. "A family emergency has come up, so I can't be here tomorrow. Could you prepare lunch for the children? Since you've helped me in the kitchen before, I think you can handle it."

"Sure," Nolan replied. "I'd be glad to help."

Mrs. Andrews looked relieved. "Good. Here's the menu—hamburgers, vegetable sticks, applesauce, and milk. Remember to put the ground beef in the refrigerator to thaw before you leave tonight. Thanks so much—I'm sure you'll do a fine job." With that, Mrs. Andrews hurried out the door.

The next day, Nolan arrived early. When he checked on the meat in the refrigerator, he realized it wouldn't be enough. "I guess I should have pulled two packages out of the freezer yesterday instead of just one," he told Clarisse.

"You've got hours before you have to start cooking," Clarisse said. "If you set the other package out on the counter now, it might thaw in time."

Nolan shook his head. "No, that's too risky. The kids could get sick, and it would be my fault. Looks like I'll have to make a quick trip to the store."

The rest of the day, including lunch, went well. When Mrs. Andrews returned, Nolan told her what had happened. She smiled and said, "I've forgotten to thaw meat a few times myself. The important thing is that you followed food safety rules. I knew I could count on you."

Your Analysis

1. Why do you suppose Mrs. Andrews chose Nolan to be in charge of lunch? How does this relate to the definition of responsibility?

2. What indications do you have that Nolan is a responsible person?

3. What are some different ways a less responsible person might have handled this situation? Why did Nolan reject those choices?

4. What are some other examples of how people show responsibility on the job?

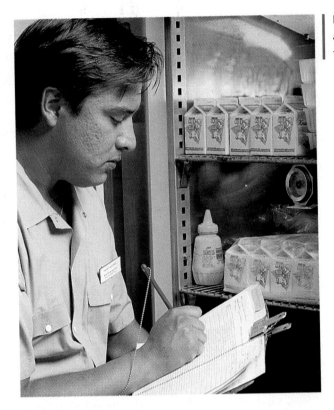

Health inspectors make regular visits to all food service operations. What do you think this inspector is checking for?

State laws usually require child care programs to be regularly monitored by the local health department. Programs are checked periodically by **health inspectors**, *health department representatives who observe and evaluate a program's health practices.* This protects children by making sure proper food safety is practiced by meal service personnel. Health inspectors check for many things. They check to make sure food is stored and served at safe temperatures. They notice if a food preparer is wearing the required hair net, which keeps hair from accidentally falling into food. They check to see if a food handler's cuts or wounds are covered with plastic gloves when handling food. (Otherwise, disease-causing agents from the wound could enter the food and cause illness.) Health departments also provide the child care staff with training in food safety and sanitation.

- Be sure food is cooked thoroughly. Meat and poultry should be cooked to an internal temperature of at least 160°F (71°C). Leftovers should be thoroughly reheated to an internal temperature of 165°F (74°C). Once you begin to cook the food, continue until it is completely done.
- When serving a meal or snack, keep hot foods hot and cold foods cold. Otherwise, bacteria will grow rapidly as the food reaches room temperature.
- After a meal, refrigerate or freeze any leftovers promptly. If perishable food has been left sitting out for more than two hours (one hour in very hot weather), discard it.

Tip
F R O M   T H E
Pros

*W*hen serving beverages to young children, fill cups only half full. This reduces the chance of spills. When spills do occur, there is less to wipe up.

Serving Meals and Snacks

At lunch time in a typical child care program, you might see a scene like this. Three tables are each set with six place settings, including cups, spoons, napkins, and child-size plates. On each table is a platter of sandwiches made with turkey, lettuce, and whole-wheat bread. The sandwiches are cut into quarters. Other serving dishes hold peas, sliced peaches, carrot sticks, and green pepper rings. Milk is served as a beverage. After children and teachers wash their hands, they sit together and begin eating the meal.

Preventing Tooth Decay

An eating pattern of frequent small meals and snacks is fine for nutrition but can be hard on the teeth. Food particles react with bacteria in the mouth, resulting in acid that attacks tooth enamel. For good dental health, encourage children to brush their teeth after meals and snacks.

Getting a meal on the table is only one part of the effort. The other is making meal time enjoyable. To make it so, most programs have basic rules. Typically, children are expected to:

- Help set the table before meals.
- Participate in meal preparation whenever possible. For example, they might make a salad as an activity with the teacher.
- Wash hands before setting the table, helping prepare meals, or eating.

- Begin eating only after everyone has arrived at the table.
- Sit appropriately in chairs while eating.
- Serve themselves reasonable portions of each food choice.
- Say "please" and "thank you" when requesting and passing food.
- Enjoy quiet, pleasant conversation during the meal.
- Use napkins appropriately.
- Clean up their own place setting and spills.

Peeling and slicing fruit for a salad gives these children a sense of accomplishment. In what other ways does helping prepare a meal benefit children?

- Wait to leave the table until everyone is finished.
- Wash hands and brush teeth after eating.

Teachers must also follow certain rules at mealtime. They should set a good example by following the same guidelines that the children are expected to follow. They should never withhold food as punishment, offer food as a reward, or force children to clean their plate. These practices interfere with teaching good eating habits.

TEACHING NUTRITION CONCEPTS

You can provide children with the right foods, but until they learn how to choose them on their own, your job isn't done. Nutrition education should be one of the goals of any child care program.

Through nutrition education, children learn that food does more than just satisfy hunger. This learning process can be extended to the home and parents as well.

Food Experiences for Children

Just because a food is green or has lumps in it doesn't make it bad. Getting children to see that they can enjoy and benefit from all kinds of foods is not always an easy task. A menu with variety exposes children to many foods, some of which may be new to them.

Children should be encouraged to take at least a small taste of each food; however, they should never be pressured or forced to taste a food they dislike or are suspicious of. A new food may need to appear on the menu several times before a finicky child finally accepts it. Putting a new food on a plate with a popular food item is often helpful. Presenting unfamiliar foods in a positive way not only helps children learn about food but also lets them become more comfortable with trying something new.

FOCUS ON INFANT PROGRAMS

Parents usually provide formula for their infants. They may ask you to warm the bottle of formula before giving it to the baby. Do not heat formula in a microwave—parts of the mixture could become dangerously hot while the rest feels only lukewarm. Instead, use a bottle warmer, or heat the filled bottle in a pan of water on the range. Shake a few drops of formula onto your wrist to be sure it is lukewarm, not hot.

When feeding babies, hold them in a nurturing manner. Never leave a bottle propped in a baby's mouth while you attend to other business. This could cause digestive problems, ear infections, or even choking. If the baby wants a sucking device at nap time, provide a pacifier instead of a bottle.

When it is time to offer children solid food (usually after six months of age), follow parent's recommendations for introducing baby cereals, strained fruits and vegetables, and pureed meats. Introduce new foods one at a time. Closely observe children for signs of an allergic reaction, such as a rash or diarrhea.

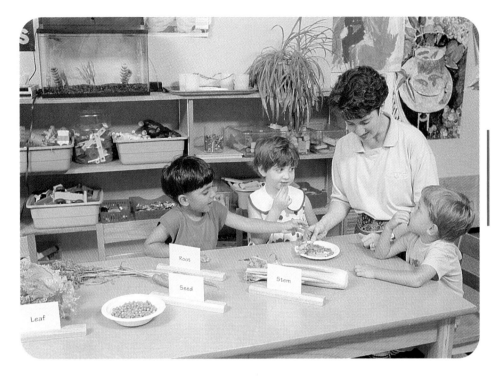

Most children are interested in learning about different types of food and where they come from.

Preschoolers are not too young to begin learning some basic nutrition concepts. Here are some concepts that can be understood by young children:

- Food is fuel for the body. It helps people grow and gives them energy.
- People should eat a variety of foods every day. This keeps bodies healthy. It helps fight off illness.
- People need to drink several glasses of water every day.
- Food comes from plants and animals.
- People eat different parts of plants, including stems, roots, leaves, and seeds.
- Most food is grown on the farm and then taken to a supermarket.
- People can grow their own food in gardens.
- People from different parts of the world eat different foods.
- Food can be cooked in many different ways.

Nutrition concepts can be taught to children through food experiences. Many teachers conduct food preparation activities with children as young as two years of age. The younger the child, the simpler the food project. Two-year-olds may begin by spreading peanut butter on crackers. As children gain experience in food preparation, more complex recipes can be prepared. They might like to make granola or vegetable soup. Conduct the activity at a child-size table over an easily cleaned surface. Talk about the smell, taste, and appearance of the food while preparing it.

Other activities, such as reading books, can often be linked with nutrition education. Reading the story "Goldilocks and the Three Bears" in the morning can be followed by preparing porridge with the children in the afternoon.

Puzzles and matching games about food are also worthwhile activities. They help children identify and label food choices. Table games encourage older children to

Insuring Safety

Follow these safety tips whenever allowing children to help prepare food:

- Always try out a recipe before making it with children. Be sure it is not too difficult and presents no undue safety hazards.
- Teach children safety rules and be sure they are followed. Supervise constantly.
- Have children wash hands before working with food and practice sanitary habits during the activity.
- Use plastic bowls and utensils when possible to prevent injury if accidents should occur.
- Limit the use of electrical appliances.

classify food into food groups. Some teachers have younger children sort pictures according to food and nonfood.

Field trips are another method of nutrition education. The class might visit a pizza parlor, supermarket, orchard, farm, restaurant, vegetable stand, farmer's market, or ice cream store.

Puzzles and other activities can help reinforce what children have learned about food.

FOCUS ON SCHOOL-AGE PROGRAMS

School-age children want more freedom of choice in their food selections. Offer nutritious options so that any choice is a healthful one.

Allow school-age children to help plan, purchase, and prepare some of their daily snacks. These projects help them feel important and responsible. Most school-age children enjoy preparing food. They can become very creative and develop new recipes of their own.

Creative teachers use songs, records, finger plays, poems, flannel board stories, bulletin boards, and puppet shows to teach good eating habits. The public library is generally a good source for these materials.

The U.S. Department of Agriculture funds agencies called Nutrition Education Training (N.E.T.) centers. These N.E.T. centers provide a wealth of activity ideas for nutrition education, usually free of charge.

Nutrition Education for Parents

Parents are role models for their children's eating habits. The more parents know about nutrition, the more likely they are to provide healthful meals at home and to set a good example when it comes to food choices. Child care providers can look for opportunities to educate parents on nutrition. For example, they might:

- Ask parents to join the class for a snack or lunch.
- Send home nutritious recipes in newsletters.
- Host a potluck meal featuring healthful foods.

- Invite parents on nutrition-related field trips.

Some parents may need extra assistance with nutrition. These parents may be referred to a federally funded nutrition program called the **Women, Infants, and Children (WIC) Program.** *This program provides nutrition advice and low-cost food, including infant formula. It is available to low-income pregnant and breast-feeding women, infants, and children up to five years old.*

FOOD FOR THOUGHT

Nutritionists believe that eating habits learned in early childhood continue into adulthood. If children learn to choose wisely and moderately from the food groups, they are likely to add quality and length to life. By providing nutritious meals and snacks plus food-related learning activities, a child care program can help foster good eating habits now and in the years to come.

Chapter 13 Review

Chapter Summary

- Good nutrition is important to physical, intellectual, and emotional development.
- The body needs these nutrients: carbohydrates, proteins, fats, vitamins, minerals, and water.
- To plan meals and snacks that provide the right amounts of all necessary nutrients, use the Food Guide Pyramid.
- Children's meals should have variety and appeal in addition to being healthful and nutritious.
- Proper food safety and sanitation practices prevent food-related illness.
- Guidelines should be set up for mealtimes to help insure enjoyable meals.
- Children benefit from nutrition education. Parents should also be educated about nutrition.

Reviewing the Facts

1. Explain the importance of good nutrition.
2. What is the function of carbohydrates?
3. Give three examples of foods that supply carbohydrates.
4. What is the role of proteins in nutrition?
5. Why is it important to eat a variety of foods daily?
6. Name the groups in the Food Guide Pyramid.
7. Should children be served the same quantity of food that adults are served? Explain your answer.
8. What is the CACFP and what is its role?
9. Give three examples of foods that could cause young children to choke.
10. List three ways a meal can be made appealing to children.
11. Briefly describe four procedures meal preparers should follow when working in the food area.
12. When serving meals, why is it important to keep hot foods hot and cold foods cold?
13. Describe three educational food experiences for children.

Thinking Critically

1. Why might children be more willing to try new foods if they have helped prepare them?
2. What link might there be between good nutrition and good self-esteem?
3. What might be some advantages of using plant food combinations, such as beans and rice, as a source of protein?
4. Suppose a parent or teacher regularly tells a child, "No dessert until you eat all your vegetables." What does this teach the child about the relative value of desserts and vegetables? What problems might this cause in the long run?
5. As a caregiver, suppose you discover that several children are not eating breakfast. Some are eating inappropriate foods for breakfast. What steps could you take to encourage families to have a nutritious breakfast each morning?

Activities and Applications

1. **Parent Interview.** Ask the parent of a young child about the child's eating habits. What techniques has the parent used to introduce new foods?
2. **Recipe File.** Collect at least ten nutritious snack recipes for preschoolers. Be sure to include finger foods and "fun" foods.

3. **Supermarket Visit.** Take a young child with you to the supermarket. Which foods catch the child's eye? Why are the foods attractive to the child? Are they nutritious?

4. **Activity Planning.** Create an activity that could help preschool children learn about food and nutrition. For example, you might make a set of food flash cards or write a puppet show.

Your Professional Portfolio

Imagine that you are in charge of food service for a child care center that operates from early morning through evening hours. Plan one day's menu for preschool children, including breakfast, lunch, dinner, and two snacks. Also write an explanation of why your menu is nutritious and appropriate for preschoolers. Place the completed menu and explanation in your portfolio.

Observing and Analyzing

Looking at Lunches

The lunches that children have in a child care program are usually either prepared at the school or sent from home. Some lunches, however, are cooked at another school or in a central kitchen for delivery to several sites. Occasionally programs contract out to community restaurants or caterers for daily deliveries.

When convenience is a concern, a parent may appreciate having the lunch provided or available for purchase at the school. To save costs or to control what is eaten, a parent may prefer to send lunch from home. If you ask children which they prefer, most would choose the lunch that tastes best, regardless of the source. The most important issue for all, however, should be making sure the meal is a nutritious one. Try the observation ideas below to explore this thought.

- **Public Programs.** Observe a public school or government-subsidized program for school-age children and record what is served, what is eaten, and what is thrown out barely eaten or untouched. Was the food prepared in an appetizing manner? Also record the children's comments. Were they favorable or unfavorable? What suggestions, if any, would you make?

- **Private Programs.** Visit two private programs, one that provides lunch prepared in the program's kitchen and another where the children bring their lunches from home. Make the same observations mentioned above.

- **Nutritional Value.** After observing the lunches served in the two activities above, analyze them for nutritional value. Which was the most nutritious? Which looked the most appealing? Which foods were the best liked, and which were the least popular?

- **Commercials.** Observe commercials shown during Saturday morning television programming for children. Make a list of the food-related items shown. Which items are wholesome, healthful choices? Which are not nutritious? Which commercials are shown more, the healthful choices or the less nutritious? Why? How do you think exposure to these commercials affects children?

Career Profile

Meet Consuella Martinez, child care program director. As director, Consuella manages a staff of twenty people. Together they tend to the various needs of ninety children ages six weeks to ten years.

Why did you choose this career?

"I've always liked children. I babysat often during junior high school. During high school I volunteered in a child care center. The center's director suggested I attend college to become qualified to work in the child care profession. Thanks to her interest and encouragement, here I am today!"

What education and skills do you need?

"After high school I studied two years to obtain an associate's degree in child care. After working several years as a child care teacher I completed two more years of college to obtain my bachelor's degree in early childhood education. That qualified me to be a child care director.

"Directors need lots of different skills. Some days I feel pulled in ten directions at once. Good communication and problem-solving skills are essential. It's also important to work well with all kinds of people.

"As director, I use management skills like any other businessperson. I manage our budget and maintain records on staff and children. A role I take very seriously is insuring a safe and healthful environment for our children and staff. In addition, I'm expected to maintain good relationships with parents. Last, but not least, I have to operate our program legally at all times. It's very important to abide by state laws and to cooperate with state officials."

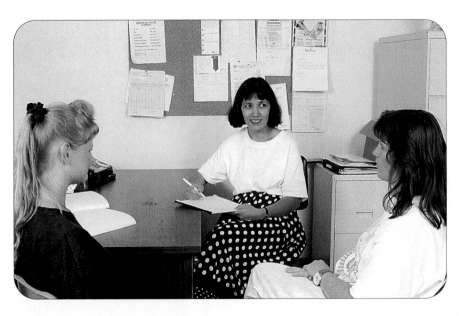

What is a typical day on the job like?

"No day is really typical for me! Directors have to be flexible. We do whatever it takes to keep the whole program running smoothly. Most mornings I greet families as they arrive. Later I visit each classroom to observe teachers and offer a helping hand. After lunch time I take kindergartners to school. Later I return phone calls and do billing or payroll. Around three o'clock I pick up school-age children from their schools. When it's needed, I also care for an ill child, substitute for a teacher, purchase supplies, or interview someone for a position."

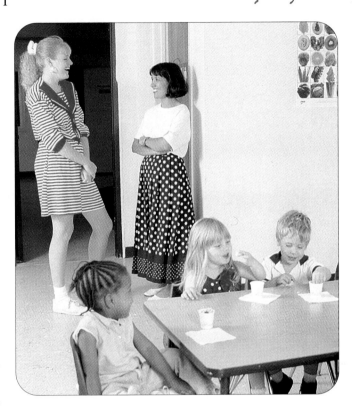

What is most challenging about your job?

"Working with people can be the best and the worst part of my job. For instance, it's hard telling an employee her work is poor. It's even harder to fire someone. Reminding parents to pay overdue bills is never fun. Interviewing and training new employees is time consuming. I wish we could pay people more than we are able to, but fortunately, enough people put a high priority on their desire to work with children. After all, caring for children is an important job!"

What is your favorite part of the job?

"Actually, I have many favorites. I love to see how children mature and grow. I enjoy conducting staff training workshops. Organizing parent programs is a creative part of my job. We offer 'family nights' where children, parents, and child care staff get together for fun and games. This helps build a partnership between parents and the child care center staff."

SHARE YOUR THOUGHTS

1. What personal qualities might help a person be an effective child care director?
2. Identify one of the challenges Consuella mentioned. Offer suggestions for making the task less difficult.
3. What part of being a director sounds most rewarding to you? What part would you like least?

SKILLS ON THE JOB

Reflections

"I'll never forget the first time I saw Corey. He was so thin. His nose was running, and he had no energy. Corey never smiled during the early weeks that he spent at our child care center. He didn't even talk much. When the other children were having fun, he was distanced from them—and from the staff. There was something about Corey, though, that touched me. I just had to get through to him, and I was sure I could. Not a day went by that I didn't make at least some small effort. Corey and I shared crackers and apple slices. Sometimes I sat close by during naptime. I read to him and hugged him. I showed him how to put log blocks together. Then one day I took out a little clown puppet. Corey's eyes widened as I spoke to him through the clown. A smile like I had never seen before came over his face. That was another day I'll never forget, because the world seemed to change for Corey from that day on—and it changed for me too."

—Erika

Chapter 14

Developing Professional Skills

CHAPTER OBJECTIVES

■ Describe the traits of a responsible employee.

■ Explain the importance of professional ethics.

■ Discuss guidelines for getting along with others on the job.

■ Give suggestions for managing time effectively.

■ Identify steps to take in solving problems.

■ Cite methods of handling stress.

Terms to Learn

- confidentiality
- dress codes
- professional
- professional ethics
- self-control
- time management

mi Komuro sat apart from the others, collecting her thoughts and calming the butterflies in her stomach. In a few moments, she would give the farewell speech honoring Lida Johnson. "What should I say?" she asked herself. Now that the evening had arrived, the words she had prepared didn't seem right. They seemed too formal, too impersonal.

Emi looked around the room, which was festive with balloons and streamers. On one wall, a banner proclaimed "Little Friends Preschool Honors Lida Johnson." A large cake, decorated with flowers and the words "Happy Retirement," was waiting to be served. Teachers and parents milled about, talking and laughing. At the center of it all, a silver-haired woman with an orchid corsage and a bright smile accepted their congratulations.

Like everyone else, Emi had grown to love Lida. She could list all kinds of qualities Lida had that people admired. "But it's more than that," Emi thought. Images started coming back to her—of Lida's arm around her shoulders after Emi made a serious mistake as a beginning teacher; of Lida's eyes watching her intently as she explained a problem; of the tears of laughter that came when she and Lida shared stories one evening after the children had gone home.

As Emi sat deep in thought, her eyes came to rest on one of the children's books displayed in the book rack. It was one of Lida's favorites. In it a little rabbit taught the other animals in the forest a message about love and communication. "Say what's in your heart," the rabbit had said. At that moment, Emi found the words she wanted.

THE IMPORTANCE OF WORKPLACE SKILLS

Throughout her career in child care, Lida Johnson became more than just an employee. She brought character, warmth, and knowledge to her work. She became a true **professional**. In other words, *she not only possessed the expertise to do her job well, but she also had the skills and qualities that gained her the respect of employers and coworkers.*

What are the specific skills and qualities needed by child care professionals? One obvious answer is child care abilities. You need to be able to read a story to children in a way that captures their attention. You need to be able to plan a science activity that is organized and teaches a concept. While these abilities are certainly essential, you may be surprised to learn that other types of skills are just as important for success. They include the ability to maintain a positive attitude, get along with coworkers, manage your time, and solve problems. These and other workplace skills will help you every day on the job.

YOUR RESPONSIBILITIES

As a child care professional, you have a responsibility to the people you work for. In return for giving you pay and benefits, your employer has the right to expect certain things from you. One expectation, of course, is that you will perform the duties of your job to the best of your ability.

You are also expected to follow any guidelines and rules, such as those found in an employee handbook. Good employees do not ask for special favors, nor do they make excuses for not following the rules.

You must also meet certain basic expectations that apply to any job, whether they are spelled out in a handbook or not. Here are some examples.

A Positive Attitude

Among the best workers are those who have a positive attitude. People who have a positive attitude are energetic and enthusiastic. They look on the bright side of situations rather than focusing on the negative. Instead of complaining about problems, they view them as challenges to be met. They take pride in the quality of their work and are always looking for ways to improve.

A positive attitude is particularly important in the child care field. As a child care professional, you set the tone for children's daily experiences. A positive attitude provides children with an uplifting experience. In addition, staff and parent relationships go more smoothly if you have a "can do" attitude.

Dependability

How do people show dependability? Stella, a child care aide, has this quality. She leaves for work about 15 minutes early each day. That way she always arrives at the center on time, even if traffic is moving slowly.

In order for a child care program to run smoothly, every employee needs to be dependable. What are other examples of dependability on the job?

She knows the children look forward to seeing her each morning and would be disappointed if she were not there to greet them.

Stella also knows that when she is absent, the other employees have to work that much harder. If she cannot work when she is scheduled to, she lets the director know as far in advance as possible. Stella, however, is rarely absent. That pleases the director, who needs employees that can be counted on. The parents, too, appreciate Stella's attendance. They know their children are getting consistent care.

FOCUS ON INFANT/TODDLER PROGRAMS

Being a dependable employee is especially important in infant and toddler programs. At this critical stage of life, forming a close attachment to a primary caregiver is essential for emotional and social development. Such an attachment can be formed only when an employee accepts the responsibility of regular work attendance.

Stella is a reliable and dependable employee. Would an employer be able to say the same about you?

Appropriate Dress and Grooming

Your appearance makes a statement. It shows how you feel about yourself and your job. Proper dress and grooming convey a professional image to your employer, coworkers, parents, and program visitors.

A professional appearance starts with good grooming. You should arrive at work clean, with teeth brushed and hair neatly combed. A well-groomed appearance provides children with a healthy role model.

Dress codes, or *rules for workplace dress*, vary from one program to another. In general, clothing should be clean and in good repair. It should also provide adequate coverage for modesty. If T-shirts are allowed, avoid those with inappropriate pictures or slogans. For example, a shirt advertising alcohol or cigarettes should not be worn in a child care facility.

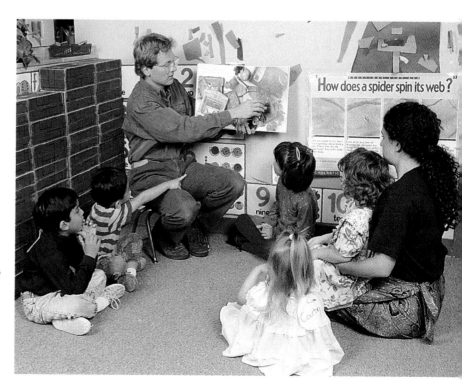

Appropriate dress combines a professional image with the demands of the job. Each program sets its own standards.

Clothing worn to work should also be practical. Because you may spend time on the floor playing with children, your clothing should allow you to move comfortably. It should be easily cleaned so that you do not have to worry about sand and playground dirt. Avoid jewelry that poses a safety hazard, such as a long necklace or hoop earrings that a child could pull.

Honesty

Suppose you were the director of a child care center. How would you feel if you found out that one of the teachers had lied on her job application? You would probably wonder what else she had lied to you about. You would wonder if she could be trusted to work with children.

Lying is one example of dishonest behavior that can lead to dismissal from a job. Stealing is another. Working for a business does not give you the right to "borrow" from the cash register or take company supplies for your personal use.

Some dishonest workers steal their employer's time. They spend time daydreaming, gossiping, or tending to personal business when they should be working. Remember, you are paid to do your job for a certain number of hours each day. During that time, you should be productive. While you are at work, give full attention to your duties. Save personal business for breaks, lunchtime, and nonwork hours.

Initiative

Workers who show initiative are valued. They have a willingness to perform tasks without being told. When people with initiative notice that something needs to be done, they go ahead and do it. For instance, Alissa noticed that some of the children's smocks had tears in the seams. The next day, she arrived a few minutes early with a needle and thread and repaired the smocks. The other teachers appreciated Alissa's quick action.

You might show initiative by volunteering to take on additional responsibilities, such as creating a new bulletin board. You can also show initiative by attending workshops or college classes to acquire new knowledge and skills.

Initiative is not always appropriate, however. If you see that something needs to be done, ask yourself whether you have the skills, experience, or authority to do it yourself. If not, you should notify your supervisor of the situation.

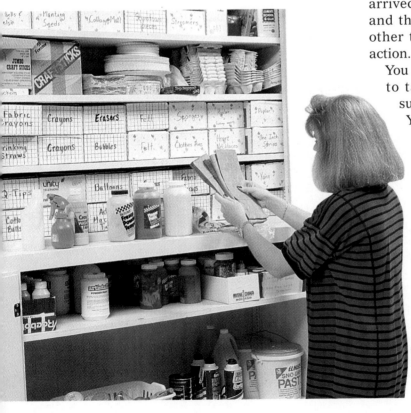

What would happen if no one took the initiative to straighten the supply room or check for broken toys?

What kinds of confidential information might be available to only a few staff members?

Professional Ethics

As a child care professional, you will sometimes have to make a choice based on moral principles and values. Kayla, for example, faced such a situation one afternoon shortly after she began working at a child care center. Most of the children were already gone when one of the parents, Mr. Fischer, stopped to talk. "I live next door to Joshua Reed's family," he said. "Gee, it's too bad about Joshua. I mean, it's pretty obvious something's wrong with him. It's some kind of emotional problem, right?"

"Well, actually. . . " Kayla began, then stopped herself. She had been about to explain that Joshua wasn't really emotional-ly disturbed, even though his behavior was sometimes a problem. Then she had remembered an important guideline for child care professionals. "Actually, it's not right for me to talk about that," Kayla continued. "I'd be happy to discuss any questions you have about your child's behavior, but I have to keep information about other children private. I'm sure you understand."

Kayla had to choose between showing a helpful attitude toward Mr. Fischer and protecting the privacy of the Reed family. Her decision was made easier by her clear sense of professional ethics. **Professional ethics** refer to *standards of right and wrong that apply to your behavior as a professional.* The way you conduct yourself on the job and carry out your responsibilities should be guided by professional ethics at all times.

Ethical standards are like road signs. When faced with a dilemma, a clear set of guiding principles can point you toward the right path. In Kayla's situation, the guiding principle was **confidentiality**, or *maintaining the privacy of others.* Kayla understood that personal information about children, families, and coworkers should not be shared without their consent.

The National Association for the Education of Young Children (NAEYC) has developed a written ethics statement called the "Code of Ethical Conduct." The code addresses four areas: responsibilities to children, to families, to colleagues, and to the community and society. Some examples of the principles set forth in the code are on page 274.

Excerpts from the Code of Ethical Conduct
National Association for the Education of Young Children

Section I: Ethical Responsibilities to Children

- Above all, we shall not harm children. We shall not participate in practices that are disrespectful, degrading, dangerous, exploitative, intimidating, psychologically damaging, or physically harmful to children...

- We shall involve all of those with relevant knowledge (including staff and parents) in decisions concerning a child...

- When, after appropriate efforts have been made with a child and the family, the child still does not appear to be benefitting from a program, we shall communicate our concern to the family in a positive way and offer them assistance in finding a more suitable setting...

- We shall be familiar with the symptoms of child abuse and neglect and know community procedures for addressing them...

Section II: Ethical Responsibilities to Families

- We shall not deny family members access to their child's classroom or program setting...

- We shall inform families of program philosophy, policies, and personnel qualifications, and explain why we teach as we do...

- Families shall be fully informed of any proposed research projects involving their children and shall have the opportunity to give or withhold consent...

- We shall not use our relationship with a family for private advantage or personal gain...

- We shall maintain confidentiality and shall respect the family's right to privacy...

Section III: Ethical Responsibilities to Colleagues

- When we have a concern about the professional behavior of a coworker, we shall first let that person know of our concern and attempt to resolve the matter...

- When we do not agree with program policies, we shall first attempt to effect change through constructive action within the organization...

- Employees who do not meet program standards shall be informed of areas of concern and, when possible, assisted in improving their performance...

- Hiring and promotion shall be based solely on a person's record of accomplishment and ability to carry out the responsibilities of the position...

Section IV: Ethical Responsibilities to Community and Society

- We shall communicate openly and truthfully about the nature and extent of services that we provide...

- We shall cooperate with other professionals who work with children and their families...

- We shall not participate in practices which are in violation of laws and regulations that protect the children in our programs...

Certain ethical standards apply to any profession, whether or not they are part of a written code of conduct. What happened to Bob, a kindergarten teacher, is an example. One day he and Sheila, another teacher at the school, discussed several ideas for a musical presentation to be given on Parents' Night. Later, Sheila described one of the ideas to the principal. Although Bob had originally suggested the idea, Sheila chose not to mention this. When the principal complimented her for being so creative, Sheila just smiled and thanked him. What do you think of Sheila's professional ethics? Would you want her for a coworker?

Child care professionals who abide by ethical standards earn the respect of the people they work for, coworkers, parents, and community members. They are able to respect themselves as well.

GETTING ALONG ON THE JOB

*M*any employees do not realize that "people skills" are just as important as technical skills. The fact is, your ability to work well with others has a great deal to do with your success on the job. This is true in any occupation, but especially in a child care setting.

Communication

Have you ever been angry or hurt over something a friend said, only to discover later that it was all a misunderstanding? Most likely, what your friend meant and what you thought you heard were two different things. Good communication skills can help prevent such problems. That's important to remember when you converse with your supervisor, coworkers, parents of children in the program, and anyone else.

Communicating effectively includes the ability to express yourself clearly. Speak distinctly in a pleasant tone of voice. Put yourself in the listener's place and provide enough information for clear understanding.

Equally important is the ability to listen. Let the person speak without interruption. Focus on what the speaker is saying, and show genuine interest. When the speaker has finished, summarize what was said to be sure you understand the message. By brushing up on your speaking and listening skills, you can help pave the way for smooth working relationships.

Unlike most occupations, the child care profession requires that you communicate well with children as well as adults. Understanding children's

If you have difficulty remembering what you are told, slip a notepad and pen in your pocket to jot down reminders. In many situations, such as giving medication to a child, following through accurately is essential.

THE MULTICULTURAL CLASSROOM

A true professional knows how to work well with people of all cultures. This may mean becoming familiar with other customs and standards. If you don't, miscommunication may lead to negative feelings.

In some cultures, for example, looking into a teacher's eyes when the teacher is speaking to you is thought to be disrespectful. Contrast this to the North American practice of establishing eye contact when communicating with others. Likewise, body language is not universal. A gesture that has an "obvious"

meaning to you may have an entirely different meaning in another culture. The hand motion for waving good-bye in some parts of Mexico looks like the "come back" gesture to the North American. In some Asian cultures, it is considered extremely rude to point a finger at someone, even if you are counting children or making motions to a song.

Interpreters can help identify what might cause confusion. You can also read about other cultures as well as keep the lines of communication open with families.

needs, desires, and moods calls for careful listening and observation. What you say to children, and how you say it, affects both their behavior and their emotional well-being. Chapter 15 gives guidelines to help you interact with children effectively.

Communicating with parents is another important responsibility of child care professionals. You can find suggestions for communicating with parents on pages 278-279.

Cooperation and Teamwork

A basketball or soccer team wouldn't win many games if one player was sent out to do all the work. Similarly, a child care program cannot run smoothly without the cooperation of all staff members. They must work together as a team to accomplish more than any of them could alone.

As a member of the team, you must be willing to do your fair share of the work. Perform the tasks that are assigned to you to the best of your ability, without stalling or

complaining. Offer to assist others if you see they could use some help.

Communication and teamwork go hand-in-hand. Child care professionals who take the time to communicate with each other tend to work together better. Regular staff meetings are the most effective way to insure ongoing communication. All staff members must understand how tasks are being divided and what their assignments are. They must also make sure they are in agreement about general matters, such as the goals of the program. Meetings also give staff members a chance to share ideas and stay informed about new developments.

Teams often work best when they rotate weekly responsibilities so that no one person tires of a particular job. For instance, team members may take turns reading at story time. Cleaning the sand and water play area and creating bulletin boards are other jobs that can be rotated. This style of cooperation shows consideration for all staff members.

Building Professional Skills

Diplomacy

WHAT IS DIPLOMACY?

Diplomacy is the ability to communicate without causing anger, hurt feelings, or other negative reactions. Diplomacy requires both personal and technical skills. You must be able to understand how others feel about your message and to anticipate possible responses. You must also be able to express yourself well, using honest but not offensive statements. The reward of learning diplomacy is better personal and professional relationships.

Diplomacy in Action

Daniel loaded the last of the soccer equipment into his car. Nearby the father of one of his young players waited. Daniel collected his thoughts, and then approached him.

"Hello, Mr. Hesketh. You know your son is turning into quite a soccer player."

"Well, he should be," Mr. Hesketh replied. "I make sure he practices at least three times during the week and on the weekend too."

"Your support is important," Daniel said. "I know it means a lot to Ross."

Mr. Hesketh appeared slightly embarrassed. "I just want him to do well. Sometimes that means pushing him a little. He has so much potential."

"He sure does," Daniel agreed. "In fact, sometimes I have to keep myself from overcoaching him."

"Overcoaching?" Mr. Hesketh repeated slowly.

Daniel nodded. "That's a mistake I've made too often. When you see someone as good as Ross is, you want to do everything to help him be the best. You push him a little harder, because you want him to succeed. Sometimes, though, kids get confused and frustrated from trying to do everything right, all at once. They get hurt physically or forget that other things are important, like family and friends. Either way, it all works against us in the end. So sometimes I have to remind myself that Ross has plenty of time to learn."

Mr. Hesketh looked thoughtful. "That's an interesting point."

Just then Ross joined them. "I shouldn't have missed that goal," he began. "I let their guys get me out of position and . . ."

"Don't worry about it," his father interrupted. "You're learning. These things take time." He and Daniel exchanged knowing smiles.

Your Analysis

1. What concern was Daniel trying to express to Mr. Hesketh? Why did he need diplomacy to explain this concern?

2. Cite two specific examples of Daniel's use of diplomacy. For each example, give one way he might have expressed himself that would have produced a negative response in Mr. Hesketh.

3. Describe a situation in your own life when you had to use a diplomatic approach.

Communicating with Parents

Children benefit when child care professionals and parents work as a team by sharing information. Parents want to know how their children are getting along at the center, what they have accomplished, and whether there are any special problems. Caregivers need insight into how home life may be affecting classroom behavior. Through regular communication, a trusting relationship builds between parents and staff.

There are many ways to communicate with parents. Here are some of the most common methods, along with suggestions for their use.

INFORMAL CONVERSATION

Arrival and departure times are ideal opportunities for brief, informal conversation with parents. At arrival time, parents may have helpful information to share—for example, "Nikki's grandparents were visiting last night, so we let her stay up a little later than usual." At departure time, let parents know how the day went. You might say "Jeremy tied his shoes without help today" or "Katrina is eager to tell you about how we planted flower seeds." Remember that the child, as well as other children and parents, may be listening. Avoid making negative comments or discussing confidential matters.

BRIEF NOTES

In some situations, you may also need to give parents a written note when they come to pick up their child. For example, if a child has a bruised knee after a fall on the playground, the parent needs an accurate report of what occurred. Informal notes may be written daily to expand information given in conversation.

PARENT-TEACHER CONFERENCES

More formal meetings between parents and child care professionals should be scheduled on a regular basis, such as once or twice a year. These conferences give the teacher a chance to share information about the child's progress and any areas that need improvement. They also give parents an opportunity to ask questions and discuss any concerns of their own.

Here are some guidelines for conducting a parent-teacher conference:

- Try to find a time that is convenient for the parents.

- Let parents know that they will be able to bring up any questions or concerns they may have.

- Prepare for the meeting by reviewing records of the child's behavior and progress. Identify the topics you would like to discuss.

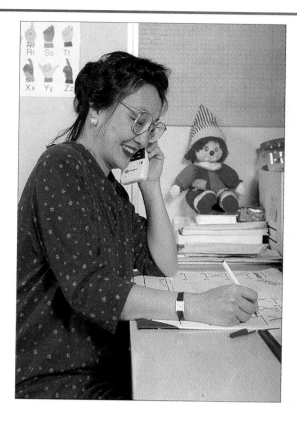

- At the meeting, help parents feel at ease by greeting them in a friendly, respectful manner.

- Start by focusing on the child's strengths. Discuss areas in which the child is doing well or has shown improvement. Share specific examples to illustrate your points.

- When bringing up problems or concerns, avoid labeling the child or criticizing the parent. If you say, "Paige is a troublemaker who has obviously been allowed to run wild," the parent will probably take offense. It is much better to say, "Paige finds it difficult to sit and listen quietly during story time." Not only is this statement more positive, it is more clear.

- Suggest ways that the parents and child care staff can work together to help the child improve.

- Listen carefully to what parents have to say. Make sure you understand their concerns. For example, one father told his son's child care teacher, "Malcom says the other kids make fun of the way he talks." The teacher responded, "Are you concerned about the fact that Malcom is being teased?" The father replied, "A little, but I'm more worried that Malcom may have a speech problem." Knowing this, the teacher was better able to respond in a way that would reassure the parent.

- Take the opportunity to learn more about the child and the parents. Ask such questions as, "Does Mei-ling seem to look forward to coming to the center each day?"

- End the discussion on a positive note. Be sure to thank parents for coming.

TELEPHONE CALLS

Between regularly scheduled conferences, occasional telephone calls can help keep caregivers and parents in touch. Telephone calls are a good way to share brief, positive messages. When a teacher calls just to say "I'm proud of the way Jorge is improving at getting along with others," both the parent and the child feel encouraged.

NEWSLETTERS

Many child care programs send home a weekly "Dear Parents" letter. This is a good way to keep all parents informed of the program's activities. A typical letter might include a list of learning experiences and special events planned for the coming week. It might also suggest activities for parents and children to enjoy at home. In addition to providing weekly letters, some child care programs publish a larger monthly newsletter.

You will receive feedback on your work in many ways—through formal reviews, comments from parents and coworkers, and by observing how children respond to your care.

Respect and Courtesy

You won't get very far in any job if you treat your supervisor in a disrespectful or rude manner. The same is true of your relationship with your coworkers. Treat them with professional respect, just as you would like to be treated.

The parents of children enrolled in the program also deserve your courtesy. If you need to discuss a problem with a parent, be tactful. Don't say, "You've done a terrible job of teaching your child manners." Instead, you might say, "I've noticed that Jacob doesn't want to sit at the table for meals. We have a rule in the center that says children must sit down to eat. I'd like to discuss some ways we might work together to change Jacob's behavior."

Accepting Feedback

As part of your job, you will periodically receive feedback, or comments on your work performance, from your supervisor. Feedback can be very helpful to you. It is one way for you to judge how well you are doing your job. It also gives you an opportunity to learn how you can improve.

One child care aide in a preschool sought feedback to make improvements. Becky was reading the children a story during group time. Her supervisor, Mr. Rodriguez, sat quietly in the background and watched. Halfway through the story, the children became restless and distracted. Afterwards, Becky wondered whether Mr. Rodriguez would think she was not very good at working with children. Rather than worrying about it, however, she decided to ask Mr. Rodriguez to give her suggestions for improvement. Mr. Rodriguez shared several helpful tips for making stories more interesting to children. Not only did Becky learn new methods for effective storytelling, she also showed Mr. Rodriguez that she is willing to develop her skills.

If your supervisor criticizes some aspect of your work, resist the urge to become angry or defensive. Remember, the criticism is not meant as an attack on you personally. It is intended to help you learn and improve.

Listen carefully and try to understand the reasons behind the comments. If something is not clear to you, politely ask for further explanation. At the end of the conversation, say something like, "Thank you for bringing this to my attention. From now on, I'll be more careful about how I set up the learning centers." Then follow through.

Giving Feedback

Remember that it is up to the supervisor, not you, to evaluate your coworkers. If a coworker asks you for feedback, however, you may offer helpful suggestions. Express your thoughts and feelings in a positive, nonjudgmental way. Avoid demeaning or attacking the person.

Suppose one of your coworkers said to you: "You're so irresponsible. You never put the art materials back where they belong. Because of you I won't be able to do my art activity today." Your feelings would probably be hurt right away. Comments like these don't encourage you to remedy the problem very quickly. On the other hand, suppose your coworker said: "It's frustrating when I can't find the art materials I need for activities. Can we all agree to make a bigger effort to put them back in the right places?" In this case, you would probably be more willing to cooperate to solve the problem. Since your character wasn't attacked, the relationship between you and your coworker will likely remain friendly and respectful. Follow this approach when you give feedback to others.

Remember, feedback can include compliments as well as criticism. Anytime you notice that a coworker is doing an especially good job, let the person know. A sincere word of

praise goes a long way in establishing a good working relationship. Simply taking the time to say, "I really admired the way you encouraged Lonnie to come out of his shell today," lets coworkers feel appreciated and valued. Everyone needs a pat on the back sometimes.

Minimizing Conflict

Almost nothing ruins the positive atmosphere of a workplace faster than a disagreement between workers. If two employees are constantly snapping at each other, or have stopped speaking at all, everyone suffers. These suggestions can help minimize conflict:

- Keep lines of communication open.
- Resolve small differences right away, before they can grow into major conflicts.
- Keep discussions positive. Address issues, not personalities.
- Don't jump to conclusions. Give people a chance to explain their side of the story.

While working in a preschool program, for example, Isaiah had trouble getting along with one coworker. Fran treated him abruptly and never had a kind word to say. They often came close to arguments in front of the children. Finally, Isaiah suggested that they meet after school one day to talk. Through frank discussion, they resolved some issues on their own. Now their regular pizza night each month gives them a chance to work through problems. With greater understanding between them, they have more respect for each other when their points of view differ.

Tip FROM THE *Pros*

*W*hen addressing a problem with a coworker, pick a good place and time for the discussion. Find a private area where you can talk freely. Select a time that will not interfere with your work responsibilities. Make sure you will have adequate time for each of you to express your views.

Have you ever forgotten to do an important task, or suddenly realized you need to be in two places at once? Time management skills can help you avoid such problems.

FACING DAY-TO-DAY CHALLENGES

*T*he child care profession is a rewarding one, but it is also full of challenges. The days are often hectic. The outdoor game you plan may have to be cancelled because of rain. One child may accidentally knock a jar of paint to the floor while another is having a temper tantrum. You may feel tired and frustrated. After the children have gone home for the day, you somehow have to find time to plan the following week's activities.

Every job has its especially challenging times. The key is to find effective ways to meet the challenges. The sections that follow suggest strategies that can help.

Managing Your Time

"Oh no—I'm late for work again!" Tony hurried out the door with his shoes untied and his shirt untucked. He had thought that getting up at 6:30 a.m. would give him plenty of time. That was before he remembered his promise to give his plans for a woodworking activity to the director today. "I would have been on time if I hadn't had to work on those plans," he decided. "It's not really my fault I'm late." What do you think of Tony's excuse?

Tony could have avoided this problem if he had been more skilled in using his time wisely. He needs to learn about **time management**—*planning to make the best use of time in order to accomplish goals.*

Time management is an important job skill. It helps you prepare for tasks, meet deadlines, and make a larger contribution to your workplace. Time management is also important in your personal life. It allows you to fit in all the people and activities that are most important to you and still have some time just for yourself.

Everyone has the same 24 hours in a day. Those who accomplish the most in those hours have learned to spend their time wisely. To manage your time successfully, try these tips:

- **Set specific goals.** Write down what you need or want to accomplish. Your list will probably include both short-term goals (things to do tomorrow or this week) and long-term goals (what you want to accomplish in the coming months or years).

- **Plan how to meet your goals.** For instance, a child care director might plan to send a classroom newsletter to parents. To do this, the director selects a specific date to sit down and create the newsletter. A deadline, a week before this date, is also set for all teachers to submit classroom news.

- **Use a calendar.** Write down due dates for school and work assignments as soon as they are given to you. Make a note of meetings, appointments, and other events scheduled for a particular time.

- **Make a "to do" list.** Each evening, make a list of the tasks you will try to accomplish the next day. Assign each item a priority— "A" for tasks that *must* be done that day, "B" for tasks that *should* be done if at all possible, and "C" for tasks that *may* be done if you have time. The next day, focus on getting the "A" tasks done first. As you complete each task, cross it off your list. This gives you a great feeling of accomplishment.

- **Eliminate the "time-wasters" in your life.** Have you ever spent an hour flipping television channels, even though you were bored by the programs? Could you have put that time to better use? Identify what activities waste your time and try to eliminate them.

- **Combine activities when possible.** For instance, Aleta Brown, a child care teacher, writes notes to parents during the children's nap time. She plans the next week's lessons while she is at the laundromat. Combining activities helps her use time more efficiently.

When you make the most of all your waking hours, you are able to accomplish more. By using time well, you will be able to meet your employment obligations and still have a rewarding personal life.

Staying Flexible

"The one thing you can count on is that you can't count on anything." This saying is humorous, but it illustrates an important point. No matter how carefully you plan the day's activities, something may happen that you didn't expect. Sudden changes in plans require flexibility on your part. You must be willing and able to adapt to new situations.

Flexibility calls for quick thinking. It also calls for preparedness. Successful people learn to anticipate possible problems and have a backup plan in mind. For instance, when Seth planned a field trip for his preschool class and it was time to leave, the school bus had not yet arrived. Seth kept the children occupied with a guessing game and a song. Fifteen minutes later, the bus finally arrived and the field trip went on as planned. If Seth had not been prepared for the delay, the children would probably have become restless and out of control while they waited for the bus. Planning and preparation allow child care professionals to handle the unexpected with confidence.

Maintaining Self-Control

Everyone experiences strong emotions at times. How would you feel if a child called you a name and kicked you on the shin? Most people would feel hurt and angry. If you saw smoke and flames coming from the room across the hall, you would have feelings of fear and alarm. There is nothing wrong with such feelings—they are natural under the circumstances.

Part of being a professional, however, is learning how to practice self-control in situations such as these. **Self-control** is *the abili-*

> Child care professionals must learn to respond to children's anger without becoming angry themselves.

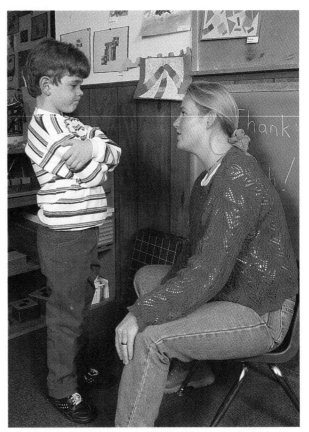

ty to react to difficult situations in a calm, productive manner instead of an emotional one. Self-control does not mean that you don't have negative emotions. It simply means that you, not your emotions, are in control of how you behave.

During an emergency, such as a fire, self-control helps you stay calm. It enables you to think clearly and take the appropriate action. Seeing that you are calm and confident, children feel more secure. If, on the other hand, your reaction is one of panic and confusion, the situation only becomes worse.

When you are angry, self-control can keep you from doing something hurtful that you would regret later. *Never take your anger out on a child.* The child who kicks you on the shin is dealing with his or her own anger and frustration in the only way the child knows how. You, however, are mature enough to practice self-control. As a professional, you must learn to react in a calm, but firm manner. (Chapter 15 provides information on appropriate ways to respond to a child's misbehavior.)

If you feel yourself starting to lose your self-control, stop and take a deep breath. Then think before you act.

Using Problem-Solving Skills

The ability to solve problems is important in every job. When working in child care, problems arise every day. Some are large problems, such as how to calm parents when their child has been bitten by a two-year-old. Others are small, such as not having enough napkins for lunch time.

Most problems require fast thinking and a quick solution. This is why it is so important for caregivers to have training before they become responsible for a group of children. Quick decisions will be wiser decisions if you have been adequately educated and prepared to face problems typically encountered in child care.

To help you meet challenges more effectively, remember this six-step problem-solving process:

1. ***Identify the problem.*** What is happening? Assess the situation quickly and calmly. Carefully listen to what is being said or observe what is being done.

2. ***Explore possible solutions.*** Think of several ways the problem might be solved.

3. ***Evaluate each possible solution.*** Anticipate the positive and negative effects of each course of action.

4. ***Choose the best solution.*** Decide which possibility will best solve the problem with the fewest negative effects.

5. ***Carry out the solution.*** Sometimes this can be done quickly and easily. In other cases, you may need to develop a plan of action.

6. ***Evaluate the solution.*** Has your solution improved the situation? Has it created new problems? You may have to choose another solution and try it out.

Now you have an organized way to meet the challenges you face in child care. Before trying to solve a problem, be sure you have the authority, knowledge, and experience to make the necessary decisions. If you don't, obtain assistance from a coworker or the director as soon as possible.

Handling Stress

Whenever you experience tension, worry, strain, or even intense excitement, you are experiencing stress. Stress can result from many different situations in life, both positive and negative. Worrying about an upcoming test, ending a close relationship, and moving to a new town are all examples of stressful situations. The everyday challenges of working in a child care program can also be stressful at times.

In itself, stress is not necessarily bad. In fact, life without stress of any kind would be bland and dull. When stress is continuous or severe, however, it can lead to health problems. People who are under a lot of stress may have frequent headaches, backaches, or neck pain. They may lose their appetite or have digestive trouble. Some people become moody or depressed and find it hard to concentrate. If stress becomes overwhelming, job performance may be impaired. In child care, this could put children at risk.

You cannot avoid all stressful situations; however, you can learn to cope better with stress so that it does not affect your physical and emotional health. Here are some suggestions for handling stress:

- ***Practice good health habits.*** Be sure to eat right, get enough sleep, and exercise regularly.

- ***Find time to relax.*** Use the time management skills you read about earlier. Even a ten-minute break of peace and quiet can help give you a new outlook.

- ***Maintain at least a few close friendships.*** Talking to a friend who really cares can work wonders.

- ***Don't expect too much of yourself.*** Be realistic about what you can accomplish with the time, energy, and abilities you have. Ask others to lend a hand when needed—they will probably be glad to help.

- ***Look for ways to reduce unnecessary stress.*** For example, if you are bothered by excess noise and chaos during play time, talk to the director. Perhaps the schedule or learning centers need to be organized differently.

- ***Seek help when stress becomes overwhelming.*** Talk to your physician or a professional counselor. They can offer many helpful suggestions. (Students can be helped by school counselors.)

Remember, everyone experiences stress at one time or another. If you learn to handle stress well now, you will be better equipped to handle stress in a child care setting. You will be glad you did.

YOUR PROFESSIONAL SUCCESS

As you have probably realized, you will not achieve professional success overnight. Fortunately, you are not expected to. Rather, the skills and traits that lead to professional success are acquired like any other: through time, commitment, and practice. Each day offers more opportunities to refine these qualities. Make the most of them.

Chapter 14 Review

Chapter Summary

- Employees who demonstrate a positive attitude and a sense of responsibility to their employer are valued in the workplace.
- Professionals conduct themselves according to a code of ethics.
- Getting along with others on the job requires communication, cooperation, and respect.
- Time management skills can help you meet professional and personal obligations.
- Solving problems is easier with a step-by-step approach.
- Flexibility, self-control, and the ability to cope with stress are important for child care professionals.

Reviewing the Facts

1. Why is it especially important for child care professionals to have a positive attitude?
2. How does an employee show initiative?
3. What is meant by professional ethics? Give an example of behavior addressed in a code of ethics.
4. Name two ways to encourage cooperation and teamwork among child care professionals.
5. How should you react if your employer offers you a suggestion for improvement?
6. List four tips for effective time management.
7. Why must child care professionals practice self-control?
8. List the six steps in the problem-solving process.
9. Name three possible symptoms of excessive stress.
10. Give three guidelines for coping with stress.

Thinking Critically

1. Identify some "symptoms" of a negative attitude. How might these affect the children at a center? How might it affect other workers?
2. Suppose you were the director of a child care center. One of your employees does an excellent job but is often late. How would you react?
3. Do you think dress codes are necessary in child care programs? Why or why not?
4. Why is initiative valued by employers?
5. What principles would you include in a code of ethical conduct? Why?
6. Suppose you are one of two teacher's aides in a child care classroom. You feel the other aide is not doing her fair share. When two children have a conflict, for instance, she pretends not to notice or to be busy with something else. You are growing tired of handling every situation yourself. The teacher does not seem to be aware of the problem. To whom would you bring up your concern, and why? What would you say? What if that did not solve the problem?
7. When budgeting your time, why is it wise to set both short-term and long-term goals?

Activities and Applications

1. **Want Ad.** Assume you are the director of a child care center. Create a want ad describing the qualities you desire in an employee.

2. **Positive Communication.** Work in teams to create a skit portraying positive communication skills between a caregiver and parent.

3. **Coping with Stress.** Using current magazines and newspapers, locate articles on methods of identifying and coping with stress. Report your findings to the class.

Your Professional Portfolio

During a job interview, you may be asked to describe your strengths and weaknesses. Start preparing now by writing a self-analysis. First, describe in writing three characteristics or skills that you feel are your strong points. Then choose a characteristic that is one of your weaker areas. List at least three steps you can take to improve in this area. Place the completed self-analysis in your portfolio. Refer to it periodically to check your progress.

Observing and Analyzing

Professionals at Work

Reading about professional skills is a good way to learn about them. Seeing them demonstrated in real life, however, can make you appreciate them even more.

Much of what you learn comes from experience and observation. When you see the way other people handle things, you discover what works well and what does not. You learn that some qualities and actions are worth imitating. Following the examples of successful people that you admire can contribute to your own success.

You can use your observation skills to help you achieve a very useful goal—becoming a valued employee. Look for the lessons that go on around you in everyday life. Then use them to your advantage. The ideas below will get you started:

- **Identifying Skills and Qualities.** Think of three or more people you admire that you are around on a regular basis while they are working. These might be people like school personnel, store clerks, medical professionals, and people you work with if you have a part-time job. For each

person, begin a list of specific actions you see that demonstrate the skills described in this chapter. Add to the lists for a designated period of time, perhaps two to four weeks. Then analyze your observations. What qualities, actions, and skills that you would like to imitate stand out in your mind?

- **Professional Skills.** Observe the staff at a child care facility. Record examples of any of the following positive work habits that you see: appropriate dress; initiative; good communication skills; cooperation; respect or courtesy; giving or accepting feedback; flexibility; and self-control.

- **Communicating with Parents.** Observe a child care program at arrival or departure time. Record the types of information shared by parents and teachers and the words used by both. Note the reactions as messages are received. Review your findings and look for a relationship between ways of communicating and the responses they produce.

Chapter 15

Guiding
Children

CHAPTER OBJECTIVES

- Identify the goals of classroom guidance.
- Describe effective techniques for communicating with young children.
- Distinguish between punishment and positive discipline.
- Distinguish between effective and ineffective methods of discipline.
- Describe ways in which caregivers can guide children's emotional, social, and moral development.
- Suggest approaches for guiding especially troubled children.

Terms to Learn

- active listening
- body language
- consequences
- I-message
- positive discipline
- positive reinforcement
- redirection
- self-discipline
- time out

Just as Larry heard the laughter, he felt the water droplets on his arm. Larry Dunbar was a teacher's aide in the Carlyle County Preschool. Turning toward the source of the laughter, he saw two four-year-olds at the nearby water table.

"Your baby needs a shower," Tyler said as he splashed water toward Brittany and her doll.

"Your baby's in the rain," Brittany laughed as she sent back a spray of water with equal vigor.

The water play was obviously fun, but it was getting out of hand. Larry had to step in.

"Guess what, Brittany—Tyler?" Larry said. "Rain is for outdoors and showers are for bathrooms. This is the water table. What's it for?"

"Not for splashing," Brittany responded.

"That's right," Larry continued calmly. "We have some rules, don't we? Can you tell me what they are?"

"The water stays in," Brittany answered.

"Wipe up spills," added Tyler.

"You know what to do," Larry said matter-of-factly. He watched the two children as they took paper towels to dry off the floor and the edge of the table. "That's nice and dry," he said with a smile when the children were done. "No one will slip on this floor. Now, these babies of yours need to either finish their bath without splashing or put on some warm clothes. Which will it be?"

GOALS FOR GUIDANCE

Brittany and Tyler are not "bad" children. Like all young children, they are just beginning to learn acceptable ways of behaving. They must struggle to cope with their emotions and control their impulses. Along the way, they need the guidance of caring adults.

In the child care setting, guidance serves several purposes. One is to maintain safety and order in the classroom. This might be considered the short-term goal of classroom guidance. For example, establishing a rule against running indoors helps insure that no one gets hurt. It also contributes to an appropriate atmosphere for learning.

Guidance also has long-term goals. Children need guidance so they can learn to share, take turns, and resolve conflicts peacefully. Positive guidance helps children develop such traits as kindness, courtesy, respect for themselves and others, cooperation, independence, and responsibility. One of the most important goals of positive guidance is to help children develop **self-discipline**—*the ability to guide one's own behavior without help from others.* As you can see, guidance is closely related to emotional, social, and moral development.

Classroom Goals

*W*hen deciding how to guide behavior, teachers think about their goals for children. The staff may discuss and agree on specific goals, perhaps a list like this one.

Children will . . .
- Not engage in any activity that might cause harm to themselves or to others.

- Respect their own rights and the rights and feelings of others.
- Treat classroom equipment and materials with care.
- Learn to make some decisions for themselves.
- Learn that they can solve some problems and conflicts on their

own instead of asking an adult to do it for them.
- Develop self-control so that words, instead of hitting, are used to solve problems and express emotions.
- Maintain positive self-esteem.

COMMUNICATING WITH CHILDREN

*T*o provide guidance, caregivers must know how to communicate with children effectively. Skilled child care professionals are able to relate to children in a warm, natural way.

Talking to Children

The way you speak to children can make a difference in their behavior, their relationship with you, and their feelings about themselves. When talking to children, follow these guidelines:

- Kneel or sit at the children's eye level. This helps hold their attention and allows them to see your facial expressions.
- Maintain eye contact.

When you position yourself at the children's level, you can communicate with them more effectively.

- When giving a child directions or asking a question, first address the child by name. This will gain the child's attention for more purposeful listening.
- Speak in a clear, respectful, and expressive voice. A "sing-song" or "sugar-coated" voice is not appealing.
- When responding to inappropriate behavior, use a calm, direct, matter-of-fact tone. Do not shout or speak harshly to children.
- Use simple words and short sentences. When messages are too long or complex, children have difficulty understanding.
- Use positive statements whenever possible. Children quickly become discouraged if everything they are told begins with "Don't..." or "Stop..." or "You shouldn't..." Some examples of positive communication are provided below.

Listening to Children

Listening to children is a delightful experience. Their voices and faces are full of expression. The older they become, the more eager children are to share thoughts and ideas. The more you let them share, the more skilled they become at communicating.

Listening to children involves more than hearing what they say. To understand what children are thinking and feeling, also watch their **body language**—*the gestures, body movements, and facial expressions that help convey meaning.* A child who stops working on a jigsaw puzzle, frowns, folds his or her arms, and stomps away is sending a message. It may be: "I'm frustrated by this puzzle, and I don't want to work on it anymore." The saying "actions speak louder than words" is especially true of young children. Understanding children's nonverbal messages requires that you become a keen observer.

Active Listening

Imagine that you are four years old. You're painting a picture—the best one ever, and it's almost finished. You can't wait to

Positive Messages

SAY THIS. . .	INSTEAD OF THIS. . .
Hold on tightly.	Don't fall.
You may run *outside*.	Stop acting hyper.
Chairs are for sitting on.	Quit acting like you live in a zoo.
When you use your regular voice, I'll get your ball for you.	Don't whine like a baby.
Turn the pages gently.	Stop crumpling the pages.
Use your quiet voice.	No yelling!
When the blocks are on the shelf, we will go outside.	Quit dawdling.
The red brush goes in the red paint cup.	Don't you know how to do anything?

Focus on INFANT/TODDLER PROGRAMS

Infants communicate through crying and body language. Just as caregivers learn to distinguish what different cries mean, they can also interpret motions. When infants are tired of being held, for example, they turn their head away from the face of the caregiver to show disinterest. A responsive caregiver follows this cue and places the infant in a new situation. Caregivers who do not "read" cues accurately can frustrate babies.

Communicating to infants is also important. Talk to babies frequently, using exaggerated facial expressions. Applaud each achievement, whether it is taking a first step or finding a big toe for the first time. This builds the infants' self-esteem.

Toddlers are just beginning to speak with words. Much of their communication is still through body language. Raising the arms usually means a one-year-old wants to be picked up. Scrunched-up faces tell adults when toddlers don't like particular foods. To understand these messages, child care professionals must observe carefully.

take it home and show your family. Suddenly, somehow, a big blob of paint drips down the front of your picture. It's completely ruined. In your frustration, you scream, "I hate painting! I hate it!" and begin to sob. Which of the following would you want to hear from your teacher?

- "You don't mean that."
- "You should have been more careful."
- "It doesn't matter. You can paint another picture."
- "Crying about it won't help."
- "Cheer up—it doesn't look that bad."

Statements like these are not very comforting, are they? These messages are telling you what you *should* have done or what you *should* be feeling. They don't acknowledge what *did* happen and what you *are* feeling.

When children are upset, they want someone to respond with understanding and acceptance. Teachers can provide that acceptance with a technique called **active listening**. It involves *responding with a description of what you think the other person is feeling, and why*. For example, in the painting situation, a better response is: "It sounds like you're really upset because the paint spilled on your picture. You worked so hard on it." Another situation might call for a response like: "It must feel a little scary to come here for the first time. It's hard to have fun here when you don't know any of us yet." Still another example is: "It looks like you feel frustrated at having to wait so long for your turn. You really want to show everyone what you brought, don't you?"

Active listening helps children cope with their feelings. They learn that it's okay to feel angry, scared, or frustrated, and that other people sometimes feel the same way. Often children begin to feel calmer as soon as they realize that someone understands them. The next time you are faced with comforting a distressed child, try active listening.

Positive discipline involves guiding children through a learning process. What are some of the things children must learn along the way?

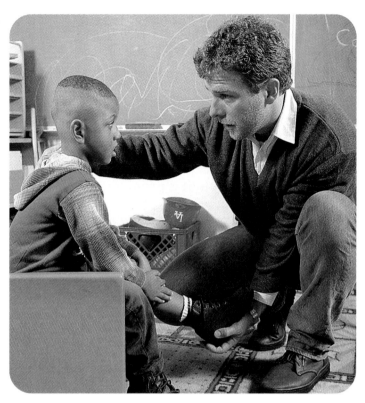

A POSITIVE APPROACH TO DISCIPLINE

Most teachers and parents would agree that in order to guide children's behavior, some form of discipline is necessary. What does that mean?

The word "discipline" means different things to different people. Many people associate discipline with punishing children when they misbehave. Others feel that the term has a broader meaning.

To avoid confusion, child care professionals often refer to **positive discipline**. By this, they mean *the process of teaching children acceptable behavior without harming them physically or emotionally*. Positive discipline sometimes includes appropriate punishment, but it also includes much more. As you will see, positive discipline involves:

- Having reasonable expectations for children's behavior.
- Letting children know how you want them to behave.
- Taking steps to encourage good behavior and prevent misbehavior.
- Reacting to misbehavior in appropriate ways.

Thinking About Your Expectations

Before you can begin to practice positive discipline, you should examine your own expectations for children's behavior. If those expectations are unrealistic or unjust, both you and the children will become frustrated.

Understanding Children's Behavior

Sometimes people mistakenly believe a child is misbehaving when, in fact, the child's actions are simply typical of the developmental level. For example, most children do not easily share until about age three. A two-year-old who refuses to let a playmate use a favorite toy should not be punished. The child is simply behaving as any typical two-year-old would.

Children are naturally energetic, spontaneous, curious, and adventurous. They may climb so high on the jungle gym that they can't get down, or they may ask endless questions that try the patience of adults. Wise caregivers realize that such incidents are not misbehavior. They simply reflect children's natural, healthy desire to learn about and enjoy their world.

Caring adults also understand that many factors can contribute to misbehavior. Though it may sometimes seem otherwise, children who misbehave are probably not doing so just to aggravate you. They may be bored, frustrated, hungry, tired, or ill. They may feel a need for more adult attention. They may be experiencing problems at home, such as fighting between parents or a parent's alcoholism. All of these situations can greatly affect children's behavior. This does not mean that misbehavior should be excused. If you are aware of these factors, however, you will be more likely to guide behavior effectively.

Allowing for Mistakes

No matter how hard children try, they can never be perfectly well-behaved. A child who is excited at being asked to water the plants may accidentally knock one of the pots over. In a crowded hallway, one child may cause another to trip without meaning to. Mistakes are part of being human. When what the child did was clearly an accident, it should not be considered misbehavior.

Similarly, children should not be punished for doing something that they could not have known was wrong. For example, on her first trip to an art museum, Sondra tried to climb on a piece of sculpture. She had not yet been told that the museum exhibits were just for looking, not touching.

The Danger of Labels

Just as adults should not expect too much of children, they should also not expect too little. What happened to five-year-old Chloe is an example of this. Unlike her older sister, Chloe didn't like to talk to people she didn't know very well. Her parents noticed the contrast. Whenever her father introduced Chloe to an adult, he would say something like "Chloe is the quiet one of the family" or "She's our shy girl." The more Chloe heard this message, the more she thought of herself as shy. By the time she entered first grade, Chloe had to be coaxed to speak up in class.

A child who is labeled "troublemaker" or "bully" tends to confirm the label by giv-

Lauren's teacher knows that her fine motor skills are still developing. That's why she asked Lauren to wipe up the spill instead of punishing her.

THE MULTICULTURAL CLASSROOM

Think for a moment about the different cultural and ethnic groups you are familiar with. Are there certain general behaviors or qualities that you associate with these groups? If your answer is "yes," you need to analyze your thinking.

To explore this idea, use your imagination to create a culture called the Green people. Suppose that some individuals believe the Green people are hot-tempered. If you accept this as a child care professional, what happens when a four-year-old Green child enrolls in your classroom? If the child has temper tantrums, you might excuse them because your thinking says this behavior is "natural" for a Green person. On the other hand, you might have immediate negative feelings about the Green child because you believe, even before you see evidence, that this child is going to be troublesome. You might expect negative reactions and overreact to behavior that you believe is heading toward a temper tantrum when it really isn't. Over time you may even "teach" the Green child that you expect negative behavior, and the child may learn to conform to that image.

In the multicultural classroom, there is no room for stereotypes. Each child, regardless of background, is unique and deserves a chance to be treated that way. Viewing videotapes of positive discipline situations that feature adults and children of many ethnicities can be a good starting point for discussing stereotypes. These tapes may be located through libraries, catalogs, and colleges.

---

ing adults just what they expect. In addition, such negative labels as "stupid" and "clumsy" are hurtful and damaging to self-esteem.

Labels do not need to be spoken aloud to have an effect. Your tone of voice, your facial expression, the toys you offer, how you react to misbehavior—all can be influenced by the mental category in which you have placed a child. Children pick up on these subtle differences. As a child care professional, guard against tagging children with unflattering labels.

Establishing Classroom Rules

Children cannot learn to behave appropriately if they do not understand which behaviors are appropriate. Thus, the next step in positive discipline is to let children know what you want them to do. The simplest way is to give them rules they can easily understand and follow.

Rules vary from one child care program to another. The important thing is that staff members agree on them. A good place to start is by thinking about the purpose of rules. Rules are set up to protect:

- Every child's safety and well-being.
- Other children's rights and feelings.
- Classroom materials and property.
- The learning atmosphere.

With this in mind, the teachers in a child care setting can begin to identify whether or not specific behaviors are acceptable. They will probably agree that some behaviors, such as hitting, are not acceptable under any circumstances. Other behaviors may be acceptable only at certain times and places. For instance, loud voices may be used outdoors but not in the classroom.

A long list of guidelines for acceptable behavior would be overwhelming to children. Most teachers decide to give children a limited number of rules, such as three to five for each area or activity within the child care setting. (A small number of general rules may also be needed.) The rules that are chosen should be important ones that children can reasonably be expected to follow. For instance, the rules for finger painting might be:

- Wear a smock.
- Clean up spills right away.
- Paint on your own paper.

Tip FROM THE Pros

*P*ublish classroom rules in your program's newsletter. Encourage parents to adopt the same rules at home.

Choose rules that you will be able to apply consistently. Of course, flexibility sometimes calls for changing or bending the rules to fit new circumstances. In general, however, the same rules should apply every day and to everyone, including adults.

Once the rules have been chosen, they must be communicated to the children. Children will be more likely to understand and follow rules if you phrase them in a way that is simple, positive, and specific. A rule for arrival time might be "Hang your coat on the hook." This is much clearer than saying "Don't leave coats lying around everywhere." It also tells children what they *can do* instead of what they *can't* do.

When introducing rules to children, explain the reasons for each rule. You might say, "When we're indoors, we walk with quiet feet. If we run indoors, someone could fall and get hurt." The younger the child, the simpler the explanation should be.

To help children learn and remember the rules, display them on a poster in each learning center. Use pictures to clearly illustrate the rules.

Promoting Good Behavior

Wise caregivers do not simply wait for children to misbehave before they intervene. Instead, they do whatever they can to help children behave appropriately. They prevent situations

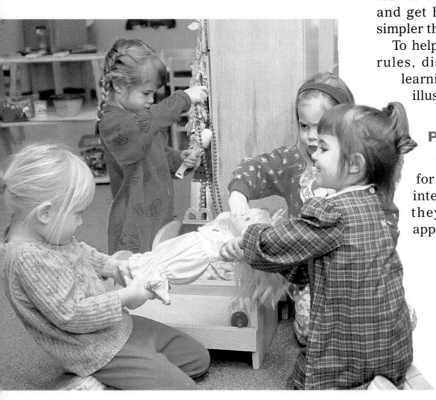

At age three, disputes over toys are still common. By setting, explaining, and enforcing classroom rules for use of toys, children learn important social skills. What are some of these skills?

Courtesy of Lakeshore Learning Materials

Predictable routines give children a feeling of stability. However, children also need challenging new experiences to stimulate learning. When they are interested in activities, they are less likely to misbehave.

that lead to misbehavior, offer choices, set a good example, and are generous with praise.

Planning to Prevent Problems

Many potential behavior problems can be prevented through careful planning. By structuring the schedule and the environment to minimize boredom, frustration, and conflict, you can reduce the likelihood of misbehavior. Specifically:

- **Plan a wide variety of interesting activities.** Children who are constructively occupied are less likely to misbehave. Unit 5 will help you plan an interesting curriculum.
- **Make sure activities are at the appropriate level.** If activities are too difficult, children will become frustrated and may resort to aggressive behavior. If activities are too easy, children may become bored and aimless.
- **Provide enough equipment.** One preschool classroom had ten children, but the block center had only enough blocks for one child to build a structure. This set the stage for frequent fights as children competed for blocks.
- **Arrange the physical environment so children can meet your expectations.** For instance, when toy shelves are within children's reach, they are able to obey rules about putting toys away. Materials not meant for use by children should be stored out of sight to avoid temptation.

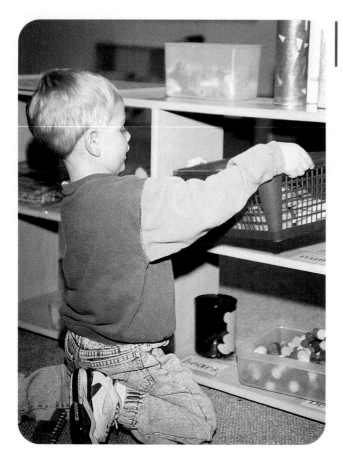

Low shelves with specific places for toys help children participate more actively and willingly in cleanup.

children won't have to misbehave to get a teacher's attention.

Offering Choices

Another way to help children behave appropriately is to offer them choices. Children (like adults) often resist direct commands. Giving children opportunities to make decisions for themselves helps prevent power struggles between teacher and child.

Be sure the choices you offer are real ones. Whichever option the child chooses, you must be willing to follow through. If the child is getting ready to go outdoors on a cold day, asking "Would you like to put on your coat?" is not appropriate. Instead, you might say, "Here's your coat. Which arm is going in the sleeve first?"

Giving children a choice shows that you respect their opinions and independence. This builds self-esteem. Can you think of some other opportunities for choice in the classroom?

Setting an Example

Young children learn by imitating adults. When you work with young children, you are a role model. To encourage good behavior, provide children with a positive example to follow. Obey classroom rules, just as you expect the children to. Model desirable social skills in your dealings with both children and adults. If you would like children to say "please" and "thank you," for instance, make a habit of doing so yourself.

- *Plan a balanced schedule.* Provide for both quiet time and active play. Children who are either overly tired or full of pent-up energy find it hard to behave appropriately.

- *Follow a consistent schedule.* Children find security in a predictable schedule. Secure children follow rules more easily.

- *Keep the schedule flowing smoothly.* Children become frustrated if they must wait too long.

- *Provide individual attention.* Plan times when children can interact with teachers one-to-one or in small groups. That way

Tip FROM THE Pros

*W*hen offering choices, present only two or three alternatives. More than that can be confusing to children.

Positive Reinforcement

Positive reinforcement is *a response that rewards a particular behavior, making it more likely to be repeated.* Praise, attention, and smiles are all examples of positive reinforcement.

Children bloom when given honest and thoughtful praise. On the other hand, the wrong type of praise can do more harm than good. Compare the following two examples:

- "Great job, Rodrigo. You're such a good boy!"
- "Rodrigo, I'm so pleased that you put all the blocks on the shelf. You didn't leave a single one on the floor!"

The first example is positive but vague. Descriptions such as "great job" and "nice work" are so general that they often sound insincere. Rodrigo may be left wondering just what he did that was so wonderful. He may even begin to feel anxious, because he wants to keep on being a "good boy" but does not know how. In addition, children who hear Rodrigo being called a "good boy" may conclude, "The teacher thinks I'm not as good as he is."

The second example of praise is much more effective. It shows Rodrigo that the teacher sincerely noticed his hard work and values thoroughness. When you praise children, always remember to be specific and sincere.

Responding to Misbehavior

Despite your best efforts, children misbehave at times. When you respond to misbehavior, your choice of words and actions deserves careful thought. It is not necessary to hurt, frighten, threaten, or demean a child who has misbehaved. You simply want the child to understand that the misbehavior is unacceptable and cannot be permitted to continue. You also want the child to see himself or herself as a worthwhile person who is capable of doing better in the future. In short, your goal is to discourage the misbehavior without discouraging the child.

Good teachers know that responding positively to good behavior encourages children to repeat it. Positive reinforcement also builds self-esteem.

Poor Methods of Discipline

- Shouting, scolding, yelling
- Telling children they are bad, naughty, or failures
- Calling children names
- Using sarcasm

- Embarrassing or humiliating children
- Making children promise to be good
- Bribing children to behave
- Threatening children with loss of affection

- Punishing out of a desire to make children suffer
- Hitting or hurting children

There are a number of effective ways to respond to misbehavior. Which you choose depends on the situation. A combination of methods may be needed.

Ignoring

Sometimes children misbehave just to get attention. The best response may be to ignore the misbehavior, as long as it is not harmful to anyone.

During an art activity, a group of children were cutting shapes out of construction paper. One boy, Shane, kept putting the scissors up to his head, acting as though he were going to cut his hair. Each time, he looked at the teacher and paused to see what would happen. The teacher wisely concluded that Shane was just hoping for a reaction, so she ignored him. When Shane saw that his actions did not bring the desired results, he went back to cutting paper. The teacher then went over to Shane and commented on how well he had used the scissors to cut shapes. In that way, she rewarded Shane for his positive behavior rather than his inappropriate behavior.

Giving Reminders

Young children are forgetful and easily distracted. When their behavior momentari-ly slips, they may simply need a reminder to follow classroom rules. Try to give reminders in a way that does not sound like nagging or blaming. You might say, "Youssef, where do we put the costumes when we're finished playing with them?" or "Hannah, did you remember to wash your hands before coming to the table?"

Using "I-Messages"

Suppose that at meal time, a teacher and several children are passing bowls of food around the table. Ms. Bartolo is just about to serve herself some peaches when four-year-old Bobbie Jo grabs the bowl from her hands. Although there is no specific rule about taking food without asking, Ms. Bartolo wants to discourage Bobbie Jo's behavior. What do you think she should say?

Some people might be tempted to say, "Give me back the peaches," or "That was rude," or "Don't be so greedy." These statements are not likely to be effective. The first is a direct command, which Bobbie Jo is likely to resist. The other two attack Bobbie Jo with negative labels that say "you are rude" and "you are greedy."

A better approach is to respond with what psychologist Thomas Gordon calls an **I-message**. This is *an honest description of the behavior, how it affects you, and your feel-*

ings about it. Ms. Bartolo might say, "Bobbie Jo, when you grab the bowl away from me, I can't serve myself some peaches. That hurts my feelings. Besides that, I'm disappointed because I really wanted some peaches."

This response does not attack Bobbie Jo. Instead, it helps her see why her behavior is a problem. It also gives Bobbie Jo the opportunity to change her behavior on her own. Many teachers have found I-messages to be very effective in situations such as this.

Redirection

Redirection involves *steering a child who is misbehaving to a different, acceptable activity.* For example, Terrence and Karla were throwing blocks at a tower they had built, trying to see who could knock it down first. The teacher interrupted their game, saying, "Remember our rule: blocks are for building, not throwing. If you want to play a throwing game, you may toss these bean bags into the bucket." The teacher recognized the children's desire for an active game and provided a safe alternative.

FOCUS ON INFANT/TODDLER PROGRAMS

Regardless of what you might hear people say, infants do not misbehave. Some infant behavior, such as crying, may be annoying to adults, but this can hardly be considered misbehavior. Babies do not cry intentionally to grate on the nerves of their caregivers. Cries are based on need, sometimes just for comfort. Giving an infant comfort does not "spoil" the child. In fact, it contributes to the infant's sense of well-being and positive emotional development.

As infants and toddlers learn to crawl and walk, they delight in exploring everything they can. Instead of restricting them, concentrate on clearing a safe path. Make sure there is nothing in their reach that may harm them or that they may accidentally damage. This will not only keep them safe but will also prevent both you and the children from being worn down by endless repetition of "no—don't touch." If infants become fascinated with something that is dangerous or forbidden, try distracting them with an appealing, safe object or activity.

During the toddler stage, children learn they can assert their will by saying "no." This struggle for independence is normal and desirable but can be frustrating at times. Toddlers want to do as much as possible for themselves and at their own pace. When caregivers allow children independence appropriate to their level of development, self-confidence grows.

Temper tantrums are more common at this age than any other. Some occur when toddlers become so frustrated and angry that they lose control of themselves. A caregiver who is calm and understanding can help restore peace. Tantrums can also be a deliberate attempt to control others. For instance, a child who has been denied candy may scream in an attempt to get it. In this case, the best response is to ignore the tantrum. Giving in only teaches the child that tantrums are a good way to get whatever is wanted.

Time out can be used effectively to help children learn that misbehavior has consequences. What are the potential problems with using time out?

Enforcing Consequences

In the previous example, what if Terrence and Karla decided not to play with the bean bags and soon began to throw the blocks again? In that case, they must learn to accept the consequences. **Consequences** are *events that occur as the result of a particular behavior.* When children realize their actions may have negative consequences, they are motivated to control their own behavior.

Caregivers should select consequences that are suitable for the child's age and developmental level. Here are three types of consequences commonly used by child care professionals:

- ***Natural Consequences.*** Sometimes the natural results of an action are enough to discourage the behavior from being repeated. For instance, Yolanda was reminded to put her painting in her cubby, but she did not. As a result, the painting got stepped on and torn. Natural consequences can be effective but should be used only if they do not endanger the child or others.

- ***Withdrawal of Privileges.*** Another approach is to deny the child a privilege for a short time. If possible, the privilege being taken away should be directly related to the misbehavior. That way the consequences will be more meaningful to the child. For example, if Terrence and Karla continue to throw blocks, they might be denied access to the block area for the rest of the morning. They should then be directed to another activity where they may start fresh.

- ***Time Out.*** In some child care settings, a child who continues to be very disruptive may be given a **time out.** This is *a short period of time in which the child must sit apart from the other children and activities.* Time out can be effective but must be used with care. It should never be treated as a "jail sentence" or a way to humiliate the child. The proper use of time out is to let the child calm down and regain self-control. For preschoolers, time out should last no longer than three to five minutes.

Whatever consequences you choose, here are some guidelines for enforcing them:

- Don't make the incident the center of attention. Speak privately to the child who misbehaved.

- Give the child a chance to correct the behavior, but clearly identify the consequences if he or she does not. Offer a choice: "You may play with the puzzle as long as you keep the pieces on the table, or you may find something else to do. If you continue to throw the pieces on the floor, the puzzle will have to be put away."

- Once you decide to enforce the stated consequences, take action as soon as possible. If you wait until later, the child will not be able to associate the consequences with the misdeed.

- Be consistent. If you enforce rules only some of the time, children can become confused. They may purposely misbehave in order to learn what is allowed.

- Be prepared for some unpleasantness. If the child cries, sulks, or says "I hate you," remain calm but firm. Giving in only teaches the child to use the same tactics next time.

- Establish a definite ending time for consequences: "You may not ride the tricycle for the rest of the day."

- Express your trust in the child to behave more appropriately in the future: "I'm sure that tomorrow you'll be able to play more safely with the tricycle."

Focus on SCHOOL-AGE PROGRAMS

School-age children have more fully developed intellectual skills than preschoolers. In a way, this makes discipline easier because teachers can better reason with children this age. On the other hand, school-age children sometimes use their advanced verbal skills to test and challenge caregivers. Maintaining a relationship of mutual respect is very important.

School-age children can be quite sensitive, taking every teacher comment personally. They are acutely aware of issues of fairness, protesting when they feel someone has received favored treatment. Be sure to apply positive discipline in a consistent, impartial way.

To ensure greater cooperation, let school-age children become involved in creating rules. You can use a class meeting to discuss what the rules should be. Provide posters and markers for the students to create signs outlining the rules.

School-age children are more likely than preschoolers to tease and call each other names. Address these issues directly so everyone understands feelings are to be protected.

Provide plenty of new and challenging projects to keep school-age children constructively occupied. They are eager to take responsibility for classroom jobs, such as feeding animals, helping to prepare snacks, and organizing games.

After sitting all day in school, children have pent-up energy that sometimes results in misbehavior. Provide opportunities for them to release energy constructively, by running on a playground, hiking to a park, or playing basketball, for instance.

Building Professional Skills

Consistency

WHAT IS CONSISTENCY?

Consistency is acting in predictable ways in similar situations. This does not mean that your response is always the same regardless of the circumstances. Rather, consistency lets others know what to expect from you. Behaving consistently shows that you have well-thought-out beliefs about what is important and acceptable. When you work with children, a consistent approach helps them understand and conform to what you expect of them.

Consistency in Action

Paulette sighed as she bent down to pick up the books. Three of them remained on the floor where Heidi had just been looking at them. Several yards away, Heidi glanced over her shoulder to see Paulette placing the books back on the shelf. Heidi scurried on to her next activity.

"Just last week I talked to Heidi about putting the books back when she's done," Paulette said to Mrs. Wheeler, the director of the preschool program, "but she doesn't pay attention to me. One day I stood right beside her while she returned them to the shelf."

"What happened yesterday?" Mrs. Wheeler asked.

"I just put them away myself," Paulette answered. "It was easier than fighting with her over it. And today she got away before I noticed that the books were on the floor."

"I think I can help you," Mrs. Wheeler said. "Let's plan a response to Heidi's behavior that will be the same every day until she realizes that she must put the books away or always face the same consequence. I think Heidi is trying to control the situation. If she thinks she can get away with something once, she will keep trying. A consistent approach to Heidi is going to make a difference. We'll talk about it again after school today."

Your Analysis

1. What was inconsistent about Paulette's handling of Heidi?

2. What messages did Heidi get from Paulette about putting the books away?

3. What dangers lie in the attitude that it is easier to do it yourself than confront a child over an issue?

4. How will a consistent approach to Heidi's behavior help both Paulette and Heidi?

5. What response do you think Mrs. Wheeler might suggest that Paulette use consistently with Heidi?

GUIDING CHILDREN IN OTHER WAYS

*P*ositive discipline is an important aspect of guidance, but it is not the only one. Child care professionals influence children's emotional, social, and moral development in many ways throughout the day. It's up to you to make sure that the guidance you provide is positive. Here are just a few examples of ways a supportive teacher can provide positive guidance:

- *Offer encouragement.* Show a child who has just mastered a new skill that you share in the excitement. Tell a struggling child, "I'm proud of the way you keep trying."

- *Foster independence.* Let children accomplish as much as they can without adult help. When appropriate, suggest that children help one another.

- *Provide assurance.* A smile, a warm welcome, a touch on the shoulder, or a hug can let children know they are valued.

- *Help children cope with their feelings.* Use active listening to encourage children to express their emotions. Help them vent their feelings through such activities as pounding clay, painting a picture, or playing with puppets.

- *Promote respect for others.* Be a role model by treating children the way you would want to be treated. Plan a curriculum that teaches children to value people of different cultures, age groups, genders, and abilities. When children try to exclude others from play, remind them, "Everyone is welcome here."

How might you encourage this child to join in classroom activities without making him feel pressured?

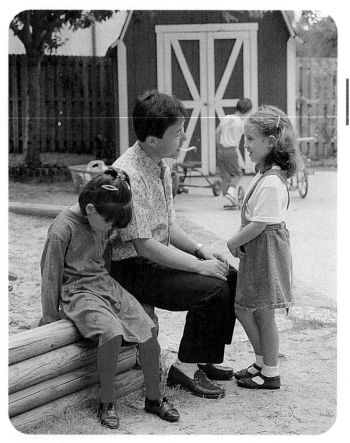

Why is it important for caregivers to help children develop empathy? How can this be done?

Helping Children Solve Problems

When children learn to solve simple problems, they are better able to solve bigger ones later in life. Allow children the opportunity to think for themselves instead of doing the thinking for them. This is what Mr. Seawell did when his class faced a problem.

Following a field trip to an apple orchard, six children were busy cutting apple shapes out of red construction paper. After a while, Melissa came to Mr. Seawell to report, "We can't make any more apples." Casually, he led the children through the problem-solving strategy that you read about in the last chapter.

1. *Identify the problem.* Mr. Seawell returned with Melissa to the table where the children were working. After listening to the children's explanations, he summarized them: "I see. You can't make more apples because the red paper is gone."

2. *Explore possible solutions.* Mr. Seawell asked, "What do you think you should do?" Several children had ideas. (If the children had not come up with any ideas, he might have said, "Let me make some suggestions.")

3. *Evaluate each possible solution.* "Now let's talk about what you think of each idea," Mr. Seawell said. He listened respectfully to each child's point of view.

- *Help children develop empathy.* Empathy is not a word that most children know, yet they can learn to understand another person's feelings. Even very young children can offer aid and comfort to someone who is sad or hurt. You can help children relate to the feelings of others: "Joni feels sad right now, just like you did when your hamster died."

- *Coach children to improve their social skills.* If Brock is shy, for example, you might show him how to use such openings as "What's your name?" and "I'd like to play, too."

Caregivers can also help children develop two abilities that will be valuable throughout life. These are the abilities to solve problems and resolve conflicts.

He asked questions at times but avoided imposing his own opinion.

4. ***Choose the best solution.*** Mr. Seawell could have asked the children to vote by hand for their favorite solution. In this case, however, it seemed acceptable to let each child decide.

5. ***Carry out the solution.*** Some children took crayons and began drawing apples on white paper. Others made apples from green and yellow construction paper.

6. ***Evaluate the solution.*** When the apples were finished, Mr. Seawell asked, "What do you think of the way you solved your problem?" All agreed that both solutions worked out well.

You need not insist that children go through these steps every time a problem arises. When children see the problem-solving process in action, however, they are more apt to remember and use it on their own.

Helping Children Resolve Conflicts

Conflict is a natural and common occurrence in a toddler or preschool-age program. Two children may have a tug-of-war over a toy truck, each shouting, "I had it first!" Another child may sit on the ground crying after being pushed from the tricycle seat. Children even fight over who gets to sit in the teacher's lap at story time. Learning how to resolve conflicts in a positive manner—without physical reactions and name-calling—is a major challenge of childhood.

Although children must learn to resolve their own conflicts, they need the help of caregivers to do so. Resolving conflicts involves many social skills: communication, negotiation, cooperation, and the ability to stand up for one's own rights while respecting the rights of others. A supportive teacher can help children acquire these skills.

As a child care professional, what should you do when conflict occurs? The answer

Children need to learn acceptable ways to settle disputes. They can do so only if caregivers guide them through the process when needed.

depends on the situation. If a child is being physically harmed or endangered, immediately take action. Stop the child who is doing the hurting, and then comfort the one who is hurt. If the situation poses no immediate danger, simply move closer and remain observant. This lets children know that you are aware of what is going on.

If the children seem to need help resolving their conflict, provide only as much guidance as necessary. Try these ideas:

- Signal your availability to help by making a neutral comment: "It looks like you cannot agree on who will play with the truck."

- Encourage each child to relate his or her point of view. Ask such questions as "What happened next?" and "How did you feel about that?"

- If children find it difficult to express their feelings, you may need to coach them: "Maybe you feel mad because Sonia took the tricycle away from you. It's okay to tell her that makes you mad."

- Remind children of the problem-solving steps. Encourage them to think of many possible solutions. These might include sharing, taking turns, trading, or choosing another activity.

- Help the children negotiate a solution that is acceptable to everyone involved: "Eddie says he will let you use the truck if you give him the bulldozer. What do you think of that idea?" Don't pressure children to agree to a solution that is not acceptable to them.

- As a last resort, if the children still cannot resolve the conflict, do it for them. You might say, "This is a tough one. I'll help you decide this time."

Teaching children how to resolve conflicts on their own takes more time than solving the problem for them. In the long run, however, it is much better for the children.

MEETING SPECIAL CHALLENGES

Following the guidelines discussed in this chapter will help you go a long way toward maintaining a safe, orderly classroom. You should realize, however, that practicing positive guidance will not eliminate all misbehavior. Developing self-discipline and social skills is a long process. All children have occasional difficulties along the way.

Some children seem to have more difficulties than others. Carlo, for example, appears unusually tense and must frequently be stopped from punching and kicking other children. Deanna seems determined to break every rule and tells teachers, "I don't have to do what you say!" Behavior problems such as these may last only a few days or weeks, or they may continue for a long time. Either way, they can present a significant challenge for child care professionals.

If you have observed a pattern of behavior problems, set up a parent conference. Be careful not to use negative labels or sound as though you are placing blame. Explain that you are concerned about the child's behavior and want to work together to find a solution. Some of the questions you may want to ask are: Have there been behavior problems at home? If so, when did they begin? How do you handle them? Is there something in the child's life that might be upsetting him or her right now?

As you read earlier, behavior problems can sometimes be traced to difficult situations in the child's home life. Examples range from the death of a beloved pet to violence in the home or neighborhood. You may be able to suggest measures for the parents to try. For example, a child's anxiety over divorce may be eased if the parents talk to the child in a reassuring way. You may also need to refer the parents to another source of help, such as a family counselor or social worker.

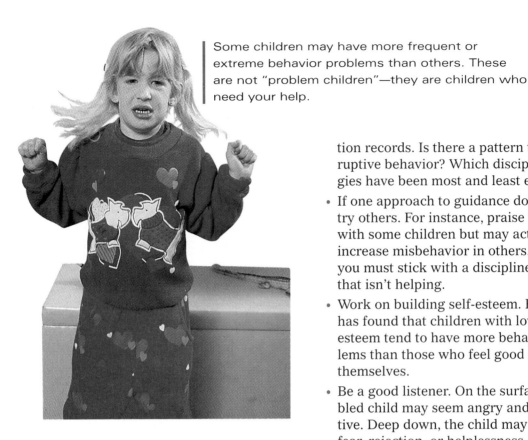

Some children may have more frequent or extreme behavior problems than others. These are not "problem children"—they are children who need your help.

A child who is extremely withdrawn, depressed, or aggressive may have an emotional or behavioral disorder. This child needs the help of a professional who is trained to deal with these problems.

Whether or not the parents seek help for their child, you may still have to deal with the problem behavior in your classroom. The guidance techniques discussed in this chapter apply to troubled children as well as typical children. In addition, you can turn to these suggestions:

- Try to avoid labeling the child as a troublemaker. If adult and child become adversaries, the roles are not easy to escape. Instead, think of the child as one who needs extra help and guidance.
- Make objective observations of the child's behavior. Periodically review the observa-tion records. Is there a pattern to the dis-ruptive behavior? Which discipline strate-gies have been most and least effective?

- If one approach to guidance doesn't work, try others. For instance, praise is effective with some children but may actually increase misbehavior in others. Don't feel you must stick with a discipline method that isn't helping.

- Work on building self-esteem. Research has found that children with low self-esteem tend to have more behavior prob-lems than those who feel good about themselves.

- Be a good listener. On the surface, a trou-bled child may seem angry and destruc-tive. Deep down, the child may be feeling fear, rejection, or helplessness. By using active listening, you can encourage the child to express painful emotions with words instead of misbehavior.

IMPROVING YOUR SKILLS

*G*uiding children is a skill that comes with practice. Child care professionals must think before they speak and act. With experience comes an increasing ability to respond appropriately to the many situa-tions that arise. You can learn so much from those who have been there before. Stop, look, and listen to the experts in your field. They can help you help children feel good about themselves and get along better with others. This is one of the greatest rewards of the child care profession.

Chapter 15 Review

Chapter Summary

- Guidance is needed for children's safety and personal growth.
- Caregivers must be skilled at communicating with children.
- Positive discipline helps children learn acceptable behavior without physical or emotional harm.
- Caregivers must have realistic expectations for children's behavior.
- Clearly stated rules help children behave appropriately.
- Teachers can encourage good behavior by preventing problem situations, offering choices, setting a good example, and providing positive reinforcement.
- Possible responses to misbehavior include ignoring, giving reminders, using "I-messages," and redirection.
- Consequences for unacceptable behavior should be appropriate and consistent.
- Supportive teachers can help children develop positive social traits and skills.
- Troubled children can benefit from extra guidance and outside help.

Reviewing the Facts

1. How can positive guidance lead to self-discipline?
2. What is active listening?
3. Contrast punishment with positive discipline.
4. What are the dangers of labeling children?
5. Name three guidelines for phrasing rules effectively for children.
6. How does positive reinforcement affect behavior?
7. What are "I-messages"?
8. Why is consistency so important when enforcing consequences?
9. Name three inappropriate methods of discipline.
10. Describe three ways a teacher might react when conflict occurs.
11. Give two situations in which a troubled child may need outside help.

Thinking Critically

1. Why would a "sugar-coated" voice be ineffective for disciplining children?
2. Should adults ever make negative statements to children, such as "stop hitting" or "no pushing"? Why or why not?
3. Why is the saying "actions speak louder than words" especially true of young children?
4. Identify some possible long-term consequences if a child is continually punished for typical childhood behavior.
5. What is a "self-fulfilling prophecy"? How does it relate to guiding children?
6. Explain which guidance technique(s) to use if: a) a two-year-old child bites another child; b) a five-year-old child uses an obscenity, enjoying the shocked reaction it produces.

Activities and Applications

1. **Active Listening.** Think of three situations in which a teacher could use active listening with children. Write a script that shows what might happen in each, including the teacher's responses.
2. **Rules for Children.** Write three rules you would want children to follow in each of these learning centers: dramatic play; active play; outdoor active play; language arts;

blocks. (For a description of these learning centers, see pages 174-175 in Chapter 9.) Phrase the rules appropriately.

3. **Preventing Abuse.** From a family services agency, obtain literature on using positive discipline and preventing child abuse.

4. **Discipline and the Law.** Interview a child care licensing agent about state laws that address discipline in a child care program.

SCHOOL TO WORK

Your Professional Portfolio

Write and illustrate a story for preschoolers that focuses on how two children solved a problem or resolved a conflict. Keep the story simple and brief enough to hold children's interest. If possible, use a tape recorder or video camera to record yourself as you read (or pretend to read) the story to a group of children. Follow the guidelines for good communication. Place the story and the tape recording in your portfolio.

Observing and Analyzing

Choosing Effective Techniques

One of the most difficult parts of learning to use guidance techniques is deciding what to use when. What works in some situations may not work in another. Some children are more responsive to one approach than others. Children might not even react the same way from day to day, depending on their moods, health, and sense of well-being. All of this can make choosing the right technique for the moment a challenge.

Your skill in guiding behavior will improve through trial-and-error. To reduce the negative impact of error, however, you can watch what other people do to see what works and what doesn't—what seems right and what seems wrong. By shaping your thinking *before* you have to act, you can be better prepared to give children the kind of guidance that builds their self-esteem rather than tears it down.

To get started, learn to recognize positive techniques in action. Compare these to the negative approaches you see some people take. Use these activities as a basis for your observations:

- **Watching Behavior.** Observe adults dealing with children's behavior in public settings, such as a store, restaurant, or supermarket. Make notes on the situations, the responses, and the outcomes. Analyze what you observed. Describe in writing two positive situations you observed. What made them positive? Describe two negative situations. Recommend a positive approach that would have been more effective.

- **Identifying Techniques.** Visit a child care program and observe as child care professionals guide behavior. Look for situations in which the adults use techniques described in the chapter. Look for examples of active listening, enforcing consequences, I-messages, offering choices, positive reinforcement, ignoring negative behavior, giving reminders, and redirection. Evaluate the effectiveness of the techniques you observed. Were there situations in which a technique worked with one child but not another?

Chapter 16

Learning Through Observation

CHAPTER OBJECTIVES

- Explain why child care professionals observe and record children's behavior.

- Discuss the benefits and drawbacks of specific approaches to observation.

- Describe methods for recording observations.

- Give guidelines for using observation records.

- Identify behaviors to look for when assessing children's development.

Terms to Learn

- anecdotal record
- checklist
- event record
- frequency count
- naturalistic observation
- participant observer
- rating scale
- running record

'd better make a note of that," Charlene thought as she reached for one of the index cards in a large pocket of her smock. She always wore this smock while she was teaching in the preschool because the pockets were so handy. Besides that, it also protected her clothes. She noted the date and time on the card and wrote Quinn's name at the top.

"Shortly after arriving, Quinn crawled under a table and stayed there for ten minutes," Charlene wrote on the card. She then placed the card back in her pocket.

A little later she noticed how well Yokita was doing as she used the scissors to cut out shapes. Charlene pulled out another index card and noted Yokita's progress on it.

Clay had been watching her. "Is that going to be a story?" he asked.

"In a way it is," she replied.

"Is it going to be about me?" Clay wanted to know.

"Yes, I think I will write about you—and a cat," Charlene responded patiently.

"I have a cat. His name is Ripples. Will you write about him too?"

"I certainly will, Clay," Charlene said. "I'll write about you and Ripples." She reached into her pocket for a fresh index card and began to write.

"What does the story say?" Clay asked.

"It says: 'Once upon a time there was a boy named Clay and a cat named Ripples, and they were *very* curious fellows.'" With a smile, Charlene looked expectantly at Clay. She waited for the next question that she knew would come.

WHY OBSERVE CHILDREN?

By this time in your study, you have probably spent a large amount of time observing. That's part of being a student. It's also part of being an employee in the field. People who go on to work in child care don't stop observing. If anything, they work at refining the skill and continually use it to be effective on the job.

When systematically gathered, the information collected through observation has multiple uses. As a student, you observe so that you can learn about children and the child care field. As a child care professional, however, you will observe for other reasons. You will want information about children so that you can use it in their behalf. The reasons why child care professionals observe and record children's behavior include:

- **To get to know individual children.** Observations help teachers determine a child's abilities, interests, and level of development. Activities can then be planned with the child's needs in mind.

- **To identify special needs.** Observation records can help determine whether a child needs specialized services or programs, such as speech therapy, counseling, a gifted program, or remedial education.

Listening

WHAT ARE LISTENING SKILLS?

Listening involves more than simply hearing words. It requires paying attention to facial expressions, tone of voice, and word choice. You can test your listening skills by repeating the message in your own words to make sure you understand. Well-developed listening skills allow you to hear not only what is said but also what is felt.

Listening Skills in Action

As Howard Kereotes glanced over at the swings, he saw Gina sitting alone. She had been there yesterday too. As her teacher, Howard knew that this was unusual, and he was concerned.

"May I join you, Gina?" he asked. He made a show of trying to get comfortable in the swing's small seat. "Ouch! I thought these were one-size-fits-all." He copied Gina's slouched shoulders and slumped head. He asked, "Are we having fun yet?"

Gina shrugged. "I like this. It's nice and quiet."

"Yes, the world can be a noisy place," agreed Howard. "Traffic, TVs, radios, teachers . . ."

"And babies," Gina muttered. "Babies are the worst."

"That's right," Howard recalled. "You have a new little brother, don't you?"

"Sister," Gina corrected emphatically. "And can she cry! All day, in the middle of the night, when she's hungry, or wet, or tired, or . . . just because. All she does is make noise, but everybody thinks she's wonderful."

"Yes, they're very demanding, considering they don't do anything."

"That's for sure," Gina exclaimed. "And she's in my room most of the time. It used to be nice in there, but not anymore. I didn't ask for a little sister!"

"No, you didn't," Howard agreed. "It must feel pretty unfair, when you didn't have a say in the matter."

"That's right. That's just how it feels."

"Did I ever show you a picture of my little sister, Gina?" Howard asked, as he pulled out his wallet and revealed two photos. "That's her when she was around your age. Here she is with me last year during the holidays. She brought me that hat from out West where she lives now. I hardly ever get to see her anymore." There was a note of regret in his voice.

Gina studied the photos for a long moment. "I like her smile," she said. Suddenly, she turned and gave Howard a smile of her own.

Your Analysis

1. Identify the clues that Howard observed in order to understand how Gina was feeling.

2. How did Howard encourage conversation with Gina?

3. In what ways was Howard skillful at helping Gina?

A lot goes on in a child care setting each day. The practice of observing and recording behavior helps focus your attention on details that might otherwise be missed.

THE MULTICULTURAL CLASSROOM

If someone were to observe your classroom or program, would they see signs of an ongoing multicultural curriculum?

- Do the pictures or posters on the wall feature children of different ethnicities?

- Do dolls and their clothing represent a variety of cultures?

- Are there musical instruments played and songs sung that come from other countries?

- Do classroom books provide an assortment of positive images for both genders and many different age and cultural groups?

- Does the dramatic play area include play foods, utensils, furniture, and dress-up clothing of different cultures?

- Most importantly, are the above examples available at all times? A "tourist" approach with a short-term "children of the world" theme is soon forgotten.

- **To address specific problems.** Observation can help teachers plan a strategy for dealing with problem behavior. For instance, Monique often bites other children, despite all efforts to get her to stop. Before deciding what to try next, Monique's teacher will review the observations and look for patterns. Does Monique target any child in particular? Is there a certain time of day that the biting tends to occur? What kinds of things happen just before and after a biting incident? The answers may provide important clues to a solution.

- **To document progress.** Teachers and parents want to know how children are progressing in their development. When observation records are kept, it is easier to notice changes that occur over time.

- **To evaluate the program.** Observations of all the participants in a child care program over a period of time can reveal whether the program is meeting its goals. Observation of the environment itself gives clues to its effectiveness and any need for improvement.

- **To learn about child development.** Even the most experienced child care specialists gain a deeper understanding of children from firsthand observation.

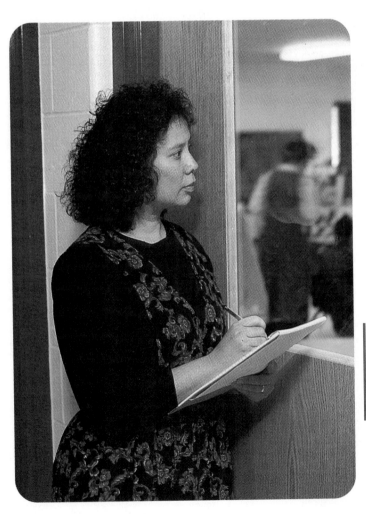

THE ROLE OF THE OBSERVER

Observing is a purposeful, structured activity. It can be accomplished in multiple ways. Researchers sometimes place children in special situations to see how they react; however, you are more likely to use a different approach, called **naturalistic observation**. This means *observing children as they behave naturally in their everyday environment.*

A one-way mirror allows observers to see into the classroom without distracting children from their normal activities. What are some possible disadvantages of this method?

One way to make naturalistic observations is to be a **participant observer**, *someone who interacts with children while observing*. This is the method used by Charlene, the teacher who made observation notes at the beginning of the chapter. As a participant, Charlene talks to the children and leads them in activities. As an observer, she notices details about the children's behavior and records them on her index cards.

Charlene's method is a convenient one for many child care teachers, but it also has several drawbacks. When you interact with children, you become a part of the situation you are observing. This makes it impossible to "step back" and see the situation as an outsider would. In addition, thinking about what you are *doing* can distract you from what you are *observing*. Finally, you may not have time to record your observations right away or in as much detail as you would like.

For these reasons, observations are often made by someone who is strictly an observer. This person might be one of the classroom teachers, who is temporarily assigned to observe rather than participate. It might also be a child care student, like you, who is visiting the classroom for the purpose of recording observations.

There is one potential problem with this approach. If an observer hovers over children with a clipboard, they will know that something unusual is going on. Some children may become shy and embarrassed, while others may show off for their "audience." This defeats the purpose of naturalistic observation. Therefore, the observer must make his or her presence felt as little as possible.

Sometimes the observer actually sits in another room and watches children through a one-way mirror. This is a special type of window that the observer can see through, but that looks like a mirror to the children on the other side. More often, the observer has no choice but to sit in the same room with the children. In that case, the observer must take care to stay in the background as much as possible.

If you are an observer in this type of situation, follow these guidelines to avoid drawing attention to yourself:

- Sit in a low chair.
- Position yourself off to the side, but where you can still observe easily.
- Wear simple, appropriate clothing.
- Do not start a conversation with children or make eye contact.
- If a child asks what you are doing, give a brief but honest answer. You might say, "I'm writing down how children play so I can remember it later."
- Do not interfere in what is going on *unless* a child is in immediate danger and no other caregiver is available.

RECORDING YOUR OBSERVATIONS

How will you record your observations? You have several choices. They range from simple counts and checklists to detailed descriptions of behavior. The method you choose depends on your purpose for observing. Some commonly used methods are described and illustrated here. Note that the examples in the illustrations are incomplete. They are intended to give you an idea about what these records are like.

No matter which type of recording method you use, the following guidelines apply:

- Include your name so that others will know who made the observation.
- Note the date and the beginning and ending time.
- List the children involved and their ages. Also note any adults involved.

- Identify the setting.
- Be careful not to record behaviors that you did not actually observe. If Salina tells a teacher, "Joey hit me," simply record what Salina said. Don't record that Joey hit Salina unless you actually saw it happen.
- Record events as they happen or soon afterward, while the details are fresh in your mind.

Anecdotal Record

An **anecdotal record** (ANN-ik-DOH-tul) is *a written description that focuses on a particular incident*. The description includes where and when the incident took place, who was involved, and what was said and done. For instance, you might write an anecdotal record about the interaction between several children in the dramatic play area on a particular day. You would describe everything the children do and say, including tone of voice, facial expressions, and body language.

An anecdotal record can be written about one child. You may simply jot down observations informally as you make them. The observations that Charlene made at the beginning of this chapter were anecdotal ones. She was not looking for anything specific. Rather, she randomly noticed behavior and activities that were significant enough to remember, and she recorded each one on an index card.

Event Record

Sometimes a specific situation or behavior needs tracking. For example, a teacher who believes that too many problems are occurring in the block center may want to know what is causing the trouble.

An **event record** can help provide information. *With this record, the observer identifies a specific situation and describes what is going on each time that situation occurs over a period of time.* First, a time frame is selected, perhaps one or more days. If a form is used, it includes space for short descriptions. The observer makes notes every time the situation occurs during the time frame. Although this type of record keeping can be time-consuming, it often provides useful information.

To solve the problems in the block center of one preschool, for example, the teacher

---

Anecdotal Record

Date: _9/23_   **Time:** _11:15 a.m._

Setting: _Dramatic Play Center_   **Observed by:** _Crystal_

Child: _Courtney, age four_

Observation: *After Courtney played alone in the dramatic play center, she started to leave. All of the dress-up clothes she had used were on the floor. When reminded of the rule for putting things away,* *Courtney walked away. After a second reminder, Courtney said, "I don't have to." Miss Winn responded, "You'll miss out on snack time. When you pick up the clothes, you can join us."*

Event Record

Date: _4/23_   **Time:** _8:00 a.m.—5:00 p.m._
Setting: _Block Center_   **Observed by:** _Tia_
Focus of Observation: _Problems in Block Center_

TIME	OBSERVATION
8:35 a.m.	Steve and Cory played with blocks until Steve's building fell over. Steve's blocks hit Cory's building and knocked it over too. Cory shoved Steve.
10:15 a.m.	Isaac and Anna May built a block road for their toy car to travel on. As Miranda returned her blocks to the shelf, she tripped on the block road. Isaac and Anna May yelled at Miranda.
11:30 a.m.	Tanya made a "house." To complete it, she pushed some of Porter's blocks out of the way. Porter hit Tanya.

decided to make observations all day long on three separate days of the week. Each time children had a conflict or other problem in the center, the teacher made notes. Later the notes were analyzed to discover what steps should be taken to correct the situation.

Frequency Count

A quick way to observe events is to maintain a frequency count. A **frequency count** is *a record of how many times a particular behavior or situation occurs during a specific period of time.* A tally sheet is used for recording this information. The observation

Frequency Count

Purpose: _To see how many picture books were used during free play_
Date: _10/17_   **Time:** _2:00–2:30 p.m._
Setting: _Language area_   **Observed by:** _Naomi_

CHILD'S NAME AND AGE	FREQUENCY (NUMBER OF BOOKS)
Gretchen (4 yrs. 2 mos.)	II
Alex (4 yrs. 5 mos.)	
Cassie (3 yrs. 11 mo.)	IIII

Running Record

Date: _11/3_

Time Segment: _10:00—10:10 a.m._   **Gender:** _male_   **Age:** _2 1/2_

Child Observed: _Nathan S._   **Observed by:** _April_

TIME	OBSERVATION
10:00—10:01 a.m.	Nathan walked over to the sand and water table. He picked up a cup and dipped some water and poured it out. Nathan repeated this action two more times.
10:01—10:02 a.m	Nathan switched from dipping water to dipping sand. After spilling out the first cup of sand, Nathan looked inside the cup and said, "Sand stuck." He put the cup back into the sand.
10:02—10:03 a.m	Nathan crawled over to the block center. He took a block from Julie, who was already playing in the center. Julie cried. Nathan gave the block back.
10:03—10:04 a.m.	Nathan walked over to the shelving where blocks are stored and took several blocks off the shelf. He stacked the blocks on the floor and then knocked them over. He stacked the blocks again.

Checklist

Child's name: _Randy_   **Age:** _3 yrs. 5 mos._

Date: _1/25-1/27_   **Observed by:** _Jarod_

Setting: _Preschool Lab_

Development Observed: _Large Motor Development_

- ✓ Runs
- ✓ Skips
- ✓ Jumps with two feet
- ✓ Hops on one foot
- ___ Balances on one foot
- ✓ Alternates feet going up stairs
- ___ Alternates feet going down stairs

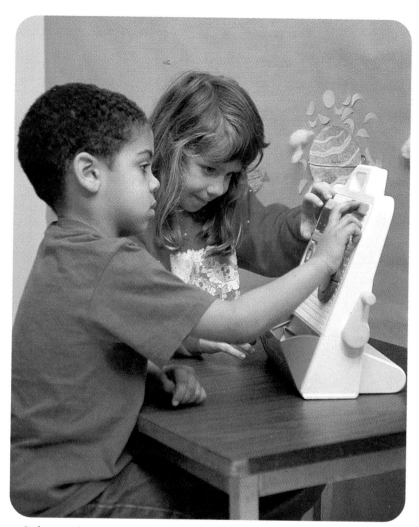

A running record is a good way to track what a specific child does throughout the day. How might you use this information?

od was three minutes long. No notes were made; only a tally mark indicated each hitting episode. Totaling the tally marks gave an indication of how serious the problem was. Later, after further investigation and corrective measures, another frequency count showed that the number of hitting incidents had decreased.

Running Record

With a **running record**, the observer creates *a sequential record of anything that happens during a specific period of time.* The time period may be as short as ten minutes or may last all day. The observer may write down everything that happens during the time period or may observe and record at specific intervals within the time period.

For example, a teacher may want to identify a toddler's developmental abilities. The teacher decides to observe for ten minutes, with a written observation on whatever the toddler is doing recorded each minute. When completed, the observation notes provide insight into the child's current skills.

may focus on one child or include several children. Repeating the frequency count at a later date can help you see whether the behavior is occurring more or less often than before.

To find out how often hitting incidents occurred on the playground, for example, one preschool teacher made five observations during the day. Each observation peri-

Checklist

A **checklist** is simply *a list of specific information that the observer is looking for.* It can be used to study the environment, but more often a checklist identifies behavior or skills that children are expected to develop. When the child demonstrates a behavior or skill, the teacher either makes a check mark or writes the date next to the appropriate

Rating Scale

Child's name: _JaNelle_   **Age:** _3 yrs. 2 mos._

Date: _4/16_   **Time:** _9:00-9:30 a.m._

Observed by: _Celia_   **Setting:** _Preschool Lab_

Skill Observed: _Language Skills_

SKILL	ALWAYS	SOMETIMES	NEVER
Speaks clearly enough to be understood		✓	
Uses past tense verbs correctly			✓
Uses correct word order when asking questions		✓	
Joins in conversations with other children		✓	

item on the list. Additional space may be provided for comments or descriptions.

Some teachers update each child's checklist weekly. Others may do so only twice a year. Checklists are useful for parent-teacher conferences because they can give parents a picture of how their child is developing.

Rating Scale

On a **rating scale**, the observer records *a verbal or numerical evaluation of listed items. The listed items might forcus on children's abilities or behaviors or characteristics of the center's environment.* For example, the observer might be asked to rate the child's skill in performing a certain task on a scale of 1 to 5. As with checklists, rating scales are often used periodically throughout the year to give an overall picture of a child's development. Checklists and rating scales may be developed by teachers for their specific use or purchased from suppliers of educational materials.

Objective Descriptions

Several of the observation techniques you have just read about require that you describe situations. Remember that these need to be objective, not subjective. As you read in Chapter 3, an objective description is based on facts alone. An objective observation might say: "Shannon

> ### Tip FROM THE Pros
>
> **A**dd detail to your descriptions by choosing words with specific meanings. Instead of writing "Thomas went to the science center," tell whether he ran, shuffled, skipped, marched, walked quickly, or wandered slowly. Action words and descriptive phrases can help you record not only what children did, but *how* they did it.

walked into the room with her head held down. She was dragging her sweater on the ground behind her." A subjective description, on the other hand, is based on personal judgments. It might state: "Shannon was depressed as she came into the room."

While you are observing, your job is to record facts. Later on, you can think about your impressions of what took place. Was Shannon depressed, or was she tired, ill, lonely, or disappointed? Do you have enough information to decide? Others may want to read what you have recorded and draw their own conclusions. They can only do so if descriptions are accurate and objective.

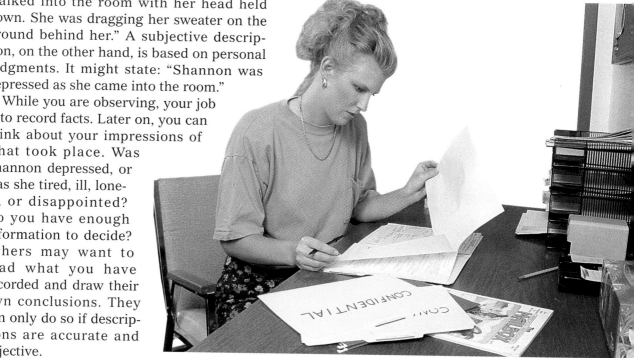

What problems might occur if observation information is not kept confidential? As a student, how should you insure confidentiality?

USING OBSERVATION RECORDS

*O*nce observations have been written down, the records should be filed for later reference. Several easy systems can be used for keeping observations organized.

All records that pertain to individual children need to be placed together under each child's name. Some teachers keep a file folder for each child. Others place observation records in an accordion file or tabbed ring binder. Teachers should review the records periodically to make sure they are collecting adequate information about each child in the program.

Observation records that deal with situations can be categorized and filed in some systematic manner. For example, a study of how often children use a particular piece of play equipment on the playground might be filed under "active play."

Maintaining Confidentiality

To insure that the privacy of child and family is not invaded, always keep observation records confidential. They should never be left in open view. If observations will be made available to a researcher or person other than the teacher, written permission must be obtained from those who have legal custody of the child. Signed and dated permission slips should be placed in files before any observation takes place.

If observation records are used in research, care should be taken to provide false names or identifiers for children who have been observed. Observers sometimes refer to children by their initials to protect their identity.

Interpreting Observations

Observations are of little use if they are just filed away and never used. When reviewed and interpreted, however, they give information that can be helpful. To interpret something is to explain its meaning. When interpreting observations, child care professionals look for patterns and try to draw conclusions about the causes and meaning of behavior.

Interpretations must always be made with care. Experienced child care professionals resist jumping to conclusions based on a single observation. Instead, they review a series of observations collected over several days, weeks, or months. They base their interpretations on facts, experience, and training, not personal likes and dislikes. Even then, wise teachers realize that their interpretation is only an educated guess.

Monique's teacher, Ernesto, made an educated guess about why Monique persisted in biting other children. He began by reviewing event records of biting incidents. Most of the incidents occurred shortly before nap time and involved conflicts over sharing toys. Ernesto's interpretation was that Monique was getting overtired, and so found it especially difficult to cope with frustration. Ernesto decided to try steering Monique toward quiet, solitary activities, such as looking at books in the reading corner, at the time of day when biting tended to occur. After several weeks, a frequency count showed that the number of biting incidents had indeed gone down. If it had not, Ernesto would have needed to rethink his interpretation of Monique's behavior.

As a child care student, you will be given many opportunities to practice your observation skills. Sometimes you will be expected to leave the interpretation up to others. If you are asked to draw your own conclusions, be sure to keep these comments distinct from the observation itself. Clearly label both the observation and the interpretation.

ASSESSING CHILDREN'S DEVELOPMENT

As you have read, some of the reasons for conducting observations are to identify a child's abilities, needs, and rate of progress. In order to get a clear picture of a child's overall development, teachers should conduct observations in a variety of situations over time. They should take care to collect information about all areas of development, including physical, intellectual, social, emotional, and moral. Your knowledge of development, based on information in this text and any other classes and resources, will help you learn what to look for. Some of the basics are described here.

Observing Physical Development

Clues to physical development include the child's appearance, health, and physical abilities. Observe and record:

- Signs of health: smooth, soft skin; clear, bright eyes; nose not runny or breathing blocked; clean teeth; firm, clean gums.
- Any evidence of illness or injury.
- Changes in napping, toileting, or eating habits.
- Stamina and energy levels.
- Evidence of large and small motor skills.
- Evidence of eye-hand coordination (when using blocks and puzzles, for example).

Observing Intellectual Development

To observe intellectual development, note how children think and cope with daily experiences. When observing, pay attention to the child's:

- Ability to cope with problems. Is the child able to think of possible solutions, or does the child rely on others to solve problems?

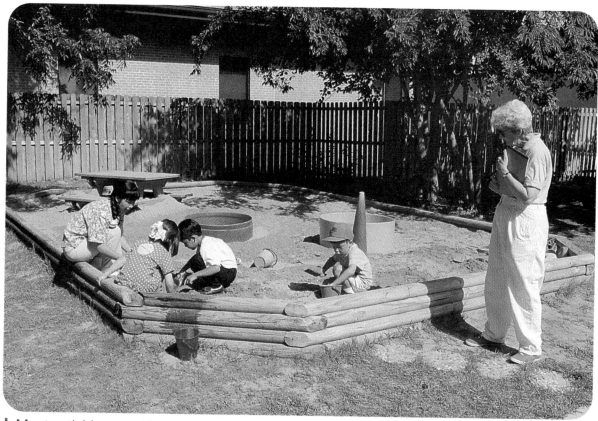

Most activities provide opportunities to observe and assess several areas of development. What areas might you observe during sandbox play?

- Ability to make identifications. Can the child recognize shapes, colors, numbers, sizes, and spatial relationships?
- Language skills. This includes vocabulary development and the ability to communicate effectively. Is the child understood by most people?
- Use of imagination and creativity. Examine all types of activities, especially art, language, and dramatic play.

Observing Social Development

Observation can also give clues to children's social development. Observers should note:

- Achievements relating to social skills, such as sharing, cooperation, and taking turns.
- How aggressive the child is. Does the child go after what he or she wants to the point of causing conflict with others?
- How assertive the child is. Will the child speak up or take action to get what he or she wants in an acceptable, agreeable manner?
- How passive the child is. Does the child allow others to dominate him or her? Is the child unwilling to stand up for what is important and proper?
- Situations in which the child is a leader or a follower.

Trust and bonding are important parts of children's emotional development.

- Whether the child seems to play as well alone as in a group.
- Whether the child plays well with both boys and girls.

Observing Emotional Development

Children give hints about their current level of emotional development through their behavior. Observations should include:

- Evidence of the child's self-identity. For instance, is the child able to see himself or herself as distinctly separate from the parent? How easily does the child separate from the parent at the beginning of each day?

- Examples of how the child copes with frustration. Note situations in which the child shows self-control (or lack of it), such as in a conflict with another child.
- Evidence of trust and bonding. Does the child have a favorite teacher to turn to for comfort and affection? Does the child show signs of trusting others, especially when ill or hurt? Does the child appear relaxed and confident when in your care?

Observing Moral Development

Moral development can be observed through both the behavior and attitudes that children are developing. As children make progress in this area, you will note whether they have:

- A willingness to follow rules.
- An increasing awareness of basic principles concerning what is right and wrong.
- A willingness to accept responsibility for their own actions.
- An increasing awareness of, and desire to avoid, actions that are harmful to people, animals, and property.
- A sense of remorse (regretfulness) displayed when they know they have caused injury or ill will.

Other Ways to Assess Children's Development

Observation is one way to gather information about children's level of development. Another is by collecting samples of their work. For example:

- Completed art projects show evidence of creativity, as well as children's ability to coordinate the small muscles that handle brushes and other tools.
- Audio tapes of stories that have been dictated to a teacher demonstrate children's language, vocabulary, and ability to apply concepts.
- Videotapes of children at play in the dress-up area allow observers to witness imagination and emerging social skills.
- Snapshots of children's block buildings exhibit children's understanding of size, shape, and spatial relationships.

BUILDING OBSERVATION SKILLS

*B*ecoming a skilled observer takes practice. The more often you observe, the more effective you will become at noting and recording the details of children's behavior. If you continue in the child care field, you will gain the knowledge and experience required to make sound judgments when interpreting observations. Firsthand observation of children will help give you the insight needed by a child care professional.

By observing this situation, what might you learn about Carrie's development?

Chapter 16 Review

Reviewing the Facts

1. Give three reasons why teachers observe children.
2. What is naturalistic observation?
3. Name one advantage and one disadvantage of the participant observer approach.
4. Why should a nonparticipating observer try to stay in the background?
5. What type of information is included in an anecdotal record?
6. Describe a frequency count.
7. What is the difference between a checklist and a rating scale?
8. What is meant by interpreting observations?
9. List two things you might note when assessing social development and two things you might note when assessing intellectual development.

Thinking Critically

1. Identify the advantages and disadvantages of naturalistic observation as compared to setting up special situations to observe children's reactions.
2. A parent asks whether you think her child is ready to learn to write her own name. What information would you use to help you answer this question?
3. Objectivity is important when describing behavior. Is it also important when using other recording methods, such as a checklist or frequency count? Explain.
4. How might personal likes and dislikes influence a teacher's interpretation of observation records?

Activities and Applications

1. **Descriptive Writing.** Write the word "run" across the top of a piece of paper. List as many words and phrases as you can to describe different ways children run. What does this tell you about recording observations accurately?
2. **Objective Writing.** With a partner use pictures from magazines to write objective descriptions of what you see. After you both look at the same picture, write separate observations. Then compare and analyze what you have each written, looking for any subjective observations. Rewrite these to make them objective.

3. **Running Record.** Observe and record a young child's behavior for ten minutes while a classmate does the same. Use the running record method. Compare your observations with your classmate's. Do your descriptions give the same basic picture of the child's behavior as your partner's? What conclusions can you draw about recording behavior?

SCHOOL TO WORK

Your Professional Portfolio

As you observe children for the remainder of this course, collect samples of the observation records you create. Sort through these, looking for the best examples of your work. Put two or three of the best in your portfolio. Make sure they show your skill at making objective observations.

Observing and Analyzing

Practicing Your Observation Skills

You don't need to be in a child care setting to practice using your observation skills and tools. Anywhere you have the opportunity to watch and listen, you can work at improving your observation abilities.

- **Observation Techniques.** Practice observation techniques with the following exercises:
  a. Act as a participant observer at your family's next meal.
  b. Use anecdotal records to describe one of these situations or another situation of your choosing: a customer paying for purchases at a store; birds gathering at a bird feeder; people waiting at a bus stop.
  c. Use a frequency count to determine the popularity of a certain food at the school cafeteria.
  d. Write objective descriptions of scenes in a television program.
  e. Watch a videotape—of children at play, of a sporting event, or of a nature program—and practice writing accurate and objective descriptions of some of the actions you observe.

- **Observation Tools.** Practice making and using observation tools by:
  a. Making a checklist of all the steps in one of your regular routines, such as getting dressed in the morning or preparing a meal. Check off each step, recording the time, as you complete it.
  b. Creating a rating scale that lists the qualities of an appealing, healthful meal. Use it to rate the food choices of a friend or classmate at lunch time.

Career Profile

Meet Karen Carnegie, a teacher's aide in a nursery school. Karen works along with a teacher in a classroom of twelve two- and three-year-old children.

Why did you choose this career?

"I've always had fun playing with my younger brothers, sisters, and cousins. Our child care class in high school included a six-week volunteer program in a preschool. Working with so many children at one time was a new experience for me. I found that I felt more confident assisting the teacher than I did leading the group on my own. Once I graduated, I decided to apply for a teacher's aide position, and I got the job."

What education and skills do you need?

"My state doesn't require formal training for a teacher's aide position. I did have to prove that I was at least eighteen years old and had never been convicted of child abuse or neglect. My employer requires me to continue learning. I attend one professional conference every year, as well as local affiliate meetings of the National Association for the Education of Young Children. Once a month my program director invites speakers to our nursery school to conduct staff training meetings. Topics range from children's health to creative art for young children. Opportunities like these help me be the best teacher's aide possible.

"I know that someday I will want to be the lead teacher in a classroom. To prepare for this, I have enrolled in community college to obtain a two-year associate's degree in early childhood care and education. While completing that course work, I can also work on obtaining my Child Development Associate credential.

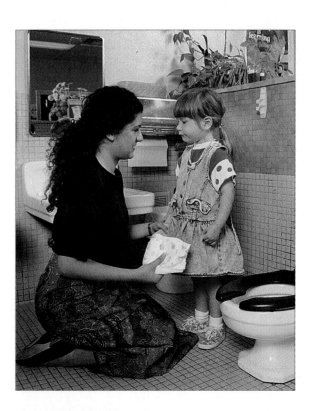

"Working as a team member is a very important skill for me. Cooperation among all adults who work with the children makes the days go more smoothly for everyone. I have to take the initiative when I see that things need to be done, such as cleaning paint brushes or helping a child who has had a toileting accident. My job requires that I be organized and plan ahead. It's my responsibility to have play materials available and set out before children come to participate in an activity. Chaos can break out if children have to wait a long time because I've forgotten to prepare materials.

"I've learned from staff training that being skilled in positive discipline makes me a more effective teacher's aide. When a teacher is reading a story, for example, I can sit beside a child who may need extra help paying attention in order to help the child focus on the activity."

What is a typical day on the job like?

"Just like the teacher, I arrive before the children do. I review the teacher's lesson plans and help assemble needed materials. I help the teacher greet children and parents. Throughout the day I do a variety of things. I play outside with the children, prepare tables for snacks, help children clean up, and read stories to small groups of children. Most days I spend time in each of the learning centers, playing with children to guide their learning, while the lead teacher conducts an activity in another center."

What is most challenging about your job?

"Most of the drawbacks I notice are linked to the fact that I'm an aide rather than a teacher. Parents seem to have a little more respect for the teachers. Also, I have to do more of the cleanup work in the center. My salary is lower, too. These are all reasons why I'm continuing my education so that I can get a better position someday."

What do you like best about your work?

"I really enjoy working with my lead teacher. We agree on how young children should be taught, and I'm learning a lot. Most of all, we have fun together. We both love laughing with the children. We are often amazed at how much children grow and develop."

SHARE YOUR THOUGHTS

1. If you were a teacher's aide, what kind of classes or workshops would you attend to become better at your job?

2. Why do you think it is important to have a good teacher's aide in an early childhood classroom?

3. What part of being a teacher's aide sounds most interesting to you? What part would you like the least?

CURRICULUM PLANNING FOR PRESCHOOLERS

Reflections

"It's when the light dawns for a child that I have my best moments when working with preschoolers. It might be when a little boy successfully writes his name for the first time, or a little girl suddenly realizes what numbers stand for. The other day I watched a child cross the balance beam after she had been trying for weeks. There was a look of pure joy on her face. I do everything I can to help children have moments like these. They are as special for me as they are for the children."

—Lamont

Chapter 17

Teaching and Learning

CHAPTER OBJECTIVES

- Describe the qualities of a strong curriculum.
- Create a lesson plan.
- Apply principles of how children learn when planning lessons.
- Explain the impact of teaching style on learning.
- Describe effective teaching techniques.

Terms to Learn

- bias
- chronological grouping
- close-ended materials
- developmental grouping
- facilitate
- family grouping
- focus object
- lesson plan
- manipulatives
- open-ended materials
- open-ended questions
- teachable moments
- thematic unit

T hat's interesting, Caroline," Marguerite Reilly, the teacher's aide, said to one child as she stopped at the table where several children were drawing. They had been asked to draw a place that was very special to them.

Then Marguerite glanced at Peter's work. Instead of a drawing, his paper was covered with a series of bluish-green streaks. Marguerite watched as he systematically took blue and green crayons and blended them in different combinations on the paper. Curious about his efforts, Marguerite said, "Blue is my favorite color."

Peter sighed. "I want to draw the beach and the ocean," he explained, "but I can't get the color of the water right. I think it looks kind of like that." He pointed to one blur. "And kind of like that." He pointed to another. "But I can't remember exactly."

"Sometimes things just don't turn out the way we want them to," Marguerite said with understanding, "but at least. . ."

Suddenly Peter exclaimed, "That's what it looked like!" He pointed to the stone in Marguerite's ring.

"Why, you're right, Peter," she responded with excitement. "This stone is called an aquamarine. 'Aqua' means water and 'marine' means the sea. So this stone is supposed to look like ocean water."

Peter beamed. "I *knew* it!" he said.

Marguerite hesitated, then took off the ring and set it on the table. "If you are very careful with this," she told him, "I'll leave it here for a few minutes so you can look at it and get the color just right."

Ten minutes later, Peter held his paper up for Marguerite to see. "I got it!" He pointed proudly to one blue-green patch.

Marguerite compared them admiringly. "Yes, that's a perfect match. Good for you, Peter!"

As Peter went back to his drawing, Marguerite slipped the ring on her finger. Later her husband would enjoy hearing how his gift had served a very special function that day.

WHAT WILL YOU TEACH?

L ike Peter, most children are eager to explore and make discoveries. They need these opportunities in order to grow and learn. Without them, development suffers. Children can easily fall behind and develop problems. As a child care professional, an important part of your job is to promote child development through learning activities—but what will you teach and how will you teach it? That's what this unit of your text is all about.

Anyone who works with children needs plenty of activity ideas. There are many hours to fill during the weeks and months in child care. Your journey through this unit will equip you with many ideas, but an idea is of little use without a plan for implementing it. This chapter will show you how to turn an idea into reality.

Becoming skillful at planning and carrying out activities is a worthwhile goal. You can use the tried-and-true ideas of others, but you can also learn to adapt ideas and create your own. The child care professional who has this ability is highly valued in the field.

BUILDING A STRONG CURRICULUM

*I*n a good preschool program, activities don't just happen. They are carefully developed as part of the curriculum, which provides a plan for giving children educational experiences.

When teachers develop the curriculum, they begin with the philosophy and goals of the program. To accomplish goals, they break them down into manageable parts. For example, one part of a goal that aims at developing children's social skills would be learning cooperation. Activities can then be chosen that help children practice cooperation.

What makes a curriculum strong? The key is well-planned activities. First of all, they need to be stimulating and varied, not repetitive and boring. They should capture children's interest, giving them information and encouraging them to think.

When well planned, curriculum activities are geared to the children's abilities and level of development. If they are too easy, children become bored and restless. They may turn to disruptive behavior to make things interesting. If activities are too diffi-

In a well-planned curriculum, each day's activities help to meet the program's goals. Active involvement can increase learning.

cult, children become frustrated. If they develop a sense that they can't learn, self-esteem suffers. The ideal, of course, is a curriculum that challenges children yet enables success.

A strong curriculum is also balanced. In other words, it includes activities that address all areas of development, as well as different subject areas. Typically, the curriculum is divided into subject areas that correspond to the learning centers in the classroom. The chapters in this unit describe learning centers that are typically included. Remember, however, that activities can also be created for any other learning centers a program might have.

Finally, a strong curriculum meets all program goals. Activities in different subject areas work together to support the goals.

Planning Skills

WHAT ARE PLANNING SKILLS?

Planning skills are those abilities needed for successfully arranging events, activities, and projects. Qualities needed for planning include organization, resourcefulness, and logic. To plan well, you must know what you want to accomplish—your purpose for the activity—as well as the abilities and limitations of the people and circumstances involved.

Planning Skills in Action

"I think we can do this," Debra said to her class of second graders. They were talking about preparing and hosting a luncheon for grandparents and other special older adults. "You know what it will take, though—" she added, "careful planning and lots of cooperation."

With assurances that the students wanted to make the effort, Debra first sought permission from the school principal. Once this was secured, she selected a time and date for the event. The children's usual lunch hour seemed a natural choice. She chose a date several weeks away, when the school's conference room would be available.

Next, she and the children needed a menu they were capable of preparing. After a class discussion, they decided on soup, sandwiches, and fruit salad. She then assigned specific preparation tasks, including sending out invitations, based on each student's interests and abilities.

With the menu settled, Debra spoke to the head cook about where the food could be obtained and how much it would cost. She placed the food order as soon as all the responses to the invitations had been returned.

Debra's biggest concern was about the food preparation itself. She found several parents and kitchen staff members who volunteered to oversee the students as they prepared the meal.

On the day of the luncheon, everything—and everyone—was ready. "I really enjoyed sharing this experience with Jimmie," one grandparent told Debra. As they left, other adults and the children,

too, made equally favorable comments.

"This just might become an annual event," Debra thought to herself. Already she was thinking about a few things that they could do more efficiently the next time.

Your Analysis

1. Identify, in order, the steps Debra took to organize the lunch. Was this order logical? Why or why not? Explain or give examples.

2. What human resources—people and their talents—did Debra rely on to carry out the plan?

3. What limitations did she have to consider?

4. How might Debra improve upon this experience?

Can you think of at least eight possible activities that you could use in a thematic unit about apples?

For example, "to foster creativity and imagination" is a goal of many programs. To meet this goal, teachers plan activities not just in art but also in music, creative movement, dramatic play, and other subject areas to encourage children to work with their own ideas and to be expressive.

Curriculums are planned and implemented with care by creative, involved child care professionals. Although classroom teachers do most of the planning, the director may also become involved. Final approval of the curriculum comes from the director.

Thematic Units

Often the curriculum activities that teachers plan are based on a theme. A **thematic unit** is *one central topic, or theme, about which children will learn.*

THE MULTICULTURAL CLASSROOM

Teachers today are not as likely to use multicultural themes as a basis for units as they once were. Instead, they weave projects, toys, and props that promote understanding and appreciation of different cultures into the entire curriculum throughout the school year. To offer them as a novelty or one-time experience only marks them as "foreign" and "different," not as part of a truly multicultural society.

For example, Mr. McGuire noticed children collecting leaves while on a walk. The children's interest motivated him to plan a thematic unit on trees. The children took a field trip to a tree nursery. In the art area, they made a "forest" of different kinds of trees, using real leaves and bark. To learn math concepts, they counted and sorted acorns from an oak tree. For science, they observed a tree in the play yard and identified all the animals and insects that live in it. For a snack, the class baked apples with dates and walnuts—all of which grow on trees. At story time, Mr. McGuire read books about trees.

As you can see, this approach gave the children all kinds of knowledge about trees. Weaving a single topic into several subject areas helps children learn how knowledge overlaps in real life.

Thematic units can be developed around hundreds of different topics. Creative teachers like to think of new units each year. Organized teachers keep lists of theme ideas and activities that correspond to them. Such lists make a handy reference in the future.

Scheduling Curriculum Activities

As activities are planned, they are incorporated in the daily schedule. In Chapter 12 you saw how schedules work. Regular routines, including arrival, meals, snacks, naps, toileting, and departure, form the core of the schedule. The rest of the time is reserved for activities. You can't just drop them in without some forethought, however.

Tip FROM THE Pros

*C*hildren enjoy the props, room decor, and activities that accompany a thematic unit. Try planning activities based on these appealing themes: colors, celebrations, transportation, gardens, cartoon characters, numbers, insects, animals, space travel, dinosaurs, families, friends, community helpers, occupations, seasons, sounds, water, weather, bridges, libraries, and musical instruments.

When placing activities in the schedule, look at timing. Will there be enough time to accomplish what you want to do? Is this the best time of day for the children to do this activity? Will the activity interfere with anything else going on in the center? Answering questions like these ahead of time will help the schedule flow more smoothly.

DEVELOPING LESSON PLANS

*I*t takes more than just an idea to make an activity happen in the classroom. Each one must first be developed into a lesson plan. A **lesson plan** is *a detailed, written explanation of an activity, including the purpose, any materials needed, and the step-by-step method for carrying out the activity.*

Why do you suppose people need and use lesson plans? Lesson plans are an organization tool. They force you to think ahead about what you want to accomplish and why. They enable you to think through what you will do. They can also be saved for future use and reference.

Imagine what would happen if you had to walk into a preschool classroom right now and teach a group of children about gravity. Without materials and a procedure, you would probably flounder. You might waste time and bore the children while quickly trying to come up with appropriate ideas of what to do. You probably would not have the items you need to give the children a hands-on experience. You might take one direction and then realize afterwards that you left out something important or interesting that should have been done.

At first, developing lesson plans may seem time-consuming and unnecessary. The process will go more quickly with experience, and you will soon see the benefits of careful pre-planning.

Lesson plans enable teachers to work through their ideas mentally and on paper before they are enacted. By doing so, teachers have a clear understanding of the purpose behind each activity. They can assemble the right materials in the right quantity. They can set up a logical procedure, without missing or out-of-sequence steps. They are prepared to make good use of available time.

Many teachers use a preprinted form for preparing lesson plans. If you were making a lesson plan, you would fill out the form as shown in the completed sample on page 339. Although there may be some variations, the basic information that you record on a lesson plan includes:

- **Target Age Group.** Record the age or level of development of the children.
- **Theme.** Enter the central topic for the lesson.
- **Title of Lesson.** Give the lesson an appropriate title.
- **Purpose.** Briefly state the overall objective of the lesson.
- **Concepts to Develop.** List exactly what you want the children to learn. It may be one concept or several. For example, if the children are going to play at the water table with many objects, they might learn that some items sink and some float.
- **Skills to Develop.** Identify any abilities that children will acquire or strengthen. Skills developed during a music activity, for instance, might include keeping a steady beat and following directions.
- **Materials Required.** List all materials needed, including quantities.
- **Procedures.** Outline the steps for conducting the activity. Put them in order. Try to be as thorough as possible in breaking the sequence down. Well-planned activities begin with a short introduction that motivates children. You might use a question or show an object to create interest. The activity should be completed with something that brings it to closure. A question that generates thought or conclusions may be enough. A transition to the next activity on the schedule may also be included at the end.

Sample Lesson Plan

Target Age Group: *Four- and five-year-olds*
Theme: *Our Senses*   **Title of Lesson:** *Touch and Tell*
Purpose: *To help children develop their sense of touch and language skills*

CONCEPTS TO DEVELOP	SKILLS TO DEVELOP	MATERIALS REQUIRED
• Objects vary in size, shape, and texture. • Objects can be identified by touch. • Objects have different characteristics that can be described.	• Gathering information through touch. • Descriptive language and vocabulary.	• Empty, clean, decorated coffee can. • Large box filled with familiar toys, plastic fruit, blocks, etc., that will fit individually in can. • Blanket to cover box. • Carpet squares.

Activity Procedure

1. Have children sit in a large circle on carpet squares.
2. **Introduction.** Ask the children to touch some items around them, such as their hair, clothing, or shoes. Then ask them to tell how these items feel.
3. Tell children they are going to learn how to gather information using just their sense of touch.
4. Place an object from the box in the coffee can. Use the blanket to keep all children from seeing the object.
5. Invite one child at a time to play the game as follows:
   • Have the child reach into the can and feel the object without looking.
   • Ask the child to describe what he or she is feeling without telling what it is.
   • The class then tries to guess what object is in the can.
6. Once the object is identified, repeat Steps 4 and 5 until all the children have had several turns.
7. **Closure.** Remind children that many objects around them are interesting to touch. Can they name any items that they especially like to touch? Can they think of objects that are not safe to touch?

QUESTIONS TO GUIDE LEARNING	POSSIBLE FOLLOW-UP ACTIVITIES
1. How does the object feel? 2. What shape is the object? 3. Is the object hard or soft? 4. How might this object be used?	1. Sorting fabrics of different textures. 2. Texture rubbings art project. 3. Texture collage art project. 4. Touch-and-feel board in science center for Jesse and Bonita.

Evaluation

Six of the eight children were successful with this activity. Be sure to include a few less familiar objects to challenge the more developmentally advanced children. Begin activity with easier objects to identify. Allow 30 minutes the next time the activity is used.

- *Questions to Guide Learning.* List questions that will focus a child's thinking. By asking, "What are some ways we can sort these buttons?" a teacher encourages the child to identify different ways of categorizing.

- *Possible Follow-Up Activities.* Either before or after conducting the lesson, make note of any follow-up activities that would be appropriate. Sometimes teachers identify the children who would benefit most from a follow-up activity.

- *Evaluation.* Briefly assess the effectiveness of the lesson. Include information about the number of children who were successful. Think about questions like: What adaptations need to be made for different ability levels? How could the lesson be improved? Would you use the lesson again? Some teachers write down specific questions on the form before beginning the lesson.

HOW CHILDREN LEARN

The better you understand children, the better able you are to create effective lesson plans. Lessons are aimed at learning. Your lesson plans need to take into account how children learn.

Do you think children learn in the same way that adults do? In some ways, the answer is "yes." Children, however, are not miniature adults. They don't have all the skills that adults and older children have. Therefore, they cannot learn in exactly the same way.

Think about how you learn best. Suppose you needed to learn a new soccer or basketball play. Would you rather hear an explanation, see a diagram, or try it yourself? You might want some combination of hearing, seeing, and doing. Someone else on your team may learn the same play in a different way than you do. Remember that there is no single right way to learn. Everyone has his or her own style.

Although young children do learn by hearing, seeing, and doing, they don't do so in the same way that adults and older children do. So much can get in the way. Vocabularies are limited. Attention spans are short. Motor skills are still developing. Many concepts are not understood. For reasons like these, child care professionals plan lessons carefully. They keep these principles in mind:

- *Children learn best by doing.* They cannot learn just by listening to explanations. They need hands-on experiences. For this reason, teachers provide many **manipulatives**. These are *toys and materials children can operate and change with their hands.* Clay, dough, sand, and snap beads are examples. Manipulatives help children develop fine motor skills as they learn concepts. Objects of many shapes, sizes, and colors also stimulate their thinking.

- *Children learn best when using their senses.* Sensory experiences—seeing, touching, hearing, smelling, and tasting—capture children's attention and maintain their interest. Children develop concepts about the properties of the world by exploring them with their senses.

- *Children often learn through trial and error.* Like young scientists, children actively explore and experiment when interacting with their environment. They learn what works and what doesn't. Making mistakes and learning from them is a natural part of the learning process.

- *Children learn best when all areas of development are nurtured.* Activities that aim at intellectual, physical, emotional, social, and moral development are needed for children to become well-balanced

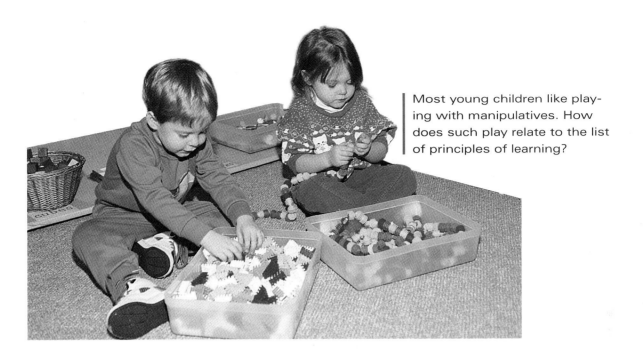

Most young children like playing with manipulatives. How does such play relate to the list of principles of learning?

adults. Remember that these areas are interrelated. Progress in one area usually means progress in another.

- *Children learn through positive reinforcement.* The child who works hard to balance a tall block building is immediately "rewarded" for learning about the principles of weight and gravity, because the building stands. Praise and recognition from caregivers when children learn something new makes them feel good. The joy, pride, and feelings of success that come from new accomplishments are reinforcing to children. They make children *want* to continue learning.

- *Children acquire and experiment with new behaviors through imitation and role modeling.* The significant people in children's lives provide them with words and actions to learn. It is not unusual for parents, caregivers, and teachers to see themselves reflected in the behavior of children.

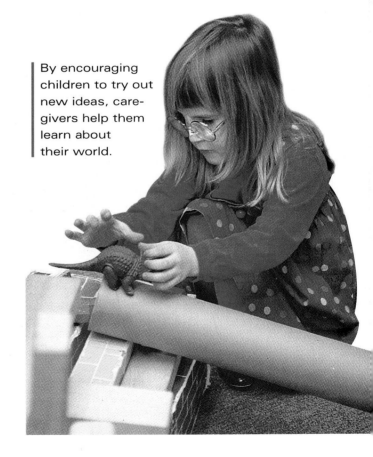

By encouraging children to try out new ideas, caregivers help them learn about their world.

Learning Through Play

Is learning work or play for you? For young children, learning is play. Living and learning are inseparable. Many experiences are new to them, so learning is a continual process. Early childhood specialists agree that play has a major role in learning. Playful interactions with peers, adults, and materials in the environment add to a child's store of knowledge about the world. Through activities that involve play, children grow in all areas of development.

The Role of Play Materials

Some toys and play materials promote learning better than others do. Even those that contribute to learning do so in different ways. When analyzed as teaching tools, play materials are said to be either open-ended or close-ended. Effective teachers make sure that both types are included in their lesson plans.

Open-ended materials are *items that can be used in a variety of ways, with no single "correct" outcome expected.* In other words, the child decides what to do with them. Open-ended materials allow for plenty of creative input from children. With them, children develop independence, decision-making skills, problem-solving skills, and imagination. Many art materials are open-ended. Paints and doughs are two examples. Water and sand toys as well as blocks can be used in an open-ended manner. With these toys, children think for themselves about what they will do with the toys as they play.

Close-ended materials, or structured materials, are *items that are meant to be used in primarily one way, with an expected result.* These materials are less open to input from the child. They help children learn how to follow directions. They also help develop sensory perception and motor skills. Examples include puzzles, matching games, snap beads, stringing beads, and sewing cards. As you can see, the outcome when using toys and materials like these is known ahead of time, but the processes that children go through to use them are useful for learning.

A water table is a popular piece of equipment in many centers. Why do you think young children are drawn to this type of play?

Getting Bias out of the Classroom

*F*or some reason that she did not understand, five-year-old Elizabeth didn't think her teacher liked her. Perhaps Elizabeth was mistaken. On the other hand, perhaps the problem was bias.

Bias is *any attitude, belief, or feeling that results in unfair treatment of an individual because of his or her identity.* People with biases judge others negatively. They look at a person's size, appearance, abilities, gender, economic status, social position, or ethnic background and decide the person isn't worthwhile. They may act on their biases by excluding, ignoring, or mistreating the person. Such behavior is wrong. It doesn't belong in society—or in the early childhood classroom.

People who work with children need to identify their own biases and eliminate them. At the very least, they cannot act on them. If they do, they risk hurting children very deeply. Child care professionals must also teach children to think and act without bias. Gentle guidance and good role modeling are keys to doing this. In addition, child care professionals need to eliminate biased toys and materials from the classroom. Books that send inappropriate messages, dolls that represent only select groups, and posters that give incorrect portrayals of ethnic backgrounds and roles are all a problem. Through increased awareness and sensitivity, teachers can create an environment in which biases are unwelcome.

PUTTING LESSONS INTO ACTION

*C*hildren learn with help from adults. Lesson plans come to life in the hands of teachers. A good lesson plan may not be effective when poorly presented. On the other hand, a weak lesson plan may be saved by a skillful teacher. The manner a teacher uses to teach a lesson is called teaching style. The tools and methods used are called techniques. Teachers combine both of these to make lessons worthwhile for children.

Teaching Styles

Just as personalities are different, teaching styles are too. As a student, you are definitely familiar with all kinds of teaching styles. Through your own classes, you have met some teachers who conduct class with theatrical energy and others who are calm and relaxed. Some teachers have very precise expectations about behavior, while others allow informality. Some teachers prefer structured, orderly lessons; others are more spontaneous.

When working with children, a child care professional's teaching style becomes integrated with the activity. In fact, a teacher often plans the activity to fit with his or her teaching style. For example, Mrs. Rooney is dramatic and expressive. After reading a story about a monkey, she joined the children as they all walked around the room like monkeys. Ms. Tuttle has a more quiet manner. After reading the same story, she showed pictures of different kinds of monkeys and led a discussion about going to the zoo.

Teaching styles hinge on more than just personality. The teacher's own learning style

This teacher has chosen a unique way to present an activity. How does it reflect the individual's teaching style? What are some other approaches that different teachers might take?

is a factor. A person who learns by doing, for example, is more likely to teach others by using a hands-on approach. A teacher who learns well visually might attach flannel cutouts to a story board in order to illustrate an idea.

Beliefs also affect teaching style. What a teacher believes about children and how they learn has impact. Suppose teachers are working with two children who are shy. The children are afraid of making mistakes. One teacher might believe that a gentle approach is the best way to gradually build their self-confidence. Another teacher who believes the same children need to be drawn out might take an outgoing approach, using humor.

One teaching style is not necessarily better than another. Children can benefit from all types. Some children may relate better to one style than another. A child who likes action, for example, might love to run around like a monkey but become impatient with talk about the zoo. On the other hand, the need to sit still and practice listening as others talk about the zoo may help the energetic child learn some control. When teachers with different styles interact with children throughout the day, children have opportunities to learn in different ways and adapt to varied situations.

Experienced, sensitive teachers are aware of their teaching style. Those who are partic-

ularly skilled know how to adapt it when necessary. They may have to change to meet children's needs or to handle the activity. With sharp observation skills, a versatile person does what is necessary when the situation demands it.

Teaching Techniques

When working with children, teachers not only form a style of teaching, but they also choose techniques to use. Skilled teachers have tools and methods that work. They know from experience. Some of the proven techniques that teachers use are described here.

Arranging the Environment

Effective teachers make sure the physical surroundings promote success rather than interfere with it. What if children are expected to put toys away, for example, but there isn't enough room for storage? How can children comply with the rule? When the environment is a stumbling block, children are not able to learn effectively.

Setting the Stage

To begin an activity, teachers help children get into the proper frame of mind. Before reading a story about a lost puppy, for example, Mrs. Plummer asked, "Have you ever been somewhere with your family and gotten separated from them? How did you feel when you looked around and you couldn't find them? What did you do? In this story . . ." This opener attracts the children's interest and lets them know what to expect. It also prepares them to empathize with the puppy.

Teachers may also set the stage by using a **focus object,** *an item that is related to an activity and helps introduce it.* For example, before having children plant seeds in cups, one teacher showed garden tools and led a discussion about gardens.

Handling Play

Since children learn through play, teachers need to handle play activities carefully. Teachers should **facilitate** play, or *help bring it about without controlling it.* This skill comes with experience. For example, a teacher who tells the children to make a train with the empty boxes controls play. A teacher who puts the boxes out and says, "What can be done with these?" facilitates play.

With the right attitude and actions, you can help children get the most out of play. Give children some freedom to choose play materials and use them in ways that suit them. An open-minded approach to play gives children a chance to be creative and independent.

By interacting with children in play situations, teachers are less likely to miss opportunities for growth and learning. They recognize **teachable moments,** *unplanned opportunities for learning.* They also become skilled at interpreting the thoughts and feelings children express through play.

Grouping Children

When planning an activity, teachers must think about the mixture of children that will be involved. The number of children, their age range, and their ability level all affect teaching and learning.

Grouping begins with how children are placed in classrooms. Many programs do this by *placing children of the same age together.* This is called

By using a focus object, you can help attract the children's attention. Here every child gets a close-up look at the sprouting seed.

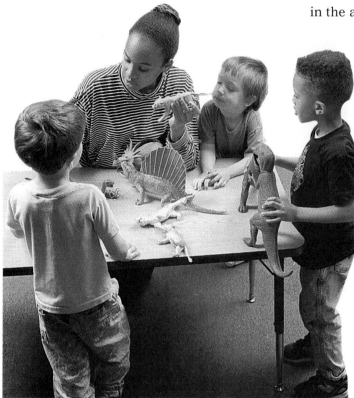

What are some advantages of working with children in small groups?

chronological grouping. With **developmental grouping**, *children are placed in classrooms according to ability*. Some programs use **family grouping**, in which *children of a certain age range are placed in the same classroom*. Three- through five-year-olds might be grouped together, or six- through eight-year-olds.

Each method has its pros and cons. When children of the same age or ability level make up the classroom, it is easier to plan activities that will be suitable for all. However, children miss the opportunity to relate to those of other ages and abilities. Family grouping can be a challenge because teachers must consider a wider range of developmental needs. An inappropriate activity will leave older or younger children in the age range feeling left out and learning little. On the other hand, the right activity can give younger children a chance for learning that they might not have had in chronological grouping. It can give older children the chance to relate positively with younger ones, increasing their self-esteem by letting them feel "grown up."

Often teachers use the technique of dividing the class into smaller groups for specific activities. Teachers determine group size according to how much personal attention an activity requires. During some parts of an activity, especially when children are learning new skills, teachers may divide the class into smaller groups to give more one-on-one attention to each child. Later, when children are more confident and competent in their abilities, the teacher may have them work in larger groups.

Some activities are better suited to a certain group size. Most team sports, for example, are more fun with the required number of players. Some art and science projects, on the other hand, are more manageable when conducted in small groups.

Generally, groups should be small enough to prevent overcrowding. A child can feel overwhelmed or "lost" in a group that is too large. Some children misbehave under the same circumstances. Usually, the younger the child, the smaller the group size should be.

Using Concrete Objects

Children are in the early stages of intellectual development. Their ability to imagine and form concepts is limited. Suppose you were trying to describe the seashore to young children. Which would the children understand better, hearing that sand is "pale," "gritty," and "grainy," or seeing and feeling a handful of sand? Because children have limited experiences, descriptive phrases often have little meaning for them. Concrete objects, ones that can be seen and touched, are much easier for them to understand.

Asking Questions Correctly

Open-ended questions are *those that require more than a yes or no answer.* As with open-ended play materials, there is no right or wrong response. Open-ended questions are excellent tools for encouraging children to express feelings, explain ideas, and relate experiences. They stimulate both the creativity and the intellectual skills needed for language development.

Other Techniques

Teachers have many techniques for helping children learn. Bulletin boards that involve children can reinforce concepts. For example, you might create one that challenges children to match shapes. Puppets at story time capture attention. Music and recorded stories add variety to activities. Some teachers use videotapes featuring animation of classic children's books to spark interest in literature.

Experienced teachers are a good resource for teaching techniques. They may not be able to list everything they do in a conversation. If you watch them work, however, you will discover many ideas worth trying when you are in charge of lessons.

APPLYING YOUR KNOWLEDGE

Building lesson plans for the activities that make up a curriculum is a challenge. Now that you know the basics, you can step up to the challenge. It's time to call on your own creativity. It's time to see what you can do when it comes to helping children learn. The rest of this unit has all kinds of information about activities for different learning centers. Take what you have learned in this chapter and apply it as you move forward.

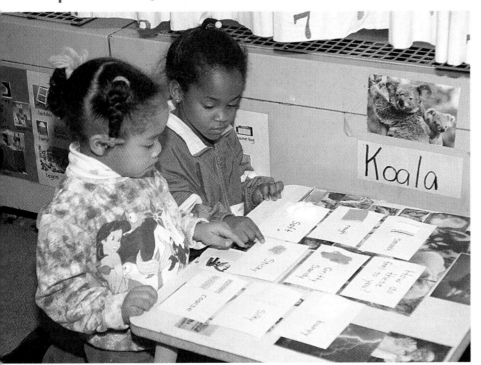

Think of all the words language uses to describe textures. Children need to actually feel those textures before the words have meaning for them.

Chapter 17 Review

Chapter Summary

- An early childhood curriculum provides a plan for giving children educational experiences.
- The philosophy and goals of a program form a basis for building the curriculum. Goals are broken down so that specific lessons can be planned.
- For good organization, teachers use lesson plans that guide them as they carry out activities with the children.
- Teachers can plan a number of activities as part of one thematic unit.
- To plan appropriate activities, teachers must understand how children learn.
- Play has a special role in children's learning. Play materials can be open-ended or close-ended.
- Teaching styles affect how activities for children are handled.
- Teachers use many different techniques to make activities interesting and effective for children.

Reviewing the Facts

1. Identify three qualities of a strong curriculum.
2. What is a thematic unit? Give an example and explain how the theme could be developed through different areas of the curriculum.
3. What is a lesson plan?
4. Why do teachers use lesson plans?
5. List the components that should be included in a lesson plan.
6. Identify six principles that explain how children learn.
7. What are open-ended and close-ended play materials? Give an example of each.
8. Explain how personality and beliefs affect teaching style.
9. Name and briefly describe three teaching techniques.

Thinking Critically

1. Do you think some teachers can handle certain activities without a lesson plan? Explain your answer.
2. Can the principles of how children learn also be applied to adults? Why or why not?
3. Can teachers learn through teaching? Explain your answer.
4. What types of play activities might help children grow in all areas of development: physical, intellectual, emotional, social, and moral?
5. Which of your personality traits do you think would most strongly influence your teaching style? What kinds of activities might you plan as a result?

Activities and Applications

1. **Thematic Units.** Suppose you were planning a thematic unit on birds. List four activity ideas that might work with this theme. (If you wish, choose a different theme to work with.)
2. **Play Materials.** With a partner, make lists of play materials that are close-ended and open-ended. Compare your lists with others in the class.
3. **Focus Objects.** In writing describe two activities that might be planned for children in a preschool and explain how a specific focus object could be used with each.

4. **Open-Ended Questions.** Select a children's book suitable for preschoolers. Write five open-ended questions about the story that you might ask the children.

5. **Lesson Plans.** Create a lesson plan based on one of these ideas or an idea of your own: learning to zip, button, and snap clothing; learning about shadows; matching colors; how maps are used.

SCHOOL TO WORK

Your Professional Portfolio

Begin a list of ideas for thematic units. To get started, use those listed in the "Tip from the Pros" feature on page 337. You may be surprised at how many possibilities there are for a list like this. Once your mind gets on the theme track, ideas will be triggered by all sorts of objects and events that go on around you. Keep notes as the ideas surface. Maintain the list in your portfolio file.

Observing and Analyzing

Techniques: Mix and Match

Knowing *about* teaching techniques is only the first step to using them effectively. Equally important is knowing when and how to use each one.

Effective teachers learn how to recognize what will work and what won't, depending on the circumstances. For example, they might choose a bigger focus object for a large group than they would for a small group.

Observation can help you identify teaching techniques and evaluate them. What you learn will be helpful to you if you work with children someday. Increase your understanding and awareness of teaching techniques with the following activities:

- **Observing in Your School.** As you attend classes, note the different techniques teachers use. Without using names, keep a list of different techniques you notice. Along with each technique, include observations about its effectiveness.

- **Observing in a Child Care Setting.** Visit a preschool or kindergarten classroom. Observe and make notes regarding the following:

  1. What do you see about the environment that increases children's chances for success? Is the arrangement of furnishings and equipment effective? What use is made of the walls? How do teachers make use of the environment?

  2. Did the teacher use focus objects? What were they? When were they introduced? What were the children's responses?

  3. Did the teacher discover and use any teachable moments? Describe how they arose and how they were used for learning.

  4. Did the group size change while you were present? How?

  5. What concrete objects were provided? What concepts were they used to teach? How did the children respond?

  6. Did the teacher use any open-ended questions? What topics did they relate to? How did the children respond to them?

Afterwards, review your notes. Did the teacher favor one technique more than others? Were there variations in how the technique was applied? Did the children's responses indicate that the technique was effective? Use your findings to draw some conclusions about what you learned from this observation.

Chapter 18

Art

Activities

CHAPTER OBJECTIVES

- List the goals of an art curriculum.

- Describe the stages of children's artistic development.

- Plan an art learning center for preschoolers.

- Explain appropriate methods for guiding children's art experiences.

- Plan and lead art activities for children.

t went really high, and I got to hold the string," Kimi said to her father with excitement. He had just picked Kimi up from preschool. "Miss Noreen brought it. It was pink and purple and looked like a giant butterfly. When it was really high, it was just a little butterfly."

Kimi's father smiled as she chattered away about this event that seemed to have made her day. Noreen Applegate, Kimi's preschool teacher, had brought the kite and shown the children how to fly it. She had given each child a chance to hold the string. As Kimi described how the wind had carried the kite, she talked about the motions the kite made and the feel of the wind tugging at the string when it was her turn to hold it.

"The kite even had a really long tail," Kimi said. "Miss Noreen said the tail helped the kite fly."

"I see a tail on your kite too," Kimi's father said. Kimi looked with pride at the kite she had made from yellow construction paper. She held it carefully with both hands. It was decorated with shiny red sequins, hand-drawn hearts, and a bright green bow. Colored ribbons and yarn formed the long tail.

"Yes, but my kite's not for flying," Kimi said firmly. "It's just to look at."

"Well, when we hang it on the refrigerator door," her father replied, "it just might look like it's flying."

Kimi's eyes widened as she smiled back at her father. She rather liked that idea.

GROWING THROUGH ART

Kimi's experience shows that art can be much more than learning to stay within the lines when coloring a picture. **Art** is *the use of skills and creative imagination to produce something pleasing.* Art can give children the chance to exercise their language skills and creativity. It can teach them how to work together. It can even introduce them to some basic scientific principles. When you understand the opportunities for growth that art experiences provide, you can make them an effective and enjoyable part of a preschool curriculum.

GOALS OF THE ART CURRICULUM

At first glance, a toddler's scribbles and a preschooler's drawings may not seem important. Children's art, however, provides a special way to promote growth and development during early childhood. Well-planned art activities give children opportunities to practice skills, express thoughts and feelings, and experience achievement. The benefits include:

- *Developing Physical Skills.* Children practice eye-hand coordination and fine motor skills through coloring, cutting, and pasting.

- *Developing Social Skills.* Many art activities can easily be turned into cooperative efforts. Children learn to work together and see how each individual's contribution adds to the final product.

- *Encouraging Creativity and Decision Making.* Imagination and independent thinking skills grow when children use many different materials to create and decorate projects of their own design.

- *Boosting Self-Confidence.* Children learn that they can create something of their own. With encouragement, they gain confidence in their abilities to think of, and carry out, plans.

- *Building Basic Concepts.* Art activities can be related to many topics. Coloring with charcoal becomes a lesson in nature when the teacher talks about where charcoal comes from. Making a hat can teach history and culture.

ARTISTIC DEVELOPMENT

As with walking and talking, children go through predictable stages in learning to create art. Experts have identified a general age range for each stage, but you need to remember that *children progress through these stages at individual rates*. Depending on physical maturation and how often art activities are experienced, any particular child may be advanced or delayed in relation to the age ranges outlined here:

THE MULTICULTURAL CLASSROOM

Young children may not be able to grasp the finer points of artistic expression. However, they can learn to appreciate what artists demonstrate about their culture through art. Find examples from different cultures and time periods: a Rubens painting; an Aztec calendar; a Chinese kite; a Ukrainian decorated egg. Talk about the colors and materials and how they are used. Discuss the scenes depicted and the purpose served by each creation. You can use art as a basis for simple lessons in history, geography, and social studies. Then ask the children to relate the artwork to their own lives: If you were a painter, what would you care enough about to paint? How could you make a practical item more attractive? In short, try to communicate that art is a window into the values and ideas of the culture in which it is created.

At the scribble stage, children don't yet realize that their movements control the design they make. Later in this stage, children begin to make basic shapes such as circles and squares.

- **Scribbles (Ages one-four).** During this stage, children progress from random scribbling to more deliberate patterns, such as zigzags and spirals. Children gain control of shoulder muscles before they control the smaller muscles in the wrist and fingers. Therefore, early drawings tend to sprawl in wide loops over an entire piece of paper.
- **Symbolic (Ages four-six).** At this stage, drawings may resemble real objects. Details, such as eyelashes, begin to appear. Children frequently repeat shapes to create patterns.
- **Realistic (Ages five-ten).** Children make increasingly complex designs, spending more time on each drawing. They are concerned about making people and objects look "real." Drawings reflect more accurate details and **proportion**, or *the size relationship of the parts.*

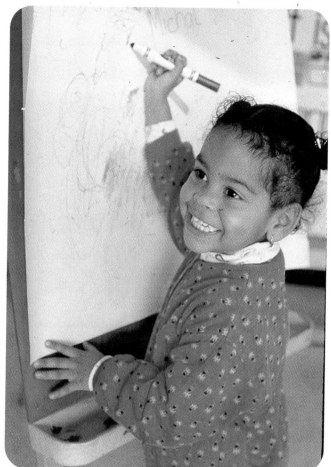

THE ART CENTER

All good early childhood classrooms include a well-stocked art learning center. This invites children to select art activities on their own during free play or at choice time according to what interests them. Many different materials are provided, with new ones substituted from time to time. They can be stored on labeled shelves. Materials should fit the abilities and interests of the children who use the center.

The center is best located in an uncarpeted area. Having a sink nearby is very helpful for cleanup. Children need room to work without bumping others and damaging their projects. Shelves, tables and chairs, easels, and drying racks should be easy to clean.

Safety

Be cautious about the art materials you provide. Some are hazardous. Such substances as spray paints and liquid dyes can trigger allergic reactions or asthma attacks.

Make sure art supplies, especially safety scissors, are in good repair. Supervise activities continuously when using objects small enough to put in the nose, ears, or mouth. Buttons and seeds are examples.

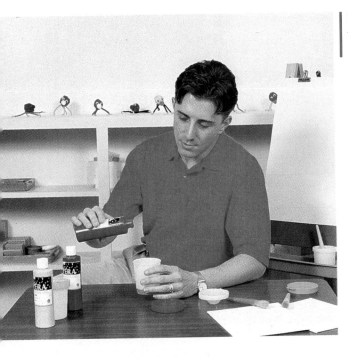

Most toddlers and preschoolers love art activities. However, it is essential that the materials used be safe and appropriate.

- Buy water-based glues, pastes, markers, and paints. These materials should be labeled nontoxic.
- Don't let children use paints or markers on their skin. Wash promptly after activities.
- Make sure your art center has good ventilation. Use a fan to circulate air if needed.
- Use a vacuum or a wet mop to clean up dusty debris. Sweeping stirs up dust.

Other important safety tips include:

- Buy premixed clays that are talc-free. Powdered clay may contain asbestos, a substance that has been linked to cancer.

GUIDING ART EXPERIENCES

Although children enjoy working on their own in the art center, some art activities are led by the teacher. Thinking ahead about some basic principles can make these activities more effective.

Insuring Safety

The Arts & Crafts Materials Institute (ACMI) is a nonprofit group of art supplies manufacturers that analyzes products for safety for adults and children. Products reviewed by the ACMI receive one of the following labels:

- AP (Approved Product) Nontoxic: safe for adults and children.
- CP (Certified Product) Nontoxic: safe and meets certain quality standards.
- Health Label (HL): has been properly tested and labeled for safety. This label is followed by either the word "nontoxic" or a specific warning.

If you have older art supplies that have not been labeled, dispose of them as directed.

Value the Process

Which is more important, the art project created or the process that a child goes through to create it? Most educators believe that *what children learn through the process of creating art is just as important, if not more important, than what they produce.* This art teaching principle is referred to as **process versus product.** What it means is that development occurs when children experience the creative process. The quality of the product doesn't matter.

Two children who use clay to make an animal, for example, practice the same skills. Even if one animal looks more realistic than the other, both children have still benefited from the experience. Making both children feel good about their efforts is part of the teacher's responsibility. When the emphasis is on process, not product, art experiences are less apt to aim for a specific result. They allow children to have input and make decisions about what they want to do.

Build Creativity

An activity that requires children to assemble a product that looks exactly like the teacher's example is simply follow-the-directions art. There is no room for creativity. Instead, the teacher, not the child, practices making decisions. The child simply learns to copy someone else's work. Although some skills may be practiced, children don't get a chance to think for themselves.

Although two preschoolers painted these rainbows, each child took a different approach. Encourage creativity when you work with children.

Building Professional Skills

Creativity

WHAT IS CREATIVITY?

Creativity is experimenting with possibilities. Everyone works with the same tools of creation—words, colors, shapes, function—and faces the same boundaries—limitations of time and other resources. Creative people, however, learn to put things together in new ways to achieve desired effects. They arrange words in new ways to express feelings. They even find more efficient ways of doing things, such as moving furniture. Creativity isn't only an "artistic" value; it is valuable for completing practical tasks as well.

Creativity in Action

Two days after their field trip to the farm, the first-graders were still talking about it. They seemed especially impressed with Bud, the horse they had ridden around the barn.

"I wish we could have brought Bud back with us," Amanda sighed.

Stephen, their teacher, saw the opportunity for an art project. "We can't keep Bud here," he agreed, "but maybe we could make a horse that looks like him to remind us of how much fun we had. What did Bud look like?"

The responses came quickly. "Big." "Brown." "Long, pointy ears."

"Good." Stephen wrote all their descriptions on the board and then read them back. "Now what do we have in this room that might look like Bud?"

The children scanned the room. Carlos pointed to an old teacher's desk in the corner. "That desk is big and brown—and it has legs."

"Sure enough, Carlos!" Stephen said. "How can we make it look even more like a horse?"

With Stephen's guidance, the children were soon re-creating their "horse." Two children made ears from brown paper grocery bags. Two others drew eyes and nostrils on the cup sections of an egg carton and glued them onto a shoe box "head." Stephen fit the shoe box on one end of an old broomstick. Then he attached this "neck" to the desk with a suction cup.

The children watched as he assembled the rest of their work and transformed the desk into the horse of their imagination.

"That," Stephen pronounced, "is the most beautiful horse I've ever seen."

Your Analysis

1. What "problem" did the children face? How did they solve it creatively?

2. Give two examples of how the children "recycled" materials for their project. How does reusing items in this way require creativity? How is it a practical skill?

3. Identify two ways that Stephen encouraged creativity in the children.

Regularly including open-ended art activities encourages creativity. Children have greater control over products and methods. Suppose a class is putting on a puppet play about family pets. The teacher asks a small group of children to go to the art center to make puppets for the play. The center is well equipped for puppet making. It contains small paper bags, socks, plastic foam balls, glue, an assortment of fabric scraps, paper, sequins, yarn, crayons, markers, and paint. Children are allowed to use any or all of the materials to create their puppets, and no two need look the same. The children have no model to guide them, so the products are as varied as the children who created them. By providing an open-ended activity, the teacher has helped the children develop their imaginations.

Respond Appropriately

When a child proudly presents you with a picture or painting, it is tempting to ask, "What is it?" This question can result in a silent, blank stare from a disappointed child who thinks, "Can't you tell?" If this awkward situation happens frequently, children may conclude that they are not good at creating art. To avoid discouraging young artists, a better response would be, "My, how hard you've worked. Would you tell me about your picture?" This response recognizes children's efforts and encourages them to interpret their work to you and practice their language skills at the same time. If vocabulary is limited, don't pressure children to say too much. Let their enthusiasm in the conversation be your guide.

Be accepting and appreciative of children's art. Focus on the learning process that the child has experienced without passing judgment. How might a child benefit from hearing remarks like these: "I see you have learned to draw a zigzag line!" "What an interesting border you've created on your picture." "I can see you like the color red very much." "What did you like to draw the most in your picture?"

Needless to say, in the early childhood years, it is inappropriate to grade children's art or to label it as bad or ugly. These practices lower self-esteem and can stifle interest and creativity.

Respect Children's Art

Because young children are just learning to draw, their pictures are not usually accurate in terms of perspective and proportion. With years of experience, children do improve their accuracy. In the meantime,

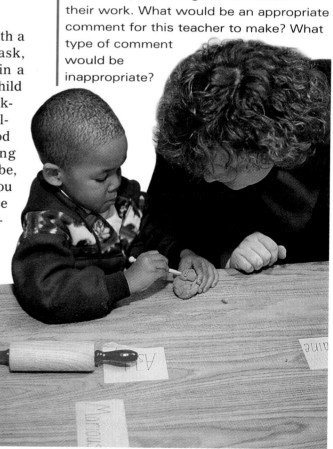

Children appreciate genuine interest in their work. What would be an appropriate comment for this teacher to make? What type of comment would be inappropriate?

Children feel special when their art projects are displayed. Why is it important to change art displays often?

Display Children's Art

Children beam when their works of art are posted. Self-esteem is built when a caring teacher says, "Thank you for showing me your painting! It's very special! May I hang it on the wall for everyone to see?" When displaying art, write the artist's name in an upper corner, using capital and small letters. Whenever possible, hang the art at children's eye level. Rotate items often to show appreciation for every student's effort and to maintain interest. Return art to the artists to display at home.

ACTIVITIES FOR THE ART CENTER

What happens in the art center? Many art activities can be part of the regular list of options for children at choice time or during free play. Drawing and painting materials, for example, may always be available. Other materials, such as modeling clay or glitter for gluing, may be provided only at specific times. Special art projects may be one-time events.

As teachers plan art activities, they think about how many children will use the center. Since some activities require more supervision than others, this also affects plans. Each type of art activity has certain considerations of its own that should be part of the planning process.

Drawing and Coloring

Although some children like coloring books, they are not the best choice for an early childhood education program. When

teachers should not redraw, touch up, or complete what a child has created. Instead, help the child take pride in his or her own accomplishments. Making changes or doing parts of the project for the child only sends the message that the child can't do it right. Self-esteem suffers in these instances.

Sometimes a child will ask, "You draw a horse for me; you do it better." A good response would be: "I want you to draw your own horse. Since I'm older than you are, I've had lots of practice drawing. If you keep practicing, you'll learn to draw a horse to look just the way you want." Patiently provide encouragement by helping the child remember what a horse looks like: "Is a horse big or small? How many legs does it have? Where does its tail go? What colors of horses have you seen?"

FOCUS ON INFANT/TODDLER PROGRAMS

The purpose of art for infants is mainly stimulation and skill building. Show them bright colors and patterns. Let them sort, stack, and place objects in a random pattern to develop eye-hand coordination. They need this skill before they can hold and control a drawing implement. Simply making water marks on blank paper helps infants notice shape and design and demonstrates cause and effect.

Toddlers can participate more fully in art. They can make prints and string beads. Toddlers enjoy finger painting. Since they still like to put things in their mouths, use homemade, edible finger paint. Try instant pudding (mixed with water instead of milk) and partially set flavored gelatin.

The same mixtures can be thinned to use as easel paint. When working with easel paint, toddlers are more comfortable with large brushes, 1 to 1 1/2 inches (2.5 to 4 cm) wide.

you provide art activities, you will want to choose those that make a strong contribution to learning. Providing an outlined form for children to color has definite limitations. For one thing, it is *not* the best way to build eye-hand coordination. In addition, many experts agree that overexposure to traditional coloring books and preprinted pages limits creativity.

Without a preprinted picture, children draw for themselves. When someone draws a picture for children, the children are deprived of the chance to develop their *own* thinking skills. When children draw a flower, for example, they use memory and observation skills. They practice decision making as they plan how to use the space on the paper. They become aware of a flower's specific characteristics. Coloring the flower still enables them to practice fine motor skills and eye-hand coordination. Filling in someone else's drawing in a coloring book offers far fewer learning opportunities.

Instead of coloring books, provide different sizes, shapes, and colors of paper so children can express their own perceptions

Tip FROM THE Pros

*T*raditional paintbrushes are fine, but what else could children use as painting tools? Try pot scrubbers, dish mops, sponges, toothbrushes, leaves, chopsticks, eyedroppers, twigs, whisk brooms, yarn pompons, roll-on bottles, and flyswatters (clean and unused). Instead of regular paper, try using sandpaper, computer paper, aluminum foil, manila paper, paper sacks, wallpaper samples, and meat trays (unused or thoroughly washed).

and ideas. Supply plenty of crayons, chalk, colored pencils, and markers, including numerous duplicates of each color to avoid conflicts.

Painting

Children love to create art with paint and brushes. Painting gives them a way to express their emotions. With limited vocabularies, they may be able to "speak" through their artwork. Simply exploring the different consistencies of paint is exciting for them. Through painting, they learn to blend primary colors into secondary colors. Painting is sometimes a forbidden activity in the home because it can be messy—all the more reason to provide it in the classroom. For painting activities, the art center should include:

- *Paint.* Water-based tempera paint is inexpensive, washable, and nontoxic. It comes in ready-to-use and powdered forms. To help prevent spills, pour only small amounts of the paint into individual containers. Clean, empty orange juice cans make good containers for paint. (For younger children, provide only two colors at a time.) Store extra paint in a labeled, tightly covered container out of children's reach.

- *Easels.* These slanted boards hold paper for painting. Adjust the easels to children's height. In group care, it is best to have easels that allow two to four children to paint at once.

- *Paper.* Newsprint, the type of paper used for newspapers, is good for easel painting. Clip a large sheet of paper to each easel. For variety, provide old sheets of wallpaper, discarded cardboard, and poster board.

- *Tools for Painting.* For easel painting, use long-handled brushes 1/2 to 1 inch (1 to 2.5 cm) wide. Younger children may need wider brushes. Place one brush in each paint container and remind children to put each brush back in its own container when finished. Also experiment with other objects for applying paint, such as feathers, cotton swabs, cotton balls, and sponges. After painting, be sure to wash brushes and other painting tools thoroughly. Children usually enjoy helping with this task.

- *Cover-Ups.* Plastic aprons and old shirts can be used to keep children's clothes clean during painting. Help the children roll up long shirt sleeves on their clothes before they begin to paint.

Many children have their first painting experience with a brush and easel in a child care program. Notice Sara's concentration.

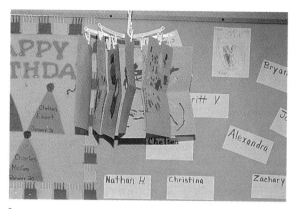

This drying rack keeps art projects out of the way while they dry. What other methods of drying have you observed? Which seem to work best?

Do not leave paintings on an easel to dry. This prevents another child from using the easel. Instead, find a place just for drying paintings. Some classrooms use a drying rack, an indoor or outdoor clothesline, or a spare table.

Finger Painting

The sensory experience of finger painting can be very soothing to children. It helps them release tension and relax. Some children may be hesitant to try finger painting at first. Encourage them to watch others or to begin by painting with one finger only. Most quickly come to enjoy the activity. Since finger painting can be messy, follow the same principles for cover-ups that you would use with other types of painting activities.

Slick, glossy paper is needed for finger painting. Finger paint can be purchased ready-to-use. Recipes for homemade finger paint may be found in art resource books for teachers. Simple substitutes for finger paints can be made by adding food coloring to cold cream, hand lotion, shaving cream, or liquid soap.

Print Making

Print making is another creative technique children can explore in the art center. Simple **print making** consists of *placing an object in a small amount of paint and then pressing the object onto paper or another material.* An impression of the object is then left on the paper. You can make prints from almost any object—from hands and feet, to nuts and bolts, to leaves and flowers. Try making scenes composed entirely of prints, such as a tree made from prints of leaves and twigs.

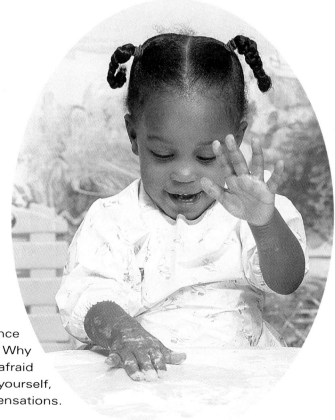

Finger painting is an art experience that most young children enjoy. Why do you think some children are afraid of it at first? Try finger painting yourself, concentrating on the physical sensations.

Modeling and Shaping

Using dough or clay, children can create shapes and objects that are **three-dimensional,** *having height, width, and depth.* Doughs, which are softer and easier to work than clays, can be made inexpensively from ingredients such as flour or cornstarch, salt, and water. Clays must usually be purchased rather than made.

As they shape and mold the dough or clay, children practice fine motor skills and eye-hand coordination. Through pounding, rolling, twisting, and squeezing the materials, children learn through their senses while having fun. Playing with dough or clay is also a great stress reliever for children as they take out aggressive feelings by punching and squeezing the material.

Include many objects and utensils for cutting and shaping. Cookie cutters and rolling

Explain why your choice of utensils and objects for playing with dough would depend upon the ages of the children and whether the play is supervised by a caregiver.

pins are two common choices. Interesting designs can also be made with bottle caps, a garlic press, buttons, coins, and shells.

Cutting and Tearing

Cutting activities help develop fine motor skills and eye-hand coordination. Toddlers can develop these skills by simply tearing pieces of paper. For cutting activities, provide safety scissors for children. Right- and left-handed scissors should be available.

Many materials are excellent for small children to cut or tear. Magazines and flower catalogs are colorful favorites.

Pasting, Gluing, and Attaching

Children like to attach objects to each other. Glue sticks, tape, staples, paper clips, string, yarn, hook-and-loop tape, and brass paper fasteners can all be used to attach objects to paper. Supervise these activities carefully. Some children like the taste of glue and paste, but these materials may contain substances that should not be consumed.

After they master cutting and pasting techniques, children can practice making choices by making a collage. A **collage** (kuh-LAHZH) is *a picture or design made by gluing or pasting many different pieces of material to a backing.* Many materials work well in collages. Pictures, paper, and fabric scraps are often used. You might also offer colored string, paper doilies, and different types of seeds. Varying the size, shape, colors, and textures of materials makes the experience interesting and stimulating to the senses. The arrangement of the materials is up to the artist.

The backing material for the collage must be heavy enough to support the weight of all the glued materials. Heavy construction paper, poster board, and cardboard are good choices. Store items for collages in separate, labeled containers in the art center so children may use them when they wish.

Can you identify some of the materials that were used to make this collage? What other materials might find new uses in art projects?

BECOMING A SCAVENGER

There's nothing like working with children on art projects to turn a person into a dedicated scavenger. Once the mind is set for planning art activities, a teacher seldom wants to throw anything away. A common thought is: "I'll bet the children could use that to make something." Egg cartons, wrapping paper, magazines, boxes, tubes, spools, and sewing trims all inspire ideas. That's the mindset you will want to adopt. When you do, you won't even be tempted to resort to coloring books. Instead, your own creativity will be the foundation for promoting creativity in the children under your guidance.

FOCUS ON SCHOOL-AGE PROGRAMS

School-age children enjoy more challenging versions of the same activities as the younger child. They are ready to use smaller brushes, 1/8 to 1/4 inch (3 to 6 mm) wide, for easel painting. Expect to see more realism and detail in their work. They can use clays or doughs to make more intricate projects, such as necklaces, pins, and flower vases. Cutting activities should also include more detail and smaller items.

Weaving, sewing, stitchery, woodworking, and assembling model kits are all creative crafts school-age children enjoy. These activities require more skill, concentration, and patience. They maintain interest while providing a developmentally appropriate challenge.

Older children can make items for room decoration. They might try these projects:

- A **mobile** is *a collection of items or pictures suspended on wire by string.* Once all items on the mobile balance, it is hung from the ceiling. Children might make a mobile of paper songbirds to hang in the science center.
- **Origami** (OR-uh-GAH-mee) is *a Japanese art form in which squares of tissue paper are folded into representational forms, such as birds.*
- **Dioramas** (DY-uh-RA-muhs) are *three-dimensional pictures made with small, cut-out designs.* Making a large, detailed diorama can be a group effort.
- A **mural** is *a long, continuous painting or drawing on one very large piece of paper.* It is displayed on a wall and is another good group project.

Chapter 18 Review

Chapter Summary

- Through art, children learn to express feelings and ideas, practice skills, develop self-esteem, and develop creativity.
- Art activities should be appropriate to children's age and level of development.
- Artistic ability develops in stages.
- In art, children need positive guidance and encouragement, not criticism.
- The art center should be stocked with a variety of art materials that give children choices.
- Common art activities include coloring, painting, finger painting, print making, modeling with dough or clay, cutting, pasting, and making collages.

Reviewing the Facts

1. List four goals of the art curriculum.
2. Identify and describe the three stages of artistic development. Include the general age range for each stage.
3. Describe an art learning center.
4. Give three safety suggestions for preschool art activities.
5. Why is the process of an art activity more important than the product of the activity?
6. Give two examples of how a teacher should respond to children's art.
7. Why do many experts find coloring books inappropriate for art centers?
8. How do children benefit from finger painting?
9. Discuss three reasons for using clay and dough activities with preschoolers.
10. What is a collage? Identify two benefits of making collages.
11. What is a diorama? For what age group is making a diorama best suited?

Thinking Critically

1. What field trips or visitors might stimulate a young child's interest in art?
2. Suggest two ways that math or science concepts can be taught in an art activity.
3. When schools need to make budget cuts, art programs are often the first targeted. Why do you think this is so? How can schools support art programs in tight financial times?
4. What might be some benefits of encouraging young children to value process as well as product?

Activities and Applications

1. **Reusable Art.** Make a list of possible art activities that use "recycled" materials.
2. **Process Versus Product.** With a partner, make a list of comments that an adult might use to convey to children that the process of creating art is as important as the finished product.
3. **Homemade Doughs.** Demonstrate how to make homemade dough. Compare the cost of making it to that of purchased modeling compound.
4. **Book Review.** Review an art activity resource book for preschool teachers. What are its strengths? Weaknesses? Would you recommend it for purchase? Why or why not?

Chapter 18 Review

5. **Learning Center.** Draw your own design for an art learning center. Provide details that show contents and arrangement.

6. **Planning an Activity.** Plan an art activity for preschoolers. Develop a lesson plan around your idea. Then carry out the activity with a group of preschoolers.

Your Professional Portfolio

Develop your own card file of activity ideas, using large index cards. Keep them in a shoe box or file card box. Categorize them according to subject areas, including those presented throughout this unit of your text. Write down as much information about each idea as you have, so that you can later develop lesson plans around the ideas.

Observing and Analyzing

Process Versus Product

An emphasis on process over product is not always easy to put into practice. Adults are used to giving and accepting criticism. They tend to be goal-oriented. Children quickly learn that making the best product possible is often the goal. Because adults are looking for progress, they may subtly push children to improve on their efforts each time they create something. It can be difficult to put aside this attitude when helping children with art activities.

Do early childhood teachers communicate to children that the creative process is more important than the finished product? If so, how? For some answers to these questions, try the following activities:

- **Recording Reactions.** Look for one or more opportunities to observe how parents and other adults react to displays of children's art. Try to include times when the artists are present and when they are not. To help you think of ways to observe this, consider: parent's night (or some other function) at school; one of your siblings and an adult; or a young sibling of one of your friends.

- **Preschool Art Activities.** Observe an art activity in a preschool classroom. Describe the activity. List the supplies made available to the children, noting whether materials are open or close ended. Identify the different skills children practiced while working on their projects. Record the teacher's comments to the children as they worked.

After completing one or both of the activities, review your findings. Based on what you have read in this chapter, draw conclusions about how successful teachers and other adults were at emphasizing process over product.

Chapter 19

Language Activities

CHAPTER OBJECTIVES

- Explain how the preschool environment can promote development of language skills.

- Plan a language arts learning center for preschoolers.

- Assess the suitability of specific books for children.

- Demonstrate the ability to read a story effectively to preschoolers.

- Explain how to prepare children for reading and writing.

- Plan and lead language arts activities.

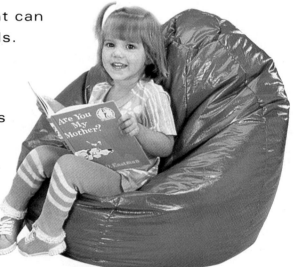

Courtesy of Lakeshore Learning Materials

Terms to Learn

- bilingual
- emergent literacy
- finger plays
- flannel boards
- invented spelling
- language arts
- language chart
- literate
- native language
- print-rich environment
- storytelling
- visual discrimination
- whole language

t's big!" Jeremy said.

"It's orange," added Rosie.

"I think it's bumpy," Ellie noted.

The preschoolers were gathered around the pumpkin Mrs. Heinrich had brought to class. She had asked them to describe it in different ways. As they responded, she wrote their comments on a chart she was holding. "Pumpkins are fully grown and ready to pick from the vine in the fall. That's why this is a good time for us to look at a real one in class. Would you like to see the inside of the pumpkin?" she asked the group.

As they responded eagerly that they would, Mrs. Heinrich carefully cut around the top of the pumpkin. Lifting the top, she said, "Tell me how you think this smells."

"Yummy," Carson said.

"It smells funny," Jeremy pronounced as he wrinkled his nose.

Next, Mrs. Heinrich had each child pull out some seeds and describe how the pumpkin felt inside. "Stringy," "slimy," and "wet" were among the responses. She added each answer to her chart. Finally, she gave a small piece of pumpkin to each child. "How does it taste?" she asked, again adding their comments to the chart.

"Now let's carve a face on our pumpkin. I have a feeling that this pumpkin wants to have a happy face." As Mrs. Heinrich carved the face, the children watched, chattering with her about the expression that was forming.

"There," she said at last. "The carving is done. And now, Ms. Pumpkin, would you like to know what the children said about you?" Lifting her chart, she began to read all the comments. The preschoolers listened eagerly for their own responses.

"I think she likes what we said," Sherrie pointed out with a gleam in her eye. "She's still smiling."

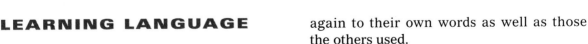

LEARNING LANGUAGE

As Mrs. Heinrich worked with the children, she did more than just carve a pumpkin. She taught language skills. By writing responses on a **language chart**, *a large paper where children's responses are recorded*, she created a written record of what went on. She also reinforced the children's language practice as they listened again to their own words as well as those the others used.

Infants first begin to learn about language as they mimic sounds. When exposed to language on a daily basis, children gradually acquire an understanding of their **native language**. This is *the language spoken in the home, which children learn first.* Children who are *able to speak and understand two languages* are said to be **bilingual.**

Building Professional Skills

Communication Skills

WHAT ARE COMMUNICATION SKILLS?

Think of all the ways you have of communicating ideas: spoken and written words; tone of voice; facial expressions; posture; eye contact; physical distance. All of these elements help you send and receive messages. Skilled communicators realize they are using these channels. They also consider their audience and how signals might be interpreted. They control the elements of communication to express just what they mean.

Communication Skills in Action

Damon, a teacher's aide, was watching some preschoolers in the play yard when Mrs. Owen arrived from work to pick up her daughter Claire. When Claire appeared, her usually neat braids were loose and messy. Her hands, face, and clothes were stained with damp earth.

"Mommy, I was chasing a rabbit," Claire began, breathless and excited. "We read *Alice in Wonderland* today, and she chased a rabbit and . . ."

"I know about *Alice in Wonderland*," her mother interrupted. "Just get in the car and try not to get it dirty. We still have to pick up Daddy, and then I'll have to clean you up before I can start dinner."

Damon winced. He could understand how, after a long day at work,

Mrs. Owen would be upset. When he saw the look of dismay on the child's face, however, he had to act. He knelt down and looked in her eyes, neither smiling nor scowling.

"Claire, we understand why you wanted to chase that rabbit—and I'm glad you listened to the story so well. But the rabbit led you into the dirtiest part of the play yard. Your mother has worked hard today, and now she has extra work to do. Can you give her some help when you get home?"

Claire nodded sheepishly. She said nothing.

Then Mrs. Owen knelt and kissed Claire's forehead. "It's all right, sweetie. No more animal chasing today, though, okay? Now, go wash your hands and face, and then

you can tell me all about the rabbit and the story."

Your Analysis

1. What attitude did Mrs. Owen's initial reaction communicate to Claire? Why did Mrs. Owen respond as she did?

2. What attitude did Damon communicate to Claire? How would you evaluate his communication skills?

3. Compare Mrs. Owen's first response with her second. Explain what caused the change.

4. How was Claire's self-esteem preserved in this scene?

5. Why is it important for early childhood professionals to communicate well with both children and adults?

Children who have a different native language find bilingual materials especially helpful. How can they benefit all the children in a classroom?

In infancy, children understand much more language than they can speak. During toddlerhood, language production increases rapidly. Children chatter away to their toys and themselves. The preschooler has an expanding vocabulary and is interested in talking about everything. Preschoolers need opportunities to use their language skills with other children. They also need adults who will listen to them, react with interest, and respond through conversation.

THE LANGUAGE ARTS CURRICULUM

Language arts includes *activities that teach children to listen, speak, read, and write.* The goal is to help children learn to communicate effectively with others. Children need approximately two years of experience making the sounds of a language and listening to others make sounds before they can speak understandably. The ability to read and write language takes even longer. Teachers help children work toward these goals by providing an environment and a learning center that focus on building language skills.

A Language Arts Environment

If you never heard a word spoken, could you learn to speak? You could, but it would be very difficult. That's why early childhood classrooms need to be filled with language opportunities. Teachers should model proper language usage throughout the day. Meal and snack times offer many opportunities to

FOCUS ON INFANT/TODDLER PROGRAMS

Infant and toddler programs should provide sensory activities to give children plenty to talk about. With toddlers, nouns are of primary importance. They love to name everything. Stories should be read to one or two children at a time. Use books with pictures of objects for children to point to and name.

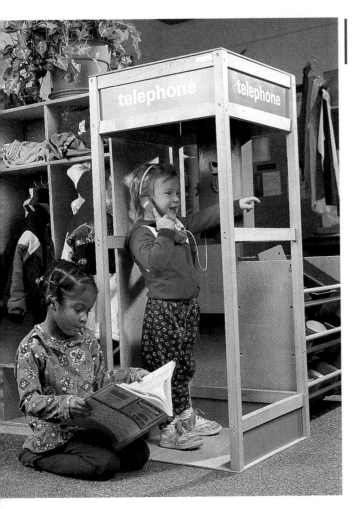

Children love to mimic adults. Using a "phone booth" makes Abigail feel grown up while she practices her speaking skills.

encourage conversation. Story time develops listening skills. Even a simple, practical experience like teaching children to tie their shoes can teach communication skills. The children listen as you explain the procedure. They increase their vocabulary as you name the different parts of a shoe. Asking such questions as "What other kinds of shoes have you seen?" "Who wears them?" and "Why do they wear them?" encourages children to use verbal skills. Listing the different types of shoes for the children to see promotes reading skills.

Early childhood teachers further encourage language skills by creating a **print-rich environment**, *a setting in which printed materials are used throughout the classroom in meaningful ways.* When playing "restaurant," for example, children can use a telephone book to "look up" a telephone

enrich language. Teachers who involve children in writing a letter to an ill classmate help children understand how reading and writing fit into their everyday lives.

Effective teachers encourage language usage in all classroom activities. Toy telephones placed in the dramatic play center

When a library area is arranged in an inviting way, it is used more frequently. One of James' favorite activities is to listen to a tape while following along with the story in the book.

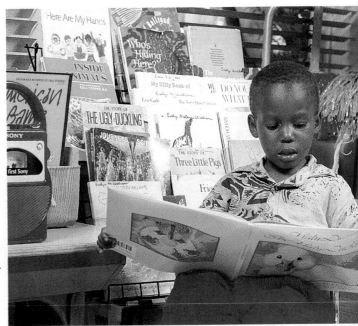

number to make reservations. Menus in the play restaurant help children understand how reading is used in everyday life. Books can be placed in the dramatic play center so children can "read" on the sofa as their parents do. The science center should be stocked with accessible nature books. *Including reading and writing in all classroom activities* in this manner is practicing **whole language.**

The Language Arts Center

While language skills can be practiced in all learning centers, the language arts learning center is specifically planned for this purpose. The center should be quiet and well lighted. It includes a library corner, a storytelling area, and a writing area.

- *Library Corner.* A library corner should be a warm and cozy spot. Rugs or carpeting, child-size rocking chairs, and stuffed animals all help make reading an enjoyable experience. Displaying book jackets on low bulletin boards and hanging mobiles help build interest in reading. Books themselves should also be promi-

nently displayed. The focal point, of course, is a well-stocked book shelf. A record or tape player with story recordings and books is also helpful, especially for visually impaired children.

- *Storytelling Area.* Here children should find items for acting out stories. These include puppets, a stage for puppet plays, and doll houses with dolls of different ethnic backgrounds and both genders. Pictures that stimulate ideas and a cassette recorder with blank tapes encourage children to invent stories and tell about personal experiences.

- *Writing Area.* Preschoolers can practice their budding writing skills at a writing area. Stimulate their interest in, and appreciation for, words with alphabet and number books, cookie sheets with magnetic letters, and writing toys, such as stencils for tracing letters. Provide children with child-size tables and chairs and plenty of writing tools and paper. Include envelopes and play stamps for letter writing. Computer programs with developmentally appropriate word games may also be provided.

Finding the Best

*E*very year, the American Library Association honors excellence in children's literature with two prestigious awards. The Caldecott Medal is given to the illustrator of the year's best children's picture book. Past winners include *Mirette on the High Wire,* illustrated by Emily Arnold McCully; *Black and White,* illustrated by David Macaulay; and *Song and Dance Man,* illustrated by Stephen Gammell. The Newbery Award is given to the author of the year's outstanding

children's book. Recent winners include *Missing May* by Cynthia Rylant, *Maniac Magee* by Jerry Spinelli and *Joyful Noise: Poems for Two Voices* by Paul Fleischman. Some past Newbery Award winners, such as *Sounder* by William H. Armstrong, *Island of the Blue Dolphins* by Scott O'Dell, and *The White Stag* by Kate Seredy, are considered classics. While each book must be individually judged for appropriateness, these awards can be guides in finding good books for children.

THE MULTICULTURAL CLASSROOM

The classics in children's literature have earned their enduring popularity by appealing to children for many generations. Some of these stories, however, are biased regarding age, gender, and ethnicity. How can a teacher who wants to share these classics with children overcome this drawback?

First, look for newer editions of the books, with illustrations featuring characters of varied ethnicity. You can also provide your own nonbiased illustrations with multicultural puppets and flannel board figures. Also, balance favorites from this country with classic tales from other parts of the world. Find out what folklore is passed on to children in North Africa or the Philippines. Parents, libraries, and international studies programs at colleges and universities are good sources for these stories.

Even if the bias remains, the story may still have merit for older children. Explain that it was written in a time when such attitudes were not challenged. You might even ask children to retell the story in a way that shows greater respect for all people.

READING ACTIVITIES

Good children's books motivate children to want to learn to read. They like to look at books themselves and practice early reading skills. Hearing a story read or told, however, is a special pleasure that captures imaginations and carries children to worlds that are new to them.

Providing Books for Children

Anyone who has been around an infant or a toddler knows what can happen when the child "reads" a book with paper pages. Missing and torn pages are testimony to the fact that books need to be chosen with age in mind.

Even a good story won't capture children's interest unless it is handled skillfully. What signs do you see of this reader's skill?

Board books, those with sturdy cardboard pages, hold up best to wear and tear from toddlers. Even before children read, teachers can promote interest in literature with *picture books.* These are books with large, often full-page, illustrations to keep the interest of children who are not yet able to read. Each page has anything from no words to a few sentences. The plot of a good children's book is simple enough that it can be told in pictures. The words and pictures are matched carefully. This shows children that words can create images to tell a story. *Big books* are oversized picture books, sometimes as large as 24 by 36 inches (60 by 90 cm). This enlarged format enables children in groups to see the pictures much better.

As you might expect, the type of story is as important as the physical structure of the book. When choosing books, be sure to think about the interests of each age level:

- *Infant/Toddler.* Infants and toddlers enjoy picture books with large illustrations and bright colors. Books for toddlers should emphasize words they already know. Toddlers enjoy stories about others their own age. Animal and vehicle books that emphasize sound words are other favorites. Rhythm, rhyme, and repetition make story time fun.

- *Preschool.* Preschoolers prefer books that cater to their need for security and their growing imagination. They like books about familiar characters and experiences. Stories about other children, family, and community workers, such as police officers and doctors, appeal to them. At the same time, they are intrigued by make-believe and the world of talking animals. Preschoolers also enjoy nonsense books with funny situations, surprises, and exaggeration.

Signs of Good Literature

*H*ow can you tell whether a book is worthwhile for children? Look for these qualities:

- A simple, understandable plot.
- Characters that interest young children—such as children, families, and animals—or to whom they can easily relate.
- A focus on familiar topics that build on a child's firsthand knowledge of the world, such as home life.

- A theme appropriate for young children, such as friendship.
- Illustrations that clearly depict the plot and characters' actions.
- No more than five sentences per page.
- Basic but descriptive vocabulary.
- Predictable phrases, repetition, and rhymes that encourage children to read along.

- Humor and suspense to maintain interest.
- Make-believe that does not frighten young children.
- Current, accurate information in nonfiction books.
- Characters of different cultural backgrounds.
- Respectful treatment of all people, regardless of gender, nationality, disability, religious beliefs, or age.

• **School-Age.** The reading tastes of school-age children are as varied as their interests. Books and children's magazines about nature, science, and community life are popular. School-age children like fantasy and humor. Although their attention span is increasing, most of these children still prefer short stories.

Reading to Children

What do you like when you listen to a story? An expressive reader? Humorous characters? Skillful building of suspense? A surprise ending? Children like the same things. If you've ever tried to read a story before a group, however, you know that it takes skill to maintain their interest—skill that comes from practice.

Prepare for story time by selecting an appropriate book and reading it aloud several times to yourself. As children gather for the story, you might sit in a rocker or sing songs with children. Introduce the story with a technique or prop that arouses interest. You might show children the jacket cover. Can they guess what the story will be about? Read the book title and the name of the author and illustrator before beginning to read.

Before you begin to read, be certain that all children can see the book. You may want to hold it open beside you and facing the children as you read, or you can read a page

Tip FROM THE Pros

*C*hildren's magazines are a source for good literature. Favorites of younger children include *Sesame Street*, *Turtle,* and *Your Big Backyard.* Older children enjoy *Cricket, Playmate,* and *National Geographic World.*

or two and then turn the book so children can see. Children may need reminders not to sit on their knees, so that all can see.

Reading with expression and enthusiasm captures children's interest. A lifeless monotone makes it seem like you are bored. Maintain interest by using different voices for the characters in the story. Whisper, talk louder, or include a child's name in the story to keep the attention of the group. Look at the book and then at the children as you read, making eye contact with each one at times.

When the story is finished, don't miss the opportunity to develop language skills with follow-up activities. Ask questions to help children review the plot sequence and the feelings and actions of characters. Have the children retell the story or act it out. Sing songs that relate to the story or do a special art project. Other follow-up activities are more elaborate. After reading *Goldilocks and the Three Bears,* children

A visit from the book's main character—a beautiful insect—prepares the children to listen carefully to the story.

might make oatmeal ("porridge") and serve it as a snack. They might see real bears in a zoo or wildlife park. They could visit a carpenter's shop to see wooden chairs being made. Regardless of their resources, good teachers find ways of answering the question, "What else can children learn from this experience?"

Telling Stories to Children

Some people read stories, and some people tell them. **Storytelling** is a skill. *Instead of reading from a book, the person tells the story from memory.* Accomplished storytellers practice to perfect their skill. They have learned to follow these guidelines:

- Choose a simple story with an interesting, well-paced plot.
- Plan a short introduction and ending.
- Memorize basic scenes and key phrases, not exact words.
- Rehearse the story in front of a mirror before presenting it.
- Use colorful and descriptive vocabulary.
- Include comical characters, humor, and suspense when possible.
- Use your facial expressions to convey meaning.
- Vary vocal rhythm to maintain interest.
- Repeat predictable phrases so children can join in.
- Add a surprise ending for fun.
- Don't be afraid to make mistakes. Children are very forgiving.

Did you realize that reading readiness is linked to visual discrimination activities?

Preparing Children to Read

Before children can learn to read themselves, they must understand that letters are combined to create words, and words represent thoughts and ideas. Gradually, through many different language experiences, children learn to recognize language symbols (letters and words) and to understand their meaning. When this meaning is understood, children are considered **literate**, or *able to read.* During early childhood, *the gradual process of learning to read* is called **emergent literacy**.

If a child can't see the difference between a "b" and a "d" or an "m" and an "n," reading isn't easy. Seeing differences is one skill that children need in order to read. **Visual discrimination** is *the ability to notice similari-*

ties and differences in colors, shapes, and designs. Visual discrimination lets children notice the differences between letters.

Teachers can provide many activities to help preschoolers develop skills needed for reading. These include assembling puzzles; matching shapes and colors; creating patterns with beads or blocks; categorizing objects according to shape, number, or size; creating "books" of their own in the art area; and dictating stories to the teacher.

LISTENING AND SPEAKING ACTIVITIES

Some children have little to say, yet others talk as though they were wound up like a toy. All children need practice—with talking *and* with listening. Paying attention at story time develops listening skills. Other techniques that promote listening and speaking skills are:

- *Sound-Matching Games.* Listening skills are developed when teachers ask children to match sounds they hear. To make a sound game, provide pairs of plastic eggs (all one color) that contain identical materials. You might use rice, pebbles, and beans. When children shake the plastic eggs, they match up pairs by sound. Toy catalogs sell games that have animal noises recorded on a tape. Children match an animal picture with the sound the animal makes. Music activities are also great ways to encourage children to listen to sounds.

- *Finger Plays, Nursery Rhymes, and Songs.* The playful rhythms, patterns of repeating phrases, and rhyming of words make language fun. Children hear the parts of words (syllables) as they are stressed and stretched to the rhythm of the song or rhyme. **Finger plays** add a visual element to the words by *accompanying a song or chant with specific hand motions.*

- *Sharing Time.* Preschoolers love to talk about themselves—their pets, families, and activities. It is, after all, one thing they are experts on. By encouraging children to share this information during group conversations, teachers promote self-confidence and self-esteem

From what you know about preschoolers, why do you think finger plays are so appealing to them?

Preschoolers often treat puppets as if they were real people or animals. This interaction provides real opportunities for practicing both talking and listening skills.

along with communication skills. They also encourage children to take an interest in others. With open-ended questions, children give more complete answers.

- ***Puppetry and Dramatic Play.*** When groups of children play with puppets, they learn to listen as well as talk. Dramatic play characters that promote language skills include newspaper and television reporters, weather announcers, radio announcers, postal carriers, and waiters and waitresses.

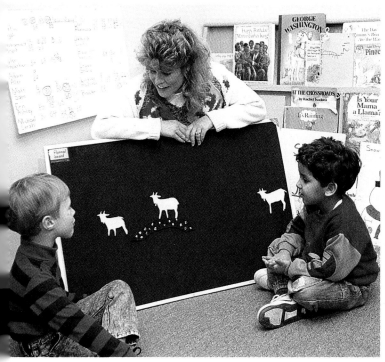

- ***Flannel Board Play.*** Children and teachers tell stories when using **flannel boards**. These are *large pieces of cardboard or wood covered with flannel or felt.* They range in size from twelve-inch (30-cm) square lap boards to those as large as a bulletin board. Small figures, such as people or animals, are cut from flannel or felt of different colors. These figures stay in place when placed against the flannel board but can be easily repositioned. The storyteller moves the figures on the board as the story progresses.

How might your use of a flannel board differ with a small group of children or a large group? What advantages would a flannel board have in each situation.

FOCUS ON SCHOOL-AGE PROGRAMS

To encourage reading, provide school-age children with paperback books and a quiet place to read them. To promote writing skills, provide paper and envelopes for letters to pen pals. School-age children can also make holiday cards and write creatively on computers and typewriters. Language arts comes to life when you take school-age children on field trips to a television station, radio station, newspaper office, or live stage theater.

WRITING ACTIVITIES

Preschoolers love to pretend to write. You may see them "write" a letter that contains zigzag markings that represent words. These early steps are important preliminaries to real writing.

Beginning to Write

Watch a child who is beginning to write letters, and you will likely see deep concentration as the child works to control the writing tool. Line lengths and directions are not easy to manage when the muscles in the hand and fingers are not fully developed.

As fine motor skills develop, the hand gains better control of a pencil. Playing with dough or clay and manipulative toys, such as pegboards and connecting blocks, helps this skill develop. Using safety scissors, crayons, markers, and paintbrushes during art also prepares children to use writing tools.

Eye-hand coordination is another skill needed for writing. To form letters and words, children have to make the hand and eye work together. Stringing beads and working puzzles develop this skill.

As with other developmental skills, not all children begin to write at the same time. When children

Writing letters depends on coordinating many different skills. Individual help and encouragement are keys to success.

are ready for writing, provide them with examples of how printed letters (unconnected ones) are made. Several *manuscript systems*, or methods for printing letters and numbers, are used successfully with children. Find out which one is used in your program and follow it. Practice your own printing skills to provide a good model.

Generally, the first word children print is their own name. Help them recognize their names by printing them on paintings, name tags, and cubbies. Provide children with properly printed copies of their names and encourage them to practice copying the letters. Remember that mastery comes only with practice. Children need patient support.

Expressing Ideas Through Writing

Young children can express ideas through writing by dictating their thoughts to a teacher, who writes them on paper. Children five years and older enjoy writing words themselves. This is a positive, significant step in children's literacy development and should be encouraged.

The rules of spelling can be confusing and difficult for children to remember. They often bypass these rules and use **invented spelling**, *spelling a word the way it sounds*. Be patient with children's invented spelling. If you do not understand what a child has written, ask the child to read it to you. The more children write, the more concerned they will become about writing accurately. Be sure to spend time with children who want help with spelling and writing. Remember to reinforce writing efforts by asking children to share their writing during group times.

Children can become "authors" even before they can write well. Shari drew the pictures for her book and her teacher wrote down the words for Shari's story.

EMPHASIS ON READINESS

*R*eadiness" is a key word as far as preschoolers and language arts are concerned. Although some caregivers take great pride when a child reads or writes at an early age, this is not the goal of a preschool program. Formal lessons come with later schooling. The wise child care professional knows that preschoolers don't need the frustration and stress that can come with pressure to learn language skills too soon. The teacher who creates interest in children, instills confidence in them, and helps them develop coordination and fine motor skills gives children a strong foundation for successful learning of language skills when the time is right.

Chapter Summary

- Language development begins in infancy.
- There are four main language arts components: listening, speaking, reading, and writing.
- Language arts learning centers include a library corner, a storytelling area, and a writing area.
- Language should be emphasized throughout the daily schedule.
- Children's literature encourages interest in reading.
- Children's books should be carefully selected.
- Finger plays, rhymes, songs, dramatic play, and storytelling develop children's language skills.
- Children must master certain intellectual and physical skills before they can read and write.

Reviewing the Facts

1. When does language development begin?
2. What is the goal of a language arts curriculum?
3. What is a print-rich environment and why is it needed in an early childhood program?

4. Briefly describe a language arts learning center.
5. Briefly describe the characteristics of books that appeal to infants and toddlers, to preschoolers, and to school-age children.
6. Explain how to read a story effectively to children.
7. Give three tips for effective storytelling.
8. Define emergent literacy.
9. Identify a skill children need before they can read. Name an activity that helps develop the skill.
10. Describe two activities that promote listening skills.
11. Identify two skills children need before they can write. Name an activity that helps develop each skill.

Thinking Critically

1. What advantages in learning language skills might children in preschool have over those who stay home?
2. Many people believe that technology has provided children with so much entertainment, such as television and video games, that language skills suffer. How might technology be used to encourage language skills?
3. Why might it be harmful to push children to learn to read or write too soon?
4. What might happen if a preschooler does not develop the fine motor skills and eye-hand coordination needed to hold a pencil before entering formal schooling?

Activities and Applications

1. **Childhood Books.** If possible, bring to class one of your favorite books from childhood. Explain to the class why it was appealing to you.
2. **Story Time Skills.** Demonstrate your reading or storytelling skills for the class. Have class members identify your strengths and offer suggestions for improvement.
3. **Follow-Up Activities.** Choose a children's book and describe three suitable follow-up activities.
4. **Finger Plays.** Demonstrate a finger play

Chapter 19 Review

(or a song or nursery rhyme). Discuss the learning skills involved in the activity.

5. **Learning Center.** Draw your own design for a language arts learning center. Provide details that show contents and arrangement.

6. **Planning an Activity.** Plan a language arts activity for preschoolers. Develop a lesson plan around your idea. Then carry out the activity with a group of preschoolers.

Your Professional Portfolio

Prepare a flannel board story to use with preschoolers. Choose a story with only a few characters. Select colorful pieces of felt to make the characters. Flannel fabric tends to ravel and not be as durable as felt. Store the felt characters, along with a copy of the story, in a file folder or file pocket with your portfolio. Also include ideas for an introduction, telling the story, and follow-up activities.

Observing and Analyzing

Speaking of Language Skills

You can learn much by observing the resources that children use to learn language skills and the techniques that adults employ to help them. Studying how children use language skills as they develop also gives you information that will help when you work with them. Try these ideas in order to improve your awareness and knowledge of children and language skills:

- **Observing Preschoolers.** Listen to preschoolers that you encounter. Possibilities are siblings of friends; relatives; children in your neighborhood; and children in stores, restaurants, parks, and libraries. How do these preschoolers express themselves? Do they use complete sentences? Do they talk freely? What ages are they? How do adults respond to them? As you observe many children, do you see any link between the type of interaction with adults and the language skills of the children? Summarize what you observe in writing.

- **Children's Programming.** Watch a children's program on television that is considered to be high quality. How are language skills promoted? List specific techniques.

- **Story Time.** Observe story time at a library or preschool. Describe how the reader or storyteller presented the story. In what ways was it effective? How might it have been improved?

- **Library Observation.** Visit the children's section of a library. Watch as preschoolers select books. What interests them? Watch the interaction as adults help make choices. Look at the books yourself to find some that you think are the best. Choose one to review.

- **Toy Departments.** Visit the toy department in a store. Write descriptions of five toys that you think would be the best at promoting preschool language skills.

- **Writing Samples.** Obtain six or more samples of children's writing at different preschool ages (three to five). You might ask children you know (relatives, neighbors, siblings of friends) to write their name. Show your samples to the class, explaining how they show the different developmental levels of the children.

Chapter 20

Dramatic Play Activities

CHAPTER OBJECTIVES

■ Explain how dramatic play encourages growth in all developmental areas.

■ Plan a dramatic play learning center for preschoolers.

■ Describe how teachers encourage dramatic play.

■ Plan items for a prop box.

■ Explain how children benefit from play with puppets.

■ Describe how to make and use puppets.

■ Plan and lead dramatic play activities.

Terms to Learn

• prop box
• props
• role play
• spontaneous dramatic play

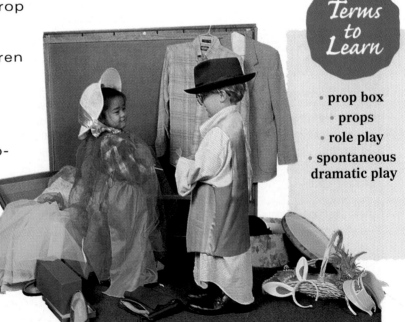

Look out! Here comes the water! Swishhh!" five-year-old Francine called out. She held the end of a short rope in front of her and moved it from side to side, then up and down.

"Don't worry. I'll save you," Blake said confidently. His firefighter hat slipped down over his eyes as he rushed toward Earl in order to bring him to safety.

As Mica, the teacher's aide, walked into the preschool classroom, the "fire" was in full blaze, or so the children pretended.

Mica heard Eddie repeating with urgency into a toy telephone, "Emergency! Emergency! 9-1-1! 9-1-1!"

Excitement mounted as the children scurried about, taking on roles in the dramatic scene. Then Mica noticed one little girl standing at the edge of the action. She held a short rope in her hand, but she didn't seem to be involved. She didn't move at all. Mica wondered if Nicky felt left out. She was often quiet during preschool. Now, there she was holding a "fire hose," but she wasn't quite assertive enough to join in the fire fighting. "Maybe she needs some encouragement," Mica theorized.

With that thought in mind, Mica walked over to Nicky and knelt down. "I think the firefighters could use some help," she said to Nicky. "Shall we join them?"

"Oh, no," Nicky replied very seriously. "I can't. I'm the fire hydrant."

THE WORLD OF MAKE-BELIEVE

Their ability to engage in make-believe is one of the most endearing qualities of children. Adults often admire the innocent, enthusiastic way children plunge into a world of their own making. This play is more than an amusing pastime, however. Through dramatic play, children find avenues of expression. They develop skills and explore possibilities that will eventually become very significant in their lives.

WHAT IS DRAMATIC PLAY?

As you know, creating realistic or fantasy situations and acting them out is known as dramatic play. In dramatic play, children often imitate adults and act out situations they observe or imagine. Like Nicky, they may even take on the role of inanimate objects or animals. Dramatic play allows children to explore safely what they are too young to—or cannot ever—experience in real life.

In dramatic play, preschoolers often imitate the parts of their lives that are most familiar. This time, though, they get to be the parents.

Some authorities use the term "dramatic play" only when they are referring to a single child acting out a situation. They use the term "sociodramatic play" to describe two or more children acting out situations together. In this text, "dramatic play" can refer to either solitary or group play.

As part of dramatic play, children **role play**, or *assume the identity of someone else.* They "become" people or characters they find fascinating, such as parents, community helpers, and cartoon heroes. (Remember that to preschoolers, cartoon heroes can be as real as parents.) This most often occurs as **spontaneous dramatic play**, meaning that children *engage in dramatic play without the suggestion or direction of adults.*

Dramatic play can take place anywhere. Children may prepare and serve "dinner" in the housekeeping center or build a train and take a "vacation" in the block center. Sandboxes, water tables, and outside playgrounds are other common sites for dramatic play.

FOCUS ON INFANT/TODDLER PROGRAMS

Infants first learn about dramatic play through simple games like "This Little Piggy Went To Market." The caregiver provides the drama through facial expressions and tone of voice. Eventually, infants start imitating these. Although infants can't use puppets, they love a show put on by others.

For toddlers, dramatic play is either solitary or parallel. It rarely involves interaction with other children. Duplicate toys, such as telephones, cash registers, and baby buggies, help prevent problems with sharing. "I had it first" has little meaning to a toddler. During toddlerhood children begin to understand how to use puppets. Their skills become much more refined after age three.

PROMOTING DEVELOPMENT

*L*ike real life experiences, dramatic play helps children develop skills in all areas:

- **Physical.** Dramatic play can be as physically active as "real" play. When children button dress-up clothes and use plastic eating utensils, they develop fine motor skills. Chasing "villains" uses large muscle movement.

- **Intellectual.** Children use language skills to suggest and plan their dramatic play scenes (often changing plans as they go). They develop problem-solving skills and imagination—especially symbolic thought—as they try to create settings with the materials at hand. They show memory skills as they reenact scenes they have witnessed or experienced.

- **Emotional.** Dramatic play is one avenue children have for confronting and trying to understand their feelings and fears. In family scenes, they may act out sibling rivalry. In a wading pool, they can pretend to be accomplished swimmers, when in fact they may be frightened of water. Dramatic play allows children to try out all kinds of emotions, which is a good rehearsal for dealing with them later. They learn about empathy as they put themselves in the places of other people. Make-believe also allows children to experience a sense of control and power.

- **Social.** All interaction is an opportunity for social growth. In dramatic play, children work together to conceive and carry out a story. They follow each other's lead as the play progresses, sometimes compromising to work out small problems. They assume social and employment roles by pretending to be husband and wife or doctor and patient. They learn to appreciate the clothes and customs of other cultures. Budding relationships strengthen into friendships.

- **Moral.** Through dramatic play, children put the rules and values they are beginning to learn into practice. Rescuing a kitten from a tree and playing "superhero" show that children have started to absorb some ideas of right and wrong. Although they may not realize it, they are forming a code of conduct.

Dramatic play satisfies a need children have to figure out how the world works. In doing so, they learn the importance of cooperation.

A dramatic play center should be inviting. Why would a full-length mirror be a good addition?

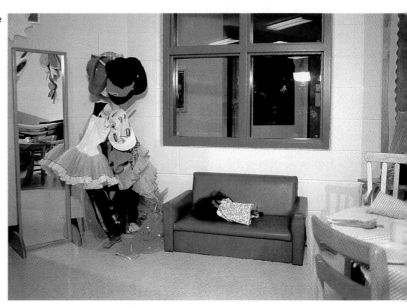

THE DRAMATIC PLAY LEARNING CENTER

Although dramatic play goes on everywhere, the dramatic play learning center is designed specifically for this purpose. You may see dress-up clothes hanging on hooks and child-size furnishings. Dolls and stuffed animals who "live" in the center quickly become characters in whatever drama is taking place.

What you see going on in this center one day may not be the same on another. Skilled teachers "set the stage" for play by creating different themes throughout the year. For example, the center could focus on family living and be arranged into one or more rooms of a home. At other times the center might be equipped as a post office, campsite, florist shop, jewelry store, or supermarket. By rotating play themes regularly, teachers encourage creativity and prevent children from losing interest.

THE MULTICULTURAL CLASSROOM

Setting up an exciting multicultural dramatic play area does not have to be expensive or cumbersome. Invite parents to help. Use catalogs, magazines, costume books, and library references for ideas. Donated fabrics and trims can be used to dress and accessorize homemade or purchased dolls and puppets of many ethnicities.

Donated clothing, obtained from families, cultural centers, and community members, is always fun. Imagine what the children could do with a French beret, a Greek captain's hat, an English bowler, a Chinese cap, a Russian babushka, or a turban from India. Add to these a cowboy hat, baseball cap, and spring bonnet for photo opportunities. Don't forget to include a full-length mirror.

Even equipment can be multicultural. For example, a wok in the housekeeping center is a subtle reminder of the Asian-American culture. Setting place mats from a Japanese restaurant on the housekeeping kitchen table casually exposes children to Japanese art and alphabet characters.

FOCUS ON SCHOOL-AGE PROGRAMS

Advanced skills allow school-age children to enjoy more complicated dramatic play. They may write out plots and scenes before acting them out. They like to make special props. Puppets created by school-age children may become childhood keep-sakes. Unlike younger children, who usually shy away from "public" performances, school-age children love it. They will make elaborate plans to act out a play or present a puppet show. Making and selling tickets and preparing popcorn increase enthusiasm.

ENCOURAGING DRAMATIC PLAY

Because dramatic play is beneficial to children, effective teachers look for ways to include and encourage it in their daily activities. Several techniques may be used for this.

Scheduling

Children need ample time for dramatic play. They must decide on a theme and their roles, put on costumes, enact the scene, and then put away the equipment and materials. Children need at least a 45-minute block of time for dramatic play. Some teachers provide an hour.

Developing Prop Boxes

Teachers create collections of **props**, *items that suggest themes for dramatic play*. Children use props to add realism and interest to pretend play. A **prop box** is *a container for storing items used in a specific theme*. What theme is suggested by a prop box that includes a lab coat, a stethoscope, and an eye chart?

Props trigger the imaginations of children. With a sense of realism and some hands-on items, children can create their own actions and words.

Props bring realistic detail to children's play. For instance, how might you emphasize that firefighters need oxygen to stay alive when working in smoke? One way is to provide face masks (perhaps from discarded scuba diving gear) and make-believe air tanks (oatmeal boxes covered with aluminum foil and strapped on with elastic). Children quickly see that these are important safety items for firefighters.

Using prop boxes to follow up a story or help children explore a particular concept is another example of how dramatic play can be encouraged. After reading a book about astronauts, one teacher put helmets (made from cardboard boxes) and other space-related items in a prop box. Using props, children develop a deeper understanding of the information in the story.

Teachers create community helper prop boxes so that children learn about jobs in society. These boxes might focus on medical professionals, firefighters, police officers, judges, and veterinarians. Prop boxes that emphasize fun and entertainment are also popular. These include items for portraying dancers of all kinds, clowns, singers, and artists.

Tip FROM THE Pros

*M*any different themes can be used for prop boxes. Here are some possibilities: airline attendant, airline pilot, artist, baker, ballet dancer, barber, bride and groom, business executive, carpenter, child care director, computer operator, cook, dentist, disc jockey, farmer, forest ranger, hairstylist, nurse, plumber, photographer, race car driver, scientist, and teacher.

When selecting materials for prop boxes, choose safe, clean, durable items that are easy to use and familiar to the children. When possible, choose real props rather than toy ones. Parents, secondhand stores, and garage sales are possible sources for props. Props should be accessible to all children regardless of gender, race, or physical ability. Wise teachers put at least two of each prop in a box. This encourages cooperative play and reduces the risk of conflict over popular props.

Participating in Dramatic Play

Children like to have teachers join in their play from time to time; however, the teacher should follow the children's lead and resist taking over. Participation allows teachers to model appropriate play skills for children who are very aggressive or have trouble cooperating with others. By observing a teacher, children can also learn how to handle real-life roles correctly. For example, when the children were playing "library," Miss Carmichael said very softly to the "librarian," "I need a book about trains. Could you help me find one, please?"

Insuring Safety

*I*n case of an outbreak of head lice, remove all hats and clothing from the dramatic play center and treat them for lice infestation. The health department can explain how to do this. Once the outbreak has been controlled, the items may be returned to the center.

Enthusiasm

WHAT IS ENTHUSIASM?

Enthusiasm equals effort plus enjoyment. When you are enthusiastic about an activity, you don't do things halfway. You put all your energy into it; you truly care about the outcome. People are typically enthusiastic about something they enjoy. Enthusiasm is also "catching." Your excitement and involvement in a project can spark someone else's.

Enthusiasm in Action

Vice-principal Evans raised his head at the muffled commotion. Trooping past his office came Matty Novak and her kindergarteners, all dressed in yellow and black, construction paper wings taped between their shoulders and pipe cleaner antenna tied around their heads.

"What's going on?" he asked one student.

"We're bees!" she replied. "We're going to gather nectar!"

Mr. Evans followed and watched silently from the sidewalk outside. Matty led the children along the play yard fence, over a tree stump, twice around the bushes, and back to the middle of the field. "Okay, swarm. What have we found?"

"Flowers! Nectar!" the children exclaimed.

"Right! What kind of flowers?"

"Pretty ones! Smelly ones! Clover!"

"Yes! We bees like all of those. Show me what we do now."

She and the children bent over the imaginary flowers and began "drinking" the "nectar" until Matty called, "Now we're stuffed full of nectar. What do we do next?"

"Go back to the hive! To make honey!"

"Such smart bees!" Matty began skipping back toward the school. Passing the vice-principal, she called over her shoulder, "Care to join us for honey on whole wheat bread, Mr. Evans?"

"Don't mind if I do," he laughed as he joined them, skipping along behind the last "bee" in the line.

Your Analysis

1. What evidence of enthusiasm do you notice in this scene?

2. In what ways was the enthusiasm "catching"?

3. What benefits are the children getting from dramatic play in this activity?

4. What personal qualities do you think help someone feel or show enthusiasm?

Teachers can enter dramatic play as a way of helping children who may have a difficult time joining the activity. For instance, a group of children were acting out a camping scene while a shy student looked on. One sensitive teacher decided to say, "What would you do if two big bears came into camp? Come on, Suni, let's be bears." This provided an easy way for Suni to join the play.

OBSERVING DRAMATIC PLAY

*B*y observing dramatic play, child care professionals gain understanding of children's development, abilities, and personal interests. This information is helpful when planning developmentally appropriate activities. For instance, a teacher noticed that Walt liked to dig in the sandbox. Frequently, Walt pretended to be a scientist digging for dinosaur bones. Making the most of Walt's interest, the teacher planned simple science activities related to archeology. The teacher's observations provided valuable insight for planning a successful curriculum.

Documenting Play

When teachers observe play, they often use anecdotal records. They write descriptions of children's behavior during play, noting the date and time. Significant abilities are noted so that teachers can assess growth over time.

Teachers gain valuable insight into a child's thinking when play is purposefully observed. Five-year-old Joleen, for example, was scheduled to have her tonsils removed. During play, Joleen repeatedly "operated" on the legs of the baby dolls and then pretended they couldn't walk anymore.

Joleen's teacher suspected that this was her way of trying to understand what was going to happen at the hospital. He talked to Joleen about her upcoming hospital stay, explaining in simple terms what it would be like. He assured her that her legs would not be operated on and that she would still walk afterwards. He then documented what had happened for future reference. He also shared his observations with Joleen's parents to help them prepare her for surgery.

Through children's dramatic play, you have unique opportunities to learn more about them. Documenting specific incidents or examples of development can help you identify both problems and progress.

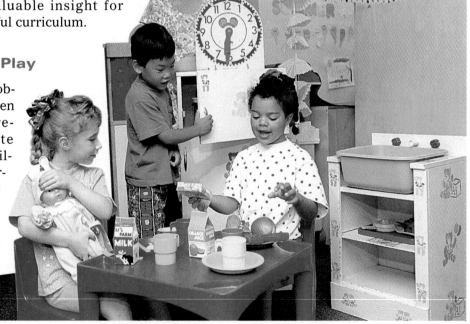

What to Observe in Dramatic Play

*C*hildren reveal themselves through dramatic play. Here are some things to notice:

• Does the child participate regularly and easily in dramatic play?

• Are there recurrent themes?

• How does the child solve conflicts in dramatic play?

• Can the child be a leader as well as a follower in dramatic play?

• Does the child accept the ideas of others? Does the child refuse to participate when peers do not go along?

• Does the child depend excessively on one playmate?

• Does the child use verbal and nonverbal communication skills effectively?

• What attitude does the child display? Boldness? Weakness? Combativeness? Daring? How does this compare to the child's usual attitude?

• Do other children choose this child as a playmate?

• Does the child prefer to play with peers or adults?

• Does the child use props creatively? Does he or she only copy peers?

• How involved does the child become in the play's plot? Does he or she contribute to the main action or simply move in and out of the play area?

• Are the child's play skills typical, advanced, or delayed as compared to those of peers?

• Are there behaviors that might warrant your concern for the child's physical or emotional well-being?

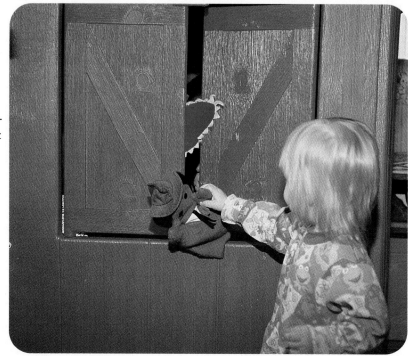

Children who are normally shy often find it easier to respond to puppets. Why do you think this is true?

USING PUPPETS

*P*reschool children love puppets. With puppet in hand, they can easily slip into the character of an alligator, a dog, or a chef. Playing with puppets develops many skills; it is an important part of the dramatic play experience.

Development Through Puppet Play

Playing with puppets has specific developmental benefits for children. Among them are:

- **Physical.** Children use both the large muscles in the arm and the small muscles in the fingers when playing with puppets. Eye-hand coordination is also practiced.
- **Intellectual.** Puppets push children to listen, talk, and share. Children try to give their puppets personality, calling for imagination and creativity.
- **Emotional.** Children express their feelings through puppets. Negative emotions, especially, are more easily shown through the safety and security of a puppet's character.

- **Social.** Puppets help children share and play with others. Children use cooperation and teamwork to create plots and interact with another child's puppet. Shy children talk more freely through a puppet. Gradually these children gain the confidence to speak for themselves.
- **Moral.** As with other dramatic play activities, puppet play allows children to act out acceptable and unacceptable behavior. They can show their basic understanding of moral concepts, such as right and wrong or reward and punishment.

Puppet Activities

Children usually step into the world of fantasy with ease. They can use puppets to act out nursery rhymes and folktales. They also enjoy using puppets to act out the lyrics of songs and finger plays during music time. Simply making conversation with another child and his or her puppet may be pleasure enough.

A Puppet Stage

Children don't have to have a stage to play with puppets. It does add to the sense of theater, however, and gives children a way to separate themselves from the action. Anything that children can safely stand or crouch behind could be used for a stage. Discarded appliance boxes make sturdy, inexpensive puppet stages. Cutting a hole out of the front so the box resembles a television or stage adds to the appeal.

Putting on a Show

Puppets are not just for children's play. Teachers use them, too, to tell stories and interact with children.

A good puppet show begins with a story theme. Choose a theme that you could build a simple story around. You may want the story to teach a lesson. Think about what you might do with a theme on safety, following rules, manners, family life, or friendship.

Once a theme is chosen, the story can be developed. The characters need to be involved in a series of events that surround a problem and solution. Try to build suspense. Bring the story to a clear and logical ending.

In a puppet show, the way puppets move adds to the enjoyment. Puppets that simply bob up and down are ineffective. You can do much more. With a hand puppet, wrist movements can make the puppet turn, bow, and sit. Movements of the arm can make the puppet run, hop, walk, fly, and fall. By using the fingers, all sorts of gestures are possible. You can make the puppet nod and point. Can you think of emotions that could be expressed too?

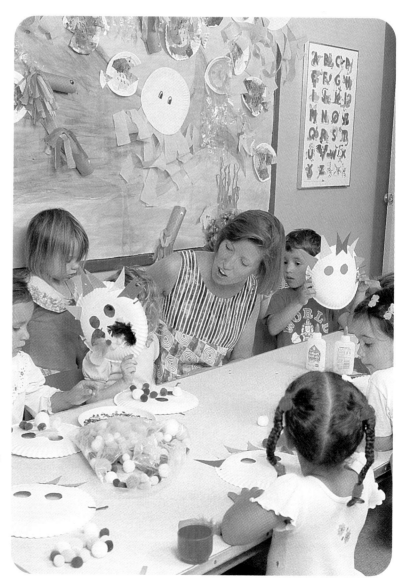

Simple paper plate masks also make good puppets. Children enjoy making these themselves.

Of course, when you put on a puppet show, you need a special voice for each character. Your own voice won't do. Make the voices distinctive, perhaps one high and one low in pitch. Match them to the characters. A scary bear, for example, might have a gruff voice.

The more experienced you become at puppetry, the more elaborate you can make your performances. Try adding sound effects and even props. Let your imagination and your skills be your guide.

What qualities does a successful puppet show include? Why do you think they appeal to young children?

LEARNING ABOUT LIFE

One of the joys of childhood is dramatic play. Nearly everyone has memories of those exciting moments when all things were possible—when the world of make-believe offered experiences that might never be equaled in the real world. Such adventures are part of the privilege of childhood and the responsibility. What better way is there for children to test their skills and experiment safely with life? What better way is there for adults to "see" what is going on in the minds of children and enable children to learn about life's experiences before they actually live them?

Types of Puppets

Puppets come in all shapes and sizes. All should be well made and colorful, with no detachable or sharp parts that might cause choking or injury. Children like to make puppets themselves. They learn from the process and feel proud of their efforts. Popular, easily made puppets include:

- **Stick Puppets.** Use a craft stick with a cut out character glued to the stick. Children can hold and move the stick to act out a story.

- **Sack Puppets.** A small, brown paper sack works well for this puppet. The flap is decorated with paper, fabric, ribbons, and other trims to make the character.

- **Glove Puppets.** A garden glove, mitten, or child's knit glove can be used. Attach a face to each fingertip, or make a face on the back of the hand while the fingers become the legs or hair.

- **Sock Puppets.** These are made with a sock and decorated with buttons, felt, yarn, moveable eyes, and other craft items. (Make sure children are old enough to use small objects without danger of choking.)

- **Hand Puppets.** Made from a simple pattern and fabric, these puppets can be sewn by hand or machine or glued with fabric glue. Attach a face directly to the puppet, or decorate a plastic foam ball to use as its head.

- **Finger Puppets.** Small pieces of felt or construction paper, folded to slip over a finger, are colored and decorated.

- **Mask Puppets.** These are made from paper plates decorated to resemble faces. A rubber band or paper strip can be attached to the back to make a place for the child's hand to slip through.

- **Puppet-in-a-Cup.** Stick puppets are used with a decorated paper cup. The sticks are pushed through the bottom of an inverted cup and moved up and down as needed during the story. The cup becomes the puppet stage.

Chapter 20 Review

Chapter Summary

- Dramatic play helps children experience and practice different roles.
- Dramatic play fosters development in all areas; it is an important way for children to learn.
- The teacher uses many techniques to facilitate dramatic play experiences.
- Dramatic play learning centers and prop boxes use themes to stimulate pretend play.
- Puppet play can contribute to all areas of development.
- Puppets and puppet stages can be made inexpensively.

Reviewing the Facts

1. What is dramatic play?
2. Explain spontaneous dramatic play.
3. What is role playing? Give an example.
4. Explain how dramatic play can contribute to growth in any three areas of development.
5. Describe what a dramatic play learning center is like.

6. How can teachers facilitate learning through dramatic play?
7. What caution should teachers follow when participating with children in dramatic play?
8. Why do teachers make formal observations of dramatic play?
9. List five things a teacher might look for when observing children in dramatic play.
10. How can teachers use dramatic play to foster cultural acceptance?
11. Citing any three developmental areas, give examples of how children benefit from puppet play.
12. Identify and describe three types of puppets that can be made easily by teachers and children.

Thinking Critically

1. What dramatic play themes did you enjoy as a child? What roles did you practice? What did you learn from these experiences?
2. How might dramatic play and puppet play be especially beneficial to children in times of crisis?

3. What effect do you think television might have on children's dramatic play?
4. How does dramatic play as described in this chapter differ from scripted, rehearsed plays? What benefits might written plays provide?
5. Suppose a child consistently showed attitudes during dramatic play that were very different from those he or she showed at other times. What might be the reason for this? What action—if any— would you take?

Activities and Applications

1. **Dramatic Play Follow-up.** Suggest three props you would provide for dramatic play after reading: a story about farmers; a book about a train engine; a poem about cats.
2. **Teacher Participation.** With a partner, demonstrate how a teacher might join children's dramatic play to model a positive social skill.
3. **Puppet Play Adaptations.** Select well-known folktales, fables, or nursery rhymes. Describe how

you would adapt them for puppet play.

4. **Learning Center.** Draw your own design for a dramatic play learning center. Provide details that show the basic arrangement. List and/or draw the contents you would include to go along with a specific theme.

5. **Planning an Activity.** Plan a dramatic play activity for preschoolers. Develop a lesson plan around your idea. Then carry out the activity with a group of preschoolers.

Your Professional Portfolio

Select a theme to use in a dramatic play center. On an index card, write down the following items: ways to set the stage for this particular dramatic play theme; items you might put together in a prop box for this theme; ways to encourage children to get involved in dramatic play activities. File your theme card under dramatic play in the activity file you developed earlier.

Observing and Analyzing

Discovering More about Dramatic Play

Through observation, you can learn much that will help as you guide the dramatic play of children. Try these ideas:

- **Expression.** In school and other locations, observe the way people use their voices and faces for expression. Also note their body language. You might watch teachers, adults in your family, people on television, public figures, and people on the job. What techniques capture attention? What techniques are ineffective? How does what people do in performance differ from their expressiveness in real life?

- **Props.** Throughout your daily routine, observe people that you see on the job. What props would be typically associated with the professions you see? Prepare lists of the props that go with each of several careers.

- **Children at Play.** Watch children who are playing dramatically. You might observe neighborhood children or children at a family or public gathering. Note what the children play and how they go about it. How real does the play seem to them? What props do they create for themselves?

- **Television Puppetry.** Watch a puppetry segment of a quality children's program on television. What type of puppets were used? What purpose was intended? Did the puppet(s) gesture, cry, point, run, fall, sleep, nod, faint, or act surprised, sad, happy, fearful, or loving? How were these actions and emotions conveyed? Did the voices match the characters? Were the voices carried out consistently?

- **Your Puppetry Skills.** Obtain or make one or more puppets. Use the puppet(s) informally with a child. You might interact with a family member or a child in your neighborhood. You can plan a theme or just converse with the child. Experiment with your technique and voice. What reactions do you get from the child? Analyze what worked well and what didn't. If possible, practice your skills (you could use a mirror) and try them out again with another child.

Chapter 21

Social Studies
Activities

CHAPTER OBJECTIVES

■ Identify goals of a social studies curriculum.

■ Plan a social studies learning center for preschoolers.

■ Describe how each of these areas is part of a social studies curriculum for young children: learning about self, family, and community.

■ Explain how aging and environmental issues can become part of the social studies curriculum.

■ Identify methods of helping children become socially responsible citizens.

■ Plan and lead social studies activities.

Terms to Learn

• social responsibility
• social studies

t's dry and white and you use it to make bread," Madeline Ingersoll said to the kindergarteners seated around her. "And here's what we're going to use to make it." Madeline pointed to the items she had brought with her. She was a guest in the class that day.

For a long moment puzzled expressions on the faces of the children greeted her. Finally Carlita exclaimed, "Flour!"

"But you buy flour at the store," protested Stefan.

"You're both right," Madeline responded. "You can buy flour in the store, but it starts out as something else." She explained how wheat is grown in huge fields and then harvested. "The berries are removed from the plant and ground very fine to make flour. Then it's packaged in bags and taken to the store," she added.

As she spoke, Madeline passed around wheat stalks and wheat berries that she had brought with her for the children to see, touch, and smell. Then she used her wheat grinder to process some berries into flour. After each child held a small amount, they talked about how smooth it felt.

"Why do you make flour?" Stefan asked. "You could buy it like my grandmother does."

"My mother taught me how to make flour," Madeline replied. "We're Mormons. That's our religion, just like some people are Catholic or Muslim or Protestant or Jewish. We believe that eating healthful food that we make ourselves is very important. Besides," she added with a smile, "I enjoy showing school children how flour is made!" With that, Madeline gave each child a piece of whole wheat bread freshly baked in her kitchen.

"I like it," Travis announced. "It's brown and round and different, but it's the best bread I ever tasted!"

WHAT IS SOCIAL STUDIES?

Like sponges, children are ready to absorb information. Among the most interesting lessons they have to learn are those about people, places, and events. When Madeline Ingersoll visited kindergarten, the children learned about why wheat is grown, about how food gets to market, and about people and their beliefs. Tasting homemade bread was only part of the lesson.

Although young children are still basically self-centered, they can begin to learn about the world that is beyond their everyday experience. Technology has already done much to increase their awareness. Television, for example, provides a window on the world. Modes of transportation allow people to travel outside their immediate surroundings with ease, speed, and frequency. In a world that gets "smaller" all the time, people have a greater need for understanding than ever before. For children, lessons in understanding begin with social studies.

Social studies is *the part of a curriculum that teaches children about themselves as well as their family, community, and the world.* Through social studies, children discover that the world is a fascinating place in which people are similar, yet different. Through knowledge, children develop understanding, and through understanding, they learn acceptance. No social studies curriculum would be complete without such a purpose.

GOALS OF THE SOCIAL STUDIES CURRICULUM

Planning the social studies curriculum presents one problem. You may be frustrated because time limits what you can do. Subjects like history, economics, geography, government, current events, and careers are all covered under the social studies umbrella. Simple lessons related to all of these are possible for young children. You want children to gain knowledge about the world, but you also want to teach them how to get along within it. To accomplish this, you first set goals like the ones listed here:

- Help children develop a positive attitude toward themselves and others.
- Help children understand their role within the family unit.
- Encourage children to recognize and appreciate how individuals and families are alike and different.
- Introduce children to the community and its services.
- Spark children's interest in how people in their community work and live.
- Help children acquire positive social behaviors so they may live happily within the family, community, and society.
- Enable children to see that people of all backgrounds bring special qualities and contributions to the world.
- Help children become aware of climates and environments on earth.
- Help children learn to manage and conserve the earth's resources.

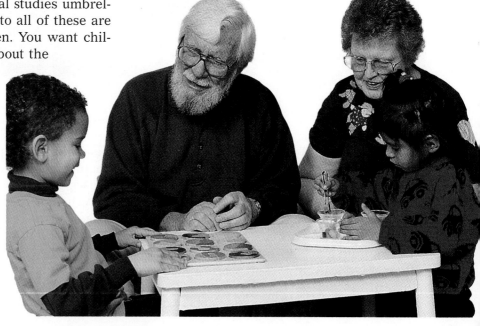

Attitudes toward older people begin to form early in a child's life. How might an early childhood program encourage a positive attitude?

THE SOCIAL STUDIES LEARNING CENTER

*D*iscoveries about the world are made in the social studies center. Here children learn about other people, including the aging and people of varying ethnic backgrounds. You might find maps, a globe, and multicultural items. Any props or games that relate to people, communities, and getting along with others could be placed in this center. Sometimes the social studies center is combined with another. When space is a problem, placing it with the language arts center is a good solution.

SOCIAL STUDIES ACTIVITIES

*T*o achieve the goals of the social studies curriculum, teachers include many different topics in their plans. Like all learning, social studies should start with what is most familiar to children. Thus, effective early childhood teachers begin their social studies curriculum with activities that help children learn about themselves.

Heritage can be a source of pride. Encourage children to share their own with the class.

Tip
FROM THE
Pros

*P*osters that highlight social studies concepts suitable for young children can be obtained from fire stations, libraries, police stations, service organizations, and state departments of conservation.

Learning about Self

Children are strongly individualistic. Gradually they learn to act as members of families, neighborhoods, and communities. Understanding and liking oneself is the first step in developing a well-rounded personality and being able to function productively in society.

People who have high self-esteem—who accept and value their own traits and abilities—tend to participate more fully in life and get along better with others. Therefore, teachers can help children become good community members by helping them develop self-esteem. They do this by planning activities in which children can succeed. They acknowledge strengths and positive traits. They provide activities that explore children's likes, abilities, and interests.

The toys included in the classroom should reflect the diversity of society. This is one element of promoting self-esteem.

Through class activities, children can learn that families are not all the same, but they are all important.

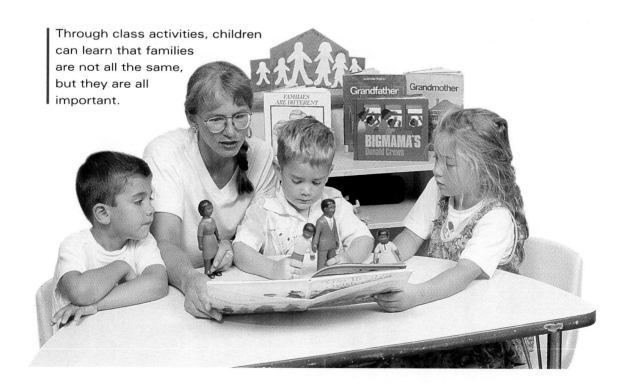

Showing respect and appreciation for children's heritage helps develop self-pride. You can include items from different cultures in the classroom environment and curriculum. Respect for ethnic groups, for example, can be promoted with a collection of dolls that have different skin tones, features, and hair and eye colors. Dolls should have hairstyles and clothing that is typical of what people wear in everyday life, not costumes that are outdated or incorrect.

Learning about Families

After self, family is the next most familiar social concept to children. Through social studies activities, they can learn about different families. Examples can be found in most schools. There are children from traditional nuclear families and single-parent homes. Some children may live in households that include members of the extended family—grandparents, aunts, uncles, and cousins. Some children have siblings; others have none. Sharing their own varied experiences of family life with each other teaches children about the diversity of families.

Children can also learn that family types and roles vary among different cultures. Through pictures, stories, and guest speakers, they can see that family members have different jobs and expectations according to their culture.

Possibly the most important thing young children can learn about families is that strong families are necessary to individuals and to society. Families take care of their members physically and emotionally. They teach them some of the skills they need to be personally happy and productive in society. Moreover, they make an effort to build family strength by following traditions and showing commitment.

Learning about Community

Thinking abstractly is difficult for young children. For this reason, learning about people and places beyond their own family and home is more difficult. The progression from street address to city to state to country is very hard for children to grasp. In fact, when asking preschoolers what town they live in, you are likely to hear such responses as "Greenview Apartments," "Illinois," and "the United States."

Because of these developmental limitations, exploring community life with children should begin with their home and immediate neighborhood. Take walks around the neighborhood. Talk with people who live there. Discuss what makes a neighborhood strong and why this is important.

Next, you can invite children to explore neighborhoods beyond their own. As a class, ride the bus on community routes. Point out businesses where parents and neighbors might work. Notice places of worship, libraries, museums, parks, the fire station, and schools. These activities gradually introduce children to the world beyond their own homes.

Books and films are a good starting point for exploring the concept of community with children. Field trips to sites away from the classroom also broaden children's experiences and awareness of the world. A special visitor, a guest invited into

Tip FROM THE Pros

*F*or young children, the world away from their homes and the child care program is a new and exciting place. Field trips to locations like these offer interesting experiences and opportunities for growth: airport, bank, courthouse, doctor's office, fire station, hospital, humane society, library, museum, nature preserve, newspaper office, park, police station, radio station, recycling center, schools, supermarket, and television station.

THE MULTICULTURAL CLASSROOM

Skin tone is an ethnic difference that children readily see in each other. Make skin tone a source of interest and pride with this activity. Have an adult trace each child, or have the children trace each other, on large paper. Then let children decorate the tracings.

After a lesson on skin tones, have the children mix their own. Premixed, ready-to-use, skin-toned paint is available through many catalogs and school sup-ply businesses. Mixing it individually, however, is more fun and allows for creativity. One way of achieving varied skin tones is to start with a basic brown (mix red with green, blue with orange, or yellow with purple). Then add that to containers of white. Add more red, yellow, etc., to create individual hues. Margarine cups are good mixing containers and will hold leftover paint for the next project.

---

the classroom to share a talent or skill, can help children appreciate the different jobs in society and the people who perform them.

Community Helpers

Police officers, firefighters, doctors, nurses, and life-guards are just a few examples of community helpers, people whose jobs involve helping others within the community. Because children are fascinated by community helpers, teachers often plan units of study around the topic. When planning a unit on community helpers, use a variety of activities, such as books, special visitors, field trips, puppets, flannel board stories, finger plays, and prop boxes.

For example, Mr. Gilmore introduced a study of subway engineers as community helpers by reading a book about subways. He invited an engineer to class. He even scheduled a ride on the subway. Follow–up activities included writing a thank you note to the engineer and setting out subway engineer prop boxes for dramatic play. Providing experiences like these helps children understand the place each person has in making a community work.

When a real doctor visits the classroom, children can ask questions and learn in a nonthreatening setting. Parents are often willing to visit the classroom and talk about their jobs.

Diversity in the Community

In the past, people might never have encountered anyone from another country or culture unless they were wealthy enough to travel. Today's children live in a multicultural world. They routinely see similarities and differences in people's music, dress, food, celebrations, art, and appearance. Creative teachers make learning about other people and their customs an exciting adventure. They encourage a positive attitude as they marvel at differences while celebrating a spirit of unity with all people.

When many cultures are represented in a program, you have built-in resources for classroom activities. Parents and family members may be surprised when you ask them to share their culture with children, but they are likely to be flattered. If you don't have this kind of resource, contact colleges and high schools to see if they know of faculty members or foreign exchange students who can be of help.

The following ideas will help you introduce children to their wide, wonderful world. Regardless of the methods you choose, be sure to include as many hands-on activities as possible. Remember, that's how children learn best.

- Provide books that include children from a variety of cultures and races.
- Invite special visitors with different cultural backgrounds to visit the classroom. Ask them to talk about and demonstrate some of their customs.
- Serve ethic foods regularly as part of meals, snacks, and cooking activities.
- Provide instruments from different cultures in the music center. At music time play folk songs and other ethnic music. Occasionally watch a video tape of cultural dances. Teach children simple cultural songs and dances.
- Celebrate holidays of different cultures. Have children make holiday decorations. Include cultural foods, songs, dances, and other appropriate activities.

As children learn about other people in a multicultural society, be sure to stress the ways in which people are all alike. This is one of the most important purposes of social studies in the preschool curriculum.

The themes you include in your curriculum can be incorporated into all types of activities. Music lends itself to learning about other cultures.

Learning about Aging

Just as positive images of different cultures need to be incorporated in the classroom, so do the images of aging. Misconceptions about aging form when children have little opportunity to interact with older adults. Given information and closer contact, children learn to be comfortable with the appearance of age. They discover that aging can mean wisdom, patience, and tenderness. They learn to be sensitive to the problems associated with aging. Even more important, they develop a desire to interact with older adults. In exchange for conversation, knowledge, and caring, they give back all of these plus helpfulness.

As lifespans increase, the number of older people in society is growing. With understanding, children are more likely to be responsive to the needs of this expanding segment of society. They will also have fewer fears about growing older themselves.

Contact is the key to bridging the gap between generations. Teachers can arrange visits to retirement homes and senior citizen centers. Older adults who have time to spare can also be invited to volunteer in the early childhood classroom.

Learning about the Environment

Children enjoy learning about the different environments on planet Earth. Begin teaching about your own local environment before introducing unfamiliar ones, such as tropical rain forests and Arctic zones.

When focusing on environments, teach children about land characteristics, plants, and animals. Social studies concentrates on how these impact people's lives. To begin a study with children, take a walk around your child care facility. What types of trees are there? What kinds of plants and animals? Are there mountains or flatlands around you? What is the weather like? How do all these features of the environment affect children's lives? Discussions about climate and details about specific lifestyles, such as desert living, are beyond the understanding of preschoolers. By helping them see that people do not all live in the same environment, however, you begin to open their eyes to the planet's diversity.

Conserving Resources

Children can learn to care for the environment and conserve community and world resources if adults show them the way. Even preschoolers can learn such principles. The much-publicized campaign of "Reduce, Reuse, and Recycle"—the three Rs—is an effective concept that can be made simple enough for young children. As a class, go outside to watch a garbage truck making its rounds. Explain that the garbage will be buried in the earth. As children begin to learn that trash doesn't just disappear, they will understand the purpose for practicing the three Rs.

Next, provide classroom opportunities to put the ideas into practice. Children can conserve paper by coloring on both sides. Remind them that running a small stream of water when washing hands reduces the use of water. Conserving electricity means turning off classroom lights and computers when not in use.

Also demonstrate how to reuse items. If clean, computer paper, egg cartons, and packing materials can be reused in art projects. If children bring lunches or snacks from home, encourage them to reuse paper and plastic bags.

Establish classroom recycling centers. By sorting recyclable materials, children learn to classify as well as conserve resources. Children can bring castaway items to the classroom and then earn money from the recycling center. To help children learn that trees are a renewable resource, use the money earned from recycling to purchase a tree for the play yard.

Many centers have their own recycling centers and actively teach children about the environment and recycling. Do you think such lessons, taught at an early age, will have an effect on later behavior? Why or why not?

SOCIAL RESPONSIBILITY

*W*hen people make a positive contri-bution to the community and obey *community laws*, they practice **social responsibility.** To become productive mem-bers of society, children should learn from an early age to accept basic responsibilities. These range from respecting property to vot-ing regularly in democratic elections.

Encouraging Social Responsibility

Through daily classroom routines, children learn attitudes and behaviors that prepare them to be active, respon-sible citizens. By following these prac-tices, teachers show children that social responsibility is important to a fair, orderly society:

- *Expect children to obey rules.* Children can follow basic rules related to self-respect and respect for others. Insist that children settle problems with words rather than by hitting. Never allow them to hurt another's feelings through teasing. Require that children put away toys once they are finished playing with them. Have them assist in cleaning up after art projects and meal time.

- *Have children help with classroom tasks.* Children develop pride when they contribute to the overall wel-fare of the class by performing rou-tine jobs that need to be done. They can water plants, feed pets, and set tables for snack time.

- *Give children opportunities to make deci-sions.* Although many citizens do not real-ize it, their right to vote in a democracy is rare in today's world. If they were aware of this fact, they might not take the privi-lege for granted. Allowing children to vote on some classroom matters shows them that by expressing their preference, they can make a difference. This may encourage them to exercise their right to vote more responsibly when they are adults. Classroom voting opportunities can be found in any situation with more than one acceptable option. Children can vote on which storybook they would like to hear or what song they would like to sing. Other voting activities include choosing a class mascot, a favorite video, or a preferred snack.

Building Professional Skills

Respect

WHAT IS RESPECT?

Respect is awareness of how important people and things are. Because of respect, you believe other people are equal to you—even if they are very different from you—and you treat them that way. You are careful with the property of others because it may have value to them even if it doesn't to you. Respecting other people and their possessions also makes you see that you are worthy of the same consideration. Those who respect others generally receive respect in return.

Respect in Action

To help pass the time, Jill did some hand sewing as she sat on the park bench. Periodically, she looked up to keep an eye on Lindsey, the eight-year-old she watched for the O'Malleys.

After a while, Lindsey ran up to her from the swings. "What's that man doing?" Lindsey asked.

Jill looked to where she pointed. An older man was gathering aluminum cans in a large, plastic bag.

"He's collecting cans," Jill explained. "Later, he'll sell them to some people who can make them into something else. That way he can make some money and the park stays clean."

Lindsey said authoritatively, "My friend Danny say people who do that are poor and live in a bad part of town."

Jill thought for a moment. "Not everyone who collects cans is poor. He may be, but if he is, at least he's trying to make some money honestly. And we don't know where he lives. In fact, we don't know anything about him. How would you feel if someone said that about you, just because of what somebody else told them?"

Lindsey shook her head. "I wouldn't like it."

"What about me?" Jill held up her sewing. "I wore a hole in these jeans, so I cut off the legs to use as rags, and I can wear the pants as shorts. Does that make me poor? Do I live in a bad part of town?"

"No!" Lindsey laughed. "You live next to me!"

"That's right. If you tried to judge me by appearances, you might be wrong."

Lindsey looked again at the older man. "If he is poor," she said slowly, "we should do something to help him."

Jill smiled. "Good idea. Let's talk about what we can do."

Your Analysis

1. Was Lindsey being intentionally disrespectful? Explain.

2. What was the effect of Jill using herself as an example?

3. Identify the actions that showed respect in this story. For what or whom was respect shown?

How are responsibilities for classroom tasks assigned in centers you have visited? Which do you think is the best method?

A STRONG IMPACT

*T*he impact of the social studies curriculum is like no other. As a young person who is close to reaching adulthood, you are, no doubt, well aware of many of society's problems. Gangs, violence, hatred, and crime are all too common. These are destructive forces that cannot be allowed to grow. Your work with young children is crucial in this effort.

Caring is at the heart of the social studies curriculum. Young children must first learn respect for themselves before they can extend the same regard to others. They see that they are worthwhile and important but that the world contains many other people who are too. Gradually, children look beyond themselves and, with guidance, they develop a sense of responsibility for what happens in the world.

As a child care professional, you will have an opportunity to shape the way children think. Research shows that attitudes form at an early age. It is much easier to mold the mind of a young child than it is to change it once destructive thinking has taken hold. Through a well-planned social studies curriculum, you can provide lessons that give children a foundation for getting along in the world and also for making it a better place.

FOCUS ON SCHOOL-AGE PROGRAMS

*S*ocial studies for school-age children should be project-oriented. The more hands-on and practical the experience, the better. Involve school-age children in community projects, such as planting a butterfly garden or making decorations for residents of nursing homes.

School-age children can learn social responsibility by occasionally helping with the care of younger children. Reading stories and singing songs with preschoolers give school-age children a sense of pride and leadership.

Chapter 21 Review

Chapter Summary

- Early childhood social studies focuses on children learning about themselves, their family, and their community.
- The goals of social studies include helping children like themselves and take pride in their culture.
- Learning about diverse ethnic groups and customs broadens children's views of the world.
- Field trips, special visitors, storybooks, music, and prop boxes are ways to help children learn about the community and community helpers.
- Children can help conserve community and world resources by learning to reduce, reuse, and recycle materials.
- Teaching social responsibility starts in the early childhood years.

Reviewing the Facts

1. What is social studies?
2. List six specific goals of a social studies curriculum for young children.
3. Briefly describe a social studies learning center.
4. How do teachers promote self-esteem through social studies?
5. Identify two basic concepts about families that young children can learn.
6. Why should the study of community begin with a child's own neighborhood?
7. Give five examples of community helpers. How do children benefit from learning about community helpers?
8. Identify three ways of teaching children about different cultures and customs.
9. What can children learn through contact with aging adults?
10. What basic concept about the world's environment can young children be taught?
11. Suggest four ways children can become involved in conserving resources.
12. What is social responsibility? Name two things teachers can do to encourage children to be socially responsible.
13. What is the potential impact of a well-planned social studies curriculum?

Thinking Critically

1. How might a preschool social studies curriculum differ from one for older children?
2. What are the dangers if a child care professional believes that some ethnic groups and cultures are better than others?
3. How would you respond to a preschooler who says, "I can't play with her because she's . . ." (the child names a specific ethnic background)?
4. Describe stereotypes that are often applied to older people.
5. What can child care professionals do to reduce or prevent young children's mistrust of people who are different from themselves?

Activities and Applications

1. **A Simple Field Trip.** A field trip could be as simple as a walk in the neighborhood. With a partner, make a list of theme ideas that could give the same route new interest. For example, children could look for shapes one time and colors the next.

Chapter 21 Review

2. **Most Important Idea.** Write down what you believe the most important idea in this chapter is. Share opinions with the rest of the class.

3. **Learning Center.** Draw your own design for a social studies learning center. Provide details that show the basic arrangement. List and/or draw the contents you would include.

4. **Planning an Activity.** Plan a social studies activity for preschoolers. Develop a lesson plan around your idea. Then carry out the activity with a group of preschoolers.

SCHOOL TO WORK

Your Professional Portfolio

Spend some time in the children's section of a library. Browse the books to find several with multicultural themes. Write reviews of at least three to place in your portfolio. You might also begin a list of such books to maintain for future use when working with children.

Observing and Analyzing

Increasing Your Awareness

Your awareness of what goes on around you can help form the basis for creating an early childhood curriculum. This principle is especially true with social studies. What do you notice that would be good for children to learn? How can your observations be translated into activities for children? Try these suggestions to get yourself in the habit of noticing social studies lesson ideas for children:

- **How People Get Along.** Pay attention to any problems your friends and family members have in their relationships. Look at the characteristics that cause difficulties. What could you teach young children that would help them in this area?

- **Current Events.** Read the newspaper, listen to news programs on the radio and television, and listen to people talk about what's going on. Evaluate the difficulty level of these situations for preschoolers to understand. Are there basic principles or pieces of information that children could learn as a start?

- **Multiculturalism.** Notice positive and negative attitudes that people have toward different cultures and ethnic backgrounds. What stereotypes do you see promoted? What would you like children to learn?

- **Citizenship.** All around you are examples of good and poor citizenship. Notice how laws and rules are observed. What are the effects? Are there lesson applications for children in the preschool classroom?

- **Environmental Concerns.** Take a close look at your school building, the grounds, public buildings, and all parts of your neighborhood. Notice signs that indicate how much people care about their environment. Do you see litter; graffiti (drawings on public surfaces); wasted energy and materials; dangers; or neglected property? How might you convert what you notice into simple lessons for young children?

As you can see, the world around you is filled with opportunities for children to learn. Just as the newspaper reporter develops a "nose for news," you too can develop an awareness of ideas for teaching. Make sure you adapt your ideas for children's understanding. For example, they may not understand the term "ecology," but they can put litter from the play yard into sacks for disposal in order to keep the area clean, safe, and pleasant for play. Such lessons are the foundation for more complicated messages as children grow older.

Chapter 22

Music and Movement Activities

CHAPTER OBJECTIVES

- Identify the benefits of music to children.

- Plan a music learning center for preschoolers.

- Explain the teacher's role in music.

- Describe how basic skills and concepts are reinforced through music activities.

- Plan and lead music and creative movement activities.

Terms to Learn

- action verses
- beat
- call-and-response songs
- creative movement
- echo method
- improvisation
- lyrics
- melody
- pitch
- rhythm instruments
- tempo

he song!" five-year-old Marcus exclaimed. "Hurry!" Caleb watched as Marcus, Peter, and Roseanne scurried through the door of the child care center. Each day Caleb transported them to the center after their kindergarten class was over. Like the children, he could hear the lively tune coming from one of the classrooms. Curious, he followed them as they scurried down the hall.

As he peered through the doorway, Caleb watched the children join the others in a semicircle around the teacher. She played the guitar while the children sang.

After the first verse, the teacher called out, "Now sing like Martians." The children sang the next two lines in a squeaky, shrill chorus. "Now like bullfrogs," the teacher directed, and the children dropped their voices to their lowest octave. Caleb chuckled. Not only were the children thoroughly enjoying themselves, but they had made the transition from kindergarten to child care without a second thought.

"That teacher," he said to himself, "knows what she's doing."

BENEFITS OF MUSIC

Through music in early childhood education, children learn to produce and order sounds and tones with their voices and musical instruments. They also learn to appreciate musical compositions and move creatively to them.

Musical expression begins early. Children seem to have an inborn desire to make noise and listen to sounds. Music can be a joyful experience for children. Through exposure to music, they learn to recognize and enjoy all kinds of music as well as musical instruments. They may even create music themselves. As with art activities, the process of exploring and experimenting with music is more important to development than actual performance.

Music activities benefit a child's development in a number of ways:

- **Physical Development.** As children move rhythmically to music, they develop their large muscles and refine their motor coordination skills. Hopping, wiggling, swaying, bouncing, stomping, and twirling to music are all healthful and acceptable ways to release their seemingly endless supply of energy. To play basic instruments, such as drums or tambourines, children use fine motor skills. Learning to handle these instruments demands eye-hand coordination.

- *Intellectual Development.* Language skills develop as children sing. Memory is challenged as they learn **lyrics**—*words to songs*—and follow directions to musical games. Vocabularies grow and concepts become clearer as children sing songs about shape, color, and size. Listening skills develop too. Children have to listen carefully to the sounds, words, and music before they can respond appropriately. Attention span lengthens and concentration improves. In addition, children learn about music itself. They identify **tempo**, *the speed at which a song is sung*, as well as **beat**, *the recurring pulse that gives a song rhythm.* To sing tunefully, children must be able to recognize **pitch**, *the highness or lowness of musical sounds*, and to listen for **melody**, *the tune of a song.* Putting all of these together in order to make music and move to it causes children to use reasoning skills. As musical skills improve, thinking skills do too.

- *Emotional Development.* Music can calm frustration as well as provide an outlet for anger. Children express and cope with their own emotions through music. They gain self-confidence by successfully participating in musical activities. Their cultural heritage is affirmed when songs from their family's background are shared.

- *Social Development.* In music learning centers, children learn to obey rules and share materials. Playing instruments in harmony requires cooperation and waiting for a turn. Group singing promotes feelings of togetherness and belonging that help friendships develop. Social awareness is encouraged when music of other cultures is explored. Folk songs from all countries pass on important social values, such as friendliness, cooperation, honesty, and caring for family. Cultural songs that tell exciting tales of heroes and heroines help children understand what people in other times and places valued.

With well-planned activities, an enthusiastic teacher can both instill a love of music and enhance development.

THE MULTICULTURAL CLASSROOM

Introducing music from around the world can be accomplished in many ways. Music in different languages has been recorded by many children's musicians, including Raffi; Steve and Greg; Sharon, Lois, and Bram; Ella Jenkins; and Marcia Berman, and by such folk singers as Peter, Paul, and Mary; Pete Seeger; and James Taylor. You can find songs recorded in French, Spanish, Japanese, and Hebrew, as well as songs from English-speaking countries with cultures and traditions of their own (Jamaica, Ireland, Trinidad, and England). Classical and contemporary music from many countries is available in most public libraries and music stores. The families in your community might share music from their own collections.

Some simple, multicultural musical instruments can be made from reusable materials. Look for ideas for making them in *Hands Around the World*, by Susan Milord, Williamson Publishing Co., Charlotte, Vermont.

THE MUSIC LEARNING CENTER

A music center is an area in the classroom set aside just for music experiences. It should be available to children during free play. There they can explore the sounds that instruments make and listen to recorded music, perhaps with headphones to avoid disturbing others. In addition, teachers conduct small group activities in the music center and use materials from the center for large group activities.

Recordings and a machine for playing them are basic to the music center. A well-stocked center has a wide variety of recorded music, from relaxing melodies to fast-paced music for active play. Suitable music should be available for group sing-alongs and chants, as well as musical games (such as "The Farmer in the Dell"), dancing, and other movement activities. Be sure to include folk music of many cultures.

Children understand beat and tempo before they master the more difficult skills of following a melody or singing on pitch. Therefore, the music center should have child-size versions of **rhythm instruments**, *musical instruments that allow children to experiment with making their*

Rhythm instruments are part of every culture. Can you think of at least three different lessons you could teach using authentic cultural instruments such as these?

own rhythms. Maracas and drums are two simple rhythm instruments that children can master.

Most child care programs also have musical instruments for teachers to use as they lead activities. These might include a piano, guitar, or zither. The zither, a stringed instrument that is played with a pick and fingers, is portable and easily mastered. One type of zither, the Autoharp®, has buttons for playing chords.

THE TEACHER'S ROLE

*T*he success of musical activities depends on teachers. Teachers collect music ideas by using resource books, attending conferences, and exchanging with other teachers. They know that repetition is good, but at some point it results in boredom.

Teachers find ways to incorporate music into classroom routines. Greeting and farewell activities are good times to include music. Songs may be used as a calming transition from outside play. At nap time, children are eased into sleep with lullabies and other soft music.

Appreciation for music of all kinds grows when teachers include many types of music in the day. Playing light classical music during nap time can help children appreciate its soothing qualities. Listening to calypso music during lunch would encourage children to associate it with friendship and informality.

If certain children do not eagerly take part in music, the teacher can help. Some children take longer than others to feel at ease in group activities. Asking parents what music the children listen to at home and then using that music in activities is helpful. Working with children individually and in small groups in the music center often helps them overcome their reluctance. Some children feel more secure and confident when they have an instrument to play; they focus on the instrument instead of themselves. Sitting near hesitant children shows support, and giving them an extra bit of praise can boost their confidence.

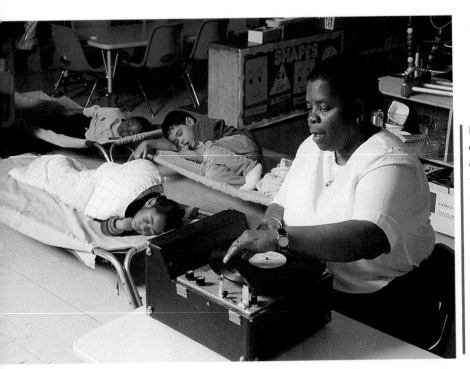

Music serves many purposes. A caregiver's job can be easier when music is used to signal certain activities and encourage specific reactions in children. At nap time music has a calming effect on these children. The soft sounds tell them that it is time to rest. At the same time, the children learn to appreciate the light classical music selected by the caregiver.

Resourcefulness

WHAT IS RESOURCEFULNESS?

Resourcefulness is the ability to meet your needs by using what you have. Resourcefulness is actually a twin skill. The first part is knowing what tools— resources—are available to you. The second, and often more challenging, part is thinking of ways to use whatever is available to accomplish your goal. Often you may lack resources, such as money or time, that seem essential to reaching goals. Instead of giving up, look for "hidden" resources and find creative ways to use them. That's resourcefulness.

Resourcefulness in Action

Lyle was growing frustrated. The children in his music classes were so enthusiastic and eager to learn. If only they could afford more and better instruments, who could tell what might happen? Some might become truly gifted musicians. At the very least, they would all increase their enjoyment of music.

Watching a travel documentary one day, Lyle saw island children "playing" conch shells by blowing into them. That gave him an idea. The next day he came to class with a large sack. "Today," he told the children, "I have some new instruments for you." He poured the sack's contents onto his desk. Out tumbled two dozen margarine tubs, their lids securely sealed—some half-filled with small rocks, some with toothpicks, and some with plastic beads. The children looked bewildered, but Lyle explained, "What is music but a combination of sounds? And what are musical instruments but things that produce sounds? You don't need money to make music— just imagination and feeling."

Over the next few days, the children learned to play their "instruments." They shook them. They scraped the sides. They tapped the tops. They learned which contents produced which sounds. By the end of the week, they were performing original compositions written just for margarine-tub bands.

"I never realized there were so many sounds in the world," Jermaine said.

"I wonder what else we can make music with."

Your Analysis

1. What were Lyle's goals? What resources for reaching his goals did he lack? What available resources did he use instead?

2. How did Lyle's resourcefulness inspire the children?

3. Have you heard of people making music by humming through wax paper, playing spoons, and tapping bottles that contain different amounts of water? What other creative ways are there to make music?

4. How are creativity and imagination related to resourcefulness?

MUSIC ACTIVITIES

Music is much more enjoyable for children when there is variety. Singing is not the only way to spark their interest, as you will see when you read on.

Exploring Sounds

Before learning about music specifically, children need to learn about sounds in general. After becoming aware of familiar sounds, children enjoy creating new sounds through music.

Teach children about sounds by going on listening walks. What sounds of nature can they identify? Are there birds, frogs, or crickets? What sounds of the city do they hear? How does a train's whistle differ from a truck's horn? Listen for quiet sounds, harsh sounds, pretty sounds, and scary sounds. Can children guess how these sounds are made?

Explore how sounds are used in daily life. Clock buzzers wake them up; kitchen timers tell them when food is ready; alarms warn of fire and storms; and sirens tell of a police officer in a hurry. What other sounds can children remember hearing?

Children should explore sounds they can make with their own bodies. They can slap, clap, snap, hum, or stamp to a tune.

Help children identify different ways music is used: on car radios, in places of worship, in elevators, in a baby nursery, on a television program or commercial, in a movie. Can they guess why music is used in these ways? After becoming good listeners, children enjoy specific music activities.

Singing with Children

The human voice is the finest musical instrument of all. Young children love to sing and have a charming way of making up their own songs. They are masters of **improvisation**, or *creating a melody and lyrics as the mood strikes*. They sing as they bathe, dress, eat, and play. Musical improvisation should be encouraged in children. It fills a basic need for self-expression.

The ability to sing in tune develops slowly. Children have a limited singing range, which gradually widens as they grow older. They learn to sing by imitating others.

Beginning at age three, children like to sing in groups. When choosing songs for group singing, consider developmental level and interests. Select a simple melody within voice range. Make sure the song has an

Musical skills develop after children improve their awareness of sounds. As Ben listens to the tape of sounds that animals make, he marks the corresponding pictures. This game helps improve his ability to discriminate sounds.

FOCUS ON INFANT/TODDLER PROGRAMS

Even at two months of age, infants begin to tell the difference between musical sounds and other sounds. Infants enjoy hearing music. Some show preference for music by lying very still while listening or turning their head toward the music's source.

Early in life infants begin to make sounds. They soon realize these sounds get reactions from adults. By six months of age, infants may string a series of sounds together. Researchers believe this may be an infant's first attempt at producing music.

Music can be part of basic caregiving routines. Caregivers can sing to infants as they bathe and diaper them or rock them to sleep.

Toddlers are too young to participate in a large group music activity. They do enjoy singing alone as they explore making sounds. They experiment with sound by playing with objects in their environment—pounding on empty oatmeal boxes, banging on pots and pans, and jingling keys.

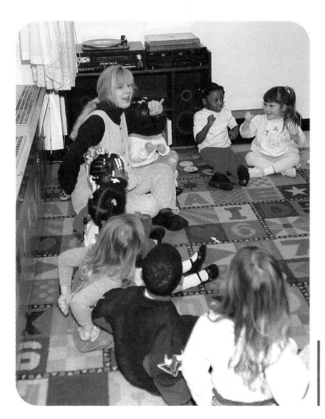

identifiable beat or rhythm. Children enjoy songs that have an interesting story to tell. Humor and surprise are especially appealing. Look for songs with verses that repeat predictably and have understandable vocabulary. **Call-and-response songs**, in which *an adult sings questions and children sing back the answers*, are popular. If the song lends itself to accompanying hand or body motions, so much the better.

Teaching Songs to Children

When teaching songs, first let the children listen to the complete song. Some teachers use the echo method in teaching.

Even if you aren't known for your singing ability, you can still teach songs to preschoolers. Just show them how much fun singing can be.

With the **echo method**, *children first listen as a line or verse is sung and then repeat it.* This continues until the entire song is completed. If the song is well chosen, children usually learn it with ease. Keeping songs simple and repeating them frequently aid the learning process. Pairing certain parts with motions and providing plenty of facial expression also helps children memorize songs.

Many teachers are not musically inclined. This doesn't have to limit their students' musical experiences. Most songs can be sung without instrumental accompaniment. Children's records are also helpful to teachers who do not play an instrument. A teacher's singing need not be perfect. Enthusiasm and love of music will come through.

Guidelines for Presentation

As with any other activity, planning and know-how make music activities more effective. Follow these guidelines when presenting singing activities to children:

- *Be comfortable.* Choose songs you enjoy and feel confident presenting.
- *Plan ahead.* Plan music time for no more than 15 to 20 minutes. Begin with energetic songs that grab attention. Finish with slower songs to help children calm down.
- *Know the songs.* Practice the actions and verses so you can present a song without looking at notes.
- *Use voice and face expressively.* Vary your voice by speaking slower, faster, softer, and louder. Use facial expressions to maintain interest and show enthusiasm.

Tip FROM THE *Pros*

Musical instruments are easily stored on Peg-Board®, with separate pegs for each instrument. Draw the outline of each instrument below the peg so children can put the instrument back by matching the shape to the outline on the board.

- *Accompany singing with an instrument when possible.* Although they are not necessary, musical instruments add a special element to activities. Rehearse the songs until you are comfortable singing and playing at the same time, or ask someone else to accompany you.
- *Vary music activity locations.* Music can take place in different places. Just for fun, conduct music activities outside under a tree, inside a tent, or in a play loft.

Playing Instruments

Children love to play simple rhythm instruments, such as triangles and wood blocks. These materials may be purchased or can be made inexpensively. Many multicultural rhythm instruments are available. They can be exciting additions to music centers.

To make sure instruments have a long life in the classroom, introduce them a few at a time. Demonstrate how to use each instrument appropriately so it does not break. Show children where and how instruments are stored. Set basic rules for playing with instruments. Children who misuse an instrument, for instance, will have to give it up until they are ready to handle it correctly. Planning interesting activities reduces the temptation to misuse musical instruments.

Activities with Instruments

Even simple instruments can be part of musical activity. Here are some ways that you might include them in the daily routine:

- Use instruments in a marching parade.
- Give children instruments to use as sound effects during stories. Before the story

Learning to play a song together can give young children a real sense of accomplishment. Can you identify the instruments these children are using?

- Experiment with tempo and volume by asking children to follow your lead. Can they play loud, soft, slow, and fast?
- Ask one child to hide in the room and play an instrument quietly. Have the other children find their playmate by following the sound.
- Provide instruments so children can pretend to put on a band performance.

Moving to Music

Moving to music is fun. Children can be expressive, active, or even silly, as the mood strikes them. **Action verses**, *songs for which children act out the motions described in the lyrics*, require children to use their minds and their bodies. In the song "Grey

begins, identify when each child should play an instrument. Give cues as needed.

- Behind a screen, play an instrument familiar to the children. Have the children guess what instrument it is.
- Play a tune on an instrument. Have the children guess what song it is.
- Play instruments while singing a favorite song. Ask children to express different moods the song inspires in them.
- Create a pattern of beats with a drum. Have the children repeat your pattern, using their own instruments. Vary the patterns of beats to add challenge. Let children take turns playing patterns for others to follow.

Action verses appeal to preschoolers because they combine body movements with a song. Keep in mind that these take practice for children to learn.

Recycled Rhythm: Homemade Rhythm Instruments

INSTRUMENT	MATERIALS	PROCEDURE
Shakers and Rattles	Plastic eggs, salt and pepper shakers, or 35 mm film canisters; buttons, raw rice, dried beans, or corn.	Fill containers with varying amounts of buttons, rice, beans, or corn; secure lids or seams with tape.
Sandpaper Blocks	Two wooden blocks, about 3 by 5 by 2 inches (7.5 by 12.5 by 5 cm); two 3- by 5-inch (7.5- by 12.5-cm) rectangles of coarse sandpaper.	Glue sandpaper onto blocks; replace sandpaper as needed.
Drum	Cylinder-shaped snack container, oatmeal canister, or coffee can with snug-fitting plastic lid; strip of nylon or other sturdy fabric.	Attach fabric strip to can; sling over shoulder so drum can be carried on opposite hip and played with both hands.
Tambourine	Embroidery hoop, paper plate, or aluminum pie tin; small bells; string or pipe cleaner	Attach bells to hoop, plate, or pie tin with string or pipe cleaner.
Cymbals	Two aluminum pie tins; two empty thread spools.	Glue spools to center of insides of pie tins; use spools as handles.
Wrist and Ankle Bells	Elastic strips, about 2 inches (5 cm) wide; small bells.	Measure and cut elastic to fit wrists and ankles; sew on bells; sew elastic into bands.

Squirrel," for example, children sing about a squirrel collecting acorns for the winter. The song lyrics give children cues on how to imitate the squirrel's actions. Pairing music with action in this manner helps increase attention span and helps children learn more quickly.

Teachers encourage children to interpret music through movement. Props stimulate imagination. Scarves, leis (Hawaiian flower necklaces), tutus (ballerina skirts), hoops, top hats, streamers, pompons, wands, and grass skirts all encourage creative expression.

Musical games also promote active involvement. Such songs as "Did You Ever See a Lassie," "London Bridge," and "Hokey Pokey" allow children to explore the many movements their bodies can make. Keep musical games very simple. Young children have trouble remembering complicated rules and waiting too long for a turn. Remember that small groups are easier to manage and motivate than larger ones.

Other Ways to Enjoy Music

Music activities need not be limited. Prop boxes for dramatic play can have a musical theme. Creative teachers also explore music through field trips and special visitors.

Where might you take children on a field trip to see music in action in the community? A radio station, music store, recording studio, and dance studio are possibilities. If there are theater productions for children, you might arrange for children to watch one. Could you take children to see an orchestra or high school band rehearse? In some areas you might even be able to visit businesses that repair or manufacture instruments. A watchful eye on what is going on in the community may give you other ideas for introducing music to children.

Even when you can't take children out, you may be able to bring music into the classroom. Look for musicians who are willing to share their talent and expertise. Singers, folk musicians, a string quartet, madrigal singers, dancers, a barber shop quartet, a disc jockey, and a recording studio technician are a few ideas.

LASTING APPRECIATION

Music is for everyone, not just the musically talented. So often people think of music as an art form. That may be true, but for most people it is simply a source of pleasure. Those who acquire an appreciation of music from an early age grow up knowing how to fit music into their lives. They may like to create music, dance to it, or simply listen to it. Whatever the decision, music brings a special dimension to daily living.

FOCUS ON SCHOOL-AGE PROGRAMS

If provided with a solid foundation of music experiences in early childhood, school-age children may be ready for formal instruction. This is typically provided through schools or private teachers. In a child care center, school-age children may be given time to practice lessons.

School-age children still enjoy using basic rhythm instruments to create music. They are interested in putting on musical shows. Field trips to musical sights are especially beneficial for this age group. Such a trip might motivate a child to begin music lessons. Listening to music in the music center helps school-age children relax.

Creative Movement with Young Children

Active participation is the key to teaching young children. That's what **creative movement**—*responding to music through physical movement*—is all about.

To be successful with creative movement activities, prepare carefully. Provide an adequate supply of suitable, creative instruments and props. Children need a large open space with secure footing, away from windows and glass doors that

they might run into. Teacher participation—to serve as models for activities and to share the fun—is recommended, but children need to move and interpret music according to their own creative impulses.

The elements that make up creative movement are: body awareness, force and time, space, locomotion, weight, and moving in groups. Here are some ideas to use with children as you explore each of these elements:

Body Awareness. These activities familiarize children with the parts of their body and their range of movement.

- Play music with different tempos. Have children move parts of their bodies to the beat—first the head, then arms, legs, fingers, toes, and finally the entire body.

- Have children dance with props to encourage expression and creativity in movement. Streamers, scarves, grass skirts, leis, boas, pompons, veils, and hats are a few examples.

- Play soothing instrumental music. Have the children pretend to be a sprouting seed. Verbally guide the children into pretending to be a sapling and then a mature, leafy tree. How would they move in a gentle breeze? In a storm? If a bird landed on one of their branches?

- Have children move to music while balancing a beanbag on their head, arm, knee, elbow, etc.

Force and Time. Force describes strength of movements. Time refers to how quickly or slowly children move.

- Have children respond to music with varying tempos, such as a wedding march and Irish jig. Notice how their movements change.

- Adjust the volume of the music. How do children respond to louder music? To softer music?

Space. These activities encourage children to explore the use of physical space.

- In a large, open area, play a steady drum beat. Encourage children to move to the beat—forward, backward, sideways, and in circles.

- Play circus music while children move through an obstacle course. Have them go under a plank, around a table, and up and down steps.

Locomotion. With locomotion, children experience different ways to move from one place to another.

- Have children mimic animal movements. Ask them to gallop like ponies, slither like snakes, or crawl like turtles. Play appropriate music for each movement.

- Playing suitable music, have children mimic human movements. Can they march like a band leader? Sneak like a spy?

Weight. In these activities, children learn how weight affects body movements.

- Tell children to imagine they are carrying a heavy backpack. How would they walk going up a steep hill? Going down?

- Have children participate in a simple musical game, such as "Hokey Pokey," first holding streamers and later holding bottles or cartons filled with sand. Ask them to compare their movements in each case.

Moving in Groups. This requires personal coordination and coordinating movements with others.

- Playing music with a rapid tempo, have groups of children form themselves into a type of food, such as a bunch of bananas or a branch of cherries.

- Play musical "Follow the Leader." Have children take turns setting a beat with a tambourine, drum, or rhythm sticks. The "leader" also selects the movement the others make to the beat.

Chapter 22 Review

Chapter Summary

- Music activities benefit children's overall development.
- Good teachers create music learning centers and carefully plan and prepare activities.
- Music activities include listening to sounds, singing, playing musical instruments, and moving to music.
- You don't have to be musically talented to carry out music activities with children.
- Using a musical instrument gives a child a hands-on experience that contributes to enjoyment and involvement.
- Musical instruments for young children can be made inexpensively.
- Children can make music and also learn to move creatively to it.

Reviewing the Facts

1. In general, how does music benefit children?
2. Name one way music activities can aid each of these areas of development: physical, intellectual, emotional, and social.
3. Describe a typical music learning center.
4. Suggest two strategies for involving hesitant children in music activities.
5. List four ways to help children explore sounds.
6. Describe four guidelines for preparing to present a singing activity.
7. What is the "echo method"?
8. Describe how to make two simple rhythm instruments.
9. List four props that teachers can provide to encourage children to move to music.
10. What are the elements of creative movement?

Thinking Critically

1. Do you recall any songs you learned as a child? What social or cultural messages did they give? Would you recommend these songs for children today? Why or why not?
2. What musical activities did you participate in as a child? How did they aid your physical, intellectual, emotional and social development?
3. Why might some children be hesitant to participate in music activities? Do you think this tendency increases or decreases as children grow older? Explain your answer.
4. What musical sounds might appeal most to infants? Why do you think they would enjoy these sounds? What are some ways you might incorporate musical sounds into the daily routine of an infant?

Activities and Applications

1. **Choosing Music.** With a partner, make a list of songs or types of music that would be suitable foreach of the following: mealtime; nap time; transition from physical play to story time. Give reasons for your selections to the class.
2. **Music Review.** Visit the children's section of a library. Listen to three musical recordings for children. Write a review of each recording and present it to the class.
3. **Rhythm Instruments.** Work in groups to make rhythm instruments. Find and perform a song using these instruments.

Chapter 22 Review

4. **Learning Center**. Draw your own design for a music learning center. Provide details that show the basic arrangement. List and/or draw the contents you would include.

5. **Planning an Activity.** Plan a music or creative movement activity for preschoolers. Develop a lesson plan around your idea. Then carry out the activity with a group of preschoolers.

SCHOOL TO WORK

Your Professional Portfolio

Select an age-appropriate action song for preschoolers and plan a presentation. On an index card, write down the lyrics, leaving one or two spaces between lines. In a contrasting color of ink, use the blank spaces to write down actions (and sketches) for each line of lyrics. Present your song with actions to your class for evaluation. Place an improved version in your portfolio activity file.

Observing and Analyzing

Many Uses for Music

Music can be interwoven throughout the day in a preschool setting. Music is spontaneous when the teacher starts a song that fits the mood ("It's raining, it's pouring . . ." or "I'm going to shake, shake, shake my sillies out . . .," a Raffi classic). Music provides transitions and reminders ("Who has left their sweater, their sweater, their sweater?"). Music can follow children anywhere: on the way to lunch, onto the school bus, and as they march to the playground. A creative mind finds many ways to make music a frequent addition to the activity in a classroom.

Try these observation suggestions in order to become more familiar with how experienced teachers use music with children:

- **Children's Programming.** Watch a quality television program for children, such as Sesame Street. Notice how and when music is used in the program. Is it blended throughout the program? Are special music activities included? What purposes do different kinds of music serve? Can a television program do more with music than might be possible in a preschool?

- **Community Programs.** Check the newspaper, library, and other public agencies for musical programs scheduled for children. Attend one of these events. Take notes and report back on what the program was about, how it was handled, and the reactions of the children. Evaluate the effectiveness of the event.

- **Early Childhood Programs.** Spend some time visiting programs for different age groups, and see how music fits into the schedule and routines. Were music activities planned or spontaneous? Did you see improvisation? What kinds of musical activities were used? How did children respond to the music? What skills did the teachers demonstrate in presenting musical activities? How did the teacher encourage involvement?

Chapter 23

Science and
Math Activities

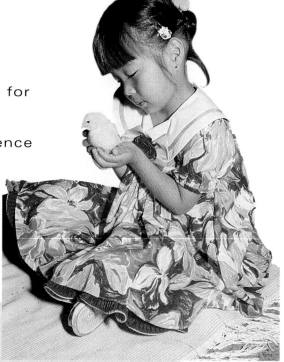

CHAPTER OBJECTIVES

- Explain how science and math activities benefit children.

- Describe the goals of science and math curricula.

- Plan a science and math learning center for preschoolers.

- Explain the teacher's role in making science and math interesting and enjoyable for children.

- Plan and lead science and math activities.

Terms to Learn

- hypothesis
- mathematical vocabulary
- mathematics
- numerals
- rebus recipe
- science
- sensory table

"r. Rockwell, look what we found!"

That exclamation was often heard on Louis Rockwell's nature walks. He always encouraged his inquisitive four-year-olds to notice sights, sounds, and smells. He wanted them to ask questions.

"Those are woolly caterpillars," he said as he carefully placed the wriggling insects in a jar with air holes. "Who can find some leaves for food and a stick for the caterpillars to climb on? The stick has to fit in the jar," he said to the children.

That afternoon the children carefully examined the caterpillars in the science center.

"Look! That one's hungry," Trent pointed out.

"They wiggle funny," Latisha noticed.

With Louis's guidance, they looked at the tiny jaws and legs through a magnifying glass. As Louis held the caterpillars, the children lightly touched their fuzzy bristles. They measured length and width to determine which caterpillar was the longest, the shortest, the fattest, and the thinnest. Louis read the class a description of woolly caterpillars in a book about native insects. Later, they made caterpillars from egg cartons as an art project.

"And now it's time to return the caterpillars to their home outdoors," Louis told the children. "That's where they belong. And then one day, they will turn into something very special."

"They will?" Latisha said with surprise.

"Yes," Louis answered. "Butterflies."

Latisha's eyes grew very wide, and Louis knew that another fascinating lesson was just waiting to be learned.

ENCOURAGING CURIOSITY

Louis Rockwell understands something about children. He knows that when they learn to appreciate the wonders of the world at a young age, they will later be excited about exploring that world through more advanced studies of math and science. It may seem that four-year-olds are not old enough to grasp math and science concepts.

It's true that much information is beyond them, but it's not too early to lay a foundation of curiosity and confidence that children can carry with them.

As technology plays a greater and greater role in society, excellence in science and math becomes increasingly important. In the future, many more jobs will require technical knowledge and skills. Children who are raised to see math and science as exciting and interesting have a definite advantage.

By making intriguing science and math materials available, you encourage children to explore on their own. Jeff is comparing the weights of various gourds by using a balance.

BENEFITS OF SCIENCE AND MATH

*I*ntellectual skills are sharpened through science and math activities. Math activities strengthen abstract thinking. In science activities, children learn to make accurate observations. They learn to recognize and classify objects according to similar characteristics. In doing a simple science experiment, they first make a **hypothesis**, *a possible explanation based on observable facts.* Then they draw conclusions from the experiment and communicate results. All are important mental abilities. Both math and science also teach logical thinking and problem-solving skills.

As with other types of learning, science and math exploration benefits the whole child. Physical development is aided when children use fine motor skills and eye-hand coordination to count, sort, measure, and weigh small items. They exercise their large muscles on nature walks. Emotional growth occurs as children gain confidence and self-esteem by learning new skills and concepts. Science projects offer excellent opportunities for social development as children work together. Recycling projects encourage social awareness as children discover the importance of creating and protecting healthful environments.

GOALS OF A SCIENCE CURRICULUM

*S***cience** is *a system of knowledge covering general truths and laws about the physical world.* When you think about it, that is one of a child's primary tasks in the early years—learning how the world works. A science curriculum in a child care setting simply expands this natural tendency.

Goals for a science curriculum include:

- Fostering children's appreciation of nature and themselves.

Computers and Preschoolers

*E*ven preschoolers are not too young to use computers. Early exposure to computers has several benefits. Children become comfortable with their use. Once familiar with the simple operational tasks they need to know, they can often work independently. Moreover, they take first steps to computer literacy, which is important with today's technology. Choose programs for preschoolers carefully. They need instructional materials that are easy to use, suitable for their age, and that reinforce basic concepts.

- Nurturing curiosity and providing opportunities to explore the world.
- Encouraging children to investigate the world, using their senses.
- Providing children with hands-on experiences that develop basic science concepts.
- Increasing children's ability to observe, describe, classify, see relationships, and solve problems.

THE MULTICULTURAL CLASSROOM

*O*ne built-in feature of a multicultural approach is that it is multifaceted. It can be incorporated into any aspect of life because it concerns itself with all of them. Math and science are not exceptions. Activities that teach science and math concepts also present opportunities to explore the history, geography, and culture of other lands. Does a cooking activity include stir-frying? Explain that this method of cooking became popular in China and Japan because the scarcity of firewood meant that food had to be cooked quickly. Are you growing corn plants as a science activity? Describe how corn is prepared in different cultures. Are children learning to write numerals? Find examples of how different cultures have created numerals within their own languages. Provide examples of different ways of writing today's date, and let the children write their own birthdays in different numeral styles.

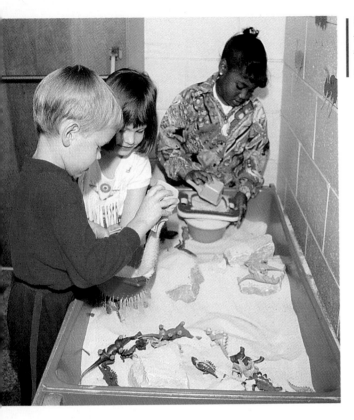

Sand and other sensory materials lend themselves to dozens of different activities. How many can you identify? What can be learned from these activities?

shape bingo games, puzzles, kaleidoscopes, and different objects to count and sort.

Sometimes the **sensory table** is placed in the science learning center. This is *a table with a boxlike, hollow top that can hold water, sand, beans, or other substances for children to play with.* The substance contained in the table can be changed periodically. Pitchers, funnels, rustproof spoons, shovels, pails, measuring cups, boats, and trucks are among the equipment children might use at the sensory table.

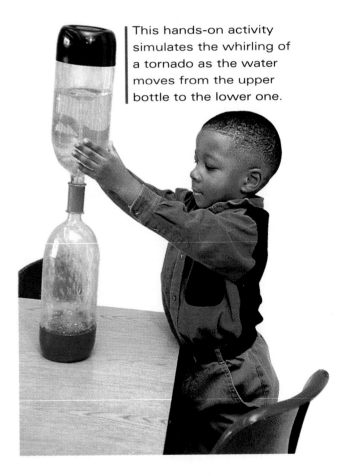

This hands-on activity simulates the whirling of a tornado as the water moves from the upper bottle to the lower one.

THE SCIENCE AND MATH LEARNING CENTER

*I*nvestigations of math and science may be made in one center or two separate ones. When planning a center, include at least one table and a set of chairs. Display science collections on a low table or shelf. If live animals are included in the program, they may be housed in this learning center.

Since science and math activities sometimes require a group effort, provide enough materials for at least four children to use the center at once. When looking for materials for science and math centers, include items from nature—leaves and twigs, nuts and seeds, shells, fossils, rock and mineral kits, and ant farms. Also provide measuring devices (rulers, yardsticks, balance scales), play money and cash registers, color and

SCIENCE ACTIVITIES

What happens when a person tries to learn something that is just too difficult? Chances are, enthusiasm for learning is lost. Before you can develop science activities for children, you need to be sure that the concepts are understandable. You want to spark interest, not eliminate it. A hands-on approach does this best. Relate principles to everyday life. Some favorite topics are the earth and sky; properties of air, soil, and water; and characteristics of plants, animals, and humans.

Teachers usually organize concepts around broad themes. "All About Fish" and "All About Rain" are two that children enjoy. Other common themes are the four seasons; animals in the zoo, ocean, desert, or forest; insects; colors and how they are made; rocks and minerals; food and nutrition; sounds and noises; how the body works; transportation; and plants and trees.

Young children can practice many skills through science activities. They like to collect, observe, and touch objects, plants, and animals. As they do, have them describe what their senses discover. Encourage them to question and think. Through exploration, they can compare and classify materials. They also note relationships like cause and effect. In addition, they notice similarities and differences in objects, plants, and animals. They use experimentation to test and retest scientific principles, such as what sinks and what floats.

Cooking Activities

The kitchen is almost a laboratory in itself. Its contents and the chemical processes that go on there make it so. Most children are familiar with at least some of the equipment and procedures used in cooking. They can carry out many tasks themselves. Cooking is a highly sensory experience,

---

Science Made Simple

Science activities need not be long-term. Some require little planning or preparation, yet are rich with potential for learning. Think of the science concepts you could explore through the following activities:

- Show children how to feel their pulse and heartbeat. Have them do this before and after a vigorous physical activity.

- Watch popcorn popping.

- Give children magnets of varied shapes, sizes, and strengths. Have them experiment with objects to find out what the magnets can and cannot pick up.

- Make a rainbow by spraying water from a garden hose in the sunshine.

- Place a bird feeder just outside the classroom window. Experiment to see what foods the birds prefer.

- Use objects to make shadows with a flashlight in a darkened room. Move them closer to and farther from the light. Hold the flashlight at different angles to the objects.

- Make static electricity. Rub an inflated balloon with a wool cloth. Under some conditions, such as dry winter weather, static electricity can also be produced by running a comb through your hair. Darken the room for maximum effect.

Even though most preschoolers cannot yet read, they can follow recipe directions that include drawings and symbols. Why would it be better to use such a recipe rather than just telling the children what to do?

with many opportunities to observe, taste, smell, and handle ingredients and utensils. The fact that the "science project" produces a tasty treat adds to children's interest and enjoyment.

Cooking activities lend themselves easily to a number of themes. They can be part of units on vegetables, farming, and homes. An activity for a unit on farm animals might be churning cream into butter. To illustrate the theme "All About Vegetables," you might have children combine the vegetables and mix the dressing ingredients for a tossed vegetable salad. Print the recipe in large, bold letters on poster board. You may wish to make a **rebus recipe**, *a recipe that illustrates ingredients and directions with picture symbols*, to help the children follow the steps.

Cooking Guidelines

For a successful cooking experience with young chefs, remember these guidelines:

- Look for simple recipes that illustrate the concept to be taught.
- Choose cooking activities that are related to other classroom activities. You might make carrot salad after reading "Peter Rabbit" during story time.
- Make cooking activities a multicultural experience by preparing simple foods, enjoyed in other parts of the world, such as baked plantain, a tropical fruit similar to a banana.
- Use only "foolproof" recipes. Test them yourself before having children prepare them.

- Beginning cooks often spill things. It's best to prepare foods over an easily cleaned surface, such as a tile floor. Lay a sheet of plastic over carpeting to catch spills.
- Limit group size to no more than six children and supervise them at all times.
- Avoid using kitchen appliances if possible. Without them, there are more opportunities for hands-on learning and fewer safety hazards.
- Make sure everyone follows the rules of safety and sanitation described in Chapter 13. Wear aprons to keep clothing clean.
- Allow plenty of time. Hurrying can lead to carelessness and accidents. It can also hinder learning.
- Let each child participate in some way.

Classroom Pets

Howard is one of the most popular members of Glenda Janssen's preschool class. The children bring him grass and carrots, watching in fascination as his tiny but powerful jaws churn the food. They take turns helping Glenda when she cleans his cage and takes him to the play yard for exercise. They like to gently stroke his soft fur. They giggle as they try to imitate the constant twitching of his pink nose.

Howard, of course, is a rabbit. He is also an ongoing science project, teaching the children many basic facts about the natural world. Through Howard, and from books and movies Glenda has found, they know that rabbits can move very fast by hopping. They have learned that wild rabbits live mostly in fields and prairies because they like to hide in tall grass. They know that newborn rabbits stay in a nest that the mother digs in the ground and covers with grass and fur. They have also discussed how rabbits are similar to, and different from, people and other common pets. Howard is a living laboratory for the basic principles of biology.

Howard has also allowed the class to become scientists. They discovered he likes to eat many kinds of plants, but not meat—they conducted an experiment. They have also noticed that Howard moves his ears toward the source of sounds. From this and other evidence, they concluded that he has a keen sense of hearing.

Caution and good judgment are part of having animals in the classroom. The animal must be healthy and nonthreatening, in appearance as well as reality. Many states require a veterinarian to certify that classroom pets are in good health. Be sure none of the children are allergic to the pet. Also be sure that the animal is cared for, either by yourself or the children. "Low-maintenance"pets, such as fish and gerbils, are good choices. If you cannot keep an animal in the classroom, have students share their pets for a day. Some animal welfare agencies also bring pets to "visit" classrooms.

Learning with Plants

Plants may not be as much fun as animals, but they do have several advantages as science projects. Their great diversity makes it easy to teach different concepts. Their growth is quick and dramatic enough for young children's limited patience. Foods from plants are readily available and easily investigated in a classroom setting. Plants are easy to find in nature and to grow indoors or outdoors.

From plants, children can learn about the life cycle, the stages that living things go through during a lifetime. First, they can find the seeds in different fruits, vegetables, and flowers. Then they can see the seeds

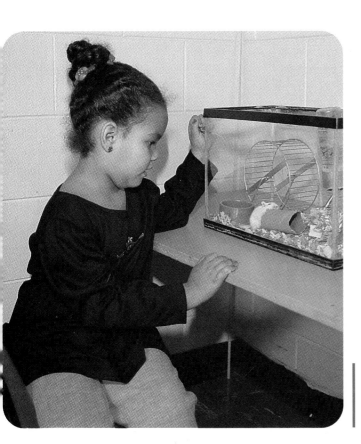

Having a pet in the classroom helps children observe changes day to day. They also learn the responsibility daily care of a pet requires.

Building Professional Skills

Attention to Detail

WHAT IS ATTENTION TO DETAIL?

Paying attention to detail is a balancing act. You may be tempted to disregard the details of a project because one or two "little things" don't seem to make much difference. No product, however, is any better than its parts. On the other hand, becoming too concerned with detail can lead to frustration and wasted effort. You need to identify important details and give them priority. They are the ones that will show in the end.

Attention to Detail in Action

Celeste was leading the school-age children who attended an after-school program at her church in a new project: planting and tending their own flowers. She watched as the children enthusiastically dug holes, dropped in the seeds, pounded dirt over them, and splashed them with water. One boy, however, sat staring at his seed packet. After a few minutes, he looked about thoughtfully. He seemed confused.

"How's it going, Ian?" Celeste asked him.

Ian shook his head. "I'm not sure I should plant my flowers here." He showed Celeste the back of the packet. "When my father plants flowers, he always looks at the back of the package. I think this says the flowers should have some shade, but there's no shade here. Will they get too much sun?"

Celeste hadn't thought of that. Now she looked around, too. "Why don't you plant them in that corner of the yard? Then the bushes will give them shade in the afternoon." Ian brightened. He went off to the corner with his seeds and watering can.

Celeste scanned the group of young gardeners. "They will be disappointed if their flowers don't grow," she thought. Then an idea formed. "Tomorrow I'll have them plant more seeds over by Ian's. As the flowers grow, we can compare how well they do in the two locations. That should be an interesting science experiment. Ian's attentiveness just may have saved this project."

Your Analysis

1. What detail did Celeste overlook?

2. What might have been the outcome if Ian had not noticed and dealt with the problem?

3. Assess Celeste's handling of the situation. How effective will it be? What do you think she will say to the children? What did she learn from the incident?

4. Why do people sometimes miss significant details?

5. Why are details especially important to math and science?

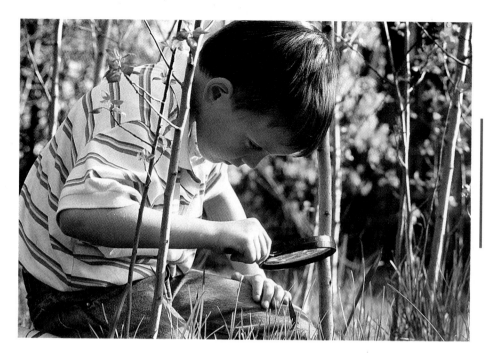

Although science activities can be successful indoors, outdoor exploration can spark curiosity and awareness in unexpected ways.

sprout by placing them on moist paper towels or in a jar of water When the sprouts are planted, children witness the rest of the growth process.

Other projects demonstrate different aspects of plant life. Placing a celery stalk in a jar of colored water shows children how plants "drink." Find a branch with buds that are about to bloom and place it in a vase of water. Let children watch the buds blossom. Explain the purpose of flowers on plants. Of course, you must always make sure children work only with nonpoisonous plants.

If space and season permit, older children can plant gardens. Food from their gardens can be used in cooking activities. This extends the concept of a natural cycle and introduces children to the idea of a food chain.

Nature walks are another good way to teach science with plants. Children can watch bees pollinate flowers—from a safe distance. They can collect, observe, feel, and smell colorful autumn leaves as the teacher explains why leaves change color and fall to the ground. By observing the natural world, children—and teachers—learn that science is all around them.

GOALS OF A MATH CURRICULUM

Mathematics is *the study of numbers and their functions, and of shapes.* Children experience math concepts daily without realizing it. They ask for *more* milk; they see *many* flowers in a field; they discover an object is *heavier* than it looks. All these general ideas become part of their **mathematical vocabulary**, *words that express numbers or quantities.* This everyday exposure to concepts of measurement and comparison is their first lesson in mathematics. Children who see and hear these terms used frequently—"We make a sandwich with *two* slices of bread and *one square* slice of cheese"—become "fluent" in math.

True understanding of math does not develop until children are between ages five and seven, in the middle to later part of the preoperational stage of intellectual development. The goal of a math curriculum in preschool is to provide an environment that nurtures the development of math skills. These include:

- Identifying and classifying shapes.

- Understanding concepts of size and space.

- Sorting objects based on specific characteristics.

- Using math vocabulary that relates to number and establishes relationships between objects.

- Mastering one-to-one correspondence, which will lead to the ability to count.

- Organizing mathematical information and relating it in an understandable way.

- Establishing relationships between objects through comparison.

- Using math concepts and applying them to everyday life.

MATH ACTIVITIES

Would you give a preschooler math workbooks with exercises to complete? Other activities are much better. When children group, sort, measure, weigh, and compare objects, they see how math skills apply to daily life. Children see math as a way of organizing and communicating information.

Teachers highlight math concepts through theme planning. For example, Miss Romero emphasized math in a unit on supermarkets. As her preschoolers played in the "supermarket" they found in the dramatic play center, they had to answer math-related questions. What quantity and volume of food should they buy? What do the fruits and vegetables weigh? How much does the food cost? Some children even counted the items in their cart to see if they could get into the "express lane." Themes that stress science skills generally lend themselves well

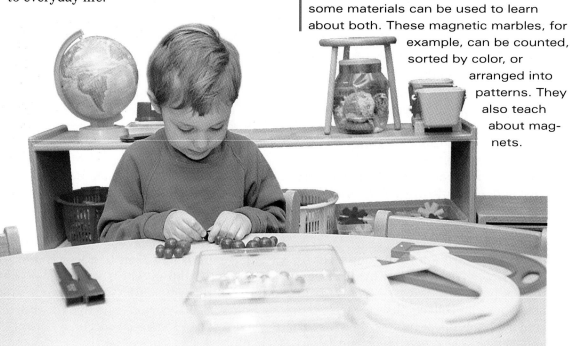

Math and science are closely linked and some materials can be used to learn about both. These magnetic marbles, for example, can be counted, sorted by color, or arranged into patterns. They also teach about magnets.

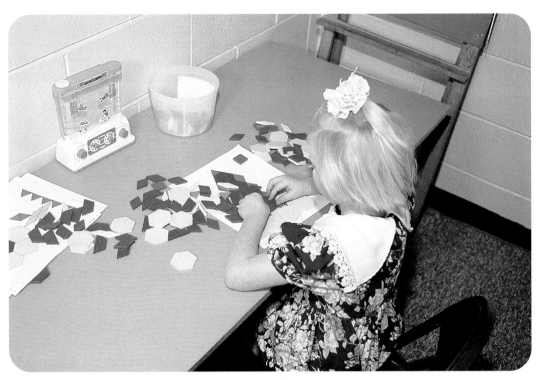

Pattern blocks help children recognize and use shapes. They can be combined to make patterns or pictures of objects. What other uses for them can you think of?

to math skills also, but math concepts can be included in almost any thematic unit.

Varying activities to suit themes maintains interest. Children can learn sorting with different colors of Indian corn in the fall and different kinds of flowers in the spring.

Recognizing Shapes

Children begin to notice different shapes as infants. By the preschool years, they are ready for activities that help build this skill. At snack time say, "Please put the round crackers on the square tray." Show children how different shapes can be put together—a triangular roof on a rectangular house with square windows. Encourage them to see relationships between shapes by giving them colorful paper shapes to use in creating their own designs and patterns. Matching games, either purchased or homemade, are also good for teaching children about shapes and related concepts.

Sorting

Matching shapes is one way of sorting, or classifying objects according to one or more characteristics. Children notice similarities and differences in objects, a valuable reasoning skill for both math and science. They

---

Tip FROM THE Pros

Cleanup time can be used to teach about shapes, sizes, and sorting. Have one child put away the curved objects and another, the objects with square edges. Ask children to put away all the blue items first and then the red ones.

can sort clothes when "doing the laundry" in the dramatic play center. Have them sort tableware for meals. Give children small plastic animals and have them create barnyards and zoos by including only those animals appropriate to each setting. Remember that at this age, children are capable of sorting by a single characteristic only. Don't ask them to separate blue socks from a pile of blue socks, red socks, and blue mittens.

Seriation

Identifying size relationships between objects is another important skill for understanding math processes. As you may recall, seriation is organizing objects according to increasing or decreasing size. While children look at a picture book about farming, the teacher might ask, "Which is taller—the farmer or the barn?" In the dramatic play center, the teacher could instruct, "Put the dishes away with the smaller ones on top of the bigger ones."

Any time you can make a comparison, you can teach seriation. Children can make Valentine's Day decorations by forming a pattern with hearts of different sizes cut from doilies or construction paper. They can help with a cooking activity by setting out measuring cups and spoons from smallest to largest.

Counting

Many complex mental processes are used in learning to count. By age three, most children are capable of rote counting. They can recite numbers in order, but the words have no meaning for them. To truly understand what numbers and their names represent, children must master rational counting. They must also learn to recognize numerical symbols and place them in order.

Rational Counting

Rational counting requires the understanding of one-to-one correspondence. Children learn to assign one and only one number to each object counted. Teachers

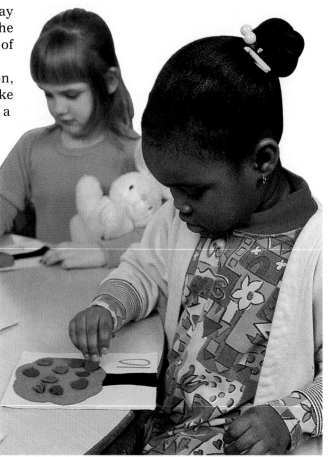

Many activities offer opportunities to learn math principles. What math skills might Veronica practice during this art project?

encourage this skill by counting objects with the child as each object is touched. You can count steps as the class goes up or down them. You can count graham crackers as the child places them on a tray at snack time. This is double reinforcement as the child realizes that the number of crackers corresponds to the number of students.

Specific activities also teach counting skills. Fill a basket with small items and tell each child to pick out a different amount. Make counting a physical activity by having children clap their hands, stomp their feet, or jump in place a certain number of times. Make a paper chain calendar, adding a link at the beginning of each day. Have the children count the number of links.

Recognizing Numerals

Once children understand rational counting, they can learn to recognize **numerals**, or *written symbols that represent numbers.* Teachers can help them make this association through simple activities. Mark bushel baskets with a numeral and have children place the corresponding number of apples in each one. Have children shape numerals from clay and then roll small bits of clay into the matching number of balls. Take photographs of the children in groups of different sizes. Provide them with numeral cards and have them pair the cards with the pictures showing the same number of children.

Ordering Numerals

As children advance intellectually, they combine their ability to count with their recognition of numerals. They order numerals, or place them in the correct sequence. Many activities help strengthen this skill. For instance, you could paint numerals on toy cars and have the children race the cars, finishing in numerical order. Children could place leis, each with a different number of flowers, around each other's necks in

sequential order. You might draw or bring in automobile license plates and have the children arrange the numbers in each from least to greatest.

THE TEACHER'S ROLE

*P*erhaps more than in any other curriculum area, teachers need to guard against doing too much for children during science and math activities. Showing children how to use some pieces of equipment and how to treat animals and plants is necessary. So is guiding investigation by supplying facts and suggesting questions for children to answer. Providing helpful materials and encouraging children to use them is also important.

Equally important, however, is letting children explore and discover on their own. The more children participate in learning, the more they learn. Even activities that do not produce the expected results are not failures; they are learning experiences too. Teachers help children understand what has happened, while allowing them to know the excitement and pride that come with discovery.

A Fresh Approach

To maintain interest, teachers continuously collect new activity ideas. They read education resource books, talk with other teachers, plan with coworkers, observe other teachers' classrooms, and reflect on personal experiences. Teachers often share their hobbies, such as rock collecting or gardening, with children. A teacher's enthusiasm for math and science can be catching.

Field trips show children math and science in action. Even a short walk provides learning opportunities. During these outings, children can observe nature or gather leaves, flowers, rocks, nuts, or shells to

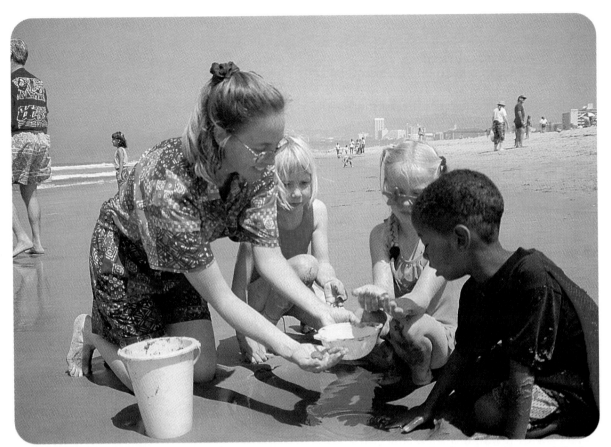

Successful teachers expand the world for children. They also help them understand that learning is a natural, ongoing part of life.

FOCUS ON INFANT/TODDLER PROGRAMS

For infants and toddlers, learning about science and math is very subtle. Children at these ages increase their awareness through their senses. Helping them use their senses sets the stage for more advanced observations and understandings later on. Stimulate their senses by giving them room to move and use their bodies. Vary their visual perspective and environment frequently. Allow them to explore concepts of cause and effect by giving them crib mobiles to hit and water tubs to splash around in. Let them see gravity at work by returning toys to them to drop again and again.

FOCUS ON SCHOOL-AGE PROGRAMS

For school-age children, science and math lessons belong in the formal school day, not in child care. In child care, provide informal chances to explore science and math.

Children enjoy science and math hobbies. Rock collecting and photography are possibilities. Children who like to draw might observe or read about animals and then draw them in their natural surroundings. With wood-working, needle crafts, and building model cars and ships, children apply math concepts.

Take children to a veterinarian's office, an airport, a bank, or a floral shop. Schedule visits by a firefighter, a beekeeper, an athlete, or an athletic trainer. What science and math principles are used in these fields to make life safer, easier, and more enjoyable?

bring back to class. There they can examine, count, classify, and categorize what they found.

Materials throughout the classroom show children how math and science relate to all subject areas. Nature magazines might be found in the language center. A calendar on the wall teaches counting and sequence. Building blocks can be used to demonstrate size, shape, weight, and balance.

Teachable Moments

Watch and listen carefully for teachable moments. They occur more frequently than you may realize. Children learn about evaporation as their easel paintings dry. Mixing paint from powdered tempera introduces the concept of ratios (number relationships). The concept of gravity is clearer when children discover that blocks always fall down and never up. Children learn that air moves when watching flags waving in the breeze. When you sharpen your own interest in the world around you, teachable moments become more obvious.

INTEGRATING SUBJECTS

Science and math have a strong link to life. Lessons in these areas explain what is happening in the world and why. They give children tools for managing better. They can even lead children toward careers and interesting leisure pursuits in the future. Effective teachers help children understand the relationship between life and learning.

Effective teachers also show children how science and math relate to each other. How can a person work with a recipe without having the math skills to measure accurately? How can someone plant a garden without calculating the purchase of supplies and the number of rows and seeds to plant? As you know, what children learn in one area often has impact on another.

If you help children see these principles, you just might set them on a more positive course for learning. Their appreciation for learning will grow, as will their desire to learn more. Instilling these attitudes in children should be a high priority.

Chapter 23 Review

Chapter Summary

- Science and math activities strengthen important intellectual skills.
- A science curriculum encourages children to explore and analyze their world.
- Cooking activities are interesting, enjoyable ways for children to apply science concepts.
- Animals and plants can teach children about biology and the life cycle.
- Math concepts can be taught in daily routines and through a variety of curriculum activities.
- Children learn science and math best through active participation.
- Teachers should look for opportunities to keep science and math activities interesting and relevant.

Reviewing the Facts

1. Name three ways in which science and math activities benefit children.
2. Identify three goals of a science curriculum.
3. Briefly describe a science and math learning center.
4. List four skills that children can practice through science activities.
5. Give three reasons why cooking activities are a good way to teach science concepts.
6. Identify two advantages of keeping classroom pets to teach science concepts.
7. How might plants be used to illustrate the life cycle?
8. Identify four goals of a math curriculum.
9. Identify an activity that teaches each of the following math skills: recognizing shapes; sorting; rational counting; recognizing numerals; and ordering numerals.
10. What is the teacher's role in teaching science and math activities to preschoolers?
11. Give three ways that teachers can keep science and math activities new and interesting.

Thinking Critically

1. How could you use these materials to teach preschoolers science and math principles: a box of buttons; pictures from magazines; colored chalk; straws; a mirror; rulers; sponges?
2. While playing with water at the sensory table, several children tell you they think big things sink and small things float. How would you help them consider factors other than size when deciding what will sink or float?
3. Why would it be better to ask a preschooler, "What do you see happening?" than "Did the water turn blue?"

Activities and Applications

1. **Dramatic Play Link.** Suggest two science-related and two math-related dramatic play themes. For each theme, list three suitable props.
2. **Brainstorming.** With a partner, make two lists, one of simple adjectives (such as big, soft, round, and loud) and one of simple nouns (such as boat, balloon, and bubbles). Use words that would be understandable and interesting to young children. Then discuss with your partner how you might use several words from each list to teach lessons to preschoolers.

Chapter 23 Review

3. **Locating Resources.** Scan the telephone directory for community resources. Which sites could be used as field trips to stimulate interest in science and math?

4. **Learning Center.** Draw your own design for a science and math learning center. Provide details that show the basic arrangement. List and/or draw the contents you would include.

5. **Planning an Activity.** Plan a math or science activity for preschoolers. Develop a lesson plan around your idea. Then carry out the activity with a group of children.

SCHOOL TO WORK

Your Professional Portfolio

Develop a hands-on bulletin board centered around a science or math concept. After putting up the bulletin board, take a picture to include in your portfolio. Also include an index card with a brief description of the bulletin board, its purpose, and the materials that you used.

Observing and Analyzing

Ideas All Around You

Through observation, you can acquire a long list of ideas for teaching children math and science concepts. Try the suggestions listed here. Keep records of what you find. They could come in handy someday if you work with children.

- **Ideas from Texts.** Browse through your own math and science books as well as those of younger siblings and friends. As you note the lessons taught, think about the underlying simple concepts that a young child could learn. For example, if a science book talks about Arctic climates, you might teach children about freezing water. They could learn that ice can be picked up and that it melts when it becomes warm.

- **Ideas around You.** Begin to think like a preschool teacher. So much that you see has potential for teaching preschoolers. Look around you right now. What do you notice? Sunbeams through a window? Wheels, hinges, knobs, or handles? Different textures? Different voices? A spider on the wall? A clock? A light bulb? Do you see things that roll, turn, spin, tip, or float? What concepts and lessons could you build around these? Try increasing your awareness wherever you go. You may be surprised at how skillful you can become at coming up with ideas.

- **Ideas in Stores and Catalogs.** Many toys and educational materials are designed to teach science and math principles to young children. Look through catalogs and sale flyers to find those that you believe would be effective. Browse toy departments, too, for ideas. Some malls even have stores that sell only scientific items. Could you adapt any of the ideas with homemade versions?

- **Ideas in Classrooms.** Visit a preschool classroom to see how teachers actually incorporate math and science. Do you see a calendar, a weather chart, height and weight charts, classroom surveys (who has a dog, cat, etc.), a poster of daily attendance, a balance scale, a sensory table, magnifying glasses, magnets, and classroom pets? What other items do you see? How are they used?

Chapter 24

Activities for Active Play

CHAPTER OBJECTIVES

- Explain how active play benefits all areas of development.
- Plan active play learning centers (indoor and outdoor) for preschool children.
- List ways of insuring children's safety during active play.
- Identify creative resources for active play.
- Plan and lead active play activities.

Terms to Learn

- active play
- maze
- parachute play

t's still raining," four-year-old Cherrie lamented to her mother as she looked out the window. "Is it ever going to stop?"

"It might clear up," Anita Sapinski said to her daughter, a note of doubt in her voice. "Now let's get going. We're late for preschool."

It was Monday morning. The rainy weather had kept active, energetic Cherrie inside over the whole weekend. Anita felt a bit sorry for the preschool teachers who would have to deal with a classroom full of four-year-olds after such a dreary weekend.

Later that day, Anita returned to the preschool to pick up Cherrie. She had gotten off work early and decided to take Cherrie with her to the store. As she shook the rain from her umbrella, she could hear squeals of delight coming from inside the center. She opened the door to see furniture from the learning centers pushed up against the walls. In the open area in the middle of the room, Cherrie and her classmates were batting balloons to each other. They leaped, twisted, and laughed as they tried to keep the balloons aloft. Cherrie's teacher and the aide were on their knees, joining the fun. One child dove for a balloon but missed. It bounced along the carpet.

A chorus of groans arose, but Cherrie's teacher said, "Good try, Tomas. You almost had it." She quickly tapped the balloon back into the air, and the game began anew.

It was a full five minutes before Cherrie noticed her mother at the door. The little girl was flushed and breathless, but grinning. "Mama!" she called. "Watch this!" She laughed with delight as she and her friends batted the balloons back and forth.

"I see!" Anita exclaimed. "Good for you!"

Anita continued to watch the action. "No more worrying about rainy days," she thought. "After this, Cherrie may even look forward to them."

ENCOURAGING ACTIVE PLAY

Boundless energy and enthusiasm are hallmarks of childhood. Children seem fueled by the excitement of discovering how fast they can run and how far they can jump. *Activities that are primarily physical* are referred to as **active play**. Those who plan the preschool curriculum make sure that active play is included.

BENEFITS OF ACTIVE PLAY

Participating in active play benefits children's overall health and well-being. It helps them develop in all areas.

- ***Physical Development.*** The most obvious benefit of active play is to the body. Children learn to move and control their arms and legs. Acquiring new skills, they strengthen muscles, both large and small. They improve physical coordination and balance. Even a simple game of catch requires the complex physical and mental coordination of perceptual motor skills. The brain enables a child to judge the distance to another child. It activates the muscles needed to grip the ball, swing the arm, and release the ball into the air. Meanwhile, the catcher perceives the ball and the speed of travel. The brain sends messages to shoulders, arms, hands, and fingers. It coordinates all the muscles needed to produce the quick reflexes for catching a moving object.

Regular physical activity has other less obvious but long-lasting benefits. It plays a major role in the functioning of the immune system, so that the body can fight off diseases. Physical activity strengthens the heart and lungs and helps control weight—all important factors in maintaining good health.

- *Intellectual Development.* Active play often means playing games, which includes learning rules. Remembering rules and acting accordingly show intellectual growth. Many games use language skills as children sing chants and talk to each other. Older preschool children play games that call for strategy. This leads to complex thinking skills as children solve problems and set goals.

- *Emotional Development.* As children master control and coordination of their body, self-confidence and self-esteem grow. Daily opportunities for active play give children a constructive outlet for excess energy, which relieves tension and stress. Stress can be harmful to children's mental and emotional well-being. A build-up of tension and stress can damage physical health too.

- *Social Development.* When children play games, they learn to work well with others and to abide by the rules. By playing team games, children develop a sense of unity and belonging. They learn to cooperate with others to achieve common goals, a skill they will apply in their future work and family lives.

- *Moral Development.* Older children who play team sports learn positive character traits, such as fairness, honesty, and doing your best. They are given the chance to act on these qualities and put their values into practice.

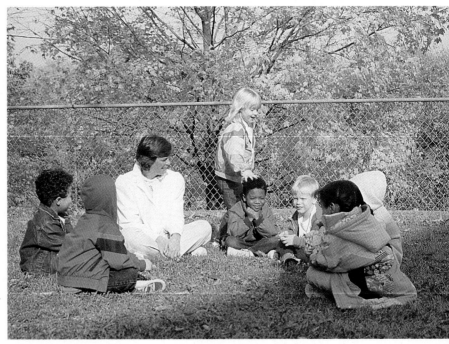

Action games like "Duck, Duck, Goose" can give practice in all areas of development, not just physical.

Focus On SCHOOL-AGE PROGRAMS

School-age children need their own active play space, especially outside. Equipment that challenges their more advanced skills should be provided.

School-age children love group games and team projects. Choose activities that encourage cooperation. Active play for school-age children may include opportunities to ice skate or roller skate and play baseball, soccer, or basketball. Contact sports, such as rugby, boxing, and football, are not recommended for young school-age children. These sports can cause serious injuries that interrupt normal bone and muscle development.

Visiting instructors may provide lessons in tap dancing, folk dancing, clog dancing, tennis, or gymnastics. Parents are sometimes charged an extra fee for these activities.

ACTIVE PLAY LEARNING CENTERS

Children need adequate space to run and play freely. Ideally, a program has a spacious outdoor play yard as well as an indoor active play area. Unfortunately, not all centers have these. Play yards are often too small, which results in overcrowding. Classrooms rarely have adequate space to create a separate room for active play. As a child care professional, perhaps you will take up the challenge of insuring that, in the future, more children are provided with adequate play areas.

Outdoor Areas

Having separate play areas for infants and toddlers, preschoolers, and school-age children is best. Fewer accidents and conflicts occur.

An outdoor play yard should have grassy areas for running and playing games and hard surface areas for wheel toys. Sand and water areas add interest and variety to active play.

Fencing is required around the play area in most states. Ideally, the yard has an open area in the center, with activity areas placed around it. Traffic patterns should allow children to move freely without having to run through one activity area to get to another.

Play yards should have plenty of climbing equipment scaled to children's sizes. Climbing equipment may include plastic and wooden structures. The landing areas around these structures should be covered with 8 to 10 inches (20 to 25 cm) of impact-absorbing material, such as shredded tires or sand.

Play yard equipment should be versatile. A climbing structure with a suspended wooden bridge and firefighter's pole, for example, can be used for climbing as well as for dramatic play.

Except for swings and slides, equipment should accommodate more than one child at a time. This gives more play opportunities for everyone. Pass up the rocking horse

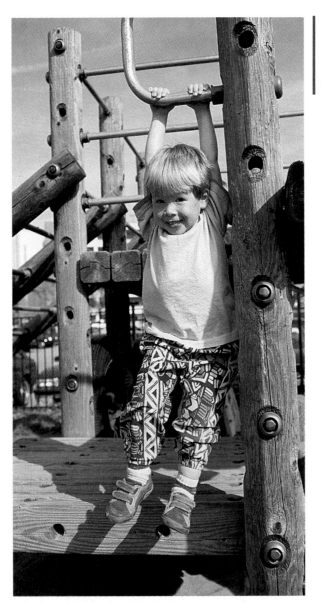

Children love to climb and test their muscles. This sturdy, wooden climbing structure has sand underneath to cushion any falls. What other safety features can you identify?

mounted on stationary springs in favor of a climbing dome or jungle gym.

Teeter-totters, merry-go-rounds, swinging exercise rings, and high slides have been associated with many injuries to preschoolers. These and other similar items should not be included in the play yard.

Indoor Areas

If you are fortunate, the program in which you work will have a separate room for indoor active play. Some rooms are even large enough for children to play on riding toys.

When there is a separate room for active play, equipment may include small-scale wooden climbers with mats placed underneath for safety in case of falls. Mats are often provided in other areas, too, for rough-and-tumble play.

Programs without separate indoor facilities depend on clever teachers to provide children with active play experiences. The staff must be creative, finding physical activities that can be enjoyed in a limited space. They may make space by moving classroom

Insuring Safety

When pushing children on swings, push only from the front. This encourages children to learn to pump and lessens the chance of pushing them off the swing.

furniture to the side walls. Using soft, flexible items, such as sponge toys and balloons, prevents damage to classroom materials.

Programs located in areas that experience harsh winters or frequent rains should make providing indoor active play space a high priority, since weather conditions limit outdoor play. To do this, programs often request play space in the gym of a nearby school, recreation center, YMCA, or YWCA.

Tip
FROM THE
Pros

*T*o keep children safely distanced on climbing equipment, paint each part with a different color. Tell children that only one person is allowed on each color at a time.

Play areas should also be free of items that could hurt children. Make daily checks for such dangers as broken glass, splintered climbing equipment, and tacks on the floor.

Children should have easy access to drinking water during and after play to replenish fluids lost through perspiration. During warm weather outdoor active play should be conducted in shaded areas. Water play helps children keep cool during warm months.

KEEPING PLAY AREAS SAFE

*W*hether active play occurs indoors or outdoors, children need plenty of open space to move freely. A child who cannot ride a tricycle without danger of running into a swing set may be discouraged from physical activity. If children often receive bumps and bruises from hitting the corner of a toy shelf during indoor active play, their adventurous spirit will be inhibited.

The highest point on outdoor climbing equipment should be no more than 4 feet (1.2 meters) from the ground. Anchor swings and climbing equipment securely to prevent tipping. In unpaved play yards, equipment legs should be sunk deeply into the ground so they are not uprooted during play. Padding under climbers and swings cushions falls. Indoors, covering overhead lights with wire mesh prevents breakage from high-flying balls or bean bags.

When you have new equipment or when new children enter the program, be sure to teach the rules for safe play. Note that shredded tires are used beneath this slide.

Teaching Safety Rules

Active play is energetic and exuberant. Unfortunately, in the less restricted environment of active play, children tend to be less careful. Teachers need to remind them about the rules that help prevent accidents and injuries. Explain these clearly and in positive terms. In this way, children see that they are learning about positive behavior rather than being warned against negative behavior.

Tell children these rules about climbers:

- Only one person may be on each part of the climber at a time.
- Play on the climber only when it is dry.
- Hold on with both hands. Use the *lock grip* (hands on both sides of the bar with fingers interlaced).

With swings, children should learn these rules:

- Only one person may use a swing at a time.
- Hold on with both hands while swinging.
- Sit in the middle of the swing with knees bent and feet down.
- Only an adult may push a child in a swing.
- Stop the swing before getting off.
- Walk far around children who are swinging.

Teach children these rules about slides:

- Only one person may slide at a time.
- Hold onto the sides with both hands until you are ready to slide.
- Check that no one is at the bottom of the slide before going down.
- Slide in a sitting position with feet first.
- Move away from the bottom of the slide when you reach the ground.

Even though rules are stressed, remember to keep a close eye on children during active play. They easily forget the rules at times.

CHOOSING RESOURCES

Safety is only one factor to consider when providing resources—equipment, toys, and materials—for active play. The best active play resources are not only safe, but

Children need to understand a few clear and simple rules about using active play equipment. What would you teach children about the use of these toys?

they also give children an opportunity to develop a whole range of physical skills, as well as the chance to have fun.

Many toys and games meet these criteria. Rubber balls, beach balls, sponge balls, bean bags, flying discs, and balloons all help refine eye-hand coordination, perceptual motor skills, and gross motor skills. Scarves, streamers, and strips of crepe paper encourage running and creative movement. Pinwheels and kites add variety to active play. Wheel toys, such as tricycles and scooters, build strong leg muscles. Such games as hopscotch, rim ball (a basketball hoop placed low for preschoolers), and bowling with plastic balls and pins also help develop gross motor and perceptual motor skills.

Wagons, wheelbarrows, two-seater riding toys, and rocking boats encourage large muscle development as well as cooperation. Balance beams and hoops help develop balance and coordination.

Resources can be purchased from commercial vendors; however, many items can be made by parents and teachers at lower costs. Either type is a good choice if it helps children develop desired skills.

PLANNING ACTIVE PLAY ACTIVITIES

*P*laying the same games over and over again is not fun for children. They like new experiences. Start with simple activities and then gradually include more challenging ones as skills develop. In reading the fol-

Playing "Catch" with a parachute adds excitement. A team effort is needed to pull the fabric down quickly and catch the person running under it.

lowing activity suggestions, challenge yourself to think of variations to keep them new and interesting.

Parachute Play

With **parachute play**, *a group of children use a large circle of nylon fabric for active play.* The nylon circle should be between 6 and 12 feet (1.8 and 3.7 meters) in diameter. Some have handles. Parachute play is especially good for developing muscles in the arms and shoulders. Parachute play activities include:

- *Bounce-the-Balls.* Have the children firmly grip the "parachute" around the edges and pull it tight. Toss five to ten sponge balls in the middle of the parachute. Have the children see if they can move the nylon sheet to make the balls jump like popcorn.

- *Catch.* With children holding the "parachute" on all sides, ask them to reach as high as possible toward the sky. Call out the name of a child, who runs under the parachute from one side to the other. As the child crosses, the other children pull the parachute toward the ground, trying to "catch" the child. Repeat until all children have had a turn.

- *Ring-Around-the-Rosie.* With each child holding onto the edge of the parachute, play "Ring-Around-the-Rosie." Have children circle in different directions each time.

Bean Bag Play

Bean bags are inexpensive play materials that can be used in many ways, indoors and out. Some simple games that use bean bags include:

- *Target Toss.* Children toss bean bags into empty coffee cans, laundry baskets, plastic buckets, or plastic dish pans.

- *Moving Target.* Using a sturdy rope, suspend a tire from a tree limb. Push the tire gently. Children try to toss the bean bag through the hole of the moving tire.

- *Balancing.* Encourage children to walk around the room while balancing bean bags on their feet, elbows, shoulders, or head.

Balloon Play

Balloons are another inexpensive choice for active play. They are best suited for indoor play. (Remember to blow up balloons yourself and throw away any broken pieces. Choking is always a possibility with balloons and children.) Games using balloons include:

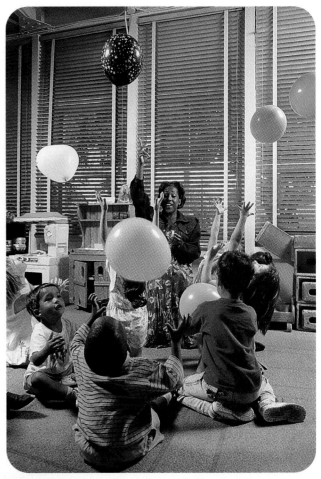

Children love the challenge of keeping balloons afloat in the air. They soon discover that light taps provide the best chance for control.

- *Balloon Volleyball.* Stretch a string across the room. Divide children into two teams. Have them bat balloons over the string to each other.

- *Balloon Ping-Pong.* Children can bat balloons to each other using nylon paddles. Bend a wire clothes hanger to form a circle. Straighten the hooked end to form a handle, taking care not to leave any sharp edges. Pull a nylon stocking tightly over the wire circle to create a paddle, allowing some of the stocking to come down onto the handle. With duct or electrical tape, attach the nylon to the handle and then wrap the handle completely with the tape.

- **Float the Balloons.** Provide up to six balloons. Set a stopwatch. Have the children see how long they can keep the balloons in the air without letting any touch the ground.

Rope Play

Jumping rope is a longtime favorite activity, especially for school-age children. Ropes, however, also have other uses in active play. These include:

- **Tightrope.** Stretch a rope out on the floor. Children can pretend to be tightrope walkers as they walk along it.
- **Long Jump.** Lay two ropes parallel and close to each other. Allow each child to jump over the ropes. Gradually make a larger space between the ropes. Challenge children to see how far they can jump.
- **Follow the Wavy Line.** Attach long pieces of rope together. Lay the rope throughout an area in a wavy design. Challenge children to follow the wave in different ways. Can they slither along the wave? Slide? Walk backwards?

Balance Beam Play

Provide several balance beams across a room, about 4 inches (10 cm) off the ground. Have children first walk forward, then backward, then sideways along the beam. After they master these feats, have them carry a bean bag on their head or shoulder while walking on the beam.

In other activities, children can see how many times they can jump over the beam. Have them try walking with one foot on the beam and one foot on the ground.

Hoop Play

Large plastic hoops can be used as originally intended, which is to swivel the hips and abdomen to keep the hoop revolving around the waist. They can also be used in other activities, including:

- **Hoop Hop.** Place six to ten hoops on the floor throughout the classroom. Children must hop from one hoop to the next.
- **Hoop Walk.** Provide each child with a hoop. Call out directions for them to follow. For example: Walk around your hoop; skip around your hoop; hop on one foot in and out of your hoop.
- **Raise the Hoop.** Pairs of children stand in a hoop. Challenge the children to lift the hoop off the floor and over their heads without using their hands.
- **Roll the Hoop.** In pairs, have children roll hoops back and forth to each other.

Courtesy of Lakeshore Learning Materials

A balance beam requires good muscle control and balance. How could you help a child who is unsuccessful on the balance beam develop the necessary skills?

Obstacle Courses and Mazes

Obstacle courses provide opportunities to strengthen large muscle groups in all parts of the body. You can create an obstacle course from items already on hand. Children can crawl under tables, creep through tunnels, step in and out of tires, and hop over block walls.

A **maze**—*a deliberately confusing series of pathways*—can be created with large plastic or cardboard boxes. Children may walk, skip, and hop through the maze or, if there is enough space, drive through it on riding toys. Make the maze as challenging as space and materials allow, with twists, turns, and dead ends. Build intellectual skills by marking the walls with numbers or different colored flags. Give directions for negotiating the maze, such as, "Keep the red flags to your left and the blue flags to your right."

Games

Like mazes, games offer mental as well as physical exercise. These games are especially good for developing eye-hand coordination and perceptual motor skills:

- **Simon Says.** Challenge children with directions that focus on parts of the body as well as positions. For example: Put your hand beside your ear; put your elbow on your knee; touch one foot to one elbow.
- **Mirror Game.** Two children face each other. One child tries to copy the exact movements of the lead partner. Children take turns being leader.

> When you teach children simple games they can play among themselves, you are also developing the social skills needed inside and outside the classroom. The "Mirror Game" being played here requires only two willing people.

- **Color Touch.** Form groups of four to six children. Direct children to touch someone wearing red. While still touching that person, they must touch someone wearing blue. Children may touch with hands, fingers, feet, knees, and head. Continue with as many colors and positions as possible.
- **Human Scarf.** Have children stand in a circle. Stand in the middle and hold a long scarf up for everyone to see. Gracefully move the scarf from side to side. Ask the children to imitate the scarf movements with their body. Vary the scarf movements from slow and smooth to fast and jerky. Bend the scarf into different shapes. How closely can the children move and bend like the scarf? Let the children take turns being the leader with the scarf.
- **Hide and Seek.** Wind up a music box and hide it. Let the children try to find the music

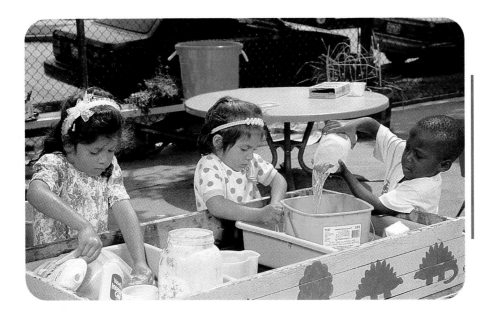

The ideal place for water play is outdoors on a warm day. A sensory table filled with water can provide endless play opportunities. When possible, try to include water activities of other types too.

box by following the sound. See if they can find it before the song ends. An alarm clock can also be used.

- *Gold Hunt.* Paint medium-sized rocks with yellow tempera paint. When they are dry, hide the "gold nuggets" in the sand, dirt, or gravel. Let children dig for the hidden treasure.

- *Freeze (or Statue) Tag.* This is similar to regular tag, except that when touched by the person who is "it," children must freeze their body position (or turn into a statue). The game continues until all children are "frozen," or until the teacher asks another child to be "it." In another version, children can be "unfrozen" by a child who has not been tagged.

- *Shadow Tag.* The person who is "it" tries to touch another person's shadow rather than the person's body.

Active Water Play

Children really enjoy water play during very warm weather. They can stay cool while still having fun. Children delight in simply running and playing under a sprin-

kler. You might provide plastic squirt and spray bottles for children to play water tag. You can also fill balloons with water, tie the ends, and then let the children play catch with the water-filled balloons. You might even set up a "car wash" for riding toys by providing a hose, soap, sponges, and rags. With any water play, make sure children dress appropriately.

Active Snow Play

In cold climates, winter snow doesn't have to spell the end of outdoor active play. In fact, it can provide opportunities for new experiences. As with water play, make sure children are properly dressed.

- *Snow People and Animals.* Children can express their creativity, learn about shape and size, practice memory skills, and strengthen muscles by building snow people and animals.

- *Shoveling.* Snow shoveling lets children feel helpful and grown-up while engaging in active play. Provide child-size snow shovels. Have children make paths for people to walk on or clear an area to

THE MULTICULTURAL CLASSROOM

Ring-Around-the-Rosie" began as a childish interpretation of the Great Plague in Europe in the Middle Ages. "London Bridge Is Falling Down" commemorates the keeping of prisoners in the Tower of London during the same era. Games from parents' childhood may not have quite the dramatic history that these do, but they can still bring new cultural flavor to the activity in a classroom.

Ask parents and grandparents if they can remember some favorite games from their youth. Invite them to visit the class to teach these games to the children. Videotape the lessons to preserve them for future classes. Encourage parents and grandparents to share other memories as well. Use these to encourage children to think about how and why games have changed over the generations. Hardly anyone rolls hoops for fun today. Why not? Is hopscotch as popular among children today as it was with parents? Children may learn something about their families, and you may acquire some "new" games for your files.

sprinkle bird seed and corn for squirrels. Children can also work singly or together to create designs or mazes.

- **Snow Bricks.** Gather empty rectangular milk cartons made of wax-coated cardboard. Make sure they are clean and well rinsed. Show children how to pack the cartons tightly with snow and then turn them upside down to shake loose the "bricks." Bricks can be stacked to make walls and forts.

- **Treasure Hunt.** Have children go outside and make tracks in newly fallen snow. Give them each a "treasure" to hide at the end of their tracks. Let children "track down" each other's treasures.

Looking for Ideas

The lists of activities in this chapter are by no means complete. As you begin to collect ideas, you will see that active play can be filled with variety. Whenever you think of something new or see a good idea in action, make a record for future reference.

Children's pleasure in active play depends on your dedication to finding and implementing ideas that capture the interest of each child at one time or another.

THE LONG-TERM IMPACT

*I*n today's world, it's far too easy for people to get in the habit of inactivity, like sitting in front of the television. Many never develop a desire for physical exercise. The result is often health and weight problems.

How can this syndrome be avoided? The best method is to start children very young with regular exposure to an active lifestyle. They need to be active early so that they learn to appreciate the good feelings that come with physical exercise. Through regular encouragement and opportunity, children can feel a need for exercise. When you make physical activity a regular part of a child's life right from infancy, the child is likely to maintain that interest for life.

Building Professional Skills

Safety Consciousness

WHAT IS SAFETY CONSCIOUSNESS?

Safety consciousness is the awareness of hazards or dangers. This includes not only obvious problems but also potential threats. The safety conscious person is knowledgeable, alert, and imaginative. You must be familiar with the things and people you are dealing with; you must be watchful of surroundings; and you must be able to imagine how these elements might contribute to a hazardous situation.

Safety Consciousness in Action

"You mean you let them go?" Mrs. Calderon asked.

"Well, yes, I thought you said the park district said the ice was thick enough," Ms. Santini replied.

"No, I said that it *wasn't* thick enough yet. We'll have to send someone to call them back right away."

While this conversation was going on, Levi Irby, the teacher's aide, was headed toward the park with five children from the after-school child care program. They were going to ice skate. As they approached the pond, Levi noticed that only two people were skating at the far end. "That's odd," he thought. "Usually it's pretty crowded once the ice is ready for skating."

While the children put on their skates, Levi began to walk around the pond, looking at the ice. He found a place where a tree limb was sticking through the ice and making cracks. Something was bothering him about this. He decided to walk out on the ice himself. Choosing a spot that looked strong and that he knew was shallow, he stepped out. As he walked slowly nearer to the middle, he felt the ice move a little. It didn't look right either.

"Wait!" he called out to Robin. She was getting ready to join him on the ice. "I don't like the way this ice looks. Guess what? We're going to build a snow fort instead."

At that moment, Ms. Santini came running up. "I was wrong," she called out. "The ice isn't ready for skating."

Levi smiled. "That's okay," he called back. "We changed our minds. We've got a new plan in the works."

Your Analysis

1. How did knowledge, alertness, and imagination affect Levi's actions?

2. How did Levi avoid disappointing the children?

3. Explain how the saying, "An ounce of prevention is better than a pound of cure," applies to safety consciousness.

Chapter 24 Review

Chapter Summary

- Active play stimulates overall development and contributes to children's health and well-being.
- Children require safe and spacious indoor and outdoor active play areas.
- Some centers do not have the space they need to provide adequate indoor and outdoor activity.
- Resources provided for active play should develop a wide range of physical skills.
- Teachers must plan many different active play experiences to stimulate overall development.
- Children who learn to appreciate physical activity at an early age are more likely to carry that interest into adulthood.

Reviewing the Facts

1. Name one way active play benefits each area of development: physical, intellectual, emotional, social, and moral.
2. Describe what an outdoor active play learning center should be like.
3. What types of equipment should not be provided in an outdoor play area?
4. Name two ways that programs can provide indoor active play when they have no separate indoor facilities.
5. Identify three safety features to look for in an active play area.
6. Identify three active play resources that can help children develop both gross motor skills and eye-hand coordination.
7. What is parachute play? Describe two types of parachute play.
8. Briefly describe one type of active play experience that uses each of the following items: bean bags; balloons; ropes; hoops.
9. Describe two games that provide active play experiences.
10. Give three examples of active water play experiences and three examples of active snow play experiences.

Thinking Critically

1. A number of recent studies show that many children in the United States are in poor physical shape. As an early childhood professional, what would you do to improve this situation? What action would you take locally? Nationally?
2. How structured do you think active play periods should be? What are some benefits of structured play periods? Of unstructured active play?
3. Children who are less athletic and coordinated often develop a poor self-image when they compare themselves to more physically gifted children. How might this be prevented or minimized?
4. How might you incorporate physical activity in an infant's schedule?
5. Do children need expensive equipment for active play? Explain your answer.

Activities and Applications

1. **Toy and Game Critique.** With a partner, list ten toys or games for active play that are popular with young children. (You may want to look through store catalogues or newspaper advertisements for ideas.) Describe how—or whether—these items promote physical, intellectual, emotional, social, and moral development.

2. **Learning Center.** Draw your own design for an indoor active play learning center. Provide details that show the basic arrangement. List and/or draw the contents you would include. Evaluate the cost effectiveness of your plan.

3. **Planning an Activity.** Plan an active play activity for preschoolers. Develop a lesson plan around your idea. Then carry out the activity with a group of preschoolers.

Your Professional Portfolio

Draw a design for an ideal outdoor active play learning center that is safe for preschoolers. Include imaginative ideas, such as tricycle paths, wooden bridges, tunnels, and rolling hills. You may want to include pictures of outdoor play equipment that young children especially like. Store your plans in your portfolio.

Observing and Analyzing

Children at Play

Observation can prove to you just how important activity is to children. Try these suggestions for increasing your awareness and your ability to analyze:

- **The Children Around You.** What can you learn by watching the active play of children in your family, neighborhood, and in public settings? Some communities have a business that charges a fee for children to come into a large building and use the creative active play equipment provided. Amusement parks often have special active play areas for small children. Parks and school playgrounds also offer opportunities to watch children at play. Observe children in such settings or anyplace where children are active. First, notice how much energy they have. Is it more than adults have? Are some children more active than others? Why? What will happen if children lack opportunity to be active? Second, notice how children use their energy? Do you see aggressiveness, passiveness, danger, injury, cooperation, leadership, creativity, dramatic activity, and pleasure? What impact does each of these have on a caregiver's approach to planning active play?

- **Active Play Equipment.** If there is a park or school playground close to you, stand by and watch how children use the equipment. Are the children supervised? Is the equipment safe? What equipment is the most popular? Do children use equipment as it was intended to be used or do they find other uses?

- **Catalogues.** Look through catalogues that sell play equipment appropriate for preschoolers. Suppose that you could choose only three items to include in an active play area. Which three would you choose and why?

- **The Preschool Setting.** Visit a preschool. Find out how much of the schedule is devoted to active play. Do the children play indoors and/or outdoors? What provisions are made for those days when the weather limits outdoor activity? How involved are caregivers in active play? Do they supervise or participate? If possible, watch a group game. Is it cooperative or competitive? Evaluate its effectiveness.

Meet Antoin Brouette, an early child-hood teacher in a child care center. Antoin teaches in a classroom of three-year-olds. He is assisted by a teacher's aide.

Why did you choose this career?

"I've always been fascinated by how children learn. I enjoy helping them explore the world around them. With three-year-olds everything is new, so they're excited about learning."

What education and skills do you need?

"My state requires a minimum of one year of college with at least two courses in child development or early childhood education. I've found I still need to know more about how children think and learn, so I'm taking night classes at our community college. Soon I'll have my two-year associate's degree in child development. I also participate in at least 15 hours of in-service training every year. Through these workshops, I've learned more about giving first aid, teaching creative art, and using positive dis-cipline. This helps me be a better teacher now and will help in the future if I decide to become qualified as an early childhood curriculum coordinator.

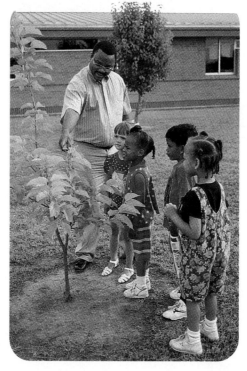

"Patience and understanding are valuable traits to have when working with three-year-olds. Sometimes children throw tantrums or have trouble following directions. That's when patience really comes in handy. Understanding what children are typically like at this age helps me handle their behavior better.

"A good teacher has to be organized. For example, I plan classroom activities two weeks in advance so I have time to gather necessary materials and be prepared for the children each day.

"I also need to know how to work well with my teacher's aide. That means respecting her skills and abilities. My aide's ideas and work make a strong contribution to my effectiveness as a teacher.

"A positive attitude and a good sense of humor are also useful to me. A person who doesn't think children are fun to be around won't like being an early childhood teacher. In fact, enjoying children's company is the one trait that all the other qualities grow from."

even after closing time, to pick up children. Leaving a child who is ill at the center is also a problem. These are the times when I try to be understanding and tactful. I try to remind myself of the difficulties parents face and the other responsibilities they have."

What is a typical day on the job like?

"I need some time in the morning before the children arrive to prepare for the day. I review my lesson plans, gather materials for the day, and set toys on the play tables so the room looks welcoming. I greet the children and talk with parents when they arrive.

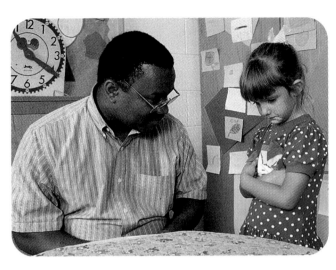

"Throughout the day my teacher's aide and I work with the children individually and in small groups. We conduct many different activities, such as science experiments and field trips. Twice each day I gather the group together to read stories or sing songs. I also eat lunch and snacks with the children. Amidst all of this activity, I help them settle disputes, put ice on minor bumps, and provide a hug when needed."

What is most challenging about your job?

"Helping a child learn to behave acceptably can be very hard. Young children need frequent coaching to help them learn how to settle arguments with words rather than fists. Since I like things to go smoothly, it can be frustrating when they don't. For example, sometimes parents arrive late,

What do you like best about your work?

"I really enjoy getting to know the children as individuals. When children attend our program for more than one year, I can see them grow as people. It reminds me that the early experiences that I provide are very important to them.

"I've found that working with children gives me a chance to see the world with new eyes. Everything is fresh and exciting to small children; they notice everything! Teaching children helps me celebrate the small things in life, such as the first butterfly of spring or the first snowfall of winter."

SHARE YOUR THOUGHTS

1. How would you describe Antoin's attitude toward learning? How might this attitude help him to be an effective teacher?
2. What might be some consequences if a teacher lacks organizational skills?
3. What part of being an early childhood teacher sounds most rewarding to you? What part would you like the least?

Unit 6

OTHER CHILD CARE CHALLENGES

Reflections

"My summer as a camp counselor was a turning point for me. That's when I met Isaac. He was one of two campers with disabilities. Isaac wasn't able to communicate very well. Even though he couldn't answer in words, I always talked directly to Isaac, not around him or about him. Part of my job was including him in our activities. One of the things I noticed about Isaac was how excited he got when the other children played any games that involved a ball. His eyes grew bright, and I sensed an eagerness in him. That's when I decided to invent a ball game just for Isaac. One day I sat him in my lap and placed a rubber ball in his. I said "Let's see if you can hit the ball off your lap, Isaac." With my help, he did just that, and he loved it. Isaac and I played that game a lot that summer. It was pure joy for him and inspiration for me. That was when I realized that I wanted to work with children who have disabilities. You wouldn't believe how often I look into the eyes of one of my children now, and I see Isaac all over again."

—Laura

Chapter 25

Infant Care Programs

CHAPTER OBJECTIVES

- Describe traits required of infant caregivers.
- Plan activities and interactions that help infants to develop physically, intellectually, emotionally, and socially.
- Identify special features and requirements of infant programs.
- Suggest ways to communicate effectively with parents.

Terms to Learn

- Caregiver Report Form
- on demand
- Parent Report Form
- staff turnover
- texture quilt

He'll be just fine," Olivia Ferguson said with reassurance.

Grace gazed wistfully at her six-month-old son Ellery as Olivia held him. Ellery reached up, trying to touch Olivia's glasses. "My glasses are shiny, aren't they, Ellery?"

Olivia looked back at Grace. "Why don't you walk around with us for a few minutes before you head off for work, Grace? I was going to show Ellery some things, but maybe you'd like to go with us. Do you have a few minutes?"

Grace nodded and smiled as she followed Olivia. This was Ellery's first day in an infant care center. Grace felt some pangs of regret at leaving her son there. "What *is* this?" she wondered to herself. "Fear? Guilt? Sadness?" Grace wasn't sure.

"Look, Ellery," Olivia was saying as Grace's attention returned. "See this mirror? It has the best babies in the world in it!" Olivia showed Ellery his reflection, and he stared in fascination.

As Olivia walked around the room, she chatted amiably with the mother and son. All the time Ellery's eyes darted from one interesting thing to another, but it was the bear that intrigued him the most. It was huge and stuffed and sat smiling broadly in a corner of the infant's room.

Grace laughed. "That bear looks like a smaller one that Ellery has at home. No wonder he can't take his eyes off it. I think Ellery's ready to stay now," Grace said, "and I'm ready to head for the office. I can see Ellery's in good hands—and paws."

A GROWING NEED

Ellery is one of many infants who spend time with caregivers on a regular basis. Many of today's families are headed by single parents or dual-earner couples. Seeking outside help with infant care is often a necessity. The result is a great demand for high-quality infant care services. Leaving an older child in a program can be difficult for parents. It is even harder to leave an infant.

Knowing that an infant will be well cared for is very reassuring to a family.

One of this country's biggest challenges is recruiting and training enough talented people to meet the growing need for quality infant care. Sensitive, well-educated professionals understand that infant care involves more than feeding and diapering. They bring love and concern for development to the job.

TRAITS OF GOOD INFANT CAREGIVERS

Watch talented infant caregivers at work and try to determine what makes them so good at their job. Competence in changing a diaper? Patience in feeding an infant? Knowledge in creating a stimulating environment? Caring for infants involves so much that a wide variety of skills and personal qualities are needed. Some of the basic qualifications that an employer might look for are shown on page 471.

Success as an infant caregiver starts with understanding the basics of infant development. Providing for infants requires much more, however. Caregivers must be warm, gentle, and responsive. They must be able to relate to and understand infants' needs and feelings. They must appreciate each child's unique temperament and approach to the world.

Outstanding caregivers are skilled at interpreting the cues babies give them. They can distinguish a "hungry" cry from a "change-me" cry and attend to both as quickly as possible. Cries for help or attention are quickly met with the caregiver's comforting arms and soft, familiar murmurs.

Good infant caregivers take great interest in babies' emerging skills. Their knowledge of child development makes them appreciate the great time and effort an infant puts into developing each new skill. Caregivers are proud of each new accomplishment and praise the infant with enthusiasm.

Infant caregivers must be careful and exact about observing and recording behavior. Infant care requires a surprising amount of paperwork. Detailed records must be maintained daily. This is time-consuming, but necessary for monitoring children's well-being and development. Taking care of this paperwork also requires good organizational skills.

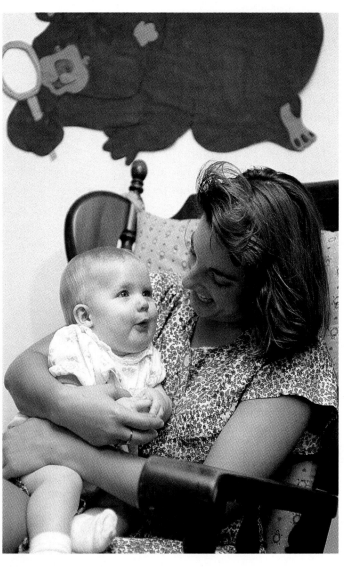

Infants need consistent care and comfort. Remember that it is in the first months of life that babies need to feel secure and learn to trust.

Qualifications of Infant Caregivers

*H*ere are the qualifications that one employer expects infant caregivers to have. Other employers may have slightly different requirements depending on company policy and state and local regulations.

- Associate's degree in child care and development.

- At least eighteen hours in child development course work. Six of these hours must specifically address infant development. Formal training in early childhood health, nutrition, and safety is preferred.

- Knowledge of proper food and health sanitation procedures.

- Current first aid and CPR certification.

- Doctor's exam stating good health, including required immunizations, absence of communicable diseases, and proof of a negative tuberculosis test.

- Absence of physical ailments that would limit one's ability to pick up and carry infants.

- Clearance from a child abuse and neglect tracking system.

- Three written, professional references testifying to competency in infant caregiving.

NURTURING INFANTS' DEVELOPMENT

*A*s you know, humans experience their fastest rate of growth and development during infancy. New skills and abilities emerge daily. Development in one area affects development in another. Quality infant programs are planned around the developmental needs of children in this exciting time of life.

As a caregiver, you can do much to encourage an infant's physical, intellectual, emotional, and social development. Caregivers get to know each baby in a very personal way. If they feel an infant is lagging in some area of development, they provide activities to help the child achieve the proper level of development. They refer

With experience, you will find it easier to judge whether a child's development is appropriate for his or her age. If you are less experienced and suspect a baby is not developing appropriately, what would you do?

families to necessary services whenever normal growth and development are at risk.

Nurturing Physical Development

During the first year of life, muscle growth and coordination are the major goals for physical development. Infants are developing perceptual motor skills, which require them to coordinate vision, intellect, and movement to achieve a task. Caregivers do not teach these new abilities to infants. Rather, they plan an environment that allows the infants to develop these skills at their own rate.

Birth to Four Months

Three-month-old Elinor's world is a place of constant wonder. On the walls beside her crib hang calendar photos of brightly colored flowers and portraits of her family. Elinor is fascinated by them, especially the pictures of human faces. Overhead, red and blue circus animals dangling from a mobile dance in a circle and lightly chime when she bats them. The motion and high, tinkling sound make her thrash with delight. As she

Mobiles encourage young infants to kick and reach.

kicks her legs, Elinor's eyes are drawn to the deep green booties on her feet, which she is just beginning to realize are her own.

The decoration of Elinor's room is no accident. Her family and care-givers purposely included these items to stimulate her physical development. Even at three months of age, she is being encouraged to be physically active: to focus her eyes, to reach for objects, to move her legs, to become aware of her body. Mastering these seemingly simple tasks is an important accomplishment for a very young infant.

Four to Eight Months

Four- to eight-month-olds enjoy toys they can use to bang and hit. Six- to eight-month-olds like shaker toys and squeeze toys that make sounds. The sounds from all these toys are reinforcing. Since infants enjoy noises, they bang, hit, shake, and squeeze the toys even more. All of these motions help develop large motor skills. Grasping helps develop small motor skills.

Insuring Safety

Crib mobiles pose a risk of strangulation if not used properly. Strings should be no longer than 12 inches (.3 m). Fasten the mobile securely so that the infant cannot pull it into the crib. When the infant becomes able to pull or push up on hands and knees, mobiles should be removed.

A texture quilt appeals to a baby's sense of touch, but what other sense might be stimulated?

Around age six months, babies begin to roll themselves over. Provide open space on carpeting so this skill can be practiced. Toys that roll, such as soft sponge balls, are good for infants this age.

Six- to eight-month-old babies strengthen their legs for walking by crawling and creeping. Encourage them by laying a texture quilt on the floor. A **texture quilt** is a *quilt made from scraps of fabrics of different textures.* You might use terry cloth, corduroy, velvet, and denim, to name just a few. As babies feel the different textures, they move themselves about to experience each one. If you make a texture quilt, make sure all the different fabrics you use are washable so that the finished quilt will be too.

Eight to Twelve Months

Eight- to twelve-month-olds are just learning to stand and balance themselves. They like to "dance" with adults by holding onto both hands, and they enjoy climbing on and off furniture. Provide low, soft chairs or sofas to help prevent injuries. Infants this age also enjoy "cruising"—holding on to furniture for balance as they practice their walking skills. Sturdy handrails mounted securely to walls can also be used for cruising. As babies begin to walk, provide open space and expect plenty of falls. Allowing infants to go barefoot gives them better footing and more confidence.

In this center, infants can use the handrails to pull themselves up. The ducks, made from different textures of carpet, are placed low enough for crawlers to reach, too.

By this age, babies begin to control the muscles needed to pick up small items with their thumb and forefinger. Encourage this development by allowing them to feed themselves small pieces of cereal. Providing infants eight to twelve months old with stacking and nesting toys helps develop perceptual motor skills.

Nurturing Intellectual Development

You may recall that infants are in the sensorimotor period of learning. In other words, they learn about the world by using their senses and their motor abilities. For intellectual development to take place, infants need a stimulating environment. They need interesting objects to look at, touch, taste, smell, and listen to, as well as grasp, push, pull, and kick. Infants should have a variety of stimulating toys to provide these experiences. However, the most stimulating element of an infant's world is a caring adult. Language development in particular depends on an infant's interactions with caregivers.

Language Development

By two months of age, babies make vocalizations—they "babble" in imitation of adult language. Caregivers should respond to the infants, using the very same sounds. Learning that their sounds bring a response, babies begin to understand the purpose of language long before they can speak.

To learn to talk, babies need a language-rich environment. Use language frequently. Explain what you are doing: "We turn on the water. We fill up the tub." Comment on things the baby is seeing or hearing: "That's a red bird." "Listen! There's the doorbell." Sentences should be short at first, just three or four words. Facial expressions and a lively tone of voice help babies understand word meanings.

Another way to help infants develop language is to show them pictures and books. Name the objects in pictures as you point to them. Let the baby turn the pages of thick cardboard books. Books with thick plastic pages hold up well under infants' use, and they can be washed.

Puppets and stuffed animals stimulate a baby's language skills. A favorite stuffed panda can "explain" what it's like to climb a tree and eat bamboo shoots. Don't forget singing as a

Talking to infants is essential to their development of language skills. Remember to use short sentences, speak with expression, and avoid baby talk.

Tip
FROM THE
Pros

Some strollers are made to accommodate up to six infants at once. This is a great advantage for caregivers in a group setting.

type of verbal communication. The variety of pitch and inflection, as well as the repetition of sounds and choruses, adds to the infant's interest and enjoyment.

New Experiences

Imagine how boring it would be to view the world around you from only one position. When babies are too young to sit up on their own, pick them up and carry them around frequently. This gives them new views of their surroundings. Vary the direction that infant chairs face so that babies can observe what is happening.

Take babies outside for strolls so they can enjoy the different sights and sounds. Such experiences keep the mind alert and also promote language development.

Games and Toys

Between eight and ten months, infants discover that objects continue to exist even though they are out of sight. This understanding of object permanence makes new games possible. Infants this age enjoy playing "hide-and-seek" and "peek-a-boo."

Toys with different shapes, colors, and textures stimulate thinking abilities. Provide infants with toys they can manipulate and investigate. Plastic blocks, nesting toys, and stacking rings are good choices.

Toys that teach the principle of cause and effect can also increase self-confidence. In learning that some of their actions will produce certain results, infants begin to develop a sense of control. Noise-making toys, such as xylophones and pounding toys, are good for this. Inexpensive drums can be made from a pan or metal container. You could use

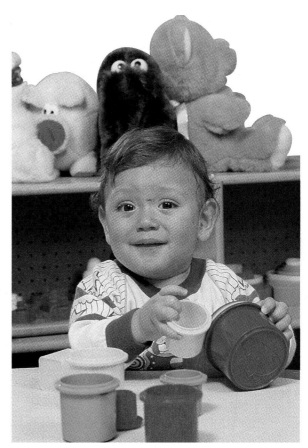

Simple, brightly colored toys are best for babies. These containers fit into one another, encouraging development of eye-hand coordination and fine motor skills.

a clean coffee can that has no sharp edges and a wooden spoon. Infants can drop wooden or plastic clothespins into the same metal container to create intriguing noises. Rolling a ball back and forth with an adult is a much quieter activity that helps babies experience cause and effect.

Nurturing Emotional Development

Emotional development takes place when babies bond with caregivers. This happens when an infant has a primary caregiver who

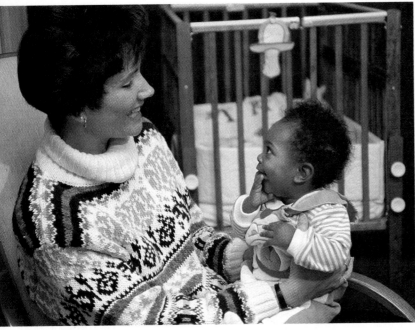

When babies are cared for by many different caregivers, it is difficult for them to form emotional bonds. In an infant care program, each baby should have one primary caregiver. How would this be an advantage for the caregiver as well as the infant?

employees leave their jobs, creating the need for new employees to be hired. When staff turnover is high, infants don't have a chance to bond with one caregiver. Infants need familiar and predictable care. Too much change is upsetting to them and can hinder their development.

A responsive adult builds a sense of trust in children, which is crucial for emotional development. Respond immediately to crying infants. This does *not* spoil them. Hold, cuddle, and rock infants frequently to provide feelings of caring, closeness, and security. To show affection and interest, spend time interacting with

is in charge of feeding, diapering, and all other basic caregiving routines.

The administrative staff should make every effort to limit staff turnover in infant rooms. **Staff turnover** is *the rate at which*

THE MULTICULTURAL CLASSROOM

Infants are constantly absorbing information about the world. Because they learn from their environment, you can inspire appreciation for cultural variety even at this early age. Simply add a multicultural twist to the usual items and practices found in the program.

Don't limit room decorations to the traditional pink and blue. Choose brightly colored curtains, floor pillows, and wall hangings made of batik and other ethnic fabrics.

Babies are fascinated by pictures of other babies. Find drawings or photographs depicting infants of varied ethnic backgrounds. Laminate them to keep them clean and then put them up at children's eye level. Place art work on the ceiling above the changing table.

Many mail-order music catalogs offer lullabies from around the world. The soothing voices and melodies of different lands can add variety and culture to nap routines.

infants—talking to them, reading or telling them stories, and playing with them.

Activities offered to infants should be challenging but within their capabilities so they do not become frustrated. Activities geared to each child's development help babies understand they can be successful. Caregivers should be enthusiastic cheerleaders when babies develop new skills. Praise helps build a sense of pride and self-esteem.

Establishing a regular pattern of routines and rituals also gives infants a sense of comfort and security. When you put an infant down for a nap, you might draw the blinds, wrap the baby in one special blanket, and sing a song that you use only for naps.

Nurturing Social Development

Infants are egocentric—they see the world from their own point of view only. Because of this, social development proceeds slowly during infancy. There are several ways, however, to move the process along.

Feedings should be social times. Infants should always be held when given a bottle. Do not overstimulate a baby, but do quietly talk to the baby while feeding. When infants begin feeding from a high chair or eating at the table, allow time for friendly conversation. Diapering can also be a social time if the pace is leisurely. Talk to the baby while diapering. When the baby smiles, be sure to smile back. Tickle the baby's tummy and you'll be rewarded with an endearing giggle.

Snuggle in a soft chair together to read a book or look at a photo album. Talk about what you see. Play give-and-take games, such as "pat-a-cake." Hand objects back and forth to each other. Reinforce imitation by playing "copycat." Make a movement or a sound as the baby tries to mimic you.

Babies don't actually play with one another. If allowed to play near each other, however, they will make casual contact. Supervise them carefully. Babies don't understand that they can hurt other people and may do so unintentionally.

OPERATING PROGRAMS FOR INFANTS

Like programs for older children, infant care programs must follow rules established by state licensing laws. Each state has specific licensing standards for infant care.

Infants thrive on adult attention. They can also keep caregivers very busy. For these reasons, there are fewer children per care-

This center currently has a ratio of three caregivers to five infants, somewhat lower than many infant care programs. Infant care costs parents more than care of preschoolers primarily because of the need for more individualized attention. How do costs compare in your area?

Building Professional Skills

Efficiency

WHAT IS EFFICIENCY?

Efficiency is accomplishing tasks with as little effort or time as necessary. Like many qualities, efficiency is born of other traits, such as preparation, organization, and experience. Being efficient makes any task easier. Efficient people are valued employees.

Efficiency in Action

"How do you manage to look after three babies at once? When mine were that age, I had my hands full with one!"

Hollie was about to reply to Liz's remark when one of the infants began to fuss. "Excuse me," she said. "That's Tiffany. She takes a bottle around this time every day."

Hollie washed her hands and took a baby bottle and box of dry formula from the cabinet near the sink where they were kept together. She mixed up the formula and began feeding Tiffany, cooing and talking to her softly.

As she was about to sit down with Liz, another infant started whimpering. "Manuel," Hollie explained. "He usually needs a diaper change after he wakes up." Still cradling Tiffany, she grad-

ually laid out a fresh diaper, cleaning towelettes, and baby powder from a shelf near the changing table. As Tiffany finished her bottle, Manuel began to cry in earnest. Hollie sang to him as she changed him, then laid him back in his crib.

Going to the sink to wash her hands, Hollie saw that Christopher, the third infant in her care, had dropped his set of plastic keys on the floor. She picked them up and dropped them into a tub of sanitizing solution beside the sink. She rinsed the keys after washing her hands and gave them back to Christopher. She jingled them and laughed with him as he grabbed them from her hand.

Liz chuckled as Hollie sat down again. "So *that's* how you manage."

Your Analysis

1. What signs of preparation and organization do you find in this story? How does this contribute to Hollie's efficiency?

2. How did Hollie's experience with the infants help her save time and energy?

3. Does being efficient necessarily mean being impersonal or uncaring? Illustrate your answer with examples from the text.

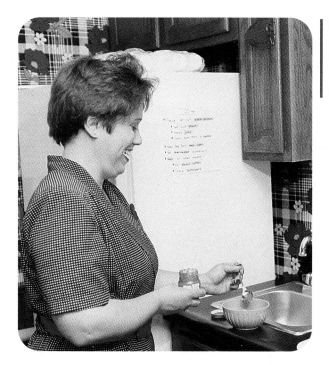

Unless special care is taken, contaminated food can cause babies to become ill. When using jars of baby food, be sure to feed from a bowl rather than the jar and dispose of any uneaten food left in the child's bowl.

giver in an infant care program than in a program for older children. In addition, the maximum number of infants in the group is smaller than with older children. When placed in a large group, infants easily become overstimulated. A typical group might have six to eight infants with two or three caregivers. However, state requirements vary.

Health and Safety

Infants are especially vulnerable to illness and accidents. Staff members must take every possible precaution to help insure the health and safety of the infants in their care.

Infants spend a lot of time on the floor, so make sure it is clean and free of cold drafts. Remember to follow the cleanliness guidelines discussed in Chapter 11. Toys should be sanitized daily. Before and after diapering an infant, wash your hands thoroughly and clean the diapering surface with sanitizing solution. Also wash your hands before and after feedings and sanitize the equipment used.

To prevent food from being contaminated with bacteria during feeding, follow these guidelines:

- Remove only a small portion of solid food from the jar at a time and place this in a bowl.

- If you need to transfer more food from the jar to the bowl, get a clean spoon. Do not use a spoon that has been in the infant's mouth or you will transfer bacteria into the jar.

- After feeding, discard any food remaining in the bowl. Do not put it back into the jar.

- Tightly cover, label, and refrigerate any food that is left in the jar. Use it within three days or discard it.

- Discard any formula left over from a feeding.

Such equipment as cribs, changing tables, and feeding chairs must be carefully screened for hazards. Check for splinters, sharp corners, removable parts, toxic paint, and pinching hinges. Make sure equipment won't tip over or collapse if an infant uses it to pull up to standing position.

Choking and suffocation are very real dangers at this age. Continuously monitor classroom floors for small objects that crawling infants may put into their mouths. Cribs should be free of thin plastic coverings, pillows, and any other items that could possibly lead to suffocation. Also eliminate dangling cords or strings that could cause an infant to be strangled. Make sure cribs and gates do not have openings in which an

Caring for Infants Safely

*T*o keep infants safe follow these guidelines:

- When using a changing table, keep one hand on the baby at all times.
- Keep baby lotion, ointments, and powders tightly closed and out of infants' reach.
- Put safety latches on doors and cabinets.
- Cover unused electrical outlets.
- Keep all areas clear of small, sharp objects, such as tacks, staples, and pins.

- Remove torn or loose carpet so beginning walkers do not trip.
- Keep babies away from doors that open.
- Lock all fences and gates.
- Store medicines and other potentially toxic items out of infants' reach.
- Never drink hot beverages while working with babies. These beverages may accidentally be spilled.
- Never leave infants unsupervised.

- Practice emergency evacuation procedures. (Mobile cribs allow several infants to be transported at once.)

infant's head could become trapped. The information above gives other tips for providing infants with a safe environment.

Daily Routines

Infant and preschool programs differ in the way daily routines are handled. In a preschool program, a schedule is set and maintained by the caregivers. For instance, all the children eat lunch at a specific time. In an infant care center, routines should be conducted **on demand**, or *according to each child's individual needs*. Each infant has an "inner clock" of his or her own. Each requires food, sleep, and diapering at different times. Infant caregivers should never schedule group times for feeding, napping, or diapering. Instead, they must be alert for

each baby's signals and provide appropriate care when it is needed.

Caring for a group of infants is different enough without trying to remember all the details of this care for every child. To help, caregivers fill out a **Caregiver Report Form**, *a form used to organize and record the routine care provided*. This form includes such information as:

- The amount of liquid and solid food served.
- The number of diapers changed.
- The number and consistency of bowel movements.
- The length and quality of naps.
- Any accidents that occurred and the treatment provided.

Every infant has his or her own internal schedule. Why is it so important for caregivers to provide care on demand rather than according to a set schedule?

being. Important information can be shared with parents by providing them with a copy of the daily Caregiver Report Form. Parents, in turn, can fill out a **Parent Report Form** each morning. This form *details the infant's activities and behavior before arrival at the center.* Having this information can help caregivers better care for the infant.

Show parents photos of their children at play. This gives parents a sense of how their child's day is spent. Invite parents to visit frequently. Involve them in the center in any way possible. Share parenting information from articles, videotapes, or books. Ask parents to help you think of new experiences to offer their baby. Keeping in regular contact with parents is one way of providing stability between the home and infant care center.

- Any signs of illness and any medicine given.
- The infant's overall mood and activity level.

BECOMING PARTNERS WITH PARENTS

Establishing a friendly relationship with parents is a must for caregivers. Parents and caregivers should meet daily to discuss the infant's overall health and well-

LOOKING AHEAD

Infant care outside of the home is a relatively new but rapidly growing field. As more is learned about infants and their development, new ideas about caring for them and encouraging their growth will come to light. Perhaps someday you will be a caregiver who puts these ideas into practice.

Chapter 25 Review

Chapter Summary

- The demand for high-quality infant care programs and qualified infant caregivers is increasing.
- Good infant caregivers are thoroughly knowledgeable about all areas of development. They are also enthusiastic, understanding, patient, warm, gentle, caring, responsive, good observers, good planners, and well-organized.
- Caregivers plan a variety of activities to nurture infants' physical, intellectual, emotional, and social development. Positive interaction between caregivers and infants stimulates all areas of infants' development.
- Care must be taken to insure that the environment provided for infants is a safe and healthful one.
- Infants' daily routines should be conducted according to their own individual needs rather than a group schedule.
- Written records must be kept so that infants' health and development can be monitored.

Reviewing the Facts

1. Why is it important for infant caregivers to be enthusiastic? Responsive? Well-organized?
2. What is a texture quilt? How does it help encourage an infant's physical development?
3. Discuss three ways to help infants develop language.
4. Identify two toys or games that aid the intellectual development of infants. Briefly outline how they help development.
5. What is staff turnover? How is it related to infants' emotional development?
6. Discuss two ways caregivers can nurture infants' social development.
7. How does the staff-to-child ratio for an infant program differ from that for older children? Why?
8. What hazards should you look for when checking equipment used for infant care?
9. What kind of information is recorded on a Caregiver Report Form?
10. Give three suggestions that can help caregivers maintain a good relationship with the parents of the infants they care for.

Thinking Critically

1. Identify the three traits that you think are most important in an infant caregiver. Give reasons for your selections.
2. An infant begins swinging her arms from side to side. What activities might you design to encourage this skill?
3. Why do you think infants prefer pictures of human faces to others?
4. Why must infants understand the concept of object permanence before they can enjoy games of hide-and-seek?
5. What information, besides that included in the Caregiver and Parent Report Forms, might be helpful if shared between parents and caregivers?

Activities and Applications

1. **Infant Toys and Equipment.** Obtain a catalog that sells infant toys and equipment. (If one is not available in your

Chapter 25 Review

classroom, you may need to contact a local child care center and ask to borrow a catalog.) What items are offered? How are they developmentally appropriate? Which items promote development in more than one area?

2. **Talking to Infants.** Show how a caregiver might stimulate language development by talking to an infant during everyday situations. Use a doll to represent the infant.

Your Professional Portfolio

To prepare yourself for caring for infants, take a trip to the library and research appropriate books for infants. Prepare an alphabetized bibliography of the best books that you find. Be sure to include the author's name, title, publisher, and a brief description of each book. Place your bibliography of books for infants in your portfolio for future use and reference.

Observing and Analyzing

Infant and Caregiver Interaction

Good caregivers are sensitive to infants' signals. As you have read, they can usually tell by the sound of a cry whether the infant needs food, a diaper change, or just some soothing and cuddling. This knowledge comes from experience. Each baby's "language" is different, but it can be learned by caregivers who are observant and responsive.

Experienced caregivers also know that interacting with infants helps their development. Infants need to be held, talked to, and played with. Following the baby's lead is important here, too. Infants send signals in many ways, not just by crying. A smile and eye contact can mean "I'm glad you're talking to me." Looking away can mean "I've had enough for now."

The following observations can give you some insight into how caregivers and infants respond to one another. Each observation can be conducted in either an infant care center or an infant's home. Focus on one caregiver as he or she interacts with an infant in these situations:

- **Responding to Cries.** Observe and record what happens when the infant starts crying. How long does it take before the caregiver responds? What does the caregiver do to comfort the baby? How long does the infant continue to

cry? Did the caregiver seem to know what to do right away, or did he or she have to try several different strategies to stop the crying?

- **Chatting with an Infant.** Note situations when the caregiver has a "conversation" with the infant. What does the caregiver say? Describe the caregiver's facial expression and tone of voice. How does the infant respond? Is there eye contact? How long does the "conversation" last?

- **Playing Games.** If possible, observe the caregiver playing a game with the infant, such as "peek-a-boo" or "pat-a-cake." Note the same information as described under "Chatting with an Infant" above.

- **Offering Toys.** Count the number of times the caregiver offers the infant a toy. Note the situation each time. What was the baby doing before the toy was offered? What type of toy is it? How does the baby react? Does the caregiver play with the toy too, or simply observe the infant's play?

Afterward, analyze what you observed. In general, did the caregiver seem to provide the right amount of interaction? Would you say this caregiver was sensitive to the baby's signals? Why or why not?

483

Chapter 26

Caring for Toddlers

- Identify features of programs that serve toddlers.

- Plan a safe, healthy, and developmentally appropriate environment for toddlers.

- Describe how to nurture physical, intellectual, emotional, social, and moral development in toddlers.

- Suggest ways to handle common challenges of the toddler years.

Terms to Learn

- negativism
- productive language
- receptive language
- separation anxiety
- temper tantrum

This is where you'll play outside, Ryan." Mrs. Lund held her son's hand as they stepped out to the toddler's play yard. She and Esteban, a teacher's aide, were helping Ryan get acquainted with the corporate child care center.

For a few minutes Ryan clung to his mother's leg, watching the other toddlers. Two of them ran from opposite directions toward a soccer ball. One stumbled, fell, and picked himself up, but it was too late. "*My* ball!" he shouted angrily, watching the other toddler carry it away.

"Here, Tad. You can have this ball instead." Esteban handed him another one. Tad clutched the new ball. The other toddler looked at it with interest.

Suddenly Ryan pointed to a piece of play equipment. "What?" he asked.

"That's called a tunnel, Ryan," Esteban explained. "Look, Marla is going through the tunnel." A little girl about Ryan's size, wearing a hooded sweatshirt, crawled through the colorful plastic tube. "Tuhll," said Ryan.

"That's right, a *tun-nel*. Would you like to try it?"

Cautiously, Ryan followed Marla through the tunnel. He emerged with a grin of triumph and ran back to the other end. "Me tuhll! More!"

Marla ran up to Esteban, her cheeks flushed. "Coat off?" she said.

"Okay, I'll take your coat off." Esteban knelt down to help her.

"No! Me do." Marla pulled away and fumbled with the zipper.

"Oh, I see. You just wanted to know if it would be all right to take your coat off." Esteban waited patiently while Marla turned around several times, looking for a way to get her arms out of the sleeves. "You've almost got it," he said, giving her cuff a tug when she wasn't looking. "There! You did it!"

Mrs. Lund shook her head, smiling, as Marla trotted off. "Why do kids this age always have to do everything themselves?"

Esteban smiled back. "Just because they *can*."

THE CHALLENGE OF TODDLERHOOD

Ryan and the others demonstrate all that is exciting—and sometimes trying—about being a toddler. Toddlers emerge from infancy with a sense of competence and a spirit of adventure. They take unmistakable delight in new accomplishments. At times, however, their newly expanding world seems like more than they can deal with on their own. Toddlers are also discovering that their desires and those of other people are not always in agreement. They must begin to learn a degree of obedience and self-control. Encouraging development while channeling behavior is the special challenge of child care programs for this age.

PROGRAMS FOR TODDLERS

*T*oddlerhood lasts from the time children learn to walk—usually around twelve months—until their third birthday. Some programs place one-year-olds and two-year-olds in the same classroom. Others have a separate classroom for each age level. Although state requirements vary, an ideal program might have eight toddlers and two adults per classroom.

As with children of other ages, successful programs for toddlers consider all elements of care. They provide a safe, developmentally appropriate environment to nurture children's overall growth and well-being. They are staffed by skilled, understanding caregivers who provide the balance of discipline and free-

The toddler stage is one of constant change and development. Toddlers who are almost three are much more capable than those who have just celebrated their first birthday.

dom needed in this exciting but challenging time of life.

Much of the information in earlier chapters—on topics such as setting up learning centers, providing for health and safety, establishing routines, and planning a curriculum—also applies to programs for toddlers. This chapter includes some important reminders but also points out developmental needs and challenges unique to the toddler years.

The Toddler Classroom

Have you ever tried to grow flowers indoors from seed? You soon discover that as the plant grows, it must be transplanted into a larger flowerpot. It needs more room for its roots to spread and more soil to provide nutrients for the roots to absorb. Otherwise the plant cannot become strong and produce blossoms.

A good physical environment for toddlers is also one that allows them to grow and "blossom." It reflects their new abilities. During the toddler stage, high chairs are replaced by low tables and small chairs. Toddlers move from cribs to small cots. Baby swings give way to rocking horses, wheeled toys, and low climbing equipment so children can practice their increasing physical skills.

At the same time, the atmosphere should be homelike and friendly. Soft sofas and rockers allow for relaxing with a book or cuddling with a teacher. Pillows, large stuffed animals, and bean bag chairs help create a comfortable environment.

Tip
FROM THE
Pros

*I*f too many different kinds of toys are provided in each learning center, toddlers can become overwhelmed. Provide a modest variety of toys instead. Try rotating them. Include plenty of duplicates to minimize conflict.

Toddler classrooms are usually divided into learning centers. These may include many of the same types as provided in a preschool classroom—blocks, science or nature, music, dramatic play, art, active play, and language arts. Of course, the equipment in each center should be geared to a toddler's size and abilities. In place of a math center, most toddler classrooms have a manipulatives center. This area is stocked with toys that require use of eye-hand coordination and fine motor skills. Examples include pop beads, puzzles, and snap toys.

Daily Routines

As toddlers grow, they are increasingly able to follow daily routines as a group. The major routine activities in most toddler programs are meals and snacks, toileting, one to two hours of napping, story time, music time, and outdoor play. During the remainder of the day, children can typically choose from several

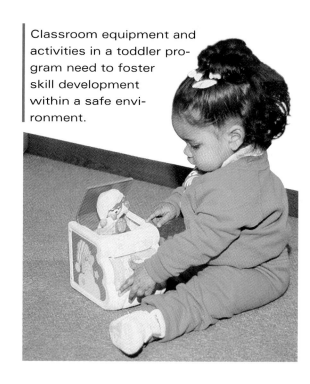

Classroom equipment and activities in a toddler program need to foster skill development within a safe environment.

small group activities planned and led by teachers.

Following a consistent schedule helps toddlers become comfortable with daily routines. The familiar repetition, along with

Can you explain why routines help to give children a sense of security? What other purposes do they serve?

trusted caregivers, helps them feel secure. When it is almost time to begin a new activity, let children know so they can complete their current activities. Transitions, such as songs and finger plays, help children move from one activity to another.

In all routines, emphasize self-help skills. Toddlers are very proud of their new skills, such as learning to use a spoon and fork and to take off a coat without help. Since their skills are not yet perfected, however, toddlers need plenty of time to complete tasks. Allow toddlers to help with simple jobs, such as passing out supplies for an art activity. Generous praise helps children take pride in their "grown-up" responsibilities.

Tips for Teaching Toileting Skills

Children usually learn toileting skills sometime during the toddler stage. Awareness of bodily functions is one sign of readiness. Children may gesture to show when their diaper needs changing. Their facial expression may show awareness that elimination is about to occur.

Never try to force a child to learn toileting skills. For learning to be successful, the child must have achieved development of the sphincter muscles that control elimination. Training that starts too early will be unsuccessful and frustrating for both child and adult.

As children begin to learn, ask parents to dress them in elastic-waist, pull-down pants for easy removal. Be alert for signs that children need to use the toilet, such as tugging at their pants. When you notice such signs, remind the child that this feeling means it is time to use the toilet. Take the child to the toilet as frequently as needed. If caregivers and parents are consistent, children eventually associate the toilet with needing to eliminate.

Some child care centers have toddler-size toilets. If these are not provided, special child-size seats or chairs may be used. If a child doesn't urinate or have a bowel movement within five minutes of sitting on the toilet, allow the child to resume play. Never leave a child on a toilet for extended periods of time.

When children are developmentally ready, the learning process usually takes only a few weeks or even days. However, newly trained children usually do not stay dry during naps. Provide diapers or a rubber mat as long as necessary. Even during waking hours, occasional accidents occur. Accept these in a calm, matter-of-fact way.

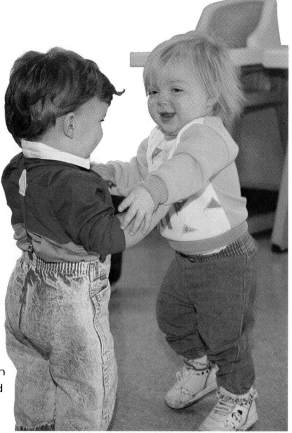

Pants with elastic waistbands help toddlers become more independent in toileting. Parents and caregivers need to coordinate their efforts during the learning process.

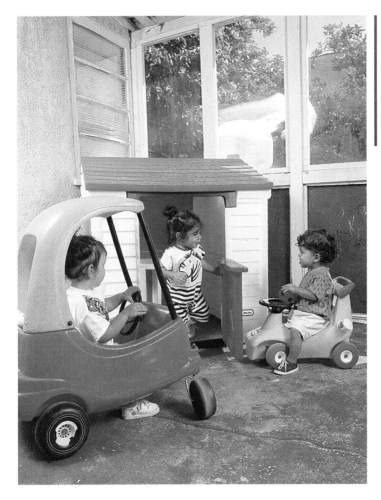

This center includes a covered play area with large windows. It provides a space for play with wheel toys that is away from the congestion of the main classroom area. This area is also used for large group activities when the weather doesn't allow outdoor play.

Health and Safety

Sanitation is as important at this age as any other. Children and teachers must wash their hands before and after eating and toileting. Teachers should also follow the universal precautions described in Chapter 11, including the use of disposable gloves when diapering children. Regular sanitizing of surfaces and toys is another part of the daily routine.

The growing curiosity and mobility of toddlers make it essential that you eliminate as many hazards as possible. Be sure medicines and toxic substances, such as cleaning agents, are locked away. Also lock the classroom refrigerator. Children have suffocated after crawling into a refrigerator and becoming trapped when the door closed behind them. Continue to keep small objects that could cause choking out of toddlers' reach. Examples include buttons, hard candies, and uninflated or broken balloons. Toys should be chosen with safety in mind and checked daily for loose or broken parts.

To reduce accidents and injuries, outdoor play space for toddlers should be separate from that for older children. Of course, all outdoor gates and fences must be locked.

Although toddlers are growing rapidly, their bodies are still relatively immature and require careful handling. For example, toddlers' arms are easily dislocated if they are jerked or pulled.

NURTURING TODDLERS' DEVELOPMENT

Like all child care programs, those for toddlers must be designed around their growth and developmental needs. To better understand and meet these needs, many programs ask parents for detailed information about their child's developmental history. The history may be collected on a form or through an interview. It may include such information as:

Active play equipment, sized for toddlers, helps the development of gross motor skills. This wheel toy is small enough to allow toddlers to climb on and off themselves. What other characteristics make it appropriate for a toddler classroom?

- The extent of the child's vocabulary.
- The primary language spoken in the home.
- Whether the child has toileting skills. How does the child communicate the need to use the toilet?
- The child's gross motor and fine motor skills.
- Special rituals parents use to help the child go to sleep.
- The child's typical behavior.
- Recent experiences that might affect behavior.
- The extent of contact the child has had with other children.

This information helps the program provide individualized care and activities to nurture all areas of development.

Nurturing Physical Development

Gross motor skills are developing quickly in toddlers. Children just learning to walk enjoy toys to push and pull, especially when they make noise. Small wheel toys and wagons are good choices. Older toddlers need plenty of opportunities to run, jump, and climb. Encourage coordination skills with low swings and climbers, obstacle courses, and tunnels (or large boxes) to crawl through. Toddlers also enjoy balls that they can safely kick, roll, and toss.

Manipulative toys help build fine motor skills and eye-hand coordination. Provide small blocks for stacking, nesting barrels, simple puzzles, sewing cards, snap beads, and beads for stringing. Inexpensive household objects can also be used as manipulative toys. For example, let

Most toddlers like the challenge and possibilities manipulative toys provide. At first you may need to show a child how toys such as beads or blocks or puzzles can be used. Soon they will discover new options for themselves.

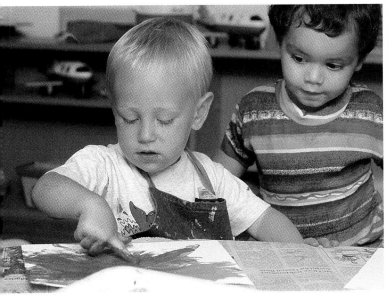

Many children have their first experience with finger painting in a toddler or preschool classroom. Why do you think finger painting appeals to young children?

basic colors and shapes. Provide safe objects to sort and classify, such as large poker chips.

Blocks of all kinds stimulate learning through trial and error. Concepts related to balance, size, shape, and weight can be "researched." Light cardboard and plastic blocks are best for beginning builders.

Provide nature items to stimulate curiosity. Let children handle pine cones, flowers, leaves, and sea shells. Use a magnifying glass to capture interest. An aquarium set at toddlers' eye level can be

toddlers practice twisting and untwisting the covers on plastic jars. They can also use metal tongs to put cotton balls into empty oatmeal boxes. For active outdoor play during warm months, squirting water from empty dish detergent bottles strengthens muscles while providing fun.

Creative activities also encourage fine motor skills. Toddlers enjoy scribbling, finger painting, painting with brushes, cutting with scissors, and molding dough. For practical experience in both fine motor and self-help skills, let children practice working zippers, buttons, and snaps. Sandboxes and sensory tables provide opportunities for learning to pour and scoop.

Nurturing Intellectual Development

Toddlers continue to learn best by using their senses. They develop understanding of concepts by exploring and experimenting with hands-on materials.

When toddlers begin to notice similarities and differences—around age two—they are ready to play matching games. Begin with

The simplicity of building toys makes them good tools for all types of learning—physical skills, intellectual development, creativity, self-esteem, and often social skills as well.

intellectually stimulating and physically relaxing.

Toddlers learn by watching as well as doing. Don't be overly concerned if a child spends a lot of time observing others playing. He or she may simply be gathering new information about the world before participating in it.

Language development plays a large role in intellectual growth. Young children understand much more language than they actually speak. *The ability to understand words spoken by others* is called **receptive language**. *The ability to use words to express oneself* is called **productive language**. Toddlers have more receptive language than productive language.

Nurture all language, especially productive language, by modeling. Throughout the day, use language to label, describe, and explain. Read books and tell stories. Invent conversations for puppets and doll house people. Label and count objects that are part of everyday life. Although your sentences should be short and simple, avoid "baby talk." Gradually make your language more complex, using more adverbs and adjectives.

Creativity develops through dramatic play activities. Puppet play, doll house play, creative movement, and art activities are all excellent ways to nurture budding imaginations.

Nurturing Emotional Development

While their lives may seem carefree, toddlers can undergo difficult times emotionally. They are experiencing new feelings that they may not understand. They are coping with fears. They are struggling with the unfamiliar practice of self-control.

Effective teachers can do much to ease children's emotional development. They can help toddlers identify their feelings—both positive and negative—and deal with them in appropriate ways. To help toddlers deal with fears, for instance, teachers should show sympathy and understanding. At the same time, they can gently encourage children to overcome their fears. Many children's books are written for just this purpose. The information on page 493 gives other suggestions for helping toddlers deal with fears.

Building self-esteem is another high priority. Teachers can plan positive experiences that give toddlers opportunities to succeed.

THE MULTICULTURAL CLASSROOM

A toddler's growing language skills can present a challenge to teachers if the child's first language is different from that spoken in the program. Resourceful teachers, however, can turn obstacle into opportunity.

Ask parents of non-English-speaking children for translations of helpful words and phrases. Include not only basics, such as "hello" and "good-bye," but other necessary information, such as "Do you feel sick?" and "Do you need to use the toilet?" Spell the words phonetically on index cards and tape them over the child's cubby for easy reference. Speak to the child in both English and the native language whenever possible. A bilingual approach eases the transition between languages. It also broadens your own education and can spark other children's curiosity about different cultures.

Responding to Toddlers' Fears

DON'T . . .

- Make fun of fears.

- Become angry or scold the child.

- Shower the child with too much sympathy— "You poor thing, that big mean dog scared you!" You'll just convince the child that there really is something to fear.

- Try to explain too much. Toddlers won't understand.

- Force the child to confront the fear.

DO . . .

- Stay calm and confident.

- Avoid the fearful object or situation, if possible. If a child is afraid of a dog on your daily walk, explore a different route.

- Try to distract the child. You might offer a favorite toy, sing a special song together, or talk about an activity the child enjoys.

- Help the child act out whatever is causing the fear. "Becoming" a monster can convince the child that monsters aren't so scary after all.

By encouraging self-help skills and offering developmentally appropriate toys and tasks, you can help toddlers feel good about their accomplishments.

Perhaps most important, teachers who are warm, loving, and comforting can help children become emotionally secure. Being "huggable" won't appear on any job description, but it's an important quality for teachers of toddlers.

Separation Anxiety

Two-year-old Lakisha was usually a happy, friendly child. When her father dropped her off at the child care center, however, she clung to him until the last possible minute. Lakisha was experiencing **separation anxiety**, *a child's fear or stress at being separated from familiar people.* Separation anxiety is typical when a child first begins child care. It may recur in times of stress, such as when a new baby is born into the family or parents experience a divorce.

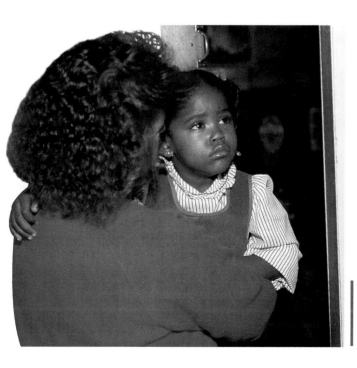

Separation anxiety is not uncommon during the toddler stage. Most of the time, though, toddlers are anxious to begin play and are content with a good-bye hug.

Building Professional Skills

Understanding

WHAT IS UNDERSTANDING?

Understanding is a two-layered quality. First, it means comprehending, having an intellectual awareness of something. It also has a deeper meaning. After you comprehend a fact intellectually, you can feel and act with empathy, compassion, and patience. Your knowledge enables you to see why children do what they do.

Understanding in Action

Doug and the two-year-olds in his child care group had just sat down to lunch. As they began to eat, Doug noticed that Gustavo was having trouble with the green beans. He seemed determined to spear them with the fork he held awkwardly in his fist, but the beans split in half every time. Instead of offering to help, Doug began to eat his sandwich, but he kept an eye on Gustavo's progress.

Brendan, meanwhile, relished in his skills. He stabbed each bean and raised it into the air and then to his mouth with great flourish. In contrast, Midori ignored her beans completely as she dawdled over her meal.

"Don't you like green beans, Midori?" Doug asked. She shook her head vigorously.

"Have you ever tried green beans?" Again came the defiant toss of the head.

"I think you would like them," he said. "Maybe we'll plant some in our garden next month."

Gustavo was still trying to chase each bean half around his plate. Doug began to wonder whether it was time to step in. Just then, Gustavo solved the problem himself. It seemed that green beans made a good finger food.

Brendan was taking a particularly dramatic bite when he knocked over his glass of milk. He shrieked and began to cry.

"Don't worry, Brendan. It was an accident," Doug reassured him. "Let's just clean it up." He gave Brendan a sponge to wipe up the milk and a towel to dry the table. "It's good to enjoy your food, but remember to be careful."

Out of the corner of his eye, Doug spotted Midori cautiously nibbling a green bean. She took another bite, then another. Doug pretended not to notice.

Lunch time was nearly over. Gustavo captured the last green bean and triumphantly popped it into his mouth. Doug gave him a big grin. He told the children, "This was a very good lunch."

Your Analysis

1. Cite examples of how Doug showed understanding for the children. What knowledge of toddlers did he show in each instance?

2. How might someone without understanding react to Midori's refusal to try the green beans? To Gustavo's eating with his fingers? To Brendan's spilling milk?

When Lakisha began crying as her father left, her teacher Ms. Miller knelt down and said softly. "I know you miss your daddy. If you like, I'll sit with you here in the rocker for a while." Lakisha crawled in Ms. Miller's lap and let herself be gently hugged and rocked. In a few minutes the tears stopped. Lakisha began looking over toward the dress-up area, where several hats were hanging from low pegs. Ms. Miller asked, "Shall we try on some hats?" Soon she and Lakisha were having fun together.

Separation anxiety can be as difficult for parents as it is for children. In a meeting with Lakisha's father, Ms. Miller explained that separation anxiety is actually a sign of positive emotional development. It shows that children have developed a strong emotional bond with their parents or other primary caregivers. Lakisha's father was relieved to know that his daughter's crying lasted only a short time each morning. Ms. Miller also reassured him that separation anxiety usually lasts only a few weeks.

Negativism

Toddlers often show **negativism** by *refusing to do what is asked or doing just the opposite.* Saying "No!" is a way for them to assert their own will. Negativism does not mean that the child is "bad" or will grow up to be defiant. It is simply a healthy sign of growing independence. However, it can be trying for adults. To reduce negativism, give toddlers plenty of opportunities to show independence in other ways. Then they will feel less need to rebel.

Crying can turn into a full-blown temper tantrum. As a caregiver, you can minimize tantrums through activities and an environment that promotes success. You also need to know how to cope with temper tantrums when they do occur.

Temper Tantrums

If you've ever seen a toddler denied a much-wanted toy or treat, you've probably witnessed a **temper tantrum.** This is *an episode in which children show anger or frustration in an aggressive or destructive way.* They may scream, kick, throw themselves on the floor, or hold their breath. Tantrums are an upsetting occurrence for everyone in a classroom.

Tantrums typically occur during the toddler stage. If you put yourself in a toddler's place, it's easy to see why. Compared to infants, toddlers are much more independent. They want to do as much as possible for themselves and make their own choices. At the same time, toddlers face many limitations. Their newfound skills are not fully developed. They don't always get what they want. Adults often tell them what to do. As a result, toddlers become frustrated. Because they do not yet have the coping skills to handle frustration, they vent their feelings physically.

Good teachers do all they can to minimize toddlers' frustration. They provide activities

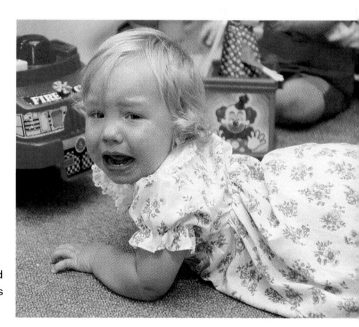

that are not too easy or too difficult so that toddlers can experience success. They offer reasonable choices and let toddlers do as much as possible for themselves.

If a child does have a tantrum, react calmly. Take the child to another room or area. Some children need to be held and comforted until they calm down. Others simply want to be left alone. However, keep an eye on the child at all times. During a tantrum, tell the child you understand how very angry he or she is. Then offer a tissue or a glass of water to signal it is time to end the tantrum.

Some children have such severe tantrums they become exhausted. In this case, move the child to a cot. Notify the parents at the end of the day and ask how tantrums are handled at home.

Frequent tantrums could be a sign of emotional difficulties. Before jumping to this conclusion, however, check for other problems, such as illness.

Nurturing Social Development

During the toddler stage, children move from solitary play to parallel play. Two-year-olds, for example, may dig in the sandbox side by side. As children approach age three, they begin to interact with one another in cooperative play. Cooperative play should not be forced, but encouraged through a carefully arranged environment. By providing toy wag-

ons, for instance, you encourage children to cooperate by pulling and pushing each other.

Toddlers are just beginning to learn to share. Introduce sharing while children are playing in small groups, such as in a learning center. Toddlers share more easily with two or three others than with a large group.

Disputes are bound to occur among toddlers. When conflicts arise, teachers can distract, divert attention, or redirect the child to a different, acceptable activity.

Toddlers begin to understand the limits set for social behavior. Outline a few simple rules. As children get older, these can become more specific. Always state rules positively. Say, "When you're angry with people, tell them so," instead of "Don't hit people when you're angry." Guide them by telling them what to do.

Biting

Biting is a particularly difficult problem among toddlers. Most children do not bite, but a typical classroom has at least one child who does.

Children who bite usually do it out of frustration or anger. They have not yet learned to express these feelings in words. Others seem to do it for entertainment—they want to get a reaction. Biting may sometimes be an attempt to relieve pain as new teeth come in. In other cases, children are simply copying another's behavior.

If one child does bite another, attend to the victim first. Otherwise you teach the aggressive child that biting is

Young toddlers begin to play next to other children but with little interaction. This is called parallel play.

a good way to get attention. (The same advice holds for children who hit or kick others.) After giving the victim first aid and comfort, firmly tell the biter that biting is not permitted. If necessary, remove the biter from the group for a time to protect the other children. At the end of the day, consult with parents about the problem.

As with any discipline problem, observation may give you clues to a solution. Certain situations may seem to lead to biting. If so, take steps to reduce or eliminate those situations. Perhaps there is too much pressure to share when the child is not developmentally ready. The child may need to be redirected to quiet, solitary activities at certain times of day. If a solution has not been found after several weeks of trying, perhaps the biter is not ready for group care. Advise parents to find a child care situation with fewer children. Children who continue to bite need more individual attention than can realistically be provided in group care.

Nurturing Moral Development

Moral development is limited in toddlers. Intellectually, they remain focused on themselves (egocentric). They are only beginning to realize that others have different needs and desires. Emotionally, they are still learning to identify feelings and control reactions. This lack of development limits toddlers' ability to understand and act according to ideas of right and wrong.

At this age, moral guidance is linked to promoting positive social skills. When you encourage children to share, you help them begin to think of others as well as themselves. By establishing a classroom routine, you help children learn to accept adult guidance. By praising children for following simple rules, you help them recognize that some actions are desirable because they please others. While these concepts are simple, they help set the stage for later development of positive moral values.

What qualities are most needed by someone who works with toddlers?

JOINING THE TEAM

Of all the qualities teachers need, patience is one of the most important. It takes a patient person to tolerate children as they assert their independence and to deal with their fears and other emerging emotions. It takes patience to let toddlers do things for themselves, even though it would be much faster—and less messy—to do it for them.

For all its challenges, teaching toddlers is an experience that some child care professionals would not trade for any other. Toddlerhood is that first step away from infancy and toward independence. Each child's potential begins to show. Encouraging and guiding development at this unique juncture takes someone who is equal parts coach, referee, and cheerleader. Perhaps you see these qualities in yourself.

Chapter 26 Review

Chapter Summary

- Group size in programs for toddlers should be small, with a high ratio of adults to children.
- Environments for toddlers should be designed to meet the needs and abilities of children this age.
- Consistent daily routines help toddlers feel secure. Self-help skills should be emphasized.
- Toilet training can begin when children show signs of being developmentally ready.
- Health and safety precautions are a daily concern in programs for toddlers.
- A developmental history form or interview helps teachers meet each child's individual needs.
- Teachers plan activities that nurture physical, intellectual, emotional, and social development in toddlers.
- Teachers must learn to deal with problems common to children this age, such as fears, separation anxiety, negativism, temper tantrums, and biting.
- Good social skills become the basis for later moral growth.

Reviewing the Facts

1. What is the ideal group size and number of teachers for a toddler classroom?
2. Contrast the equipment needed in infant and toddler programs.
3. How can caregivers know when children are ready to begin toilet training?
4. List three precautions for keeping toddlers safe.
5. Name three items of information that may be part of a developmental history form or interview.
6. Identify three activities that help children develop large muscles.
7. What is the purpose of manipulative toys? Give an example of such a toy.
8. What is the difference between receptive and productive language?
9. Name two positive effects of encouraging toddlers' self-help skills.
10. What is separation anxiety?
11. What is negativism? How can it be reduced?
12. Explain how teachers should deal with temper tantrums.
13. How can cooperative play be encouraged?

Thinking Critically

1. What might be the effect on toddlers if a teacher is too distant and unemotional? Too close and "chummy"? How might teachers be able to tell if they are too much one or the other?
2. Why might some adults push children to learn toileting skills before they are ready? What do you think the result might be?
3. Why do parents and caregivers sometimes give in to temper tantrums? What message does this send the child? What about other children who witness it?

Activities and Applications

1. **Obstacle Course.** Design an obstacle course to help toddlers develop physical skills.
2. **Matching Games.** List five common household items that could be used for matching games for toddlers. Explain how they would be used.
3. **Temper Tantrums.** With a partner, write a skit showing a caregiver deal-

ing with a child having a tantrum. Have the caregiver demonstrate either effective or ineffective tactics. Have the rest of the class critique the caregiver's response and suggest improvements.

Your Professional Portfolio

Complete an anecdotal record of a toddler that you have observed. (If you need to review the format for an anecdotal record, see Chapter 16.) Remember to keep your observation objective, based on fact rather than opinion. Then write an interpretation of the behavior you observed. Have your teacher critique your work. Place the observation and interpretation in your portfolio as an example of your observational skills.

Observing and Analyzing

A Helping Hand

Allowing toddlers to practice self-help skills has several advantages. The most obvious is that children learn to perform basic tasks necessary for independent living. They also grow in self-esteem, gaining confidence in themselves and eagerly seeking new challenges. See how self-help skills are included in the daily routines of toddlers by observing the following situations at a child care center or in the home.

- **Mealtime.** Observe toddlers prepare for and eat a meal. What preparation tasks are the children allowed to perform? What self-feeding skills are they capable of? What cleanup tasks are they responsible for? What items or practices are used at mealtime to help insure success? What physical, intellectual, and social skills are the toddlers practicing?
- **Dressing.** Observe toddlers dressing for outdoor play. Notice which articles of clothing seem easiest and most dif-

ficult for them to put on by themselves. What physical skills seem most necessary for self-dressing? What do teachers or parents do to help make self-dressing successful?
- **Cleanup Time.** Watch toddlers help clean up after an activity. What items are they allowed to put away? What items do teachers or parents put away? How is the room arranged physically to encourage success? What physical, intellectual, and social skills are the children exercising?

Chapter 27

Caring for School-Age Children

CHAPTER OBJECTIVES

■ Explain the need for school-age child care programs.

■ Describe an appropriate environment for school-age children.

■ Discuss considerations in planning schedules, routines, and activities for this age group.

■ Identify ways to nurture the physical, intellectual, emotional, social, and moral development of school-age children.

Terms to Learn

- latchkey children
- on-site
- tutor

Nine-year-old Angelo woke to his mother's kiss on his forehead. "Time to get up," she whispered.

It had been six months since Angelo and his mother, Joanna, moved to the city. Angelo was comfortable with the routine by now. He got up each weekday morning at 6:15, giving him just enough time to have a glass of juice, wash up, and get dressed. Then his mother drove him to the child care center on her way to work. During breakfast at the center, Angelo liked to joke with the other children and his favorite teacher, Jim. Afterward he would brush his teeth and do his classroom job. This week it was feeding the fish. Usually Angelo had time to play a game or read a little before the van took him and the others to school. At three o'clock, the same van brought them back to the center.

"How was your day?" Joanna asked when she came to get Angelo at five.

"It was great," Angelo said. "Allison helped me review fractions before school, so I think I did pretty well on the math test. We practiced free throws after school. And a chef from one of the hotels showed us how to make omelets. Can I make us an omelet for breakfast on Saturday?"

"Sounds great, sport," Joanna replied. "You know, maybe I should start coming to the center with you. Then I'd get to shoot free throws and make omelets, too."

"No way, Mom!" Angelo grinned. "Keep your job. Leave that other stuff to me!"

MEETING A NEED

Families like Joanna and Angelo are lucky. They have access to a child care program designed specifically for school-age children. Millions of children in the United States who need care outside of school hours are left without adult supervision. *Children who stay home alone before and after school* are sometimes called **latchkey children**. This is because they carry a door key to let themselves in when no one else is at home. Children who are unsupervised can become bored and aimless. Even worse, in the event of an accident or emergency, they would be in real danger.

The need for more child care programs for school-age children is great. Such programs offer children a safe "home away from home." They also bring peace of mind to parents.

SCHOOL-AGE PROGRAMS

Most of the children in school-age programs are between six and ten years of age. However, some may be as old as twelve. A typical program operates before school from 6:00 a.m. to 9:00 a.m. and after school from 2:00 p.m. to 6:00 p.m. On school holidays and during summer vacation, programs must be open all day.

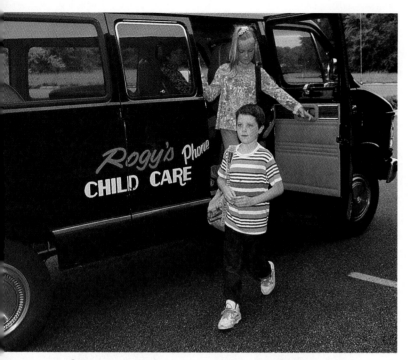

Many parents need a school-age program that transports children to and from school. What additional safety issues does this raise? What safety problems can such transportation solve?

Many school-age programs are part of a child care center, such as one operated by a day care chain, YWCA, or religious organization. A bus or van takes children from the center to school in the morning and returns them in the afternoon. Increasingly, elementary schools are offering **on-site** school-age child care programs, or programs *located on the premises*. On-site programs are very convenient for children and parents.

Ideally, a school-age group includes no more than about twenty children, though some states do allow more. Many states require only one teacher per twenty children. However, one teacher for every ten children is much more desirable. School-age children deserve a reasonable chance to receive personal attention. Being able to share the day's events with an adult helps

them build self-esteem and cope with the pressures they often face.

School-age children's growth and development is enhanced in child care settings, but in a less structured manner than in the classroom. Quality programs for school-age children provide opportunities for fun as well as for learning. They encourage growth without demanding it. They are safe but not stifling, stimulating but not high-pressure.

The Environment

Classrooms in good school-age programs, like those for younger children, are casual and comfortable. A relaxed, quiet atmosphere helps children get their day off to a good start. It also helps them unwind after a long and sometimes stressful day at school.

A well-planned classroom includes learning centers where many interesting activities are offered. There are also private areas where children can curl up with a book, listen to music, or talk with a friend. Furnishings include soft sofas or bean bag chairs as well as tables or desks for doing homework.

Learning centers for school-age children should not be simply larger versions of those created for preschoolers. Titles of some learning centers may be the same, but materials and activities must be geared to six- to twelve-year-olds. An arts and crafts area might include materials for not only drawing, painting, and pasting, but also weaving, jewelry making, and photography. To keep noise levels down, dividers between learning centers should be high and thick enough to serve as sound barriers.

Ideally, programs provide both indoor and outdoor areas for active play. On-site programs usually have ready access to the school gymnasium or activity room, playing fields, and sports equipment.

The environment of a center sets the mood. Children who have been in school all day need surroundings that offer plenty of activity choices.

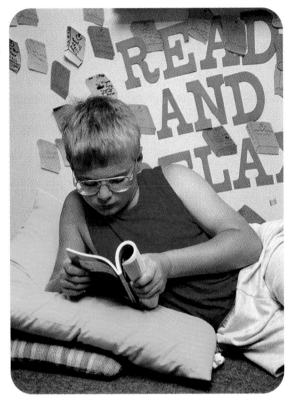

Schedules and Routines

Like everyone else, school-age children need some predictable routines in their day. However, they also need variety and choices. As children get older, they must learn to make good use of their own time rather than having all their activities planned for them. Thus, programs for school-age children should strike a balance between the familiarity of routines and the freedom of unstructured time.

Daily routines include arrival and departure time, both in the morning and in the afternoon. The arrival routine includes a greeting and a health check. Younger children may enjoy a song to begin the day.

After arrival, most programs schedule a planning time. Children hear about the activity options for the day so they can make choices. One or more group activities may be offered, such as woodworking instruction and a soccer game. In addition, blocks of time are set aside for children to do as they wish—whether that means playing checkers with a friend, reading for pleasure, or climbing on outdoor play equipment. Leisure time is especially necessary in the afternoon, after children have spent the day in the structured environment of school.

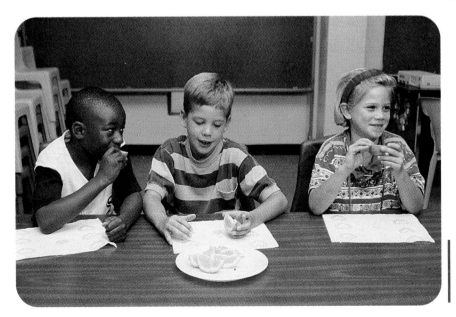

Afternoon routines for school-age children should include a nutritious snack.

Meals are a large part of daily routines. Breakfast gets the day off to a good start. A healthful snack in the afternoon satisfies a child's hunger after school and helps meet nutritional needs. During the summer and on holidays, most programs serve breakfast, lunch, and two snacks. Meal routines should be calm and leisurely. To build skills and a sense of responsibility, children can help prepare food, set tables, and clear dishes.

All-day programs generally provide a rest time, especially for children six and seven years old. Grooming and hygiene are other regular routines. Each child needs a personal toothbrush and comb for daily use.

Planning Activities

When it comes to planning activities, school-age programs share some qualities with programs for younger ages. Teachers must be sure to nurture all areas of development instead of focusing on just one or two. The program should also provide a reasonable balance between quiet, active, indoor, outdoor, large-group, and small-group experiences.

However, there are some differences. Teachers in school-age programs spend less time directing specific activities. A preschool teacher might plan that during small group time on a particular day, children can make collage pictures of farm animals. School-age children would find this too restrictive. They need the freedom to decide not only whether to make a collage, but also what type of collage to make and how to go about it.

Still, it is up to the teachers to provide stimulating options. Creative teachers enjoy sharing their own hobbies, such as cooking, computers, or dance. They also like to discover new interests along with the children. They use their creativity and flexibility to expand on the activities that children find most appealing. Although they encourage children to participate, they never require it. If some activities are unpopular, or certain children always seem bored, sensitive teachers take note. They drop what doesn't work and provide new alternatives to capture interest.

Another difference between school-age programs and those for younger children is that a much wider age range is served. The needs, interests, and abilities of a six-year-old are much different from those of a twelve-year-old. Accommodating both, and all the ages in between, can be a challenge. Sometimes dividing into groups of younger and older children works best. However, children also benefit from mixed-age group-

Some activities, such as playing computer games, may be an everyday option in a school-age program. Adding special activities, like T-shirt painting, to the schedule helps spark interest and allows children to develop new interests and skills.

This museum contains prehistoric animals, such as woolly mammoths and saber-toothed tigers that were caught in a tar pit. What related activities might you, as a teacher, plan around a field trip?

ings. Younger children look up to older ones and enjoy learning from them. Older children gain a sense of responsibility by watching out for younger ones and helping to plan activities for them. Many experiences, such as a nature walk, can interest both younger and older children as long as teachers are sensitive to the needs of each age group.

Field Trips

During school vacations, when children attend the child care program all day, field trips can stimulate interest and provide new experiences. Explore your community for good resources. Museums, aquariums, and zoos are natural choices. The list does not stop there, however. Children might also enjoy visiting an ethnic restaurant, a factory, an airport or train station, a utility company, a recycling center, a bank, a plant nursery, or a bicycle shop. Of course, a trip to a park, swimming pool, or other recreational facility is always welcome.

Invite parents to attend field trips whenever possible. Taking field trips to parents'

workplaces is also a good way to encourage parent involvement in the program.

Clubs and Special Activities

Some programs for school-age children form clubs around a special theme. Clubs are a great way to foster interests and build friendships. You might form clubs for children interested in creative writing, photography, collecting stamps or trading cards, bird watching, pen pals, drama, or art. A survey of children's interests can help you decide which clubs to offer.

Many programs also offer weekly or twice-weekly special activities, such as gymnastics, swimming lessons, or organized sports. Usually, parents must pay an extra charge for these activities.

NURTURING DEVELOPMENT

School-age children do not need the constant supervision required for younger children. Keeping up with their developmental needs, however, more than makes up for it. Children this age need plenty of opportunities to be active and to investigate their world. They also need support from caring adults as they develop maturity and expand their horizons.

Outdoor games and activities are excellent for improving both physical and social skills. Having fun should be stressed more than winning.

Nurturing Physical Development

Sadly, many children do not have opportunities or encouragement to participate in physical activities. Recent studies show that over half of all school-age children in the United States do not meet even minimum fitness standards.

School-age child care programs can help young people become and stay physically fit. Large motor skills are called upon when children play tag and other active games, hold relay races, or play team sports, such as T-ball, softball, and volleyball. Noncompetitive activities also aid development. Children enjoy jumping rope, skating, using outdoor play equipment, and creative movement.

Fine motor skills and eye-hand coordination become more refined as children grow older. These abilities can be strengthened with arts and crafts, such as needlework, pottery, basket weaving, woodworking, and building models. In all activities, stress enjoyment as much as skill development.

Insuring Safety

Although school-age children are more mature than preschoolers, they are still vulnerable to accidents. Supervise them closely when they use climbers, swings, and other play yard equipment; ride bikes or take walks on community streets; swim or play near water; and use woodworking tools or kitchen appliances. Teach safety rules and encourage children to help you spot hazards.

Nurturing Intellectual Development

Mental growth should not be limited to the structured hours of the school day. School-age programs can provide enjoyable, interesting ways for children to use their minds.

School-age children like group games that challenge them to think and solve problems. Many popular card and board games stimulate thinking skills while providing fun. You may even want to design some of your own. Educational computer games are another possibility.

Microscopes, magnets, magnifiers, and prisms can encourage exploration into the natural world. Provide books for children to

Tip
FROM THE
Pros

Ask school-age children to write articles for the program's newsletter. Not only is the effort creative and fun for the children, but it's also a great way to keep parents informed.

use as references to identify native trees, flowers, butterflies, and birds. Plant flowers and vegetables in an indoor or outdoor garden. Support their interest in scientific studies, especially if it relates to a topic studied in school.

Language skills can be nurtured by creating quiet areas for leisure reading. Provide a library of paperback books for children to exchange.

Encourage children to apply creativity and imagination to all areas of life. Let them experiment with art materials. Ask them to arrange flowers, make centerpieces, and help decorate the classroom. Encourage them to make new types of structures with building blocks. Give them opportunities to write stories, poems, songs, and plays. Older children might put on a puppet show for younger ones, using a script they write themselves and puppets they make.

Homework and Tutoring

Children in before- and after-school programs should have the opportunity to do homework if they choose. However, doing homework while at the child care center should not be a requirement. Good communication between parents, teachers, and children is needed so that all agree on the expectations regarding homework.

An advantage of doing homework at the center is that children can work together. Adults can also provide explanations and assistance when needed. Of course, "helping" with homework does not include doing the work for the child.

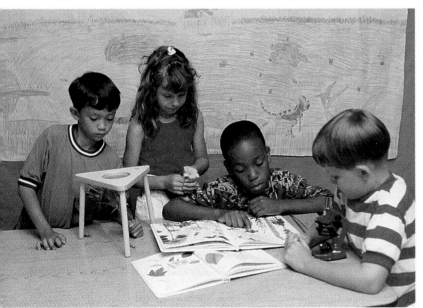

With equipment, supplies, and encouragement, children are usually eager to learn on their own. They also teach each other about their discoveries. What are the benefits of this type of learning?

Children may benefit from having a **tutor**, *someone who provides individual instruction on a regular basis.* A teacher may offer to tutor children who need help mastering certain subjects. A child who is especially good at math might help explain difficult concepts to others. Older children can tutor younger ones. In addition to benefiting the child who receives help, such an arrangement aids the social and intellectual development of the child who does the tutoring.

Nurturing Emotional Development

It is not always easy for school-age children to sort through the wide variety of emotions they experience. Teachers should be available to listen to school-age children's thoughts, feelings, and fears. In particular, teachers can be a valuable resource for children who are confused about peer relationships.

Sensitive teachers provide school-age children with opportunities to examine their emotions. A good way to accomplish this is through drama and other creative activities. School-age children may start a diary or record their feelings on a tape recorder. (Insure privacy when this is done.) Teachers can also provide many good books dealing with school-age emotions.

Building Self-Esteem

As children grow older, they are capable of making more decisions and assuming greater responsibilities. Giving them opportunities to do so builds self-esteem. Younger school-age children might be given a choice of snacks from a selection of nutritious foods. An older child could be responsible for picking up and organizing books in the reading area.

Encouraging pride in children's cultural background is another way to boost self-esteem. Invite children to share foods, cele-

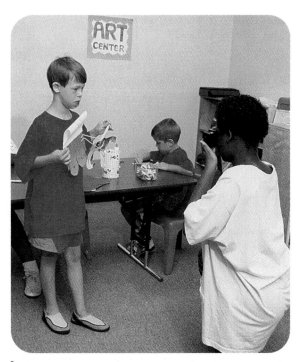

In child care programs, videotaping and taking photographs are techniques useful for a variety of purposes. This caregiver is documenting the best work of each child. How could this boost self-esteem?

brations, history, and other aspects of their cultural heritage. Children who become secure in their cultural identity in this way tend to be more accepting of other cultural groups.

Finally, build self-esteem by modeling it. Be positive about yourself. Take pride in your appearance and show security in your values. Insist that the children treat you and each other with the proper respect. In this way, children learn to respect themselves as well.

Nurturing Social Development

Cooperative projects are a good way to help children develop social skills. They might work together to paint a mural or build a replica of a famous landmark. They

Dealing with Bullies

Some children with low self-esteem become bullies who taunt and threaten their classmates. Deep down, they lack confidence and fear they will not be liked. To prove—especially to themselves—that they are superior, they intimidate other children. Caregivers need to treat bullies firmly, but with compassion. Make it clear that bullying behavior is not acceptable. At the same time, look for opportunities to praise and encourage these children's positive qualities.

could construct an enormous papier-mâché dinosaur or prepare a meal together. Planning parties—including decorations, refreshments, and games—is also a good exercise in cooperation and teamwork.

In addition to observing all types of holidays, children can make up their own celebrations. One program declared a "Wacky Week." One day they tried to do everything backwards; the next day they wore bizarre clothing. They read newspapers and magazines for "strange but true" stories. The fun broke down barriers and inspired much creative thinking.

Field trips can expand children's awareness of their community. Inviting visitors to the classroom is another method. Guests might range from the mayor to a construction worker to a dance instructor. A variety of visitors shows children the diversity of

THE MULTICULTURAL CLASSROOM

The school-age years present a challenge to multicultural acceptance—and an opportunity. Attending school, children are exposed to differing attitudes regarding other cultures. At the same time, they are beginning to make decisions and form attitudes of their own. Even a child raised to value all people regardless of background may develop biases.

Wise teachers take advantage of school-age children's growing intellectual and social skills to instill a deeper appreciation of cultural diversity. Teachers can provide historical information about other nations and peoples. Bookshelves should include biographies of noteworthy figures of various cultures. A child who is interested in science can learn of the Native Americans' contributions to medicine and the ancient Aztec grasp of astronomy. A child who enjoys poetry should find selections by African, Latin American, and Russian authors as well as other poets. Like all aspects of education, teaching respect for other cultures must become more involved and stimulating to keep up with children's ability to understand.

the world and may inspire an interest in a certain field. Include parents as guest speakers—not only can they share information about their work, but they will also enjoy the chance to visit their child's classroom.

Guidance and Discipline

The principles of positive discipline discussed in Chapter 15 apply to all age groups. However, teachers must take the child's level of development into account. School-age children need fewer restrictions than preschoolers. Still, as children experience more independence, they are likely to test the limits set for them. Teachers must establish clear, firm boundaries for acceptable behavior.

School-age children are more likely to follow classroom rules when they have been given a say in creating them. Discussing and voting on rules teaches children to consider the needs and wishes of others. They also learn to negotiate and compromise in order to reach an agreement.

Nurturing Moral Development

To help children this age grow morally, teachers should continue to encourage positive social attitudes. They can also expect more responsible behavior. All children, for example, can be taught to respect the property of others. For younger children, this might mean asking before playing with another child's game. Older children can see how this principle requires them to take care of the program's equipment so that all can enjoy it.

School-age children are better able to understand the larger world. Encourage them to think about how their actions, attitudes, and decisions affect others. Children this age may be influenced by peer pressure to do things that are hurtful, such as teasing an overweight child. If they have been taught concern for others, they are less likely to engage in such behavior.

Moral guidance can be incorporated into already existing activities. In the library offer stories, fictional or true, about children faced with moral dilemmas. In food preparation and eating areas, hang posters reminding children to use resources wisely, show good table manners, and avoid littering.

BRIDGING THE GAP

School-age child care programs can be viewed as bridging the gap between time spent at home and at school. In a way, they bridge another gap as well. By providing positive experiences and guidance, a quality program can smooth the transition from the early years to the even more complex stage of adolescence.

When children engage in projects or games that require cooperation, they learn essential social skills. How would you, as a caregiver, react when disputes occur?

Building Professional Skills

A Positive Role Model

WHAT IS A POSITIVE ROLE MODEL?

You know that a role model is someone whose behavior and attitudes others imitate. A positive rode model displays qualities that contribute to a rewarding, productive, happy life: honesty, decency, generosity, humor, industriousness, and many others. Positive role models are living examples of positive values.

A Positive Role Model in Action

Vada Hinckley looked forward to her twice-weekly craft classes at the child care center. The children really seemed to enjoy making things and listened with genuine interest when Vada talked about her life as a young girl, a mother, and a school teacher. She never realized the impact of her stories, however, until a teacher showed her an essay one of the students had written for school.

The assigned subject was "I Want to Be Like..." The girl had written, "I want to be like Mrs. Hinckley. She grew up in the Depression. She had to work hard and didn't have much money, but she still has happy memories of her childhood. Later she raised a family and taught school. Wives weren't supposed to work, but she wanted a career helping people. Now she is retired, so she volunteers a lot. She is a strong person who doesn't let trouble get her down and doesn't make excuses for herself. Mrs. Hinckley has really lived."

Vada was both surprised and touched. "I never meant to brag about my life," she said. "I was just doing the best I could."

Your Analysis

1. What positive values are evident in Vada's life?

2. Vada hadn't realized the children were paying such close attention. Do you think this is typical of role models? Explain your answer.

3. What role models do children have today? Are these role models positive ones? Explain.

Chapter 27 Review

Chapter Summary

- Programs for school-age children provide care during times when children are not in school and parents cannot be with them.
- School-age children need less supervision and structure than do preschoolers. However, personal attention is still important.
- Quality programs provide a safe, interesting, and relaxed environment for school-age children.
- In daily routines and schedules, school-age children are given a reasonable amount of freedom to choose their own activities.
- Field trips, clubs, and other special activities can add interest to the program.
- Physical, intellectual, emotional, social, and moral development can be nurtured in school-age child care programs.

Reviewing the Facts

1. What happens when child care programs for school-age children are not available? Why is this a problem?
2. What is an ideal group size and number of teachers for a school-age program?
3. How do learning centers for school-age children differ from those for preschoolers?
4. Why is it appropriate to give children more freedom in choosing activities as they grow older?
5. Describe how effective teachers respond to children's cues when providing activity options.
6. Give four examples of businesses that school-age children might enjoy visiting on a field trip.
7. Name three safety precautions necessary in school-age child care.
8. Identify five types of activities that can help school-age children develop intellectually.
9. Explain the general policy regarding homework in a typical school-age child care program.
10. What are three ways teachers can help school-age children build self-esteem?
11. What can teachers do to counteract the negative influence of peer pressure?

Thinking Critically

1. Do you think a single program can effectively meet the needs of both younger and older school-age children? If so, how? If not, why not? What alternatives would you suggest?
2. Besides furniture, what items might you include in a child care environment to make it appealing and relaxing for school-age children?
3. Compare teachers of school-age children with those of preschool children. What qualities do you think both should possess? What qualities might be more important for school-age teachers than for preschool teachers? Why?

Activities and Applications

1. **Child's Viewpoint.** Interview a school-age child who attends a child care program. Ask the child what he or she likes and dislikes about the experience. Have the child suggest improvements.

Chapter 27 Review

2. **Board Games.** With a partner, make a list of five popular board games for school-age children. Analyze what specific skills each game is designed to develop.

3. **Latchkey Children.** Write a paragraph that begins as follows: "Life for latchkey children is. . . ."

SCHOOL TO WORK

Your Professional Portfolio

Plan a day of "Junior Olympics" for children in an after-school child care program. What events might you include in the Junior Olympics? List equipment or training that the children might need to participate in these events. Note any safety concerns and how these should be addressed. Record your plans on index cards and place them in your portfolio activity file.

Observing and Analyzing

Expanding Young People's Horizons

Some workers in a school-age child care program may be tempted to think of their job as essentially "babysitting"—simply watching children and keeping them out of trouble. They may see the children only an hour in the morning and again in the afternoon, and they think that little can be accomplished in such a short time. They may feel that children already have enough to do between school and home responsibilities—why push them to get involved with more? As a result, they offer few options for children, or inappropriate choices that don't maintain a young person's interest.

This attitude can do children a great disservice. As you have read in this chapter, a before- and after-school program should do much more than house children as they wait for a ride home or to school.

How do programs for school-age children in your community measure up? Visit one, if possible, using the following ideas to guide your observations.

- **Learning Centers.** Is the classroom clearly organized into learning centers? If so, what are they? What types of materials are provided in each one? If the classroom does not have learning centers, how is it organized?

- **Self-Directed Activities.** How much freedom do children have to choose their own activities? (If possible, obtain a copy of a typical day's schedule.) During free time, do most of the children seem able to find an activity that holds their interest? How do the children use the learning centers and materials provided? What role do teachers play in guiding or directing activities?

- **Responsibilities.** Note any evidence that children are given responsibilities. For example, is there a sign posted to show job assignments? Do children help with tasks, such as serving snacks and cleaning up?

Afterward, analyze what you have observed. Do you feel this program is successful in providing a relaxed, yet enriching environment for school-age children? Why or why not? What specific improvements can you suggest?

Chapter 28

Caring for Children with Special Needs

CHAPTER OBJECTIVES

■ Explain what inclusion means and why it is practiced.

■ Discuss how to encourage a classroom atmosphere of acceptance and respect for individual abilities.

■ Outline ways to adapt a child care program to meet special needs.

■ Describe some specific needs of children with disabilities and gifted children.

Terms to Learn

- accessible
- gifted children
- inclusion
- Individualized Education Plan (IEP)
- learning disability
- special needs

rs. Martino, look what Erik has!"

Lena Martino turned to see three of the boys in her preschool class, their eyes shining with excitement. One of them carefully handed her a glittering chunk of quartz rock.

"That's a beautiful rock, Erik," Lena said. "Thank you for showing it to me. Where did you get it?"

Erik's hands and fingers moved in rapid rhythm. His interpreter said, "My parents bought that for me at the Grand Canyon."

"I've been there," the third boy said. He remembered to face toward Erik when speaking. "We were at the same place."

"Erik showed us this, too," Robert said, handing Lena a smooth black rock. "He said he found it at the beach. He's going to ask his dad to take us there."

"My, that would be fun!" Lena smiled. She was glad that after a week of shyness, Erik and the other children were finally warming up to each other.

Erik turned to his interpreter and signed emphatically. She laughed and signed a reply. Turning to Lena, she explained, "He told me I was right. Children who can hear are just like him!"

DEFINING SPECIAL NEEDS

By now, you know that every child in a classroom has individual needs. A child may be ahead in some areas of development and lag behind in others. Children who are coping with a family crisis or who speak another language also have individual needs. Caring, sensitive teachers do all they can to provide experiences suited to each child's unique stage of development.

Some children have special needs that go even further. In this chapter, the term **special needs** refers to *circumstances that cause development to vary significantly from what is considered average.* For instance, children who learn and develop much more quickly than others fall into one category of special needs. This category, called giftedness, will be discussed at the end of the chapter. Other types of special needs are due to disabilities. Examples include vision problems, limited mobility, and difficulty in learning.

No matter what special needs a child may have, remember that in all other ways he or she is no different from anyone else. Like other children, those with special needs require a secure, stimulating environment in which to develop to their fullest ability.

ONE CLASSROOM, DIFFERENT ABILITIES

*T*he education of children with special needs has changed greatly over the past few decades. Once they were automatically assigned to special classes or special schools. For some, that remains the best option. More and more, however, people are recognizing the value of **inclusion**. This means *combining children with average abilities and children with special needs in the same classroom as much as possible.* Sometimes the word "mainstreaming" is used instead of "inclusion," but the philosophy is the same.

The practice of inclusion is supported by research and reflected in current law. In 1975, Public Law 94-142, the Education for All Handicapped Children Act, was passed. (Its name was later changed to the Individuals with Disabilities Education Act, or IDEA.) This federal law states that children who have disabilities must be educated with children who are not disabled whenev-

er possible. The Americans with Disabilities Act (ADA) of 1990 further insures equal opportunities for people with disabilities in all public accommodations. These laws mean that infants and children with disabilities cannot legally be excluded from public child care programs. Private programs have the same obligation unless the cost of accommodation is financially impossible.

Providers need to explore resources for help in securing what children who have disabilities need. The Easter Seal Society is one source of information, assistance, and referral. Volunteers, training programs, and special funding may be among the services available.

Benefits of Inclusion

Inclusion is practiced for several reasons, not just because it is the law. Children with and without special needs benefit from it.

Inclusion encourages children to value diversity. They learn to be compassionate, respectful, and appreciative of those different from themselves. By developing personal relationships with one another, they learn that people are more alike than they are different.

Without inclusion, "average" children may grow up without ever having the experience of getting to know people who are different. Later in life, when they do encounter people with disabilities, they may feel uncomfortable or fearful. They

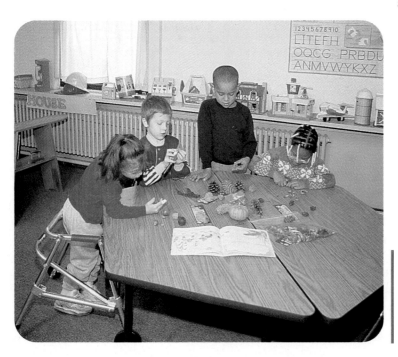

Inclusion of children with disabilities in regular classes can have real benefits for all involved. The keys to success are flexibility, creativity, and a positive attitude.

may have stereotyped beliefs about what disabled people are like. Inclusion helps to prevent this pattern of thinking.

By attending regular classes, children with special needs learn to function as normally as possible in the "real" world. They can attend a school or child care facility in a convenient location rather than traveling long distances to a special school. In the past, many children with special needs did not have the opportunity to attend any type of educational program until school age. Including these children in infant, toddler, and preschool care programs provides them with enriching experiences they might otherwise miss.

Inclusion can also help the parents of children with special needs. These parents, like their children, can too easily become isolated from others. Associating with parents of nondisabled children allows them to share concerns and experiences that all parents have. Of course, they still have the option to join or form specialized parent groups as well.

Respecting Abilities

Successful inclusion begins with a positive attitude on the part of teachers. Teachers who accept and respect children with special needs serve as a model for others. Their attitude sets the tone for the classroom, helping to create a comfortable atmosphere for everyone.

Good teachers find out what children with disabilities *can* do and encourage them to do it. They focus on abilities, not disabilities.

> In some schools, puppet shows are used to help teach children what it is like to have a disability. Why might this be an effective teaching technique for this subject?

As much as possible, treat a child with special needs as any other. Expect no more or less than the child is capable of. Show patience and understanding, but not pity. As with other children, avoid labeling. Children should not be defined by their disability. It is only part of who they are.

Encouraging Acceptance

When children encounter something new, they are usually curious about it. They may also be fearful at first. Meeting someone who has a disability is no different. A person who wears leg braces, or someone whose speech is slurred because of a mental disability, would seem strange and puzzling to many young children. Teachers can minimize these natural reactions by helping children better understand disabilities.

At the beginning of the chapter, you read about Erik, who has a severe hearing impairment. Before Erik joined the class-

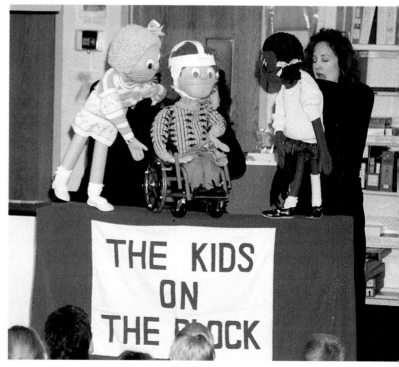

THE KIDS
ON
THE BLOCK

Empathy

WHAT IS EMPATHY?

Empathy is the ability to put yourself in other people's positions and understand what they are experiencing. When you empathize, you really share someone's feelings, almost as if they were your own. Empathy can be a powerful motivating force. Understanding what another person is facing can inspire you to make the situation better.

Empathy in Action

Mr. Barclay watched as his fifth grade students left the room for recess. Most were chattering and giggling—all except Alex, who rolled silently out the door in his electric wheelchair.

"Could I please see you a minute, Ryan?" Mr. Barclay called to the last departing student. When the others had left, he said, "I'd like to ask a favor. Alex has been in our school for almost a month, and he's still lonely. I wondered if you could take the lead and try to include him more. Then maybe the other kids will too."

"Sure," Ryan answered. "But I don't think Alex wants any of us to be friends with him."

"Why do you say that?"

"I don't know. He just acts stuck up." Ryan thought a moment. "He always eats lunch way off by himself. And in the before-school program, I used to say 'Hi' every morning but he never answered, so I quit."

"I can see why you'd give up after a while," Mr. Barclay observed. "It's not easy to keep being friendly to someone who ignores you."

"Yeah, exactly."

"But have you thought of it from Alex's point of view?" Mr. Barclay continued. "Right now, he's the new kid. Remember how you felt when you moved here?"

Ryan nodded. "It wasn't easy," he admitted.

"Do you think Alex might be feeling the same way?"

"He probably is." Ryan spoke slowly, thinking aloud. "He's new, so he feels different. Plus he's the only one who uses a wheelchair, so that makes him different too. He probably misses his old friends, like I did."

"Sounds like you and Alex have some things in common. Maybe even more than you realize. Did you know he collects baseball cards?"

"Really? I wonder if he knows I do." Ryan looked toward the door. "I've got to go now. Thanks, Mr. B!"

Your Analysis

1. For whom did Mr. Barclay show empathy?

2. How did empathy help Ryan accept Alex as a person?

3. How might the students in Alex's classroom help him get over his feelings of being different?

room, Mrs. Martino helped the rest of the class learn more about him. She told them that Erik had been very sick as a baby, and now he could hear very little. She was careful to explain, however, that Erik was no longer sick and that common illnesses don't cause people to lose their hearing. She also stressed that except for his hearing problem, Erik was no different from them. To help the children understand what Erik's impairment was like, Mrs. Martino let them wear ear plugs. She showed them a hearing aid similar to Erik's and explained how it works. Another day, Erik's interpreter visited the class and explained how people communicate with sign language. Lena and the children learned to sign "hello," "goodbye," and "thank you." In these ways the children not only became more understanding of Erik's disability, but were able to help Erik feel more comfortable and accepted when he joined the classroom.

Teachers can promote understanding in many ways. Books are available to help children of various ages understand disabilities. Puppet programs have been developed that feature characters who talk about their disabilities. In one outreach project, dolls with specific special needs "visit" nondisabled children and their families for a weekend. They are accompanied by letters in which the dolls describe their special needs and suggest things the family can do to make their stay more pleasant.

In addition to learning about disabilities, children need to see that people with disabilities are part of everyday life. Display posters and pictures that show children of varying abilities playing together. Provide storybooks that acknowledge disabilities without making them the main focus of the plot. The dramatic play area can include dolls, puppets, and doll house figures that represent children with special needs. When inviting adults to the program as guest speakers—to talk about careers, for example—include people with disabilities. This lets children see that people with disabilities can lead independent and successful lives.

As they learn about disabilities, young children sometimes make comments or ask questions that adults consider embarrassing. John Thomas, a preschool teacher, remembers the day a librarian who uses a wheelchair visited his classroom for the first time. One boy asked the visitor, "Are your legs broke?" Another told her, "I can walk and you can't." A girl who was fascinated by the wheelchair said, "Get up and let me have a turn." John and the librarian were both understanding enough to realize that the children did not mean to be rude. They simply needed more information. By giving the children simple, honest answers, John and his visitor helped the children learn about more than just library books that day.

STRATEGIES FOR MEETING SPECIAL NEEDS

When planning a program that will include children with special needs, child care professionals have much to think about. Later you will read about some of the approaches needed for specific special needs. For now, here are some general principles.

Staffing the Classroom

Children with special needs may require individual instruction. Some need assistance with basic care routines. For these reasons,

---

Tip **FROM THE** *Pros*

*C*hild advocacy groups are good sources of volunteers to work in classrooms. Check with social service agencies to locate child advocacy groups in your area.

A higher staff-to-child ratio may be needed when a class includes children with special needs. What factors should be considered when making this decision?

extra teachers, aides, or volunteers are often needed in the classroom.

Children with severe impairments may need to be assisted or taught by someone with specialized education and training. Many colleges have courses and degree programs relating to children with special needs.

Working with Parents

Parents of children with special needs are a valuable resource for teachers. They are familiar with their child's history, habits, and day-to-day changes. They can provide much information to help meet the child's individual needs.

In return, teachers must keep parents informed. Parents naturally want to know what the program is doing for their child and how their child is progressing. They also have a right to take part in decisions regarding their child's care and education. Encourage parents to observe the program regularly. After observation times, a parent-teacher conference allows questions to be answered and insights shared.

Parents of children with special needs have many concerns. They may worry about their child being rejected by others. They may wonder whether they are doing everything they can to help their child. They may have to make difficult decisions about care, educa-

Close communication with the parents of children with special needs can help a child care experience be a more positive one for children, staff, and parents. How might each of these benefit from such dialogue?

tional programs, and medical treatment. Good teachers are sensitive and supportive as they listen and respond to parents' concerns. They also refer parents to appropriate sources of help and information. These might include parent support groups, local agencies, and national organizations, such as the March of Dimes.

Adapting the Environment

The most caring, enriching program in the world won't benefit a child whose wheelchair doesn't fit through the classroom door. Making sure that the physical environment is **accessible**, or *easily used by those with disabilities,* is often one of the first concerns that must be addressed. Teachers, children, parents, and others should work together to identify and remove barriers and safety hazards.

Tip FROM THE Pros

*T*oys adapted for use by children with special needs can be obtained from toy lending libraries. Some Easter Seals Rehabilitation Centers lend such toys through Lekotek programs, named after the Swedish term for play library.

Adapting the Curriculum

Simply being able to attend the program is not enough. Children with special needs must also benefit from it. Like all children, they need activities and experiences designed to nurture their physical, intellectual, emotional, social, and moral development.

Whenever possible, avoid planning separate activities for children with special needs. Doing so emphasizes their differences from other children, making them feel left out. Instead, plan activities that all children can participate in to some degree. To accommodate individual children, modify the activity, the equipment, or the teaching method as needed. For example, Sara Cheng's preschool class includes a girl who has little control over the muscles in her arms and legs. Sara often leads creative movement activities by saying something like "Pick a part of your body to move to the music" or "Use your body to show how the music makes you feel." This approach lets every child take part in his or her own way.

In public school programs, administrators, parents, teachers, and specialists work together to create an Individualized Education Plan for each child with a special need. An **Individualized Education Plan (IEP)** is *a written plan that outlines how to encourage development in a child who has special needs.* It is required by Public Law 94-142 and must include the following information:

This center has two floors. The elevator gives children with mobility problems access to both levels.

- Current level of the child's abilities.
- Annual goals for the child's development.
- Short-term educational goals.
- Educational services to be provided.
- Degree to which the child will be included in a regular classroom. For example, some children may need to spend part of the day receiving special services from a therapist.
- The procedure for determining whether the plan's goals are being met.

Adapting Schedules and Routines

Routines such as eating, dressing for outdoor play, toileting, and transitions can be especially time consuming for children with disabilities. Allow for the extra time needed when you plan the schedule. As with all children, independence and self-

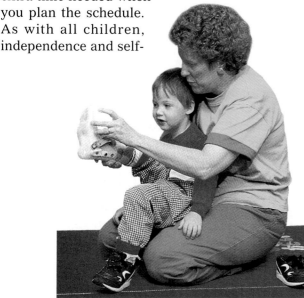

All children need the sense of accomplishment and independence that mastering self-help skills provides. Each child's abilities and needs will determine which skills are most important and how they can best be taught. Would a child with a disability necessarily need special help with all skills?

help skills should be strongly encouraged among children with special needs. Other children in the classroom may try to be helpful by doing things for the child who has a disability. Remind them that people like to do as much as possible for themselves.

Some children require special health care. This may include medicine, emergency treatment, or some form of therapy. Teachers should request specific written instructions from parents.

SPECIFIC DISABILITIES

The following suggestions will help you make adaptations for children with specific disabilities. Of course, these are only a sampling of the different kinds of special needs. As a child care professional, you may encounter many others. Remember, too, that each child is different. Talking with the child's parents, doctors, and therapists and observing the child yourself are the best ways of finding out what specific changes need to be made.

Many children with hearing impairments use more than one method of communication. This teacher is both signing and speaking clearly to help the child read her lips.

Hearing Impairments

Difficulty in hearing can range from mild impairment to total deafness. Hearing problems interfere with language development and other areas of learning. They also make social relationships more challenging, since hearing and nonhearing people communicate in different ways.

Some hearing impairments can be lessened or corrected with hearing aids. If so, teachers should ask parents to teach them how to handle the device properly. Hearing aids have a limited range. A child who uses one cannot be expected to hear a teacher who is at the other end of the room or play yard. Also remember that hearing aids make all sounds louder. Reduce distracting background noise whenever possible.

Several visual methods for communicating with the hearing-impaired have been developed, including American Sign Language. If a child uses one of these methods, the program may need to provide an aide to act as an interpreter. In addition, the other teachers and children should try to learn at least a few common phrases.

Children with hearing impairments often enjoy being able to teach others their communication method.

Some children who are hearing-impaired read lips. When this is the case, make sure the child can see your face when you speak. Bend down to eye level and face the light if possible. Lipstick helps draw attention to a female teachers' lips. Male teachers should be clean-shaven so that lips can be easily seen. Lip movement should be distinct but natural. Children who read lips should sit directly in the front of the teacher during story time and group activities. Facial expressions and frequent gestures can also help you communicate.

Props, pictures, and hands-on experiences help children with hearing impairments (and others) learn concepts. You might illustrate a story's plot on a flannel board as you read it, for example. During music time, let a child with a hearing impairment feel the vibration of the musical instrument. Combining movements, such as clapping, with music lets the child see a song's rhythm. When signaling transitions from one activity to another, combine visual cues, such as turning overhead lights on and off, with ones that can be heard.

Vision Impairments

As with hearing impairment, vision impairment ranges from mild to complete. Children with severe vision impairment need a classroom that is accessible to them. They often memorize room arrangement to help identify clear pathways. In such cases, classroom furniture should not be moved

Many children with disabilities can participate in the same activities that other children enjoy. What differences might you expect in the way Miranda handles this activity as compared to others in her group?

frequently. If it is moved, give the children a "tour" of the new placement. Some teachers paint the edges of furniture in a high-contrast color so that it is more easily seen by children with poor vision. Keep items such as toys and games in the same places every day. To help children who can read identify objects by feel, use plastic labels with raised print or label them in Braille, the system of writing for the blind. Cubbies can be marked with bows, feathers, or large buttons.

When You Suspect a Problem

As a child care professional, you will often work with children who have already been identified as having special needs. You may also be the one who first notices signs that a special need exists. Knowledge of child development helps teachers identify children who may have special needs. So do keen observation skills and carefully kept records. This was the case when Whitney, a preschool teacher, observed a four-year-old girl in her classroom. Over a period of several weeks, Whitney noted that Cynthia's behavior was changing. Sometimes Cynthis didn't respond when Whitney spoke to her. The child also had trouble following directions. Based on what she observed, Whitney suspected a hearing problem. She did not jump to conclusions, however, but shared the information with the preschool director and the child's parents. When a problem is suspected, teachers refer parents to professionals who can identify the problem and suggest a course of action. In Cynthia's case, a physical exam did reveal a hearing problem. After she was fitted with a hearing aid, the problems disappeared. If Whitney had not been so observant, however, Cynthia's development and self-esteem might have suffered lasting damage.

Encourage children to find their way around by using their other senses. Point out that the paints and clays make the art center smell different from the dramatic play center, where you can hear the traffic from the street outside. Mark different parts of the room with items that can be felt, heard, or smelled.

Vision impairment interferes with the learning process by limiting the associations that can be made. Children with severely impaired vision cannot learn what a giraffe is by associating the sound of the word with a picture of a giraffe. Instead, they must associate the word "giraffe" with other words they understand, such as "long neck" and "four legs." Impaired vision or hearing can dampen curiosity as well. Children who can't see or hear new things have less reason to explore. Physical and intellectual growth may be hindered as a result. To counteract this, caregivers must use the child's other senses to motivate learning.

To adapt activities, use words and hands-on experiences as much as possible. During a gardening activity, let the child touch and smell the soil and the seeds. Guide the child's hand as you dig with the spade, all the while describing what is happening. Let the child hear and feel droplets from the watering can. In the classroom, provide toys of many different shapes, textures, and weights, especially ones that move or make sounds. Art activities can be enjoyed for the movement and physical sensations involved. Use touch and motion to explain concepts such as "circle." To encourage large motor development, provide safe, open areas for running and jumping.

Many books and games are available in large-print versions to benefit children with partial vision. Some classroom materials may be enlarged with a photocopier. Children who are blind can listen to stories recorded on cassettes. They can also use Braille books and games after they learn to read with this system.

Other Physical Impairments

Some children have physical conditions that affect their gross or fine motor abilities. They may use crutches, a walker, or a wheelchair to get around. They may have poor muscle control or be missing part of an arm. All of these conditions create challenges, but none should prevent a child from participating in a program.

The goal of inclusion is to involve children with special needs as completely as possible in all classroom activities. Jason cannot walk but has some use of his hands. Why is this large peg board a good toy for improving his fine motor skills?

The first step is to insure that the building itself is accessible. If a child uses a wheelchair, for instance, doors and pathways need to be wide enough for easy access. If a child has limited use of the hands, faucets in hand washing areas must be easy to operate. The goal is to provide all children in the classroom with the same level of independence.

Adaptations may also be needed in classroom routines, play equipment, and activities. For example, you may need to provide double-handled cups and bowls to use at mealtime. Puzzle pieces can be fitted with large knobs for easier handling. Suction cups attached to the bottom of a toy can help hold it steady. A sandbox could be raised to accommodate children in wheelchairs. If some children cannot easily sit in chairs, you might equip chairs with straps or do more activities on the floor. Long pieces of string can be attached to bean bags to make them easier to retrieve when playing target games. As you can see, many solutions do not require much time or expense—just some creative thinking.

Mental Impairments

Like physical impairments, mental impairments may be mild, moderate, or severe. Children who are mentally impaired are slower to develop than others. Their intellectual skills, such as the ability to understand cause and effect, are diminished. Their attention span is usually shorter than average. Motor skills and eye-hand coordination are often affected. They may show less emotional control and fewer social skills than other children.

Children with mental impairments can be successfully included in regular child care programs. They should be placed according to their developmental ability, not their chronological age. These children respond well when given short, clear directions. You may need to break down activities into small, orderly steps and guide the children more closely. Demonstrate and repeat activities as often as possible.

Seeing other children easily master skills that they find difficult can be very frustrating for children who are mentally impaired. To counteract this, give them as many opportunities as possible to be successful. Such questions as "What is your favorite animal?" permit all children in the classroom to give a "right" answer, regardless of mental ability.

Learning Disabilities

A **learning disability** is *a disorder that affects the way the brain processes information.* It is not the same as a mental impairment. In fact, many children with learning disabilities are above average in intelligence. However, because they cannot use information from the senses in a normal way, learning is hindered.

Many specific types of learning disabilities exist. Some affect the ability to use or understand spoken language. For example, a child may have difficulty naming objects or understanding even simple directions. A child with a reading disorder (called *dyslexia*) may have trouble learning to recognize letters of the alphabet. To the child, the letters may at times appear backwards or jumbled, or even seem to move around on the

page. Another type of disorder relates to arithmetic skills. The child may be unable to count objects or recognize basic shapes. In many cases, more than one type of disorder is present.

Learning disabilities often go unrecognized, especially in young children. Parents and educators may believe that such children are simply developing more slowly than their peers and will catch up later. Another common reaction is to think that the child is not trying hard enough or not paying attention. Children may blame themselves for being "dumb" or "lazy," not realizing the true nature of their problem.

Learning specialists are professionals trained to identify learning disorders and help children overcome them. They can help children learn to use different ways of gathering, organizing, and interpreting information. Counselors can help children deal with behavioral and self-esteem problems associated with learning disabilities. Regular classroom teachers must work closely with parents and specialists to determine what techniques best meet the child's needs.

Learning specialists have special training for diagnosing and treating learning disorders. Often, however, it is parents or caregivers who first recognize that a child has difficulty learning. Early diagnosis and treatment help minimize the effects of a learning disability.

Behavioral and Emotional Disorders

All children occasionally have trouble relating to others or coping with their emotions. Their behavior may be aggressive or overly active at times. With some children, however, emotional or behavioral problems are frequent and extreme—so much so that they interfere with learning. Such children may be diagnosed as having a behavioral or emotional disorder.

One of the most common behavioral disorders is called ADHD, which stands for *attention deficit* (DEFF-uh-sit) *hyperactivity* (HY-puhr-ak-TIV-uh-tee) *disorder*. Some children with ADHD have difficulty paying attention and following instructions. Others are aggressive, impulsive, and overly active—they "can't sit still." Still others show a combination of these symptoms. As with learning disabilities, the problem seems related to how the brain functions. In fact, ADHD and learning disabilities often occur together.

Other types of behavioral and emotional disorders vary widely. Children may be withdrawn, depressed, unusually fearful, or violent. In each case, the problem is more severe and continual than the normal emotional ups and downs of childhood.

Children with behavioral and emotional disorders require professional help. Medication may be prescribed to control the symptoms. Therapy can also be beneficial. Teachers should work with professionals and parents to provide the best classroom atmosphere for the child. Often this is a calm, consistent, orderly environment with plenty of individual attention.

GIFTED CHILDREN

Gifted children are *those who are extraordinarily talented or excel in one or more areas*. Some children are intellectually gifted. Others excel in some form of artistic expression, such as music or painting. Exceptional athletes and dancers are physically gifted.

Signs that may indicate giftedness include:

• Advanced vocabulary and language skills.

THE MULTICULTURAL CLASSROOM

For gifted children, as well as others, a thematic unit that explores another country can be enlightening. To make the experience more personal, have children exchange letters with international pen pals. Writing to pen pals from other countries can not only satisfy active, curious minds, but it can also open the door to friendship and genuine cross-cultural understanding. Contact these organizations for more information:

World Pen Pals
1694 Como Avenue
St. Paul, MN 55108

International Friendship League
55 Mount Vernon Street
Boston, MA 02108

- Developmental skills acquired earlier than most peers.
- Walking and talking earlier than usual in infancy.
- Creativity in inventing and problem solving.
- Intense curiosity.
- Advanced attention span.
- Ability to concentrate on and persist in complex tasks.
- Unusual attention to detail.
- Perfectionism.
- Good memory.
- Preference for company of older playmates and adults.
- Good sense of humor.
- Ease in grasping new concepts and ideas.
- Talent for making plans and organizing tasks.

Gifted children need programs that challenge them at their advanced developmental level. Otherwise they lose interest and don't bother to do their best. They may misbehave out of boredom.

Teachers can respond to the special needs of gifted children in many ways. Enrichment activities that explore concepts in more depth should be planned. Gifted children may also enjoy helping to organize and plan group projects. Field trips and special visitors can help satisfy a gifted child's intellect, as well as stimulate and motivate other children.

Because they pay close attention to detail, gifted children often take longer to complete projects to their satisfaction. Allow them large blocks of time to thoroughly investigate topics. Avoid rushing them through art projects or block building.

Children who excel in a particular area, such as dance or music, should be given plenty of opportunity to develop their skills. If lessons or experiences outside the program are not available to the child, a volunteer talented in that area may be recruited.

Many gifted children show great curiosity at an early age. Remember, though, that giftedness does not mean that a child shows unusual talent in *every* area.

EVERYONE GAINS

*I*t may have occurred to you that many techniques for working with children who have special needs—encouraging the use of all the senses, promoting self-reliance, focusing on the child's abilities—apply equally to other children. Practicing these techniques could make you a better, more sensitive teacher. This lends weight to the argument of those who support inclusion in education: that special children can teach as much as they learn.

Chapter 28 Review

Chapter Summary

- Special needs occur when development varies significantly from what is considered average.
- Including children with special needs in regular classrooms can benefit the children, their classmates, their parents, and their teachers.
- A positive attitude calls for focusing on children's abilities rather than their disabilities.
- Teachers can help children understand disabilities and accept differences.
- Meeting special needs may require additional staff as well as changes in the environment, curriculum, and schedule. Working with parents is essential.
- Gifted children need additional enrichment in their learning environment.

Reviewing the Facts

1. Name four examples of special needs.
2. What is inclusion? Describe three specific benefits it has.
3. How should teachers treat children with special needs as compared to other children?
4. List three ways a teacher could help nondisabled children understand and accept others' disabilities.
5. In what way can parents of children with special needs help teachers? In what way can teachers help parents?
6. What does IEP stand for? What is the purpose of this document?
7. What should be emphasized when adapting activities for children with limited vision?
8. What is the best way to teach a skill to a child with a mental disability?
9. What is the difference between a mental disability and a learning disability?
10. Should gifted children be given less time than others to complete projects? Explain.

Thinking Critically

1. What concerns might some people raise about inclusion? What could be done to address these concerns?
2. What role has technology played in allowing people with disabilities to participate in society?
3. Suppose some five-year-olds in a child care program were teasing a child who had a disability. What would you do?
4. Why do you think some learning disabilities are not identified even in school-age children? What could be done to improve the situation?

Activities and Applications

1. **Wheelchair Tour.** Take a tour of your school in a wheelchair or on crutches. What obstacles do you encounter? How might they be eliminated?
2. **Understanding Others.** Write a brief story or puppet show script that could be used to help preschoolers learn about a specific disability.
3. **Experiencing a Learning Disability.** Copy a sentence from a book or write a line from a poem or song. Reverse some of the letters and write some words backwards to make them appear as they would to a child with dyslexia. Exchange papers with a classmate

and try to read what the other has written. Next, hold a strip of paper up to your forehead using the hand you usually write with. With your other hand, write your first name across the strip of paper using a crayon or marker. What feelings did you experience? How might your feelings be similar to or different from those of a child with a learning disability struggling to do a task?

Your Professional Portfolio

Select a specific activity that a preschool teacher might use—perhaps one you developed for an earlier chapter. Identify two types of special needs that would require you to adapt the activity. For each special need, decide how you would modify the activity by making changes in the equipment or your teaching technique. Create adapted lesson plans and place them in your portfolio.

Observing and Analyzing

Beyond the Classroom

Great strides have been made in people's understanding of those with special needs. Public facilities have a legal—and ethical, some would say—obligation to accommodate people with special needs in whatever way possible. Gradually, the general public is becoming more aware of the needs and rights of people with disabilities.

There is a saying, however, that "you can't legislate feelings." In other words, laws can change people's behavior, but not their attitudes. Children with special needs—like all others—need to see that they are genuinely valued and accepted for themselves, not simply included because the law requires it.

Have people with disabilities been accepted as "part of the landscape" in society? Are they included in those areas not covered by the law? The following observations can help you gain insight:

- **Catalog Survey.** Look through a catalog from a seller of clothing or children's products. Count the number of children or adults with special needs that appear in the photographs. How does this compare to the total number of people shown?

- **Book Survey.** Search the library for examples of children's books that feature characters with disabilities. In how many instances is the disability the main focus of the story? Are the characters portrayed as complete persons apart from their disabilities? Are adults with disabilities seen fulfilling multiple roles, such as parent, spouse, and productive worker?

- **Television Survey.** Over the course of a week, record instances in which children or adults with disabilities appear in television programs that you normally watch. Describe their role in the program, referring to the questions listed under "Book Survey" above.

From the information you have gathered, draw some conclusions about society's voluntary inclusion of people with special needs. How would you rate the general public's image and awareness of those with disabilities?

Meet Catherine Ing, an infant caregiver in a child care program. Catherine and two other caregivers share the responsibilities of caring for the twelve infants in their room.

Why did you choose this career?

"Babies are fascinating to me. The amount of growth and change that infants go through is amazing. When I learned that infancy is the period of greatest development for children, it confirmed what I already believed. I felt it would be worthwhile to influence that development. Of course, there's something very sweet and loveable about infants too."

What education and skills do you need?

"My position requires a four-year bachelor's degree in early childhood education. I am also certified in first aid and infant/toddler CPR. Because I feed and diaper children so many times a day, I also have a sanitation certificate from the health department. To earn that certificate, I had to learn

techniques for preventing the spread of contagious diseases.

"Since infants can't talk to you, observation skills and good record keeping are absolutely essential. Observation tells me when a child is ill. I have to 'read' behavior to understand how an infant is feeling. Trained observation is also needed to detect crisis situations, such as child abuse.

"Good observation skills allow me to keep the detailed, accurate records needed to track infants' daily development. Although I don't plan the kind of curriculum that a teacher would for preschoolers, I do make sure the infants have stimulating activities that are right for them every day. I know what to do based on what skills I see them testing and mastering. Planning activities that are not too easy or too hard is my goal.

"Attention to detail is important. For instance, I sanitize the diapering table and meal service surfaces each time I use them. With infants, little things like that can make a big difference.

"To nurture children emotionally and socially, infant caregivers need to be patient, warm, and loving. My coworkers and I find it easy to build the self-esteem of our babies because we genuinely enjoy them. Hugging and cuddling the babies seems natural and it's very important for their emotional well-being."

What is a typical day on the job like?

"Since babies have their own schedules, I'm constantly busy—giving a bottle to one child, changing another child's diaper, soothing someone to sleep, or playing games. At feeding times I feel like I'm working in a fast food restaurant!

"In the classrooms with older children, teachers can sometimes take a break when the children take naps. In the infant room, the children don't all nap at the same time. Someone usually keeps us on our toes.

What is most challenging about your job?

"The job involves more physical labor than you might think. I lift and carry babies—from cribs, from diapering tables, from the floor—more times than I can count. That can be hard on the back and shoulders.

"Fighting illness is another concern. Since I feed infants, wash them when they spit up, and change diapers hourly, I'm very close to them all the time. It's easy to catch something. Some illnesses you become immune to, but not all of them."

What do you like best about your work?

"Infants discover something new every day. I love their responsiveness and enthusiasm. If you give them a chance, they will investigate anything—although you have to make sure they do so safely. Infants develop so quickly. It's great to be the one who applauds their hard work when they accomplish something new.

"The unconditional love children give helps me have a positive attitude about life. Babies are very accepting.

"I also take pride in being the first caregiver to help parents in their demanding job of raising children. They often ask my advice about infant development. I like working with parents who really want the best for their children."

SHARE YOUR THOUGHTS

1. What "milestones" would you "celebrate" with an infant?
2. What kinds of concerns do you think parents bring to their infant's caregiver? How might the concerns of first-time parents differ from those of parents who have had children before?
3. What would be the most rewarding aspects of being an infant caregiver for you? What would be the drawbacks of the position?

LOOKING AHEAD

Reflections

"The thing I remember most is the feeling I had as I was walking up to the door of the child care center. It was only the third job interview I'd ever had in my life, and I was scared. I was fresh out of a community college training program, and I really wanted this job. My knees were shaking, and I just knew I was going to say all the wrong things. Then I looked up at the window of the center and saw two little faces peering out at me. One nose was pressed flat against the pane. As I returned the children's gaze, they greeted me with smiles. One child waved cautiously. That was the moment that turned everything around for me. I smiled and waved back, and the feeling of apprehension lifted. I did get the job, and those two children are now special friends of mine. They have no idea what they did for me, but I'll always remember."

—Diana

Chapter 29

Finding Employment in Child Care

CHAPTER OBJECTIVES

- ■ Locate sources of job possibilities.

- ■ Write an effective letter of application and resumé.

- ■ Explain how to present yourself well in a job interview.

- ■ Give tips for succeeding as a new employee.

- ■ Identify suggestions for handling a job change appropriately.

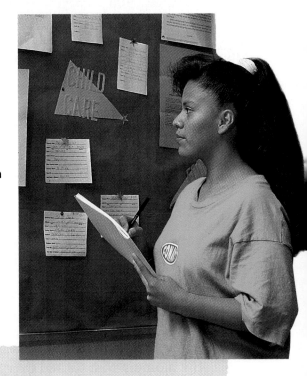

Terms to Learn

- confirmation letter
- cover letter
- criminal background check
- interview
- letter of application
- letter of inquiry
- networking
- recruit
- references
- resumé

nly three months left," Jim thought to himself. "I can hardly believe it." In twelve short weeks Jim would be graduating from high school. His senior year was quickly sailing by. Soon, if all went as planned, he'd be on his way to a career in the child care field.

"I just hope I can find a job," Jim said to his mother during lunch one day. "I really want to work part-time as a child care aide while I take my community college classes."

"Don't worry. You've got plenty of experience," his mother pointed out. "You've been a camp counselor, and you've also worked in the preschool program at your school. Besides that, you've even volunteered in the day care center at church. If I were the director of a program, I'd hire you in a second."

"That's great, Mom. When can I start?" Jim teased. To himself, he thought, "Too bad it's not quite that easy." He knew it would take more than experience alone to get the job he wanted. The jobs wouldn't come looking for him; he would have to look for them. Then would come the process—perhaps a long one—of filling out applications and going on interviews.

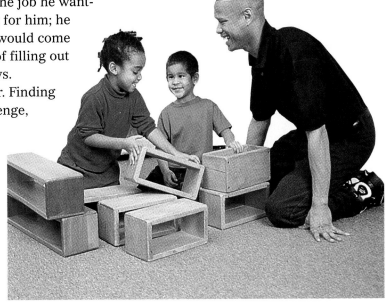

Jim remained confident, however. Finding a job in child care would be a challenge, but not an overwhelming one. His experience was a good beginning. He loved children, he could work hard, and he was willing to learn. "I know I'll make a good aide," he thought. "Now I just have to make sure that employers who have job openings know it, too."

LOOKING AHEAD TO EMPLOYMENT

Will I get the job, or will someone else?" This question is likely to be on Jim's mind in the near future. It may be on yours, too. Although there is no insurance when it comes to job hunting, you can take action that will increase your chances for success. Not everyone has a positive attitude, and not everyone makes the effort to be prepared. The person who does, however, has an edge in the job market. Will that be you?

FINDING JOB OPENINGS

You can't get a job unless you first figure out where the openings are. People use several methods to learn about job opportunities.

Making Inquiries

You never know what might be available until you ask. Some job hunters contact employers to find out about openings. What businesses and organizations might employ child care personnel in your area? The list of places on page 45 in Chapter 2 will give you ideas. You can also check the Yellow Pages of your telephone directory under such general listings as child care, schools, and social service organizations.

Once you have identified a possible employer, you can send a **letter of inquiry**. This is *a short letter sent to a potential employer to ask about job openings.* Send your letter to the program director or person in charge of personnel. In a few sentences, tell a little about yourself, giving your employment objective and inquiring about possible openings. When Ashley began her job search, she sent out several letters of inquiry. She wrote: "As a graduating high school senior, I have experience and training in child care. I am seeking a position as a teacher's aide or assistant in a preschool program. Do you have such an opening, or will you possibly have one in the near future?"

If you prefer more personal contact, you can call potential employers on the phone. You may receive a simple "yes" or "no" answer from the person you reach, or you may be referred to someone else. Sometimes it takes several calls to locate the right person.

If you learn about a job opening, be prepared with a few questions about the position. Ask how you may apply for a job that sounds suitable.

Keeping a job search notebook helps you stay organized. Important information learned in telephone conversations, such as where and to whom you must apply, can be recorded in the notebook. Be sure to write down the name of the contact person in case you need it again.

Randomly inquiring about jobs has both advantages and disadvantages. On the one hand, an employer may be impressed by your initiative and desire. On the other hand, the method can be time-consuming. You may have to contact many businesses before finding one that has an opening for a position that meets your qualifications. You will also find that some employers do not accept job inquiries unless they are already advertising an opening.

Recruiting

When employers have openings, they often **recruit**, or *actively seek*, new employees. Job openings may be publicized through one or more of the following avenues:

- ***Newspaper Classified Ads.*** The Sunday edition of a large metropolitan newspaper usually carries the most complete help-wanted ads. Each ad usually identifies the employer, the position, some of the most

A Sample Classified Ad

*T*eacher's Aide needed for day care and pre-kindergarten program at Wildwood Early Childhood Learning Center. High school diploma, some experience with preschool-age children desired. Paying $6/hour, benefits. Ten-hour day, four-day work week. Contact Mrs. Marla White, Director, 555-1278.

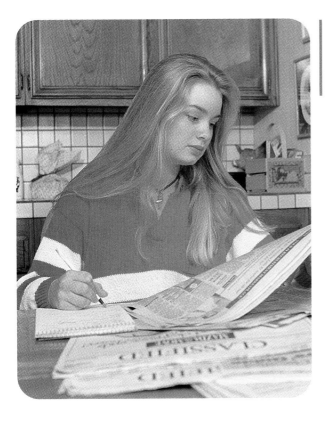

If you see a classified ad for a job that interests you, take careful note of the information in the ad. Some request that you respond with a phone call or letter. Others may ask that you apply in person.

ment-supported and free of charge. Private agencies charge a fee to the applicant, the employer, or both. Sometimes each party pays half the fee when the applicant is hired. The fee is usually computed as some portion of the job's salary. Terms of fee payment are described in a contract, which applicants must sign before the agency accepts them as clients.

• *School Counselors and Placement Offices.* While high school counselors cannot get you a job, they are usually good sources of information about

important duties and requirements, and sometimes the salary. A sample classified ad is shown on page 538. Even if you are not currently looking for a job, reading the ads introduces you to the job market. You will see what kinds of jobs are available and where they are located.

• *Employment Agencies.* These businesses operate by matching employers with job hunters. Applicants fill out forms, describing their skills, interests, and training. They are notified if and when the agency learns of a job that seems suitable. Employment agencies may be either public or private. Public agencies are govern-

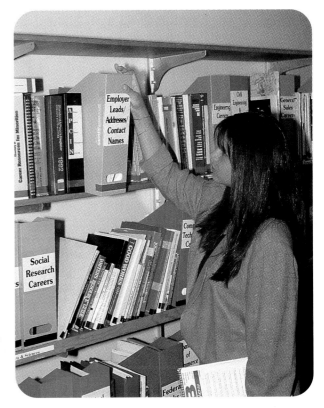

Placement offices have many resources to help you learn more about not only careers, but also specific employers. How might you use this information?

specific job openings and the job market in general. College and university placement offices can sometimes provide the same information, although they primarily serve their own students. Community colleges may be more accessible to non-students.

Networking

"He got that job because he knows someone." Have you ever heard someone make a statement like that? It's true that knowing someone can be a useful key to landing a job. Awareness of this principle can help you.

Networking is *making and maintaining contact with others in order to exchange information and services. Within a profession, people commonly network to find and fill jobs.* Here's how it works. An employer lets others in the profession know that the business has an opening. A person who is networking hears about the opening through contacts in the profession and applies for the job. Word often spreads during meetings of professional organizations. People in the child care field, for example, might network at a meeting of the National Association for the Education of Young Children.

Networking can be more informal. If you are looking for a job, you might ask friends and acquaintances for leads. Even when they don't know about a specific job, they might do some asking or listening for you.

It pays to develop a network. High school and college students can get to know counselors, teachers, and business people who may be able to help them. Establishing a positive relationship with such people and talking to them about future plans is a smart move.

Other Methods

What other ways might you use to find out about available jobs? Individuals and small companies sometimes advertise job openings on bulletin boards in supermarkets, places of worship, libraries, and other community buildings. Schools and public service groups occasionally sponsor job fairs where employers set up information booths. Just as a journalist develops a "nose for news," you can sharpen your awareness so that opportunities don't go unnoticed.

APPLYING FOR A POSITION

Once you have identified a position that you are interested in and qualified for, the application process begins. The first step is usually preparing a resumé.

The Resumé

A **resumé** is *a written summary of your education, work experience, and any special talents or skills.* This information is listed under distinct headings, letting potential employers quickly find out what they need to know about you. A sample resumé is shown on page 541.

Your resumé should make a positive impression on an employer. It needs to be organized and have a professional appearance. Keep your resumé short, preferably one typed page and no more than two. Busy employers do not have time to read the details that long resumés contain. Choose a format that is clean and clear. Books on resumé writing give samples of different styles.

Tip
FROM THE
Pros

When filling out a job application, ask for two copies or make a photocopy of the original. Fill out the copy in pencil as a rough draft. Submit the other, polished copy to the employer.

A Sample Resumé

Maria Anita Hernandez
981 W. Warnal St., Apt. 2-D
Memphis, TN 38173
(615) 555-1872

EMPLOYMENT OBJECTIVE
To obtain a teacher's aide position in a preschool program.

SPECIAL SKILLS
Have proven ability to teach young children new games and lead them in the games they know; was in charge of the bulletin board display at Riggs High School Lab School for 1994 and 1995; can speak and write Spanish and some French.

EDUCATIONAL BACKGROUND
Riggs High School, graduating May, 1995
CPR training, Metro YMCA, June, 1994

WORK EXPERIENCE
Teacher's Aide. Riggs High School Lab School. August, 1994—present. Have worked with the children of students and faculty in this preschool program for approximately 10 hours per week.

Babysitter. Have been a regular babysitter (10-20 hours per month) for three families with children ages two to ten since June, 1992, to the present.

Aide. Pine Hills Baptist Church Day Care Center. Worked as an aide from June through August, 1993 and 1994.

ACTIVITIES AND INTERESTS
For the past two years, have played on the YMCA senior girls' softball team; member of the Photography Club and Spanish Club at Riggs High School for four years; enjoy cooking and needlework.

Creating a well-written, neatly prepared resumé (or letter of application) is well worth the time and effort. If your resumé (or letter) contains careless errors, what message are you sending potential employers?

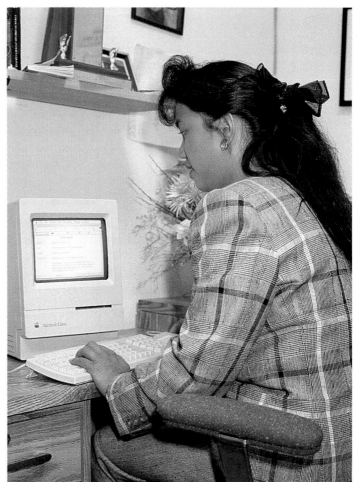

If you have work experience, put the most recent job first and list any others in reverse chronological order. If you haven't had much work experience, you may worry that your resumé looks "skimpy" and unimpressive. Look for ways to emphasize the skills and qualities that you would bring to the job. Include volunteer work, relevant classes you have taken, and awards you have received, keeping the page limit in mind. These show your interest and involvement in work and community, even if you have limited experience.

Most employers ask for **references**. These are *people who know you well and can provide information about your character and work habits*. A reference can be a teacher, an employer, a club advisor, a coach—anyone who can honestly recommend you.

Some people include references on their resumé. It is more professional, however, to supply these when an employer requests them. When asked to provide references, give name, title, full address, and phone number. You should have at least three references. Be sure to ask permission before you use a person as a reference. You might also explain the type of job you are applying for so they can be prepared with some relevant details for your potential employer.

A resumé is a valuable employment tool throughout your working life. Update it regularly as you gain more experience, education, and training.

The Letter of Application

A **letter of application** is *a letter sent to a potential employer to apply for a specific position*. A sample is shown on page 543. In the letter, you describe your qualifications and ask for an interview. *When the letter accompanies a resumé*, it is referred to as a **cover letter**.

A letter of application introduces you to an employer. Unless it makes a good impression, you have little chance of getting

A Sample Letter of Application

March 23, 19—

Mr. Will Hyer
The Learning Center
22 E. Grace Street
Memphis, TN 38156

Dear Mr. Hyer:

I am writing to inquire about the opening for a teacher's aide position at The Learning Center. My guidance counselor at Riggs High School, Mrs. Andrea Taylor, suggested I contact you. Please consider me an applicant for this position.

At the end of May I will be graduating from Riggs High School. For the past two school years, I have worked in the preschool at Riggs. My experience also includes babysitting and day care work. I enjoy children and have many interests and abilities that are valuable assets in an early childhood education position. My resumé is enclosed.

In the future I plan to continue my education and get my CDA. I hope to be a preschool teacher someday. May I have an interview? I would be glad to talk with you at your convenience. My home telephone number is 555-1872.

Thank you for your time and consideration. I will look forward to hearing from you.

Sincerely,

Maria Hernandez
981 W. Warnal St., Apt. 2-D
Memphis, TN 38173

beyond this step. Make sure the letter is well written and neatly typed. If you have trouble with spelling, grammar, or punctuation, get help with writing your letter. If you are not a good typist, ask someone to type it for you.

As you begin your letter, try to personalize the greeting ("Dear . . . .") by using the name of the person responsible for hiring employees. If necessary, you may call the business to get the name.

Use a positive tone in your letter. Focus on your qualifications and assets rather than on areas in which you are lacking. Include any training, education, abilities, and experience that indicate your suitability for the job. Try to be thorough, but avoid irrelevant information. Don't speak poorly of your former or current employer or coworkers. This holds true during the entire job-hunting process. If you send the letter with a resumé, summarize your qualifications in a few sentences and mention that the resumé is enclosed.

Proofread your letter before mailing it, and, if possible, have someone else proof it too. Sign it neatly in black ink.

The Interview

If all goes well on your job hunt, an interview is the next step. An **interview** is *a meeting between a job applicant and a potential employer. At this time the employer learns more about the applicant and the applicant learns more about the job.* Interviews are critical. In a short span of time, impressions are made that strongly influence whether you get the job.

Arranging for the Interview

When setting up an interview, try to select a date that gives you time to prepare. Ask how much time you should allow for the interview. (Most require about thirty min-

THE MULTICULTURAL CLASSROOM

Experience with a multicultural approach can be a selling point with potential employers. First, develop your ability to serve a wide range of children, and then make sure your skills are apparent on your resumé and during interviews.

Being bilingual is an asset. If you can speak, read, or write a second language, be sure to mention this fact. On your resumé list any workshops with multicultural themes that you have attended. Also note any experience you have had in working with children from varied backgrounds. In an interview, state your personal philosophy about respecting each child's uniqueness. When discussing your experience, stress the skills you gained, as well as any ideas you have, for promoting a multicultural perspective in the curriculum.

Your portfolio is the place to illustrate your abilities. Include photographs that show you leading multicultural activities that you planned. Include sheet music with examples of multicultural songs or finger plays that you put together from library research. List your favorite multicultural books and activity resources. All of these can be impressive when you present yourself to a potential employer.

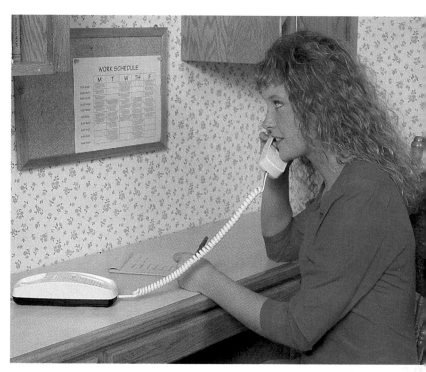

Why is it a good idea to have a calendar or schedule handy when you call to set up an interview?

utes to an hour.) Ask how many people will be interviewing you and whether you should bring along any specific materials.

If you sense that the employer would appreciate the formality, you may send a **confirmation letter**, *which verifies your agreement to meet at a certain time and date.* Thank the interviewer for agreeing to see you, and say that you are looking forward to the meeting. This demonstrates a professional attitude and helps create a favorable impression even before the interview itself.

Preparing for the Interview

For most people, an interview is a major hurdle on the way to employment. Concerned about making the best impression possible, they are quite naturally nervous.

Thorough preparation can help you relax. You will be at your best if you know what to expect and what is expected from you. Remember these tips:

- *Learn about the business.* Learn all you can about the employer before the interview. Read company newsletters and brochures, and talk to someone who is familiar with the business. If possible, tour the facility. All the information you gather will help you converse with ease. Showing interest is a good way to make a positive impression.

- *Anticipate interview questions.* Familiarize yourself thoroughly with the information in your resumé so that you

can answer questions about it. Applicants are also routinely asked such questions as these: "How did you become interested in the field of child care?" "What do you have to offer our program?" Interviewers may set up imaginary situations and ask how you would react. For example, one situation might be: "A child is frustrated because she finds it difficult to complete a coloring task. What words of encouragement would you give her?" Another example is: "A child brings a magnet to school for show and tell. Describe some simple activities with the magnet that would help the children learn about magnetism."

Some questions may be more difficult to answer. An interviewer might say, "Tell me about a time when your work was criticized," or "Why should I hire you?" These are not attacks; they are meant to reveal something about your personality. Be honest when answering such questions, but try to emphasize the positive.

Whether you are making a speech, entering a competition, or going for a job interview, careful preparation helps. You will be more at ease and confident if you plan ahead. What preparations could you make that would be useful during an interview?

in child care does not require a business suit, but blue jeans and a T-shirt are not appropriate for an interview either. Clothing should be clean and neatly pressed. Choose a conservative hairstyle and use cologne sparingly. For females makeup should not be overdone.

Keep in mind that some questions are illegal for an interviewer to ask. Asking for information that could be used to discriminate against you is not appropriate. Questions about age, marital status, and religion are examples. If you are asked a personal question that makes you uncomfortable, you might say something like: "That information is personal to me and really has no influence on my ability to perform the job."

- *Assemble examples of your work.* This is when the care you have put into your portfolio pays off. You may have awards and certificates, newsletters, video tapes, lesson plans, toys, and photographs to present. Select those items that give a clear picture of your abilities and interests and that illustrate your best work.

- *Dress and groom properly.* Your appearance creates a powerful impression. Dress as you would for the job itself. A position

Completing the Application Form

You may be asked to fill out a job application form before the interview or when you arrive for the interview. To complete the application, you will need your driver's license and social security card, plus a copy of your resumé and list of references.

Read the entire application form before you begin. Fill it out neatly, completely, and honestly. Print your answers, using ink. Watch your spelling, punctuation, and grammar. If you are completing the application on site and do not have the information required, ask if you may provide it on the following work day. If a question does not apply to you, write "NA" (not applicable) or draw a short line in the space. This lets the employer know that you have not overlooked or intentionally omitted the question.

Some states require prospective child care employees to consent to a **criminal background check**. This is *an investigation to*

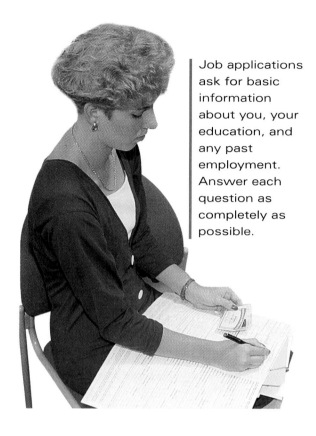

Job applications ask for basic information about you, your education, and any past employment. Answer each question as completely as possible.

Handling the Interview

Interview day can be a stressful one. Always arrive for a job interview ten to fifteen minutes early. If you are unsure about where you are going, make a trial run before the day of your interview. Time the trip so you will know how long it takes.

Bring your job search notebook with you so that you can write down information you learn at the interview. You may want to prepare a list of questions about the job beforehand to make sure you find out everything you need to know.

These tips can also help you interview well:

- Shake hands only if the interviewer offers to shake hands first. Use a firm, but not overpowering, grasp. Smile.
- Stand until you are asked to take a seat. Use good posture.
- Take a deep breath. Try to maintain a relaxed sitting position.

determine if an applicant has been convicted of a crime. Employers are especially concerned about crimes against children, which disqualify an applicant from employment. A request to complete criminal background check forms should not alarm you. It is designed to protect children.

Look on the job interview as an opportunity for you and the interviewer to get to know one another. Focus on making a good impression, but also remember to relax and be yourself.

- Speak clearly and loudly enough to be easily heard. Use correct grammar, not slang.

- Make eye contact with the interviewer and smile easily as you speak and listen.

- Answer all questions directly, completely, and honestly. Be positive in your responses. Avoid the temptation to criticize, especially if the question is somewhat difficult or embarrassing to answer.

- Be enthusiastic. Show that you are interested in, and excited by, the job.

- If your mouth becomes dry as the interview continues, politely ask for a glass of water.

- Do not eat or chew gum during the interview.

Once the interviewer has gained enough information, you will have the opportunity to ask questions about the job. You may be curious about job-related duties, hours, and benefits, if these topics have not yet been discussed. Do not ask about salary or benefits early in the interview. This can give the impression that financial concerns are more important to you than anything else.

Ending the Interview

The interviewer provides a cue when the interview has ended, probably by standing up and offering to shake hands. At this time, stand up, shake hands, and thank the interviewer. Offer to submit further information if necessary. Asking when a decision on the position will be made is appropriate.

If you are confident about your ability and you are applying for a position as an aide or a teacher in a child care program, offer to volunteer in one of the program's classrooms for a day. This gives you an opportunity to demonstrate your skills. If you currently work with children, invite the interviewer to visit and observe you at work.

Following Up

Forgetting information that you might need after an interview is easy to do. After leaving, jot down anything important that you might want to refer to later. Some possibilities are:

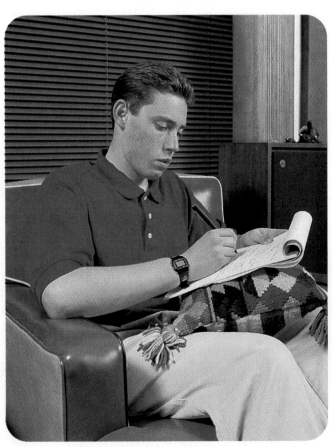

During a job interview, you gather information that you may need later. Write this down so it isn't forgotten. Comparing jobs and taking follow-up action is easier when you have made notes for later reference.

- Name and title of the interviewer
- Details of the job description
- Pay and benefits
- Date position is to be filled
- Advantages of the job, such as paid courses, on-site training, and conference attendance
- Your impressions of the job (perhaps including program, staff, children, and facility)

Send a thank you note to the interviewer (to each one if there were several). Thank the interviewer again for seeing you, and say that you look forward to hearing from him or her. You may be asked back for another interview before a final decision is made.

THE JOB OFFER

If all goes well, you may receive a job offer. Will you take the job or not? For each person, different factors enter into the decision. Do you need a job right away? Are you likely to get other offers? How strong is your interest in this job? Are you well suited for the job? Whatever the situation, each person needs to think carefully in order to reach a decision.

Keep in mind that job stability looks good on a resumé. If you resign after a short time, you may be viewed as a poor risk for future jobs. The more often this happens, the worse it looks. Try to take a job that you can be committed to for a reasonable time.

If you are lucky enough to have more than one job offer, you may request time from employers to make your choice. You may want to tell them—without applying pressure—that you are considering other job offers. To help in making your decision, write down the pros and cons of each job. Use the notes you made during and after each interview.

Finding a job isn't always easy. Sometimes offers don't come along, or it takes a long search to get one. Don't give up. Instead, try to turn the situation around. First, think positive and let your upbeat attitude show. If you do, you will gain admiration and interest from others, including employers and people who can help you. Keep in mind that even people who have become highly successful have experienced rejection.

Second, analyze your approach. Are you the best candidate for a job that you can be? You may need to take classes to improve your job skills. Polishing your job-hunting skills may be necessary too. Putting your best foot forward takes effort, but the results can make it all worthwhile.

ON THE JOB

Starting a new job can be a little frightening. You have new things to learn, in a new situation, and with people you may never have met before.

On the first day of work, plan to arrive a few minutes early. Find out in advance where you should go and to whom you report. Bring any documents or information you need to complete insurance and tax withholding forms.

Be an observant, active learner. Ask questions and follow directions carefully. Don't be afraid to show inexperience or lack of knowledge. Other workers know you are new on the job. They will respect you for your willingness to learn and your interest in doing the best job possible. If you notice anything that you would like to do differently, save your ideas. They will be more acceptable to others later, after you have gained their trust.

As you learn, be patient with yourself. Pat yourself on the back when you perform well. When you do not, make a mental note about

Self-Confidence

WHAT IS SELF-CONFIDENCE?

Self-confidence is belief in your ability to handle situations well. Having self-confidence allows you to try new things, to take reasonable risks, and to risk failure. Experience and knowledge help you feel self-confident, but how you feel about yourself is even more important. When you like yourself and believe you have something to offer, you feel confident, even in unfamiliar or challenging situations.

Self-Confidence in Action

Troy looked out on the rows of anxious young faces. "Good morning," he began. "I'm Mr. Miller. I know this classroom is new to all of you, and I'm a new teacher for you too. This is even a new school for some of you. I know how it feels to be new, because this is my first year here." Troy paused, noticing the serious expressions on the first-graders' faces.

"I'll tell you what," he continued. "I'll help you if you help me. Then being new will be easier on all of us. We have plenty to do this year, and I'm excited about it, because I love children and I love to teach. You're going to learn a lot in the days and weeks ahead, but do you know who's going to be the first one to learn something? Me. I have to learn who you are. Let's

do this. When I call your name, I want you to stand up and tell me one thing about yourself that makes you happy."

The first name Troy called was Vinnie Harper. A boy stood up and said nothing. He looked at the floor.

"So you're Vinnie Harper," Troy said with a smile. "*The* Vinnie Harper? The one I've heard so many good things about? Tell me one thing about yourself and then I'll know."

The boy looked up and said quietly, "I have a dog named Spunky."

"You *are* the one," Troy said enthusiastically. "I can see that this is going to be a great class. We have at least one terrific student—and who knows how many more that I don't even know about yet!"

The other children smiled and Vinnie relaxed as a pleased expression crept over his face. When Troy called the next name, Jennifer quickly stood up. She was eager to tell everyone about the oatmeal cookies she and her grandmother had made over the weekend.

Your Analysis

1. How did Troy reveal self-confidence in talking to his class?

2. How did Troy's self-confidence help him inspire self-confidence in his students?

3. Describe the relationship between self-confidence and self-esteem.

4. How can self-confidence be beneficial when a person works with children?

doing better in the future. Acknowledge your mistakes, but don't dwell on them. Remember that the only people who never make mistakes are those who never do *anything*. Mistakes are inevitable in the learning process.

Get to know the people you work with. If you are not introduced to everyone, make the effort to introduce yourself. Identify the jobs of other employees, and learn how their jobs relate to yours. Remember that first impressions are often wrong. Reserve judgments about people until you really get to know them.

Begin right away to build good relationships with others. A friendly approach helps. You can show respect by listening and being considerate. Avoiding conversations that focus on gossip is a good idea. By pitching in to help and following the rules, you practice cooperation. Getting along well with others helps make going to work a pleasure and is an important key to keeping a job.

CHANGING JOBS

The average worker changes jobs over half a dozen times in his or her working life. People leave jobs for many reasons. They may want a better job or one that they enjoy more. Whatever the reason, certain guidelines make job changes go more smoothly.

Make sure you leave a job on the best terms possible. Since your record does follow you, it pays to do all you can to leave on a positive note. Here are some suggestions for these situations:

- Do your job searching on your own time, not your current employer's.
- Continue to work hard even when you are looking for another job.
- As you talk to prospective employers, refrain from expressing any complaints about your current job. Otherwise, you may put yourself in a negative light.
- Give at least a two-week notice before you leave.
- When appropriate, volunteer to help find and train your replacement.

Taking notes when you're new on the job can be helpful. It shows others that you take your responsibilities seriously.

YOUR CAREER AHEAD

As a young person, most of your life is still ahead of you. Work is likely to be a significant part of those years. Now is when you set the stage for what your life's work will be. If you learn what it takes to land the job you want and you put that knowledge into practice, you will make progress toward a bright future.

Chapter 29 Review

Chapter Summary

- You can learn about job openings through many different sources.
- The application process may include writing a letter of application, sending a resumé, filling out an application, and going for an interview.
- Prepare ahead for the interview to improve your chances of being hired.
- Answer interview questions honestly. Be positive and enthusiastic.
- Consider carefully before accepting a job offer and when choosing from more than one.
- The first weeks on a new job can be challenging because you have much to learn in a new situation.
- If you decide to change jobs, try to leave your current job on good terms.

Reviewing the Facts

1. How is a letter of inquiry different from a letter of application?
2. How can a job search notebook help you?
3. Give three ways that you can use to find out about employers' recruitment efforts.
4. How does networking help people find jobs?
5. What information should you include on your resumé if you don't have much work experience? Why is this helpful?
6. What is the purpose of a job interview?
7. Identify and briefly describe four things you can do to prepare for an interview.
8. Give five tips for conducting yourself during an interview.
9. What should your reaction be if you don't get a job offer?
10. Suggest three ways to be successful when you are new on the job.
11. Why should you leave a job on the best terms possible?

Thinking Critically

1. Suppose you send out several letters of inquiry and get no responses. What might have happened? What would you do?
2. Why do such things as a neat appearance and well-written letter and resumé make a difference when job hunting?
3. Some people look at an interview that didn't go well as a good experience. What good might come from such an interview?
4. How are good communication skills (reading, writing, speaking, and listening) useful in a job search?
5. What kinds of questions do you think would be inappropriate in an interview? How would you respond to a question you were uncomfortable answering?
6. Should you ever take a job that doesn't really appeal to you? Explain your answer.

Activities and Applications

1. **Interview Preparation.** Tape or video record yourself answering the following question: Why do you want to work with young children? Play the tape and evaluate your answer. Was your answer clear and convincing? Did it make sense?
2. **Interview Practice.** With a partner, assume that

you are each going to interview for a position as a teacher's aide in a child care program. Individually, prepare questions that an interviewer might ask. Then take turns interviewing each other for the position.

3. **Newspaper Research.** Clip and collect newspaper advertisements for jobs in child care. Analyze whether you would be a qualified applicant for any of the jobs after high school graduation, and if not, why.

SCHOOL TO WORK

Your Professional Portfolio

Try writing your own resumé. Type it on good quality typing paper. Make any corrections as neatly as possible after proofreading. If possible, use a computer to prepare and store the resumé so that it can be easily updated. Keep your resumé in your portfolio.

Observing and Analyzing

Observation and the Job Hunt

As you near the end of this course, your observation skills should be sharpening. Much of the time you have observed in order to learn about children. You can also use your powers of observation to gain information that will help you in other ways.

Think about this statement: The more observant you are, the better chance you have of getting a job. Do you agree? Try these ideas to discover how observation can help you find and land a job:

- **Looking for Leads.** Some communities have places where job leads are posted. Have you noticed any in yours? Where are public bulletin boards available? Do they contain job leads? Locate one or two boards if you can, and note the kinds of jobs advertised.

- **Networking Possibilities.** Begin a list of people that you would like to add to your personal network. Consider including school personnel, business people, and community leaders. How could you get to know some of these people better? Are there meetings you could attend or organizations you could join? Make

an effort to build one or two new relationships that might be helpful to you.

- **Proofreading Skills.** How observant are you when it comes to finding errors in written material? Remember that letters of inquiry and resumés need to be free of errors, including typographical ones. Try exchanging typed writing samples with a partner and reading them carefully to find problems. (You might each create a typed sample with intentional errors.) Your success with finding the errors will indicate how important it is for you to have someone else proofread your letter and resumé after you create them.

Chapter 30

Growing as a Professional

CHAPTER OBJECTIVES

- Devise a plan for making and meeting career goals.

- Identify and describe sources of information about careers.

- Give examples of personal considerations that affect career choice.

- Describe opportunities for continuing education in the child care field.

- Give strategies for balancing work and personal life.

- Explain how a child care professional displays character.

Terms to Learn

- burnout
- career path
- character
- conferences
- continuing education
- entrepreneur
- occupational briefs
- professionalism

To sum up, I've been very pleased with your performance," Mrs. Snyder said. "We're happy that you joined our staff, Colleen."

Colleen had been working as a teacher's aide for six months. Earlier in the morning she had felt a little nervous at the prospect of her first performance review. Then Mrs. Snyder's reassuring smile let her know she had nothing to worry about.

"Now I'd like to hear what you have to say," Mrs. Snyder continued. "How do you feel things have been going?"

"Well, it's been challenging at times, but I really enjoy my job." Colleen thought for a moment. "I guess my favorite part is helping to plan activities—like the time you asked me to come up with a special theme for the week."

"Under the Sea Week was the most fun we've had around here in a long time," said Mrs. Snyder. "The children learned a lot, and they loved it. So did the parents and staff. And most of the credit goes to you, Colleen. You came up with some unique activities and managed to pull all the resources together. Maybe you should give some thought to being a curriculum coordinator."

The director's praise gave Colleen something to think about. Organizing a theme week had given her a great sense of accomplishment. Now, the director's confidence that she could tackle bigger challenges made her feel genuinely valued and respected as well. Colleen felt herself becoming a vital part of the child care center—and of the child care profession.

BECOMING A PROFESSIONAL

As a young person just starting out, Colleen has a sense of something special ahead. She wants to do more than just work at a job. She wants to be a professional.

You have seen the word "professional" used throughout this text. In Chapter 14, you read about many personal qualities that are part of being a child care professional—but there is more.

A professional makes work a meaningful part of life. Work becomes not just something to do, nor is it just a way to earn a living. A professional makes an effort to build a career that brings satisfaction along with challenge. He or she displays **professionalism**, *a sense of commitment, enthusiasm, and responsibility associated with a career.* To put professionalism into action, a person:

- Creates and pursues a career plan.
- Continues to learn.
- Balances work with personal life.
- Develops character.

CREATING A CAREER PLAN

*I*f you don't know where you're going, you may end up someplace else." This saying can easily be true of a person's career. Your career is your life's work within a certain field of employment. If you know where you want your career to head, you are likely to get there. Ignoring the future, however, and neglecting to set goals may set you adrift. Your decisions remain unguided. Your career may never take the right directions.

Some people begin their career with goals firmly in mind. Others gradually clarify their goals as they work toward them. Either way, it takes planning to get from where you are now to where you want to be. Part of that effort is developing a **career path**, *a plan for each step that will take you to your career goals*. To sketch out a career path, you need information. You must take a close look at what opportunities are available. Then you need to evaluate how well the options suit you before you begin to plan.

Researching Careers

By this time in your study, you should have some ideas about careers that sound interesting. Follow up on your interests by talking to professionals themselves, if possible. They can give you the clearest idea of what the careers are really like.

Libraries are another source of information about careers. Most libraries have trade magazines of various professions. These magazines have information about different careers in specific fields. Some libraries also have pamphlet files that contain **occupation-**

al briefs, or *summaries of specific jobs*. These files are indexed in the card catalog. The librarian can show you how to locate them.

Libraries usually carry three other publications that are also valuable resources for career research:

- **The Occupational Outlook Handbook (OOH).** This book gives information about a job's potential for growth in the future. (Remember that while child care is a rapidly expanding field, the demand is greater for some positions than others.) In addition, the *OOH* tells about job duties, working conditions, levels and places of employment, possibilities for advancement, education and training requirements, and average salary. It also lists sources of additional information. Be sure to use the most recent edition of the *OOH*, since salaries and job outlooks can change.

- **The Dictionary of Occupational Titles (DOT).** Here you will find detailed descriptions of the duties and responsibilities of more than 20,000 jobs. It does not tell about the education or training required for them, however. Be sure to read the instructions on how to use the *DOT*. If you need assistance, ask the librarian.

- **The Guide for Occupation Exploration (GOE).** This guide organizes jobs according to interest categories, including artistic, mechanical, plants and animals, and humanitarian. These categories are further broken down into worker trait groups, with jobs listed according to the traits that are most helpful to job performance. Under each worker trait group,

Tip FROM THE *Pros*

*A*ttitude toward the job affects employee stress and job burnout. Loving your work, thinking of your career as a vocation or calling, and looking forward to each day— these are defenses against burnout. Explore career options until you find the career that's right for you. It can make a big difference in your life.

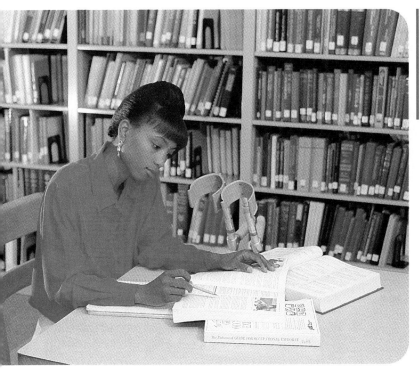

Library resources are a good source of information about careers. Where would you look to learn what jobs match your specific interests? To find out whether demand for a particular job is expected to grow in the future?

care might best "fit" you, take a personal inventory.

First, review what you read in Chapter 2 about choosing a child care career. Does the field still appeal to you? If so, what positions would you like to aim for, now and later? Do these agree with your values and priorities? To find out, examine your thoughts about such things as work schedules and income.

you will find a job description, plus information about required skills, education, and training. The *GOE* also suggests interests and aptitudes that go along with jobs.

Taking a Personal Inventory

Have you ever tried on clothes that were fashionable and fit your body, but didn't suit *you*? A career can be like that. Although a career may seem very attractive at first glance, you won't be comfortable with it unless it complements the real you. To find out how a career in child

Before a career choice is made, people need to examine their personal skills and interests. How might someone use artistic talent in a profession that relates to children?

Next, think about your personal strengths and characteristics. You already know the qualities of a successful child care professional—flexibility, creativity, and many others. You probably also have interests and talents that would help you be more successful in one child care career than in another. Would you enjoy the planning, problem solving, and management required of an administrative position, or does caring for individual children and developing personal relationships with them sound more rewarding?

Finally, consider training and education. How much of either of these are you willing or able to pursue? Some jobs require only a high school diploma; others take two or more years of advanced education. Jobs with more responsibility and greater income potential call for training and education in your career plan.

Entrepreneurship

As you examine your interests and abilities, you may discover things about yourself that open up other possibilities for your career. Perhaps you could be a successful entrepreneur. An **entrepreneur** (AHN-truh-pruh-NUR) is *someone who owns and operates a business.* Here are questions to ask yourself if this sounds appealing to you:

- Do I have the necessary experience and knowledge of children and child care itself?
- Do I have, or can I get, the financial backing to start a business?
- Am I willing to become informed about laws related to operating a business, such as those concerning taxes, employee rights, safety regulations, and zoning?
- Do I have the time and energy to start the business and maintain it on a daily basis?
- Am I mature enough to accept ultimate responsibility for a business?

- Do I have the patience and commitment to see a business through problems and difficult times?
- How will running a business affect my family and personal life?

Entrepreneurship can be exciting, but there are risks as well as rewards. The satisfaction of being your own boss is a plus. So is the freedom you have to use your talents and ideas as you see fit. On the other hand, if the business fails, the loss is yours, not someone else's.

Making a Plan

Suppose you have identified a career that appeals to you. In many ways it seems right for you. How do you use what you know about the career to develop a career path?

When Colleen's director suggested that she become a curriculum coordinator, Colleen researched the position. She found that she would need a bachelor's degree in early childhood education, followed by three years of experience teaching and planning the curriculum in an early childhood classroom. In addition she would need experience working with a team of professionals and also with children who have special needs.

Colleen used that information to devise a career path. She outlined the plan this way:

- Enroll part-time in a college program to obtain a bachelor's degree.
- Continue to work part-time as a teacher's aide in order to pay for education and stay current in the field.
- Upon graduation, teach in an early childhood program that includes children with special needs.
- After three years, seek a position as a curriculum coordinator.

Remember that traveling on your career path may take longer than you expect, and

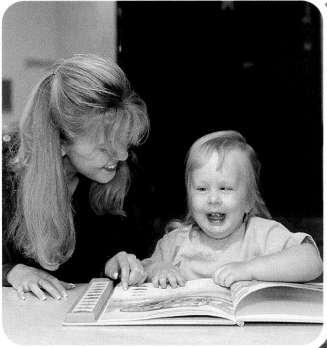

Having a career plan can help you decide what steps to take. It can motivate you to acquire the education and experience you need to qualify for the position you hope to hold someday.

you may have to take some detours. You may even change your mind somewhere along the way in order to pursue a different goal. That's okay. The plan is what's important because it guides you. Having a plan is vital to achieving your goals for professional growth in the child care field.

CONTINUING TO LEARN

*T*he world is a quickly changing one, full of new information and new processes. Keeping up with the latest developments requires continual learning. Through **continuing education** *people acquire new knowledge and experience, even after obtaining a career position. Continuing education refines and updates job skills.* It may also help rekindle diminishing interests and spark new ones. All of these benefits are of concern to the person who wants to grow as a professional.

Continuing education takes different forms. Some are single events, and some ongoing experiences. They may be free of charge or involve costs. Child care professionals are always looking for continuing education opportunities that fit their needs as well as their budgets. They might:

- Attend a class on new children's literature at a community college.

- Take classes that lead to a degree.
- Learn first aid and CPR.
- Observe teachers in other programs.
- Attend a weekend workshop on discipline, curriculum, or administration.
- Travel to another country to visit early childhood programs.

One simple and relatively inexpensive way to continue education is to join organizations in the field and subscribe to their periodicals. These magazines are a good resource for new ideas and products.

Conferences

As part of their continuing education, many professionals attend conferences. **Conferences** *are large gatherings at which members of a specific profession exchange information about the latest findings, developments, and practices in their field.*

The National Association for the Education of Young Children hosts a yearly conference of about 20,000 early childhood

Training in first aid techniques could help someone qualify for a position as an infant caregiver. What other types of continuing education might be needed?

Viewing product displays is just one of the ways to gain information at a professional conference, such as the annual meeting of NAEYC.

professionals. It lasts four days. At this conference, people within the profession attend workshops conducted by their peers. Experts speak on subjects of importance to child care professionals. Businesses display the latest in early education and child care materials and equipment.

Other child care groups that sponsor conferences include the American Association of Family and Consumer Sciences, The Children's Defense Fund, and the Association for Childhood Education International. Many organizations also plan local conferences that you can learn about by calling your local child care and referral agency.

CDA Certification

Earning the Child Development Associate (CDA) credential is another type of continuing education. (In Chapter 2 you read about the CDA and how to obtain more information on it.) One of the requirements for receiving this credential is the completion of 120 hours of formal education in several subject areas. The subject areas are related to the six competencies listed in the appendix at the back of this text. Courses may be offered by colleges and universities or by organizations recognized for early childhood teacher preparation.

Pursuing the CDA credential benefits candidates. It lets them measure their own skills and knowledge against a national standard. It gives them feedback from peers and authorities in the field, which they can use to grow as professionals. Because the CDA credential is a valued award, it provides incentive to learn new skills or fine-tune existing ones in order to be accredited.

BALANCING WORK AND PERSONAL LIFE

As you can see, professionals strive to become the best that they can be in their work. Sometimes, however, they go too far. They may focus solely on their career at the expense of personal life. The result is often **burnout**. People with this problem are *physically and emotionally exhausted from too much time and attention spent on the job.* They lose energy and enthusiasm, leaving them drained and bored. Whether labeled as burnout or not, excessive career pressures can limit personal time or make it less enjoyable.

Just as disturbing is what happens when people have too much responsibility and commitment in their personal lives. Overburdened, they may be tired and unable to function as they should. The effect easily carries over to their work life.

Professionalism doesn't survive well when either one of these situations continues. Successful people learn to manage their work and personal lives so that they are complementary.

Concern about how to balance work and personal life has grown over the years. Both women and men have careers outside the home today. Careers can be time-consuming. For married as well as single people, busy personal schedules add to the challenge of managing daily life. When children are part of a family, additional responsibilities exist.

People need methods for making their lives run smoothly. Many ideas are available. In Chapter 14 you read about some that focus on time and stress management. Here are some additional strategies to use:

- **Set priorities.** Seldom is there time to accomplish everything you want to do, at work or at home. Decide what is most important and do that first.

- **Divide responsibilities.** Work with others to determine how tasks can be shared. At work, a coworker might create a bulletin board while you plan an activity. In a family setting, you might have a family meeting to discuss what needs to be done and who will take care of each task. When responsibilities are divided among family members, everyone has a chance for some free time.

- **Include time for fun.** People schedule their work hours, so why shouldn't they make time for fun? Leisure activities help you release tension from the pressures of career and other responsibilities. Plan time for personal activities that you enjoy. Families also need to include time for fun

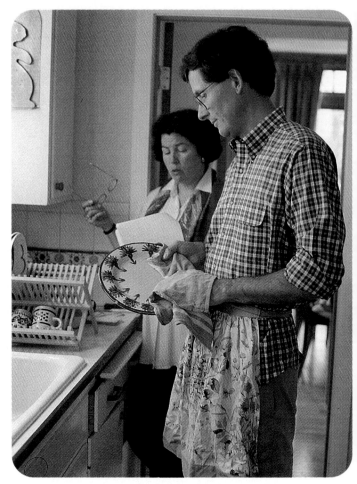

Household work is time-consuming. An employed person who has most of the household responsibilities as well has little time left to relax. That can lead to stress and other problems. How might families remedy such a situation?

together. Relationships improve and families grow stronger when family members share pleasurable moments.

- **Get involved in the community.** Look for opportunities to help others and make improvements in your community. You will be reminded that work is not all that's important in life. You may also develop a sense of pride and satisfaction with your efforts. Be careful, however, that community involvement does not demand too much from limited reserves of time and energy.

- *Develop a spiritual side.* Everyone needs time for reflection and meditation, whether you find it while walking on the beach, reading poetry, or attending worship services. Staying in touch with your beliefs and attitudes can help you keep your goals and values in clear focus.

- *Solve problems.* Since problems in either work or personal life can cause problems in the other, solutions are needed. Problems can be anything from too many household jobs to do, to a need for child care, to family violence. Resolving or avoiding problems takes the effort of everyone involved—the professional, the family, and the employer. When problems are serious ones, such as alcoholism and marital difficulties, professional counselors may be needed.

Many employers take a supportive role in helping employees manage work and personal life. Some allow flexibility in work hours so that people can tend to important personal concerns. Other creative ways for employers to accommodate employees are needed.

THE MULTICULTURAL CLASSROOM

When something interferes with your ability to give children the best possible start in life, change is necessary. That's part of growing as a professional. Do you have biases that need to be corrected? Admitting to having biased views about other cultures and groups in society is not a failure. It is, in fact, a step toward personal and professional growth. The National Association for the Education of Young Children offers these suggestions for evaluating your own attitudes about gender, culture, and differences:

- Write a description of your own ethnic identity. Which elements of your background are relevant to your personal identity? Which are not?

- Make a list of behaviors that you consider acceptable and unacceptable for males and females.

- Rewrite a fairy tale with traditional, clearly defined gender roles, switching the genders of the characters. How comfortable are you with this new version?

- List disabilities that make you feel comfortable and uncomfortable. Are some disabilities more difficult for you to deal with? If so, why?

An honest assessment of your own biases can make you more sensitive in promoting multiculturalism. Three valuable resources for learning more about teaching respect and appreciation for people of all cultures are *Hands Around the World* by Susan Milord (Charlotte, VT: Williamson Publishing, 1992); *Roots & Wings: Affirming Culture in Early Childhood Programs* by Stacey York (St. Paul, MN: Red Leaf Press, 1991); and *Anti-Bias Curriculum* by Louise Derman-Sparks and the ABC Task Force (Washington, DC: National Association for the Education of Young Children, 1993).

Building Professional Skills

Confidentiality

WHAT IS CONFIDENTIALITY?

As you know, professional ethics require child care professionals to withhold confidential information about the child and his or her family from other people. This is a protection for everyone involved and is critical in promoting good communication between the home and the facility.

Confidentiality in Action

Lisa, a teacher's aide, was helping her class of four-year-olds get ready to go home. Joey's mother, Mrs. Redmond, had arrived a little early. She drew Lisa aside for a chat.

"That Russell keeps bothering Joey. Every day, Joey comes home with a different story about Russell, about his terrible behavior. What's wrong with Russell anyway? Why is he like that?"

Russell's problem, Lisa knew, was a disordered home life. His parents were divorcing. His father was an alcoholic, and his mother was having a difficult time dealing with the situation. Lisa told Mrs. Redmond none of this, however.

Instead, she said, "We are aware of the problem with Russell, Mrs. Redmond, and we're working on it. We feel confident that things will smooth out shortly. I'll pay close attention to how Russell and Joey interact and look for some ways to improve the situation. "

As Lisa turned, she noticed that Russell's mother had just walked in the door. Lisa smiled warmly, hoping that Russell's mother had not overheard Mrs. Redmond's comments.

Russell's mother smiled back self-consciously and busied herself with gathering her son's art papers. The conversation had reached her ears. She felt concern for Russell's behavior, but she also felt relief. She was relieved that Lisa had said nothing about her problems. Knowing she could trust the center's staff with personal information gave her some peace of mind at a time when she needed it the most.

Your Analysis

1. Why didn't Lisa just tell Mrs. Redmond all of the truth?

2. How might Russell's mother have reacted if Lisa had told Mrs. Redmond about her family problems? How might this have affected Lisa? How might it have affected the center? What effect could it have on Russell?

Even in a field like child care, where budgets are often low and children need constant care, solutions can be found. One mother of a three-year-old, for example, solved her need for child care through an arrangement with her employer. Since she worked in a child care center, she brought her son to the site where she worked. Solving her child care problem gave her peace of mind and allowed her to focus her full attention on her duties as a child care professional.

DEVELOPING CHARACTER

*W*hat is the mark of a true professional? Some might say dedication. Some might say knowledge of the field. Others might say achievement. Opinions may vary, but most would agree that character, as much as any other quality, earns respect and admiration. It is a quality worth developing.

Character is *what people have when they are morally strong*. Their decisions and actions are based on clear principles of right and wrong. In other words, they operate under a code of ethics, as you read in Chapter 14.

If you become a child care professional, how will you demonstrate character? What does it mean to have character in such a profession? It means that you take your responsibilities seriously. You genuinely care about doing your job well. You are concerned about the image of child care and those who work with children. You realize that your behavior and attitude reflect on the profes-

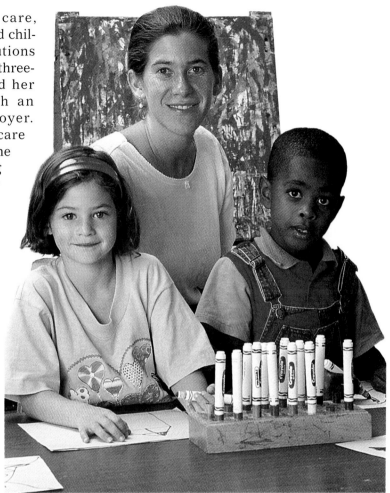

Children are the future. As they are shaped, so too is the society of tomorrow. Child care professionals have a serious, yet fulfilling, mission ahead of them. Can the profession count on you to join in that mission?

sion as a whole, and you act accordingly. Fairness, honesty, and consideration mark your behavior. Above all, you respect children and want the best for each and every one. You are proud to be recognized as a child care professional—and it shows. If you are to be a true professional, it is goals like these that will guide you.

Chapter 30 Review

Chapter Summary

- As a professional, you need to think about your long-term role in the child care field.
- When exploring careers, consider your values and personal traits, and look for employment opportunities that suit them.
- Professionals who are willing to take the risks of entrepreneurship can find opportunities in child care.
- Continuing education is necessary for maintaining skills and growing in the profession.
- Professionals can develop coping strategies to avoid burnout and balance work and personal life.
- A true professional develops character and demonstrates it in his or her career.

Reviewing the Facts

1. What does it mean to be a professional?
2. Why is a career path important to a professional?
3. Identify the *OOH* and the *GOE*. Briefly explain how each is used.
4. Explain three personal considerations when choosing a career.
5. What is an entrepreneur?
6. Give three suggestions for continuing your education after you've started to work.
7. Describe three ways that seeking the CDA credential benefits candidates.
8. What is job burnout? What causes it?
9. List four strategies for balancing work and personal life.
10. How does a child care professional show character?

Thinking Critically

1. In planning a career path, why is it important to find out in advance all requirements of your chosen position?
2. Tammy wants to work in her career for a while and then get married and stay home for a few years to raise her children. Do you think she needs a career plan? Explain your answer.
3. What is the relationship between professionalism and the level of quality in child care programs throughout the country?
4. What might happen when a professional neglects continuing education? What effect might this have on a career? On coworkers? On the people the professional serves?
5. Explain this irony of job burnout: Those professionals who are most prone to it are the ones that the profession can least afford to lose.
6. Suppose that you talk to a professional about a career that interests you. The person tells you about some poor experiences he or she has had. How will this information affect your thinking about the career?

Activities and Applications

1. **Career Exploration.** Use one or more of the career reference books described in the chapter (*OOH*, *DOT*, and *GOE*) to learn more about child care careers that sound interesting. Narrow your selection to two careers and summarize information on each in paragraph form.

Chapter 30 Review

2. **Delegating Family Responsibilities.** Working with a partner, make a list of tasks that must be done regularly in a household. Create an imaginary family and decide how responsibilities might be divided among the members.

3. **Complete the Sentence.** Assume that you are headed for a career in child care. In writing, complete the following sentence: "I will be considered a professional because . . ." Use additional sentences if you wish.

SCHOOL TO WORK

Your Professional Portfolio

Choose a career in the child care field that interests you. Write a career plan that could lead you to this career. Include the amount of time that would be involved at each step. Place the plan in your portfolio.

Observing and Analyzing

Observation Continues

As this course comes to a close, think about how your observation skills have developed. You began by simply sharpening your ability to notice what was going on around you. Then you learned to watch children for specific purposes. What you learned in the course became more real to you and more understandable through firsthand observation.

Just because this course is over does not mean that your opportunity to observe has come to an end. In fact, this is just the beginning. The future holds much for you in terms of observation. Whatever career direction you take, you can use the skills you have learned. Observation skills will help you in your professional, as well as personal, life. Using them will make you more aware of what people around you are doing and thinking. Your relationships with coworkers and others can thrive when you pay close attention to their words and actions and then base your responses on what you have observed.

If you decide to become a child care professional, part of your growth will depend on your ability to be a competent observer.

Continue to evaluate your skills by asking yourself questions like the ones below. The answers will keep you in touch with your abilities and help you become the best child care professional that you can be.

Ask yourself:

- Do I demonstrate my concern for children by taking time to observe them?
- Am I willing to listen as much or more than I speak?
- Have I developed an awareness of details?
- Am I willing to take advice from others on how and what to observe?
- Do I record what I actually see rather than my opinions?
- Do I place value on the observations that others make?
- Do I form opinions only by listening to someone else, or do I make my own observations too?
- Am I careful about what I say to others about my observations?
- Do I respond to children, not just direct them?
- Do I act on my observations in an appropriate manner, so that children can benefit from what I discover?

Career Profile

Meet Marlina Vladamir, who operates a family day care program in her home. Marlina currently cares for six children, ages six months to ten years.

Why did you choose this career?

"I have to say that I do enjoy working with young children and their families, but there's a practical side to my career choice too. I used to work in a nursery school. When I had a child of my own, I decided to start a family day care business. Now I can stay at home with my child and earn an income at the same time."

What education and skills do you need?

"In my state I don't need any particular certificate or college degree to operate a home day care business. I would have really had a tough time, however, without my training and experience working at the nursery school. I've had college courses in early childhood education and four years of training in the nursery school job. I continue to attend family child care conferences to keep up with new curriculum ideas.

"I did have to have a background check to prove that I've never been convicted of child abuse. This is something that is routinely done to protect children.

"Since I'm running my own business, I had to educate myself on what's involved. The course I took on financial management from our Small Business Administration office was very useful. My home needed a 'diploma,' too—certificates showing that it meets fire, safety, and health codes. This allows me to be licensed by the state, which gives parents confidence in my program.

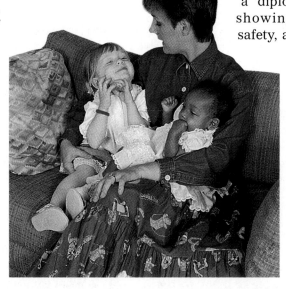

"As far as skills are concerned, I need the same ones that any other person who cares for young children should have. I need patience in guiding behavior and enthusiasm in leading learning activities. Since I care for younger and older children in one group, I have to work with all ages very well.

"Strong organization and management skills serve me well. I'm responsible for keeping all kinds of paperwork in order—insurance forms, tax returns, and bills to send to parents. I have to manage my space efficiently, too, since my business is also my family's home."

What is a typical day on the job like?

"I have a longer day than most people who work in child care. Parents begin bringing children around 6 a.m., and some are still here at 6 p.m. That means I must be ready early—and my home must be too. I follow a basic schedule of breakfast, then quiet indoor play, followed by active play, and then lunch. After lunch we have nap time, then an art or science project, more active play, and then stories until the parents arrive. I keep my schedule flexible so I can handle the needs of different age groups. If I'm caring for infants, I have to allow for frequent naps and feedings. If I have more toddlers, I count on more time for developing self-help skills. The activities I plan vary also, but they are similar to those found in a larger child care program."

What is most challenging about your job?

"Caring for children of such a wide age span is a daily challenge. I have to plan activities for all ages, from infants to ten-year-olds. I have to keep the house safe for creeping infants and active toddlers.

"Running my business from my home has other drawbacks. For instance, I work to balance my family's need for privacy with my client children's need for play space. More importantly, I have to balance my attention between my own child and the other children. My daughter has to 'share' Mommy with so many others. I try to understand when she seems jealous or possessive. If I can let her know she's special without making the other children feel less important, I've accomplished something."

What do you like best about your work?

"Working with just a few children in my own home, I become very close to their families. My clients and I are closer than some neighbors. We're almost an extended family. Sharing our experiences as parents helps us all to be better at caring for children. It also helps my own child's social development to become friends with such a variety of other children."

SHARE YOUR THOUGHTS

1. What type of child might benefit most from a family day care setting?
2. What might be some challenges in making a home safe for an infant, a toddler, and a school-age child?
3. What would you enjoy about operating a family day care program? What would you find difficult?

Appendix

CDA Competency Goals and Functional Areas

Candidates for the CDA credential are assessed according to CDA competency standards. These national standards are the criteria used to evaluate a caregiver's performance with children and families. The standards are summarized in the chart below. The chart shows six competency goals that are subdivided into 13 functional areas. Each task or function described must be carried out by the caregiver in order to accomplish the competency goals. Additional information on these standards can be obtained from The Council for Early Childhood Professional Recognition, 1341 G Street, NW, Suite 400, Washington, DC 20005-3105.

CDA COMPETENCY GOALS	FUNCTIONAL AREAS
I. To establish and maintain a safe, healthy, learning environment.	1. Safe: Candidate provides a safe environment to prevent and reduce injuries. 2. Healthy: Candidate promotes good health and nutrition and provides an environment that contributes to the prevention of illness. 3. Learning Environment: Candidate uses space, relationships, materials, and routines as resources for constructing an interesting, secure, and enjoyable environment that encourages play, exploration, and learning.
II. To advance physical and intellectual competence.	4. Physical: Candidate provides a variety of equipment, activities, and opportunities to promote the physical development of children. 5. Cognitive: Candidate provides activities and opportunities that encourage curiosity, exploration, and problem solving appropriate to the developmental levels and learning styles of children. 6. Communication: Candidate actively communicates with children and provides opportunities for support for children to understand, acquire, and use verbal and nonverbal means of communicating thoughts and feelings. 7. Creative: Candidate provides opportunities that stimulate children to play with sound, rhythm, language, materials, space and ideas in individual ways and to express their creative abilities.

III. To support social and emotional development and provide positive guidance.	8. Self: Candidate provides physical and emotional security for each child and helps each child know, accept and take pride in himself or herself and to develop a sense of independence.
	9. Social: Candidate helps each child feel accepted in the group, helps children learn to communicate and get along with others, and encourages feelings of empathy and mutual respect among children and adults.
	10. Guidance: Candidate provides a supportive environment in which children can begin to learn and practice appropriate and acceptable behaviors as individuals and as a group.
IV. To establish positive and productive relationships with families.	11. Families: Candidate maintains an open, friendly, and cooperative relationship with each child's family, encourages their involvement in the program, and supports the child's relationship with his or her family.
V. To ensure a well-run, purposeful program responsive to participant needs.	12. Program Management: Candidate is a manager who uses all available resources to ensure an effective operation. The Candidate is a competent organizer, planner, record keeper, communicator, and cooperative coworker.
VI. To maintain a commitment to professionalism.	13. Professionalism: Candidate makes decisions based on knowledge of early childhood theories and practices. Candidate promotes quality in child care services. Candidate takes advantage of opportunities to improve competence, both for personal and professional growth and for the benefit of children and families.

Glossary

A

accessible. Easily used by those with disabilities. (28)

accident log. A written record of all injuries as they happen. (10)

accident report form. A form used to record specific information about any accident involving a child. (10)

accommodation. A change in thinking that makes new information fit into what a person already knows and understands. (5)

action verses. Songs for which children act out the motions described in the lyrics. (22)

active listening. Responding with a description of what you think another person is feeling, and why. (15)

active play. Activities that are primarily physical. (24)

advisory board. A group of people, often parents, community members, or people in early childhood careers, who help directors develop and implement center policies. (8)

anecdotal record. A written description that focuses on a particular incident. (16)

antibodies. Substances produced by the immune system that when released into the blood help destroy disease-causing organisms. (11)

art. The use of skills and creative imagination to produce something pleasing. (18)

assimilation. Taking in new information and trying to make it fit with what is already known and understood. (5)

attachment behavior. When an infant shows signs of pleasure at the appearance of a caregiver and signs of distress when that person leaves. (4)

attention span. The ability to focus on a specific activity for a period of time. (5)

au pair. (oh PARE). A person who comes from one country to live with a family in another country, exchanging housework and child care for room and board. (1)

autonomy. (aw-TAHN-uh-mee). Independence. (5)

B

beat. The recurring pulse that gives a song rhythm. (22)

bias. Any attitude, belief, or feeling that results in unfair treatment of an individual because of his or her identity. (17)

bilingual. Ability to speak and understand two languages. (19)

body language. Gestures, body movements, and facial expressions that help convey meaning in conversation. (15)

bonding. Forming a strong attachment to, and preference for, the primary caregivers. (4)

burnout. Physical and emotional exhaustion from too much time and attention spent on the job. (30)

C

CDA advisor. An individual who counsels candidates and provides specific training for the CDA (child development associate) credential. (2)

call-and-response songs. A song in which an adult sings questions and children sing back the answers. (22)

cardiopulmonary resuscitation (CPR). (CAR-dee-oh-PULL-muh-NAIR-ee ree-SUH-suh-TAY-shun). A life-saving technique used when the heartbeat and/or breathing has stopped. Gentle puffs of air are given to the person while forcing the heart to pump blood by applying gentle pressure to the chest. (10)

career path. A plan for each step that will lead to career goals. (30)

Caregiver Report Form. A form used to organize and record the provision of routine care. (25)

centration. A term coined by Piaget to refer to how children in the preoperational period can focus on only one characteristic at a time when they sort objects. (6)

cephalocaudal. (SEF-uh-luh-KAWD-ull). A principle of development in which children master body movement and coordination from the head downward. (3)

character. A quality exemplified by moral strength. (30)

checklist. Specific information that an observer looks for while observing children. (16)

child abuse. Nonaccidental injury inflicted on a child. (11)

Child and Adult Care Food Program (CACFP). A federally funded program that helps provide healthful meals and snacks in child and adult care facilities. (13)

child care. A broad term that describes any situation in which children are provided with supervision, support, and sometimes training by individuals outside the child's immediate family. (1)

child care resource and referral specialist. An individual who works mainly on the telephone to assist parents in making child care arrangements. (2)

child development. The pattern of change that occurs as children grow from birth to adolescence. (3)

Child Development Associate (CDA) credential. Awarded to an applicant after the person demonstrates competency skills in specific areas of child care. (2)

child development consultants. Individuals who give child development advice to people who create children's products. (2)

child neglect. Failure to provide a child with the basic necessities of life, including food, clothing, shelter, and medical care. (11)

choice time. A technique used to let children decide which activity they would like to participate in next. (12)

chronological grouping. Placing children of the same age together. (17)

classification. Mentally grouping objects into categories according to similarities. (6)

close-ended materials. Items that are meant to be used in primarily one way, with an expected result. (17)

cognitive development. Intellectual development that occurs as children think, understand, reason, and use language. (3)

collage. (kuh-LAHZH). A picture or design made by gluing or pasting separate pieces of material to a background surface. (18)

communicable diseases. Infectious diseases that are passed from person to person. (11)

compassion. Recognizing when others are having problems and wanting to be of help. (2)

concepts. General ideas formed from other information. (5)

concrete operations period. A period of intellectual development identified by Piaget during which children (ages seven to eleven) think logically and relate logic to actual objects and experiences. (7)

conferences. Large gatherings at which members of a profession exchange information about the latest findings, developments, and practices in their field. (30)

confidentiality. Maintaining the privacy of others. (14)

confirmation letter. A letter that is sent to a potential employer in order to verify an agreement to meet at a certain time and date. (29)

conscience. (KAHNT-shunts). Attitudes about right and wrong that guide behavior. (6)

consequences. Events that occur as the result of a particular behavior. (15)

conservation. The understanding that an object's physical dimensions remain the same even when its appearance changes, a concept Piaget linked to the preoperational stage of intellectual development. (6)

continuing education. Acquiring new knowledge and experience, even after obtaining a career position. Continuing education refines and updates job skills. (30)

cooperative play. Playing together and agreeing on play themes and activities. (6)

cover letter. A letter of application that accompanies a resumé. (29)

creative movement. Responding to music through physical movement. (22)

criminal background check. An investigation to determine if an applicant has been convicted of a crime. (29)

cubby. A small space for storage of personal items. (9)

curriculum. A long-range plan of activities and experiences for children. (1)

custodial needs. Physical needs, such as toileting, hand washing, eating, napping, and resting. (9)

D

deficiency. Severe shortage. (13)

depth perception. The ability to judge distance and see objects in perspective. (7)

developmental grouping. Placing children together according to their ability. (17)

developmentally appropriate curriculum. Activities that are geared to different levels of ability and development in order to accommodate all children in a program. (1)

dioramas. (DY-uh-RA-muhs). Three-dimensional pictures made with small, cut-out designs. (18)

director. A key person in most child care settings. The director may work with children but has the primary responsibility of management. The director manages daily operations and guides the staff. (2)

diversity. The term often used today when talking about all the qualities people have that make them different from one another. (7)

dramatic play. The imitation of real-life situations during play. (6)

dress codes. Rules for dress in the workplace. (14)

E

early childhood. The years between birth and age eight. (1)

early childhood education. Child care programs that promote development through formal teaching and learning experiences for children up to age eight. (1)

early childhood professionals. People who work in early childhood programs. (2)

echo method. A method of teaching songs in which the children first listen as a line or verse is sung and then repeat it. (22)

egocentric. (ee-go-SEN-trick). Seeing everything from a person's own point of view. (4)

emergency treatment waiver form. A statement that is signed by a parent or legal guardian and gives permission to secure emergency medical treatment for a sick or injured child. (10)

emergent literacy. The gradual process of learning to read. (19)

emotions. Feelings about self, others, and the world. (3)

empathy. The ability to recognize and understand the feelings of others. (6)

entrepreneur. (AHN-truh-pruh-NUR). Someone who owns and operates a business. (30)

environment. Everything—objects, conditions, atmosphere—that makes up the surroundings. (1)

event record. A record that identifies a specific situation and describes what happens each time that situation occurs over a period of time. (16)

extended family. A description of family that includes relatives other than parents and children. (1)

eye-hand coordination. The ability to move the hands and fingers precisely in relation to what is seen. (4)

F

facilitate. To help bring about something without controlling it. For example, teachers facilitate children's play. (17)

family grouping. Placing children of a certain age range (including several different ages) in the same classroom or group. (17)

fine motor skills. Skills that require use of the small muscles, as in the fingers, wrists, and ankles. (5)

finger plays. Specific hand motions that accompany a song or chant. (19)

flannel board. A piece of cardboard or wood covered with flannel or felt and used to tell a story by attaching fabric pictures. (19)

focus object. An item that is related to an activity and helps introduce it. (17)

Food Guide Pyramid. A guide to daily food choices based on the recommendations of nutrition experts. (13)

frequency count. A record of how many times a particular behavior or situation occurs during a specific period of time. (16)

G

gender identity. The awareness of being male or female. (6)

gender role. The behavior and responsibilities expected of a man or woman in the family and society. (1)

gifted children. Children who are extraordinarily talented or excel in one or more areas. (28)

grand mal seizure. A complete loss of consciousness, with stiffening, jerking, or thrashing of the body. (11)

gross motor skills. Skills that use the large muscles of the back, legs, shoulders, and arms. (5)

growth plateau. A period of relatively slow and steady growth. (7)

H

health inspectors. Health department representatives who observe and evaluate a program's health practices. (13)

Heimlich maneuver. (HIME-lick muh-NOO-vur). A technique used in response to choking by applying pressure on the body to dislodge an object that is blocking air through the windpipe or throat. (10)

home visitor. A parent educator who goes into the child's home to teach the parent how to guide the children's learning and to answer parents' questions. (2)

hormones. Growth-regulating chemicals that are produced by the body and carried in the blood. (7)

hypothesis. A possible explanation based on observable facts. (23)

I

I-messages. An honest description given by a person in order to say how he or she is affected by and feels about certain behavior. (15)

immune system. A bodily system that produces antibodies that resist disease. (11)

immunization. A vaccine given orally or through a shot to protect the person from a particular disease. (11)

improvisations. Creating a melody and lyrics as the mood strikes. (22)

inclusion. Combining children with average abilities and children with special needs in the same classroom. (28)

Individualized Education Plan (IEP). A written plan that outlines how to encourage development in a child with special needs. (28)

industry. The desire to perform skills, succeed at tasks, and make social contributions. (7)

infancy. The time between birth and twelve months of age. (4)

infectious diseases. Illnesses that are caused by organisms that enter the body and damage tissue. (11)

inferiority. A feeling of not having met expected standards. (7)

initiative. (ih-NIH-shuh-tiv). Motivation to accomplish more. (6)

interview. A meeting between a job applicant and a potential employer. At this time the employer learns about the applicant and the applicant learns about the job. (29)

invented spelling. Spelling a word the way it sounds. (19)

isolation room. A separate, cozy, comfortable place to rest when children become ill while attending a child care program. (9)

J, K

job board. A device that shows jobs that children should do. (12)

job jar. A container filled with pieces of paper that show pictures of activities or jobs. (12)

L

language arts. Activities that teach children to listen, speak, read, and write. (19)

language chart. A large paper where children's verbal responses are recorded. (19)

latchkey children. Children who stay home alone before and after school. (27)

learning centers. Areas that are clearly defined for specific types of play and are organized around a theme or curriculum topic. Examples are music, science, and language arts. (9)

learning disability. A disorder that affects the way the brain processes information. (28)

lesson plan. A detailed, written explanation of an activity, including the purpose, any materials needed, and the step-by-step method for carrying out the activity. (17)

letter of application. A letter sent to a potential employer to apply for a job. (29)

letter of inquiry. A short letter sent to a potential employer to ask about job openings. (29)

liability insurance. An insurance policy that covers costs involved in any resulting lawsuit if a program is found responsible for an injury or damages that occur at the center or in connection with center activity. Medical costs for injury can be included in this insurance. (8)

liable for negligence. Held accountable in a court of law if found negligent in preventing an accident or handling an emergency in a responsible manner. (10)

licensing laws. Rules and regulations that early childhood programs must follow as outlined by individual state laws. (8)

literate. Able to read. (19)

lyrics. Words to songs. (22)

M

manipulatives. Toys and materials children operate and change with their hands. (17)

mathematical vocabulary. Words that express numbers and quantities. (23)

mathematics. The study of numbers and their functions, and of shapes. (23)

maturation. The gradual process of growth as each stage of development unfolds. (3)

maze. A deliberately confusing series of pathways. (24)

melody. The tune of a song. (22)

mobile. An art project made with a collection of items or pictures suspended on a wire by string. (18)

motor skills. Abilities that depend on the use and control of muscles. (3)

mural. A long, continuous painting or drawing on one very large piece of paper. (18)

N

nanny. Someone trained in child care and employed to go into the home to care for children. (1)

native language. The language spoken in the home and first learned by children. (19)

naturalistic observation. Observing children as they behave naturally in their everyday environment. (16)

negativism. Refusing to do, or doing the opposite of, what is asked. (26)

networking. Making and maintaining contact with others in order to exchange information and services. Within a profession, people network to find and fill jobs. (29)

noncommunicable diseases. Infectious diseases that do not pass from person to person. (11)

nontoxic. Not poisonous. (9)

nuclear family. A family consisting of a mother, father, and their children. (1)

numerals. Written symbols that represent numbers. (23)

nurture. (NUR-chur). To provide love, support, attention, and encouragement. (4)

nutrients. The substances that are found in food and used by the body to function, grow, repair itself, and produce energy. (13)

nutrition. The process through which the body utilizes the nutrients in food. (13)

O

object permanence. The understanding that an object continues to exist even when out of sight. (4)

occupational briefs. Summaries that describe specific jobs. (30)

on demand. According to individual needs. Feeding schedules of infants are on demand. (25)

one-to-one correspondence. The understanding that, when counting objects in a group, each item is counted once and only once. (6)

on-site. Located on the premises. (27)

open-ended materials. Items that can be used in a variety of ways, with no single "correct" outcome expected. (17)

open-ended questions. Questions that require more than a yes or no answer. (17)

origami. (OR-uh-GAH-mee). A special Japanese paper folding technique in which squares of tissue paper are folded into representational forms, such as birds. (18)

P, Q

parachute play. An active play activity in which a group of children participate in games based on the use of a large circle of nylon fabric. (24)

parallel play. Children playing near each other but not with each other. (5)

Parent Report Form. A form that details a child's activities and behavior before arrival at the center. (25)

participant observer. Someone who interacts with children while observing. (16)

pathogens. Disease-causing organisms, such as bacteria and viruses. (11)

perceptual motor skills. Skills that require the coordination of vision, intellect, and movement. (4)

perishable. Foods that will spoil if not refrigerated or frozen. (13)

personal hygiene (HI-jeen). Keeping the body clean in order to promote good health and prevent illness. (12)

petit mal seizures. (puh-TEE mahl). A few seconds during which consciousness is clouded and possibly a few muscles twitch. (11)

philosophy. General beliefs, concepts, and attitudes an early childhood program has about how children learn and how the program should serve and educate young children. (8)

pitch. The highness or lowness of musical sounds. (22)

policy. A statement of rules or guidelines that guide the actions and decision making of an organization. (8)

portfolio. A collection of actual samples of a person's work, put together to show his or her capabilities, often to a potential employer. The examples are assembled in a binder, folder, or some other type of container that allows for simple, attractive presentation. (2)

positive discipline. The process of teaching children acceptable behavior without harming them physically or emotionally. (15)

positive reinforcement. A response that rewards a particular positive behavior, making it more likely to be repeated. (15)

preoperational period. Piaget's second period of intellectual development that covers ages two to seven. In this period children start to think symbolically and imaginatively, relying less on motor skills and more on thinking to direct behavior. (5)

preschoolers. Children from three to five years of age. (6)

prevention. Taking action to keep something from happening. (10)

print making. Placing an object in paint and then pressing the object onto paper or another base material. (18)

print-rich environment. A setting in which printed materials are used throughout the classroom in meaningful ways; promotes language skills in children. (19)

process versus product. The belief that what children learn through the process of creating art is just as important, if not more important, than what they produce. (18)

productive language. The ability to use words to express yourself. (26)

professional. A person who possesses the education and training to perform a job well and has skills and qualities admired and respected by others. (14)

professional ethics. Standards of right and wrong that apply to a person's behavior as a professional. (14)

professionalism. A sense of commitment, enthusiasm, and responsibility associated with a career. (30)

program goals. Basic skills, concepts, and attitudes to be developed and encouraged in children; these are developed from an early childhood program's philosophy. (8)

prop box. A container for storing items used in a specific dramatic play theme. (20)

proportion. The size relationship of an object's parts. (18)

props. Items that suggest themes for dramatic play. (20)

proximodistal. (PRAHK-suh-MOE-DISS-tull). A principle of development in which children develop from the center of their body outward. (3)

puberty. A stage when boys and girls undergo a series of physical changes and develop into men and women who are able to reproduce. (7)

R

rating scale. A verbal or numerical evaluation of listed items; may be used as a technique for observing children. (16)

rational counting. The understanding that the last number counted in a group represents the entire number of objects. (6)

rebus recipe. A recipe that illustrates ingredients and directions with picture symbols. (23)

receptive language. The ability to understand words spoken by others. (26)

recruit. To actively seek, as when employers recruit candidates for a job. (29)

redirection. A guidance technique that steers a child who is misbehaving to a different, more acceptable activity. (15)

references. People who know you well and can provide a potential employer with information about your character and work habits. (29)

reflexes. Instinctive, involuntary reactions to a stimulus, such as a noise or a touch. (4)

resourcefulness. An ability to find the ways and means to do something. (2)

resumé. A written summary of education, work experience, and any special talents or skills; often prepared for a potential employer. (29)

rhythm instruments. Musical instruments, such as maracas and drums, that allow children to experiment with making their own rhythms. (22)

role model. A person whose behavior and attitude are imitated by others. (5)

role play. To assume the identity of someone else; may be part of dramatic play activities. (20)

rote counting. Reciting numbers in order without understanding that each number represents a specific amount. (6)

routine. A regular, expected procedure that is followed in order to accomplish something. Arrival, mealtime, and nap time, for example, are regular routines within a child care program. (12)

running record. A sequential record of anything that happens during a specific period of time; often used as a technique for observing children. (16)

S

safety hazards. Items, conditions, and situations that could cause physical or emotional danger. (10)

safety policy. A policy that states the rules and procedures to follow to insure physical and emotional well-being. (10)

sanitation. Practicing cleanliness to prevent the spread of illness and disease. (13)

sanitized. Cleaned in a way that will kill the organisms that can cause illness. (9)

schedule. A plan for how time will be used, placing events in the order that they will occur and indicating how long each event will last. (12)

school-age children. Children from the ages of six to twelve. (7)

science. A system of knowledge covering general truths and laws about the physical world. (23)

self-concept. The picture individuals carry in their mind of who they are, what they can do, and what they are like. (3)

self-control. The ability to react to difficult situations in a calm, productive manner instead of an emotional one. (14)

self-correcting. Educational materials that are designed to provide immediate feedback after a child correctly or incorrectly finishes the task. (8)

self-directed. When children respond on their own without having to be told what to do; leading to independence. (12)

self-discipline. The ability to guide your own behavior without help from others. (15)

self-esteem. How people feel about the image they have of themselves. (3)

self-help skills. Skills that allow children to help take care of themselves and their personal needs, such as self-feeding. (5)

sensorimotor period. (sents-ree-MOH-tur). Piaget's first stage of intellectual development, which describes the period from birth to age two when infants and one-year-olds learn by using their senses and motor abilities to gain information about the world. (4)

sensory table. A table with a boxlike, hollow top that can hold water, sand, beans, or other substances to play with. (23)

separation anxiety. A child's fear or stress at being separated from familiar people. (26)

sequence. A step-by-step pattern. (3)

seriation. Organizing objects according to increasing or decreasing size. (6)

social responsibility. The practice of making a positive contribution to the community and obeying community laws. (21)

social studies. The part of a curriculum that teaches children about themselves and their family, community, and the world. (21)

solitary play. Engaging in play alone rather than with other children. (5)

special needs. Circumstances that cause development to vary significantly from what is considered average. (28)

sphincter muscles (SFINK-tur). Muscles that surround certain body openings and have the ability to close them; control of such muscles is needed for toileting readiness in children. (12)

spontaneity. (SPAHN-tuh-NAY-uh-tee). Acting impulsively, or without taking time to use thinking and reasoning skills. (2)

spontaneous dramatic play. When children engage in dramatic play without the suggestion or direction of adults. (20)

staff-to-child ratio. The number of personnel in relation to the number of children in a classroom or group. (8)

staff turnover. The rate at which employees leave their jobs, creating the need for new employees to be hired. (25)

stereotype. A preset idea about a person or group of people based solely on one characteristic, such as gender, nationality, race, or religion. (6)

storytelling. A skill in which a person tells a story from memory instead of reading from a book. (19)

stranger anxiety. The fear of unfamiliar people, usually expressed by crying, that many infants develop. (4)

stress. Mental and physical tension and strain caused by problems, pressures, fears, or unsettling changes. (7)

syrup of ipecac. (IH-pih-kak). A substance given to cause vomiting in poisoning situations; it should only be used when vomiting the poisonous substance will not cause further internal damage. (10)

T, U

teachable moments. Unplanned opportunities for learning. (17)

teacher-directed. Activities in which a teacher leads and supervises children. (12)

temperament. A person's inborn style of reacting to the environment. (4)

temper tantrum. An episode in which children show anger or frustration in an aggressive or destructive way. (26)

tempo. The speed at which a song is sung. (22)

texture quilt. A quilt made from scraps of fabrics of different textures; infants use their sense of touch with these. (25)

thematic unit. A curriculum segment that is based on one central topic, or theme, about which children will learn. (17)

three-dimensional. Having height, width, and depth. (18)

time management. Planning to use time well in order to accomplish goals. (14)

time out. A short period of time in which a child must sit apart from other children and activities. (15)

toddler. A child between the ages of twelve and thirty-six months. (5)

toxic. Poisonous. (9)

traffic pattern. The direction of movement that children take as they move from one part of the classroom to another. (9)

transition. A short activity or technique used to help guide children smoothly from one activity or event to another. (12)

tutor. Someone who provides individual instruction on a regular basis. (27)

V

vaccine. A small amount of a disease-producing organism that is introduced into the body, usually by injection, so the body can build a resistance to it. (11)

values. Beliefs and attitudes about what is important. (3)

visual discrimination. The ability to notice similarities and differences in colors, shapes, and designs. (19)

vocalizations. Sounds infants make that imitate adult language. (4)

W, X, Y, Z

whole language. The practice of including language skill development in all classroom activities. (19)

Women, Infants, and Children (WIC) Program. A federally funded program that provides nutrition advice and low-cost food, including infant formula to low-income pregnant and breast-feeding women, infants, and children up to five years old. (13)

Index

Credits

Cover & Interior Design: William Seabright & Associates

Cover Photography: Robert F. Kusel

Illustrations:

Circle Design
  Carol Spengel: 174-175, 195
Morgan-Cain & Associates: 70-71, 203-204, 232-233
PALS Preschool & Kindergarten: 357
Jordan Parker: 175 t
Liz Purcell: 397

Photos:

Arnold & Brown: 51 t
Roger B. Bean: 20, 25, 29, 31, 40, 61 b, 64, 65 t, 67, 74 l, 81 l, 83, 85, 88, 89, 93, 97, 100, 101, 103, 106, 113, 118, 125, 136, 151, 155, 157 t, 159, 165, 166, 168, 169, 170, 173, 178, 186, 190, 194, 202, 207, 209, 211, 220, 223, 226, 228, 233 t, 234, 235, 236, 237, 238, 239 t, 246, 290, 294, 296, 298, 305, 315, 321, 327, 338, 343, 344, 346, 347, 349, 360, 363 t, 376, 377, 379 b, 381, 386, 392, 394, 406, 421, 424, 434, 437, 440, 441, 450, 452, 453, 455, 470, 471, 473 b, 474, 476, 477, 479, 480, 486 t, 487, 488, 490 b, 495, 496, 497, 499, 500, 503, 507, 508, 516, 521, 522, 523, 524 t, 525, 546, 560
Marshal Berman Photography/Design Office: 348, 379 t, 562
Keith Berry: 37, 38, 46-47, 51 b, 79, 95, 107, 112, 153, 160, 174 t tc b, 175 ct cb b, 192, 197, 200, 213 b, 224, 250, 268, 275, 316, 336, 359, 365, 372 t, 374, 378, 388, 389, 420, 423 t, 426 br bl, 427 t, 433, 436, 442, 458, 520 b, 539 b, 547 t, 553, 557 t, 559
The Bettmann Archive: 60
CLEO Freelance Photography: 80, 117, 128, 132, 134, 157 bl, 191, 514, 529

Constructive Playthings, U.S. Toy Co., Inc.: 174 cb, 448, 468, 472, 490 t, 491 b
Gail Denham: 116, 131, 135, 137, 188, 231, 248, 364, 403, 432
EF AuPair: 23
Fisher-Price: 473 t
FPG International Corp.
  Telegraph Colour Lib: 164
Cliff Gardiner, Jr.: 41 b, 121, 122, 355
Ann Garvin: 54-55, 90, 142-143, 163, 199, 244, 245, 253 t, 264-265, 271, 284, 306, 313, 330-331, 340, 353, 356, 384, 401, 402, 415, 429, 464-465, 469, 481, 532-533, 551, 568-569
Hasbro/Playskool: 176
John Hopkins: 177
Human Issues Collaborative
  Ron Chappel: 72
The Kids on the Block Inc.: 517
Robert F. Kusel: 1, 2-3, 14-15, 56-57, 144-145, 266-267, 332-333, 466-467, 534-535
Lakeshore Learning Materials, Carson, CA: 297, 368, 457
Mishima: 22 t, 65 b, 70 r, 71, 152 t, 243, 280, 299, 418, 454, 501, 506, 515, 537, 555, 565
Armando F. Mola: 380
NAEYC
  Melanie Rose White: 561
Nasco: 94, 167, 371, 404 t, 417, 426 t, 427 br
  Little Tikes®: 393
Omni-Photo Communications, Inc.
  Ann Hagen Griffiths: 98, 148
Brent Phelps: 110, 184, 241, 253 b, 259, 272, 325, 411
Photo Researchers, Inc.
  John Carter: 87
  Tim Davis: 133
  Patrick Donehue: 70 l
  Will McIntyre: 61 t
  Will & Deni McIntyre: 44 t